"Dan Wallace and his editorial team have produced an exceedingly helpful reader's lexicon on the Apostolic Fathers. This is a comprehensive and user-friendly resource for anyone studying the Apostolic Fathers or just doing some advanced Greek study. *A Reader's Lexicon of the Apostolic Fathers* is sure to be an enduring exegetical resource for future study of early Christian literature. I earnestly look forward to further volumes from Kregel publishers in this series of lexica."

—Michael F. Bird, Lecturer in Theology,
Ridley Melbourne College of Mission and Ministry.

"This lexicon offers a handy and user-friendly way into the world of the Apostolic Fathers by helping students of NT Greek use their knowledge to expand their horizons. You can never stop learning a language, and the richness of Greek is especially rewarding. This is the perfect second step for those who are ready to take it."

—Gerald Bray, Research Professor of Divinity, History and Doctrine,
Beeson Divinity School

"*A Reader's Lexicon to the Apostolic Fathers* is precisely the tool needed by students of Greek who want to begin reading the Apostolic Fathers in the original. Organized to help them as they work through these texts, students with only a year or two of Greek will begin to make headway as they read these important documents in the original. Highly recommended."

—D. A. Carson, Research Professor of New Testament,
Trinity Evangelical Divinity School

"It is gratifying to see increasing interest in the Apostolic Fathers and more tools becoming available for the study of them. This new reader's lexicon will be a very useful tool to facilitate reading what is to many Greek students an unfamiliar corpus. The lexicon is well-conceived and has been produced with commendable attention to detail and sensitivity to the context. Even in the age of digitally tagged texts, there is a secure place for a printed lexicon as a companion to Holmes's edition of the Fathers."

—Rodney J. Decker, Professor of Greek and NT,
Baptist Bible Seminary

"Clearly conceived and easy to use, *A Readers Lexicon to the Apostolic Fathers* will be an invaluable resource for beginning Greek students who are eager to read important Christian writings from just outside the New Testament. For anyone who has already learned the basics of New Testament Greek, I cannot recommend it highly enough."

—Bart D. Ehrman, James A. Gray Professor, Department of Religious
Studies, University of North Carolina at Chapel Hill

"However helpful translations may be, there is no substitute for reading works in their original language. Wallace's lexicon provides a welcome crib to assist in the study of the Apostolic Fathers in Greek. With this uncluttered guide by their side, students should be able to read, to understand, and then to interpret these important early Christian writings with a well-informed enthusiasm."

—Keith Elliott, Emeritus Professor of New Testament Textual Criticism, The University of Leeds, UK

"Daniel Wallace and his colleagues have put together an excellent tool that will facilitate the reading and study of the Apostolic Fathers, a collection of writings that New Testament scholars, as well as patristics scholars, have come to appreciate much more in recent years. Thus the publication of *A Reader's Lexicon of the Apostolic Fathers* is quite timely and will be welcomed by scholars and students alike. The purpose and principles of this new work are clearly explained. The layout is attractive and very user-friendly. Now no one has an excuse not to read the Apostolic Fathers in Greek!"

—Craig A. Evans, Payzant Distinguished Professor of New Testament, Acadia Divinity College

"For the first time a lexicon has been specifically designed to assist readers of the texts collectively known as the Apostolic Fathers. This excellent tool will assist the fluency and speed at which these texts can be read and studied. The format and contents of the lexicon have been designed primarily as a tool that enables advanced students to widen their exposure to a greater range of early Christian Greek texts. Dan Wallace, Brittany C. Burnette, and Terri Darby Moore, the editors of this volume, are to be congratulated on producing such a splendid pedagogical tool, which should assist students in developing their ability to read Hellenistic Greek."

—Paul Foster, Senior Lecturer in New Testament Language, Literature and Theology The School of Divinity, University of Edinburgh

"This resource will surely be an inducement for students, from a point relatively early in their Greek studies, to take up these valuable books of the Apostolic Fathers and read them. That can only be a good thing."

—Charles E. Hill, Professor of New Testament, Reformed Theological Seminary

"One of the best ways to improve one's understanding of the Greek of the New Testament is to read Greek outside of the NT—and the collection of early Greek texts known as the Apostolic Fathers is one of the best places to begin. *A Reader's Lexicon of the Apostolic Fathers* will surely facilitate wider engagement with these important authors, as it will enable students to spend more time reading and less time thumbing through a lexicon. This thoughtfully-designed volume is a welcome addition to my Apostolic Fathers bookshelf--a great tool for students, and a welcome resource for their teachers."

—Michael W. Holmes, University Professor of Biblical Studies & Early Christianity, Bethel University

"This thoughtfully designed work will be of great practical usefulness to students (and general readers) in becoming acquainted with the fascinating body of texts known as the Apostolic Fathers. Intended for those who have cut their teeth on the language of the Greek New Testament, this lexicon should prove very helpful in widening their knowledge of early Christian writers."

—L. W. Hurtado, Emeritus Professor of New Testament Language, Literature & Theology, University of Edinburgh

"Scholars of the New Testament and early Christian literature are blessed to have an increasing array of textual and linguistic resources. This book will enable rapid reading of the Apostolic Fathers for students of New Testament Greek who wish to further develop their language skills and get a broader sense of early Christian literature. It will be a welcome addition to the toolbox of those who are building their vocabulary of Koine Greek. The focus on words occurring fewer than thirty times in the corpus of the Apostolic Fathers keeps the book to a handy size while giving readers an easily usable tool to identify words in context."

—Roderic L. Mullen, SBL Series Editor, New Testament in the Greek Fathers

"This book provides a useful reading aid for those beginning their study of the Apostolic Fathers and who have not had the opportunity to learn their wider and distinctive vocabulary. The glosses are generally clear and concise, organized chapter by chapter according to author, and hence allow the reader to focus upon reading the Greek text, rather than repeatedly looking up words in a lexicon."

—Stanley E. Porter, President and Dean, and Professor of New Testament, McMaster Divinity College, Hamilton, Ontario, Canada

"With the publication of *A Reader's Lexicon of the Apostolic Fathers*, access to the primary texts of this vital collection of earliest Christian writings has never been faster or easier. It's like an expressway replacing a gravel road. I only wish this route had been available to me when I first read through the Apostolic Fathers in Greek over a decade ago.

This excellent resource efficiently and sufficiently defines vocabulary and idioms as well as periodically parses problematic grammatical forms. The definitions are selective enough so as not to be overwhelming but also broad enough in semantic range so as to not limit the reader's exegetical options. In short, this is a powerful tool, not a pedantic tutor.

Alphabetized lexical entries are subdivided not only by chapter but also by section or verse. The volume is flexible enough to be used in two different ways: as a means of learning unfamiliar vocabulary prior to reading the Apostolic Fathers or as a tool for looking up vocabulary while reading.

*A Reader's Lexicon of the Apostolic Fathers* is ideal for students who have completed two years of Koine Greek. Both New Testament and patristic scholars will find this to be a helpful resource both personally and in conjunction with instruction. I highly recommend this handbook for readers of the Apostolic Fathers and will use it in my own Apostolic Fathers course elective."

—Michael J. Svigel, Associate Professor of Theological Studies,
Dallas Theological Seminary

"The study of the Apostolic Father and their writings has become something of a growth industry in the last twenty years, with major volumes published in the Hermeneia series and elsewhere updating what we know about these writings. I am happy to commend Daniel Wallace's new volume, a much needed reader's lexicon, so that students of the Greek text of the Apostolic Fathers can readily access this valuable early Christian material. Like Philip who responded to the Ethiopian eunuch's question: 'How can I understand this without some help?', Wallace has now come along side our own chariots, our own studies of these ancient sacred texts, and provided a guide to translation and understanding. Highly recommended!"

—Ben Witherington III, Amos Professor of the NT for Doctoral Studies,
Asbury Theological Seminary,

"Students at evangelical seminaries receive excellent instruction in the study of the Hebrew text of the Old Testament and the Greek text of the New Testament. But an important lacuna in their training is often the neglect of the Church Fathers, as evangelicals have tended to leapfrog from the first century to the Reformation Era, leaving the study of the patristic texts to students from the Roman Catholic or Greek Orthodox traditions. This neglect is lamentable as there is so much in these writings that is indispensable for our understanding of church doctrine and practice, such as that of 'clinical" baptism,' e.g. Constantine's decision to delay baptism until he was on his death bed, and the separation of the office of the bishop (*episkopos*) from that of the elder.

The Apostolic Fathers are the earliest and most important of the patristic texts. Michael W. Holmes has provided an excellent edition of the Greek text and its translation (2007). As the result of painstaking labor, Daniel B. Wallace, Brittany C. Burnette, and Terri Darby Moore, have now provided those who wish to study the Greek text with an invaluable aid, in their *Reader's Lexicon of the Apostolic Fathers*. This should enable a new generation of evangelicals to undertake serious scholarship on these texts, the most important after the New Testament itself, for our understanding of the early church at the end of the first and beginning of the second century."

—Edwin M. Yamauchi, Professor of History Emeritus,
Miami University, Oxford, OH

# A READER'S LEXICON OF THE APOSTOLIC FATHERS

Daniel B. Wallace, Senior Editor

Brittany C. Burnette, Editor

Terri Darby Moore, Editor

Kregel Academic

*A Reader's Lexicon of the Apostolic Fathers*



Published by Kregel Publications, a division of Kregel, Inc., P.O. Box 2607, Grand Rapids, MI 49501.



The Greek font used in this book is GraecaU and is available from www.linguistsoftware.com/lgku.htm, +1-425-775-1130.

ISBN: 978-0-8254-3949-0

Printed in the United States of America
13 14 15 16 17 / 5 4 3 2 1

# Contents

Preface ..... 11

Acknowledgments ..... 15

Abbreviations ..... 19

First Clement ..... 21

Second Clement ..... 59

Ignatius to the Ephesians ..... 69

Ignatius to the Magnesians ..... 77

Ignatius to the Trallians ..... 83

Ignatius to the Romans ..... 87

Ignatius to the Philadelphians ..... 91

Ignatius to the Smyrnaeans ..... 95

Ignatius to the Polycarp ..... 101

Polycarp to the Philippians ..... 105

The Martyrdom of Polycarp ..... 109

The Didache ..... 119

The Letter of Barnabas ..... 127

The Shepherd of Hermas ..... 147

The Letter to Diognetus ..... 225

The Fragment of Quadratus ..... 237

The Fragments of Papias ..... 239

The Traditions of the Elders ..... 249

# Preface

This volume is the second in a series of reader's lexica. The first was *A New Reader's Lexicon of the Greek New Testament*, by Michael H. Burer and Jeffrey E. Miller, appearing in 2008. At the urging of the editors at Kregel Publications, principally Jim Weaver, Dennis Hillman, and Paul Hillman, I accepted the role of senior editor for this new series. Ultimately, we envision having several volumes that assist students of Hellenistic Greek in their reading of various corpora that are relevant to nascent Christianity. The lexicon of the Apostolic Fathers (AF) was chosen to be the second in this series because the AF are early and important links to apostolic Christianity, they are hotly debated as to their connection with the normative kerygma of the primitive church, and they are often disregarded in evangelical circles because they are not Scripture. We hope that this work will spur many students of the New Testament, especially evangelicals, to get into the AF and wrestle with their content, theology, praxis, use of the New Testament, and devotion to the risen Lord.

I asked two former ThM interns of mine, Terri Moore and Brittany Burnette, to be the junior editors on whose shoulders the great bulk of the work would be done. They are exacting students of Scripture whose love for the Greek text and skill in exegesis are exceptional. Brit, in fact, has taught a course at her church on the AF for a long time; Terri taught for several years as an adjunct in the New Testament Department at Dallas Seminary. Both women are currently working on their doctorates, Terri her PhD and Brit her DMin. We mapped out an approach in January 2008 and Terri and Brit attacked their assignments enthusiastically and with great care. We also asked several individuals—who are mentioned with gratitude in the Acknowledgments—to proofread the manuscript. The project took much longer than anticipated for a variety of reasons, not the least of which was the pioneering nature of this work. We are happy to finally offer it to students of the New Testament who understand the value of other ancient sources for illumination of the biblical text.

The text followed is Michael Holmes's third edition of the *Apostolic Fathers* (Grand Rapids: Baker, 2007). As in the *New Reader's Lexicon of the New Testament*, we have not listed all the words found in the AF. We have limited the vocabulary to those words that occur *thirty times or less in the NT*. The NT was chosen as the index because those who read the AF almost always first get acquainted with the Greek of the NT. The cut-off at thirty times, rather than fifty times (as in the NT reader's lexicon), was chosen on the belief that students who begin reading the AF will almost always have a better grasp on NT vocabulary than just the words that occur more than fifty times in that corpus. Admittedly, setting the bar at thirty is somewhat arbitrary; it could have been much lower. The number we set means that a vocabulary of merely 453 words is sufficient for a student to begin to read the AF with some proficiency.

A few particular features of the lexicon's layout should be noted. All vocabulary is given in its lexical form. Verbs are glossed as infinitives so as to distinguish them more easily from nouns (e.g., ἀναγκάζω is *to force* rather than *force*). Nouns are listed with their articles. Even in consecutive verses the lexicon lists every word in the AF that occurs thirty times or less in the NT. The vocabulary in each verse is laid out alphabetically. Lexical forms are given first, followed by at least two numbers and as many as four, each separated by a high dot (•). The first number indicates how many times the word appears in that book. The last number indicates how many times the word appears in the AF. For Ignatius, there are three numbers for each entry, the middle one indicating how often the word appears in all of Ignatius's letters. (No such middle number appears in *1 Clement* or *2 Clement* since the latter is authored by someone else.) Occasionally, a number in brackets precedes the other numbers. This indicates the frequency of the word in that particular verse. For examples of this layout, consider the following:

*1 Clement* 16.10:
**ἀντί** [2] 4 • 15 *instead of, in place of*
The word occurs twice in *1 Clement* 16.10, four times in *1 Clement*, and 15 times in the AF.

Ignatius to the *Romans* 7.1:
**διαφθείρω** 1 • 3 • 12 *to deprave, ruin*
The word occurs once in *Romans*, three times in Ignatius, and twelve times in the AF.

*Shepherd of Hermas* 10.4 (Hv 3.2):
**πύργος, ὁ** 147 • 148 *tower*
The word occurs 147 times in *Hermas* and once elsewhere. It should be noted that although this word occurs almost 150 times in the AF, since it appears only four times in the NT, it is included in the reader's lexicon.

Here are a few interesting statistics on the vocabulary of the AF:

- The AF collectively are 47 percent the size of the NT (66,263 and 138,158 words respectively).
- Exactly 4966 different words occur thirty times or less in the

NT; for the AF the same list (including words that do not occur at all in the NT) comes to 4052.

- The rich vocabulary of the AF can be seen by comparison with the NT: even though the AF comprise less than half the number of words of the NT, there are 4296 different lexical forms in the AF compared to 5420 in the NT. In other words, the AF vocabulary stock is nearly 80 percent of that of the NT.

- The most common word listed in this lexicon is πύργος (*tower*), a word that occurs 148 times, all but once in the *Shepherd of Hermas.*

- The most frequently occurring words in any verse are ἐγκρατεύομαι (*to abstain*)—six times in *Hermas* 38.2, Ἰακώβ (*Jacob*)—six times in *Barnabas* 13.5, and πτελέα (*elm tree*)—five times in *Hermas* 51.3.

- The verse with the most vocabulary in the lexicon is *Diognetus* 7.2 (34 words, with two of them occurring twice in the verse).

The glosses are contextually determined. The editors employed the third edition of Bauer's *A Greek-English Lexicon of the New Testament and Other Early Christian Literature* (Chicago: University of Chicago Press, 2000), by Frederick Danker (BDAG); G. W. H. Lampe, *A Patristic Greek Lexicon* (Oxford: Clarendon, 1961); *A Greek-English Lexicon* by H. G. Liddell, and R. Scott, 9th ed. with supplement; rev. by H. S. Jones (Oxford: Oxford University Press, 1968); J. B. Lightfoot, *The Apostolic Fathers: Clement, Ignatius, and Polycarp*, five vols.; reprint ed. (Grand Rapids: Baker, 1981); and Michael Holmes's translation in his third edition of the *Apostolic Fathers*. No attempt has been made to cite these sources except on rare occasions (mostly dealing with idioms). Occasionally, the glosses listed in all these works are found to be contextually questionable. In such instances the editors have added their own gloss while also retaining the gloss from one or more of the standard sources.

The glosses are at times mixed with definitions. What we put in italics are the basic glosses that can be used in translation. We are not strictly following BDAG in terms of italicizing only the glosses since the more expanded definitions are also helpful for translation. Consider, for example, ἐναλλάξ in *1 Clement* 12.4. The definition/gloss in BDAG says "**in the opposite direction, *crosswise***"; BDAG's general definition is "in the opposite direction" while their gloss is "*crosswise*." Because *crosswise* could be misunderstood, we have also supplied the general definition that could be used in translation as an expanded gloss. Practicality and communication were key factors in deciding which definitions to include.

There are also occasional syntactical, morphological, and idiom notes found throughout the lexicon. No attempt has been made to be systematic with these notes, and in general our policy has been to offer a bare minimum of them overall. The particular idioms in the AF can almost always be found in BDAG or Lampe; some of the unusual syntax is also discussed in *A Greek Grammar of the New Testament and other Early Christian Literature*, by F. Blass and A. Debrunner; trans. and rev. by R. W. Funk (Chicago: University of Chicago Press, 1961). In later editions of our lexicon, as readers communicate with us, we hope to expand on these notes, keeping with what we envision as the level of Greek skill that the average reader of the AF will have. Such notes will be incorporated especially in relation to the completion of the second edition of my *Greek Grammar Beyond the Basics: An Exegetical Syntax of the New Testament* (Grand Rapids: Zondervan, 1996 [first edition]), which, when published, will include extensive syntax culled from the AF.

This volume may be profitably used by students in their third or fourth semester of biblical Greek as well as by more advanced students. Professors who require that first-year students learn more vocabulary than what occurs fifty or more times may find this volume helpful to their charges once they have mastered their verb paradigms.

This reader's lexicon is not intended to supplant the standard lexica for the AF. There is a wealth of information especially in BDAG and Lampe that a reader's lexicon does not touch on. Rather, it is our hope that readers will engage the text and, in the process, interact with these standard tools for understanding this significant body of literature.

All errors—be they lexical, grammatical, or typographical—rest ultimately on my shoulders. A task as large as this undertaking will surely evidence a good number of infelicities. Input from the readers of this lexicon, therefore, will be gratefully appreciated.

Daniel B. Wallace
Senior Editor
The Feast Day of Saints Peter and Paul

# Acknowledgments

The recipients of our gratitude constitute an unusually long list. In the spring semesters of 2008, 2010, and 2012, my master's students at Dallas Seminary taking the course Advanced Greek Grammar worked on various aspects of the syntax of the Apostolic Fathers. I encouraged them to write their term papers on some feature of syntax in the AF. Notably, two term papers, each written by one of my academic interns, were later revised and published in theological journals: Michael R. Whitenton, "After Πίστις Χριστοῦ: Neglected Evidence from the Apostolic Fathers," *Journal of Theological Studies*, NS, 61.1 (2010) 82–109; and Brian J. Wright, "Greek Syntax as a Criterion of Authenticity: A New Discussion and Proposal," *Catholic Biblical Quarterly* 74.1 (2012) 84–100. Both essays are significant contributions to the relevance of the AF to the NT. Several others developed their term papers into ThM theses. I would like to think that all of the students in these classes grew in their appreciation of the AF. Luke Tsai did some proofreading, even though his work was not part of a course, as did Mike Hansen, a student at Southern Baptist Seminary. Cortney Whiting and Ambilike Mwangomo later took independent study courses on the AF and helped immensely with the proofreading and syntactical notes of the lexicon.

The Advanced Greek Grammar class of 2012 deserves special notice. Many of the students did extra credit for the course by laboring in the mind-numbing task of checking word-frequency, contextual glosses, and other proofreading duties. These include Kirby Applegate, Raymond Baclit, Kyle Hughes, Jason Stein, Jessica Tron, Nancy Turner, Derrick Varghese, Stephen Wiggins, and especially Dan Pfeifer and Alex Gonzales.

I have taught first-year Greek at Dallas Seminary for nearly three decades. Since 2001, my sections of first-year Greek have all been "Honors Greek" or, as the students prefer to call it, "Greek on steroids." Since 2007, the students have produced translation and syntactical analysis papers on portions of the AF. Their enthusiasm for this body of literature was surprising at first, but at all times encouraging. Along the way, these honors students used early drafts of the *Reader's Lexicon of the Apostolic Fathers*. The trials and errors of imposing such corpora on first-year students sensitized me to their abilities and aided immeasurably in the final form of the lexicon.

My academic interns have had a large role in the proofreading and production of this lexicon as well. Philip Miller created the initial concordance of words that would be treated in the lexicon. Stascek Bialecki, Rex Howe, Matt Larsen, Adam Messer, Matt Morgan, Tim Ricchuiti, Russell Schaffner, Paul Wheatley, and Mike Whitenton all worked on various aspects of proofreading the manuscript. Special thanks are due to Greg Rhodea and Jason Stein, my academic interns for 2011–12, who did incredibly extensive work—all in a timely manner and without a whisper of complaint—in proofing the manuscript and offering many valuable suggestions.

Of all the students who labored on the lexicon, Brian Ortner, working on his PhD in NT at Dallas Seminary, must be singled out. With no course credit but with an enlarged servant's heart, Brian helped by managing the database, guiding me through a maze of multiple master files; creating macros for Word that converted fonts with ease; double-checking contextually-sensitive glosses; formatting the master documents; and completing a good number of other thankless proofreading assignments. Without his extraordinary help and prodding, this volume would have been delayed by at least another year.

Once Brit, Terri, and I did our penultimate proofreading of the galleys, I handed the manuscript to my sweet wife, who examined every line with a critic's keen eye. Thank you, Pati, for your labor of love!

Κῦδος to all of you for your tremendous assistance in reining in a project that seemed to stretch its tentacles out in every direction!

This project could not have been accomplished without extensive use of Accordance. Not only did this software program provide us with a morphologically tagged text of the third edition of Holmes's *Apostolic Fathers* but its digital BDAG, concordance of all New Testament words occurring thirty times or less, concordance of all the AF word entries used in this lexicon, and innumerable other features saved us a significant amount of time. We are grateful to Oak Tree Software for this powerful tool.

Profound appreciation for the folks at Kregel is happily acknowledged. Jim Weaver, a longtime friend and Christian gentleman of unwavering principle and former director of academic books at Kregel, first suggested this project, met with the three editors, drew up the contract, and continued to encourage us to complete the task. To him especially we are indebted. Dennis Hillman, the publisher at Kregel, guided us with a bird's-eye view of the project and with an excellent grasp on how this tome should be packaged and marketed. Paul Hillman, the senior project manager, helped in innumerable ways with the layout and text. Laura Bartlett, Kregel's marketing manager for academic and ministry books, added creativity and almost boundless exuberance to the publication of this book.

I (Brit) want to offer thanks to Terri Moore, at whose side it was a pleasure and privilege to work. To my parents, Spencer and Carol Burnette, and my sister, Inger, thank you for your unfailing love and support. Special gratitude must also be given to Darrell L. Bock, Anastasia Beeson, Sharifa Stevens, Erin Stambaugh, and the ladies of Shabby Chic Ministries. Finally, I would like to thank the faculty and staff members of Plano Christian Academy and Dallas Christian College, most notably, Koko Carroll, Scott Harris, Lorna and Ali Beavers, Matthew Meeks, and Brett Vance.

In addition to those mentioned above, I (Terri) would especially like to thank my husband and children for their unwavering support. Darren was instrumental in convincing me to say yes to the project and in ensuring I had adequate time to finish amidst PhD studies, adjunct responsibilities, and the requirements of home life with three children. Jacob, Stella, and Alex never once complained when Mom needed just five more minutes of quiet, nor when that five minutes so often turned into many more!

We (Brittany and Terri) would both like to express our gratitude to Dan Wallace for including us on this project. True to form, he has taken two young scholars under his wing and given us the opportunity to work on a meaningful and challenging project. Such mentorship is rare and treasured.

Several people have surely gone unmentioned who deserve better. An old professor's failing memory is to be blamed for this lacuna. You know who you are and you know that, in the *eschaton*, your praise will come from Jesus Christ, to whom we all owe our deepest debt of gratitude.

Daniel B. Wallace, Senior Editor
Brittany C. Burnette, Editor
Terri Darby Moore, Editor

# Abbreviations

| | |
|---|---|
| act. | active |
| adj. | adjective |
| AF | Apostolic Fathers |
| BDAG | Danker, F. W., reviser and editor. *A Greek-English Lexicon of the New Testament and Other Early Christian Literature*, 3rd edition. Based on Walter Bauer's *Griechisch-Deutsches Wörterbuch zu den Schriften des Neuen Testaments und der frühchristlichen Literatur*, 6th edition, edited by Kurt Aland and Barbara Aland, with Viktor Reichmann, and on previous English editions by William F. Arndt, F. Wilbur Gingrich, and F. W. Danker. Chicago: University of Chicago Press, 2000. |
| BDF | Blass, F., and A. Debrunner. *A Greek Grammar of the New Testament and other Early Christian Literature.* Trans. and rev. by R. W. Funk. Chicago: University of Chicago Press, 1961. |
| *ExSyn* | Wallace, Daniel B. *Greek Grammar Beyond the Basics: An Exegetical Syntax of the New Testament.* Grand Rapids: Zondervan, 1996. |
| fig. | figurative, figuratively |
| gen. | genitive |
| indecl. | indeclinable |
| Lampe | Lampe, G. W. H. *A Patristic Greek Lexicon.* Oxford: Clarendon, 1961. |

| | |
|---|---|
| Lightfoot | Lightfoot, J. B. *The Apostolic Fathers: Clement, Ignatius, and Polycarp*, five vols.; reprint ed. Grand Rapids: Baker, 1981. |
| lit. | literal, literally |
| LSJ | Liddell, H. G., and R. Scott. *A Greek-English Lexicon.* 9th ed. with supplement. Rev. by H. S. Jones. Oxford: Oxford University Press, 1968. |
| metaph. | metaphorically |
| mid. | middle |
| NT | New Testament |
| pass. | passive |
| pl. | plural |
| subst. | substantival, substantivally |

# First Clement

## Preface

**ἁγιάζω** 3 • 16 *to consecrate, dedicate, sanctify*
**κλητός** 1 • 3 *called, invited*
**Κόρινθος, ἡ** 1 • 3 *Corinth*
**παντοκράτωρ, ὁ** 6 • 12 *Almighty, All-powerful, Omnipotent (One)*
**παροικέω** [2] 2 • 6 *to inhabit a place as a foreigner/stranger, be a stranger*
**πληθύνω** 3 • 11 *to be multiplied, grow, increase*;
  **πληθυνθείη** aorist pass. optative
**Ῥώμη, ἡ** 1 • 8 *Rome*

## Chapter 1

1 **αἰφνίδιος** 1 • 1 *sudden*
**ἀλλότριος** 2 • 14 *alien, unsuitable*
**ἀνόσιος** 3 • 3 *unholy*
**ἀξιαγάπητος** 2 • 3 *worthy of love*
**ἀπόνοια, ἡ** 2 • 2 *madness, frenzy;*
  **εἰς τοσοῦτον ἀπονοίας** *to such a level/degree/pitch of madness*
**αὐθάδης** 1 • 5 *self-willed, stubborn, arrogant*
**βραδύς** 1 • 5 *slow, rather tardy*
**ἐκκαίω** 1 • 1 *to instigate something destructive, kindle* or *start*
**ἐκλεκτός** 12 • 30 *chosen*
**ἐπάλληλος** 1 • 1 *in rapid succession, repeatedly*
**ἐπιζητέω** 1 • 9 *to discuss, debate, dispute*
**ἐπιστροφή, ἡ** 1 • 2 *turning/giving one's attention to something, attention*
**μεγάλως** 3 • 9 *greatly*
**μιαρός** 4 • 4 *abominable, foul, wretched, depraved, wanton*
**νομίζω** 3 • 10 *to think, believe, hold, consider*
**ξένος** 1 • 8 *strange, surprising, unheard of, foreign*
**περιβόητος** 2 • 2 *well known, far famed, celebrated*
**περίπτωσις, ἡ** 1 • 1 *misfortune, calamity*
**πρᾶγμα, τό** 1 • 24 *thing, matter, affair; difficulties, troubles*
**προπετής** 1 • 1 *rash, reckless, thoughtless*
**σεμνός** 6 • 12 *honorable, worthy, venerable, holy, above reproach*
**στάσις, ἡ** 9 • 9 *uprising, riot, revolt, rebellion, discord*
**συμφορά, ἡ** 1 • 1 *misfortune, calamity, disaster*
**τοσοῦτος** 9 • 38 *so great/strong, to such extent, to such a degree of*
2 **ἀσφαλής** 2 • 4 *certain*
**βέβαιος** 3 • 9 *unwavering and persistent, abiding*
**γνῶσις, ἡ** 6 • 32 *knowledge*
**δοκιμάζω** 4 • 19 *to put to the test, examine; be convinced*
**ἐπιεικής** 3 • 4 *yielding, gentle, kind, courteous, tolerant*
**εὐσέβεια, ἡ** 4 • 6 *devoutness, Christian piety, godliness*
**ἦθος, τό** 2 • 2 *custom, usage, habit*
**μακαρίζω** 1 • 5 *to call/consider blessed, happy, fortunate*
**μεγαλοπρεπής** 7 • 7 *magnificent, sublime, majestic, impressive*
**πανάρετος** 5 • 5 *most excellent*
**παρεπιδημέω** 1 • 1 *to visit (with someone)*
**σώφρων** 2 • 2 *prudent, thoughtful, self-controlled*
**τέλειος** 5 • 25 *perfect*
**φιλοξενία, ἡ** 4 • 5 *hospitality*
3 **ἁγνός** 6 • 11 *pure, holy*
**ἄμωμος** 7 • 17 *blameless*
**ἀπονέμω** 1 • 3 *to assign, show, pay, accord*
**ἀπροσωπολήμπτως** 1 • 2 *impartially*
**ἐπιτελέω** 13 • 15 *to complete, accomplish, perform, bring about*

**ἐπιτρέπω** 1 • 10 *to order, instruct*
**ἡγέομαι** 8 • 25 *to lead, guide*
**καθηκόντως** 1 • 1 *as is fitting, in accordance with obligation or duty*
**καθήκω** 3 • 3 *to come/reach to, be proper/fitting*
**κανών, ὁ** 3 • 4 *assignment, formulation*
**μέτριος** 1 • 1 *moderate;*
  **νοεῖν μέτρια** *practice self-restraint*
**νέος** 4 • 16 *young, in the early stages of life*
**νοέω** 3 • 46 *to be minded*
**νόμιμος** 3 • 4 *lawful;*
  subst. *statute, law, commandment*
**οἰκουργέω** 1 • 1 *to fulfill one's household responsibilities*
**πάνυ** 1 • 5 *altogether, very*
**σεμνός** [2] 6 • 13 *honorable, worthy, venerable, holy, above reproach*
**σεμνῶς** 1 • 4 *honorably, worthily, in a manner above reproach*
**στέργω** 1 • 2 *to love, feel affection for*
**σωφρονέω** 1 • 2 *to be reasonable, be sensible, be serious; keep one's head*
**ὑποταγή, ἡ** 2 • 4 *subjection, subordination*

## Chapter 2

1 **ἀλαζονεύομαι** 2 • 3 *to boast, be boastful*
**ἀρκέω** 1 • 5 *to be satisfied/content with something*
**ἐνστερνίζομαι** 1 • 1 *to store away within oneself*
**ἐπιμελῶς** 2 • 9 *carefully, diligently*
**ἐφόδιον, τό** 1 • 1 *travel allowance, provisions for a journey*
**ἡδέως** 3 • 10 *gladly*
**πάθημα, τό** 1 • 2 *suffering, misfortune*
**προσέχω** 4 • 25 *to pay attention to, give heed to, follow*
**σπλάγχνον, τό** 2 • 5 *heart*
**ταπεινοφρονέω** 11 • 14 *to be modest, be unassuming*

2 **ἀγαθοποιΐα, ἡ** 4 • 4 *doing good*
**ἀκόρεστος** 1 • 1 *insatiable*
**βαθύς** 1 • 1 *profound*
**ἔκχυσις, ἡ** 1 • 1 *outpouring*
**λιπαρός** 1 • 1 *bright, costly, rich*
**πλήρης** 3 • 20 *complete, full, in full*
**πόθος, ὁ** 1 • 1 *longing, wish, desire*
**ἐδέδοτο** (pluperfect of δίδωμι) *had been given*

3 **ἄκων** 1 • 1 *unwilling*
**βουλή, ἡ** 5 • 19 *plan, purpose, intention*
**ἐκτείνω** 2 • 7 *to stretch out*
**εὐσεβής** 2 • 4 *devout, godly, pious, reverent*
**ἱκετεύω** 3 • 3 *to supplicate, beseech*
**ἵλεως** 3 • 5 *gracious, merciful*
**μεστός** 1 • 4 *filled with something*
**ὅσιος** 6 • 10 *devout, pious, holy, pleasing to God, holy*
**παντοκράτωρ, ὁ** 6 • 12 *Almighty, All-Powerful, Omnipotent (One)*
**πεποίθησις, ἡ** 5 • 7 *trust, confidence*
**προθυμία, ἡ** 2 • 6 *willingness, readiness, goodwill*

4 **ἀγών, ὁ** 2 • 7 *struggle, fight*
**ἀδελφότης, ἡ** 1 • 2 *fellowship*
**ἀριθμός, ὁ** 5 • 14 *number, total*
**δέος, τό** 1 • 1 *awe*
**ἐκλεκτός** 12 • 30 *chosen*

5 **ἀκέραιος** 2 • 3 *pure, innocent*
**ἀμνησίκακος** 1 • 2 *bearing no malice, forgiving*
**εἰλικρινής** 1 • 2 *sincere, pure*

6 **βδελυκτός** 3 • 3 *abhorrent, detestable*
**παράπτωμα, τό** 4 • 10 *offense, wrongdoing, sin*
**πενθέω** 1 • 2 *to be sad, grieve, mourn*
**πλησίον** 3 • 17 *near;*
  subst. *neighbor, fellow human being*
**στάσις, ἡ** 9 • 9 *strife, discord, disunion*
**σχίσμα, τό** 5 • 10 *division, dissension, schism*
**ὑστέρημα, τό** 2 • 4 *lack, shortcomings*

7 **ἀγαθοποιΐα, ἡ** 4 • 4 *doing good*

ἀμεταμέλητος 3 • 3 *feeling no remorse, having no regret*
ἕτοιμος 1 • 9 *ready*
8 **δικαίωμα, τό** 3 • 12 *regulation, requirement, commandment*
**ἐπιτελέω** 13 • 15 *to complete, perform, accomplish, bring about*
**κοσμέω** 4 • 10 *to adorn, decorate; make beautiful or attractive*
**πανάρετος** 5 • 5 *most excellent*
**πλάτος, τό** 1 • 1 *breadth, width, from side to side*
**πολιτεία, ἡ** 2 • 5 *way of life, conduct*
**πρόσταγμα, τό** 7 • 10 *order, command(ment), injunction*
**σεβάσμιος** 1 • 1 *worthy of veneration, honorable*
**ἐγέγραπτο** (pluperfect of γράφω) *had/have been written*

## Chapter 3

1 **ἀπολακτίζω** 1 • 1 *to kick away, kick off, kick up, kick*
**ἐπιτελέω** 13 • 15 *to fulfill*
**παχύνω** 1 • 1 *to make fat, well-nourished*
**πλατύνω** 1 • 1 *to make broad, enlarge*
**πλατυσμός, ὁ** 1 • 2 *extension, enlargement, expansion*
2 **αἰχμαλωσία, ἡ** 1 • 2 *captivity*
**ἀκαταστασία, ἡ** 3 • 4 *disorder, unruliness*
**διωγμός, ὁ** 1 • 2 *persecution*
**ἔρις, ἡ** 9 • 10 *strife, discord, contention*
**ζῆλος, ὁ/τό** 22 • 25 *jealousy, envy*
**πόλεμος, ὁ** 3 • 4 *strife conflict, quarrel*
**στάσις, ἡ** 9 • 9 *strife, discord, disunion*
**φθόνος, ὁ** 4 • 4 *envy, jealousy*
3 **ἄδοξος** 1 • 2 *without reputation, obscure*
**ἄτιμος** 2 • 3 *dishonored, despised, in disrepute*
**ἄφρων** 5 • 17 *foolish, ignorant*
**ἔνδοξος** 8 • 54 *honored, distinguished, eminent*
**ἔντιμος** 1 • 2 *honored, respected*
**ἐπεγείρω** 1 • 1 *to arouse, excite, stir up (against someone)*
**νέος** 4 • 16 *young, someone in the early stages of life*
**φρόνιμος** 1 • 4 *sensible, thoughtful, prudent, wise*
4 **ἄδικος** 5 • 14 *unjust*
**ἀμβλυωπέω** 1 • 1 *to be dim-sighted, see poorly*
**ἀναλαμβάνω** 5 • 10 *to take to one's self, adopt*
**ἄπειμι** 2 • 5 *to be absent/away*
**ἀπολείπω** 4 • 6 *to put aside, give up, abandon*
**ἀσεβής** 5 • 14 *irreverent, impious, ungodly*
**βαδίζω** 1 • 1 *to walk*
**ζῆλος, ὁ/τό** 22 • 25 *jealousy, envy*
**καθήκω** 3 • 3 *to come/reach to, be proper/fitting;*
**πολιτεύεσθαι κατὰ τὸ καθῆκον τῷ Χριστῷ** *to conduct oneself in a manner that enhances the prestige of Christ*
**νόμιμος** 3 • 4 *lawful;* subst. *statute, law, commandment*
**πολιτεύομαι** 6 • 10 *to live, lead one's life*
**πόρρω** 5 • 8 *far (away)*
**πρόσταγμα, τό** 7 • 10 *order, command(ment), injunction*

## Chapter 4

1 **Ἄβελ, ὁ** 4 • 4 *Abel*
**θυσία, ἡ** 10 • 22 *sacrifice, offering*
**Κάϊν, ὁ** 6 • 6 *Cain*
**πρωτότοκος** 1 • 4 *firstborn*
**στέαρ, τό** 1 • 2 *fat*
2 **Ἄβελ, ὁ** 4 • 4 *Abel*
**δῶρον, τό** 3 • 4 *gift, present, offering*
**ἐφοράω** 1 • 1 *gaze upon*
**θυσία, ἡ** 10 • 22 *sacrifice, offering*
**Κάϊν, ὁ** 6 • 6 *Cain*
**προσέχω** 4 • 25 *to pay attention to, give heed to, follow, notice*
3 **Κάϊν, ὁ** 6 • 6 *Cain*
**λίαν** 2 • 48 *very (much), exceedingly*
**λυπέω** 1 • 17 *to become sad, be sorrowful, be distressed*

**συμπίπτω** 2 • 3 *to have one's countenance fall, become distorted, become downcast*
4 **διαιρέω** 1 • 1 *distribute, divide*
**ἱνατί** [2] 2 • 2 *why, for what reason?*
**Κάϊν, ὁ** 6 • 6 *Cain*
**ὀρθῶς** 2 • 8 *rightly, correctly*
**περίλυπος** 1 • 2 *very sad, deeply grieved*
**συμπίπτω** 2 • 3 *to have one's countenance fall, become distorted, become downcast*
5 **ἀποστροφή, ἡ** 1 • 1 *turning, return*
**ἡσυχάζω** 3 • 3 *to rest*
6 **Ἄβελ, ὁ** [2] 4 • 4 *Abel*
**Κάϊν, ὁ** [2] 6 • 6 *Cain*
**πεδίον, τό** [2] 2 • 17 *level place, plain, field*
7 **ἀδελφοκτονία, ἡ** 1 • 1 *fratricide*
**ζῆλος, ὁ/τό** 22 • 25 *jealousy, envy*
**κατεργάζομαι** 3 • 7 *to bring about, produce, create*
**φθόνος, ὁ** 4 • 4 *envy, jealousy*
8 **ἀποδιδράσκω** 2 • 2 *to run away, escape*
**ζῆλος, ὁ/τό** 22 • 25 *jealousy, envy*
**Ἠσαῦ, ὁ** 1 • 1 *Esau*
**Ἰακώβ, ὁ** 3 • 13 *Jacob*
9 **δουλεία, ἡ** 2 • 3 *slavery*
**ζῆλος, ὁ/τό** 22 • 25 *jealousy, envy*
**μέχρι** [2] 2 • 23 *to the point of*
10 **Αἰγύπτιος** 1 • 2 *Egyptian*
**Αἴγυπτος, ἡ** 6 • 9 *Egypt*
**ἀναγκάζω** 1 • 3 *to compel, force*
**ἀναιρέω** [2] 4 • 10 *to do away with, destroy*
**δικαστής, ὁ** 1 • 1 *judge*
**ἐχθές** 1 • 1 *yesterday*
**ζῆλος, ὁ/τό** 22 • 25 *jealousy, envy*
**καθίστημι** 6 • 8 *to appoint, put in charge, authorize*
**κριτής, ὁ** 1 • 6 *judge*
**ὁμόφυλος** 1 • 1 *fellow-tribesman, compatriot*
**τρόπος, ὁ** 3 • 17 *manner, way, kind, guise*
**Φαραώ, ὁ** 2 • 2 *Pharaoh*
**φεύγω** 4 • 20 *to flee*
11 **Ἀαρών, ὁ** 2 • 2 *Aaron*
**αὐλίζομαι** 1 • 2 *to live, stay*
**ζῆλος, ὁ/τό** 22 • 25 *jealousy, envy*
**Μαριάμ, ἡ** 1 • 1 *Miriam*
**παρεμβολή, ἡ** 2 • 2 *a (fortified) camp*
12 **Ἀβειρών, ὁ** 1 • 1 *Abiram*
**ᾅδης, ὁ** 2 • 3 *the nether world, Hades*
**Δαθάν, ὁ** 1 • 1 *Dathan*
**ζῆλος, ὁ/τό** 22 • 25 *jealousy, envy*
**θεράπων, ὁ** 5 • 6 *attendant, aide, servant*
**κατάγω** 1 • 1 *to lead/bring down*
**στασιάζω** 7 • 7 *to rebel*
13 **ἀλλόφυλος** 2 • 4 *alien, foreign*
**ζῆλος, ὁ/τό** 22 • 25 *jealousy, envy*
**Σαούλ, ὁ** 1 • 1 *Saul*
**φθόνος, ὁ** 4 • 4 *envy, jealousy*

## Chapter 5

1 **ἀθλητής, ὁ** 1 • 4 *contender, athlete*
**ἀρχαῖος** 2 • 12 *ancient*
**γενναῖος** 5 • 8 *noble, illustrious*
**παύω** 3 • 12 *to stop (oneself), cease*
**ὑπόδειγμα, τό** [2] 6 • 8 *example, model, pattern*
2 **ἀθλέω** 1 • 2 *to compete, contend*
**ζῆλος, ὁ/τό** 22 • 25 *jealousy, envy*
**στῦλος, ὁ** 1 • 1 *pillar, support*
**φθόνος, ὁ** 4 • 4 *envy, jealousy*
4 **ἄδικος** 5 • 14 *unjust*
**ζῆλος, ὁ/τό** 22 • 25 *jealousy, envy*
**πόνος, ὁ** 4 • 6 *pain, distress, affliction, hardship*
**ὑποφέρω** 3 • 12 *to submit to, endure*
**Πέτρον** (at beginning of verse, an acc. of reference; cf. *ExSyn* 203) *regarding Peter*
5 **βραβεῖον, τό** 1 • 2 *prize, award, reward*
**ἔρις, ἡ** 9 • 10 *strife, discord, contention*
**ζῆλος, ὁ/τό** 22 • 25 *jealousy, envy*
**ὑποδείκνυμι** 1 • 3 *to indicate, point out*
6 **ἀνατολή, ἡ** 2 • 6 *east, orient*
**γενναῖος** 5 • 8 *noble, illustrious*
**δεσμός, ὁ** 3 • 14 *bond, fetter*
**δύσις, ἡ** 2 • 3 *west*
**ἑπτάκις** 1 • 1 *seven times*
**κῆρυξ, ὁ** 1 • 4 *herald, proclaimer*
**κλέος, τό** 2 • 2 *fame, glory*
**λιθάζω** 2 • 3 *to stone*

**φορέω** 1 • 17 *to bear constantly/ regularly, wear*
**φυγαδεύω** 1 • 1 *to banish from the country*
7 **ἀπαλλάσσω** 1 • 3 *to go away, leave, depart*
**δύσις, ἡ** 2 • 3 *west*
**ἡγέομαι** 8 • 25 *to lead, guide*
**τέρμα, τό** 1 • 1 *end, limit, boundary*
**ὑπογραμμός, ὁ** 3 • 4 *example*

## Chapter 6

1 **αἰκία, ἡ** 3 • 3 *mistreatment, torture*
**βάσανος, ἡ** 1 • 18 *torture, torment*
**ἐκλεκτός** 12 • 30 *chosen*
**ζῆλος, ὁ/τό** 22 • 25 *jealousy, envy*
**ὁσίως** 8 • 9 *devoutly*
**πολιτεύομαι** 6 • 10 *to live, lead/ conduct one's life*
**συναθροίζω** 1 • 2 *to unite with, be joined to*
**ὑπόδειγμα, τό** 6 • 8 *example, model, pattern*
2 **αἴκισμα, τό** 2 • 2 *mistreatment, torment*
**ἀνόσιος** 3 • 3 *unholy*
**ἀσθενής** 4 • 12 *(physically) weak*
**βέβαιος** 3 • 9 *abiding, steadfast*
**γενναῖος** 5 • 8 *noble, illustrious*
**γέρας, τό** 1 • 1 *prize, reward*
**Δαναΐδες, αἱ** 1 • 1 *the Danaids*
**δεινός** 1 • 7 *fearful, terrible*
**Δίρκη, ἡ** 1 • 1 *Dirce*
**δρόμος, ὁ** 2 • 5 *course, goal*
**ζῆλος, ὁ/τό** 22 • 25 *jealousy, envy*
**καταντάω** 3 • 4 *to arrive at, attain, meet*
3 **Ἀδάμ, ὁ** 3 • 4 *Adam*
**ἀλλοιόω** 2 • 5 *to change, change in order to make void*
**ἀπαλλοτριόω** 2 • 2 *to estrange, alienate*
**γαμετή, ἡ** 1 • 1 *wife*
**ζῆλος, ὁ/τό** 22 • 25 *jealousy, envy*
**ὀστέον, τό** [2] 4 • 6 *bone*
4 **ἐκριζόω** 1 • 2 *to uproot, utterly destroy*
**ἔρις, ἡ** 9 • 10 *strife, discord, contention*
**ζῆλος, ὁ/τό** 22 • 25 *jealousy, envy*
**καταστρέφω** 2 • 5 *to destroy, ruin*

## Chapter 7

1 **ἀγών, ὁ** 2 • 7 *contest, race*
**ἐπίκειμαι** 2 • 6 *to confront*
**ἐπιστέλλω** 3 • 3 *to inform/ instruct by letter*
**νουθετέω** 1 • 9 *to admonish, warn, instruct*
**σκάμμα, τό** 1 • 1 *arena*
**ὑπομιμνήσκω** 3 • 4 *to remind*
2 **ἀπολείπω** 4 • 6 *to put aside, give up*
**εὐκλεής** 1 • 1 *famous, renowned*
**κανών, ὁ** 3 • 4 *rule, standard*
**κενός** 1 • 26 *empty*
**μάταιος** 2 • 14 *idle, empty, fruitless, useless, powerless, lacking truth*
**παράδοσις, ἡ** 1 • 7 *tradition*
**σεμνός** 6 • 12 *honorable, worthy, venerable, holy, above reproach*
**φροντίς, ἡ** 2 • 3 *reflection, thought, care, concern*
3 **προσδεκτός** 1 • 3 *acceptable*
**τερπνός** 1 • 1 *delightful, pleasant, pleasing*
4 **ἀτενίζω** 5 • 5 *to look intently at, stare at*
**ἐκχέω/ἐκχύννω** 2 • 6 *to pour out*
**ἡμέτερος** 3 • 13 *our*
**μετάνοια, ἡ** 9 • 72 *repentance, turning about, conversion*
**τίμιος** 1 • 3 *of great worth/value, precious*
**ὑποφέρω** 3 • 12 *to bear, bring, effect*
**χάριν** 3 • 4 *for the sake of, on behalf of, on account of*; possibly *grace* (as acc. direct object)
5 **δεσπότης, ὁ** 24 • 52 *lord, master*
**καταμανθάνω** 1 • 4 *to observe (well), notice, learn*
**μετάνοια, ἡ** 9 • 72 *repentance, turning about, conversion*
**ἐν γενεᾷ καὶ γενεᾷ** *from generation to generation*
6 **μετάνοια, ἡ** 9 • 72 *repentance, turning about, conversion*
**Νῶε, ὁ** 2 • 3 *Noah*
**ὑπακούω** 5 • 9 *to obey, follow, be subject to*

7 ἀλλότριος 2 • 14 *not one's own, strange, another's (slave), alien (to God)*
ἁμάρτημα, τό 1 • 8 *sin, transgression*
ἐξιλάσκομαι 1 • 2 *to appease*
ἱκετεύω 3 • 3 *to supplicate, beseech*
Ἰωνᾶς, ὁ 1 • 1 *Jonah*
καίπερ 2 • 7 *although*
καταστροφή, ἡ 2 • 2 *ruin, destruction*
Νινευίτης, ὁ 1 • 1 *Ninevite*

## Chapter 8

1 λειτουργός, ὁ 3 • 3 *servant, minister*
μετάνοια, ἡ 9 • 72 *repentance, turning about, conversion*
2 γνώμη, ἡ 1 • 20 *declaration, decision, resolution*
δεσπότης, ὁ 24 • 52 *lord, master*
μετάνοια, ἡ [2] 9 • 72 *repentance, turning about, conversion*
ὅρκος, ὁ 1 • 2 *oath*
προστίθημι 2 • 22 *to add, put to*
3 ἀνομία, ἡ 12 • 33 *lawlessness*
ἐπακούω 1 • 3 *to hear, listen to*
κόκκος, ὁ 1 • 1 *scarlet (color)*
μέλας 1 • 20 *black*
πυρρός 1 • 1 *fiery red*
σάκκος, ὁ 1 • 4 *sack, sackcloth*
4 ἀδικέω 2 • 7 *to do wrong to someone, treat someone unjustly*
ἀπέναντι 1 • 3 *opposite, before*
ἀφαιρέω 2 • 8 *to take away, do away with, remove*
δεῦτε 2 • 2 *Come here! Come on!*
διελέγχω 1 • 1 *to engage in dispute*
εἰσακούω [2] 4 • 4 *to obey*
ἐκζητέω 4 • 16 *to seek out, search for*
ἔριον, τό 1 • 10 *wool*
καθαρός 7 • 45 *pure, free*
κατεσθίω 1 • 3 *to devour, utterly destroy*
κόκκινος 2 • 7 *red, scarlet*
λευκαίνω [2] 3 • 3 *to make white*
λούω 1 • 2 *to wash oneself, bath oneself, cleanse, bathe*
μανθάνω 3 • 26 *to learn*
μάχαιρα, ἡ 1 • 3 *sword, dagger*
ὀρφανός 1 • 9 *without parents, orphan*
παύω 3 • 12 *to stop (oneself), cease*
πονηρία, ἡ 2 • 41 *wickedness, baseness, maliciousness, sinfulness*
ῥύομαι 12 • 19 *to save, rescue, deliver, preserve*
φοινικοῦς 1 • 1 *purple(-red) color/garment*
χήρα, ἡ 1 • 13 *widow*
χιών, ἡ 2 • 3 *snow*
5 βούλημα, τό 5 • 5 *intention*
μετάνοια, ἡ 9 • 72 *repentance, turning about, conversion*
μετέχω 1 • 4 *to share, have a share, participate*
παντοκρατορικός 1 • 1 *almighty*
στηρίζω 5 • 8 *to confirm, establish, strengthen*

## Chapter 9

1 ἀπολείπω 4 • 6 *to put aside, give up*
βούλησις, ἡ 4 • 4 *will*
ἔλεος, τό 7 • 19 *mercy, compassion, pity, clemency*
ἔνδοξος 8 • 54 *glorious, splendid*
ἔρις, ἡ 9 • 10 *strife, discord, contention*
ζῆλος, ὁ/τό 22 • 25 *jealousy, envy*
ἱκέτης, ὁ 1 • 1 *suppliant*
ματαιοπονία, ἡ 1 • 1 *fruitless toil*
μεγαλοπρεπής 7 • 7 *magnificent, sublime, majestic, impressive*
οἰκτιρμός 4 • 4 *pity, mercy, compassion*
προσπίπτω 2 • 3 *to fall down before/at the feet of*
ὑπακούω 5 • 9 *to obey, follow, be subject to*
χρηστότης, ἡ 1 • 9 *goodness, kindness, generosity*
2 ἀτενίζω 5 • 5 *to look intently at, stare at*
λειτουργέω 6 • 11 *to serve, render service*
μεγαλοπρεπής 7 • 7 *magnificent, sublime, majestic, impressive*
τελείως 1 • 8 *fully, perfectly, completely, altogether*

3 **Ἐνώχ, ὁ** 1 • 2 *Enoch*
**μετατίθημι** 1 • 9 *to put in another place, transfer, take up, translate, take away*
**ὑπακοή, ἡ** 5 • 5 *obedience*
4 **δεσπότης, ὁ** 24 • 52 *lord, master*
**διασῴζω** 3 • 4 *to bring safely through, save, rescue*
**ζῷον, τό** 6 • 8 *living creature*
**κιβωτός, ἡ** 1 • 1 *boat, ark*
**λειτουργία, ἡ** 8 • 11 *service, service to God*
**Νῶε, ὁ** 2 • 3 *Noah*
**ὁμόνοια, ἡ** 14 • 24 *oneness of mind, unanimity, concord, harmony*
**παλιγγενεσία, ἡ** 1 • 1 *renewal*

## Chapter 10

1 **προσαγορεύω** 2 • 5 *to call, name, designate*
**ὑπήκοος** 5 • 5 *obedient*
**φίλος** 2 • 8 *loving;* subst. *friend*
2 **ἀσθενής** 4 • 12 *weak, without influence*
**καταλείπω** 1 • 12 *to leave, give up*
**κληρονομέω** 4 • 11 *to acquire, obtain, come into possession of*
**συγγένεια, ἡ** [2] 3 • 3 *relationship, kinship*
**ὑπακοή, ἡ** 5 • 5 *obedience*
3 **καταράομαι** [2] 4 • 5 *to curse, execrate*
**μεγαλύνω** 3 • 3 *to make large/long, make great*
**συγγένεια, ἡ** 3 • 3 *relationship, kinship*
4 **ἀναβλέπω** 2 • 7 *to look up*
**ἀνατολή, ἡ** 2 • 6 *east, orient*
**βορρᾶς, ὁ** 1 • 1 *the north*
**διαχωρίζω** 2 • 2 *to separate*
**ἴδε** 2 • 10 *look!, see!*
**λίψ, ὁ** 1 • 1 *the southwest*
**Λώτ, ὁ** 2 • 2 *Lot*
5 **ἄμμος, ἡ** [2] 2 • 2 *sand*
**ἐξαριθμέω** [2] 3 • 3 *to count*
6 **ἀναβλέπω** 2 • 7 *to look up*
**ἀριθμέω** 1 • 1 *to count*
**ἀστήρ, ὁ** 3 • 7 *star, single star, planet*
**ἐξάγω** 3 • 7 *to lead out, bring out*
**ἐξαριθμέω** 3 • 3 *to count*
7 **γῆρας, τό** 2 • 2 *old age*
**θυσία, ἡ** 10 • 22 *sacrifice, offering*
**ὑπακοή, ἡ** 5 • 5 *obedience*
**φιλοξενία, ἡ** 4 • 5 *hospitality*

## Chapter 11

1 **αἰκισμός, ὁ** 1 • 1 *mistreatment, punishment*
**δεσπότης, ὁ** 24 • 52 *lord, master*
**ἐγκαταλείπω** 2 • 8 *to forsake, abandon, desert*
**ἑτεροκλινής** 2 • 2 *inclined to, having a propensity for*
**εὐσέβεια, ἡ** 4 • 6 *devoutness, piety, godliness*
**θεῖον, τό** 1 • 1 *sulfur*
**κόλασις, ἡ** 1 • 11 *punishment*
**Λώτ, ὁ** 2 • 2 *Lot*
**περίχωρος** 1 • 1 *neighboring*
**πρόδηλος** 4 • 4 *clear, evident, known (to all)*
**Σόδομα, τό** 1 • 1 *Sodom*
**φιλοξενία, ἡ** 4 • 5 *hospitality*
2 **ἅλς, ὁ** 1 • 1 *salt;*
**ἅλς** is the usual form in classical Greek; only the form **ἅλας** occurs in the NT.
**γνωστός** 1 • 3 *known*
**διστάζω** 2 • 10 *to doubt, waver*
**δίψυχος** 2 • 23 *doubting, hesitating*
**ἑτερογνώμων** 1 • 1 *of a different opinion*
**κρίμα, τό** 8 • 9 *judicial verdict*
**ὁμόνοια, ἡ** 14 • 24 *oneness of mind, unanimity, concord, harmony*
**σημείωσις, ἡ** 1 • 1 *sign, signal*
**στήλη, ἡ** 1 • 2 *monument, pillar*
**συνεξέρχομαι** 1 • 1 *to go out with*

## Chapter 12

1 **πόρνη, ἡ** 1 • 1 *prostitute, whore*
**Ῥαάβ, ἡ** 2 • 2 *Rahab*
**φιλοξενία, ἡ** 4 • 5 *hospitality*
2 **ἐκπέμπω** [2] 3 • 3 *to send out*
**ἥκω** 5 • 11 *to have come, be present*
**θανατόω** 2 • 7 *to put to death*
**Ἰεριχώ, ἡ** 1 • 1 *Jericho*

**κατασκοπεύω** 1 • 1 *to spy out*
**κατάσκοπος, ὁ** 2 • 3 *a spy*
**Ναυή, ὁ** 1 • 3 *Nun*
**συλλαμβάνω** [2] 3 • 11 *to seize, grasp, apprehend*
**χώρα, ἡ** 3 • 6 *district, region, place*
3 **εἰσδέχομαι** 1 • 1 *to take in*
**κρύπτω** 3 • 4 *to conceal, hide*
**λινοκαλάμη, ἡ** 1 • 1 *a stalk of flax*
**Ῥαάβ, ἡ** 2 • 2 *Rahab*
**ὑπερῷον, τό** 1 • 2 *upper story, room upstairs*
**φιλόξενος** 1 • 3 *hospitable*
4 **ἐναλλάξ** 1 • 2 *in the opposite direction, crosswise, wrong direction*
**ἐξάγω** 3 • 7 *to lead out, bring out*
**ἐφίστημι** 1 • 5 *to stand at/near*
**ζητέω** 4 • 19 *to seek, look for*
**κατάσκοπος, ὁ** 2 • 3 *a spy*
**κελεύω** 5 • 44 *to command, order, urge*
**ὑποδεικνύω** 1 • 1 *to* show, indicate
5 **διασῴζω** 3 • 4 *to bring safely through, save/rescue*
**ἐπιπίπτω** 1 • 2 *to happen to, befall*
**τρόμος** 1 • 2 *trembling, quivering*
6 **διασῴζω** 3 • 4 *to bring safely through, save/rescue*
**σός** 2 • 9 *your, yours*
**στέγος, τό** 1 • 1 *roof*
7 **ἐκκρεμάννυμι** 1 • 1 *to hang out*
**κόκκινος** 2 • 7 *red, scarlet*
**λύτρωσις, ἡ** 1 • 2 *ransoming, releasing, redemption*
**πρόδηλος** 4 • 4 *clear, evident, known (to all)*
**προστίθημι** 2 • 22 *to add, put to*
8 **προφητεία, ἡ** 1 • 4 *gift of prophesying*

## Chapter 13

1 **ἀλαζονεία, ἡ** 5 • 10 *pretension, arrogance*
**ἀποτίθημι** 3 • 13 *to take off, lay aside, rid oneself*
**ἀφροσύνη, ἡ** 2 • 11 *foolishness, lack of sense*
**ἐκζητέω** 4 • 16 *to seek out, search for*
**ἐπιείκεια, ἡ** 5 • 9 *clemency, gentleness, graciousness, courtesy, indulgence, tolerance*
**ἰσχυρός** 4 • 21 *strong*
**ἰσχύς, ἡ** 5 • 11 *strength, power, might*
**κρίμα, τό** 8 • 9 *justice*
**μακροθυμία, ἡ** 3 • 15 *forbearance, patience*
**μάλιστα** 2 • 14 *most of all, above all, especially, particularly*
**μιμνῄσκομαι** 3 • 9 *to remember, recollect, remind oneself*
**πλούσιος** 3 • 22 *rich, wealthy*
**πλοῦτος, ὁ** 1 • 15 *wealth*
**σοφός** 4 • 8 *wise, learned*
**ταπεινοφρονέω** 11 • 14 *to be modest, be unassuming*
**τῦφος, τό** 1 • 1 *delusion, conceit, arrogance*
2 **ἐλεάω** [2] 2 • 4 *to have mercy on*
**μετρέω** [2] 2 • 5 *to give out, deal out, apportion*
**μέτρον, τό** 1 • 3 *measure*
**χρηστεύομαι** [2] 3 • 3 *to be kind, be loving, be merciful*
3 **ἁγιοπρεπής** 1 • 2 *holy, proper/ fitting for one who is holy*
**παράγγελμα, τό** 2 • 2 *order, direction, instruction, precept*
**στηρίζω** 5 • 8 *to confirm, establish, strengthen*
**ταπεινοφρονέω** 11 • 14 *to be modest, be unassuming*
**ὑπήκοος** 5 • 5 *obedient*
4 **ἐπιβλέπω** 2 • 2 *to look upon*
**ἡσύχιος** 1 • 7 *quiet, well-ordered*
**λόγιον, τό** 4 • 11 *a saying*
**πραΰς** 1 • 8 *gentle, humble, considerate, meek*
**τρέμω** 1 • 3 *to tremble, be in awe*

## Chapter 14

1 **ἀκαταστασία, ἡ** 3 • 4 *disorder, unruliness*
**ἀλαζονεία, ἡ** 5 • 10 *pretension, arrogance*
**ἀρχηγός, ὁ** 3 • 4 *instigator*
**ἐξακολουθέω** 1 • 1 *to obey, follow*
**ζῆλος, ὁ/τό** 22 • 25 *jealousy, envy*
**μυσερός** 2 • 2 *loathsome, abominable, detestable*

**ὅσιος** 6 • 10 *devout, pious, pleasing to God, holy*
**ὑπήκοος** 5 • 5 *obedient*
2 **ἀπαλλοτριόω** 2 • 2 *to estrange, alienate*
**βλάβη, ἡ** 1 • 2 *harm*
**ἐξακοντίζω** 1 • 1 *to hurl out, aim at, plunge into*
**ἐπιδίδωμι** 1 • 62 *to give up/over, surrender*
**ἔρις, ἡ** 9 • 10 *strife, discord, contention*
**κίνδυνος, ὁ** 6 • 8 *danger, risk*
**ῥιψοκινδύνως** 1 • 1 *rashly, recklessly*
**στάσις, ἡ** 9 • 9 *strife, discord, disunion*
**τυγχάνω** 2 • 15 *to happen, turn out;*
**βλάβην οὐ τὴν τυχοῦσαν** (attributive participle with **οὐ** between noun and participle) *no ordinary harm*
**ὑποφέρω** 3 • 12 *to submit to, endure*
3 **γλυκύτης, ἡ** 1 • 2 *sweetness*
**εὐσπλαγχνία, ἡ** 1 • 1 *tenderheartedness, benevolence*
**χρηστεύομαι** 3 • 3 *to be kind, be loving, be merciful*
4 **ἄκακος** 1 • 7 *innocent, guileless*
**οἰκήτωρ, ὁ** 1 • 1 *inhabitant*
**παρανομέω** 1 • 1 *to break the law, act contrary to the law*
**ὑπολείπω** 1 • 1 *to leave remaining*
**χρηστός** 1 • 2 *kind, loving, benevolent*
5 **ἀκακία, ἡ** 1 • 10 *innocence, guilelessness*
**ἀσεβής** 5 • 14 *irreverent, impious, ungodly*
**ἐγκατάλειμμα, τό** 1 • 1 *remnant, posterity*
**εἰρηνικός** 1 • 1 *peaceable, peaceful*
**ἐκζητέω** 4 • 16 *to seek out, search for*
**ἐξολεθρεύω** 4 • 5 *to destroy utterly, root out;*
**Ἐξολεθρεύσαι** (voluntative optative) *May (the Lord) utterly destroy*
**ἐπαίρω** 5 • 6 *to lift up, hold up*
**εὐθύτης, ἡ** 1 • 2 *righteousness, uprightness*
**ἴδε** 2 • 10 *Look! See! Behold!*
**κέδρος, ἡ** 1 • 1 *cedar tree*
**Λίβανος, ὁ** 2 • 2 *Lebanon*
**παρέρχομαι** 4 • 12 *to go by, pass by*
**ὑπερυψόω** 1 • 1 *to raise, exalt*

## Chapter 15

1 **εἰρηνεύω** 5 • 17 *to keep the peace*
**εὐσέβεια, ἡ** 4 • 6 *devoutness, piety, godliness*
**κολλάω** 10 • 32 *to join oneself to, join, cling to, associate with unite with*
**τοίνυν** 1 • 2 *hence, so, well (then), indeed*
**ὑπόκρισις, ἡ** 1 • 13 *play-acting, pretense, outward show, dissembling*
2 **ἄπειμι** 2 • 5 *to be absent/away*
**πόρρω** 5 • 8 *far (away)*
**πού** 5 • 7 *somewhere*
**τιμάω** 4 • 12 *to honor, revere*
**χεῖλος, τό** 7 • 11 *the lips*
3 **καταράομαι** 4 • 5 *to curse, execrate*
4 **εὐθύς** 1 • 2 *proper, right, upright*
**πιστόω** 2 • 2 *to show oneself faithful*
**ψεύδω/ψεύδομαι** 4 • 6 *to tell lies to, impose*
5 **ἄλαλος** 1 • 1 *mute, unable to speak*
**ἀνομία, ἡ** 12 • 33 *a lawless deed*
**δόλιος** [2] 2 • 3 *deceitful, treacherous*
**ἐξολεθρεύω** 4 • 5 *to destroy utterly, root out*
**μεγαλορήμων/μεγαλορρήμων** 1 • 1 *boastful*
**μεγαλύνω** 3 • 3 *to exalt, glorify, magnify, speak highly of*
**χεῖλος, τό** [3] 7 • 11 *the lips*
6 **πένης** 1 • 16 *poor, needy*
**πτωχός** 3 • 9 *poor, lacking in spiritual worth*
**στεναγμός, ὁ** 1 • 2 *sigh, groan, groaning*
**σωτήριος** 2 • 2 *saving, delivering, preserving, bringing salvation*
**ταλαιπωρία, ἡ** 1 • 1 *wretchedness, distress, trouble, misery*

7 **παρρησιάζω/παρρησιάζομαι** 2 • 2 *to deal openly (boldly)*

## Chapter 16

1 **ἐπαίρω** 5 • 6 *to be in opposition, rise up*
**ποίμνιον, τό** 4 • 7 *flock;* fig. *defined group of persons*
**ταπεινοφρονέω** 11 • 14 *to be modest, be unassuming*
2 **ἀλαζονεία, ἡ** 5 • 10 *pretension, arrogance*
**καίπερ** 2 • 7 *although*
**κόμπος, ὁ** 1 • 1 *boasting, brassiness*
**μεγαλωσύνη, ἡ** 8 • 10 *majesty*
**σκῆπτρον, τό** 2 • 2 *scepter*
**ταπεινοφρονέω** 11 • 14 *to be modest, be unassuming*
**ὑπερηφανία, ἡ** 3 • 8 *arrogance, haughtiness, pride*
3 **ἀκοή, ἡ** 2 • 8 *account, report, message*
**ἀναγγέλλω** 4 • 8 *to disclose, announce, proclaim, teach*
**ἀποκαλύπτω** 1 • 23 *to reveal, disclose, bring to light, make fully known*
**ἀποστρέφω** 2 • 8 *to turn away*
**ἀτιμάζω** 1 • 3 *to dishonor/shame*
**ἄτιμος** 2 • 3 *dishonored, despised*
**βραχίων, ὁ** 2 • 2 *arm*
**διψάω** 1 • 2 *to be thirsty*
**εἶδος, τό** [4] 4 • 6 *form, outward appearance*
**ἐκλείπω** 1 • 1 *to be inferior*
**ἐναντίον** 2 • 5 *in the sight of, before*
**κάλλος, τό** 1 • 5 *beauty*
**μαλακία, ἡ** 1 • 3 *debility, weakness, sickness*
**πληγή, ἡ** 3 • 5 *blow*
**πόνος, ὁ** 4 • 6 *pain, distress, affliction*
**ῥίζα, ἡ** 2 • 8 *shoot, scion, descendant*
4 **κάκωσις, ἡ** 1 • 1 *mistreatment, oppression*
**ὀδυνάω** 1 • 1 *to suffer pain*
**πληγή, ἡ** 3 • 5 *blow*
**πόνος, ὁ** 4 • 6 *pain, distress, affliction*
5 **ἀνομία, ἡ** 12 • 33 *a lawless deed*
**ἰάομαι** 3 • 11 *to restore, heal*
**μαλακίζω/μαλακίζομαι** 1 • 2 *to be/become weak/discouraged/sick*
**μώλωψ, ὁ** 1 • 2 *welt, wale, bruise, wound*
**παιδεία, ἡ** 7 • 11 *upbringing, training, instruction, discipline, correction*
**τραυματίζω** 1 • 2 *to wound*
7 **ἀμνός, ὁ** 1 • 2 *lamb*
**ἄφωνος** 1 • 2 *silent, mute*
**ἐναντίον** 2 • 5 *in the sight of, before*
**κακόω** 1 • 1 *to harm, mistreat*
**κείρω** 1 • 2 *to shear*
**σφαγή, ἡ** 1 • 3 *slaughter*
**ταπείνωσις, ἡ** 3 • 4 *humiliation*
8 **διηγέομαι** 3 • 4 *to tell, relate, describe*
9 **ἀνομία, ἡ** 12 • 33 *a lawless deed*
**ἥκω** 5 • 11 *to have come, be present*
10 **ἀνομία, ἡ** 12 • 33 *a lawless deed*
**ἀντί** [2] 4 • 15 *instead of, in place of*
**δόλος, ὁ** 4 • 8 *deceit, cunning, treachery*
**πληγή, ἡ** 3 • 5 *blow*
**πλούσιος** 3 • 22 *rich, wealthy*
**ταφή, ἡ** 1 • 1 *burial*
11 **μακρόβιος** 1 • 1 *long-lived*
12 **ἀναφέρω** 2 • 8 *to take up*
**ἀφαιρέω** 2 • 8 *to take away, do away with, remove*
**δουλεύω** 4 • 42 *to (perform the duties of a slave) serve, obey*
**εὖ** 1 • 1 *well*
**πλάσσω** 3 • 8 *to shape*
**πόνος** 4 • 6 *pain, distress, affliction*
**σύνεσις, ἡ** 3 • 22 *intelligence, acuteness, shrewdness*
13 **ἄνομος** 5 • 17 *lawless*
**ἀντί** 4 • 15 *instead of, in the place of*
**ἰσχυρός** 4 • 21 *strong*
**κληρονομέω** 4 • 11 *to inherit*
**μερίζω** 1 • 1 *to make an allotment, distribute*
**σκῦλον, τό** 1 • 1 *booty, spoils*
14 **ἀναφέρω** 2 • 8 *to take up*
15 **ἐξουθένημα, τό** 1 • 1 *a despised thing*

**ὄνειδος, τό** 1 • 1 *disgrace, reproach, insult*
**σκώληξ, ὁ** 2 • 5 *worm*
16 **ἐκμυκτηρίζω** 1 • 1 *to ridicule, sneer*
**κινέω** 1 • 3 *to move, set in motion*
**ῥύομαι** 12 • 19 *to save, rescue, deliver, preserve*
**χεῖλος, τό** 7 • 11 *the lips*
17 **ζυγός, ὁ** 1 • 3 *yoke*
**ταπεινοφρονέω** 11 • 14 *to be modest, be unassuming*
**ὑπογραμμός, ὁ** 3 • 4 *example*

## Chapter 17

1 **αἴγειος** 1 • 2 *of a goat*
**δέρμα, τό** 1 • 3 *skin, hide*
**ἔλευσις, ἡ** 1 • 2 *coming, arrival*
**Ἐλισαιέ, ὁ** 1 • 1 *Elisha*
**Ἠλίας, ὁ** 1 • 1 *Elijah*
**Ἰεζεκιήλ, ὁ** 1 • 2 *Ezekiel*
**μηλωτή, ἡ** 1 • 1 *sheepskin*
**μιμητής, ὁ** 1 • 12 *imitator*
2 **ἀτενίζω** 5 • 5 *to look intently at, stare at*
**μεγάλως** 3 • 9 *greatly*
**προσαγορεύω** 2 • 5 *to call, name, designate*
**σποδός, ἡ** 1 • 4 *ashes*
**ταπεινοφρονέω** 11 • 14 *to be modest, be unassuming*
**φίλος** 2 • 8 *loving;* subst. *friend*
3 **ἀληθινός** 2 • 14 *true, trustworthy*
**ἄμεμπτος** 2 • 4 *blameless, faultless*
**ἀπέχω** 1 • 35 *to keep away, abstain, refrain from*
**θεοσεβής** 1 • 2 *God-fearing, devout*
**Ἰώβ, ὁ** [2] 3 • 4 *Job*
4 **καθαρός** 7 • 45 *pure, free*
**κατηγορέω** 1 • 1 *to accuse, reproach*
**ῥύπος, ὁ** 1 • 3 *uncleanness*
5 **Αἴγυπτος, ἡ** 6 • 9 *Egypt*
**αἴκισμα, τό** 2 • 2 *mistreatment, torment*
**βάτος, ὁ** 1 • 1 *thorn-bush*
**βραδύγλωσσος** 1 • 1 *slow of tongue*
**ἰσχνόφωνος** 1 • 1 *weak-voiced, having an impediment in one's speech*
**μάστιξ, ἡ** 3 • 8 *torment, suffering*
**μεγαλορημονέω** 1 • 1 *to use great words, boast*
**μεγάλως** 3 • 9 *greatly*
**ὑπηρεσία, ἡ** 1 • 2 *service*
**χρηματισμός, ὁ** 1 • 1 *a divine statement, answer*
6 **ἀτμίς, ἡ** 1 • 1 *vapor, steam*
**κύθρα, ἡ** 1 • 1 *a pot*

## Chapter 18

1 **ἔλεος, τό** 7 • 19 *mercy, compassion, pity, clemency*
**Ἰεσσαί, ὁ** 1 • 1 *Jesse*
**χρίω** 1 • 2 *to anoint*
2 **ἀνόμημα, τό** 1 • 2 *lawless action, iniquity*
**ἐλεέω** 3 • 16 *to have compassion/mercy/pity*
**ἔλεος, τό** 7 • 19 *mercy, compassion, pity, clemency*
**ἐξαλείφω** 5 • 8 *to remove, destroy, obliterate*
**οἰκτιρμός, ὁ** 4 • 4 *pity, mercy, compassion*
3 **ἀνομία, ἡ** [2] 12 • 33 *lawlessness*
**πλύνω** 2 • 2 *to free from*
4 **νικάω** 1 • 8 *to be victor, conquer, overcome, prevail*
5 **ἀνομία, ἡ** 12 • 33 *a lawless deed*
**κισ jσάω** 1 • 1 *to become pregnant (with someone), crave*
**συλλαμβάνω** 3 • 11 *to become pregnant, conceive*
6 **ἄδηλος** 1 • 1 *not clear, latent, unseen*
**δηλόω** 2 • 49 *to reveal, make clear, show*
**κρύφιος** 1 • 4 *hidden, secret*
7 **λευκαίνω** 3 • 3 *to make white*
**πλύνω** 2 • 2 *to free from*
**ῥαντίζω** 1 • 4 *to sprinkle*
**ὕσσωπος, ὁ** 1 • 1 *hyssop*
**χιών, ἡ** 2 • 3 *snow*
8 **ἀγαλλιάομαι/ἀγαλλιάω** 2 • 2 *to exult, be glad, be overjoyed*
**ἀγαλλίασις, ἡ** 3 • 5 *exultation*
**ἀκουτίζω** 1 • 1 *to cause to hear*

εὐφροσύνη, ἡ 1 • 5 *joy, gladness, cheerfulness*
ὀστέον, τό 4 • 6 *bone*
ταπεινόω 4 • 8 *to humble, make humble*
9 ἀνομία, ἡ 12 • 33 *a lawless deed*
ἀποστρέφω 2 • 8 *to turn away*
ἐξαλείφω 5 • 8 *to remove, destroy, obliterate*
10 ἐγκαινίζω 1 • 1 *to renew*
ἔγκατα, τά 1 • 1 *inmost parts*
εὐθής 1 • 1 *upright*
καθαρός 7 • 45 *pure, free*
κτίζω 3 • 25 *to create*
11 ἀνταναιρέω 1 • 1 *to take away*
ἀπορρίπτω 2 • 3 *to drive/scare away*
12 ἀγαλλίασις, ἡ 3 • 5 *exultation*
ἡγεμονικός 1 • 1 *guiding, leading*
στηρίζω 5 • 8 *to confirm, establish, strengthen*
σωτήριος 2 • 2 *saving, delivering, preserving, bringing salvation*
13 ἄνομος 5 • 17 *lawless*
ἀσεβής 5 • 14 *irreverent, impious, ungodly*
14 ῥύομαι 12 • 19 *to save, rescue, deliver, preserve*
15 ἀγαλλιάομαι/ἀγαλλιάω 2 • 2 *to exult, rejoice, be glad, be overjoyed*
αἴνεσις, ἡ 3 • 3 *praise*
ἀναγγέλλω 4 • 8 *to disclose, announce, proclaim, teach*
χεῖλος, τό 7 • 11 *the lips*
16 εὐδοκέω 2 • 2 *to be well pleased, take delight*
θυσία, ἡ 10 • 22 *sacrifice, offering*
ὁλοκαύτωμα, τό 1 • 7 *whole burnt offering, holocaust*
17 ἐξουθενέω 1 • 2 *to disdain*
θυσία, ἡ 10 • 22 *sacrifice, offering*
συντρίβω [2] 4 • 10 pass. *to be broken (with regard to an emotional state)*
ταπεινόω 4 • 8 *to humble, make humble*

## Chapter 19

1 βελτίων 1 • 6 *better*
καταδέχομαι 1 • 2 *to receive, accept*
λόγιον, τό 4 • 11 *a saying*
ταπεινόφρων 1 • 4 *humble*
τοσοῦτος 9 • 38 *so much, so great*
ὑπακοή, ἡ 5 • 5 *obedience*
ὑποδεής 1 • 2 *subservient*
2 ἀτενίζω 5 • 5 *to look intently at, stare at*
δωρεά, ἡ 4 • 7 *gift, bounty*
ἔνδοξος 8 • 54 *glorious, splendid*
ἐπανατρέχω 1 • 1 *to race*
εὐεργεσία, ἡ 3 • 5 *good deed, benefit, a kindness*
κολλάω 10 • 32 *to cling to, enter into a close relation with*
κτίστης, ὁ 3 • 3 *the Creator*
μεγαλοπρεπής 7 • 7 *magnificent, sublime, majestic, impressive*
μεταλαμβάνω 3 • 12 *to have a share in*
πρᾶξις, ἡ 2 • 50 *act, action, deed*
σκοπός, ὁ 2 • 3 *goal, mark*
σύμπας 1 • 3 *all (together), whole*
ὑπερβάλλω 2 • 4 *to go beyond, surpass, outdo*
3 ἀόργητος 1 • 3 *free from anger*
βούλημα, τό 5 • 5 *intention*
διάνοια, ἡ 8 • 22 *understanding, intelligence, mind*
ἐμβλέπω 1 • 5 *to look at, consider*
κτίσις, ἡ 3 • 19 *that which is created*
μακρόθυμος 1 • 9 *patient, forbearing, tolerant, even-tempered*
νοέω 3 • 46 *to consider, take note of*
ὄμμα, τό 1 • 1 *eye*

## Chapter 20

1 διοίκησις, ἡ 1 • 2 *administration, management*
σαλεύω 1 • 1 *to shake, cause to waver/totter, move*
2 διανύω 2 • 2 *to complete*
δρόμος, ὁ 2 • 5 *course*
ἐμποδίζω 1 • 2 *to hinder*
τάσσω 2 • 4 *to order, fix, determine, appoint*
3 ἀστήρ, ὁ 3 • 7 *star, single star, planet*
διαταγή, ἡ 1 • 1 *ordinance, direction*

**δίχα** 9 • 9 *apart from, without*
**ἐξελίσσω** 1 • 1 *to unroll*
**ἐπιτάσσω** 2 • 7 *to order, command*
**ὁμόνοια, ἡ** 14 • 24 *oneness of mind, unanimity, concord, harmony*
**ὁρισμός, ὁ** 1 • 1 *a fixed course*
**παρέκβασις, ἡ** 1 • 1 *deviation*
**σελήνη, ἡ** 1 • 7 *moon*
**χορός, ὁ** 1 • 4 *troop, band*
4 **ἀλλοιόω** 2 • 5 *to change*
**ἀνατέλλω** 1 • 6 *to cause to spring/rise up*
**διχοστατέω** 1 • 3 *to disagree*
**δογματίζω** 2 • 2 *to obligate*
**ζῷον, τό** 6 • 8 *animal*
**θήρ, ὁ** 2 • 2 *(wild) animal*
**κυοφορέω** 1 • 2 *to be pregnant, be fruitful*
**παμπληθής/πανπληθής** 1 • 1 *in full abundance, a vast amount of*
**τροφή, ἡ** 1 • 12 *nourishment, food*
5 **ἄβυσσος, ἡ** 3 • 4 *depth, abyss*
**ἀνεκδιήγητος** 3 • 3 *indescribable*
**ἀνεξιχνίαστος** 1 • 2 *inscrutable, incomprehensible*
**κρίμα, τό** 8 • 9 *judicial verdict*
**νέρτερος** 1 • 1 *lower, nether, belonging to the world*
**πρόσταγμα, τό** 7 • 10 *order, command(ment), injunction*
**συνέχω** 1 • 4 *hold together, sustain*
6 **ἄπειρος** 1 • 1 *boundless*
**δημιουργία, ἡ** 1 • 2 *creative act*
**διατάσσω** 3 • 8 *to order*
**κλεῖθρον, τό** 1 • 1 *barrier*
**κύτος, τό** 1 • 1 *hollow (place)*
**παρεκβαίνω** 2 • 2 *to go beyond, transgress*
**περιτίθημι** 2 • 6 *to put/place around/on*
**συνίστημι** 2 • 3 *to unite, collect*
7 **ἥκω** 5 • 11 *to have come, be present*
**κῦμα, τό** 1 • 1 *wave*
**συντρίβω** 4 • 10 *to shatter, smash, crush*
8 **ἀπέρατος** 1 • 1 *endless, limitless*
**δεσπότης, ὁ** 24 • 52 *lord, master*
**διευθύνω** 3 • 3 *to guide, direct, govern*
**ταγή, ἡ** 1 • 1 *command, decree*
**ὠκεανός, ὁ** 1 • 1 *ocean*
9 **ἐαρινός** 1 • 1 *of spring*
**θερινός** 1 • 1 *of summer*
**μεταπαραδίδωμι** 1 • 1 *to give place to, succeed, follow*
**μετοπωρινός** 1 • 1 *autumnal*
**χειμερινός** 1 • 1 *winter*
10 **ἀέναος** 2 • 2 *ever-flowing*
**ἄνεμος, ὁ** 1 • 4 *the four directions, cardinal points*
**ἀπόλαυσις, ἡ** 1 • 6 *enjoyment*
**ἀπροσκόπως** 2 • 3 *without stumbling, without disturbance*
**δημιουργέω** 2 • 3 *to create*
**δίχα** 9 • 9 *apart from, without*
**ἐλάχιστος** 2 • 16 *very small/short*
**ἔλλειψις, ἡ** 1 • 1 *failing*
**ἐπιτελέω** 13 • 15 *to complete, accomplish, perform, bring about*
**ζῷον, τό** 6 • 8 *animal*
**λειτουργία, ἡ** 8 • 11 *service*
**μαζός, ὁ** 1 • 1 *mamma, breast*
**ὁμόνοια, ἡ** 14 • 24 *oneness of mind, unanimity, concord, humility*
**παρέχω** 3 • 18 *to cause, make happen, offer*
**πηγή, ἡ** 1 • 7 *spring, fountain, flow*
**σταθμός, ὁ** 1 • 1 *station, weight*
**συνέλευσις, ἡ** 1 • 1 *(sexual) intercourse*
**ὑγεία, ἡ** 2 • 2 *health*
11 **δεσπότης, ὁ** 24 • 52 *lord, master*
**δημιουργός, ὁ** 5 • 7 *craftsworker, builder, maker, creator*
**εὐεργετέω** 1 • 3 *to do good to, benefit*
**οἰκτιρμός, ὁ** 4 • 4 *pity, mercy, compassion*
**ὁμόνοια, ἡ** 14 • 24 *oneness of mind, unanimity, concord, humility*
**προστάσσω** 4 • 8 *to command, order, give instructions, determine*
**προσφεύγω** 1 • 2 *to flee for refuge to*
**ὑπερεκπερισσῶς** 1 • 1 *beyond all measure, most highly*
12 **μεγαλωσύνη, ἡ** 8 • 10 *majesty*

## Chapter 21

1 **ἀξίως** 1 • 5 *worthily, in a manner worthy of, suitably*

**εὐάρεστος** 5 • 9 *pleasing, acceptable*
**εὐεργεσία, ἡ** 3 • 5 *good deed, benefit, a kindness*
**κρίμα, τό** 8 • 9 *judicial verdict*
**ὁμόνοια, ἡ** 14 • 24 *oneness of mind, unanimity, concord, humility*
**πολιτεύομαι** 6 • 10 *to live, lead one's life*
2 **γαστήρ, ἡ** 1 • 2 *belly*
**ἐραυνάω/ἐρευνάω** 1 • 3 *to search, examine, investigate*
**λύχνος, ὁ** 1 • 2 *lamp*
**πού** 5 • 7 *somewhere*
**ταμιεῖον, τό** 1 • 1 *hidden, secret room*
3 **διαλογισμός, ὁ** 1 • 1 *thought, opinion, reasoning, design*
**ἔννοια, ἡ** 2 • 4 *thought, knowledge, insight*
**λανθάνω** 2 • 7 *to escape notice, be hidden*
4 **λειποτακτέω** 1 • 1 *to turn away*
5 **ἀλαζονεία, ἡ** 5 • 10 *pretension, arrogance*
**ἀνόητος** 2 • 4 *unintelligent, foolish, dull-witted*
**ἄφρων** 5 • 17 *foolish, ignorant*
**ἐγκαυχάομαι** 1 • 1 *to boast*
**ἐπαίρω** 5 • 6 *to be presumptuous, put on airs*
**προσκόπτω** 1 • 1 *to give offense*
6 **αἰδέομαι** 1 • 2 *to respect*
**διορθόω** 1 • 1 *to set on the right path*
**ἐντρέπω** 2 • 9 *to turn toward something/someone, have regard for, respect*
**νέος** 4 • 16 *young*
**παιδεία, ἡ** 7 • 11 *upbringing, training, instruction, discipline, correction*
**παιδεύω** 9 • 13 *to practice discipline, correct, give guidance (to someone)*
**προηγέομαι** 1 • 4 *to preside*
**τιμάω** 4 • 12 *to honor, revere*
7 **ἁγνεία, ἡ** 2 • 13 *purity, chastity*
**ἀκέραιος** 2 • 3 *pure, innocent*
**ἀξιαγάπητος** 2 • 3 *worthy of love*
**ἀποδείκνυμι** 1 • 3 *to show forth, display*
**βούλημα, τό** 5 • 5 *intention, purpose*
**ἐνδείκνυμι** 2 • 4 *to show, demonstrate*
**ἐπιεικής** 3 • 4 *yielding, gentle, kind, courteous, tolerant*
**ἦθος, τό** 2 • 2 *custom, usage, habit*
**ἴσος** 1 • 3 *equal*
**ὁσίως** 8 • 9 *devoutly*
**παρέχω** 3 • 18 *to grant, show*
**πραΰτης, ἡ** 3 • 8 *gentleness, humility, courtesy, considerateness, meekness*
**πρόσκλισις, ἡ** 4 • 4 *inclination*
**σιγή, ἡ** 1 • 3 *silence, quiet*
**φανερός** 1 • 9 *visible, clear, plainly to be seen, open, plain, evident, known*
8 **ἁγνός** 6 • 11 *pure, holy*
**ἀναστρέφω** 2 • 2 *to act, behave, conduct oneself, live*
**διάνοια, ἡ** 8 • 22 *disposition, thought, mind*
**ἰσχύω** 1 • 9 *to have power, be competent, be able*
**καθαρός** 7 • 45 *pure, free*
**μανθάνω** 3 • 26 *to learn*
**μεταλαμβάνω** 3 • 12 *to have a share in*
**ὁσίως** 8 • 9 *devoutly*
**παιδεία, ἡ** 7 • 11 *upbringing, training, instruction, discipline, correction*
**ταπεινοφροσύνη, ἡ** 6 • 9 *humility, modesty*
9 **ἀναιρέω** 4 • 10 *to take away*
**ἐνθύμησις, ἡ** 1 • 5 *thought, reflection, idea*
**ἔννοια, ἡ** 2 • 4 *thought, knowledge, insight*
**ἐραυνητής/ἐρευνητής, ὁ** 1 • 1 *searcher, examiner*
**πνοή, ἡ** 2 • 3 *breath*

## Chapter 22

1 **βεβαιόω** 1 • 2 *to confirm, establish*
**δεῦτε** 2 • 2 *Come here! Come on!*
**προσκαλέω** 1 • 5 *to call (to)*
3 **δόλος, ὁ** 4 • 8 *deceit, cunning, treachery*
**παύω** 3 • 12 *to stop, cause to stop, quiet, relieve*

**χεῖλος, τό** 7 • 11 *the lips*
4 **ἐκκλίνω** 1 • 2 *to cease*
6 **δέησις, ἡ** 2 • 6 *prayer*
**ἐξολεθρεύω** 4 • 5 *to destroy utterly, root out*
**μνημόσυνον, τό** 2 • 2 *memory*
7 **εἰσακούω** 4 • 4 *to hear*
**ῥύομαι** 12 • 19 *to save, rescue, deliver, preserve*
8 **εἶτα** 8 • 48 *then, next*
**ἔλεος, τό** 7 • 19 *mercy, compassion, pity, clemency*
**κυκλόω** 1 • 3 *to surround, encircle*
**μάστιξ, ἡ** 3 • 8 *torment, suffering*

## Chapter 23

1 **ἁπλοῦς** 1 • 4 *single, without guile, sincere, straightforward*
**διάνοια, ἡ** 8 • 22 *disposition, thought, mind*
**εὐεργετικός** 1 • 1 *beneficent*
**ἠπίως** 1 • 1 *kindly*
**οἰκτίρμων** 2 • 2 *merciful, compassionate*
**προσηνῶς** 1 • 1 *kindly, gently, lovingly*
**σπλάγχνον, τό** 2 • 5 *heart (figuratively)*
2 **διψυχέω** 1 • 25 *to be undecided,* be *changeable, doubt*
**δωρεά, ἡ** 4 • 7 *gift, bounty*
**ἔνδοξος** 8 • 54 *glorious, splendid*
**ἰνδάλλομαι** 1 • 1 *to form false ideas, entertain strange notions*
**ὑπερβάλλω** 2 • 4 *to go beyond, surpass, outdo*
3 **γηράσκω** 1 • 1 *to grow old*
**διστάζω** 2 • 10 *to doubt, waver*
**δίψυχος** 2 • 23 *doubting, hesitating*
**πόρρω** 5 • 8 *far (away)*
**συμβαίνω** 1 • 7 *to happen, come about*
**ταλαίπωρος** 1 • 5 *miserable, wretched, distressed*
4 **ἄμπελος, ἡ** 1 • 16 *vine, grapevine*
**ἄνθος, τό** 1 • 4 *blossom, flower*
**ἀνόητος** 2 • 4 *unintelligent, foolish, dull-witted*
**βλαστός, ὁ** 1 • 3 *bud, sprout*
**εἶτα** [4] 8 • 48 *then, next*
**καταντάω** 3 • 4 *to arrive at, attain, meet*
**ξύλον, τό** [2] 2 • 23 *tree*
**ὄμφαξ, ἡ/ὁ** 1 • 2 *unripe grape*
**πέπειρος** 1 • 1 *ripe*
**σταφυλή, ἡ** 1 • 2 *(a bunch of) grapes*
**συμβάλλω** 1 • 4 *to compare*
**φύλλον, τό** 1 • 5 *leaf*
**φυλλοροέω/φυλλορροέω** 1 • 2 *to shed leaves, lose foliage*
**ὦ** 3 • 8 (interjection and marker of personal address) *O, O…!*
5 **βούλημα, τό** 5 • 5 *intention, will*
**ἐξαίφνης** [2] 2 • 6 *suddenly, unexpectedly*
**ἥκω** [2] 5 • 11 *to have come, be present*
**προσδοκάω** 1 • 8 *to wait for, look for, expect*
**συνεπιμαρτυρέω** 2 • 3 *to testify at the same time*
**ταχύς** [2] 3 • 13 *without delay, quickly, at once*
**τελειόω** 4 • 14 *to fulfill*
**χρονίζω** 1 • 1 *to take time, linger, fail to come or stay for a long time*

## Chapter 24

1 **ἀπαρχή, ἡ** 3 • 9 *first fruits, first portion*
**δεσπότης, ὁ** 24 • 52 *lord, master*
**διηνεκῶς** 1 • 1 *continually, without lapse*
**ἐπιδείκνυμι** 2 • 11 *to demonstrate, show*
**κατανοέω** 5 • 26 *to envisage, think about, notice*
3 **ἄπειμι** 2 • 2 *to go away, go, come*
**δηλόω** 2 • 49 *to explain, clarify, point out*
**ἐπέρχομαι** 2 • 8 *to happen, come about*
**κοιμάω** 3 • 12 *to sleep, fall asleep*
4 **σπόρος, ὁ** 1 • 1 *sowing*
**τρόπος, ὁ** 3 • 17 *manner, way, kind, guise*
5 **αὐξάνω/αὔξω** 2 • 7 *to grow, increase*
**γυμνός** 1 • 3 *uncovered, bare*
**δεσπότης, ὁ** 24 • 52 *lord, master*

διάλυσις, ἡ 1 • 1 *dissolution, decay*
διαλύω 2 • 3 *to break down, decay*
εἶτα 8 • 48 *then, next*
ἐκφέρω 2 • 3 *to produce*
μεγαλειότης, ἡ 1 • 3 *impressiveness*
ξηρός 1 • 47 *dry, dried up*
πρόνοια, ἡ 1 • 3 *forethought, foresight, providence*
σπείρω 1 • 5 *to sow seed*

## Chapter 25

1 ἀνατολικός 1 • 1 *eastern*
Ἀραβία, ἡ 1 • 1 *Arabia*
παράδοξος 1 • 4 *strange, wonderful, remarkable*
τουτέστιν 1 • 5 *this or that means, that is to say*
2 ἀπόλυσις, ἡ 1 • 1 *dissolution*
ἄρωμα, τό 1 • 2 *fragrant spice/salve/oil/perfume*
λίβανος, ὁ 2 • 2 *frankincense*
μονογενής 1 • 3 *unique (in kind)*
ὄρνεον, τό 2 • 3 *bird*
πεντακόσιοι 1 • 1 *five hundred*
προσονομάζω 1 • 1 *to name*
σηκός, ὁ 2 • 2 *burial-place, sepulcher, tomb*
σμύρνα, ἡ 1 • 1 *myrrh*
τελευτάω 3 • 8 *to die*
φοῖνιξ, ὁ 1 • 2 *the phoenix*
3 Αἴγυπτος, ἡ 6 • 9 *Egypt*
ἀνατρέφω 2 • 2 *to bring up, care for*
Ἀραβικός 1 • 1 *Arabian*
βαστάζω 1 • 24 *to carry, bear*
γενναῖος 5 • 8 *noble, illustrious*
διανύω 2 • 2 *to arrive (at)*
εἶτα 8 • 48 *then, next*
ζῷον, τό 6 • 8 *living thing/being*
Ἡλιούπολις, ἡ 1 • 1 *Heliopolis*
ἰκμάς, ἡ 1 • 3 *moisture*
ὀστέον, τό 4 • 6 *bone*
προγίνομαι 1 • 2 *to be born earlier, be done before*
πτεροφυέω 1 • 1 *to get/grow feathers/wings*
σηκός, ὁ 2 • 2 *burial-place, sepulcher, tomb*
σήπω 1 • 4 *to decay, rot*
σκώληξ, ὁ 2 • 5 *worm*
τελευτάω 3 • 8 *to die*
χώρα, ἡ 3 • 6 *district, region, place*
4 ἀφορμάω 1 • 1 *to start, set out*
βωμός, ὁ 1 • 1 *altar*
ἐπιπέτομαι 1 • 1 *to fly upon*
5 ἀναγραφή, ἡ 1 • 1 *public records*
ἐπισκέπτομαι 1 • 8 *to look at, examine, inspect*
πεντακοσιοστός 1 • 1 *five hundredth*

## Chapter 26

1 δημιουργός, ὁ 5 • 7 *craftsworker, builder, maker, creator*
δουλεύω 4 • 42 *to (perform the duties of a slave) serve, obey*
θαυμαστός 6 • 13 *wonderful, marvelous, remarkable*
μεγαλεῖος 3 • 6 *greatness, sublimity*
νομίζω 3 • 10 *to think, believe, hold, consider*
ὄρνεον, τό 2 • 3 *bird*
ὁσίως 8 • 9 *devoutly*
πεποίθησις, ἡ 5 • 7 *trust, confidence*
2 ἐξανίστημι 2 • 3 *to raise up, awaken*
ἐξεγείρω 1 • 3 *to awaken*
ἐξομολογέω 6 • 15 *to praise*
κοιμάω 3 • 12 *to sleep, fall asleep, die, pass away*
πού 5 • 7 *somewhere*
ὑπνόω 1 • 1 *to sleep, go to sleep*
3 ἀναντλέω 1 • 2 *to bear patiently*
Ἰώβ, ὁ 3 • 4 *Job*

## Chapter 27

1 κρίμα, τό 8 • 9 *judging, judgment*
προσδέω 1 • 3 *to be bound securely*
2 ἀδύνατος 1 • 11 *impossible*
ψεύδω/ψεύδομαι [3] 4 • 6 *to lie*
3 ἀναζωπυρέω 1 • 2 *to rekindle*
νοέω 3 • 46 *to perceive, apprehend, understand, gain an insight into*
4 καταστρέφω 2 • 5 *to destroy, ruin*

**μεγαλωσύνη, ἡ** 8 • 10 *majesty*
**συνίστημι** 2 • 3 *to put together, constitute, establish, prepare*
5 **ἀνθίστημι** 1 • 8 *to set oneself against, oppose*
**δογματίζω** 2 • 2 *to obligate*
**ἰσχύς, ἡ** 5 • 11 *strength, power, might*
**κράτος, τό** 5 • 7 *might*
**παρέρχομαι** 4 • 12 *to pass away, disappear*
6 **βουλή, ἡ** 5 • 19 *resolution, decision, directing counsel*
**λανθάνω** 2 • 7 *to escape notice, be hidden*
7 **ἀναγγέλλω** [2] 4 • 8 *to disclose, announce, proclaim, teach*
**γνῶσις, ἡ** 6 • 32 *knowledge*
**διηγέομαι** 3 • 4 *to tell, relate, describe*
**ἐρεύγομαι** 1 • 1 *to utter, proclaim*
**λαλιά, ἡ** 1 • 1 *speech, speaking*
**ποίησις, ἡ** 1 • 3 *doing, working*
**στερέωμα, τό** 1 • 1 *firmament*

## Chapter 28

1 **ἀπολείπω** 4 • 6 *to put aside, give up*
**ἔλεος, τό** 7 • 19 *mercy, compassion, pity, clemency*
**κρίμα, τό** 8 • 9 *judicial verdict*
**μιαρός** 4 • 4 *abominable, wretched, foul, depraved, wanton*
**σκεπάζω** 2 • 8 *to protect, shelter*
**φαῦλος** 2 • 2 *base*
2 **αὐτομολέω** 1 • 1 *to desert*
**γραφεῖον, τό** 1 • 1 *the thing written, writing*
**κραταιός** 2 • 3 *powerful, mighty*
**πού** 5 • 7 *somewhere*
**φεύγω** 4 • 20 *to flee*
3 **ἄβυσσος, ἡ** 3 • 4 *depth, abyss*
**ἀφήκω** 1 • 1 *to go away*
**καταστρώννυμι** 1 • 1 *to make a bed*
**κρύπτω** 3 • 4 *to hide*
4 **ἀποδιδράσκω** 2 • 2 *to run away, escape*
**ἐμπεριέχω** 1 • 1 *to embrace*
**ποῖ** 1 • 1 *where? whither?*

## Chapter 29

1 **ἁγνός** 6 • 11 *pure, holy*
**ἀμίαντος** 1 • 5 *undefiled, pure*
**ἐκλογή, ἡ** 1 • 3 *that which is chosen/selected;*
**ἐκλογῆς μέρος... ἑαυτῷ** *a chosen portion for himself*
**ἐπιεικής** 3 • 4 *yielding, gentle, kind, courteous, tolerant*
**εὔσπλαγχνος** 2 • 4 *tenderhearted, compassionate*
**ὁσιότης, ἡ** 3 • 4 *devoutness, piety, holiness*
2 **Ἀδάμ, ὁ** 3 • 4 *Adam*
**ἀριθμός, ὁ** 5 • 14 *number, total*
**διαμερίζω** 1 • 1 *to divide, separate*
**διασπείρω** 1 • 1 *to scatter*
**Ἰακώβ, ὁ** 3 • 13 *Jacob*
**κληρονομία, ἡ** 2 • 6 *possession, property*
**μερίς, ἡ** 3 • 3 *share, portion*
**ὅριον, τό** 1 • 2 *boundary*
**σχοίνισμα, τό** 1 • 1 *allotment*
**ὕψιστος** 6 • 7 *the Most High*
3 **ἅλων, ἡ** 2 • 3 *threshing floor*
**ἀπαρχή, ἡ** 3 • 9 *first fruits, first portion*

## Chapter 30

1 **ἁγιασμός, ὁ** 2 • 2 *holiness, consecration, sanctification*
**ἄναγνος** 1 • 1 *unchaste*
**βδελυκτός** [2] 3 • 3 *abhorrent, detestable*
**καταλαλιά, ἡ** 3 • 13 *evil speech, slander, defamation, detraction*
**μέθη, ἡ** 1 • 1 *drunkenness*
**μερίς, ἡ** 3 • 3 *share, portion*
**μιαρός** 4 • 4 *abominable, wretched, foul, depraved, wanton*
**μοιχεία, ἡ** 1 • 9 *adultery*
**μυσερός** 2 • 2 *loathsome, abominable, detestable*
**νεωτερισμός, ὁ** 1 • 1 *uprising, revolution, rebellion*
**συμπλοκή, ἡ** 1 • 1 *intimate embrace, intercourse*
**ὑπερηφανία, ἡ** 3 • 8 *arrogance, haughtiness, pride*

φεύγω 4 • 20 *to flee from, avoid, shun*
2 ἀντιτάσσω 2 • 7 *to oppose, resist*
ταπεινός 4 • 8 *humble*
ὑπερήφανος 4 • 6 *arrogant, haughty, proud*
3 ἐγκρατεύομαι 1 • 25 *to control oneself, abstain*
ἐνδύω 1 • 32 *to clothe oneself in, put on, wear*
καταλαλιά, ἡ 3 • 13 *evil speech, slander, defamation, detraction*
κολλάω 10 • 32 *to cling to, attach to*
ὁμόνοια, ἡ 14 • 24 *oneness of mind, unanimity, concord, harmony*
πόρρω 5 • 8 *far (away)*
ταπεινοφρονέω 11 • 14 *to be modest, be unassuming*
ψιθυρισμός, ὁ 2 • 2 *(secret) gossip, tale-bearing*
4 ἀντακούω 1 • 1 *to hear in turn*
εὔλαλος 1 • 1 *talkative, glib*
οἴομαι 1 • 11 *to think, suppose, expect*
5 γεννητός 1 • 2 *born*
ὀλιγόβιος 1 • 1 *short-lived*
6 αὐτεπαίνετος 1 • 1 *praising oneself*
ἔπαινος, ὁ 1 • 1 *praise, approval, recognition*
7 πρᾶξις, ἡ 2 • 50 *act, action, deed*
8 αὐθάδεια, ἡ 2 • 6 *arrogance, willfulness, stubbornness*
ἐπιείκεια, ἡ 5 • 9 *clemency, gentleness, graciousness, courtesy, indulgence, tolerance*
θράσος, τό 1 • 3 *arrogance, shamelessness*
καταράομαι 4 • 5 *to curse, execrate*
πραΰτης, ἡ 3 • 8 *gentleness, humility, courtesy, considerateness, meekness*
ταπεινοφροσύνη, ἡ 6 • 9 *humility, modesty*
τόλμα, ἡ 1 • 1 *audacity*

## Chapter 31

1 ἀνατυλίσσω 1 • 1 *to think over, call to mind again*
εὐλογία, ἡ [2] 2 • 2 *blessing*
κολλάω 10 • 32 *to cling to, enter into a close relation with*
2 χάριν 3 • 4 *for the sake of, on behalf of, on account of*
3 ἡδέως 3 • 10 *gladly*
θυσία, ἡ 10 • 22 *sacrifice, offering*
Ἰσαάκ, ὁ 1 • 7 *Isaac*
πεποίθησις, ἡ 5 • 7 *confidence*
προσάγω 1 • 7 *to bring (forward)*
4 δουλεύω 4 • 42 *to be a slave, be subjected*
δωδεκάσκηπτρον, τό 1 • 1 *scepter of the twelve tribes*
ἐκχωρέω 3 • 4 *to go out, go away, depart*
Ἰακώβ, ὁ 3 • 13 *Jacob*
Λαβάν, ὁ 1 • 1 *Laban*
ταπεινοφροσύνη, ἡ 6 • 9 *humility, modesty*

## Chapter 32

1 δωρεά, ἡ 4 • 7 *gift, bounty*
εἰλικρινῶς 1 • 1 *sincerely, candidly*
κατανοέω 5 • 26 *to envisage, think about, notice, consider, contemplate*
μεγαλεῖος 3 • 6 *greatness, sublimity*
2 ἀστήρ, ὁ 3 • 7 *star, single star, planet*
ἐπαγγέλλομαι 2 • 7 *to offer, promise;*
ἐπαγγειλαμένου τοῦ θεοῦ (probably a gen. absolute after ὡς) *since (God) promised*
ἡγέομαι 8 • 25 *to lead, guide*
θυσιαστήριον, τό 2 • 15 *altar*
λειτουργέω 6 • 11 *to serve, render service*
Λευΐτης, ὁ 2 • 2 *a Levite*
σκῆπτρον, τό 2 • 2 *tribe*
3 δικαιοπραγία, ἡ 1 • 1 *righteous action*
κατεργάζομαι 3 • 7 *to achieve, accomplish, do*
μεγαλύνω 3 • 3 *to exalt, glorify, magnify, speak highly of*
4 εὐσέβεια, ἡ 4 • 6 *devoutness, piety, godliness*
ἡμέτερος 3 • 13 *our*

**κατεργάζομαι** 3 • 7 *to achieve, accomplish, do*
**ὁσιότης, ἡ** 4 • 4 *devoutness, piety, holiness*
**παντοκράτωρ, ὁ** 6 • 12 *Almighty, All-powerful, Omnipotent (One)*
**σύνεσις, ἡ** 3 • 22 *intelligence, acuteness, shrewdness*

## Chapter 33

1 **ἀγαθοποιΐα, ἡ** 4 • 4 *doing good*
**ἀργέω** 1 • 1 *to slack off, become idle*
**γέ** 1 • 18 *at least, even, indeed*
**δεσπότης, ὁ** 24 • 52 *lord, master*
**ἐάω** 5 • 13 *to let, permit;*
**ἐάσαι** (voluntative optative) *May (the Master) permit*
**ἐγκαταλείπω** 2 • 8 *to forsake, abandon, desert*
**ἐκτένεια, ἡ** 2 • 3 *perseverance, earnestness*
**ἐπιτελέω** 13 • 15 *to complete, accomplish, perform, bring about*
**μηδαμῶς** 3 • 4 *by no means, certainly not, no*
**προθυμία, ἡ** 2 • 6 *willingness, readiness, goodwill*
**σπεύδω** 1 • 4 *to hurry, hasten*
2 **ἀγαλλιάω** 1 • 11 *to exult, be glad, overjoyed*
**δεσπότης, ὁ** 24 • 52 *lord, master*
**δημιουργός, ὁ** 5 • 7 *craftsworker, builder, maker, creator*
3 **ἀκατάληπτος** 1 • 1 *incomprehensible*
**ἀσφαλής** 2 • 4 *firm, sure*
**βούλημα, τό** 5 • 5 *intention, will*
**διακοσμέω** 1 • 1 *to set in order, regulate*
**διάταξις, ἡ** 1 • 1 *command*
**διαχωρίζω** 2 • 2 *to separate*
**ἐγκλείω** 1 • 4 *to lock up, shut up, enclose*
**ἑδράζω** 2 • 6 *to establish, fix, settle*
**ζῷον, τό** [2] 6 • 8 *animal*
**θεμέλιος, ὁ** 1 • 4 *foundation*
**κελεύω** 5 • 44 *to command, order, urge*
**κράτος, τό** 5 • 7 *might*
**παμμεγέθης** 2 • 2 *immense*
**περιέχω** 1 • 4 *to surround, encircle*
**προετοιμάζω** 2 • 5 *to prepare beforehand*
**στηρίζω** 5 • 8 *to set up, establish, support*
**σύνεσις, ἡ** 3 • 22 *intelligence, acuteness, shrewdness*
**φοιτάω** 1 • 2 *to go back and forth, move about (regularly)*
4 **ἄμωμος** 7 • 14 *blameless*
**διάνοια, ἡ** 8 • 22 *purpose, plan, intelligence*
**εἰκών, ἡ** 2 • 5 *form, appearance*
**ἔξοχος** 1 • 2 *prominent, preeminent;*
subst. *the prominent thing*
**ἱερός** 3 • 5 *holy*
**παμμεγέθης** 2 • 2 *immense;*
**τὸ ἐξοχώτατον καὶ παμμέγεθες** *the most preeminent and immense work*
**πλάσσω** 3 • 8 *to form, mold*
**χαρακτήρ, ὁ** 1 • 5 *reproduction, representation*
5 **ἄρσην** 1 • 8 *male*
**εἰκών, ἡ** 2 • 5 *form, appearance*
**ἡμέτερος** 3 • 13 *our*
**θῆλυς** 2 • 9 *female*
**ὁμοίωσις, ἡ** 1 • 3 *likeness, resemblance*
6 **αὐξάνω/αὔξω** 2 • 7 *to grow, increase*
**ἐπαινέω** 1 • 6 *to praise*
**πληθύνω** 3 • 11 *to be multiplied, grow, increase*
**τελειόω** 4 • 14 *to complete, bring to an end, finish, accomplish*
7 **κοσμέω** [2] 4 • 10 *to adorn, decorate, make beautiful or attractive (inwardly)*
8 **ἀόκνως** 1 • 1 *without hesitation*
**ἰσχύς, ἡ** 5 • 11 *strength, power, might*
**ὑπογραμμός, ὁ** 3 • 4 *example*

## Chapter 34

1 **ἀντοφθαλμέω** 1 • 2 *to look directly at*
**ἐργάτης, ὁ** 1 • 3 *worker, laborer*
**ἐργοπαρέκτης, ὁ** 1 • 1 *employer*
**νωθρός** 1 • 1 *lazy, sluggish*

**παρίημι** 2 • 2 *to be careless, be indolent*
2 **ἀγαθοποιΐα, ἡ** 4 • 4 *doing good*
**πρόθυμος** 1 • 4 *ready, willing, eager*
3 **μισθός, ὁ** 1 • 22 *recompense*
**προλέγω** 5 • 16 *to tell beforehand/in advance*
4 **ἀργός** 1 • 6 *idle, lazy*
**παρίημι** 2 • 2 *to be careless, be indolent*
**προτρέπω** 1 • 1 *to urge (on), encourage, impel, persuade*
5 **κατανοέω** 5 • 26 *to envisage, think about, notice*
**καύχημα, τό** 1 • 1 *boast*
**λειτουργέω** 6 • 11 *to serve, render service*
6 **κτίσις, ἡ** 3 • 19 *creation*
**λειτουργέω** 6 • 11 *to serve, render service*
**μυριάς, ἡ** 1 • 2 *myriads*
**μυρίος** 1 • 1 *innumerable, countless*
**πλήρης** 3 • 20 *filled, full*
**Σαβαώθ** 1 • 1 *Sabaoth, of hosts, of armies*
**χιλιάς, ἡ** 2 • 3 *a thousand*
**χίλιοι** 1 • 3 *a thousand*
7 **βοάω** 1 • 5 *to call, shout, cry out*
**ἐκτενῶς** 1 • 1 *eagerly, fervently, constantly*
**ἔνδοξος** 8 • 54 *glorious, splendid*
**μέτοχος** 1 • 3 *participating in/sharing*
**ὁμόνοια, ἡ** 14 • 24 *oneness of mind, unanimity, concord, harmony*
8 **ὑπομένω** 4 • 32 *to wait for*

## Chapter 35

1 **δῶρον, τό** 3 • 4 *gift, present*
**θαυμαστός** 6 • 13 *wonderful, marvelous, remarkable*
2 **ἁγιασμός, ὁ** 2 • 2 *holiness, consecration, sanctification*
**ἀθανασία, ἡ** 1 • 3 *immortality*
**διάνοια, ἡ** 8 • 22 *understanding, intelligence, mind*
**ἐγκράτεια, ἡ** 4 • 14 *self-control*
**λαμπρότης, ἡ** 1 • 2 *distinction, brilliance*
**πεποίθησις, ἡ** 5 • 7 *trust, confidence*
**ὑποπίπτω** 1 • 1 *to fall under/within*
3 **δημιουργός, ὁ** 5 • 7 *craftsworker, builder, maker, creator*
**καλλονή, ἡ** 2 • 2 *beauty*
**πανάγιος** 2 • 2 *all-holy*
**ποσότης, ἡ** 1 • 1 *quantity, amount*
**ὑπομένω** 4 • 32 *to stand one's ground, hold out, endure*
4 **ἀγωνίζομαι** 1 • 7 *to fight, struggle*
**ἀριθμός, ὁ** 5 • 14 *number*
**δωρεά, ἡ** 4 • 7 *gift, bounty*
**ἐπαγγέλλομαι** 2 • 7 *to promise, offer*
**μεταλαμβάνω** 3 • 12 *to have a share in*
**ὑπομένω** 4 • 32 *to stand one's ground, hold out, endure*
5 **ἀδικία, ἡ** 2 • 7 *wrongdoing*
**ἀλαζονεία, ἡ** 5 • 10 *pretension, arrogance*
**ἄμωμος** 7 • 17 *blameless*
**ἀνήκω** 3 • 10 *to refer, relate, belong*
**ἀνομία, ἡ** 12 • 33 *a lawless deed*
**ἀπορρίπτω** 2 • 3 *to drive/scare away, cast away*
**ἀφιλοξενία, ἡ** 1 • 1 *inhospitality*
**βούλησις, ἡ** 4 • 4 *will*
**διάνοια, ἡ** 8 • 22 *understanding, intelligence, mind*
**δόλος, ὁ** 4 • 8 *deceit, cunning, treachery*
**ἐκζητέω** 4 • 16 *to seek out, search for*
**ἐπιτελέω** 13 • 15 *to complete, accomplish, perform, bring about*
**ἔρις, ἡ** 9 • 10 *strife, discord, contention*
**εὐάρεστος** 5 • 9 *pleasing, acceptable*
**εὐπρόσδεκτος** 3 • 5 *acceptable*
**θεοστυγία, ἡ** 1 • 1 *hatred/enmity towards God*
**κακοήθεια, ἡ** 1 • 1 *meanspiritedness, malice, malignity, craftiness*
**καταλαλιά, ἡ** 3 • 13 *evil speech, slander, defamation, detraction*
**κενοδοξία, ἡ** 1 • 5 *vanity, conceit, excessive ambition*

**πλεονεξία, ἡ** 1 • 7 *greediness, insatiableness, avarice, covetousness*
**στηρίζω** 5 • 8 *to confirm, establish, strengthen*
**ὑπερηφανία, ἡ** 3 • 8 *arrogance, haughtiness, pride*
**ψιθυρισμός, ὁ** 2 • 2 *(secret) gossip, tale-bearing*
6 **στυγητός** 2 • 2 *loathsome, despicable*
**συνευδοκέω** 2 • 5 *to agree with, approve of, consent to, sympathize with*
7 **ἀναλαμβάνω** 5 • 10 *to take to one's self, adopt*
**διηγέομαι** 3 • 4 *to tell, relate, describe*
**δικαίωμα, τό** 3 • 12 *regulation, requirement, commandment*
8 **δολιότης, ἡ** 1 • 3 *deceit*
**κακία, ἡ** 2 • 9 *malice, ill-will, malignity*
**καταλαλέω** 1 • 6 *to speak degradingly of, speak evil of, defame, slander*
**κλέπτης, ὁ** 1 • 1 *thief*
**μερίς, ἡ** 3 • 3 *share, portion*
**μοιχός, ὁ** 1 • 3 *adulterer*
**παιδεία, ἡ** 7 • 11 *upbringing, training, instruction, discipline, correction*
**περιπλέκω** 1 • 3 *to weave/twine around*
**πλεονάζω** 1 • 3 *to bring forth in abundance, increase*
**σκάνδαλον, τό** 1 • 5 *temptation to sin, enticement*
**συντρέχω** 1 • 6 *to go with*
9 **ἄνομος** 5 • 17 *lawless*
**σιγάω** 1 • 6 *to say nothing, keep still, keep silent*
**ὑπολαμβάνω** 1 • 3 *to assume, think, believe, be of the opinion (that), suppose*
10 **ἐλέγχω** 3 • 16 *to convict, convince someone of something, point out something to someone*
11 **ἁρπάζω** 1 • 3 *to steal, carry off, drag away*
**δή** 2 • 6 *now, then, therefore*
**ἐπιλανθάνομαι** 2 • 8 *to forget*
**λέων, ὁ** 2 • 3 *lion*
**μήποτε** 1 • 22 *lest*
**ῥύομαι** 12 • 19 *to save, rescue, deliver, preserve*
**συνίημι** 1 • 21 *to understand, comprehend*
12 **αἴνεσις, ἡ** 3 • 3 *praise*
**θυσία, ἡ** 10 • 22 *sacrifice, offering*
**σωτήριος** 2 • 3 *saving, delivering, preserving, bringing salvation*

## Chapter 36

1 **ἀσθένεια, ἡ** 1 • 7 *weakness*
**βοηθός** 3 • 4 *helpful*
**προστάτης, ὁ** 3 • 3 *defender, guardian, benefactor*
**προσφορά, ἡ** 3 • 6 *offering*
**σωτήριος** 2 • 3 *saving, delivering, preserving, bringing salvation*
2 **ἀθάνατος** 1 • 5 *immortal*
**ἄμωμος** 7 • 17 *blameless*
**ἀναθάλλω** 1 • 1 *to grow up again, bloom again*
**ἀπαύγασμα, τό** 1 • 1 *radiance, effulgence, reflection*
**ἀσύνετος** 3 • 16 *senseless, foolish*
**ἀτενίζω** 5 • 5 *to look intently at, stare at*
**γεύομαι** 1 • 3 *to come to know, partake of, taste*
**γνῶσις, ἡ** 6 • 32 *knowledge*
**δεσπότης, ὁ** 24 • 52 *lord, master*
**διάνοια, ἡ** 8 • 22 *understanding, intelligence, mind*
**διάφορος** 1 • 1 *outstanding, excellent*
**ἐνοπτρίζομαι** 1 • 1 *to see (as) in a mirror*
**κληρονομέω** 4 • 11 *to acquire, obtain, come into possession of*
**μεγαλωσύνη, ἡ** 8 • 10 *majesty*
**ὄψις, ἡ** 1 • 6 *face, countenance*
**σκοτόω** 1 • 1 *to be/become darkened in mind*
**τοσοῦτος** 9 • 38 *so much, as much*
**ὑπέρτατος** 2 • 2 *uppermost, loftiest, supreme*
**ὕψος, τό** 3 • 7 *height*
3 **λειτουργός, ὁ** 3 • 3 *servant, minister*
**φλόξ, ἡ** 1 • 2 *flame*
4 **δεσπότης, ὁ** 24 • 52 *lord, master*
**κατάσχεσις, ἡ** 1 • 1 *possession, taking into possession*

**κληρονομία, ἡ** 2 • 6 *possession, property*
**πέρας, τό** 1 • 13 *end, limit, boundary*
5 **ὑποπόδιον, τό** 1 • 3 *footstool*
6 **ἀντιτάσσω** 2 • 7 *to oppose, resist*
**φαῦλος** 2 • 2 *base*
**εὔχρηστος** 1 • 14 *useful, serviceable*
**συμπνέω** 1 • 1 *to agree, coincide, coalesce*
**ὑποταγή, ἡ** 2 • 4 *subjection, subordination*
**χράομαι** 1 • 18 *to act, proceed*

## Chapter 37

1 **ἄμωμος** 7 • 17 *blameless*
**ἐκτένεια, ἡ** 2 • 3 *perseverance, earnestness*
**πρόσταγμα, τό** 7 • 10 *order, command(ment), injunction*
**στρατεύω** 2 • 4 *to wage battle, fight*
2 **διατάσσω** 3 • 8 *to order*
**εἰκτικῶς** 1 • 1 *readily yielding*
**ἐπιτελέω** 13 • 15 *to complete, accomplish, perform, bring about*
**εὐτάκτως** 2 • 2 *in good order*
**ἡγέομαι** 8 • 25 *to lead, guide*
**κατανοέω** 5 • 26 *to envisage, think about, notice*
**στρατεύω** 2 • 4 *to wage battle, fight, serve in the army*
**ὑποτεταγμένως** 1 • 1 *submissively*
3 **ἑκατόνταρχος/ἑκατοντάρχης, ὁ** 1 • 1 *centurion, captain*
**ἔπαρχος, ὁ** 1 • 1 *prefect, commanding officer*
**ἐπιτάσσω** 2 • 7 *to order, command*
**ἐπιτελέω** 13 • 15 *to complete, accomplish, perform, bring about*
**ἡγέομαι** 8 • 25 *to lead, guide*
**καθεξῆς** 1 • 2 *in order, one after the other*
**πεντηκόνταρχος, ὁ** 1 • 1 *company commander*
**τάγμα, τό** 2 • 16 *division, group*
**χιλίαρχος, ὁ** 1 • 1 *military tribune*
4 **δίχα** [2] 9 • 9 *apart from, without*
**σύγκρασις, ἡ** 1 • 1 *assemblage, combination*
**χρῆσις, ἡ** 1 • 5 *usefulness*
5 **ἀναγκαῖος** 1 • 4 *necessary*
**δίχα** [2] 9 • 9 *apart from, without*
**ἐλάχιστος** 2 • 16 *insignificant, trivial*

## Chapter 38

1 **πλησίον** 3 • 17 *near;* subst. *neighbor, fellow human being*
**χάρισμα, τό** 1 • 6 *favor bestowed, gift*
2 **ἁγνός** 6 • 11 *pure, holy*
**ἀλαζονεύομαι** 2 • 3 *to boast, be boastful*
**ἀναπληρόω** 2 • 4 *to fill a gap, replace*
**ἀσθενής** [2] 4 • 12 *weak*
**ἀτημελέω** 1 • 1 *to neglect*
**ἐάω** 5 • 13 *to let, permit*
**ἐγκράτεια, ἡ** 4 • 14 *self-control*
**ἐνδείκνυμι** 2 • 4 *to show, demonstrate*
**ἐντρέπω** 2 • 9 *to turn toward something/someone, have regard for, respect*
**ἐπιχορηγέω** 2 • 5 *to give, grant*
**ἰσχυρός** [2] 4 • 21 *strong*
**πλούσιος** 3 • 22 *rich, wealthy*
**σοφός** 4 • 8 *wise*
**ταπεινοφρονέω** 11 • 14 *to be modest, be unassuming*
**ὑστέρημα, τό** 2 • 4 *need, want, deficiency*
3 **ἀναλογίζομαι** 1 • 1 *to consider*
**δημιουργέω** 2 • 3 *to create*
**εἰσάγω** 1 • 6 *to bring or lead in/into*
**εὐεργεσία, ἡ** 3 • 5 *good deed, benefit, a kindness*
**πλάσσω** 3 • 8 *to form, mold*
**πρίν** 1 • 7 *before*
**προετοιμάζω** 2 • 5 *to prepare beforehand*
**τάφος, ὁ** 2 • 4 *tomb*
**ὕλη, ἡ** 1 • 4 *material, matter, stuff*

## Chapter 39

1 **ἀπαίδευτος** 1 • 1 *uninstructed, uneducated*
**ἀσύνετος** 3 • 16 *senseless, foolish*
**ἄφρων** 5 • 17 *foolish, ignorant*
**διάνοια, ἡ** 8 • 22 *imagination*
**ἐπαίρω** 5 • 6 *to be presumptuous, put on airs*
**μυκτηρίζω** 2 • 3 *to turn up the nose at, treat with contempt*
**μωρός** 1 • 12 *foolish, stupid*
**χλευάζω** 1 • 2 *to mock, scoff at, sneer at*
2 **γηγενής** 1 • 1 *earth-born*
**θνητός** 1 • 5 *mortal*
**ἰσχύς, ἡ** 5 • 11 *strength, power, might*
3 **αὔρα, ἡ** 1 • 1 *breeze*
**μορφή, ἡ** 1 • 8 *form, outward appearance, shape*
4 **ἄμεμπτος** 2 • 4 *blameless, faultless*
**βροτός** 1 • 1 *mortal*
**ἔναντι** 1 • 1 *before*
**ἐπινοέω** 1 • 2 *to notice*
**καθαρός** 7 • 45 *pure*
**παῖς, ὁ/ἡ** 4 • 20 *slave, servant*
**σκολιός** 1 • 2 *crooked, unscrupulous, dishonest*
5 **βοηθέω** 1 • 4 *to furnish aid*
**ἔα** 1 • 1 *ah! ha!*
**ἐάω** 5 • 13 *to let go, leave alone, not to speak of*
**ἑσπέρα, ἡ** 1 • 1 *evening*
**καθαρός** 7 • 45 *pure, free*
**παίω** 1 • 1 *to strike*
**πήλινος** 1 • 1 *made of clay*
**πηλός, ἡ** 1 • 2 *clay*
**πρωΐθεν** 1 • 1 *(from) morning*
**σής, ὁ** 1 • 6 *moth*
**τρόπος, ὁ** 3 • 17 *manner, way, kind, guise*
6 **ἐμφυσάω** 1 • 1 *to breathe on*
**τελευτάω** 3 • 8 *to die*
7 **ἀναιρέω** 4 • 10 *to do away with, destroy*
**ἄφρων** 5 • 17 *foolish, ignorant*
**ζῆλος, ὁ/τό** 22 • 25 *jealousy, envy*
**θανατόω** 2 • 7 *to bring death*
**ὑπακούω** 5 • 9 *to hear*
8 **ἄφρων** 5 • 17 *foolish, ignorant*
**βιβρώσκω** 1 • 8 *to eat, consume*
**δίαιτα, ἡ** 2 • 3 *habitation, dwelling-place*
**ῥίζα, ἡ** 2 • 8 *root*
9 **ἐξαίρετος** 1 • 2 *excepted, separated, delivered*
**ἐξαιρέω** 3 • 4 *to set free, deliver, rescue*
**ἥσσων** 3 • 3 *lesser, inferior, weaker*
**κολαβρίζομαι/κολαβρίζω** 1 • 1 *to mock, ridicule;*
**κολαβρισθείησαν** (voluntative optative) *may they be mocked/ ridiculed*
**πόρρω** 5 • 8 *far (away)*

## Chapter 40

1 **βάθος, τό** 1 • 4 *depth*
**γνῶσις, ἡ** 6 • 32 *knowledge*
**δεσπότης, ὁ** 24 • 52 *lord, master*
**ἐγκύπτω** 4 • 5 *to examine, gain an insight into, study*
**ἐπιτελέω** 13 • 15 *to complete, accomplish, perform, bring about*
**θεῖος** 1 • 16 *divine*
**κελεύω** 5 • 44 *to command, order, urge*
**πρόδηλος** 4 • 4 *clear, evident, known (to all)*
**τάξις, ἡ** 1 • 6 *order, proper procedure*
**τάσσω** 2 • 4 *to order, fix, determine, appoint*
2 **ἀτάκτως** 1 • 1 *disorderly, arbitrarily*
**εἰκῇ** 1 • 1 *without due consideration, in a haphazard manner*
**ἐπιμελῶς** 2 • 9 *carefully, diligently*
**ἐπιτελέω** 13 • 15 *to complete, accomplish, perform, bring about*
**κελεύω** 5 • 44 *to command, order, urge*
**λειτουργία, ἡ** 8 • 11 *service*
**ὁρίζω** 3 • 10 *to determine, appoint, fix, set*
**προσφορά, ἡ** 3 • 6 *sacrificing, offering*
3 **βούλησις, ἡ** 4 • 4 *will*
**ἐπιτελέω** 13 • 15 *to complete, accomplish, perform, bring about*

**εὐδόκησις, ἡ** 1 • 1 *approval, satisfaction, good pleasure*
**εὐπρόσδεκτος** 3 • 5 *acceptable*
**ὁρίζω** 3 • 10 *to determine, appoint, fix, set*
**ὁσίως** 8 • 9 *devoutly*
**ὑπέρτατος** 2 • 2 *uppermost, loftiest, supreme*
4 **δεσπότης, ὁ** 24 • 52 *lord, master*
**διαμαρτάνω** 1 • 5 *to miss the mark badly, be quite wrong*
**εὐπρόσδεκτος** 3 • 5 *acceptable*
**νόμιμος** 3 • 4 *lawful;* subst. *statute, law, commandment, ordinance*
**προστάσσω** 4 • 8 *to command, order, give instructions, determine*
**προσφορά, ἡ** 3 • 6 *sacrificing, offering*
5 **ἐπίκειμαι** 2 • 6 *to be imposed, be incumbent*
**λαϊκός** 2 • 2 *being unofficial, lay*
**λειτουργία, ἡ** 8 • 11 *service*
**Λευΐτης, ὁ** 2 • 2 *Levite*
**πρόσταγμα, τό** 7 • 10 *order, command(ment), injunction*
**προστάσσω** 4 • 8 *to command, order, give instructions, determine, assign*

## Chapter 41

1 **κανών, ὁ** 3 • 4 *assignment, formulation*
**λειτουργία, ἡ** 8 • 11 *service*
**ὁρίζω** 3 • 10 *to determine, appoint, fix, set*
**παρεκβαίνω** 2 • 2 *to go beyond, transgress*
**σεμνότης, ἡ** 1 • 12 *dignity, seriousness, probity, holiness*
**τάγμα, τό** 2 • 16 *division, group*
2 **ἐνδελεχισμός, ὁ** 1 • 1 *continuity*
**εὐχή, ἡ** 2 • 5 *vow*
**θυσία, ἡ** 10 • 22 *sacrifice, offering*
**θυσιαστήριον, τό** 2 • 15 *altar*
**λειτουργός, ὁ** 3 • 3 *servant, minister*
**μωμοσκοπέομαι** 1 • 2 *to examine for blemishes*
**πανταχοῦ** 1 • 2 *everywhere*
**πλημμέλεια, ἡ** 2 • 2 *fault, error, sin, offense*
**προλέγω** 5 • 16 *to tell beforehand/ in advance*
3 **βούλησις, ἡ** 4 • 4 *will*
**καθήκω** 3 • 3 *to come/reach to, be proper/fitting*
**πρόστιμον, τό** 1 • 1 *penalty*
4 **γνῶσις, ἡ** 6 • 32 *knowledge*
**καταξιόω** 2 • 14 *to consider worthy*
**κίνδυνος, ὁ** 6 • 8 *danger, risk*
**τοσοῦτος** 9 • 38 *so much, as much*
**ὑπόκειμαι** 1 • 1 *to be subject to, be exposed to*

## Chapter 42

1 **ἐκπέμπω** 3 • 3 *to send out*
2 **ἀμφότεροι** 1 • 21 *both*
**εὐτάκτως** 2 • 2 *in good order*
3 **παραγγελία, ἡ** 1 • 1 *order, command, precept, advice, exhortation*
**πιστόω** 2 • 2 *to feel confidence, be convinced*
**πληροφορέω** 2 • 9 *to convince fully*
**πληροφορία, ἡ** 1 • 1 *full assurance, certainty*
4 **ἀπαρχή, ἡ** 3 • 9 *first fruits, first portions*
**διάκονος, ὁ** 3 • 29 *assistant*
**δοκιμάζω** 4 • 19 *to put to the test, examine*
**ἐπίσκοπος, ὁ** 4 • 76 *overseer, supervisor*
**καθίστημι/καθιστάνω** 1 • 1 *to appoint, put in charge*
**χώρα, ἡ** 3 • 6 *country*
5 **δή** 2 • 6 *indeed, for*
**διάκονος, ὁ** [2] 3 • 29 *assistant*
**ἐπίσκοπος, ὁ** [2] 4 • 76 *overseer, supervisor*
**καθίστημι/καθιστάνω** 6 • 8 *to appoint, put in charge*
**καινῶς** 1 • 1 *newly*
**πού** 5 • 7 *somewhere*
**ἐγέγραπτο** (pluperfect of γράφω) *had been written*

## Chapter 43

1 **βίβλος, ἡ** 2 • 5 *book*
**διατάσσω** 3 • 8 *to order*
**ἐπακολουθέω** 1 • 4 *to follow*
**θαυμαστός** 6 • 13 *wonderful, marvelous, remarkable*
**θεράπων, ὁ** 5 • 6 *attendant, aide, servant*
**ἱερός** 3 • 5 *holy*
**καθίστημι/καθιστάνω** 6 • 8 *to appoint, put in charge*
**νομοθετέω** 1 • 2 *to ordain, found by law*
**προλέγω** 5 • 16 *to tell beforehand/ in advance*
**σημειόω** 1 • 1 *to note down, write*
**συνεπιμαρτυρέω** 2 • 3 *to testify at the same time*
2 **ἀποτίθημι** 3 • 13 *to put away, lay down*
**δακτύλιος, ὁ** 1 • 1 *ring*
**ἐμπίπτω** 1 • 5 *to set in, arise*
**ἔνδοξος** 8 • 54 *glorious, splendid*
**ἐπιγράφω** 1 • 4 *to write on/in*
**ζῆλος, ὁ/τό** 22 • 25 *jealousy, envy*
**ἱερωσύνη, ἡ** 1 • 1 *priestly office, priesthood*
**κελεύω** 5 • 44 *to command, order, urge*
**κοσμέω** 4 • 10 *to adorn, decorate, make beautiful* or *attractive*
**μαρτύριον, τό** 2 • 16 *tent of meeting, tent/tabernacle of testimony*
**ὁποῖος** 1 • 2 *of what sort, as*
**ῥάβδος, ἡ** 4 • 62 *rod, staff, stick*
**σκηνή, ἡ** 4 • 4 *tent, hut*
**στασιάζω** 7 • 7 *to rebel*
**σφραγίζω** 2 • 2 *to seal*
**τράπεζα, ἡ** 1 • 3 *table*
**φύλαρχος, ὁ** [2] 3 • 3 *head of a tribe*
3 **κλείς, ἡ** 1 • 1 *key*
**κλείω** 1 • 2 *to shut, lock, bar*
**σκηνή, ἡ** 4 • 4 *tent, hut*
**σφραγίζω** 2 • 2 *to seal*
**ὡσαύτως** 1 • 7 *(in) the same (way), similarly, likewise*
4 **βλαστάνω** 2 • 5 *to bud, sprout*
**ἐκλέγομαι** 4 • 15 *to select someone/something for oneself*
**ἱερατεύω** 1 • 1 *to hold the office or perform the service of a priest*
**λειτουργέω** 6 • 11 *to serve, render service*
**ῥάβδος, ἡ** 4 • 62 *rod, staff, stick*
5 **Ἀαρών, ὁ** 2 • 2 *Aaron*
**βλαστάνω** 2 • 5 *to bud, sprout*
**ἑξακόσιοι** 1 • 2 *six hundred*
**ἐπιδείκνυμι** 2 • 11 *to show, point out*
**μαρτύριον, τό** 2 • 16 *tent of meeting, tent/tabernacle of testimony*
**προαιρέω** 2 • 4 *to bring or take out*
**πρωΐος/πρωΐα, ἡ** 1 • 1 *(early) morning*
**ῥάβδος, ἡ** [2] 4 • 62 *rod, staff, stick*
**σκηνή, ἡ** 4 • 4 *tent, hut*
**συγκαλέω** 1 • 2 *to summon*
**σφραγίς, ἡ** 1 • 16 *seal*
**φύλαρχος, ὁ** 3 • 3 *head of a tribe*
**χιλιάς, ἡ** 2 • 3 *a thousand*
6 **ἀκαταστασία, ἡ** 3 • 4 *disorder, unruliness*
**ἀληθινός** 2 • 14 *genuine, authentic, real*
**μάλιστα** 2 • 14 *most assuredly, certainly*
**πρόοιδα** 1 • 2 *to know beforehand/ previously*

## Chapter 44

1 **ἐπισκοπή, ἡ** 3 • 5 *supervision*
**ἔρις, ἡ** 9 • 10 *strife, discord, contention*
2 **αἰτία, ἡ** 2 • 5 *cause, reason*
**διαδέχομαι** 1 • 1 *to receive in turn, succeed to*
**δοκιμάζω** 4 • 19 *to prove, approve*
**ἐπίμονος** 1 • 2 *lasting, continuous*
**καθίστημι/καθιστάνω** 6 • 8 *to appoint, put in charge, authorize, appoint*
**κοιμάω** 3 • 12 *to sleep, fall asleep, die, pass away*
**λειτουργία, ἡ** 8 • 11 *service*
**μεταξύ** 3 • 10 *afterwards, next*
**πρόγνωσις, ἡ** 1 • 1 *foreknowledge*
**προλέγω** 5 • 16 *to tell beforehand/ in advance*
**τέλειος** 5 • 25 *perfect*
3 **ἀβαναύσως** 1 • 1 *unselfishly, nobly*
**ἀμέμπτως** 4 • 6 *blamelessly*
**ἀποβάλλω** 3 • 36 *to remove, depose*

**δικαίως** 3 • 12 *justly, in an upright manner*
**ἐλλόγιμος** 4 • 4 *reputable, eminent*
**ἡσύχως** 1 • 1 *quietly*
**καθίστημι/καθιστάνω** 6 • 8 *to appoint, put in charge*
**λειτουργέω** 6 • 11 *to serve, render service*
**λειτουργία, ἡ** 8 • 11 *service*
**μεταξύ** 3 • 10 *afterwards, next*
**νομίζω** 3 • 10 *to think, believe, hold, consider*
**ποίμνιον, τό** 4 • 7 *flock*
**συνευδοκέω** 2 • 5 *to agree with, approve of, consent to, sympathize with*
**ταπεινοφροσύνη, ἡ** 6 • 9 *humility, modesty*
4 **ἀμέμπτως** 4 • 6 *blamelessly*
**ἀποβάλλω** 3 • 36 *to remove, depose*
**δῶρον, τό** 3 • 4 *gift, present*
**ἐπισκοπή, ἡ** 3 • 5 *supervision*
**ὁσίως** 8 • 9 *devoutly*
5 **ἀνάλυσις, ἡ** 1 • 1 *departure*
**ἔγκαρπος** 2 • 2 *fruitful*
**εὐλαβέομαι** 1 • 1 *to be concerned, be anxious*
**ἱδρύω** 1 • 2 *to be seated, sit, be established*
**μεθίστημι** 1 • 1 *to remove, depose*
**προοδοιπορέω** 1 • 1 *to die before now*
**τέλειος** 5 • 25 *perfect*
6 **ἀμέμπτως** 4 • 6 *blamelessly*
**ἔνιοι** 1 • 4 *some, several*
**λειτουργία, ἡ** 8 • 11 *service*
**μετάγω** 1 • 1 *to move, remove*
**πολιτεύομαι** 6 • 10 *to rule*
**τιμάω** 4 • 12 *to honor, revere*

## Chapter 45

1 **ἀνήκω** 3 • 10 *to refer, relate, belong*
**ζηλωτής, ὁ** 1 • 3 *enthusiast, adherent, loyalist*
**φιλόνεικος** 1 • 1 *emulous*
2 **ἀληθής** 1 • 16 *true*
**ἐγκύπτω** 4 • 5 *to examine, look at closely*
3 **ἄδικος** 5 • 14 *unjust*
**ἀποβάλλω** 3 • 36 *to reject*
**ἐπίσταμαι** 4 • 7 *to know, be acquainted with*
**ὅσιος** 6 • 10 *devout, pious, pleasing to God, holy*
**παραποιέω** 1 • 1 *to imitate, falsify, counterfeit*
4 **ἄδικος** 5 • 14 *unjust*
**ἀναλαμβάνω** 5 • 10 *to take to one's self, adopt*
**ἄνομος** 5 • 17 *lawless*
**ἀνόσιος** 3 • 3 *unholy*
**ζῆλος, ὁ/τό** 22 • 25 *jealousy, envy*
**λιθάζω** 2 • 3 *to stone*
**μιαρός** 4 • 4 *abominable, wretched, foul, depraved, wanton*
**παράνομος** 1 • 3 *lawless*
**φυλακίζω** 1 • 1 *to take into custody, imprison*
5 **εὐκλεῶς** 1 • 1 *gloriously*
6 **Δανιήλ, ὁ** 1 • 3 *Daniel*
**λάκκος, ὁ** 1 • 1 *pit, den*
**λέων, ὁ** 2 • 3 *lion*
7 **Ἀζαρίας, ὁ** 1 • 1 *Azariah*
**αἰκία, ἡ** 3 • 3 *mistreatment, torture*
**ἄμωμος** 7 • 17 *blameless*
**Ἀνανίας, ὁ** 1 • 1 *Ananias*
**δουλεύω** 4 • 42 *to (perform the duties of a slave) serve, obey*
**δράω** 1 • 1 *to do, accomplish*
**ἔνδοξος** 8 • 54 *glorious, splendid*
**ἐξερίζω** 1 • 1 *to be factious, be contentious*
**θρησκεία, ἡ** 2 • 3 *worship*
**θρησκεύω** 1 • 3 *to worship*
**θυμός, ὁ** 3 • 6 *anger, wrath, rage, indignation*
**καθαρός** 7 • 45 *pure, free*
**κακία, ἡ** 2 • 9 *baseness, depravity, wickedness, vice*
**κάμινος, ἡ** 1 • 3 *oven, furnace*
**κατείργω** 1 • 1 *to shut up, enclose*
**λατρεύω** 1 • 3 *to serve*
**μεγαλοπρεπής** 7 • 7 *magnificent, sublime, majestic, impressive*
**μηδαμῶς** 3 • 4 *by no means, certainly not, no*
**Μισαήλ, ὁ** 1 • 1 *Mishael*
**ὅσιος** 6 • 10 *devout, pious, pleasing to God, holy*
**πανάρετος** 5 • 5 *most excellent*
**περιβάλλω** 1 • 2 *to put on, put around, envelop (in torture)*
**πλήρης** 3 • 20 *filled, full*

**πρόθεσις, ἡ** 1 • 1 *plan, purpose, resolve, will, way of thinking*
**στυγητός** 2 • 2 *loathsome, despicable*
**τοσοῦτος** 9 • 38 *so great/strong, to such extent*
**ὑπερασπιστής, ὁ** 1 • 1 *protector*
**ὑπέρμαχος, ὁ** 1 • 1 *champion, defender*
**ὕψιστος** [2] 6 • 7 *the Most High*
8 **ἔγγραφος** 1 • 2 *recorded*
**ἐπαίρω** 5 • 6 *to lift up, hold up*
**κληρονομέω** 4 • 11 *to acquire, obtain, come into possession of*
**μνημόσυνον, τό** 2 • 2 *memory*
**πεποίθησις, ἡ** 5 • 7 *trust, confidence*
**ὑπομένω** 4 • 32 *to stand one's ground, hold out, endure*

## Chapter 46

1 **κολλάω** 10 • 32 *to cling to, attach to*
**ὑπόδειγμα, τό** 6 • 8 *example, model, pattern*
2 **ἁγιάζω** 3 • 16 *to consecrate, dedicate, sanctify*
**κολλάω** [2] 10 • 32 *to cling to, attach to*
3 **ἀθῷος** [2] 4 • 7 *innocent*
**διαστρέφω** 4 • 5 *to make crooked, pervert*
**ἐκλεκτός** [2] 12 • 30 *chosen*
**στρεβλός** 1 • 4 *crooked, perverse*
4 **ἀθῷος** 4 • 7 *innocent*
**ἐκλεκτός** 12 • 30 *chosen*
**κολλάω** 10 • 32 *to cling to, attach to, join oneself to, join, associate with*
5 **διχοστασία, ἡ** 2 • 6 *dissension*
**ἔρις, ἡ** 9 • 10 *strife, discord, contention*
**θυμός, ὁ** 3 • 6 *anger, wrath, rage, indignation*
**πόλεμος, ὁ** 3 • 4 *strife, conflict, quarrel*
**σχίσμα, τό** 5 • 10 *division, dissension, schism*
6 **ἐκχύννω/ἐκχύνω/ἐκχέω** 2 • 6 *to pour out*
**κλῆσις, ἡ** 1 • 4 *call, calling, invitation*
7 **ἀπόνοια, ἡ** 2 • 2 *madness, frenzy*
**διασπάω** 1 • 2 *to tear apart, tear up*
**διέλκω** 1 • 1 *to rend, tear apart*
**ἐπιλανθάνομαι** 2 • 8 *to forget*
**μιμνῄσκομαι** 3 • 9 *to remember, recollect, remind oneself*
**στασιάζω** 7 • 7 *to rebel*
**τοσοῦτος** 9 • 38 *so great/strong, to such extent*
8 **διαστρέφω** 4 • 5 *to mislead*
**ἐκλεκτός** 12 • 30 *chosen*
**καταποντίζω** 1 • 1 *to drown*
**κρείττων** 1 • 8 *more useful, more advantageous, better*
**μύλος, ὁ** 1 • 1 *millstone*
**περιτίθημι** 2 • 6 *to put/place around/on*
**σκανδαλίζω** 1 • 4 *to cause to sin*
9 **ἀθυμία, ἡ** 1 • 1 *discouragement*
**διαστρέφω** 4 • 5 *to mislead*
**δισταγμός, ὁ** 1 • 2 *doubt*
**ἐπίμονος** 1 • 2 *lasting*
**λύπη, ἡ** 1 • 24 *grief, sorrow, affliction*
**στάσις, ἡ** 9 • 9 *strife, discord, disunion*
**σχίσμα, τό** 5 • 10 *division, dissension, schism*

## Chapter 47

1 **ἀναλαμβάνω** 5 • 10 *to take in hand*
**ἐπιστολή, ἡ** 3 • 13 *letter, epistle*
3 **Ἀπολλῶς, ὁ** 1 • 1 *Apollos*
**ἐπιστέλλω** 3 • 3 *to inform/ instruct by letter*
**Κηφᾶς, ὁ** 1 • 1 *Cephas*
**πνευματικῶς** 1 • 4 *in keeping with the spirit*
**πρόσκλισις, ἡ** 4 • 4 *inclination*
4 **δοκιμάζω** 4 • 19 *to prove, approve*
**ἥσσων** 3 • 3 *lesser, inferior, weaker*
**προσκλίνω** 2 • 2 *to attach oneself to, join someone*
**πρόσκλισις, ἡ** 4 • 4 *inclination*
5 **διαστρέφω** 4 • 5 *to mislead*
**κατανοέω** 5 • 26 *to envisage, think about, notice*
**μειόω** 1 • 1 *to lessen*
**νυνί** 1 • 2 *now*

**περιβόητος** 2 • 2 *well known, far famed, celebrated*
**σεμνός** 6 • 12 *honorable, worthy, venerable, holy, above reproach*
**φιλαδελφία, ἡ** 2 • 4 *love of brother/sister*
6 **ἀγωγή, ἡ** 2 • 2 *way of life, conduct*
**αἰσχρός** [2] 2 • 3 *shameful, base*
**ἀνάξιος** 1 • 4 *unworthy*
**ἀρχαῖος** 2 • 12 *old, established*
**βέβαιος** 3 • 9 *abiding;*
**βεβαιοτάτην** (superlative adj. used elatively; cf. *ExSyn* 303) *well-established*
**Κορίνθιος, ὁ** 2 • 2 *the Corinthian*
**λίαν** 2 • 48 *very (much), exceedingly*
**στασιάζω** 7 • 7 *to rebel*
**ἀκούεσθαι** (pres. pass. infinitive of **ἀκούω**) *that it should be reported*
7 **ἀκοή, ἡ** 2 • 8 *fame, report, rumor*
**ἀφροσύνη, ἡ** 2 • 11 *foolishness, lack of sense*
**βλασφημία, ἡ** 1 • 7 *reviling, denigration, disrespect, slander*
**ἐπεξεργάζομαι** 1 • 1 *to cause besides, cause or effect in addition*
**ἐπιφέρω** 1 • 3 *to bring (on/about), inflict*
**ἑτεροκλινής** 2 • 2 *inclined to, having a propensity for*
**κίνδυνος, ὁ** 6 • 8 *danger, risk*
**ὑμέτερος** 2 • 4 *belonging to, incumbent upon you*
**χωρέω** 1 • 15 *to go, go out/away, reach*

## Chapter 48

1 **ἁγνός** 6 • 11 *pure, holy*
**ἀγωγή, ἡ** 2 • 2 *way of life, conduct*
**ἀποκαθίστημι** 2 • 4 *to restore, reestablish*
**δεσπότης, ὁ** 24 • 52 *lord, master*
**ἐξαίρω** 1 • 1 *to remove, drive away*
**ἐπικαταλλάσσομαι** 1 • 1 *to be reconciled to someone*
**ἱκετεύω** 3 • 3 *to supplicate, beseech*
**ἵλεως** 3 • 5 *gracious, merciful*
**προσπίπτω** 2 • 3 *to fall down before/at the feet of*
**σεμνός** 6 • 12 *honorable, worthy, venerable, holy, above reproach*
**τάχος, τό** 4 • 7 *speed, quickness, swiftness, haste*
**φιλαδελφία, ἡ** 2 • 4 *love of brother/sister*
2 **ἐξομολογέω** 6 • 15 *to praise*
**πύλη, ἡ** [2] 4 • 37 *gate, door*
3 **πύλη, ἡ** 4 • 37 *gate, door*
4 **ἀταράχως** 1 • 1 *without confusion, undisturbed*
**ἐπιτελέω** 13 • 15 *to complete, accomplish, perform, bring about*
**κατευθύνω** 2 • 2 *to lead, direct*
**ὁσιότης, ἡ** 4 • 4 *devoutness, piety, holiness*
**πορεία, ἡ** 2 • 3 *conduct*
**πύλη, ἡ** 4 • 37 *gate, door*
5 **ἁγνός** 6 • 11 *pure, holy*
**γνῶσις, ἡ** 6 • 32 *knowledge*
**γοργός** 1 • 1 *vigorous, strenuous*
**διάκρισις, ἡ** 1 • 1 *distinguishing, differentiation*
**ἐξαγορεύω/ἐξεῖπον** 2 • 4 *to express, proclaim*
**σοφός** 4 • 8 *clever, skillful, experienced*
6 **ζητέω** 4 • 19 *to strive for, aim (at), try to obtain, desire, wish (for)*
**κοινωφελής** 1 • 1 *generally useful*
**ταπεινοφρονέω** 11 • 14 *to be modest, be unassuming*
**τοσοῦτος** 9 • 38 *so much, as much*

## Chapter 49

1 **παράγγελμα, τό** 2 • 2 *order, direction, instruction, precept*
2 **δεσμός, ὁ** 3 • 14 *bond*
**ἐξηγέομαι** 1 • 2 *to tell, report, describe*
3 **ἀρκετός** 1 • 4 *enough, sufficient, adequate*
**ἐξαγορεύω/ἐξεῖπον** 2 • 4 *to express, proclaim*
**καλλονή, ἡ** 2 • 2 *beauty*
**μεγαλεῖος** 3 • 6 *greatness, sublimity*
4 **ἀνάγω** 1 • 2 *to lead, bring up*
**ἀνεκδιήγητος** 3 • 3 *indescribable*

ὕψος, τό 3 • 7 *height, high place*
5 ἀνέχω 1 • 7 *to endure, bear with, put up with*
βάναυσος 1 • 1 *base, vulgar, shabby*
δίχα 9 • 9 *apart from, without*
ἐκλεκτός 12 • 30 *chosen*
εὐάρεστος 5 • 9 *pleasing, acceptable*
καλύπτω 1 • 3 *to hide, conceal, keep secret, cover (up), remove from sight*
κολλάω 10 • 32 *to bind closely, unite*
μακροθυμέω 1 • 3 *to be patient, be forbearing*
ὁμόνοια, ἡ 14 • 24 *oneness of mind, unanimity, concord, harmony*
στασιάζω 7 • 7 *to rebel*
σχίσμα, τό 5 • 10 *division, dissention, schism*
τελειόω 4 • 14 *to make perfect*
ὑπερήφανος 4 • 6 *arrogant, haughty, proud*
6 δεσπότης, ὁ 24 • 52 *lord, master*
προσλαμβάνω 1 • 2 *to receive in(to) one's home or circle of acquaintances*

## Chapter 50

1 ἐξήγησις, ἡ 1 • 6 *narrative, description*
θαυμαστός 6 • 13 *wonderful, marvelous, remarkable*
τελειότης, ἡ 2 • 2 *perfection, completeness*
2 ἄμωμος 7 • 17 *blameless*
ἀνθρώπινος 2 • 7 *human*
δέομαι 2 • 7 *to ask, request*
δίχα 9 • 9 *apart from, without*
ἔλεος, τό 7 • 19 *mercy, compassion, pity, clemency*
καταξιόω 2 • 14 *to consider worthy*
πρόσκλισις, ἡ 4 • 4 *inclination*
3 Ἀδάμ, ὁ 3 • 4 *Adam*
ἐπισκοπή, ἡ 3 • 5 *visitation*
εὐσεβής 2 • 4 *devout, godly, pious, reverent*
ὅδε 2 • 7 *this*
παρέρχομαι 4 • 12 *to pass away, disappear*
τελειόω 4 • 14 *to make perfect*
χῶρος, ὁ 1 • 1 *place*
4 θήκη, ἡ 1 • 1 *grave*
θυμός, ὁ 3 • 6 *anger, wrath, rage, indignation*
μιμνῄσκομαι 3 • 9 *to remember, recollect, remind oneself*
παρέρχομαι 4 • 12 *to pass away, disappear*
ταμεῖον, τό 1 • 1 *inner room*
5 ὁμόνοια, ἡ 14 • 24 *oneness of mind, unanimity, concord, harmony*
πρόσταγμα, τό 7 • 10 *order, command(ment), injunction*
6 ἀνομία, ἡ 12 • 33 *a lawless deed*
δόλος, ὁ 4 • 8 *deceit, cunning, treachery*
ἐπικαλύπτω 1 • 1 *to cover up*
7 ἐκλέγομαι 4 • 15 *to select someone/something for oneself*
μακαρισμός, ὁ 1 • 1 *blessing*

## Chapter 51

1 ἀντίκειμαι 1 • 2 *to be in opposition to*
ἀξιόω 3 • 14 *to request, ask*
ἀρχηγός, ὁ 3 • 4 *instigator*
διχοστασία, ἡ 2 • 6 *dissension*
κοινός 1 • 15 *communal, common*
παραπίπτω 1 • 1 *to fall away, commit apostasy*
σκοπέω 1 • 2 *to look (out) for, notice*
στάσις, ἡ 9 • 9 *uprising, riot, revolt, rebellion*
2 αἰκία, ἡ 3 • 3 *mistreatment, torture*
δικαίως 3 • 12 *correctly, justly, uprightly*
κατάγνωσις, ἡ 1 • 1 *condemnation*
ὁμοφωνία, ἡ 1 • 1 *harmony*
περιπίπτω 1 • 1 *to fall in with, fall into*
πλησίον 3 • 17 *near;* subst. *neighbor, fellow human being*
πολιτεύομαι 6 • 10 *to live, lead one's life*

3 **ἐξομολογέω** 6 • 15 *to confess, admit*
**θεράπων, ὁ** 5 • 6 *attendant, aide, servant*
**κρίμα, τό** 8 • 9 *judicial verdict*
**παράπτωμα, τό** 4 • 10 *offense, wrongdoing, sin*
**πρόδηλος** 4 • 4 *clear, evident, known (to all)*
**σκληρύνω** [2] 3 • 4 *to harden*
**στασιάζω** 7 • 7 *to rebel*
4 **ᾅδης, ὁ** 2 • 3 *the nether world, Hades*
**ποιμαίνω** 1 • 1 *to shepherd*
5 **Αἴγυπτος, ἡ** [2] 6 • 9 *Egypt*
**αἰτία, ἡ** 2 • 5 *cause, reason*
**ἀναβάτης, ὁ** 1 • 1 *driver, rider*
**ἅρμα, τό** 1 • 1 *war-chariot*
**ἀσύνετος** 3 • 16 *senseless, foolish*
**βυθίζω** 1 • 1 *to sink*
**ἐρυθρός** 1 • 1 *red*
**ἡγέομαι** 8 • 25 *to lead, guide*
**θεράπων, ὁ** 5 • 6 *attendant, aide, servant*
**σκληρύνω** 3 • 4 *to harden*
**στρατιά, ἡ** 1 • 1 *army*
**τέρας, τό** 1 • 4 *prodigy, portent, omen, wonder*
**Φαραώ, ὁ** 2 • 2 *Pharaoh*

## Chapter 52

1 **ἀπροσδεής** 1 • 1 *needing nothing, self-sufficient*
**δεσπότης, ὁ** 24 • 52 *lord, master*
**ἐξομολογέω** 6 • 15 *to confess, admit*
**χρῄζω** 1 • 7 *to (have) need (of)*
2 **ἀρέσκω** 1 • 12 *to please, accommodate*
**ἐκλεκτός** 12 • 30 *elect*
**ἐκφέρω** 2 • 3 *to produce*
**ἐξομολογέω** 6 • 15 *to confess, admit*
**εὐφραίνω** 1 • 15 *to be glad, enjoy oneself, rejoice, celebrate*
**κέρας, τό** 1 • 4 *horn*
**μόσχος, ὁ** 1 • 2 *calf, young bull or ox*
**νέος** 4 • 16 *young*
**ὁπλή, ἡ** 1 • 1 *hoof*
3 **αἴνεσις, ἡ** 3 • 3 *praise*
**ἐξαιρέω** 3 • 4 *to set free, deliver, rescue*
**εὐχή, ἡ** 2 • 5 *vow*
**θυσία, ἡ** 10 • 22 *sacrifice, offering*
**θύω** 1 • 3 *to sacrifice*
**ὕψιστος** 6 • 7 *the Most High*
4 **θυσία, ἡ** 10 • 22 *sacrifice, offering*
**συντρίβω** 4 • 10 pass. *to be broken*

## Chapter 53

1 **ἀνάμνησις, ἡ** 1 • 1 *reminder, remembrance of something*
**ἐγκύπτω** 4 • 5 *to examine*
**ἐπίσταμαι** [2] 4 • 7 *to know, be acquainted with*
**ἱερός** 3 • 5 *holy*
**λόγιον, τό** 4 • 11 *saying*
2 **Αἴγυπτος, ἡ** 6 • 9 *Egypt*
**ἀνομέω** 1 • 4 *to be lawless, sin*
**ἐντέλλω** 1 • 29 *to command, order, give orders*
**ἐντεῦθεν** 1 • 1 *from here*
**ἐξάγω** 3 • 7 *to lead out, bring out*
**νηστεία, ἡ** 2 • 25 *fast*
**παραβαίνω** 1 • 3 *to go aside, deviate*
**ταπείνωσις, ἡ** 3 • 4 *self-abasement, mortification*
**τάχος, τό** 4 • 7 *speed, quickness, swiftness, haste*
**ταχύς** 3 • 13 *quick, swift, speedy, without delay, quickly, at once*
**τεσσαράκοντα/τεσσεράκοντα** [2] 2 • 6 *forty*
**χώνευμα, τό** 1 • 2 *cast image*
3 **ἅπαξ** 1 • 4 *once*
**δίς** 1 • 2 *twice*
**ἐάω** 5 • 13 *to let, permit*
**ἐξαλείφω** 5 • 8 *to remove, destroy, obliterate*
**ἐξολεθρεύω** 4 • 5 *to utterly destroy, root out*
**θαυμαστός** 6 • 13 *wonderful, marvelous, remarkable*
**σκληροτράχηλος** 1 • 1 *stiff-necked, stubborn*
**ὑποκάτωθεν** 1 • 1 *(from) under*
4 **βίβλος, ἡ** 2 • 5 *record-book*
**ἐξαλείφω** 5 • 8 *to remove, destroy, obliterate*
**μηδαμῶς** 3 • 4 *by no means, certainly not, no*

5 **ἀνυπέρβλητος** 1 • 2 *unsurpassable, unexcelled*
**ἄφεσις, ἡ** 1 • 13 *pardon, cancellation*
**ἐξαλείφω** 5 • 8 *to remove, destroy, obliterate, wipe out*
**θεράπων, ὁ** 5 • 6 *attendant, aide, servant*
**παρρησιάζω/παρρησιάζομαι** 2 • 2 *to speak freely, openly, fearlessly*
**τελειότης, ἡ** 2 • 2 *perfection, completeness*
**ὦ** 3 • 8 *o, oh, how!*

## Chapter 54

1 **γενναῖος** 5 • 8 *noble, illustrious*
**εὔσπλαγχνος** 2 • 4 *tenderhearted, compassionate*
**πληροφορέω** 2 • 9 *to fill (completely), fulfill*
2 **ἄπειμι** 2 • 2 *to go away, go, come*
**εἰρηνεύω** 5 • 17 *to keep the peace*
**ἐκχωρέω** 3 • 4 *to go out, go away, depart*
**ἔρις, ἡ** 9 • 10 *strife, discord, contention*
**καθίστημι/καθιστάνω** 6 • 8 *to authorize, appoint, put in charge*
**ποίμνιον, τό** 4 • 7 *flock*
**προστάσσω** 4 • 8 *to command, order, give instructions, determine*
**στάσις, ἡ** 9 • 9 *strife, discord, disunion*
**σχίσμα, τό** 5 • 10 *division, dissension, schism*
3 **κλέος, τό** 2 • 2 *fame, glory*
**περιποιέω** 1 • 9 *to acquire, obtain, gain for oneself*
**πλήρωμα, τό** 1 • 3 *that which fills (up)*
4 **ἀμεταμέλητος** 3 • 3 *not to be regretted, without regret*
**πολιτεία, ἡ** 2 • 5 *way of life, conduct*
**πολιτεύομαι** 6 • 10 *to live, lead one's life*

## Chapter 55

1 **ἐκχωρέω** 3 • 4 *to go out, go away, depart*
**ἐνίστημι** 1 • 6 *to be now, happen now*
**ἡγέομαι** 8 • 25 *to lead, guide*
**λοιμικός** 1 • 1 *pestilential*
**πολίτης, ὁ** 1 • 2 *fellow-citizen, compatriot*
**ῥύομαι** 12 • 19 *to save, rescue, deliver, preserve*
**στασιάζω** 7 • 7 *to rebel*
**ὑπόδειγμα, τό** 6 • 8 *example, model, pattern*
**χρησμοδοτέω** 1 • 1 *to give an oracular response*
2 **δεσμός, ὁ** 3 • 14 *bond, fetter*
**δουλεία, ἡ** 2 • 3 *slavery*
**ἐπίσταμαι** 4 • 7 *to know, be acquainted with*
**λυτρόω** 2 • 11 *to redeem*
**ψωμίζω** 1 • 1 *to feed*
3 **ἀνδρεῖος** 1 • 1 *manly, courageous*
**ἐνδυναμόω** 1 • 14 *to become strong*
**ἐπιτελέω** 13 • 15 *to complete, accomplish, perform, bring about*
4 **ἀλλόφυλος** 2 • 4 *alien, foreign*
**ἐάω** 5 • 13 *to let, permit*
**Ἰουδίθ, ἡ** 1 • 1 *Judith*
**παρεμβολή, ἡ** 2 • 2 *a (fortified) camp*
**συγκλεισμός, ὁ** 2 • 2 *confinement, encirclement*
5 **θῆλυς** 2 • 9 *female*
**κίνδυνος, ὁ** 6 • 8 *danger, risk*
**Ὀλοφέρνης, ὁ** 1 • 1 *Holofernes*
**πατρίς, ἡ** 1 • 4 *fatherland, homeland*
**συγκλεισμός, ὁ** 2 • 2 *confinement, encirclement*
6 **ἀξιόω** 3 • 14 *to request, ask*
**δεσπότης, ὁ** 24 • 52 *lord, master*
**δωδεκάφυλον, τό** 1 • 1 *the twelve tribes*
**Ἐσθήρ, ἡ** 1 • 1 *Esther*
**ἥσσων** 3 • 3 *lesser, inferior, weaker*
**κινδυνεύω** 2 • 2 *to be in danger, run a risk*
**κίνδυνος, ὁ** 6 • 8 *danger, risk*
**νηστεία, ἡ** 2 • 25 *fasting, abstention from food*

παντεπόπτης, ὁ 2 • 3 *one who sees all, one who is all-seeing*
παραβάλλω 1 • 3 *to give up*
ῥύομαι 12 • 19 *to save, rescue, deliver, preserve*
ταπεινός 4 • 8 *humble*
ταπείνωσις, ἡ 3 • 4 *self-abasement, mortification*
τέλειος 5 • 25 *perfect, complete, expert*
χάριν 3 • 4 *for the sake of, on behalf of, on account of*

## Chapter 56

1 ἔγκαρπος 2 • 2 *fruitful*
εἴκω 1 • 1 *to yield*
ἐντυγχάνω 1 • 8 *to pray*
ἐπιείκεια, ἡ 5 • 9 *clemency, gentleness, graciousness, courtesy, indulgence, tolerance*
μνεία, ἡ 1 • 3 *mention*
οἰκτιρμός, ὁ 4 • 4 *pity, mercy, compassion*
παράπτωμα, τό 4 • 10 *offense, wrongdoing, sin*
ταπεινοφροσύνη, ἡ 6 • 9 *humility, modesty*
τέλειος 5 • 25 *perfect*
2 ἀγανακτέω 1 • 2 *to be aroused, be indignant, be angry*
ἀναλαμβάνω 5 • 10 *to take to one's self, adopt*
κολλάω 10 • 32 *to bind closely, unite*
νουθέτησις, ἡ 1 • 1 *admonition, warning, reproof*
παιδεία, ἡ 7 • 11 *upbringing, training, instruction*
ὑπεράγαν 1 • 1 *beyond measure*
ὠφέλιμος 2 • 3 *useful, beneficial, advantageous*
3 παιδεύω [2] 9 • 13 *to practice discipline*
4 μαστιγόω 1 • 4 *to punish, chastise*
παιδεύω 9 • 13 *to practice discipline*
παραδέχομαι 1 • 9 *to receive, accept*
5 ἔλαιον, τό 1 • 4 *olive oil*
ἐλέγχω 3 • 16 *to reprove, correct*
ἔλεος, τό 7 • 19 *mercy, compassion, pity, clemency*
λιπαίνω 1 • 1 *to anoint*
παιδεύω 9 • 13 *to practice discipline*
6 ἀλγέω 1 • 2 *to feel pain*
ἀπαναίνομαι 1 • 1 *to reject, disown*
ἀποκαθίστημι 2 • 4 *to restore, reestablish*
ἐλέγχω 3 • 16 *to reprove, correct*
νουθέτημα, τό 1 • 1 *admonition, discipline*
παντοκράτωρ, ὁ 6 • 12 *Almighty, All-powerful, Omnipotent (One)*
7 ἰάομαι 3 • 11 *to restore, heal*
παίζω 1 • 3 *to play, amuse oneself*
8 ἀνάγκη, ἡ 1 • 11 *distress, calamity, pressure*
ἕβδομος 1 • 6 *seventh*
ἐξαιρέω 3 • 4 *to set free, deliver, rescue*
ἑξάκις 1 • 1 *six times*
9 λιμός, ὁ/ἡ 1 • 1 *famine*
πόλεμος, ὁ 3 • 4 *war*
ῥύομαι 12 • 19 *to save, rescue, deliver, preserve*
σίδηρος, ὁ 1 • 3 *iron*
10 ἐπέρχομαι 2 • 8 *to happen, come about, come (on), approach*
κρύπτω 3 • 4 *to hide*
μάστιξ, ἡ 3 • 8 *torment, suffering*
11 ἄγριος 2 • 8 *wild*
ἄδικος 5 • 14 *unjust, crooked*
ἄνομος 5 • 17 *lawless*
καταγελάω 1 • 2 *to laugh at, ridicule*
12 ἄγριος 2 • 8 *wild*
εἰρηνεύω 5 • 17 *to live in peace, be at peace*
θήρ, ὁ 2 • 2 *(wild) animal*
13 δίαιτα, ἡ 2 • 3 *habitation, dwelling-place*
εἰρηνεύω 5 • 17 *to live in peace, be at peace*
εἶτα 8 • 48 *then, next*
σκηνή, ἡ 4 • 4 *tent, hut*
14 παμβότανον, τό 1 • 1 *all (-covering), herbage*
15 ἅλων, ἡ 2 • 3 *threshing floor;* ἅλωνος (gen. of place; see *ExSyn* 124) *on the threshing floor*
θερίζω 1 • 1 *to reap, harvest*
θημωνιά, ἡ 1 • 1 *heap (of sheaves)*

**σῖτος, ὁ** 1 • 2 *wheat, grain*
**συγκομίζω** 1 • 1 *to bring in*
**τάφος, ὁ** 2 • 4 *grave, tomb*
**ὥριμος** 1 • 1 *ripe*
16 **δεσπότης, ὁ** 24 • 52 *lord, master*
**ἐλεέω** 3 • 16 *to have compassion/ mercy/pity*
**ὅσιος** 6 • 10 *holy*
**παιδεία, ἡ** 7 • 11 *upbringing, training, instruction, discipline, correction*
**παιδεύω** [2] 9 • 13 *to practice discipline*
**πόσος** 1 • 10 *how great (?)*
**ὑπερασπισμός, ὁ** 1 • 1 *protection*

## Chapter 57

1 **γόνυ, τό** 1 • 4 *knee*
**κάμπτω** 1 • 2 *to bend, bow*
**καταβολή, ἡ** 1 • 2 *foundation*
**μετάνοια, ἡ** 9 • 72 *repentance, turning about, conversion*
**παιδεύω** 9 • 13 *to practice discipline*
**στάσις, ἡ** 9 • 9 *strife, discord, disunion*
2 **ἀλαζών, ὁ/ἡ** 1 • 1 *boaster, braggart*
**ἀμείνων** 1 • 6 *better*
**ἀποτίθημι** 3 • 13 *to take off, lay aside, rid oneself*
**αὐθάδεια, ἡ** 2 • 6 *arrogance, willfulness, stubbornness*
**ἐκρίπτω** 1 • 2 *to drive out from*
**ἐλλόγιμος** 4 • 4 *included*
**μανθάνω** 3 • 26 *to learn*
**ποίμνιον, τό** 4 • 7 *flock*
**ὑπερήφανος** 4 • 6 *arrogant, haughty, proud*
**ὑπεροχή, ἡ** 1 • 1 *superiority, preeminence*
3 **πανάρετος** 5 • 5 *most excellent*
**πνοή, ἡ** 2 • 3 *breath*
**προΐημι** 1 • 1 *to bring forth, express*
**ῥῆσις, ἡ** 1 • 1 *word, expression*
4 **ἄκυρος** 1 • 1 *void, of no effect*
**ἀπειθέω** 3 • 5 *to disobey, be disobedient*
**ἀπώλεια, ἡ** 1 • 3 *annihilation, ruin*
**ἀφικνέομαι** 1 • 1 *to reach, come upon*
**ἄφνω** 1 • 1 *of a sudden*
**βουλή, ἡ** 5 • 19 *resolution, decision*
**ἐκτείνω** 2 • 7 *to draw out at length*
**ἔλεγχος, ὁ** 2 • 3 *reproof, censure, correction*
**ἐπειδή** 2 • 17 *(just) because*
**ἐπιγελάω** 1 • 1 *to laugh at*
**ἡνίκα** 1 • 1 *when, at the time when*
**θόρυβος, ὁ** 1 • 4 *confusion, unrest*
**καταιγίς, ἡ** 1 • 1 *a sudden blast of wind*
**καταστροφή, ἡ** 2 • 2 *ruin, destruction*
**καταχαίρω** 1 • 1 *to rejoice*
**ὄλεθρος, ὁ** 1 • 2 *destruction, ruin, death*
**πάρειμι** 1 • 17 *to be present*
**πολιορκία, ἡ** 1 • 1 *siege*
**προσέχω** 4 • 25 *to pay attention to, give heed to, follow*
**τοιγαροῦν** 2 • 2 *for that very reason, then, therefore*
**ὑμέτερος** 2 • 4 *belonging to, incumbent upon you*
**ὑπακούω** 5 • 9 *to obey, follow, be subject to*
5 **βουλή, ἡ** 5 • 19 *resolution, decision*
**εἰσακούω** 4 • 4 *to hear*
**ἔλεγχος, ὁ** 2 • 3 *reproof, censure, correction*
**ζητέω** 4 • 19 *to seek, look for*
**μυκτηρίζω** 2 • 3 *to turn up the nose at, treat with contempt*
**προαιρέω** 2 • 4 *to choose (for oneself), commit oneself to, prefer*
**προσέχω** 4 • 25 *to pay attention to, give heed to, follow*
6 **ἀσέβεια, ἡ** 1 • 3 *impiety*
**πίμπλημι** 1 • 3 *to satiate, satisfy*
**τοιγαροῦν** 2 • 2 *for that very reason, then, therefore*
7 **ἀδικέω** 2 • 7 *to do wrong to someone, treat someone unjustly*
**ἀντί** 4 • 15 *because of, for the purpose of*
**ἀσεβής** 5 • 14 *irreverent, impious, ungodly*
**ἀφόβως** 1 • 1 *fearlessly*
**ἐξετασμός, ὁ** 1 • 1 *examination, inquiry*
**ἡσυχάζω** 3 • 3 *to have rest*
**κατασκηνόω** 2 • 3 *to live, settle*

**νήπιος** 1 • 4 *infant, child*
**ὄλλυμι** 1 • 1 *to destroy*
**φονεύω** 1 • 4 *to murder, kill*

## Chapter 58

1 **ἀπειθέω** 3 • 5 *to disobey, be disobedient*
**ἀπειλή, ἡ** 1 • 2 *threat*
**ἔνδοξος** 8 • 54 *glorious, splendid*
**κατασκηνόω** 2 • 3 *to live, settle*
**μεγαλωσύνη, ἡ** 8 • 10 *majesty*
**ὅσιος** 6 • 10 *holy*
**πανάγιος** 2 • 2 *all-holy*
**προλέγω** 5 • 16 *to state beforehand/earlier*
**ὑπακούω** 5 • 9 *to obey, follow, be subject to*
**φεύγω** 4 • 20 *to escape*
2 **ἀμεταμέλητος** 3 • 3 *not to be regretted, without regret*
**ἀμεταμελήτως** 1 • 1 *without feeling regret*
**ἀριθμός, ὁ** 5 • 14 *number*
**δικαίωμα, τό** 3 • 12 *regulation, requirement, commandment*
**ἐκλεκτός** 12 • 30 *chosen*
**ἐκτενής** 3 • 3 *eager, earnest*
**ἐλλόγιμος** 4 • 4 *included*
**ἐντάσσω** 1 • 1 *to enroll*
**ἐπιείκεια, ἡ** 5 • 9 *clemency, gentleness, graciousness, courtesy, indulgence, tolerance*
**πρόσταγμα, τό** 7 • 10 *order, command(ment), injunction*
**συμβουλή, ἡ** 1 • 1 *advice, counsel*
**ταπεινοφροσύνη, ἡ** 6 • 9 *humility, modesty*

## Chapter 59

1 **ἀπειθέω** 3 • 5 *to disobey, be disobedient*
**ἐνδέω** 1 • 5 *to entangle, involve*
**κίνδυνος, ὁ** 6 • 8 *danger, risk*
**παράπτωσις, ἡ** 1 • 1 *wrongdoing, sin*
2 **ἀγνωσία, ἡ** 1 • 1 *ignorance*
**ἄθραυστος** 1 • 1 *unbroken*
**ἀθῷος** 4 • 7 *innocent*
**ἀριθμός, ὁ** 5 • 14 *number, total*
**δέησις, ἡ** 2 • 6 *prayer*
**δημιουργός, ὁ** 5 • 7 *craftsworker, builder, maker, creator*
**διαφυλάσσω** 1 • 2 *to guard, protect*
**ἐκλεκτός** 12 • 30 *chosen*
**ἐκτενής** 3 • 3 *eager, earnest*
**ἐπίγνωσις, ἡ** 1 • 3 *knowledge, recognition*
**ἱκεσία, ἡ** 1 • 1 *supplication*
**καταριθμέω** 1 • 2 *to count*
**παῖς, ὁ/ἡ** 4 • 20 *slave, servant*
3 **ἄβυσσος, ἡ** 3 • 4 *depth, abyss*
**ἁγιάζω** 3 • 16 *to consecrate, dedicate, sanctify*
**ἀναπαύω** 1 • 13 *to rest upon, abide*
**ἀνθρώπινος** 2 • 7 *human*
**ἀπελπίζω** 1 • 2 *to despair*
**ἀρχέγονος** 1 • 1 *original author, originator, source*
**βοηθός** 3 • 4 *helpful*
**διαλύω** 2 • 3 *to destroy*
**ἐκλέγομαι** 4 • 15 *to choose (for oneself)*
**ἐπιβλέπω** 2 • 2 *to look, gaze*
**ἐπίσκοπος, ὁ** 4 • 76 *guardian*
**ἐπόπτης, ὁ** 1 • 1 *a watchful observer*
**εὐεργέτης, ὁ** 1 • 1 *benefactor*
**κινδυνεύω** 2 • 2 *to be in danger, run a risk*
**κτίσις, ἡ** 3 • 19 *that which is created*
**κτίστης, ὁ** 3 • 3 *the Creator*
**λογισμός, ὁ** 1 • 4 *calculation, reasoning, reflection, thought*
**παιδεύω** 9 • 13 *to practice discipline*
**παῖς, ὁ/ἡ** 4 • 20 *slave, servant*
**πληθύνω** 3 • 11 *to increase, multiply*
**πλουτίζω** 1 • 5 *to make wealthy*
**πτωχίζω** 1 • 1 *to make (extremely) poor*
**σωτήρ, ὁ** 1 • 14 *savior, deliverer, preserver*
**ταπεινός** 4 • 8 *low position, poor, lowly, undistinguished, of no account, humble*
**ταπεινόω** [2] 4 • 8 *to humble, humiliate, abase*
**τιμάω** 4 • 12 *to honor, revere*
**ὕβρις, ἡ** 1 • 4 *insolence, arrogance*
**ὑπερήφανος** 4 • 6 *arrogant, haughty, proud*

**ὑψηλός** 2 • 12 *exalted, proud, haughty*
**ὕψιστος** [2] 6 • 7 *highest*
**ὕψος, τό** 3 • 7 *high position*
4 **ἀντιλήπτωρ, ὁ** 1 • 1 *helper, protector*
**ἀξιόω** 3 • 14 *to request, ask*
**ἀσθενής** 5 • 13 *sick, ill*
**βοηθός** 3 • 4 *helpful*
**δέομαι** 2 • 7 *to ask, request*
**δέσμιος, ὁ** 1 • 1 *prisoner*
**δεσπότης, ὁ** 24 • 52 *lord, master*
**ἐλεέω** 3 • 16 *to have compassion/mercy/pity*
**ἐξανίστημι** 2 • 3 *to raise up, awaken*
**ἐπιφαίνω** 2 • 2 *to show oneself, make an appearance*
**ἰάομαι** 3 • 11 *to heal, cure*
**λυτρόω** 2 • 11 *to redeem*
**νομή, ἡ** 1 • 2 *pasturage*
**ὀλιγοψυχέω** 1 • 1 *to be faint-hearted, be discouraged*
**παῖς, ὁ/ἡ** 4 • 20 *slave, servant*
**πεινάω** 1 • 6 *to hunger, be hungry*
**ταπεινός** 4 • 8 *lowly, undistinguished, of no account*
**χορτάζω** 1 • 1 *to feed, fill*

## Chapter 60

1 **ἀδικία, ἡ** 2 • 7 *wrongdoing*
**ἀέναος** 2 • 2 *eternal*
**ἀνομία, ἡ** 12 • 33 *a lawless deed*
**ἑδράζω** 2 • 6 *to establish, fix, settle*
**ἐλεήμων** 1 • 4 *merciful, sympathetic, compassionate*
**ἐνεργέω** 1 • 4 *to work, be at work, be active, operate, be effective*
**θαυμαστός** 6 • 13 *wonderful, marvelous, remarkable*
**ἰσχύς, ἡ** 5 • 11 *strength, power, might*
**κρίμα, τό** 8 • 9 *judging, judgment*
**κτίζω** [2] 3 • 25 *to create*
**μεγαλοπρέπεια, ἡ** 1 • 1 *majesty, sublimity*
**οἰκουμένη, ἡ** 1 • 6 *the whole world*
**οἰκτίρμων** 2 • 2 *merciful, compassionate*
**παράπτωμα, τό** 4 • 10 *offense, wrongdoing, sin*
**πλημμέλεια, ἡ** 2 • 2 *fault, error, sin, offense*
**σοφός** 4 • 8 *wise*
**συνετός** 1 • 7 *intelligent, sagacious, wise, with good sense*
**σύστασις, ἡ** 1 • 3 *structure, constitution, nature*
2 **ἁπλότης, ἡ** 1 • 15 *simplicity, sincerity, uprightness, frankness*
**διάβημα, τό** 1 • 1 *step*
**εὐάρεστος** 5 • 9 *pleasing, acceptable*
**καθαρισμός, ὁ** 1 • 1 *purity*
**κατευθύνω** 2 • 2 *to lead, direct*
**ὁσιότης, ἡ** 4 • 4 *devoutness, piety, holiness*
**παιδίσκη, ἡ** 1 • 3 *female slave*
**σός** 2 • 9 *your, yours*
**χρηστός** 1 • 2 *kind, loving, benevolent*
3 **ἀδίκως** 1 • 2 *unjustly, undeservedly*
**βραχίων, ὁ** 2 • 2 *arm*
**δεσπότης, ὁ** 24 • 52 *lord, master*
**ἐπιφαίνω** 2 • 2 *to show*
**κραταιός** 2 • 3 *powerful, mighty*
**ναί** 1 • 8 *yes, certainly, indeed, it's true that*
**ῥύομαι** 12 • 19 *to save, rescue, deliver, preserve*
**σκεπάζω** 2 • 8 *to protect, shelter*
**ὑψηλός** 2 • 12 *tall, high*
4 **ἡγέομαι** 8 • 25 *to lead, guide*
**ὁμόνοια, ἡ** 14 • 24 *oneness of mind, unanimity, concord, harmony*
**ὁσίως** 8 • 9 *devoutly*
**πανάρετος** 5 • 5 *most excellent*
**παντοκράτωρ, ὁ** 6 • 12 *Almighty, All-Powerful, Omnipotent (One)*
**ὑπήκοος** 5 • 5 *obedient*

## Chapter 61

1 **ἀνεκδιήγητος** 3 • 3 *indescribable*
**ἀπροσκόπως** 2 • 3 *without stumbling, blamelessly*
**δεσπότης, ὁ** 24 • 52 *lord, master*
**διέπω** 2 • 3 *to conduct, administer*
**ἐναντιόομαι** 1 • 1 *to oppose (oneself)*

εὐστάθεια, ἡ 2 • 2 *good disposition, tranquility, stability, firmness*
ἡγεμονία, ἡ 1 • 2 *chief command, direction, management*
κράτος, τό 5 • 7 *might*
μεγαλοπρεπής 7 • 7 *magnificent, sublime, majestic, impressive*
ὁμόνοια, ἡ 14 • 24 *oneness of mind, unanimity, concord, harmony*
ὑγιεία, ἡ 2 • 2 *health*
2 βουλή, ἡ 5 • 19 *plan, purpose, intention, counsel*
δεσπότης, ὁ 24 • 52 *lord, master*
διέπω 2 • 3 *to conduct, administer*
διευθύνω 3 • 3 *to guide, direct, govern*
ἐπουράνιος 1 • 11 *heavenly, in heaven*
εὐάρεστος 5 • 9 *pleasing, acceptable*
εὐσεβῶς 2 • 2 *in a godly manner*
ἵλεως 3 • 5 *gracious, merciful*
πραΰτης, ἡ 3 • 8 *gentleness, humility, courtesy, considerateness, meekness*
τυγχάνω 2 • 15 *to meet, attain, gain, find, experience*
3 ἐξομολογέω 5 • 14 *to praise*
μεγαλωσύνη, ἡ 8 •10 *majesty*
περισσός 1 • 5 *abundant, profuse*
προστάτης, ὁ 3 • 3 *defender, guardian, benefactor*

## Chapter 62

1 ἀνήκω 3 • 10 *to refer, relate, belong, pertain*
βίος, ὁ 1 • 13 *life*
διευθύνω 3 • 3 *to guide, direct, govern*
δικαίως 3 • 12 *correctly, justly, uprightly*
ἐνάρετος 1 • 2 *first-rate, high class, exceptional, virtuous*
ἐπιστέλλω 3 • 3 *to inform/ instruct by letter*
εὐσεβῶς 2 • 2 *in a godly manner*
θρησκεία, ἡ 2 • 3 *worship*
πορεία, ἡ 2 • 3 *conduct*
ὠφέλιμος 2 • 3 *useful, beneficial, advantageous*
2 ἀμνησικάκως 1 • 1 *without bearing malice*
γνήσιος 1 • 2 *genuine*
ἐγκράτεια, ἡ 4 • 14 *self-control*
ἐκτενής 3 • 3 *eager, earnest*
ἐπιείκεια, ἡ 5 • 9 *clemency, gentleness, graciousness, courtesy, indulgence, tolerance*
εὐαρεστέω [2] 2 • 6 *to please, be pleasing*
κτίστης, ὁ 3 • 3 *the Creator*
μακροθυμία, ἡ 3 • 15 *forbearance, patience*
μετάνοια, ἡ 9 • 72 *repentance, turning about, conversion*
ὁμονοέω 1 • 1 *to be in agreement, live in harmony*
ὁσίως 8 • 9 *devoutly*
παντοκράτωρ, ὁ 6 • 12 *Almighty, All-powerful, Omnipotent (One)*
προδηλόω 1 • 2 *to reveal*
σωφροσύνη, ἡ 2 • 3 *good judgment, moderation, self-control*
ταπεινοφρονέω 11 • 14 *to be modest, be unassuming*
ὑπομιμνήσκω 3 • 4 *to call to mind, bring up, suggest, remember*
ψηλαφάω 1 • 3 *to touch, handle*
3 ἐγκύπτω 4 • 5 *to examine*
ἐλλόγιμος 4 • 4 *reputable, eminent*
ἐπειδή 2 • 17 *(just) because*
ἡδέως 3 • 10 *gladly*
λόγιον, τό 4 • 11 *a saying*
παιδεία, ἡ 7 • 11 *upbringing, training, instruction, discipline, correction*
σαφῶς 1 • 5 *clearly, exactly, very well*
τοσοῦτος 9 • 38 *so much, as much*
ὑπομιμνήσκω 3 • 4 *to call to mind, bring up, suggest, remember*

## Chapter 63

1 ἀναπληρόω 2 • 4 *to fill a gap, replace;*
τὸν τῆς ὑπακοῆς τόπον ἀναπληρώσαντας *taking the attitude of obedience*
ἀρχηγός, ὁ 3 • 4 *leader, ruler, prince*

**δίχα** 9 • 9 *apart from, without*
**ἡσυχάζω** 3 • 3 *to be peaceable/ orderly*
**θεμιτός** 1 • 2 *allowed, permitted, right*
**καταντάω** 3 • 4 *to arrive at, attain, meet*
**μάταιος** 2 • 14 *idle, empty, fruitless, useless, powerless, lacking truth*
**μῶμος, ὁ** 1 • 1 *blame*
**πρόκειμαι** 1 • 4 *to lie or be set before someone*
**προσκλίνω** 2 • 2 *to attach oneself to, join someone*
**σκοπός, ὁ** 2 • 3 *goal, mark*
**στάσις, ἡ** 9 • 9 *strife, discord, disunion*
**τοσοῦτος** 9 • 38 *so much, as much*
**τράχηλος, ὁ** 1 • 3 *neck, throat;* **ὑποθεῖναι τὸν τράχηλον** *to submit the neck* (to the yoke)
**ὑπακοή, ἡ** 5 • 5 *obedience*
**ὑπόδειγμα, τό** 6 • 8 *example, model, pattern*
**ὑποτίθημι** 1 • 1 *to lay down, bow, submit*

2 **ἀγαλλίασις, ἡ** 3 • 5 *exultation*
**ἀθέμιτος** 1 • 3 *wanton, disgusting, unseemly*
**ἐκκόπτω** 1 • 3 *to exterminate, root out*
**ἔντευξις, ἡ** 1 • 18 *petition, request*
**ἐπιστολή, ἡ** 3 • 13 *letter, epistle*
**ζῆλος, ὁ/τό** 22 • 25 *jealousy, envy*
**ὅδε** 2 • 7 *this*
**ὁμόνοια, ἡ** 14 • 24 *oneness of mind, unanimity, concord, harmony*
**παρέχω** 3 • 18 *to cause, make happen*
**ὑπήκοος** 5 • 5 *obedient*

3 **ἀμέμπτως** 4 • 6 *blamelessly*
**ἀναστρέφω** 1 • 8 *to act, behave, conduct oneself, live*
**γῆρας, τό** 2 • 2 *old age*
**μεταξύ** 3 • 10 *between*
**νεότης, ἡ** 1 • 3 *youth*
**σώφρων** 2 • 2 *prudent, thoughtful, self-controlled*

4 **εἰρηνεύω** 5 • 17 *to live in peace, be at peace*
**τάχος, τό** 4 • 7 *speed, quickness, swiftness, haste*
**φροντίς, ἡ** 2 • 3 *care, concern*

## Chapter 64

1 **ἁγνεία, ἡ** 2 • 13 *purity, chastity*
**δεσπότης, ὁ** 24 • 52 *lord, master*
**ἐγκράτεια, ἡ** 4 • 14 *self-control*
**ἐκλέγομαι** 4 • 15 *to select someone/something for oneself*
**εὐαρέστησις, ἡ** 1 • 1 *being pleased*
**κράτος, τό** 5 • 7 *might*
**μακροθυμία, ἡ** 3 • 15 *patience, steadfastness, endurance*
**μεγαλοπρεπής** 7 • 7 *magnificent, sublime, majestic, impressive*
**μεγαλωσύνη, ἡ** 8 • 10 *majesty*
**παντεπόπτης, ὁ** 2 • 3 *one who sees all, one who is all-seeing*
**περιούσιος** 1 • 1 *chosen, special*
**προστάτης, ὁ** 3 • 3 *defender, guardian, benefactor*
**σωφροσύνη, ἡ** 2 • 3 *good judgment, moderation, self-control*

## Chapter 65

1 **ἀναπέμπω** 1 • 3 *to send back*
**Βίτων, ὁ** 1 • 1 *Bito*
**ἐπιπόθητος** 1 • 2 *longed for, desired*
**εὐκταῖος** 1 • 1 *prayed for, wished for*
**εὐστάθεια, ἡ** 2 • 2 *good disposition, tranquility, stability, firmness*
**Ἔφηβος, ὁ** 1 • 1 *Ephebus*
**Κλαύδιος, ὁ** 1 • 1 *Claudius*
**ὁμόνοια, ἡ** 14 • 24 *oneness of mind, unanimity, concord, harmony*
**Οὐαλέριος, ὁ** 1 • 1 *Valerius*
**ταχέως** 1 • 4 *more quickly, faster;* **θᾶττον** Attic form of **ταχέως**
**τάχος, τό** 4 • 7 *soon, in a short time*
**ταχύς** 1 • 18 *quick, swift, speedy*
**Φορτουνᾶτος, ὁ** 1 • 1 *Fortunatus*

2 **ἐπιστολή, ἡ** 3 • 13 *letter, epistle*

**Κορίνθιος, ὁ** 2 • 2 *the Corinthian*
**κράτος, τό** 5 • 7 *power, rule, sovereignty*
**μεγαλωσύνη, ἡ** 8 • 10 *majesty*
**πανταχῇ** 1 • 1 *everywhere*
**Ῥωμαῖος** 1 • 3 *Roman*

# Second Clement

### Chapter 1

1 **κριτής, ὁ** 1 • 6 *judge*
**φρονέω** [2] 6 • 17 *to think, form/hold an opinion, judge;*
**μικρὰ φρονεῖν** *to belittle*
2 **ἕνεκα** 1 • 15 *because of, on account of, for the sake of*
**πόθεν** 2 • 6 *from what place? from where?*
**ὑπομένω** 3 • 32 *to stand one's ground, hold out, endure*
**φρονέω** 6 • 17 *to think, form/hold an opinion, judge;*
**ἐν τῷ φρονεῖν ἡμᾶς μικρὰ περὶ αὐτοῦ** *when we belittle him/think little of him*
3 **ἀντιμισθία, ἡ** 5 • 5 *recompense, exchange*
**ὅσιος** 3 • 10 *devout, pious, pleasing to God, holy*
**πόσος** 2 • 10 *how many, how much?*
4 **προσαγορεύω** 1 • 5 *to call, name, designate, address*
**χαρίζομαι** 1 • 5 *to give graciously*
5 **αἶνος, ὁ** 2 • 2 *praise*
**ἀντιμισθία, ἡ** 5 • 5 *recompense, exchange*
**μισθός, ὁ** 7 • 22 *recompense, reward*
6 **ἀμαύρωσις, ἡ** 1 • 1 *darkening, dimness*
**ἀναβλέπω** 2 • 7 *to regain sight, gain sight*
**ἀποτίθημι** 1 • 13 *to take off*
**ἄργυρος, ὁ** 1 • 3 *silver*
**ἀχλύς, ἡ** 1 • 1 *mistiness*
**βίος, ὁ** 2 • 13 *life*
**γέμω** 1 • 4 *to be full*
**διάνοια, ἡ** 4 • 22 *understanding, intelligence, mind*
**θέλησις, ἡ** 1 • 1 *will*
**νέφος, τό** 1 • 1 *cloud*
**ξύλον, τό** 2 • 23 *wood*
**ὅρασις, ἡ** 3 • 13 *sight, appearance, face, eyes*
**περίκειμαι** [2] 2 • 4 *to wear something, have something on, be clothed in, be surrounded by, be blanketed in*
**πηρός** 1 • 1 *maimed, disabled, weakened, blind*
**χαλκός, ὁ** 1 • 2 *(anything made of) brass or bronze*
**χρυσός, ὁ** 1 • 3 *gold thing*
7 **ἀπώλεια, ἡ** 1 • 3 *annihilation, ruin*
**ἐλεέω** 1 • 16 *to have compassion/mercy/pity*
**θεάομαι** 2 • 4 *to see, behold perceive*
**πλάνη, ἡ** 2 • 11 *error, delusion, deceit, deception*
**σπλαγχνίζομαι** 1 • 9 *to have pity, feel sympathy*
8 **ἠθέλησεν ἐκ μὴ ὄντος εἶναι ἡμᾶς** *out of nothing he willed us into existence*

### Chapter 2

1 **βοάω** 2 • 5 *to call, shout, cry out*
**εὐφραίνω** [2] 3 • 15 *to be glad, enjoy oneself, rejoice, celebrate*
**ῥήσσω/ῥήγνυμι** 1 • 1 *to tear/break/let loose, break out in, break forth*
**στεῖρα, ἡ** [3] 3 • 4 *barren, infertile*
**τίκτω** [2] 2 • 2 *to give birth (to), bear*
**ὠδίνω** 3 • 3 *to have birth-pains*
2 **ἀναφέρω** 1 • 8 *to offer up*
**ἁπλῶς** 1 • 6 *simply, above board, sincerely, openly, wholeheartedly*
**βοάω** 2 • 5 *to call, shout, cry out*
**ἐγκακέω** 1 • 1 *to be afraid*
**ὠδίνω** 3 • 3 *to have birth-pains*
3 **ἐπεί** 1 • 35 *because, since, for*
**νυνί** 1 • 2 *now*

6 **θαυμαστός** 2 • 13 *wonderful, marvelous, remarkable*
**στηρίζω** 1 • 8 *to confirm, establish, strengthen*

## Chapter 3

1 **γνῶσις, ἡ** 1 • 32 *knowledge, what is known*
**ἔλεος, τό** 2 • 19 *mercy, compassion, pity, clemency*
**θύω** 1 • 3 *to sacrifice*
**τοσοῦτος** 5 • 38 *as strong as*
2 **ὁμολογέω** [2] 6 • 18 *to acknowledge, claim, profess, praise*
3 **μισθός, ὁ** 7 • 22 *recompense, reward*
**ὁμολογέω** 6 • 18 *to acknowledge, claim, profess, praise*
4 **διάνοια, ἡ** 4 • 22 *understanding, intelligence, mind*
**ὁμολογέω** 6 • 18 *to acknowledge, claim, profess, praise*
**παρακούω** 3 • 5 *to refuse to listen to, disobey*
**τιμάω** 2 • 12 *to honor, revere*
**χεῖλος, τό** 2 • 11 *the lips*
5 **ἄπειμι** 1 • 5 *to be absent/away*
**Ἠσαΐας, ὁ** 1 • 2 *Isaiah*
**πόρρω** 1 • 8 *far (away)*
**τιμάω** 2 • 12 *to honor, revere*
**χεῖλος, τό** 2 • 11 *the lips*

## Chapter 4

3 **ἐγκρατής** 1 • 3 *self-controlled, disciplined*
**ἐλεήμων** 1 • 4 *merciful, sympathetic, compassionate*
**ἐναντίος** 1 • 4 *opposed, contrary*
**ζηλόω** 1 • 2 *to be filled with jealousy, envy*
**καταλαλέω** 1 • 6 *to speak degradingly of, speak evil of, defame, slander*
**μοιχάω** 1 • 3 *to be caused to commit adultery, be an adulterer/adulteress, commit adultery*
**ὁμολογέω** [2] 6 • 18 *to acknowledge, claim, profess, praise*
**συμπάσχω** 1 • 4 *to have sympathy for*
**φιλαργυρέω** 2 • 30 *to love money, be avaricious*
5 **ἀνομία, ἡ** 1 • 33 *a lawless deed*
**ἀποβάλλω** 1 • 36 *to throw away, reject*
**ἐργάτης, ὁ** 1 • 3 *a doer*
**κόλπος, ὁ** 1 • 1 *bosom, breast, chest*
**πόθεν** 2 • 6 *from what place, from where?*

## Chapter 5

1 **καταλείπω** 2 • 12 *to leave*
**ὅθεν** 1 • 16 *for which reason*
**παροικία, ἡ** 1 • 3 *sojourn, stay*
2 **λύκος, ὁ** 3 • 5 *wolf*
3 **διασπαράσσω** 1 • 1 *to tear in pieces*
**λύκος, ὁ** 3 • 5 *wolf*
4 **γέεννα, ἡ** 1 • 1 *Gehenna*
**λύκος, ὁ** 3 • 5 *wolf*
5 **ἀνάπαυσις, ἡ** 2 • 3 *rest, relief*
**ἐπιδημία, ἡ** 1 • 1 *stay, sojourn*
**θαυμαστός** 2 • 13 *wonderful, marvelous, remarkable*
**ὀλιγοχρόνιος** 2 • 2 *of short duration, short-lived*
6 **ἀλλότριος** 1 • 14 *not one's own, strange*
**ἀναστρέφω** 1 • 8 *to act, behave, conduct oneself, live*
**δικαίως** 1 • 12 *correctly, justly, uprightly*
**ἐπιθυμέω** 2 • 17 *to desire, long for*
**ἐπιτυγχάνω** 1 • 23 *to obtain, attain to, reach*
**ἡγέομαι** 1 • 25 *to think, consider, regard*
**κοσμικός** 2 • 4 *earthly*
**ὁσίως** 1 • 9 *devoutly*
7 **ἀποπίπτω** 1 • 1 *to deviate, fall*
**ἐπιθυμέω** 2 • 17 *to desire, long for*
**κτάομαι** 1 • 10 *to procure for oneself, get*

## Chapter 6

1 **ἀσύμφορος** 1 • 7 *disadvantageous, harmful*

**δουλεύω** [2] 6 • 42 *to (perform the duties of a slave) serve, obey*
**μαμωνᾶς, ὁ** 1 • 1 *wealth, property*
**οἰκέτης, ὁ** 1 • 1 *house slave, domestic slave*
2 **ζημιόω** 1 • 1 *to suffer damage/ loss, forfeit, sustain injury*
**κερδαίνω** 1 • 1 *to gain*
**ὄφελος, τό** 1 • 2 *benefit, good*
4 **ἀπάτη, ἡ** 1 • 16 *deception, deceitfulness*
**ἀποτάσσω** 3 • 5 *to renounce, give up*
**μοιχεία, ἡ** 1 • 9 *adultery*
**φθορά, ἡ** 1 • 4 *ruination of a person through an immoral act, seduction*
**φιλαργυρία, ἡ** 1 • 5 *love of money, avarice, miserliness*
5 **ἀποτάσσω** 3 • 5 *to renounce, give up*
**φίλος, ὁ** 1 • 8 *friend*
**χράομαι** 1 • 18 *to make use of, employ*
6 **ἄφθαρτος** 2 • 7 *imperishable, incorruptible, immortal*
**βελτίων** 1 • 6 *better*
**ἐνθάδε** 3 • 5 *here*
**οἴομαι** 3 • 11 *to think, suppose, expect*
**ὀλιγοχρόνιος** 2 • 2 *of short duration, short-lived*
**φθαρτός** 3 • 10 *perishable*
7 **ἀνάπαυσις, ἡ** 2 • 3 *rest, relief*
**κόλασις, ἡ** 1 • 11 *punishment*
**μήγε** 1 • 2 *otherwise*
**παρακούω** 3 • 5 *to refuse to listen to, disobey*
**ῥύομαι** 4 • 19 *to save, rescue, deliver, preserve*
8 **αἰχμαλωσία, ἡ** 1 • 2 *captivity*
**Δανιήλ, ὁ** 1 • 3 *Daniel*
**Ἰεζεκιήλ, ὁ** 1 • 2 *Ezekiel*
**Ἰώβ, ὁ** 1 • 4 *Job*
**Νῶε, ὁ** 1 • 3 *Noah*
**ῥύομαι** 4 • 19 *to save, rescue, deliver, preserve*
9 **ἁγνός** 3 • 11 *pure, holy*
**ἀμίαντος** 1 • 5 *undefiled, pure*
**βάπτισμα, τό** 1 • 6 *plunging, dipping, washing, water-rite, baptism*
**βασίλειον, τό** 2 • 2 *kingdom*
**ὅσιος** 3 • 10 *devout, pious, pleasing to God, holy*
**παράκλητος, ὁ** 1 • 3 *mediator, intercessor, helper*
**πεποίθησις, ἡ** 1 • 7 *confidence*
**ῥύομαι** 4 • 19 *to save, rescue, deliver, preserve*

## Chapter 7

1 **ἀγών, ὁ** 5 • 7 *contest*
**ἀγωνίζομαι** [2] 5 • 7 *to engage in a contest*
**καταπλέω** 2 • 2 *to sail down*
**κοπιάω** 1 • 4 *to work hard, toil, strive, struggle*
**στεφανόω** 5 • 12 *to wreathe, crown*
**φθαρτός** 3 • 10 *perishable*
2 **ἀγωνίζομαι** 5 • 7 *to engage in a contest*
**στεφανόω** 5 • 12 *to wreathe, crown*
3 **ἀγών, ὁ** 5 • 7 *struggle, fight*
**ἀγωνίζομαι** 5 • 7 *to engage in a contest*
**ἄφθαρτος** 2 • 7 *imperishable, incorruptible, immortal*
**εὐθύς** 1 • 2 *straight*
**θέω** 1 • 1 *to run*
**κἄν** 3 • 8 *(even) if only, at least*
**καταπλέω** 2 • 2 *to sail down*
**στέφανος, ὁ** 1 • 7 *wreath, crown*
**στεφανόω** [2] 5 • 12 *to wreathe, crown*
4 **ἀγών, ὁ** 5 • 7 *struggle, fight*
**ἀγωνίζομαι** 5 • 7 *to engage in a contest*
**μαστιγόω** 1 • 4 *to whip, flog, scourge*
**στάδιον, τό** 1 • 9 *arena, stadium*
**φθαρτός** 3 • 10 *perishable*
**φθείρω** 4 • 10 *to violate rules*
5 **ἀγών, ὁ** 5 • 7 *struggle, fight*
**ἀφθαρσία, ἡ** 3 • 12 *incorruptibility, immortality*
**φθείρω** 4 • 10 *to violate rules*
6 **ὅρασις, ἡ** 3 • 13 *appearance, sight, spectacle*
**σβέννυμι** 2 • 5 *to extinguish, put out*
**σκώληξ, ὁ** 2 • 5 *worm*

σφραγίς, ἡ 2 • 16 *attestation, confirmation, certification*
τελευτάω 2 • 8 *to die*

## Chapter 8

2 ἀναπλάσσω 1 • 3 *to form, remold*
βοηθέω 1 • 4 *to furnish aid*
διαστρέφω 1 • 5 *to deform, become misshapen*
κάμινος, ἡ 1 • 3 *oven, furnace*
κεραμεύς, ὁ 1 • 2 *potter*
μετάνοια, ἡ 2 • 72 *repentance, turning about, conversion*
πηλός, ὁ 1 • 2 *clay*
προφθάνω 1 • 1 *to do before/ previously, already*
σκεῦος 1 • 9 *vessel, jar, dish*
συντρίβω 1 • 10 *to shatter, smash, crush, break*
τεχνίτης, ὁ 1 • 4 *craftsperson, artisan, designer*
τρόπος, ὁ 3 • 17 *manner, way, kind, guise*
3 ἐξομολογέω 1 • 15 *to confess, admit*
4 ἁγνός 3 • 11 *pure, holy*
5 ἐλάχιστος 1 • 16 *insignificant, trivial*
6 ἁγνός 3 • 11 *pure, holy*
ἀπολαμβάνω 4 • 17 *to receive*
ἄσπιλος 1 • 3 *pure, without fault*
σφραγίς, ἡ 2 • 16 *attestation, confirmation, certification*

## Chapter 9

2 ἀναβλέπω 2 • 7 *to regain sight, gain sight*
4 τρόπος, ὁ 3 • 17 *manner, way, kind, guise*
5 ἀπολαμβάνω 4 • 17 *to receive*
μισθός, ὁ 7 • 22 *recompense, reward*
7 ἀντιμισθία, ἡ 5 • 5 *recompense, exchange*
ἐπιδίδωμι 1 • 62 *to give up/over, surrender*
ἰάομαι 1 • 11 *to restore, heal*
8 εἰλικρινής 1 • 2 *pure*
9 προγνώστης, ὁ 1 • 1 *one who knows something beforehand*
10 αἶνος, ὁ 2 • 2 *praise*
προσδέχομαι 2 • 10 *to receive in a friendly manner*

## Chapter 10

1 ἀρετή, ἡ 1 • 6 *(excellence of) character, (exceptional civic) virtue*
ἀσέβεια, ἡ 1 • 3 *impiety*
κακία, ἡ 1 • 9 *baseness, depravity, wickedness, vice*
καταλαμβάνω 1 • 5 *to catch up with, seize*
καταλείπω 2 • 12 *to leave to one's side, give up*
προοδοιπόρος 1 • 1 *going before;* subst. *forerunner*
φεύγω 2 • 20 *to flee from, avoid, shun*
2 ἀγαθοποιέω 1 • 6 *to do what is right, be a good citizen*
σπουδάζω 2 • 14 *to be zealous/ eager, take pains, make every effort, be conscientious*
3 αἰτία, ἡ 1 • 5 *cause, reason*
ἀνθρώπινος 1 • 7 *human*
ἀπόλαυσις, ἡ 2 • 6 *enjoyment*
ἐνθάδε 3 • 5 *here*
παράγω 1 • 2 *to bring in, introduce*
προαιρέω 1 • 4 *to choose (for oneself), commit oneself to, prefer*
4 ἀγνοέω 2 • 11 *to not know, be ignorant (of)*
ἀπόλαυσις, ἡ 2 • 6 *enjoyment*
βάσανος, ἡ 3 • 18 *torture, torment*
ἐνθάδε 3 • 5 *here*
ἡλίκος 1 • 1 *how great*
οἷος 1 • 10 *of what sort (such)*
τρυφή, ἡ 1 • 22 *enjoyment, joy, delight*
5 ἀναίτιος 1 • 1 *innocent*
ἀνεκτός 1 • 1 *bearable, endurable*
δισσός 1 • 2 *double*
ἐπιμένω 1 • 16 *to continue, persist in, persevere*
κακοδιδασκαλέω 1 • 1 *to teach evil*

## Chapter 11

1 **δουλεύω** [2] 6 • 42 *to (perform the duties of a slave) serve, obey*
**καθαρός** 1 • 45 *pure, clean*
**ταλαίπωρος** 2 • 5 *miserable, wretched, distressed*
2 **διστάζω** 1 • 10 *to doubt, waver*
**δίψυχος** 1 • 23 *doubting, hesitating*
**προσδέχομαι** 2 • 10 *to wait for;* **ἡμέραν ἐξ ἡμέρας προσδεχόμενοι** *waiting day after day*
**προφητικός** 1 • 3 *prophetic*
**ταλαίπωρος** 2 • 5 *miserable, wretched, distressed*
3 **ἄμπελος, ἡ** 1 • 16 *vine, grapevine*
**ἀνόητος** 1 • 4 *unintelligent, foolish, dull-witted*
**βλαστός, ὁ** 1 • 3 *bud, sprout*
**εἶτα** [2] 2 • 48 *then, next*
**ξύλον, τό** 2 • 23 *tree*
**ὄμφαξ, ἡ** 1 • 2 *unripe grape*
**σταφυλή, ἡ** 1 • 2 *(a bunch of) grapes*
**συμβάλλω** 1 • 4 *to compare*
**φυλλορροέω** 1 • 2 *to shed leaves, lose foliage*
4 **ἀκαταστασία, ἡ** 1 • 1 *disturbance, tumult*
**ἀπολαμβάνω** 4 • 17 *to receive*
**ἔπειτα** 2 • 4 *then, thereupon*
5 **διψυχέω** 1 • 25 *to be undecided, be changeable, doubt*
**κομίζω** 1 • 4 *to carry off, get (for oneself), receive*
**μισθός, ὁ** 7 • 22 *recompense, reward*
**ὑπομένω** 3 • 32 *to stand one's ground, hold out, endure*
6 **ἀντιμισθία, ἡ** 5 • 5 *recompense, exchange*
**ἐπαγγέλλομαι** 1 • 7 *to promise, offer*
7 **εἰσήκω** 1 • 1 *to enter*
**ἐναντίον** 1 • 5 *in the sight of, before*

## Chapter 12

1 **ἐκδέχομαι** 2 • 5 *to expect, wait;* **ἐκδεχώμεθα οὖν καθ' ὥραν** *let us wait hour by hour*
**ἐπειδή** 1 • 17 *(just) because*
**ἐπιφάνεια, ἡ** 2 • 3 *appearance*
2 **ἄρσην** [2] 6 • 8 *male*
**ἔσω** [2] 3 • 4 *inside, within*
**ἥκω** 1 • 11 *to come*
**θῆλυς** [2] 6 • 9 *female*
**πότε** 1 • 6 *when?*
3 **ἀνυποκρίτως** 1 • 1 *with no insincerity/hypocrisy*
4 **δῆλος** 2 • 2 *clear, plain, evident*
**ἔσω** 3 • 4 *inside, within*
**τρόπος, ὁ** 3 • 17 *manner, way, kind, guise*
5 **ἀδελφή, ἡ** 3 • 10 *sister*
**ἀρσενικός** 1 • 1 *male*
**ἄρσην** [2] 6 • 8 *male*
**θηλυκός** 1 • 1 *female*
**θῆλυς** [2] 6 • 9 *female*
**φρονέω** [2] 6 • 17 *to think, form/hold an opinion, judge*

## Chapter 13

1 **ἁμάρτημα, τό** 1 • 8 *sin, transgression*
**ἀνθρωπάρεσκος** 1 • 1 *fawner, timeserver*
**ἄνοια, ἡ** 1 • 1 *folly*
**ἀρέσκω** 1 • 12 *to please, accommodate*
**ἐξαλείφω** 1 • 8 *to remove, destroy, obliterate*
**μεστός** 1 • 4 *filled (with something)*
**νήφω** 1 • 3 *to be well-balanced, self-controlled*
**πονηρία, ἡ** 1 • 41 *wickedness, baseness, maliciousness, sinfulness*
**ποτέ** 1 • 15 *at some time or other;* **ἤδη ποτέ** *now at last*
**πρότερος** 1 • 47 *former, earlier*
3 **βλασφημία, ἡ** 1 • 7 *reviling, denigration, disrespect, slander*
**ἔνθεν** 1 • 2 *from then on*
**ἔπειτα** 2 • 4 *then, thereupon*
**καταμανθάνω** 1 • 4 *to observe (well), notice, learn*
**λόγιον, τό** 1 • 11 *a saying*
**μῦθος, ὁ** 1 • 1 *tale, story, legend, myth*
**πλάνη, ἡ** 2 • 11 *error, delusion, deceit, deception*

τρέπω 1 • 2 *to turn*
4 ἀγαθότης, ἡ 1 • 1 *goodness*
καταγελάω 1 • 2 *to laugh at, ridicule*
ὑπερβολή, ἡ 1 • 2 *excess, extraordinary quality/character*

## Chapter 14

1 αἱρετίζω 1 • 1 *to choose*
κτίζω 2 • 25 *to create*
λῃστής, ὁ 1 • 2 *robber, highwayman, bandit*
πνευματικός 3 • 19 *filled with the divine spirit, spiritual*
σελήνη, ἡ 1 • 7 *moon*
σπήλαιον, τό 1 • 2 *hideout*
2 ἀγνοέω 2 • 11 *to not know, be ignorant (of)*
ἄνωθεν 1 • 8 *from above, from the beginning*
ἄρσην [2] 6 • 8 *male*
δῆλος 2 • 2 *clear, plain, evident*
θῆλυς [2] 6 • 9 *female*
οἴομαι 3 • 11 *to think, suppose, expect*
πνευματικός 3 • 19 *caused by or filled with the divine spirit, spiritual*
3 ἀντίτυπος [2] 2 • 2 *copy, antitype, representation*
ἀπολαμβάνω 4 • 17 *to receive*
αὐθεντικός 1 • 1 *original*
δηλόω 1 • 49 *to reveal, make clear, show*
μεταλαμβάνω [2] 6 • 12 *to receive, have a share in*
πνευματικός 3 • 19 *caused by or filled with the divine spirit, spiritual*
φθείρω [2] 4 • 10 *to ruin, corrupt*
4 μεταλαμβάνω 6 • 12 *to have a share in*
ὑβρίζω [2] 2 • 5 *to mistreat, scoff at, insult, abuse*
5 ἀφθαρσία, ἡ 3 • 12 *incorruptibility, immortality*
ἐκλεκτός 1 • 30 *chosen*
ἐξαγορεύω/ἐξεῖπον 1 • 4 *to express, proclaim*
κολλάω 1 • 32 *to cling to, attach to, join*
μεταλαμβάνω 6 • 12 *to receive*
τοσοῦτος 5 • 38 *so great/strong, to such extent*

## Chapter 15

1 ἀποστρέφω 1 • 8 *to turn, turn away*
ἐγκράτεια, ἡ 1 • 14 *self-control*
μισθός, ὁ 7 • 22 *recompense, reward*
οἴομαι 3 • 11 *to think, suppose, expect*
συμβουλεύω 1 • 3 *to advise*
συμβουλία, ἡ 1 • 2 *advice, counsel*
2 ἀντιμισθία, ἡ 5 • 5 *recompense, exchange*
κτίζω 2 • 25 *to create*
3 ἐμμένω 1 • 8 *to persevere in, stand by, remain true*
ὅσιος 3 • 10 *devout, pious, pleasing to God, holy*
πάρειμι 1 • 17 *to be present*
4 ἕτοιμος 1 • 9 *ready*
5 ἡδονή, ἡ 1 • 12 *pleasure, delight, enjoyment, pleasantness*
κατάκρισις, ἡ 1 • 1 *condemnation*
μεταλαμβάνω 6 • 12 *to have a share in*
παρακούω 3 • 5 *to refuse to listen to, disobey*
τοσοῦτος [3] 5 • 38 *so great/ strong, to such extent*
τυγχάνω 1 • 15 *to meet, attain, gain, find, experience*
φθονέω 1 • 1 *to envy, be jealous, begrudge*
χρηστότης, ἡ 2 • 9 *goodness, kindness, generosity*

## Chapter 16

1 ἀφορμή, ἡ 1 • 5 *occasion, opportunity*
παραδέχομαι 1 • 9 *to receive, accept*
2 ἀποτάσσω 3 • 5 *to renounce, give up*
ἔλεος, τό 2 • 19 *mercy, compassion, pity, clemency*
ἡδυπάθεια, ἡ 2 • 2 *enjoyment, comfort*

**μεταλαμβάνω** 6 • 12 *to have a share in*
**νικάω** 1 • 8 *to vanquish, overcome*
3 **καίω** 1 • 11 *to light, have/keep burning*
**κλίβανος, ὁ** 1 • 1 *an oven*
**κρύφιος** 1 • 4 *hidden, secret*
**μόλιβος, ὁ** 1 • 1 *lead*
**τήκω** [2] 2 • 2 *to melt, dissolve*
**φανερός** 1 • 9 *visible, clear, plainly to be seen, open, plain, evident, known*
4 **ἀμφότεροι** 1 • 21 *both*
**ἐλεημοσύνη, ἡ** [3] 3 • 5 *alms, charitable giving*
**καλύπτω** 1 • 3 *to hide, conceal, keep secret*
**κούφισμα, τό** 1 • 1 *lightening, alleviation*
**κρείττων** 1 • 8 *more useful, more advantageous, better*
**μετάνοια, ἡ** 2 • 72 *repentance, turning about, conversion*
**νηστεία, ἡ** 1 • 25 *fast*
**πλήρης** 1 • 20 *complete, full*
**ῥύομαι** 4 • 19 *to save, rescue, deliver, preserve*

## Chapter 17

1 **ἀποσπάω** 1 • 2 *to draw away, attract, proselytize*
**εἴδωλον, τό** 1 • 3 *idol*
**κατηχέω** 1 • 1 *to teach, instruct*
**παραπόλλυμι** 1 • 1 *to perish, be lost*
**πόσος** 2 • 10 *how great?*
2 **ἀνάγω** 1 • 2 *to restore, bring back*
**νουθετέω** 3 • 9 *to admonish, warn, instruct*
**συλλαμβάνω** 1 • 11 *to support, aid, help*
3 **ἀντιπαρέλκω** 1 • 1 *to let oneself be dragged over to the opposite side*
**ἀπαλλάσσω** 1 • 3 *to leave, depart*
**ἔνταλμα, τό** 1 • 1 *commandment*
**κοσμικός** 2 • 4 *worldly*
**μνημονεύω** 1 • 25 *to remember, keep in mind, think of, mention*
**νουθετέω** 3 • 9 *to admonish, warn, instruct*
**πειράω** 1 • 2 *to try, attempt, endeavor*
**προκόπτω** 1 • 1 *to progress, advance*
**προσέχω** 1 • 10 *to pay attention to, give heed to, follow*
**πυκνός** 1 • 3 *frequent, numerous, often, frequently*
**φρονέω** 6 • 17 *to think, form/hold an opinion, judge*
4 **ἐπιφάνεια, ἡ** 2 • 3 *appearance*
**λυτρόω** 1 • 11 *to set free, rescue, redeem*
5 **ἀναγγέλλω** 1 • 8 *to disclose, announce, proclaim, teach*
**ἄπιστος** 1 • 8 *without faith, disbelieving, unbelieving*
**βασίλειον, τό** 2 • 2 *kingdom*
**κράτος, τό** 1 • 7 *might*
**ξενίζω** 1 • 1 *to astonish, surprise*
**ὅρασις, ἡ** 3 • 13 *appearance, sight, spectacle*
**σβέννυμι** 2 • 5 *to extinguish, put out*
**σκώληξ, ὁ** 2 • 5 *worm*
**τελευτάω** 2 • 8 *to die*
6 **ἀσεβέω** 1 • 1 *to act impiously*
**παραλογίζομαι** 1 • 2 *to reckon fraudulently, defraud*
7 **ἄσβεστος** 1 • 3 *inextinguishable*
**ἀστοχέω** 1 • 2 *to miss, fail, deviate, depart, go astray*
**βάσανος, ἡ** [2] 3 • 18 *torture, torment*
**δεινός** 1 • 7 *fearful, terrible*
**δουλεύω** 6 • 42 *to (perform the duties of a slave) serve, obey*
**εὐπραγέω** 1 • 1 *to do what it right*
**ἡδυπάθεια, ἡ** 2 • 2 *enjoyment, comfort*
**θεάομαι** 2 • 4 *to see, look at, behold*
**κολάζω** 1 • 9 *to penalize, punish*
**ὑπομένω** 3 • 32 *to stand one's ground, hold out, endure*

## Chapter 18

1 **ἀσεβής** 1 • 14 *irreverent, impious, ungodly*
**δουλεύω** 6 • 42 *to (perform the duties of a slave) serve, obey*
2 **ἰσχύω** 1 • 9 *to have power, be competent, be able*
**κἄν** 3 • 8 *(even) if only, at least*

**μήπω** 1 • 1 *not yet*
**ὄργανον, τό** 1 • 3 *tool*
**πανθαμαρτωλός** 1 • 1 *utterly sinful*
**πειρασμός, ὁ** 1 • 4 *temptation, enticement*
**σπουδάζω** 2 • 14 *to be zealous/ eager, take pains, make every effort, be conscientious*
**φεύγω** 2 • 20 *to escape*

## Chapter 19

1 **ἀδελφή, ἡ** 3 • 10 *sister*
**ἔντευξις, ἡ** 1 • 18 *petition, request*
**εὐσέβεια, ἡ** 1 • 6 *devoutness, piety, godliness*
**μισθός, ὁ** 7 • 22 *recompense, reward*
**νέος** 1 • 16 *young*
**προσέχω** 2 • 25 *to pay attention to, give heed to, follow*
**σκοπός, ὁ** 1 • 3 *goal, mark*
**φιλοπονέω** 1 • 1 *to exert oneself, devote oneself*
**χρηστότης, ἡ** 2 • 9 *goodness, kindness, generosity*
2 **ἀγανακτέω** 1 • 2 *to be aroused, be indignant, be angry*
**ἀδικία, ἡ** 1 • 7 *wrongdoing*
**ἀηδῶς** 1 • 1 *to be displeased*
**ἀπιστία, ἡ** 1 • 4 *lack of belief, unbelief*
**ἄσοφος** 1 • 1 *unwise, foolish*
**διάνοια, ἡ** 4 • 22 *understanding, intelligence, mind*
**διψυχία, ἡ** 1 • 18 *indecision, doubt*
**ἔνειμι** 1 • 2 *to be in*
**ἐνίοτε** 1 • 1 *sometimes*
**μάταιος** 1 • 14 *idle, empty, fruitless, useless, powerless, lacking truth*
**νουθετέω** 3 • 9 *to admonish, warn, instruct*
**σκοτίζω** 1 • 1 *to be/become inwardly darkened*
**στῆθος, τό** 1 • 2 *chest, breast*
**ἐπιστρέφη** (conative pres.; cf. *ExSyn* 534–35) in **ἡμᾶς ἐπιστρέφῃ ἀπὸ τῆς ἀδικίας** *attempts to turn us away from unrighteousness*
3 **ἀθάνατος** 1 • 5 *immortal*
**κακοπαθέω** 1 • 1 *to suffer misfortune*
**κἄν** 3 • 8 *even if, even though*
**πρόσταγμα, τό** 1 • 10 *order, command(ment), injunction, instruction*
**τρυγάω** 1 • 2 *to harvest (grapes)*
**ὑπακούω** 1 • 9 *to obey, follow, be subject to*
4 **ἀλύπητος** 1 • 1 *without sorrow, free from sorrow*
**ἀναβιόω** 1 • 1 *to come to life again*
**ἀναμένω** 1 • 3 *to wait for, expect*
**ἄνω** 1 • 3 *above, high*
**εὐσεβής** 2 • 4 *devout, godly, pious, reverent*
**εὐφραίνω** 3 • 15 *to be glad, enjoy oneself, rejoice, celebrate*
**λυπέω** 1 • 17 *to be sad, be distressed, grieve*
**ταλαιπωρέω** 1 • 4 *to endure sorrow/distress, be miserable*

## Chapter 20

1 **ἄδικος** 1 • 14 *unjust, crooked*
**διάνοια, ἡ** 4 • 22 *disposition, thought, mind*
**πλουτέω** 1 • 6 *to be rich*
**στενοχωρέω** 1 • 2 *to be distressed*
**ταράσσω** 1 • 4 *to stir up, disturb, unsettle, throw into confusion*
2 **ἀδελφή, ἡ** 3 • 10 *sister*
**ἀθλέω** 1 • 2 *to compete*
**βίος, ὁ** 2 • 13 *life*
**γυμνάζω** 1 • 1 *to train, undergo discipline*
**πεῖρα, ἡ** 1 • 1 *attempt, trial, experiment*
**στεφανόω** 5 • 12 *to honor, reward, crown*
3 **ἐκδέχομαι** 2 • 5 *to expect, wait*
**ταχύς** 1 • 18 *quick, swift, speedy, quickly*
4 **ἀσκέω** 1 • 6 *to practice, engage in*
**βαρύνω** 1 • 1 *to burden, weigh down*

**βλάπτω** 1 • 3 *to harm, injure*
**δεσμός, ὁ** 1 • 14 *bond, fetter*
**ἐμπορία, ἡ** 1 • 1 *business, trade*
**εὐσεβής** 2 • 4 *devout, godly, pious, reverent*
**θεῖος** 1 • 16 *divine*
**θεοσέβεια, ἡ** 1 • 6 *piety, godliness*
**κερδαλέος** 1 • 1 *profitable, gainful*
**μισθός, ὁ** 7 • 22 *recompense, reward*
**συντόμως** 1 • 3 *promptly, readily*
5 **ἀόρατος** 1 • 13 *unseen, invisible*
**ἀρχηγός, ὁ** 1 • 4 *originator, founder, leader, ruler, prince*
**ἀφθαρσία, ἡ** 3 • 12 *incorruptibility, immortality*
**ἐξαποστέλλω** 1 • 4 *to send away, send off, send out*
**ἐπουράνιος** 1 • 11 *heavenly, in heaven*
**σωτήρ, ὁ** 1 • 14 *savior, deliverer, preserver*

# Ignatius to the Ephesians

## Preface

**ἀληθινός** 3 • 5 • 14 *genuine, authentic, real*
**ἄμωμος** 2 • 7 • 17 *blameless*
**ἀξιομακάριστος** 2 • 4 • 4 *most worthy of blessing*
**Ἀσία, ἡ** 1 • 4 • 10 *Asia*
**ἄτρεπτος** 1 • 1 • 1 *unchangeable*
**ἐκλέγομαι** 1 • 1 • 15 *to select/ choose (someone/something) for oneself;*
**ἡνωμένην καὶ ἐκλελεγμένην** (acc. perhaps due to attraction to previous words; feminine due to loose cataphoric reference to ἐκκλησία; lack of article suggests they are adverbial) *united and chosen*
**ἑνόω** 1 • 6 • 6 *to unite*
**Ἔφεσος, ἡ** 1 • 1 • 4 *Ephesus*
**Θεοφόρος, ὁ** 1 • 7 • 7 *Theophorus*
**Ἰγνάτιος, ὁ** 1 • 7 • 10 *Ignatius*
**μέγεθος, τό** 1 • 3 • 5 *greatness*
**πάθος, τό** 3 • 15 • 18 *suffering*
**παράμονος** 1 • 2 • 4 *lasting, constant, enduring*
**πλήρωμα, τό** 1 • 2 • 3 *sum total, fullness*
**προορίζω** 1 • 1 • 1 *to predetermine;*
**τῇ εὐλογημένῃ..., τῇ προωρισμένῃ** (feminine participles implicitly referring to the ἐκκλησία) *to her who is blessed..., who is predestined*
**πολυαγάπητος** 1 • 1 • 1 *much-loved*
**συγγενικός** 1 • 1 • 1 *related, kindred, of the same kind*
**σωτήρ, ὁ** 1 • 4 • 14 *savior, deliverer, preserver*
**τελείως** 2 • 3 • 8 *fully, perfectly, completely, altogether*
**φῦσις, ἡ** 1 • 2 • 4 *nature*
2 **ἐπιτυγχάνω** [2] 3 • 20 • 23 *to obtain, attain to, reach*
**θηριομαχέω** 1 • 3 • 4 *to fight with wild animals*
**κοινός** 3 • 9 • 15 *communal, common*
**Ῥώμη, ἡ** 2 • 4 • 8 *Rome*
**σπουδάζω** 5 • 8 • 14 *to hurry, hasten*
**Συρία, ἡ** 2 • 16 • 17 *Syria*
3 **ἀδιήγητος** 1 • 1 • 1 *indescribable, inexpressible*
**ἀπολαμβάνω** 2 • 4 • 17 *to welcome*
**ἐπεί** 2 • 12 • 35 *because, since, for*
**ἐπίσκοπος, ὁ** [2] 13 • 57 • 76 *overseer, supervisor*
**εὐλογητός** 1 • 1 • 3 *blessed, praised*
**εὔχομαι** 2 • 13 • 16 *to wish*
**κτάομαι** 4 • 9 • 10 *to possess*
**ὁμοιότης, ἡ** 1 • 1 • 2 *likeness, similarity, agreement*
**Ὀνήσιμος, ὁ** 3 • 3 • 3 *Onesimus*
**πολυπληθία, ἡ** 1 • 1 • 1 *whole (large) congregation*
**χαρίζομαι** 1 • 2 • 5 *to give graciously*

## Chapter 1

1 **ἀναζωπυρέω** 1 • 1 • 2 *to kindle into flame*
**ἀπαρτίζω** 3 • 5 • 7 *to finish, complete*
**ἀποδέχομαι** 1 • 3 • 6 *to welcome*
**κτάομαι** 4 • 9 • 10 *to possess*
**μιμητής, ὁ** 2 • 5 • 12 *imitator*

## Chapter 2

1 **ἅμα** 2 • 9 • 12 *together*
**ἀναπαύω** 1 • 7 • 13 *to cause to rest, give (someone) rest, refresh, revive*
**ἀναψύχω** 1 • 2 • 2 *to give (someone) a breathing space, revive, refresh*

**ἀπολαμβάνω** 2 • 4 • 17 *to welcome*
**Βοὖρρος, ὁ** [2] 2 • 4 • 4 *Burrus*
**διάκονος, ὁ** 1 • 18 • 29 *assistant*
**ἐξεμπλάριον, τό** 1 • 3 • 3 *(living) example, embodiment*
**ἐπίσκοπος, ὁ** 13 • 57 • 76 *overseer, supervisor*
**Εὔπλους, ὁ** 1 • 1 • 1 *Euplus*
**εὔχομαι** 2 • 13 • 16 *to wish*
**Κρόκος, ὁ** 1 • 2 • 2 *Crocus*
**Ὀνήσιμος, ὁ** 3 • 3 • 3 *Onesimus*
**παραμένω** 1 • 1 • 9 *to remain, stay on*
**σύνδουλος, ὁ** 1 • 4 • 6 *slave*
**Φρόντων, ὁ** 1 • 1 • 1 *Fronto*
**κατὰ θεόν** *by (the will of) God*
2 **ἁγιάζω** 2 • 2 • 16 *to consecrate, dedicate, sanctify*
**ἐάνπερ** 1 • 7 • 7 *if indeed, if only, supposing that*
**ἐπίσκοπος, ὁ** [2] 13 • 57 • 76 *overseer, supervisor*
**καταρτίζω** 1 • 3 • 6 *to put in order, restore*
**ὀνίνημι** 1 • 6 • 6 *to have benefit of, enjoy*
**πρέπω** 3 • 13 • 15 *to be fitting, be seemly/suitable*
**πρεσβυτέριον, τό** 3 • 13 • 13 *council of elders*
**τρόπος, ὁ** 1 • 4 • 17 *manner, way, kind, guise*
**ὑποταγή, ἡ** 1 • 4 • 4 *subjection, subordination*

## Chapter 3

1 **ἀπαρτίζω** 3 • 5 • 7 *to finish, complete*
**διατάσσω** 1 • 3 • 8 *to order, command*
**μαθητεύω** 2 • 4 • 4 *to be a pupil*
**μακροθυμία, ἡ** 2 • 2 • 15 *patience, steadfastness, endurance*
**νουθεσία, ἡ** 1 • 1 • 1 *admonition, instruction*
**οὔπω** 1 • 1 • 3 *not yet*
**προσλαλέω** 1 • 3 • 3 *to speak to, speak with, address*
**συνδιδασκαλίτης, ὁ** 1 • 1 • 1 *fellow-pupil, fellow disciple*
**ὑπαλείφω** 1 • 1 • 1 *to anoint*
**ὡς ὤν τις** (concessive participle) *as though I were someone*
2 **ἀδιάκριτος** 1 • 3 • 3 *inseparable, not divisive, impartial, nonjudgmental*
**γνώμη, ἡ** [3] 4 • 16 • 20 *purpose, intention, mind, mind-set*
**ἐάω** 2 • 2 • 13 *to let, permit*
**ἐπεί** 2 • 12 • 35 *because, since, for*
**ἐπίσκοπος, ὁ** 13 • 57 • 76 *overseer, supervisor*
**ὁρίζω** 1 • 1 • 10 *to determine, appoint, fix, set*
**πέρας, τό** 1 • 3 • 13 *end, limit, boundary;* pl. *distant lands*
**προλαμβάνω** 1 • 1 • 1 *to take it upon oneself, undertake*
**σιωπάω** 2 • 4 • 5 *to keep silent, say nothing, make no sound*
**συντρέχω** 2 • 4 • 6 *to agree with;* lit. *run together with*

## Chapter 4

1 **ᾄδω** 2 • 4 • 6 *to sing (in praise)*
**ἀξιονόμαστος** 1 • 1 • 1 *most worthy of the name*
**γνώμη, ἡ** 4 • 16 • 20 *purpose, intention, mind, mind-set*
**ἐπίσκοπος, ὁ** [2] 13 • 57 • 76 *overseer, supervisor*
**κιθάρα, ἡ** 1 • 2 • 2 *lyre, harp*
**ὅθεν** 4 • 10 • 16 *for which reason*
**ὁμόνοια, ἡ** 3 • 8 • 24 *oneness of mind, unanimity, concord, harmony*
**ὅσπερ** 2 • 5 • 10 *which indeed*
**πρέπω** 3 • 13 • 15 *to be fitting, be seemly/suitable*
**πρεσβυτέριον, τό** 3 • 13 • 13 *council of elders*
**σύμφωνος** 3 • 3 • 3 *attuned to, harmonious*
**συναρμόζω** 1 • 1 • 2 *to be associated with*
**συντρέχω** 2 • 4 • 6 *to agree with;* lit. *run together with*
**χορδή, ἡ** 1 • 2 • 2 *string*
2 **ᾄδω** 2 • 4 • 6 *to sing (in praise)*
**ἄμωμος** 2 • 7 • 17 *blameless*
**ἑνότης, ἡ** 4 • 11 • 11 *unity*
**εὖ** 1 • 2 • 4 *well*

**μετέχω** 1 • 1 • 4 *to share, have a share, participate*
**ὁμόνοια, ἡ** 3 • 8 • 24 *oneness of mind, unanimity, concord, harmony*
**σύμφωνος** 3 • 3 • 3 *attuned to, harmonious*
**χορός, ὁ** 2 • 3 • 4 *chorus, choir*
**χρήσιμος** 1 • 1 • 2 *useful, beneficial, advantageous*
**χρῶμα, τό** 1 • 2 • 5 *tone-color, key, mode*
**οἱ κατ᾽ ἄνδρα** *each one of you*

## Chapter 5

1 **ἀνθρώπινος** 1 • 2 • 7 *human*
**ἐγκεράννυμι** 1 • 1 • 1 *to mix*
**ἑνότης, ἡ** 4 • 11 • 11 *unity*
**ἐπίσκοπος, ὁ** 13 • 57 • 76 *overseer, supervisor*
**μακαρίζω** 1 • 2 • 5 *to call/consider blessed, happy, fortunate*
**πνευματικός** 6 • 12 • 19 *spiritual, pertaining to the (divine spirit)*
**πόσος** 3 • 3 • 10 *how great*
**σύμφωνος** 3 • 3 • 3 *attuned to, harmonious*
**συνήθεια, ἡ** 1 • 1 • 3 *friendship, fellowship, intimacy*
2 **ἐντός** 1 • 2 • 3 *inside, within, within the limits of*
**ἐπίσκοπος, ὁ** 13 • 57 • 76 *overseer, supervisor*
**θυσιαστήριον, τό** 1 • 6 • 15 *sanctuary*
**ἰσχύς, ἡ** 1 • 1 • 11 *strength, power, might*
**πόσος** 3 • 3 • 10 *how great*
**τοσοῦτος** 1 • 1 • 38 *so much, so great*
**ὑστερέω** 1 • 1 • 11 *to lack, be lacking, go without, come short of*
3 **ἀντιτάσσω** [2] 2 • 2 • 7 *to oppose, resist*
**διακρίνω** 1 • 1 • 7 *to evaluate, judge*
**ἐπίσκοπος, ὁ** [2] 13 • 57 • 76 *overseer, supervisor*
**σπουδάζω** 5 • 8 • 14 *to be zealous/eager, take pains, make every effort, be conscientious*
**ὑπερηφανέω** 1 • 3 • 3 *to be proud, be haughty*
**ὑπερήφανος** 1 • 1 • 6 *arrogant, haughty, proud*
**ἵνα ὦμεν θεοῦ ὑποτασσόμενοι** (the gen. here is probably a slip of the pen; some witnesses have the dat. θεῷ, which is either original or what Ignatius meant) *that we may be obedient to God*

## Chapter 6

1 **δηλονότι** 1 • 1 • 2 *clear, plain, evident*
**ἐπίσκοπος, ὁ** [2] 13 • 57 • 76 *overseer, supervisor*
**οἰκοδεσπότης, ὁ** 1 • 1 • 2 *master of the house, householder*
**οἰκονομία, ἡ** 3 • 3 • 6 *management*
**πλειόνως** 1 • 1 • 1 *even more*; **ὅσον ... πλειόνως** *the more ... the more*
**προσβλέπω** 1 • 1 • 1 *to look upon, regard*
**σιγάω** 3 • 4 • 6 *to say nothing, keep still, keep silent*
2 **αἵρεσις, ἡ** 1 • 2 • 6 *heresy, sect, party, school, faction*
**εὐταξία, ἡ** 1 • 1 • 1 *good discipline*
**Ὀνήσιμος, ὁ** 3 • 3 • 3 *Onesimus*
**ὑπερεπαινέω** 1 • 1 • 1 *to praise highly*

## Chapter 7

1 **ἀνάξιος** 1 • 1 • 4 *unworthy*
**δόλος, ὁ** 1 • 1 • 8 *deceit, cunning, treachery*
**δυσθεραπεύτος** 1 • 1 • 1 *hard to cure*
**εἴωθα** 1 • 1 • 2 *to be accustomed*
**ἐκκλίνω** 1 • 1 • 2 *to steer clear of, avoid*
**κύων, ὁ** 1 • 1 • 2 *dog*
**λαθροδήκτης, ὁ** 1 • 1 • 1 *one who bites in secret, one who bites stealthily*
**λυσσάω** 1 • 1 • 1 *to be raving, be mad*

**περιφέρω** 2 • 4 • 4 *to carry about, carry here and there*
2 **ἀγέννητος** 1 • 1 • 1 *unborn, unbegotten*
**ἀληθινός** 3 • 5 • 14 *genuine, authentic, real*
**ἀπαθής** 1 • 2 • 3 *free of suffering*
**γεννητός** 1 • 1 • 2 *born, begotten*
**ἰατρός, ὁ** 1 • 1 • 3 *physician (of the soul)*
**Μαρία, ἡ** 3 • 4 • 4 *Mary*
**παθητός** 1 • 2 • 2 *subject to suffering*
**πνευματικός** 6 • 12 • 19 *of spirit, pertaining to the divine spirit*
**σαρκικός** 3 • 9 • 10 *material, physical, human, fleshly, of flesh*

## Chapter 8

1 **ἁγνίζω** 1 • 2 • 4 *to dedicate oneself*
**βασανίζω** 1 • 1 • 18 *to torment, harass*
**διαβόητος** 1 • 1 • 1 *talked about, renowned*
**ἐνερείδω** 1 • 1 • 1 *to thrust in;* pass. *become fixed, firmly rooted*
**ἐξαπατάω** [2] 2 • 2 • 2 *to deceive, cheat*
**ἔρις, ἡ** 1 • 1 • 10 *strife, discord, contention*
**Ἐφέσιος** 2 • 7 • 7 *Ephesian*
**περίψημα, τό** 2 • 2 • 4 *dirt, off-scouring*
**κατὰ θεόν** *according to God's (will)*
2 **ἀπιστία, ἡ** [2] 2 • 2 • 4 *lack of belief, unbelief*
**πνευματικός** [3] 6 • 12 • 19 *spiritual, corresponding to the divine spirit, belong to the spirit*
**σαρκικός** 3 • 9 • 10 *material, physical, human, fleshly, belong to the flesh*

## Chapter 9

1 **ἀναγωγεύς, ὁ** 1 • 1 • 1 *one who leads upward*
**ἀναφέρω** [2] 2 • 2 • 8 *to take, lead, bring up, hoist up*
**βύω** 1 • 1 • 1 *to stop, plug*
**διδαχή, ἡ** 1 • 2 • 14 *teaching*
**ἐάω** 2 • 2 • 13 *to let, permit*
**μηχανή, ἡ** 1 • 1 • 1 *crane*
**οἰκοδομή, ἡ** 1 • 1 • 103 *building, edifice*
**παραδέχομαι** 1 • 2 • 9 *to accept*
**παροδεύω** 1 • 2 • 2 *to pass, pass by*
**προετοιμάζω** 1 • 1 • 5 *to prepare beforehand*
**σπείρω** [2] 2 • 2 • 5 *to sow seed*
**σταυρός, ὁ** 2 • 6 • 17 *the cross*
**σχοινίον, τό** 1 • 1 • 1 *rope* or *cord*
**ὕψος, τό** 1 • 1 • 7 *extent or distance upward, height*
**χράομαι** 1 • 4 • 18 *to make use of, employ*
2 **ἀγαλλιάω** 1 • 3 • 11 *to exult, be glad, overjoyed*
**ἁγιοφόρος** 1 • 1 • 2 *bearing holy things*
**ἀξιόω** 2 • 5 • 14 *to consider worthy, deserving*
**βίος, ὁ** 1 • 3 • 13 *life*
**θεοφόρος** 1 • 1 • 1 *god-bearing, inspired;* subst. *the God-bearer*
**κοσμέω** 1 • 1 • 10 *to adorn, decorate*
**ναοφόρος, ὁ** 1 • 1 • 1 *temple-bearer, shine-bearer*
**προσομιλέω** 1 • 1 • 1 *to speak to, converse with*
**συγχαίρω** 1 • 4 • 7 *to congratulate*
**σύνοδος, ὁ** 1 • 1 • 1 *traveling companion, fellow traveler*
**χριστόφορος** 1 • 1 • 1 *the Christ-bearer*

## Chapter 10

1 **ἀδιαλείπτως** 1 • 1 • 6 *constantly, unceasingly*
**ἐπιτρέπω** 1 • 3 • 11 *to allow, permit*
**κἄν** 1 • 2 • 8 *(even) if only, at least*
**μαθητεύω** 2 • 4 • 4 *to be a pupil*
**μετάνοια, ἡ** 1 • 1 • 72 *repentance, turning about, conversion*
**τυγχάνω** 1 • 5 • 15 *to meet, attain, gain, find, experience*
2 **ἄγριος** 1 • 1 • 8 *uncontrolled*
**ἀντιμιμέομαι** 1 • 1 • 1 *to follow the example (of someone)*

**βλασφημία, ἡ** 1 • 1 • 7 *reviling, denigration, disrespect, slander*
**ἑδραῖος** 1 • 2 • 2 *firm, steadfast*
**ἥμερος** 1 • 1 • 3 *gentle, kind*
**μεγαλορημοσύνη** 1 • 1 • 1 *proud/ boastful talking*
**πλάνη, ἡ** 1 • 1 • 11 *error, delusion, deceit, deception*
**πραΰς** 1 • 1 • 8 *gentle, humble, considerate, meek*
**σπουδάζω** 5 • 8 • 14 *to be zealous/ eager, take pains, make every effort, be conscientious*
**ταπεινόφρων** 1 • 1 • 4 *humble*
3 **ἁγνεία, ἡ** 1 • 2 • 13 *purity, chastity*
**ἀδικέω** 1 • 2 • 7 *to do wrong*
**ἀθετέω** 1 • 1 • 4 *to reject, not recognize, disallow*
**ἀποστερέω** 1 • 1 • 2 *to rob, steal, despoil, defraud, cheat*
**βοτάνη, ἡ** 1 • 3 • 30 *plant*
**ἐπιείκεια, ἡ** 1 • 3 • 9 *clemency, gentleness, graciousness, courtesy, indulgence, tolerance*
**μιμητής, ὁ** 2 • 5 • 12 *imitator*
**πνευματικῶς** 1 • 2 • 4 *spiritually, in a manner caused by/filled with the Spirit*
**σαρκικῶς** 1 • 1 • 1 *outwardly*
**σπουδάζω** 5 • 8 • 14 *to be zealous/ eager, take pains, make every effort, be conscientious*
**σωφροσύνη, ἡ** 1 • 1 • 3 *good judgment, moderation, self-control*

## Chapter 11

1 **αἰσχύνω** 1 • 2 • 3 *to be ashamed*
**ἀληθινός** 3 • 5 • 14 *genuine, authentic, real*
**ἐνίστημι** 1 • 1 • 6 *to be now, happen now, be present*
**κρίμα, τό** 1 • 1 • 9 *judicial verdict*
**μακροθυμία, ἡ** 2 • 2 • 15 *forbearance, patience*
2 **ἀεί** 1 • 2 • 7 *always*
**δεσμός, ὁ** 2 • 8 • 14 *bond, fetter*
**Ἐφέσιος** 2 • 7 • 7 *Ephesian*
**κλῆρος, ὁ** 1 • 4 • 8 *portion, share, class, company*
**μαργαρίτης, ὁ** 1 • 1 • 1 *pearl*
**μέτοχος** 1 • 1 • 3 *sharing/ participating in*
**περιφέρω** 2 • 4 • 4 *to carry about, carry here and there*
**πνευματικός** 6 • 12 • 19 *spiritual, pertaining to the divine spirit*
**πρέπω** 3 • 13 • 15 *to be fitting, be seemly/suitable, have attraction*
**συναινέω** 1 • 1 • 1 *to agree with, be in accord with*
**Χριστιανός, ὁ** 1 • 4 • 24 *Christ-follower, Christian*

## Chapter 12

1 **ἐλεέω** 1 • 6 • 16 *to have compassion/mercy/pity*
**κατάκριτος** 1 • 3 • 3 *condemned*
**κίνδυνος, ὁ** 1 • 2 • 8 *danger, risk*
**στηρίζω** 1 • 2 • 8 *to confirm, establish, strengthen*
2 **ἁγιάζω** 2 • 2 • 16 *to consecrate, dedicate, sanctify*
**ἀναιρέω** 1 • 1 • 10 *to do away with, destroy*
**ἀξιομακάριστος** 2 • 4 • 4 *most worthy of blessing*
**ἐπιστολή, ἡ** 1 • 3 • 13 *letter, epistle*
**ἐπιτυγχάνω** 3 • 20 • 23 *to obtain, attain to, reach*
**ἴχνος, τό** 1 • 1 • 2 *sole*
**μνημονεύω** 2 • 6 • 25 *to keep in mind, think of, mention*
**πάροδος, ὁ** 1 • 1 • 3 *passage, thoroughfare*
**συμμύστης, ὁ** 1 • 1 • 1 *fellow-initiate*

## Chapter 13

1 **εὐχαριστία, ἡ** 1 • 5 • 7 *the observance and elements of the Lord's Supper, Eucharist*
**καθαιρέω** 2 • 2 • 7 *to tear down, destroy, overpower*
**ὄλεθρος, ὁ** 1 • 1 • 2 *destruction*
**ὁμόνοια, ἡ** 3 • 8 • 24 *oneness of mind, unanimity, concord, harmony*
**πυκνός** 1 • 2 • 3 *often, frequently*
**πυκνῶς** 1 • 1 • 3 *frequently, often*

**Σατανᾶς/Σατάν, ὁ** 1 • 1 • 5 *Satan*
**σπουδάζω** 5 • 8 • 14 *to be zealous/ eager, take pains, make every effort, be conscientious*
**συνέρχομαι** 2 • 2 • 4 *to assemble, gather, come together*
2 **ἀμείνων** 2 • 5 • 6 *better*
**ἐπίγειος** 1 • 2 • 12 *earthly*
**ἐπουράνιος** 1 • 5 • 11 *heavenly, in heaven*
**καταργέω** 1 • 1 • 6 *to abolish, wipe out, set aside, bring to an end*
**πόλεμος, ὁ** 1 • 1 • 4 *strife, conflict, quarrel*

## Chapter 14

1 **ἀκόλουθος** 1 • 1 • 8 *following*
**ἑνότης, ἡ** 4 • 11 • 11 *unity*
**καλοκαγαθία, ἡ** 1 • 1 • 1 *nobility of character, excellence*
**λανθάνω** 3 • 3 • 7 *to escape notice, be hidden*
**τελείως** 2 • 3 • 8 *fully, perfectly, completely, altogether*
2 **δένδρον, τό** 1 • 1 • 28 *tree*
**ἐπαγγέλλομαι** [2] 2 • 3 • 7 *to profess, lay claim to, give oneself out as an expert in*
**κτάομαι** 4 • 9 • 10 *to possess*
**φανερός** 1 • 1 • 9 *visible, clear, plainly to be seen, open, plain, evident, known*

## Chapter 15

1 **ἀμείνων** 2 • 5 • 6 *better*
**σιγάω** 3 • 4 • 6 *to say nothing, keep still, keep silent*
**σιωπάω** 2 • 4 • 5 *to keep silent, say nothing, make no sound*
2 **ἀληθῶς** 2 • 15 • 23 *truly, in truth, really, actually*
**ἡσυχία, ἡ** 2 • 2 • 3 *silence*
**κτάομαι** 4 • 9 • 10 *to possess*
**σιγάω** 3 • 4 • 6 *to say nothing, keep still, keep silent*
**τέλειος** 1 • 9 • 25 *perfect, fully developed*
3 **δικαίως** 1 • 2 • 12 *correctly, justly, uprightly*
**κρυπτός** 1 • 3 • 4 *something hidden*
**λανθάνω** 3 • 3 • 7 *to escape notice, be hidden*
**ὅσπερ** 2 • 5 • 10 *which indeed*

## Chapter 16

1 **κληρονομέω** 1 • 2 • 11 *to acquire, obtain, come into possession of*
**οἰκοφθόρος** 1 • 1 • 1 *destroyer of houses or families*
2 **ἄσβεστος** 1 • 1 • 3 *inextinguishable, unquenchable*
**διδασκαλία, ἡ** 2 • 2 • 6 *teaching, instruction*
**πόσος** 3 • 3 • 10 *how great*
**ῥυπαρός** 1 • 1 • 3 *unclean, defiled*
**φθείρω** 1 • 2 • 10 *to ruin, corrupt*
**χωρέω** 1 • 6 • 15 *to go, go out/ away, reach*

## Chapter 17

1 **αἰχμαλωτίζω** 1 • 2 • 2 *to make captive, take captive*
**ἀλείφω** 1 • 1 • 1 *to besmear*
**ἀφθαρσία, ἡ** 1 • 4 • 12 *incorruptibility, immortality*
**διδασκαλία, ἡ** 2 • 2 • 6 *teaching, instruction*
**δυσωδία, ἡ** 1 • 1 • 1 *filth*
**μῦρον, τό** 1 • 1 • 1 *ointment, perfume*
**πνέω** 1 • 1 • 2 *to breathe something out*
**πρόκειμαι** 1 • 3 • 4 *to lie or be set before someone*
2 **ἀγνοέω** 1 • 3 • 11 *not to know, be ignorant (of)*
**ἀληθῶς** 2 • 15 • 23 *truly, in truth, really, actually*
**γνῶσις, ἡ** 1 • 1 • 32 *knowledge, what is known*
**μωρῶς** 1 • 1 • 1 *foolishly*
**φρόνιμος** 1 • 3 • 4 *sensible, thoughtful, prudent, wise*
**χάρισμα, τό** 1 • 4 • 6 *favor bestowed, gift*

## Chapter 18

1 **ἀπιστέω** 1 • 1 • 1 *to disbelieve, refuse to believe*
**καύχησις, ἡ** 1 • 2 • 3 *boasting*
**περίψημα, τό** 2 • 2 • 4 *dirt, off-scouring*
**σκάνδαλον, τό** 1 • 1 • 5 *fault, stain*
**σοφός** 1 • 1 • 8 *wise*
**σταυρός, ὁ** 2 • 6 • 17 *the cross*
**συζητητής, ὁ** 1 • 1 • 1 *disputant, debater*
**συνετός** 1 • 1 • 7 *intelligent, sagacious, wise, with good sense*
2 **κυοφορέω** 1 • 1 • 2 *to be pregnant, be fruitful*
**Μαρία, ἡ** 3 • 4 • 4 *Mary*
**οἰκονομία, ἡ** 3 • 3 • 6 *arrangement, order, plan*
**πάθος, τό** 3 • 15 • 18 *suffering*

## Chapter 19

1 **ἡσυχία, ἡ** 2 • 2 • 3 *silence*
**κραυγή** 1 • 1 • 1 *a loud (articulate) cry*
**λανθάνω** 3 • 3 • 7 *to escape notice, be hidden*
**Μαρία, ἡ** 3 • 3 • 4 *Mary*
**μυστήριον, τό** 1 • 3 • 11 *transcendent/ultimate reality, secret*
**παρθενία, ἡ** 1 • 1 • 1 *virginity*
**τοκετός, ὁ** 1 • 2 • 2 *childbearing, giving birth*
2 **ἅμα** 2 • 9 • 12 *together*
**ἀνεκλάλητος** 1 • 1 • 2 *inexpressible, indescribable*
**ἀνόμοιος** 1 • 1 • 1 *unlike*
**ἀστήρ, ὁ** [3] 3 • 3 • 7 *star, single star, planet*
**ἄστρον, τό** 1 • 1 • 3 *star, constellation, single star*
**καινότης, ἡ** [2] 3 • 4 • 4 *newness*
**λάμπω** 1 • 1 • 1 *to shine*
**ξενισμός, ὁ** 1 • 1 • 1 *astonishment*
**παρέχω** 1 • 3 • 18 *to cause, make happen*
**πόθεν** 1 • 1 • 6 *from what source? brought about* or *given by whom? born of whom?*
**σελήνη, ἡ** 1 • 1 • 7 *moon*
**ταραχή, ἡ** 1 • 1 • 1 *perplexity, disquietude*
**ὑπερβάλλω** 1 • 1 • 4 *to go beyond, surpass, outdo;*
**ὑπερβάλλων τὸ φῶς αὐτοῦ ὑπὲρ πάντα** (φῶς may be either a cognate acc., related loosely to ἀστέρι [so Lightfoot], or an acc. of reference ['with respect to its light']) *surpassing all with its light*
**χορός, ὁ** 2 • 3 • 4 *troop, band*
3 **ἄγνοια, ἡ** 1 • 1 • 3 *ignorance, unawareness, lack of discernment*
**ἀΐδιος** 1 • 1 • 1 *eternal*
**ἀνθρωπίνως** 1 • 1 • 1 *as a human being*
**ἀπαρτίζω** 3 • 5 • 7 *to finish, complete*
**ἀφανίζω** 1 • 1 • 2 *to be destroyed, perish, disappear*
**δεσμός, ὁ** 2 • 8 • 14 *bond, fetter*
**διαφθείρω** 1 • 3 • 12 *to spoil, destroy*
**ἔνθεν** 1 • 1 • 2 *from then on*
**καθαιρέω** 2 • 2 • 7 *to tear down, destroy, overpower*
**καινότης, ἡ** 3 • 4 • 4 *newness*
**κακία, ἡ** 1 • 1 • 9 *baseness, depravity, wickedness, vice*
**κατάλυσις, ἡ** 1 • 1 • 1 *dissolution, abolition, downfall*
**μαγεία, ἡ** 1 • 1 • 3 *magic*
**μελετάω** 1 • 1 • 6 *to practice, cultivate, take pains with*
**ὅθεν** 4 • 10 • 16 *for which reason*
**παλαιός** 1 • 3 • 7 *old*
**συγκινέω** 1 • 1 • 1 *to stir up, move*

## Chapter 20

1 **βιβλίδιον, τό** 1 • 1 • 5 *brief document*
**καταξιόω** 1 • 9 • 14 *to consider worthy*
**οἰκονομία, ἡ** 3 • 3 • 6 *arrangement, order, plan*
**πάθος, τό** 3 • 15 • 18 *suffering*
**προσδηλόω** 1 • 1 • 1 *to explain further*
2 **ἀθανασία, ἡ** 1 • 1 • 3 *immortality*
**ἀντίδοτος, ἡ** 1 • 1 • 1 *antidote*

**ἀπερίσπαστος** 1 • 1 • 1 *not distracted*
**ἀποκαλύπτω** 1 • 1 • 23 *to reveal, disclose, bring to light, make fully known*
**γένος, τό** 1 • 3 • 16 *descendant*
**διάνοια, ἡ** 1 • 2 • 22 *disposition, thought, mind*
**ἐπίσκοπος, ὁ** 13 • 57 • 76 *overseer, supervisor*
**κλάω** 1 • 1 • 2 *to break*
**κοινός** 3 • 9 • 15 *communal, common;*
**οἱ κατ᾽ ἄνδρα κοινῇ πάντες** *all of you, individually and collectively*
**μάλιστα** 1 • 3 • 14 *most of all, above all, especially, particularly*
**πρεσβυτέριον, τό** 3 • 13 • 13 *council of elders*
**συνέρχομαι** 2 • 2 • 4 *to assemble, gather, come together*
**ὑπακούω** 1 • 2 • 9 *to obey, follow, be subject to*
**φάρμακον, τό** 1 • 2 • 5 *medicine, remedy, drug*

## Chapter 21

1 **ἀντίψυχος/ἀντίψυχον, τό** 1 • 4 • 4 *ransom*
**μνημονεύω** 2 • 6 • 25 *to remember, keep in mind, think of, mention*
**ὅθεν** 4 • 10 • 16 *for which reason*
**Πολύκαρπος, ὁ** 1 • 5 • 39 *Polycarp*
**Σμύρνα, ἡ** 1 • 6 • 14 *Smyrna*
2 **ἀξιόω** 2 • 5 • 14 *to consider worthy, deserving*
**ἀπάγω** 1 • 1 • 4 *to lead away*
**κοινός** 3 • 9 • 15 *communal, common*
**ὅθεν** 4 • 10 • 16 *for which reason*
**Ῥώμη, ἡ** 2 • 4 • 8 *Rome*
**ῥώννυμι** 1 • 9 • 10 *to strengthen;*
**ἔρρωσθε** (perfect pass. imperative; cf. BDF §346; *ExSyn* 493) *farewell, goodbye*
**Συρία, ἡ** 2 • 16 • 17 *Syria*

# Ignatius to the Magnesians

### Preface

**εὔχομαι** 2 • 13 • 16 *to wish*
**Θεοφόρος, ὁ** 1 • 7 • 7 *Theophorus*
**Ἰγνάτιος, ὁ** 1 • 7 • 10 *Ignatius*
**Μαγνησία, ἡ** 1 • 1 • 1 *Magnesia*
**Μαίανδρος, ὁ** 1 • 1 • 1 *Maeander River*
**πρὸς Μαιάνδρῳ** *on/by the Maeander River*
**σωτήρ, ὁ** 1 • 4 • 14 *savior, deliverer, preserver*

### Chapter 1

1 **ἀγαλλιάω** 1 • 3 • 11 *to exult, be glad, overjoyed*
**πολυεύτακτος** 1 • 1 • 1 *very well ordered/disciplined*
**προαιρέω** 1 • 1 • 4 *to choose (for oneself), commit oneself to, prefer*
**προσλαλέω** 1 • 2 • 3 *to speak to, speak with, address*
2 **ᾄδω** 1 • 4 • 6 *to sing (in praise)*
**δεσμός, ὁ** 1 • 8 • 14 *bond, fetter*
**ἕνωσις, ἡ** 2 • 8 • 8 *union, unity*
**εὔχομαι** 2 • 13 • 16 *to wish*
**θεοπρεπής** 1 • 5 • 6 *worthy of God, revered, venerable, godly;*
**θεοπρεπεστάτου** (superlative adj.) *most redounding to the glory of God*
**καταξιόω** 1 • 9 • 14 *to consider worthy*
**κύριος** 1 • 1 • 1 *principal, essential;*
**τὸ δὲ κυριώτερον** *but what is more important*
**περιφέρω** 1 • 4 • 4 *to carry about, carry here and there*
**προκρίνω** 1 • 2 • 2 *to prefer*
**τοῦ διὰ παντὸς ἡμῶν ζῆν** (subst. infinitive with prepositional modifier; cf. BDF §398) *our forever/never failing life*

3 **διαφεύγω** 1 • 1 • 1 *to escape*
**ἐπήρεια, ἡ** 1 • 1 • 1 *abuse, ill-treatment*
**τυγχάνω** 1 • 5 • 15 *to meet, attain, gain, find, experience*
**ὑπομένω** 2 • 7 • 32 *to stand one's ground, hold out, endure*

### Chapter 2

1 **ἀξιόθεος** 1 • 5 • 5 *worthy of God*
**ἀξιόω** 2 • 5 • 14 *to consider worthy, deserving*
**Ἀπολλώνιος, ὁ** 1 • 1 • 1 *Apollonius*
**Βάσσος, ὁ** 1 • 1 • 1 *Bassus*
**Δαμᾶς, ὁ** 1 • 1 • 1 *Damas*
**διάκονος, ὁ** 3 • 18 • 29 *assistant*
**ἐπεί** 6 • 12 • 35 *because, since, for;* anacoluthon here: protasis is begun in v. 1 but apodosis is forgotten (Lightfoot)
**ἐπίσκοπος, ὁ** 12 • 57 • 76 *overseer, supervisor*
**Ζωτίων, ὁ** 1 • 1 • 1 *Zotion*
**ὀνίνημι** 2 • 6 • 6 *to have benefit of, enjoy;*
**ὀναίμην** (voluntative optative) *may I enjoy*
**πρεσβυτέριον, τό** 2 • 13 • 13 *council of elders*
**σύνδουλος, ὁ** 1 • 4 • 6 *slave, fellow-slave*

### Chapter 3

1 **ἀπονέμω** 1 • 1 • 3 *to assign, show, pay, accord*
**ἐντροπή, ἡ** 1 • 1 • 1 *respect, regard*
**ἐπίσκοπος, ὁ** 12 • 57 • 76 *overseer, supervisor*
**ἡλικία, ἡ** 1 • 1 • 4 *age, time of life, youthfulness*
**νεωτερικός** 1 • 1 • 1 *youthful*

**πρέπω** 3 • 13 • 15 *to be fitting, be seemly/suitable*
**προσλαμβάνω** 1 • 1 • 2 *to exploit, take advantage of*
**συγχράομαι** 1 • 1 • 1 *to take advantage of*
**συγχωρέω** 1 • 1 • 2 *to grant a little ground*
**τάξις, ἡ** 1 • 1 • 6 *arrangement, nature, manner, condition, outward aspect*
**φρόνιμος** 1 • 3 • 4 *sensible, thoughtful, prudent, wise*
2 **ἀόρατος** 1 • 6 • 13 *unseen, invisible*
**ἐπεί** 6 • 12 • 35 *because, since, for*
**ἐπίσκοπος, ὁ** 12 • 57 • 76 *overseer, supervisor*
**κρύφιος** 1 • 1 • 4 *hidden, secret*
**παραλογίζομαι** 1 • 1 • 2 *to deceive, delude;*
**τὸν ἀόρατον παραλογίζεται** (conative present; cf. *ExSyn* 534) *attempts to cheat the unseen one*
**πρέπω** 3 • 13 • 15 *to be fitting, be seemly/suitable*
**ὑπακούω** 1 • 2 • 9 *to obey, follow, be subject to*
**ὑπόκρισις, ἡ** 1 • 1 • 13 *pretense*

## Chapter 4

1 **βεβαίως** 2 • 2 • 3 *valid, proper*
**ἐπίσκοπος, ὁ** 12 • 57 • 76 *overseer, supervisor*
**εὐσυνείδητος** 1 • 1 • 2 *with a good conscience*
**πρέπω** 3 • 13 • 15 *to be fitting, be seemly/suitable*
**συναθροίζω** 1 • 1 • 2 *to gather, bring together, hold meetings*
**Χριστιανός, ὁ** 1 • 5 • 24 *Christ-follower, Christian*

## Chapter 5

1 **ἐπεί** 6 • 12 • 35 *because, since, for*
**ὁμοῦ** 1 • 2 • 5 *together at the same time (as), in company (with)*
**πρᾶγμα, τό** 2 • 3 • 23 *thing, matter, affair*
**πρόκειμαι** 1 • 3 • 4 *to lie or be set before someone*
**χωρέω** 2 • 6 • 15 *to go, go out/away, reach*
2 **ἄπιστος** 1 • 4 • 8 *without faith, disbelieving, unbelieving*
**αὐθαιρέτως** 1 • 1 • 1 *voluntarily*
**ἐπίκειμαι** 1 • 2 • 6 *to lie upon, be on*
**νόμισμα, τό** 1 • 1 • 1 *coin, coinage*
**πάθος, τό** 2 • 15 • 18 *suffering*
**χαρακτήρ, ὁ** [2] 2 • 3 • 5 *impress, reproduction, representation*
**τὸ ζῆν** (substantival infinitive; cf. BDF §398) *(his) life*

## Chapter 6

1 **γλυκύς** 1 • 1 • 6 *sweet, dear*
**διάκονος, ὁ** 3 • 18 • 29 *assistant*
**ἐπεί** 6 • 12 • 35 *because, since, for*
**ἐπίσκοπος, ὁ** 12 • 57 • 76 *overseer, supervisor*
**ὁμόνοια, ἡ** 2 • 8 • 24 *oneness of mind, unanimity, concord, harmony*
**παραινέω** 1 • 2 • 2 *to recommend, urge*
**προγράφω** 1 • 1 • 4 *to write before(hand), mention above*
**προκάθημαι** 2 • 4 • 4 *to preside (over), lead*
**σπουδάζω** 2 • 8 • 14 *to be zealous/eager, take pains, make every effort, be conscientious*
**συνέδριον, τό** 1 • 3 • 3 *council*
2 **ἀφθαρσία, ἡ** 1 • 4 • 12 *incorruptibility, immortality*
**διδαχή, ἡ** 1 • 2 • 14 *teaching*
**ἑνόω** 3 • 6 • 6 *to unite*
**ἐντρέπω** 2 • 5 • 9 *to turn toward (something/someone), have regard for, respect*
**ἐπίσκοπος, ὁ** 12 • 57 • 76 *overseer, supervisor*
**μερίζω** 1 • 1 • 2 *to divide*
**ὁμοήθεια, ἡ** 1 • 2 • 2 *similarity in character, agreement in convictions*
**πλησίον** 1 • 2 • 17 *near;* subst. *neighbor, fellow human being*

**προκάθημαι** 2 • 4 • 4 *to preside over, lead*
**τύπος, ὁ** 1 • 2 • 26 *copy, image*

## Chapter 7

1 **ἀμείνων** 1 • 5 • 6 *better*
**ἄμωμος** 1 • 7 • 17 *blameless*
**ἄνευ** [2] 2 • 6 • 12 *without*
**δέησις, ἡ** 1 • 1 • 6 *prayer*
**ἑνόω** 3 • 6 • 6 *to unite*
**ἐπίσκοπος, ὁ** 12 • 57 • 76 *overseer, supervisor*
**εὔλογος** 1 • 2 • 2 *reasonable, right*
**νοῦς, ὁ** 1 • 1 • 12 *mind, attitude*
**οὐθείς/οὐδείς** 1 • 1 • 3 *nothing*
2 **θυσιαστήριον, τό** 1 • 6 • 15 *sanctuary*
**προέρχομαι** 2 • 3 • 5 *to come forth, proceed*
**συντρέχω** 1 • 4 • 6 *to run together*
**χωρέω** 2 • 6 • 15 *to go, go out/away, reach*

## Chapter 8

1 **ἀνωφελής** 1 • 1 • 2 *useless*
**ἑτεροδοξία, ἡ** 1 • 1 • 1 *strange, erroneous opinion*
**Ἰουδαϊσμός, ὁ** 3 • 5 • 5 *Judeanism/Judaism, Judean way*
**μέχρι** 1 • 5 • 23 *until*
**μύθευμα, τό** 1 • 1 • 1 *story, fable*
**ὁμολογέω** 1 • 3 • 18 *to grant, admit, confess*
**παλαιός** 2 • 3 • 7 *old*
2 **ἀπειθέω** 1 • 1 • 5 *to disobey, be disobedient*
**ἐμπνέω** 1 • 1 • 1 *to inspire*
**εὐαρεστέω** 1 • 1 • 6 *to please, be pleasing*
**θεῖος** 1 • 1 • 16 *divine;*
**θειότατοι** (superlative adj. with elative sense) *very near to God*
**πληροφορέω** 2 • 4 • 9 *to convince fully;*
pass. *have perfect faith*
**προέρχομαι** 2 • 3 • 5 *to come forth, proceed*
**σιγή, ἡ** 1 • 1 • 3 *silence, quiet*

## Chapter 9

1 **ἀναστρέφω** 1 • 1 • 8 *to act, behave, conduct oneself, live*
**ἀνατέλλω** 1 • 2 • 6 *to rise, spring up, dawn*
**καινότης, ἡ** 1 • 4 • 4 *newness*
**κυριακός** 1 • 1 • 9 *the Lord's*
**μηκέτι** 1 • 1 • 16 *no longer, not from now on*
**μυστήριον, τό** 1 • 3 • 11 *transcendent/ultimate reality, secret*
**παλαιός** 2 • 3 • 7 *old, obsolete*
**πρᾶγμα, τό** 2 • 3 • 23 *thing, matter, affair, way*
**σαββατίζω** 1 • 1 • 1 *to keep the Sabbath*
**ὑπομένω** 2 • 7 • 32 *to stand one's ground, hold out, endure*
2 **ἀναμένω** 1 • 2 • 3 *to wait for, expect*
**δικαίως** 1 • 2 • 12 *correctly*
**πάρειμι** 2 • 5 • 17 *to be present*
**προσδοκάω** 1 • 2 • 8 *to wait for, look for, expect*

## Chapter 10

1 **ἀναισθητέω** 1 • 1 • 3 *to be unfeeling, be insensible*
**καθά** 1 • 1 • 2 *just as*
**μανθάνω** 1 • 2 • 26 *to learn, appropriate to oneself*
**μιμέομαι** 1 • 2 • 4 *to imitate, emulate, follow*
**χρηστότης, ἡ** 1 • 2 • 9 *goodness, kindness, generosity*
**Χριστιανισμός, ὁ** 3 • 5 • 6 *the Christian way, Christianity*
2 **ἁλίζω** 1 • 1 • 1 *to salt*
**διαφθείρω** 1 • 3 • 12 *to spoil, destroy*
**ἐλέγχω** 1 • 2 • 16 *to convict, convince*
**ἐνοξίζω** 1 • 1 • 1 *to become sour*
**ἐπεί** 6 • 12 • 35 *because, since, for*
**ζύμη, ἡ** [2] 2 • 2 • 2 *leaven*
**μεταβάλλω** 1 • 1 • 1 *to change*
**νέος** 1 • 1 • 16 *new, fresh*
**ὀσμή, ἡ** 1 • 1 • 3 *odor*
**παλαιόω** 1 • 1 • 3 *to make old;*
pass. *become old*

**ὑπερτίθημι** 1 • 1 • 1 *to set aside, do away with*
3 **ἄτοπος** 1 • 1 • 2 *evil, wrong, improper*
**ἰουδαΐζω** 1 • 1 • 1 *to live in Judean or Jewish fashion*
**Ἰουδαϊσμός, ὁ** [2] 3 • 5 • 5 *Judeanism, Judaism*
**Χριστιανισμός, ὁ** [2] 3 • 5 • 6 *the Christian Way, Christianity*

## Chapter 11

1 **ἄγκιστρον, τό** 1 • 1 • 1 *fishhook*
**ἀληθῶς** 1 • 15 • 23 *truly, in truth, really, actually*
**βεβαίως** 2 • 2 • 3 *certainly, truly, reliably*
**γέννησις, ἡ** 1 • 1 • 1 *birth*
**ἐκτρέπω** 1 • 1 • 1 *to turn, turn away*
**ἐμπίπτω** 1 • 1 • 5 *to fall (into/among), be caught*
**ἐπεί** 6 • 12 • 25 *because, since, for*
**ἡγεμονία, ἡ** 1 • 1 • 2 *prefecture; chief command, direction, management*
**κενοδοξία, ἡ** 1 • 2 • 5 *illusion, delusion, error*
**πάθος, τό** 2 • 15 • 18 *suffering*
**Πιλᾶτος, ὁ** 1 • 3 • 3 *Pilate*
**πληροφορέω** 2 • 4 • 9 *to convince fully*
**Πόντιος, ὁ** 1 • 3 • 3 *Pontius*
**προφυλάσσω** 1 • 3 • 3 *to be on one's guard*

## Chapter 12

1 **ἐάνπερ** 1 • 7 • 7 *if indeed, if only, supposing that*
**ἐντρέπω** 2 • 5 • 9 *to shame*
**ἐπαινέω** 1 • 2 • 6 *to praise*
**κατήγορος, ὁ** 1 • 1 • 1 *accuser*
**ὀνίνημι** 2 • 6 • 6 *to have benefit of, enjoy, have joy;*
**ὀναίμην** (voluntative optative) *May I have joy*
**φυσιόω** 1 • 5 • 6 *to puff up, make proud*
**πρὸς ἕνα τῶν ὑμῶν** *comparable to any one of you*

## Chapter 13

1 **ἀξιόπλοκος** 1 • 1 • 1 *worthily woven*
**ἀξιοπρεπής** 1 • 2 • 2 *worthy of honor*
**βεβαιόω** 1 • 1 • 2 *to establish, strengthen*
**διάκονος, ὁ** 3 • 18 • 29 *assistant;*
**τῶν κατὰ θεὸν διακόνων** *of the godly deacons, of the deacons (who live) by (the will of) God*
**δόγμα, τό** 1 • 1 • 10 *ordinance, decision, command*
**ἐπίσκοπος, ὁ** 12 • 57 • 76 *overseer, supervisor*
**κατευοδόω** 1 • 1 • 2 *to prosper*
**πνευματικός** 2 • 12 • 19 *spiritual, pertaining to the divine spirit*
**πρεσβυτέριον, τό** 2 • 13 • 13 *council of elders*
**σπουδάζω** 2 • 8 • 14 *to be zealous/eager, take pains, make every effort, be conscientious*
**στέφανος, ὁ** 1 • 1 • 8 *wreath, crown*
2 **ἕνωσις, ἡ** 2 • 8 • 8 *union, unity*
**ἐπίσκοπος, ὁ** 12 • 57 • 76 *overseer, supervisor*
**πνευματικός** 2 • 12 • 19 *spiritual*
**σαρκικός** 1 • 9 • 10 *material, physical, human, fleshly*

## Chapter 14

1 **ἀξιόω** 2 • 5 • 14 *to consider worthy, deserving*
**γέμω** 1 • 1 • 4 *to be full*
**δροσίζω** 1 • 1 • 1 *to refresh with dew*
**ἐκτένεια, ἡ** 1 • 1 • 3 *perseverance, earnestness*
**ἑνόω** 3 • 6 • 6 *to unite*
**ἐπιδέω/ἐπιδέομαι** 1 • 1 • 1 *to need, be in need*
**ἐπιτυγχάνω** 1 • 20 • 23 *to obtain, attain to, reach*
**μνημονεύω** 1 • 6 • 25 *to remember, keep in mind, think of, mention*
**ὅθεν** 2 • 10 • 16 *from where, whence, from which*
**συντόμως** 1 • 2 • 3 *briefly, concisely*

**Συρία, ἡ** [2] 2 • 16 • 17 *Syria*

## Chapter 15

1 **ἀδιάκριτος** 1 • 3 • 3 *nonjudgmental, not divisive, impartial*
**ἅμα** 1 • 9 • 12 *together*
**ἀναπαύω** 1 • 7 • 13 *to cause to rest, give someone rest, refresh, revive*
**ἐπίσκοπος, ὁ** 12 • 57 • 76 *overseer, supervisor*
**Ἐφέσιος** 1 • 7 • 7 *Ephesian*
**κτάομαι** 1 • 9 • 10 *to possess*
**ὅθεν** 2 • 10 • 16 *from where, whence, from which*
**ὁμόνοια, ἡ** 2 • 8 • 24 *oneness of mind, unanimity, concord, harmony*
**πάρειμι** 2 • 5 • 17 *to be present*
**Πολύκαρπος, ὁ** 1 • 5 • 39 *Polycarp*
**ῥώννυμι** 1 • 9 • 10 *to strengthen;* **ἔρρωσθε** (perfect pass. imperative; cf. BDF §346; *ExSyn* 493) *farewell, goodbye*
**Σμύρνα, ἡ** 1 • 6 • 14 *Smyrna*
**Σμυρναῖος** 1 • 4 • 4 *coming from Smyrna*

# Ignatius to the Trallians

## Preface

**ἀξιόθεος** 1 • 5 • 5 *worthy of God*
**ἀποστολικός** 1 • 1 • 4 *apostolic*
**Ἀσία, ἡ** 1 • 4 • 10 *Asia*
**εἰρηνεύω** 1 • 4 • 17 *to live in peace, be at peace*
**ἐκλεκτός** 1 • 2 • 30 *chosen*
**εὔχομαι** 3 • 13 • 16 *to wish*
**Θεοφόρος, ὁ** 1 • 7 • 7 *Theophorus*
**Ἰγνάτιος, ὁ** 1 • 7 • 10 *Ignatius*
**πάθος, τό** 2 • 15 • 18 *suffering*
**πλήρωμα, τό** 1 • 2 • 3 *sum total, fullness*
**Τράλλεις, αἱ** 1 • 1 • 1 *Tralles*; Even though plural, this is the usual form for the city of Tralles.
**χαρακτήρ, ὁ** 1 • 3 • 5 *distinctive mark*

## Chapter 1

1 **ἀδιάκριτος** 1 • 3 • 3 *unwavering*
**ἄμωμος** 2 • 7 • 17 *blameless*
**δηλόω** 1 • 4 • 49 *to reveal, make clear, show*
**διάνοια, ἡ** 1 • 2 • 22 *disposition, thought, mind*
**ἐπίσκοπος, ὁ** 9 • 57 • 76 *overseer, supervisor*
**Πολύβιος, ὁ** 1 • 1 • 1 *Polybius*
**Σμύρνα, ἡ** 2 • 6 • 14 *Smyrna*
**συγχαίρω** 1 • 4 • 7 *to rejoice with*
**φῦσις, ἡ** 1 • 2 • 4 *natural endowment/condition, nature*
**χρῆσις, ἡ** 1 • 1 • 5 *use, usage*
2 **ἀποδέχομαι** 1 • 3 • 6 *to welcome*
**εὔνοια, ἡ** 1 • 2 • 3 *favor, affection, benevolence*;
**τὴν κατὰ θεὸν εὔνοιαν** *(your) godly good will*
**μιμητής, ὁ** 1 • 5 • 12 *imitator*

## Chapter 2

1 **ἐκφεύγω** 1 • 1 • 6 *to escape*
**ἐπίσκοπος, ὁ** 9 • 57 • 76 *overseer, supervisor*
2 **ἀναγκαῖος** 1 • 1 • 4 *necessary*
**ἄνευ** 2 • 6 • 12 *without*
**διάγω** 1 • 1 • 1 *to spend one's life, live*
**ἐπίσκοπος, ὁ** 9 • 57 • 76 *overseer, supervisor*
**πρεσβυτέριον, τό** 3 • 13 • 13 *council of elders*
3 **ἀρέσκω** 1 • 4 • 12 *to please, accommodate*
**βρῶμα, τό** 1 • 1 • 4 *food*
**διάκονος, ὁ** [2] 4 • 18 • 29 *assistant*
**ἔγκλημα, τό** 1 • 1 • 1 *reproach*
**μυστήριον, τό** 1 • 3 • 11 *transcendent/ultimate, reality*
**ποτόν, τό** 1 • 1 • 3 *drink*
**τρόπος, ὁ** 1 • 4 • 17 *manner, way, kind, guise*
**ὑπηρέτης, ὁ** 1 • 2 • 5 *helper, assistant*

## Chapter 3

1 **διάκονος, ὁ** 4 • 18 • 29 *assistant*
**ἐντρέπω** 2 • 5 • 9 *to turn toward something/someone, have respect for, respect*
**ἐπίσκοπος, ὁ** 9 • 57 • 76 *overseer, supervisor*
**σύνδεσμος, ὁ** 1 • 1 • 2 *band, college*
**συνέδριον, τό** 1 • 3 • 3 *council*
**τύπος, ὁ** 1 • 2 • 26 *copy, image*
2 **ἄθεος** 2 • 2 • 5 *god-denier, atheist*
**ἐντρέπω** 2 • 5 • 9 *to turn toward something/someone, have respect for, respect*

ἐξεμπλάριον, τό 1 • 3 • 3 *(living) example, embodiment*
ἐπίσκοπος, ὁ 9 • 57 • 76 *overseer, supervisor*
κατάστημα, τό 1 • 1 • 1 *behavior, demeanor*
μαθητεία, ἡ 1 • 1 • 1 *lesson, instruction*
πραότης/πραΰτης, ἡ 2 • 2 • 4 *gentleness, humility, courtesy, considerateness, meekness*
3 διατάσσω 1 • 3 • 8 *to order*
κατάκριτος 1 • 3 • 3 *condemned*
οἴομαι 1 • 1 • 11 *to think, suppose, expect*
σύντονος 1 • 2 • 2 *intense desire, zeal*
φείδομαι 1 • 2 • 3 *to refrain*

## Chapter 4

1 καύχησις, ἡ 1 • 2 • 3 *boasting*
μαστιγόω 1 • 1 • 4 *to afflict, torment, mistreat*
μετρέω 1 • 1 • 5 *to measure*
προσέχω 1 • 4 • 25 *to pay attention to, give heed to, follow*
φρονέω 1 • 4 • 17 *to think, form/hold an opinion, judge*
φυσιόω 2 • 5 • 6 *to puff up, make proud*
2 ζῆλος, ὁ/τό 1 • 1 • 25 *jealousy, envy*
καταλύω 1 • 1 • 2 *to put an end to, ruin*
πολεμέω 1 • 1 • 7 *to be hostile*
πραότης/πραΰτης, ἡ 2 • 2 • 4 *gentleness, humility, courtesy, considerateness, meekness*
χρῄζω 2 • 2 • 7 *to (have) need (of)*

## Chapter 5

1 βλάβη, ἡ 1 • 1 • 2 *harm*
ἐπουράνιος 3 • 5 • 11 *heavenly;* subst. *heavenly thing*
μήποτε 1 • 2 • 22 *lest*
νήπιος 1 • 1 • 4 *infant, child*
παρατίθημι 1 • 1 • 6 *to do (to), cause harm*
στραγγαλόω 1 • 1 • 1 *to choke*
συγγνωμονέω 1 • 1 • 1 *to make allowance for, pardon*
χωρέω 1 • 6 • 15 *to accept, comprehend, understand*
2 ἀγγελικός 1 • 1 • 1 *angelic*
ἀόρατος 1 • 6 • 13 *unseen, invisible*
ἀρχοντικός 1 • 1 • 1 *commanding*
ἐπουράνιος 3 • 5 • 11 *heavenly;* subst. *heavenly thing*
καθότι 1 • 1 • 1 *because, in view of the fact that*
λείπω [2] 2 • 3 • 5 *to lack*
νοέω 1 • 3 • 46 *to perceive, apprehend, understand, gain insight to*
ὁρατός 1 • 4 • 5 *visible*
σύστασις, ἡ 1 • 2 • 3 *gathering, union, association*
τοποθεσία, ἡ 1 • 1 • 1 *placement*

## Chapter 6

1 αἵρεσις, ἡ 1 • 2 • 6 *sect, party, school, faction*
ἀλλότριος 1 • 3 • 14 *alien, unsuitable*
ἀπέχω 1 • 4 • 35 *to keep away, abstain, refrain from*
βοτάνη, ἡ 1 • 3 • 30 *plant*
τροφή, ἡ 1 • 2 • 12 *nourishment, food*
χράομαι 1 • 4 • 18 *to make use of, employ*
Χριστιανός, ὁ 1 • 5 • 24 *Christ-follower, Christian*
2 ἀγνοέω 1 • 3 • 11 *to not to know, be ignorant (of)*
ἀδεῶς 1 • 1 • 2 *without fear or disturbance*
ἡδονή, ἡ 1 • 3 • 12 *pleasure, delight, enjoyment, pleasantness*
θανάσιμος 1 • 1 • 2 *deadly*
καταξιοπιστεύομαι 1 • 1 • 1 *to impose by profession of honesty*
οἰνόμελι, τό 1 • 1 • 1 *wine mixed with honey*
ὅσπερ 1 • 5 • 10 *which indeed*
παρεμπλέκω 1 • 1 • 1 *to mix, mingle, blend with*
φάρμακον, τό 1 • 2 • 5 *poison*

## Chapter 7

1 **ἀχώριστος** 1 • 1 • 1 *inseparable*
**διάταγμα, τό** 1 • 1 • 1 *edict, command*
**ἐπίσκοπος, ὁ** 9 • 57 • 76 *overseer, supervisor*
**φυσιόω** 2 • 5 • 6 *to puff up, make proud*
2 **διάκονος, ὁ** 4 • 18 • 29 *assistant*
**ἐκτός** 1 • 1 • 6 *outside*
**ἐντός** 1 • 2 • 3 *inside, within, within the limits of*
**ἐπίσκοπος, ὁ** 9 • 57 • 76 *overseer, supervisor*
**θυσιαστήριον, τό** [2] 2 • 6 • 15 *sanctuary*
**καθαρός** [2] 3 • 5 • 45 first instance: *pure ritually and morally*; second instance: *pure, free from sin*
**πρεσβυτέριον, τό** 3 • 13 • 13 *council of elders*

## Chapter 8

1 **ἀνακτάομαι** 1 • 1 • 1 *to regain one's strength, renew one's energy*
**ἀναλαμβάνω** 1 • 1 • 10 *to take to one's self, adopt*
**ἐνέδρα, ἡ** 1 • 2 • 2 *ambush*
**ἐπεί** 1 • 12 • 35 *because, since, for*
**πραϋπάθεια, ἡ** 1 • 1 • 1 *gentleness*
**προοράω** 1 • 1 • 1 *to foresee*
**προφυλάσσω** 1 • 3 • 3 *to guard, protect*
2 **ἀφορμή, ἡ** 1 • 1 • 5 *occasion, opportunity*
**ἄφρων** 1 • 1 • 17 *foolish, ignorant*
**ἔνθεος** 1 • 1 • 1 *inspired by God*
**ματαιότης, ἡ** 1 • 1 • 3 *emptiness, futility, purposelessness, transitoriness*
**πλησίον** 1 • 2 • 17 *near*; subst. *neighbor, fellow human being*

## Chapter 9

1 **ἀληθῶς** [3] 4 • 15 • 23 *truly, in truth, really, actually*
**γένος, τό** 1 • 3 • 16 *descendant*
**ἐπίγειος** 1 • 2 • 12 *earthly*
**ἐπουράνιος** 3 • 5 • 11 *heavenly*; subst. *heavenly being*
**κωφόω** 1 • 1 • 2 *to become deaf*
**Μαρία, ἡ** 1 • 4 • 4 *Mary*
**Πιλᾶτος, ὁ** 1 • 3 • 3 *Pilate*
**Πόντιος, ὁ** 1 • 3 • 3 *Pontius*
**ὑποχθόνιος** 1 • 1 • 1 *under the earth*
2 **ἀληθινός** 1 • 5 • 14 *genuine, authentic, real*
**ἀληθῶς** 4 • 15 • 23 *truly, in truth, really, actually*
**ὁμοίωμα, τό** 1 • 1 • 3 *likeness*

## Chapter 10

1 **ἄθεος** 2 • 2 • 5 *god-denier, atheist*
**ἄπιστος** 1 • 4 • 8 *without faith, disbelieving, unbelieving*
**δωρεάν** 1 • 1 • 2 *in vain, to no purpose*
**εὔχομαι** 3 • 13 • 16 *to wish*
**θηριομαχέω** 1 • 3 • 4 *to fight with wild animals*
**καταψεύδομαι** 1 • 1 • 1 *to tell lies (against)*
**τουτέστιν** 1 • 2 • 5 *this or that means, that is to say*

## Chapter 11

1 **γεύομαι** 1 • 1 • 3 *to taste, partake of*
**θανατηφόρος** 1 • 1 • 1 *death-dealing*
**παραυτά** 1 • 1 • 1 *on the spot, at once*
**παραφυάς, ἡ** 1 • 1 • 14 *offshoot, side growth*
**φεύγω** 1 • 6 • 20 *to flee from, avoid, shun*
**φυτεία, ἡ** 1 • 2 • 2 *a plant*
2 **ἄνευ** 2 • 6 • 12 *without*
**ἄφθαρτος** 1 • 2 • 7 *imperishable, immortal, incorruptible*
**ἕνωσις, ἡ** 1 • 8 • 8 *union, unity*
**ἐπαγγέλλομαι** 1 • 3 • 7 *to promise, offer*
**κλάδος, ὁ** 1 • 1 • 6 *branch*
**πάθος, τό** 2 • 15 • 18 *suffering*
**προσκαλέω** 1 • 1 • 5 *to call (to)*
**σταυρός, ὁ** 1 • 6 • 17 *the cross*

## Chapter 12

1 **ἅμα** 1 • 9 • 12 *together*
**ἀναπαύω** 1 • 7 • 13 *to cause to rest, give (someone) rest, refresh, revive*
**Σμύρνα, ἡ** 2 • 6 • 13 *Smyrna*
**συμπάρειμι** 1 • 1 • 1 *to be together, be present with*
2 **ἀναψύχω** 1 • 2 • 2 *to give (someone) a breathing space, revive, refresh*
**δεσμός, ὁ** 1 • 8 • 14 *bond, fetter*
**διαμένω** 1 • 2 • 9 *to remain*
**ἕνεκα** 1 • 2 • 15 *because of, on account of, for the sake of*
**ἐξαιρέτως** 1 • 2 • 3 *especially*
**ἐπίσκοπος, ὁ** 9 • 57 • 76 *overseer, supervisor*
**ἐπιτυγχάνω** 3 • 20 • 23 *to obtain, attain to, reach*
**ὁμόνοια, ἡ** 1 • 8 • 24 *oneness of mind, unanimity, concord, harmony*
**περιφέρω** 1 • 4 • 4 *to carry about, carry here and there*
**πρέπω** 1 • 13 • 15 *to be fitting, be seemly/suitable*
3 **ἀδόκιμος** 1 • 1 • 1 *unqualified, worthless, base*
**ἔγκειμαι** 1 • 1 • 2 *to insist, warn urgently*
**ἔλεος, τό** 1 • 3 • 19 *mercy, compassion, pity, clemency*
**ἐπιτυγχάνω** 3 • 20 • 23 *to obtain, attain to, reach*
**εὔχομαι** 3 • 13 • 16 *to wish*
**καταξιόω** 1 • 9 • 14 *to consider worthy*
**κλῆρος, ὁ** 1 • 4 • 8 *lot, destiny*
**μαρτύριον, τό** 1 • 2 • 16 *testimony, proof*
**οὗπερ** 1 • 1 • 1 *which indeed*
**χρῄζω** 2 • 2 • 7 *to (have) need (of)*

## Chapter 13

1 **Ἐφέσιος** 1 • 7 • 7 *Ephesian*
**μνημονεύω** 1 • 6 • 25 *to remember, keep in mind, think of, mention*
**ὅθεν** 1 • 10 • 16 *from where, whence, from which*
**Σμυρναῖος** 1 • 4 • 4 *coming from Smyrna*
**Συρία, ἡ** 1 • 16 • 17 *Syria*
2 **ἀμέριστος** 1 • 2 • 2 *undivided*
**ἐπίσκοπος, ὁ** 9 • 57 • 76 *overseer, supervisor*
**πρεσβυτέριον, τό** 3 • 13 • 13 *council of elders*
**ῥώννυμι** 1 • 9 • 10 *to strengthen;*
**ἔρρωσθε** (perfect pass. imperative; cf. BDF §346; *ExSyn* 493) *farewell, goodbye*
**οἱ κατ᾽ ἄνδρα** *each one of you*
3 **ἁγνίζω** 1 • 2 • 4 to dedicate *oneself*
**αἴτησις, ἡ** 1 • 1 • 1 *request*
**ἄμωμος** 2 • 7 • 17 *blameless*
**ἐπιτυγχάνω** 3 • 20 • 23 *to obtain, attain to, reach*
**κίνδυνος, ὁ** 1 • 2 • 8 *danger, risk*
**εὑρεθείημεν** (voluntative optative) *May we be found*

# Ignatius to the Romans

## Preface

**ἀδιακρίτως** 1 • 2 • 2 *without wavering*
**ἀλλότριος** 1 • 3 • 14 *alien, unsuitable*
**ἀμώμως** 1 • 1 • 1 *blamelessly*
**ἀξίαγνος/ἀξιόαγνος** 1 • 1 • 1 *worthy of sanctification*
**ἀξιέπαινος** 1 • 1 • 1 *worthy of praise*
**ἀξιοεπίτευκτος** 1 • 1 • 1 *worthy of success*
**ἀξιόθεος** 2 • 5 • 5 *worthy of God*
**ἀξιομακάριστος** 2 • 4 • 4 most *worthy of blessing*
**ἀξιοπρεπής** 1 • 2 • 2 *worthy of honor*
**ἀποδιϋλίζω** 1 • 1 • 1 *to strain/filter, clear*
**ἐλεέω** 2 • 6 • 16 *to have compassion/mercy/pity;*
**τῇ ἠλεημένῃ ... ἐκκλησίᾳ ἠγαπημένῃ καὶ πεφωτισμένῃ** (first participle is adjectival; the other two are adverbial) *to the church that has found mercy, beloved and enlightened*
**ἑνόω** 1 • 6 • 6 *to unite*
**Θεοφόρος, ὁ** 1 • 7 • 7 *Theophorus*
**Ἰγνάτιος, ὁ** 1 • 7 • 10 *Ignatius*
**μεγαλειότης, ἡ** 1 • 1 • 3 *impressiveness*
**πατρώνυμος** 1 • 1 • 1 *named after the father*
**προκάθημαι** [2] 2 • 4 • 4 *to preside (over), take the lead;* fig. *be preeminent*
**Ῥωμαῖος** 1 • 1 • 3 *Roman*
**ὕψιστος** 1 • 1 • 7 *the Most High*
**φωτίζω** 1 • 1 • 1 *to enlighten, give light to, shed light upon*
**χριστόνομος** 1 • 1 • 1 *keeping the law of Christ*
**χρῶμα, τό** 1 • 2 • 5 *color*
**χωρίον, τό** 1 • 1 • 5 *(a city and its) environs*

## Chapter 1

1 **ἀξιόθεος** 2 • 5 • 5 *worthy of God*
**ἀξιόω** 1 • 5 • 14 *to consider worthy, deserving*
**ἐάνπερ** 4 • 7 • 7 *if indeed, if only, supposing that*
**ἐπεί** 1 • 12 • 35 *because, since, for*
**ἐπιτυγχάνω** 9 • 20 • 23 *to obtain, attain to, reach*
**εὔχομαι** 2 • 13 • 16 *to pray*
2 **ἀδικέω** 1 • 2 • 7 *to injure*
**ἀνεμποδίστως/ἀνεμποδίστος** 1 • 1 • 1 *unhindered*
**ἀπολαμβάνω** 1 • 4 • 17 *to receive, obtain*
**δύσκολος** 1 • 2 • 5 *hard, difficult*
**ἐάνπερ** [2] 4 • 7 • 7 *if indeed, if only, supposing that*
**ἐπιτυγχάνω** [2] 9 • 20 • 23 *to obtain, attain to, reach*
**εὐοικονόμητος** 1 • 1 • 1 *well-ordered*
**εὐχερής** 1 • 1 • 2 *easy*
**κλῆρος, ὁ** 1 • 4 • 8 *lot, destiny*
**φείδομαι** 1 • 2 • 3 *to spare*

## Chapter 2

1 **ἀνθρωπαρεσκέω** 1 • 1 • 1 *to court/curry the favor of (people)*
**ἀρέσκω** [2] 2 • 4 • 12 *to please, accommodate*
**ἐπιγράφω** 1 • 1 • 4 *to record, be identified (with)*
**ἐπιτυγχάνω** 9 • 20 • 23 *to obtain, attain to, reach*
**ἐράω** 2 • 3 • 3 *to have a longing for, feel fervently about*

**κρείττων** 1 • 3 • 8 *more prominent, higher in rank, preferable, better*
**ποτέ** 1 • 1 • 15 *ever, at any time*
**σιωπάω** [2] 2 • 4 • 5 *to keep silent, say nothing, make no sound*
2 **ᾄδω** 1 • 4 • 6 *to sing (in praise)*
**ἀνατέλλω** 1 • 2 • 6 *to rise, spring up, dawn*
**ἀνατολή, ἡ** 1 • 1 • 6 *east, orient*
**δύνω** 1 • 1 • 1 *to go down, set*
**δύσις, ἡ** 1 • 1 • 3 *west*
**ἐπίσκοπος, ὁ** 1 • 57 • 76 *overseer, supervisor*
**ἕτοιμος** 1 • 3 • 9 *ready*
**θυσιαστήριον, τό** 1 • 6 • 15 *altar*
**καταξιόω** 1 • 9 • 14 *to consider worthy*
**μεταπέμπω** 1 • 1 • 1 *to send for, summon*
**παρέχω** 1 • 3 • 18 *to cause, make happen;*
mid. *grant*
**σπονδίζω** 1 • 1 • 1 *to offer a libation/drink offering*
**Συρία, ἡ** 4 • 16 • 17 *Syria*
**χορός, ὁ** 1 • 3 • 4 *chorus, choir*

## Chapter 3

1 **βασκαίνω** 1 • 1 • 1 *to envy, grudge*
**βέβαιος** 1 • 3 • 9 *in force, valid*
**ἐντέλλω** 2 • 2 • 29 *to command, order, give orders*
**μαθητεύω** 2 • 4 • 4 *to teach*
**οὐδέποτε** 1 • 1 • 6 *never*
2 **ἔξωθεν** 1 • 1 • 3 *outside, outward*
**ἔσωθεν** 2 • 2 • 2 *inside, within, inward*
**Χριστιανός, ὁ** 1 • 5 • 24 *Christ-follower, Christian*
3 **μέγεθος, τό** 1 • 3 • 5 *greatness*
**πεισμονή, ἡ** 1 • 1 • 1 *persuasion, persuasiveness*
**Χριστιανισμός, ὁ** 1 • 5 • 6 *the Christian Way, Christianity*

## Chapter 4

1 **ἄκαιρος** 1 • 1 • 1 *untimely, ill-timed*
**ἀλήθω** 1 • 1 • 1 *to grind*
**βορά, ἡ** 1 • 1 • 1 *food*
**ἐάνπερ** 4 • 7 • 7 *if indeed, if only, supposing that*
**ἑκών** 2 • 2 • 4 *willing(ly), glad(ly)*
**ἔνειμι** 1 • 1 • 2 *to be possible*
**ἐντέλλω** 2 • 2 • 29 *to command, order, give orders*
**ἐπιτυγχάνω** 9 • 20 • 23 *to obtain, attain to, reach*
**εὔνοια, ἡ** 1 • 2 • 3 *favor, affection, benevolence, kindness*
**καθαρός** 2 • 5 • 45 *clean, pure*
**κωλύω** 1 • 1 • 3 *to hinder, prevent, forbid, stand in the way*
**ὀδούς, ὁ** 1 • 1 • 1 *tooth*
**σῖτος, ὁ** 1 • 1 • 2 *wheat, grain*
2 **ἀληθῶς** 3 • 15 • 23 *truly, in truth, really, actually*
**βαρύς** 1 • 1 • 1 *burdensome, troublesome*
**θυσία, ἡ** 1 • 1 • 22 *sacrifice, offering*
**καταλείπω** 1 • 1 • 12 *to leave, leave over*
**κοιμάω** 1 • 1 • 12 *to sleep, fall asleep, die, pass away*
**κολακεύω** 3 • 4 • 4 *to entice, deal graciously with*
**λιτανεύω** 1 • 1 • 1 *to pray to, petition*
**μηθέν/μηδείς** 2 • 2 • 3 *nothing*
**ὄργανον, τό** 1 • 1 • 3 *tool*
**τάφος, ὁ** 1 • 2 • 4 *tomb*
3 **ἀπελεύθερος, ὁ** 1 • 1 • 1 *freedperson*
**διατάσσω** 1 • 3 • 8 *to order, command*
**ἐλεύθερος** [2] 2 • 2 • 3 *free*
**ἐπιθυμέω** 2 • 2 • 17 *to desire, long for*
**κατάκριτος** 1 • 3 • 3 *condemned*
**μανθάνω** 1 • 2 • 26 *to learn, appropriate to oneself*
**μέχρι** 2 • 5 • 23 *until*

## Chapter 5

1 **ἀδίκημα, τό** 1 • 1 • 1 *mistreatment*
**δέκα** 1 • 1 • 10 *ten*
**ἐνδέω** 1 • 1 • 5 *to bind to*
**εὐεργετέω** 1 • 1 • 3 *to do good to, benefit, treat well*

**θηριομαχέω** 1 • 3 • 4 *to struggle with, contend with, fight with*
**λεόπαρδος, ὁ** 1 • 1 • 1 *leopard*
**μαθητεύω** 2 • 4 • 4 *to be a pupil, become a disciple*
**μέχρι** 2 • 5 • 23 *as far as*
**Ῥώμη, ἡ** 2 • 4 • 8 *Rome*
**στρατιωτικός** 1 • 1 • 1 *belonging to/composed of soldiers*
**Συρία, ἡ** 4 • 16 • 17 *Syria*
**τάγμα, τό** 1 • 1 • 16 *division, group, detachment*
**χείρων** 1 • 1 • 4 *worse, more severe*
2 **δειλαίνω** 1 • 1 • 2 *to be cowardly, be fearful*
**ἑκών** 2 • 2 • 4 *willing(ly), glad(ly)*
**εὔχομαι** 2 • 13 • 16 *to wish*
**κἄν** 1 • 2 • 8 *even if, even though*
**κατεσθίω** 1 • 1 • 3 *to eat up, consume, devour, swallow*
**κολακεύω** 3 • 4 • 4 *to entice, deal graciously with*
**ὀνίνημι** 1 • 6 • 6 *to have benefit of, enjoy;*
**ὀναίμην** (voluntative optative) *May I enjoy/have the benefit of*
**προσβιάζομαι** 1 • 1 • 2 *to compel, use force*
**σύντομος** 1 • 1 • 1 *short, brief, close at hand, ready*
**συντόμως** 1 • 1 • 1 *promptly, readily*
3 **ἀλεσμός, ὁ** 1 • 1 • 1 *grinding*
**ἀνατομή, ἡ** 1 • 1 • 1 *cutting up, mutilation*
**ἀόρατος** 1 • 6 • 13 *unseen, invisible*
**διαίρεσις, ἡ** 1 • 1 • 1 *tearing apart*
**ἐπιτυγχάνω** 9 • 20 • 23 *to obtain, attain to, reach*
**ζηλόω** 1 • 1 • 2 *to strive, desire, exert oneself earnestly, be dedicated to, attract*
**κόλασις, ἡ** 1 • 1 • 11 *punishment*
**μηθέν/μηδείς** 2 • 2 • 3 *nothing*
**ὁρατός** 1 • 4 • 5 *visible*
**ὀστέον, τό** 1 • 1 • 6 *bone*
**σκορπισμός, ὁ** 1 • 1 • 1 *scattering*
**σταυρός, ὁ** 1 • 6 • 17 *cross*
**συγγνώμη, ἡ** 1 • 1 • 1 *concession, indulgence, pardon*
**συγκοπή, ἡ** 1 • 1 • 1 *cutting to pieces, mangling*
**συμφέρω** 1 • 2 • 3 *to help, confer a benefit, be profitable/useful*
**σύστασις, ἡ** 1 • 2 • 3 *gathering, union, association, pack (of wild beasts), encounter, struggle*

## Chapter 6

1 **βασιλεύω** 1 • 1 • 4 *to be king, rule*
**ἐπίκειμαι** 1 • 2 • 6 *to confront, be upon*
**πέρας, τό** [2] 2 • 3 • 13 *end, limit, boundary*
**τοκετός, ὁ** 1 • 2 • 2 *childbearing, giving birth*
**ὠφελέω** 1 • 2 • 8 *to help, aid, benefit, be of use (to)*
2 **ἐμποδίζω** 1 • 1 • 2 *to hinder*
**καθαρός** 2 • 5 • 45 *clean, pure*
**κολακεύω** 3 • 4 • 4 *to entice, deal graciously with*
**συγγινώσκω** 1 • 1 • 1 *to have the same opinion/purpose/wish, agree, understand*
**ὕλη, ἡ** 1 • 1 • 4 *material, matter, stuff*
**χαρίζομαι** 1 • 2 • 5 *to give graciously*
3 **ἐπιτρέπω** 1 • 3 • 11 *to allow, permit*
**μιμητής, ὁ** 1 • 5 • 12 *imitator*
**νοέω** 1 • 3 • 46 *to perceive, apprehend, understand, gain insight into*
**πάθος, τό** 1 • 15 • 18 *suffering*
**συμπαθέω** 1 • 1 • 1 *to sympathize with*
**συνέχω** 1 • 1 • 4 *to seize, attack, distress, torment*

## Chapter 7

1 **βοηθέω** 1 • 1 • 4 *to furnish aid*
**γνώμη, ἡ** 2 • 16 • 20 *purpose, intention, mind, mind-set*
**διαρπάζω** 1 • 1 • 2 *to plunder thoroughly*
**διαφθείρω** 1 • 3 • 12 *to deprave, ruin*
**ἐπιθυμέω** 2 • 2 • 17 *to desire, long for*
**πάρειμι** 2 • 5 • 17 *to be present*

**τουτέστιν** 1 • 2 • 5 *this or that means, that is to say*
2 **βασκανία, ἡ** 1 • 1 • 1 *envy*
**δεῦρο** 1 • 1 • 1 *Come here, Come!*
**ἐράω** 2 • 3 • 3 *to have a longing for, feel fervently about*
**ἔρως, ὁ** 1 • 1 • 1 *ardor, fondness*
**ἔσωθεν** 2 • 2 • 2 *inside, within*
**πάρειμι** 2 • 5 • 17 *to be present*
**φιλόϋλος** 1 • 1 • 1 *loving material things*
3 **ἄφθαρτος** 1 • 2 • 7 *imperishable, incorruptible, immortal*
**βίος, ὁ** 1 • 3 • 13 *life*
**ἥδομαι** 1 • 1 • 2 *to be pleased with, delight in*
**ἡδονή, ἡ** 1 • 3 • 12 *pleasure, delight, enjoyment, pleasantness*
**πόμα, τό** 1 • 1 • 1 *a drink*
**τροφή, ἡ** 1 • 2 • 12 *nourishment, food*
**φθορά, ἡ** 1 • 1 • 4 *dissolution, deterioration, corruption*

## Chapter 8

2 **ἀληθῶς** [2] 3 • 15 • 23 *truly, in truth, really, actually*
**ἀψευδής** 1 • 1 • 2 *truthful, trustworthy*
**γράμμα, τό** 1 • 2 • 8 *letter (of the alphabet)*
3 **ἀποδοκιμάζω** 1 • 1 • 5 *to reject*
**γνώμη, ἡ** 2 • 16 • 20 *purpose, intention, mind, mind-set*
**ἐπιτυγχάνω** 9 • 20 • 23 *to obtain, attain to, reach*

## Chapter 9

1 **ἀντί** 1 • 1 • 15 *instead of, in the place of;*
**ἥτις ἀντὶ ἐμοῦ ποιμένι τῷ θεῷ χρῆται** *which resorts to/has God as its shepherd in my place*
**ἐπισκοπέω** 1 • 2 • 3 *to oversee, care for*
**μνημονεύω** 1 • 6 • 25 *to remember, keep in mind, think of, mention*
**ποιμήν, ὁ** 1 • 2 • 54 *shepherd*
**Συρία, ἡ** 4 • 16 • 17 *Syria*
**χράομαι** 1 • 4 • 18 *to make use of, employ; resort to*
2 **αἰσχύνω** 1 • 2 • 3 *to be ashamed*
**ἔκτρωμα, τό** 1 • 1 • 1 *untimely birth*
**ἐλεέω** 2 • 6 • 16 *to have compassion/mercy/pity*
**ἐπιτυγχάνω** 9 • 20 • 23 *to obtain, attain to, reach*
3 **παροδεύω** 1 • 2 • 2 *to pass, pass by*
**προάγω** 1 • 1 • 3 *to go before, lead the way, precede;*
**μοι τῇ ὁδῷ τῇ κατὰ σάρκα κατὰ πόλιν με προῆγον** *they were going before me on the physical route that was mine, from town to town*
**προσήκω** 1 • 1 • 3 *to come to, approach*

## Chapter 10

1 **ἅμα** 1 • 9 • 12 *together*
**ἀξιομακάριστος** 2 • 4 • 4 *most worthy of blessing*
**Ἐφέσιος** 1 • 7 • 7 *Ephesian*
**Κρόκος, ὁ** 1 • 2 • 2 *Crocus*
**ποθητός** 1 • 3 • 3 *longed-for, dearly beloved*
**Σμύρνα, ἡ** 1 • 6 • 14 *Smyrna*
2 **ἀναπαύω** 1 • 7 • 13 *to cause to rest, give (someone) rest, refresh, revive*
**δηλόω** 1 • 4 • 49 *to reveal, make clear, show, notify*
**πρέπω** 1 • 13 • 15 *to be fitting, be seemly/suitable*
**προέρχομαι** 1 • 3 • 5 *to come/go before, go on before or ahead*
**Ῥώμη, ἡ** 2 • 4 • 8 *Rome*
**Συρία, ἡ** 4 • 16 • 17 *Syria*
3 **ἐννέα** 1 • 1 • 1 *nine*
**καλάνδαι, αἱ** 1 • 1 • 2 *the calends, the first day of the month*
**ῥώννυμι** 1 • 9 • 10 *to strengthen;*
**ἔρρωσθε** (perfect pass. imperative; cf. BDF §346; *ExSyn* 493) *farewell, goodbye*
**Σεπτέμβριος, ὁ** 1 • 1 • 1 *September*

# Ignatius to the Philadelphians

## Preface

**ἀγαλλιάω** 1 • 3 • 11 *to exult, rejoice, be glad, be overjoyed*
**ἀδιακρίτως** 1 • 2 • 2 *without wavering*
**ἀποδείκνυμι** 1 • 1 • 3 *to make, render, proclaim, appoint*
**Ἀσία, ἡ** 1 • 4 • 10 *Asia*
**βεβαιωσύνη, ἡ** 1 • 1 • 1 *confirming, establishing, unwavering, set firmly*
**γνώμη, ἡ** 4 • 16 • 20 *purpose, intention, mind, mind-set*
**διάκονος, ὁ** 6 • 18 • 29 *assistant*
**ἑδράζω** 1 • 4 • 6 *to establish, fix, settle*
**ἐλεέω** 2 • 6 • 16 *to have compassion/mercy/pity*
**ἔλεος, τό** 1 • 3 • 19 *mercy, compassion, pity, clemency*
**ἐπίσκοπος, ὁ** 8 • 57 • 76 *overseer, supervisor*
**Θεοφόρος, ὁ** 1 • 7 • 7 *Theophorus*
**Ἰγνάτιος, ὁ** 1 • 7 • 10 *Ignatius*
**μάλιστα** 1 • 3 • 14 *most of all, above all, especially, particularly*
**ὁμόνοια, ἡ** 2 • 8 • 24 *oneness of mind, unanimity, concord, harmony*
**πάθος, τό** 3 • 15 • 18 *suffering*
**παράμονος** 1 • 2 • 4 *lasting, constant, enduring*
**πληροφορέω** 1 • 4 • 9 *to convince fully*
**στηρίζω** 1 • 2 • 8 *to confirm, establish, strengthen*
**Φιλαδελφία, ἡ** 1 • 1 • 4 *Philadelphia*

## Chapter 1

1 **ἀνήκω** 1 • 3 • 10 *to refer, relate, belong*
**ἐπιείκεια, ἡ** 2 • 3 • 9 *clemency, gentleness, graciousness, courtesy, indulgence, tolerance*
**ἐπίσκοπος, ὁ** 8 • 57 • 76 *overseer, supervisor*
**καταπλήσσω** 1 • 2 • 3 *to amaze, astound;*
**οὗ καταπέπληγμαι τὴν ἐπιείκειαν** *whose forbearance I am impressed with*
**κενοδοξία, ἡ** 1 • 2 • 5 *vanity, conceit, excessive ambition*
**κοινός** 3 • 9 • 15 *communal, common*
**κτάομαι** 2 • 9 • 10 *to possess*
**μάταιος** 2 • 9 • 10 *idle, empty, fruitless, useless, powerless, lacking truth*
**σιγάω** 1 • 4 • 6 *to say nothing, keep still, keep silent*
2 **ἀκίνητος** 1 • 3 • 4 *unwavering, steadfast;*
subst. *steadfast character*
**ἀόργητος** 1 • 1 • 3 *free from anger, free from passion;*
subst. *freedom from anger/passion*
**γνώμη, ἡ** 4 • 16 • 20 *purpose, intention, mind, mind-set*
**ἐνάρετος** 1 • 1 • 2 *first-rate, high-class, exceptional, virtuous*
**ἐπιείκεια, ἡ** 2 • 3 • 9 *clemency, gentleness, graciousness, courtesy, indulgence, tolerance*
**κιθάρα, ἡ** 1 • 2 • 2 *lyre, harp*
**μακαρίζω** 1 • 2 • 5 *to call/consider blessed, happy, fortunate*
**συνευρυθμίζω** 1 • 1 • 1 *to bring into harmony/accord with*
**τέλειος** 1 • 3 • 25 *perfect*
**χορδή, ἡ** 1 • 2 • 2 *string*

## Chapter 2

1 **κακοδιδασκαλία, ἡ** 1 • 1 • 1 *evil/false teaching*
**μερισμός, ἡ** 5 • 6 • 6 *division, separation*
**ποιμήν, ὁ** 1 • 2 • 54 *shepherd*

**φεύγω** 3 • 6 • 20 *to flee from, avoid, shun*
2 **αἰχμαλωτίζω** 1 • 2 • 2 *to mislead, deceive*
**ἀξιόπιστος** 1 • 2 • 4 *betraying confidence, pretentious, specious*
**ἑνότης, ἡ** 5 • 11 • 11 *unity*
**ἡδονή, ἡ** 1 • 3 • 12 *pleasure, delight, enjoyment, pleasantness*
**θεοδρόμος, ὁ** 1 • 2 • 2 *God's runner*
**λύκος, ὁ** 1 • 1 • 5 *wolf*

## Chapter 3

1 **ἀπέχω** 1 • 4 • 35 *to keep away, abstain, refrain from*
**ἀποδιϋλισμός, ὁ** 1 • 1 • 1 *filtering;* fig. *purification*
**βοτάνη, ἡ** 1 • 3 • 30 *plant*
**γεωργέω** 1 • 1 • 1 *to cultivate*
**μερισμός, ὁ** 5 • 6 • 6 *division, separation*
**φυτεία, ἡ** 1 • 2 • 2 *a plant*
2 **ἑνότης, ἡ** 5 • 11 • 11 *unity*
**ἐπίσκοπος, ὁ** 8 • 57 • 76 *overseer, supervisor*
3 **ἀλλότριος** 1 • 3 • 14 *alien, unsuitable, strange*
**γνώμη, ἡ** 4 • 16 • 20 *opinion, judgment, way of thinking*
**γνῶσις, ἡ** 4 • 16 • 20 *knowledge*
**κληρονομέω** 1 • 3 • 11 *to acquire, obtain, come into possession of*
**πάθος, τό** 3 • 15 • 18 *suffering*
**συγκατατίθημι** 1 • 1 • 1 *to agree with, consent to*
**σχίζω** 1 • 1 • 1 *to cause a division/schism*

## Chapter 4

1 **ἅμα** 3 • 9 • 12 *together*
**διάκονος, ὁ** 6 • 18 • 29 *assistant*
**ἕνωσις, ἡ** 3 • 8 • 8 *union, unity*
**ἐπίσκοπος, ὁ** 8 • 57 • 76 *overseer, supervisor*
**εὐχαριστία, ἡ** 1 • 5 • 7 *Lord's Supper, Eucharist*
**θυσιαστήριον, τό** 1 • 6 • 15 *sanctuary*
**πρεσβυτέριον, τό** 3 • 13 • 13 *council of elders*
**σπουδάζω** 1 • 8 • 14 *to be zealous/ eager, take pains, make every effort, be conscientious*
**σύνδουλος, ὁ** 1 • 4 • 6 *slave*
**χράομαι** 1 • 4 • 18 *to make use of, employ*
**κατὰ θεόν** *according to (the will of) God*

## Chapter 5

1 **ἀναπάρτιστος** 1 • 1 • 1 *imperfect, not perfected*
**ἀπαρτίζω** 1 • 5 • 7 *to finish, complete, make complete*
**ἀσφαλίζω** 1 • 1 • 1 *to safeguard, watch over*
**ἐκχέω/ἐκχύννω** 1 • 1 • 6 *to give oneself up to, dedicate oneself*
**ἐλεέω** 2 • 6 • 16 *to have compassion/mercy/pity*
**ἐπιτυγχάνω** 1 • 20 • 23 *to obtain, attain to, reach*
**κλῆρος, ὁ** 1 • 4 • 8 *lot, portion*
**λίαν** 1 • 2 • 48 *very (much), exceedingly*
**πρεσβυτέριον, τό** 3 • 13 • 13 *council of elders*
**προσφεύγω** 1 • 1 • 2 *to flee for refuge to*
**ὑπεραγάλλομαι** 1 • 1 • 1 *to rejoice/exult greatly; rejoice with the greatest joy*
2 **ἀναμένω** 1 • 2 • 3 *to wait for, expect*
**ἀξιαγάπητος** 1 • 1 • 3 *worthy of love*
**ἀξιοθαύμαστος** 1 • 1 • 1 *worthy of admiration*
**ἑνότης, ἡ** 5 • 11 • 11 *unity*
**καταγγέλλω** 2 • 2 • 3 *to proclaim, announce;*
**αὐτοὺς εἰς τὸ εὐαγγέλιον κατηγγελκέναι** *they directed their proclamation toward the gospel*
**κοινός** 3 • 9 • 15 *communal, common*
**συναριθμέω** 1 • 1 • 1 *to count/ number together*

## Chapter 6

1 **ἀκρόβυστος, ὁ** 1 • 1 • 1 *an uncircumcised person*
**ἀμείνων** 1 • 5 • 6 *better*
**ἀμφότεροι** 1 • 1 • 21 *both*
**ἑρμηνεύω** 1 • 1 • 1 *to explain, interpret, propound*
**Ἰουδαϊσμός, ὁ** [2] 2 • 5 • 5 *Judeanism/Judaism*
**στήλη, ἡ** 1 • 1 • 2 *monument, pillar;*
**στῆλαι τάφοι νεκρῶν** *tombstones*
**τάφος, ὁ** 1 • 2 • 4 *grave, tomb*
**Χριστιανισμός, ὁ** 1 • 5 • 6 *the Christian way, Christianity*
2 **ἀμέριστος** 1 • 2 • 2 *undivided*
**γνώμη, ἡ** 4 • 16 • 20 *purpose, intention, mind, mind-set, design*
**ἐνέδρα, ἡ** 1 • 2 • 2 *ambush*
**ἐξασθενέω** 1 • 1 • 1 *to become quite weak*
**θλίβω** 1 • 2 • 25 *to oppress, afflict*
**κακοτεχνία, ἡ** 1 • 2 • 2 *craftiness, deceit*
**μήποτε** 1 • 2 • 22 *that … not, lest*
**φεύγω** 3 • 6 • 20 *to flee from, avoid, shun*
3 **βαρέω** 1 • 1 • 1 *to weigh down, burden*
**εὐσυνείδητος** 1 • 2 • 2 *with a good conscience*
**εὔχομαι** 1 • 13 • 16 *to wish*
**κτάομαι** 2 • 9 • 10 *to bring upon oneself*
**λάθρα** 1 • 2 • 2 *secretly*
**μαρτύριον, τό** 1 • 2 • 16 *testimony, proof*
**φανερῶς** 1 • 1 • 2 *openly, publicly*

## Chapter 7

1 **διάκονος, ὁ** 6 • 18 • 29 *assistant*
**ἐλέγχω** 1 • 2 • 16 *to bring to light, expose, set forth*
**ἐπίσκοπος, ὁ** 8 • 57 • 76 *overseer, supervisor*
**κραυγάζω** 1 • 1 • 2 *to cry (out)*
**κρυπτός** 2 • 3 • 4 *(something) hidden;*
subst. *secret thing*
**μεταξύ** 1 • 3 • 10 *between, in the middle, next, among*
**πόθεν** 1 • 2 • 6 *from what place? from where?*
**πρεσβυτέριον, τό** 3 • 13 • 13 *council of elders*
**προσέχω** 1 • 4 • 25 *to pay attention to, give heed to, follow*
2 **ἀνθρώπινος** 1 • 2 • 7 *human*
**ἕνωσις, ἡ** 3 • 8 • 8 *union, unity*
**ἐπίσκοπος, ὁ** 8 • 57 • 76 *overseer, supervisor*
**μερισμός, ὁ** 5 • 6 • 6 *division, separation*
**μιμητής, ὁ** 1 • 5 • 12 *imitator*
**ὅδε** 1 • 1 • 7 *this*
**πρόοιδα** 1 • 1 • 2 *to know beforehand/previously*
**ὑποπτεύω** 1 • 1 • 1 *to suspect*
**φεύγω** 3 • 6 • 20 *to flee from, shun, avoid*

## Chapter 8

1 **δεσμός, ὁ** 1 • 8 • 14 *bond, fetter*
**ἑνότης, ἡ** 5 • 11 • 11 *unity*
**ἕνωσις, ἡ** 3 • 8 • 8 *union, unity*
**ἐπίσκοπος, ὁ** 8 • 57 • 76 *overseer, supervisor*
**καταρτίζω** 1 • 3 • 6 *to prepare, make, create, outfit, set;*
**ἄνθρωπος εἰς ἕνωσιν κατηρτισμένος** *a man set on* (lit. *prepared for*) *unity*
**μερισμός, ὁ** 5 • 6 • 6 *division, separation*
**συνέδριον, τό** 1 • 3 • 3 *council*
2 **ἄθικτος** 1 • 1 • 1 *inviolable, sacred, unalterable*
**ἀρχεῖον, τό** [3] 3 • 3 • 3 *official record, original document*
**ἐπεί** 1 • 12 • 35 *because, since, for*
**ἐρίθεια, ἡ** 1 • 1 • 1 *strife, contentiousness, selfishness, selfish ambition*
**πρόκειμαι** 1 • 3 • 4 *to lie before, be present; be at issue*
**σταυρός, ὁ** 1 • 6 • 17 *the cross*
**χριστομαθία, ἡ** 1 • 1 • 1 *discipleship with Christ, teaching of Christ*

## Chapter 9

1 **ἑνότης, ἡ** 5 • 11 • 11 *unity*
**Ἰακώβ, ὁ** 1 • 1 • 13 *Jacob*
**Ἰσαάκ, ὁ** 1 • 1 • 7 *Isaac*
**κρείττων** 1 • 3 • 8 *more prominent, higher in rank, preferable, better*;
**κρεῖσσον δὲ ὁ ἀρχιερεύς**: the neuter adj. focuses on the office of the high priest rather than his person
**κρυπτός** 2 • 3 • 4 *(something) hidden*;
subst. *something hidden, secret thought, plan, purpose*
2 **ἀπάρτισμα, τό** 1 • 1 • 1 *completion, consummation*
**ἀφθαρσία, ἡ** 1 • 4 • 12 *incorruptibility, immortality, imperishability*
**ἐξαίρετος** 1 • 1 • 2 *chosen, excellent, remarkable*
**καταγγέλλω** 2 • 3 • 3 *to proclaim, announce*
**ὁμοῦ** 1 • 2 • 5 *together at the same time (as), in company (with)*
**πάθος, τό** 3 • 15 • 18 *suffering*
**παρουσία, ἡ** 1 • 1 • 4 *coming, advent*
**σωτήρ, ὁ** 1 • 4 • 14 *savior, deliverer, preserver*

## Chapter 10

1 **Ἀντιόχεια, ἡ** 1 • 3 • 3 *Antioch*
**διάκονος, ὁ** 6 • 18 • 29 *assistant*
**εἰρηνεύω** 1 • 4 • 17 *to live in peace, be at peace*
**ἐπειδή** 1 • 2 • 17 *(just) because*
**πρέπω** 1 • 13 • 15 *to be fitting, be seemly/suitable*
**πρεσβεία, ἡ** 1 • 1 • 1 *ambassador, ambassadors*;
**εἰς τὸ πρεσβεῦσαι θεοῦ πρεσβείαν** *travel as an ambassador of God*
**πρεσβεύω** 1 • 2 • 2 *to be an ambassador/envoy, travel/work as an ambassador*
**σπλάγχνον, τό** 1 • 1 • 5 pl. *love, affection*
**συγχαίρω** 1 • 4 • 7 *to congratulate*
**Συρία, ἡ** 2 • 16 • 17 *Syria*
**χειροτονέω** 1 • 3 • 4 *to choose*
2 **ἀδύνατος** 1 • 1 • 11 *impossible*
**διάκονος, ὁ** 6 • 18 • 29 *assistant*
**ἐπίσκοπος, ὁ** 8 • 57 • 76 *overseer, supervisor*
**καταξιόω** 1 • 9 • 14 *to consider worthy*

## Chapter 11

1 **Ἀγαθόπους, ὁ** 1 • 2 • 2 *Agathopus*
**ἅμα** 3 • 9 • 12 *together*
**ἀποτάσσω** 1 • 1 • 5 *to say farewell (to), take leave (of)*
**ἀτιμάζω** 1 • 1 • 3 *to dishonor/shame*
**βίος, ὁ** 1 • 3 • 13 *life*
**διάκονος, ὁ** 6 • 18 • 29 *assistant*
**ἐκλεκτός** 1 • 2 • 30 *choice, excellent*
**Κιλικία, ἡ** 1 • 1 • 1 *Cilicia*
**λυτρόω** 1 • 1 • 11 *to set free, rescue, redeem*;
**λυτρωθείησαν** (voluntative optative) *May they be redeemed*
**Ῥαῖος, ὁ** 1 • 2 • 2 *Raius*
**Συρία, ἡ** 2 • 16 • 17 *Syria*
**ὑπηρετέω** 1 • 1 • 5 *to serve, be helpful*
**Φίλων, ὁ** 1 • 3 • 4 *Philo*
2 **ἅμα** 3 • 9 • 12 *together*
**Βοῦρρος, ὁ** 1 • 4 • 4 *Burrus*
**Ἐφέσιος** 1 • 7 • 7 *Ephesian*
**κοινός** 3 • 9 • 15 *communal, common*
**ὅθεν** 1 • 10 • 16 *from where, whence, from which*
**ὁμόνοια, ἡ** 2 • 8 • 24 *oneness of mind, unanimity, concord, harmony*
**ῥώννυμι** 1 • 9 • 10 *to strengthen*;
**ἔρρωσθε** (perfect pass. imperative; cf. BDF §346; *ExSyn* 493) *farewell, goodbye*
**Σμυρναῖος** 1 • 4 • 4 *coming from Smyrna*
**τιμάω** 1 • 3 • 12 *to honor, revere*
**Τρῳάς, ἡ** 1 • 3 • 3 *Troas, (the) Troad*

# Ignatius to the Smyrnaeans

### Preface

**ἁγιοφόρος** 1 • 2 • 2 *bearing holy things*
**ἄμωμος** 1 • 7 • 17 *blameless*
**ἀνυστέρητος** 1 • 1 • 2 *not lacking in anything*
**Ἀσία, ἡ** 1 • 4 • 10 *Asia*
**ἐλεέω** 1 • 6 • 16 *to have compassion/mercy/pity on*; pass. *to receive as a gracious gift, be favored with*
**θεοπρεπής** 3 • 5 • 6 *worthy of God, revered, venerable, godly*
**Θεοφόρος, ὁ** 1 • 7 • 7 *Theophoros*
**Ἰγνάτιος, ὁ** 1 • 7 • 10 *Ignatius*
**Σμύρνα, ἡ** 1 • 6 • 14 *Smyrna*
**χάρισμα, τό** [2] 2 • 4 • 6 *favor bestowed, gift*

### Chapter 1

1 **ἀκίνητος** 1 • 3 • 4 *unwavering, steadfast*
**ἀληθῶς** [2] 5 • 15 • 23 *truly, in truth, really, actually*
**γένος, τό** 1 • 3 • 16 *descendant*
**ἑδράζω** 2 • 4 • 6 *to establish, fix, settle*
**καθηλόω** 2 • 2 • 4 *to nail on*
**καταρτίζω** 1 • 3 • 6 *to put into proper condition, adjust, complete, make complete*
**νοέω** 1 • 3 • 46 *to observe, perceive, apprehend, understand, gain an insight into*
**παρθένος, ἡ** 2 • 2 • 62 *virgin*
**πληροφορέω** 1 • 4 • 9 *to have perfect faith*
**σοφίζω** 1 • 1 • 3 *to make wise, teach, instruct*
**σταυρός, ὁ** 1 • 6 • 17 *the cross*
2 **ἀληθῶς** 5 • 15 • 23 *truly, in truth, really, actually*
**θεομακάριστος** 1 • 2 • 2 *blessed by God*
**καθηλόω** 2 • 2 • 4 *to nail on*
**πάθος, τό** 4 • 15 • 18 *suffering*
**Πιλᾶτος, ὁ** 1 • 3 • 3 *Pilate*
**Πόντιος, ὁ** 1 • 3 • 3 *Pontius*
**σύσσημον, τό** 1 • 1 • 1 *sign, token, banner, standard*
**τετραάρχης/τετράρχης, ὁ** 1 • 1 • 1 *tetrarch*

### Chapter 2

1 **ἀληθῶς** [2] 5 • 15 • 23 *truly, in truth, really, actually*
**ἄπιστος** 2 • 4 • 8 *without faith, disbelieving, unbelieving*
**ἀσώματος** 2 • 2 • 2 *bodiless, disembodied*
**δαιμονικός** 1 • 1 • 1 *like spirits/phantoms, ghost-like*
**συμβαίνω** 1 • 1 • 7 *to happen, come about*
**φρονέω** 3 • 4 • 17 *to think, form/hold an opinion, judge*

### Chapter 3

2 **ἀσώματος** 2 • 2 • 2 *bodiless, disembodied*
**καταφρονέω** 1 • 1 • 9 *to disregard, be unafraid of, despise*
**κεράννυμι** 1 • 1 • 1 *to closely unite*; lit. *to make a mixture*
**ψηλαφάω** 1 • 1 • 3 *to touch, handle*
3 **ἑνόω** 1 • 6 • 6 *to unite*
**καίπερ** 1 • 1 • 7 *although*
**πνευματικῶς** 1 • 2 • 4 *spiritually*
**σαρκικός** 3 • 9 • 10 *material, physical, human, fleshly*
**συμπίνω** 1 • 1 • 1 *to drink with*
**συνεσθίω** 1 • 1 • 1 *to eat with*

## Chapter 4

1 ἀληθινός 1 • 5 • 14 *genuine, authentic, real*
ἀνθρωπόμορφος 1 • 1 • 1 *in human form*
δύσκολος 1 • 2 • 5 *hard, difficult*
ὅσπερ 1 • 5 • 10 *which indeed*
παραδέχομαι 1 • 2 • 9 *to receive, accept*
παραινέω 1 • 2 • 2 *to recommend, urge*
προφυλάσσω 1 • 3 • 3 *to guard, protect*
πώς 2 • 4 • 76 *somehow, in some way, perhaps*
συναντάω 1 • 1 • 1 *to meet*
2 ἔκδοτος 1 • 1 • 1 *given up, delivered up*
ἐνδυναμόω 1 • 1 • 14 *to strengthen*
μάχαιρα, ἡ [2] 2 • 2 • 3 *sword*
μεταξύ [2] 2 • 3 • 10 *among*
συμπάσχω 1 • 2 • 4 *to suffer with*
τέλειος 6 • 9 • 25 *perfect, complete*
ὑπομένω 2 • 7 • 32 *to stand one's ground, hold out, endure*

## Chapter 5

1 ἀγνοέω 1 • 3 • 11 *to not to know, be ignorant*
ἡμέτερος 1 • 1 • 13 *our*
μέχρι 2 • 5 • 23 *until*
πάθημα, τό 1 • 1 • 2 *suffering*
προφητεία, ἡ 1 • 1 • 4 *prophecy*
συνήγορος, ὁ 1 • 1 • 1 *advocate, attorney*
2 ἀπαρνέομαι 1 • 1 • 6 *to deny*
ἐπαινέω 1 • 2 • 6 *to praise*
νεκροφόρος 1 • 1 • 1 *bearing a corpse, clothed in a corpse*
ὁμολογέω 2 • 3 • 18 *to acknowledge, claim, profess, praise*
σαρκοφόρος 1 • 1 • 1 *flesh-bearing, clothed in flesh*
τελείως 1 • 3 • 8 *fully, perfectly, completely, altogether*
φρονέω 3 • 4 • 17 *to think, form/hold an opinion, judge*
ὠφελέω 1 • 2 • 8 *to benefit, help, aid, be of use (to)*
3 ἄπιστος 2 • 4 • 8 *without faith, disbelieving, unbelieving*
ἐγγράφω 1 • 1 • 5 *to write in, record*
μέχρι 2 • 5 • 23 *until*
μνημονεύω 1 • 6 • 25 *to remember, keep in mind, think of*
πάθος, τό 4 • 15 • 18 *suffering*

## Chapter 6

1 ἀόρατος 1 • 6 • 13 *unseen, invisible*
ἐπουράνιος 1 • 5 • 11 *heavenly, in heaven*
ὁρατός 1 • 4 • 5 *visible*
προκρίνω 1 • 2 • 2 *to prefer*
φυσιόω 1 • 5 • 6 *to puff up, make proud*
χωρέω [2] 2 • 6 • 15 *to grasp, accept, comprehend, understand*
2 ἀπέχω 2 • 4 • 35 *to keep away, abstain, refrain from*
γνώμη, ἡ 1• 16 • 20 *purpose, intention, mind, mind-set*
διψάω 1 • 1 • 2 *to be thirsty*
ἐναντίος 1 • 1 • 4 *opposed, contrary*
ἑτεροδοξέω 1 • 1 • 1 *to hold different,* i.e., *divisive* or *sectarian, opinions*
εὐχαριστία, ἡ [2] 3 • 5 • 7 *Lord's Supper, Eucharist*
θλίβω 1 • 2 • 25 *to oppress, afflict*
καταμανθάνω 1 • 2 • 4 *to observe (well), notice, learn*
μέλει 1 • 1 • 5 *it is a concern/care, it is of interest to someone*
ὁμολογέω 2 • 3 • 18 *to acknowledge, claim, profess, praise*
ὀρφανός 1 • 1 • 9 *without parents, orphan*
πεινάω 1 • 1 • 6 *to hunger, be hungry*
σωτήρ, ὁ 1 • 4 • 14 *savior, deliverer, preserver*
χήρα, ἡ 2 • 3 • 13 *widow*
χρηστότης, ἡ 1 • 2 • 9 *goodness, kindness, generosity*

## Chapter 7

1 **ἀντιλέγω** 1 • 1 • 3 *to refuse, oppose*
**δωρεά, ἡ** 1 • 1 • 7 *gift*
**συζητέω** 1 • 1 • 2 *to dispute, debate, argue*
**συμφέρω** 1 • 2 • 3 *to help, confer a benefit, be profitable/useful*; with the *dativus commodi* αὐτοῖς, the impersonal verb virtually has the force of a comparison: *it is better* for them
2 **ἀπέχω** 2 • 4 • 35 *to keep away, abstain, refrain from*
**δηλόω** 1 • 4 • 49 *to reveal, make clear, show*
**ἐξαιρέτως** 1 • 2 • 3 *especially*
**κοινός** 2 • 9 • 15 adv. dative: *together, collectively; in common*
**πάθος, τό** 4 • 15 • 18 *suffering*
**πρέπω** 2 • 13 • 15 *to be fitting, be seemly/suitable*
**προσέχω** 1 • 4 • 25 *to pay attention to, give heed to, follow*
**τελειόω** 1 • 1 • 14 *to fulfill*

## Chapter 8

1 **ἀνήκω** 1 • 3 • 10 *to refer, relate, concern*
**βέβαιος** 2 • 3 • 9 *in force, valid*
**διάκονος, ὁ** 3 • 18 • 29 *assistant;* **τοὺς διακόνους ἐντρέπεσθε ὡς θεοῦ ἐντολήν** *respect the deacons as the voice of God* ('voice' for ἐντολή here is suggested by Lightfoot)
**ἐντρέπω** 1 • 5 • 9 *to turn toward something/someone, have regard for, respect*
**ἐπίσκοπος, ὁ** 9 • 57 • 76 *overseer, supervisor*
**ἐπιτρέπω** 1 • 3 • 11 *to allow, permit, appoint*
**εὐχαριστία, ἡ** 3 • 5 • 7 *Lord's Supper, Eucharist*
**ἡγέομαι** 1 • 1 • 25 *to think, consider, regard*
**μερισμός, ὁ** 1 • 6 • 6 *division, separation*; referring to the dissidents who had separated themselves
**πρεσβυτέριον, τό** 2 • 13 • 13 *council of elders*
**φεύγω** 1 • 6 • 20 *to flee from, avoid, shun*
2 **ἀσφαλής** 1 • 1 • 4 *safe, secure*
**βέβαιος** 2 • 3 • 9 *abiding*
**δοκιμάζω** 1 • 2 • 24 *to accept as proved, approve*
**ἐπίσκοπος, ὁ** 9 • 57 • 76 *overseer, supervisor*
**εὐάρεστος** 1 • 1 • 10 *pleasing, acceptable*
**καθολικός** 1 • 1 • 6 *general, universal*
**πλῆθος, τό** 1 • 4 • 19 *fellowship, community, congregation*

## Chapter 9

1 **ἀνανήφω** 1 • 1 • 1 *to come to one's senses again, become sober again*
**εὔλογος** 1 • 2 • 2 *reasonable, right*
**λάθρα** 1 • 2 • 2 *without the knowledge of, behind the back of*
**λατρεύω** 1 • 1 • 3 *to serve*
**τιμάω** [2] 2 • 3 • 12 *to honor, revere*
2 **ἀμοιβή, ἡ** 1 • 1 • 1 *a return, recompense*
**ἀναπαύω** 3 • 7 • 13 *to cause to rest, give (someone) rest, refresh, revive*
**ἄπειμι** 1 • 1 • 7 *to be absent/away*
**πάρειμι** 1 • 5 • 17 *to be present*
**τυγχάνω** 2 • 5 • 15 *to meet, attain, gain, find, experience*
**ὑπομένω** 2 • 7 • 32 *to stand one's ground, hold out, endure*

## Chapter 10

1 **Ἀγαθόπους, ὁ** 1 • 2 • 2 *Agathopus*
**ἀναπαύω** 3 • 7 • 13 *to cause to rest, give (someone) rest, refresh, revive*
**διάκονος, ὁ** 3 • 18 • 29 *assistant*
**ἐπακολουθέω** 1 • 1 • 4 *to follow*
**Ῥαῖος, ὁ** 1 • 2 • 2 *Raius*
**τρόπος, ὁ** 1 • 4 • 17 *manner, way, kind, guise*

**ὑποδέχομαι** 1 • 1 • 3 *to receive, welcome, entertain as a guest*
**Φίλων, ὁ** 2 • 3 • 4 *Philo*
2 **ἀντίψυχον, τό** 1 • 4 • 4 *ransom*
**δεσμός, ὁ** 2 • 8 • 14 *bond, fetter;* fig. *imprisonment, prison*
**ἐπαισχύνομαι** 2 • 2 • 5 *to be ashamed*
**τέλειος** 6 • 9 • 25 *perfect*
**ὑπερηφανέω** 1 • 3 • 3 *to treat arrogantly/disdainfully, despise*

## Chapter 11

1 **Ἀντιόχεια, ἡ** 1 • 3 • 3 *Antioch*
**δεσμός, ὁ** 2 • 8 • 14 *bond, fetter;* fig. *imprisonment, prison*
**ἐπιτυγχάνω** 1 • 20 • 23 *to obtain, attain to, reach*
**εὔχομαι** 3 • 17 • 41 *to wish, pray*
**θεοπρεπής** 3 • 5 • 6 *worthy of God, revered, venerable, godly*
**καταξιόω** 1 • 9 • 14 *to consider worthy*
**ὅθεν** 2 • 12 • 23 *from where, whence, from which*
**σύνοιδα** 1 • 1 • 2 *to know, be conscious of;*
**ἐκ συνειδότος** *because of the witness of my own conscience*
**Συρία, ἡ** 2 • 16 • 17 *Syria*
**τέλειος** 6 • 9 • 25 *perfect*
2 **ἀποκαθίστημι** 1 • 1 • 4 *to restore, reestablish*
**ἀπολαμβάνω** 1 • 4 • 17 *to recover, get back*
**εἰρηνεύω** 1 • 4 • 17 *to live at peace, be at peace*
**θεοπρεσβυτής, ὁ** 1 • 1 • 1 *an ambassador for God*
**μέγεθος, τό** 1 • 3 • 5 *greatness*
**πρέπω** 2 • 13 • 15 *to be fitting, be proper, be right*
**συγχαίρω** 1 • 4 • 7 *to congratulate*
**Συρία, ἡ** 2 • 16 • 17 *Syria*
**σωματεῖον, τό** 1 • 1 • 1 *corporate life*
**τέλειος** 6 • 9 • 25 *perfect*
**χειροτονέω** 1 • 3 • 4 *to choose*
3 **ἐπιστολή, ἡ** 1 • 3 • 13 *letter, epistle*
**ἕτοιμος** 1 • 3 • 9 *ready, prepared*
**εὖ** 1 • 8 • 16 *well, right*
**εὐδία, ἡ** 1 • 1 • 1 *tranquility, peace*
**λιμήν, ὁ** 1 • 2 • 2 *harbor*
**παρέχω** 1 • 3 • 18 *to grant*
**πρᾶγμα, τό** 1 • 3 • 23 *task*
**συνδοξάζω** 1 • 1 • 1 *to join in praise*
**τέλειος** [2] 6 • 9 • 25 *perfect*
**τυγχάνω** 2 • 5 • 15 *to meet, attain, gain, find, experience*
**ὑμέτερος** 1 • 1 • 4 *belonging to you*
**φρονέω** 3 • 4 • 17 *to set one's mind to, be intent on*
**κατὰ θεόν** *by (the will of) God*

## Chapter 12

1 **ἅμα** 1 • 9 • 12 *together with*
**ἀμείβομαι** 1 • 1 • 1 *to reward*
**ἀναπαύω** 3 • 7 • 13 *to cause to rest, give (someone) rest, refresh, revive*
**Βοῦρρος, ὁ** 1 • 4 • 4 *Burrus*
**ἐξεμπλάριον, τό** 1 • 3 • 3 *(living) example, embodiment*
**Ἐφέσιος** 1 • 7 • 7 *Ephesian*
**μιμέομαι** 1 • 2 • 4 *to imitate, emulate, follow*
**ὅθεν** 2 • 12 • 23 *from where, whence, from which*
**Τρῳάς, ἡ** 1 • 3 • 3 *Troas*
2 **ἀξιόθεος** 1 • 5 • 5 *worthy of God*
**διάκονος, ὁ** 3 • 18 • 29 *assistant*
**ἔλεος, τό** 1 • 3 • 19 *mercy, compassion, pity, clemency*
**ἑνότης, ἡ** 1 • 11 • 11 *unity*
**ἐπίσκοπος, ὁ** 9 • 57 • 76 *overseer, supervisor*
**θεοπρεπής** 3 • 5 • 6 *worthy of God, revered, venerable, godly*
**κοινός** 2 • 9 • 15 adv. dative: *together, collectively;*
**τοὺς κατ' ἄνδρα καὶ κοινῇ πάντας** *all of you, individually and collectively*
**πάθος, τό** 4 • 15 • 18 *suffering*
**πνευματικός** 2 • 12 • 19 *spiritual*
**πρεσβυτέριον, τό** 2 • 13 • 13 *council of elders*
**σαρκικός** 3 • 9 • 10 *material, physical, human, fleshly*

**σύνδουλος, ὁ** 1 • 4 • 6 *fellow-slave, fellow-Christian*

## Chapter 13

1 **παρθένος, ἡ** 2 • 2 • 62 *virgin*
**ῥώννυμι** 2 • 9 • 10 *to strengthen*; **ἔρρωσθε** (perfect pass. imperative; cf. BDF §346; *ExSyn* 493) *farewell, goodbye*
**Φίλων, ὁ** 2 • 3 • 4 *Philo*
**χήρα, ἡ** 2 • 3 • 13 *widow*
2 **Ἄλκη, ἡ** 1 • 2 • 3 *Alce*
**ἀσύγκριτος** 1 • 1 • 2 *incomparable*
**Γαουΐα, ἡ** 1 • 1 • 1 *Gavia*
**Δάφνος, ὁ** 1 • 1 • 1 *Daphnus*
**ἑδράζω** 2 • 4 • 6 *to establish, fix, settle*
**Εὔτεκνος, ὁ** 1 • 1 • 1 as a proper name: *Eutecnus*; or an adj.: *with many children, with good children, fortunate because of children*
**εὔχομαι** 3 • 17 • 41 *to wish, pray*
**πνευματικός** 2 • 12 • 19 *spiritual*
**ποθητός** 1 • 3 • 3 *longed-for, dearly beloved*
**ῥώννυμι** 2 • 9 • 10 *to strengthen*; **ἔρρωσθε** (perfect pass. imperative) *farewell, goodbye*
**σαρκικός** 3 • 9 • 10 *material, physical, human, fleshly*

# Ignatius to Polycarp

## Preface

ἐπισκοπέω 1 • 2 • 3 *to oversee, care for*
ἐπίσκοπος, ὁ 5 • 57 • 76 *overseer, supervisor*
Θεοφόρος, ὁ 1 • 7 • 7 *Theophorus*
Ἰγνάτιος, ὁ 1 • 7 • 10 *Ignatius*
Πολύκαρπος, ὁ 3 • 5 • 39 *Polycarp*
Σμυρναῖος 1 • 4 • 4 *coming from Smyrna*

## Chapter 1

1 ἀκίνητος 1 • 3 • 4 *immovable*
ἄμωμος 1 • 7 • 17 *blameless*
ἀποδέχομαι 1 • 3 • 6 *to recognize, acknowledge, praise*
γνώμη, ἡ 5 • 16 • 20 *purpose, intention, mind, mind-set*
ἑδράζω 1 • 4 • 6 *to establish, found, ground*
καταξιόω 3 • 9 • 14 *to consider worthy*
ὀνίνημι 2 • 6 • 6 *to have benefit of, enjoy;*
ὀναίμην (voluntative optative) *May I have joy*
πέτρα, ἡ 1 • 1 • 20 *rock*
ὑπερδοξάζω 1 • 1 • 1 *to glory exceedingly, break out in rapturous praise*
2 ἀμείνων 1 • 5 • 6 *better*
ἀνέχω 1 • 1 • 7 *to endure, bear with, put up with*
βαστάζω 2 • 2 • 24 *to carry, bear*
δρόμος, ὁ 1 • 1 • 5 *course of life, mission*
ἐκδικέω 1 • 1 • 1 *to do justice to*
ἐνδύω 1 • 1 • 32 *to clothe oneself in, put on, wear*
ἕνωσις, ἡ 2 • 8 • 8 *union, unity*
ἐπιμέλεια, ἡ 1 • 1 • 1 *care, attention*
πνευματικός 2 • 12 • 19 *spiritual*
προστίθημι 1 • 1 • 22 *to add, put to; press on*
σαρκικός 2 • 9 • 10 *material, physical, human, fleshly*
φροντίζω 1 • 1 • 1 *to think of, be intent on, be careful/concerned about*
3 ἀδιάλειπτος 1 • 1 • 3 *unceasing, constant*
ἀθλητής, ὁ 3 • 3 • 4 *contender, athlete*
ἀκοίμητος 1 • 1 • 1 *always active*
βαστάζω 2 • 2 • 24 *to carry away, remove*
γρηγορέω 1 • 1 • 2 *to be on the alert*
κέρδος, τό 1 • 1 • 1 *a gain, profit*
κόπος, ὁ 1 • 1 • 8 *work, labor, toil*
κτάομαι 2 • 9 • 10 *to possess*
νόσος, ἡ 1 • 1 • 2 *disease, illness*
ὁμοήθεια, ἡ 1 • 2 • 2 *similarity in character, agreement in conviction*
σύνεσις, ἡ 1 • 1 • 22 *intelligence, acuteness, shrewdness*
σχολάζω 2 • 2 • 2 *to busy oneself with, devote oneself to, give one's time to*
τέλειος 1 • 3 • 25 *perfect, complete, expert*
τοῖς κατ' ἄνδρα *to each one individually*

## Chapter 2

1 ἐμβροχή, ἡ 1 • 1 • 1 *wet application, cold compress*
ἔμπλαστρος, ἡ 1 • 1 • 1 *a plaster, treatment* (for wounds)
λοιμός 1 • 1 • 2 *menacing;* subst. *public menace/enemy*
παροξυσμός, ὁ 1 • 1 • 1 *attack of fever, convulsion*
παύω 1 • 1 • 12 *to stop, cause to stop, quiet, relieve*

πραΰτης, ἡ 2 • 2 • 8 *gentleness, humility, courtesy, considerateness, meekness*
τραῦμα, τό 1 • 1 • 1 *a wound*
φιλέω 1 • 1 • 1 *to have affection for, like, consider someone a friend*
2 ἀεί 1 • 2 • 7 *always*
ἀκέραιος 1 • 1 • 3 *pure, innocent*
ἀόρατος 2 • 6 • 13 *unseen, invisible*
κολακεύω 1 • 4 • 4 *to entice, deal graciously with*
λείπω 1 • 3 • 5 *to be/do without, lack, be in need or want (of)*
ὄφις, ὁ 1 • 1 • 9 *snake, serpent*
περιστερά, ἡ 1 • 1 • 1 *pigeon, dove*
πνευματικός 2 • 12 • 19 *spiritual*
σαρκικός 2 • 9 • 10 *material, physical, human, fleshly*
φρόνιμος 1 • 3 • 4 *sensible, thoughtful, prudent, wise*
χάρισμα, τό 1 • 4 • 6 *favor bestowed, gift*
3 ἀθλητής, ὁ 3 • 3 • 4 *contender, athlete*
ἄνεμος, ὁ 1 • 1 • 4 *wind*
ἀντίψυχον, τό 2 • 4 • 4 *ransom*
ἀπαιτέω 1 • 1 • 4 *to demand, desire*
ἀφθαρσία, ἡ 1 • 4 • 12 *incorruptibility, immortality*
δεσμός, ὁ 1 • 8 • 14 *bond, fetter*
ἐπιτυγχάνω 2 • 20 • 23 *to obtain, attain to, reach*
θέμα, τό 1 • 1 • 1 *a prize*
κυβερνήτης, ὁ 1 • 1 • 2 *shipmaster*
λιμήν, ὁ 1 • 2 • 2 *harbor*
νήφω 1 • 1 • 3 *to be well-balanced, be self-controlled*
χειμάζω 1 • 1 • 1 *to toss (in a storm)*

## Chapter 3

1 ἀθλητής, ὁ 3 • 3 • 4 *contender, athlete*
ἄκμων, ὁ 1 • 1 • 1 *anvil*
ἀξιόπιστος 1 • 2 • 4 *trustworthy*
δέρω 1 • 1 • 2 *to beat, whip, bruise, endure punishment*
ἑδραῖος 1 • 2 • 2 *firm, steadfast*
ἕνεκα 1 • 2 • 15 *because of, on account of, for the sake of*
ἑτεροδιδασκαλέω 1 • 1 • 1 *to give divergent instruction, give divisive instruction*
καταπλήσσω 1 • 2 • 3 *to amaze, astound*
μάλιστα 1 • 3 • 14 *most of all, above all, especially, particularly*
νικάω 1 • 1 • 8 *to be victor, conquer, overcome, prevail*
τύπτω 1 • 1 • 2 *to strike, beat (with a hammer)*
ὑπομένω 3 • 7 • 32 *to stand one's ground, hold out, endure*
2 ἀόρατος 2 • 6 • 13 *unseen, invisible*
ἀπαθής 1 • 2 • 3 *free of suffering*
ἄχρονος 1 • 1 • 1 *timeless, eternal*
ἀψηλάφητος 1 • 1 • 1 *impalpable, intangible*
καταμανθάνω 1 • 2 • 4 *to observe (well), notice, learn*
ὁρατός 1 • 4 • 5 *visible*
παθητός 1 • 2 • 2 *subject to suffering*
προσδοκάω 1 • 2 • 8 *to wait for, look for, expect*
σπουδαῖος 1 • 1 • 3 *eager, zealous, earnest, diligent*
τρόπος, ὁ 1 • 4 • 17 *manner, way, kind, guise*
ὑπομένω 3 • 7 • 32 *to stand one's ground, hold out, endure*

## Chapter 4

1 ἀμελέω 1 • 1 • 3 *to neglect, be unconcerned*
ἄνευ 2 • 6 • 12 *without*
γνώμη, ἡ 5 • 16 • 20 *approval*
εὐσταθέω 1 • 1 • 4 *to stand firm; be stable, be tranquil, be at rest*
ὅσπερ 1 • 5 • 10 *which indeed*
φροντιστής, ὁ 1 • 1 • 1 *protector, guardian*
χήρα, ἡ 1 • 3 • 13 *widow*
2 πυκνός 1 • 2 • 3 *often, frequently*
3 δουλεύω 1 • 1 • 42 *to (perform the duties of a slave) serve, obey*
δούλη, ἡ 1 • 1 • 1 *female slave, bondwoman*

**ἐλευθερία, ἡ** 1 • 1 • 2 *freedom, liberty*
**ἐλευθερόω** 1 • 1 • 1 *to free, set free*
**ἐράω** 1 • 3 • 3 *to desire, have a longing for, feel fervently about*
**κοινός** 1 • 9 • 15 *communal, common;*
**ἀπὸ τοῦ κοινοῦ** *via the common fund (of the church)*
**κρείττων** 1 • 3 • 8 *more prominent, higher in rank, preferable, better*
**τυγχάνω** 1 • 5 • 15 *to meet, attain, gain, find, experience*
**ὑπερηφανέω** 1 • 3 • 3 *to treat arrogantly/disdainfully, despise*
**φυσιόω** 1 • 5 • 6 *to puff up, make proud*

## Chapter 5

1 **ἀδελφή, ἡ** 1 • 1 • 10 *sister*
**ἀρκέω** 1 • 1 • 5 *to be satisfied/ content with (something)*
**κακοτεχνία, ἡ** 1 • 2 • 2 *craftiness, deceit;*
pl. *wicked practices*
**ὁμιλία, ἡ** 1 • 1 • 1 *speech, lecture, sermon*
**προσλαλέω** 1 • 3 • 3 *to speak to, speak with, address*
**σύμβιος, ὁ/ἡ** [2] 2 • 2 • 3 *husband, wife*
**φεύγω** 1 • 6 • 20 *to flee from, avoid, shun*
2 **ἁγνεία, ἡ** 1 • 2 • 13 *purity, chastity*
**ἀκαυχησία, ἡ** 1 • 1 • 1 *freedom from boasting*
**γαμέω** [2] 2 • 2 • 8 *to marry*
**γάμος, ὁ** 1 • 1 • 1 *marriage*
**γνώμη, ἡ** 5 • 16 • 20 *approval*
**ἕνωσις, ἡ** 2 • 8 • 8 *union, unity*
**ἐπίσκοπος, ὁ** [2] 5 • 57 • 76 *overseer, supervisor*
**πρέπω** 2 • 13 • 15 *to be fitting, be seemly/suitable*
**φθείρω** 1 • 2 • 10 *to destroy*

## Chapter 6

1 **ἀντίψυχον, τό** 2 • 4 • 4 *ransom*
**διάκονος, ὁ** 1 • 18 • 29 *assistant*
**ἐπίσκοπος, ὁ** [2] 5 • 57 • 76 *overseer, supervisor*
**οἰκονόμος, ὁ** 1 • 1 • 1 *administrator*
**πάρεδρος, ὁ** 1 • 1 • 1 *attendant, assistant*
**προσέχω** 1 • 4 • 25 *to pay attention to, give heed to, follow*
**συγκοιμάομαι** 1 • 1 • 1 *to die together, rest together*
**συγκοπιάω** 1 • 1 • 2 *to labor together, unite efforts (with)*
**συμπάσχω** 1 • 2 • 4 *to have sympathy for, suffer together*
**συναθλέω** 1 • 1 • 1 *to contend/ struggle along with, compete together*
**συνεγείρω** 1 • 1 • 1 *to awaken with, get up together, rise together*
**συντρέχω** 1 • 4 • 6 *to run together, go with*
**ὑπηρέτης, ὁ** 1 • 2 • 5 *helper, assistant*
2 **ἄκκεπτα, τά** 1 • 1 • 1 *savings, back pay*
**ἀρέσκω** 1 • 4 • 12 *to please, accommodate*
**βάπτισμα, τό** 1 • 1 • 6 *plunging, dipping, washing, water-rite, baptism*
**δεπόσιτα, τά** 1 • 1 • 1 *deposits (of money)*
**δεσέρτωρ, ὁ** 1 • 1 • 1 *deserter*
**δόρυ, τό** 1 • 1 • 1 *spear*
**κομίζω** [2] 2 • 2 • 4 *to carry off, get (for oneself), receive*
**μακροθυμέω** 1 • 1 • 3 *to be patient, be forbearing*
**μήτις** 1 • 1 • 1 *no one, none*
**ὀνίνημι** 2 • 6 • 6 *to have benefit of, enjoy;*
**ὀναίμην** (voluntative optative) *May I have joy*
**ὅπλον, τό** 1 • 1 • 5 *weapon*
**ὀψώνιον, τό** 1 • 1 • 1 *pay, wages*
**πανοπλία, ἡ** 1 • 1 • 1 *full armor*
**περικεφαλαία, ἡ** 1 • 1 • 1 *helmet*
**πραΰτης, ἡ** 2 • 2 • 8 *gentleness, humility, courtesy, considerateness, meekness*
**στρατεύω** 1 • 1 • 4 *to wage battle, fight*

## Chapter 7

1 **ἀμεριμνία, ἡ** 1 • 1 • 1 *freedom from care, confidence*
**Ἀντιόχεια, ἡ** 1 • 3 • 3 *Antioch*
**δηλόω** 1 • 4 • 49 *to reveal, make clear, show*
**ἐάνπερ** 1 • 7 • 7 *if indeed, if only, supposing that*
**εἰρηνεύω** 1 • 4 • 17 *to live in peace, be at peace*
**ἐπειδή** 1 • 2 • 17 *(just) because*
**ἐπιτυγχάνω** 2 • 20 • 23 *to obtain, attain to, reach*
**εὔθυμος** 1 • 1 • 2 *cheerful, in good spirits*
**Συρία, ἡ** 3 • 16 • 17 *Syria*
2 **ἄοκνος** [2] 2 • 2 • 2 *untiring*
**θεοδρόμος, ὁ** 1 • 2 • 2 *God's runner*
**θεομακάριστος** 1 • 2 • 2 *blessed by God*
**θεοπρεπής** 1 • 5 • 6 *worthy of God, revered, venerable, godly*
**καταξιόω** 3 • 9 • 14 *to consider worthy*
**λίαν** 1 • 2 • 48 *very (much), exceedingly*
**Πολύκαρπος, ὁ** 3 • 5 • 39 *Polycarp*
**πρέπω** 2 • 13 • 15 *to be fitting, be seemly/suitable*
**συμβούλιον, τό** 1 • 1 • 1 *council session, meeting*
**Συρία, ἡ** 3 • 16 • 17 *Syria*
**χειροτονέω** 1 • 3 • 4 *to choose*
3 **ἀνήκω** 1 • 3 • 10 *to refer, relate, belong*
**ἀπαρτίζω** 1 • 5 • 7 *to finish, complete*
**γράμμα, τό** 1 • 2 • 8 *letter (of the alphabet)*
**ἕτοιμος** 1 • 3 • 9 *ready*
**εὐποιΐα, ἡ** 1 • 1 • 1 *a good deed*
**σύντονος** 1 • 2 • 2 *intense desire, zeal*
**σχολάζω** 2 • 2 • 2 *to busy oneself with, devote oneself to, give one's time to*
**Χριστιανός, ὁ** 1 • 5 • 24 *Christ-follower, Christian*

## Chapter 8

1 **γνώμη, ἡ** 5 • 16 • 20 *purpose, intention, mind, mind-set*
**ἐξαίφνης** 1 • 1 • 6 *suddenly, unexpectedly*
**ἐπεί** 1 • 12 • 35 *because, since, for*
**ἐπιστολή, ἡ** 1 • 3 • 13 *letter, epistle*
**κτάομαι** 2 • 9 • 10 *to possess*
**Νεάπολις, ἡ** 1 • 1 • 1 *Neapolis*
**πέζος** 1 • 1 • 1 *going by land;* subst. *messenger*
**πλέω** 1 • 1 • 1 *to travel by sea, sail*
**προστάσσω** 1 • 1 • 8 *to command, order, give instructions, determine*
**Τρῳάς, ἡ** 1 • 3 • 3 *Troas, (the) Troad*
**ταῖς ἔμπροσθεν ἐκκλησίαις** *to the churches in front/ahead* (referring to those churches closer to Syria [so Lightfoot])
2 **Ἄτταλος, ὁ** 1 • 1 • 1 *Attalus*
**Ἐπίτροπος, ὁ** 1 • 1 • 1 *Epitropus*
**καταξιόω** 3 • 9 • 14 *to consider worthy*
**Πολύκαρπος, ὁ** 3 • 5 • 39 *Polycarp*
**Συρία, ἡ** 3 • 16 • 17 *Syria*
3 **Ἄλκη, ἡ** 1 • 2 • 3 *Alce*
**διαμένω** 1 • 2 • 9 *to remain*
**ἑνότης, ἡ** 1 • 11 • 11 *unity*
**ἐπισκοπή, ἡ** 1 • 1 • 5 *visitation, care*
**εὔχομαι** 1 • 13 • 16 *to wish*
**ποθητός** 1 • 3 • 3 *longed-for, dearly beloved*
**ῥώννυμι** [2] 2 • 9 • 10 *to strengthen;*
**ἐρρῶσθαι** (perfect pass.) *farewell, goodbye*

# Polycarp to the Philippians

## Preface

**ἔλεος, ὁ** 1 • 19 *mercy, compassion, pity, clemency*
**παντοκράτωρ, ὁ** 1 • 12 *Almighty, All-Powerful, Omnipotent (One)*
**παροικέω** 1 • 6 *to be a stranger*
**πληθύνω** 1 • 11 *to multiply, grow, increase;*
  **πληθυνθείη** (voluntative optative) *may it be multiplied/be (yours) in ever greater measure*
**Πολύκαρπος, ὁ** 1 • 39 *Polycarp*
**σωτήρ, ὁ** 1 • 14 *savior, deliverer, preserver*
**Φίλιπποι, οἱ** 1 • 1 *Philippi*

## Chapter 1

1 **ἁγιοπρεπής** 1 • 2 *holy*
**ἀληθής** 1 • 16 *real, genuine, not imaginary*
**ἀληθῶς** 1 • 23 *truly, in truth, really, actually*
**δεσμός, ὁ** 1 • 14 *bond, fetter*
**διάδημα, τό** 1 • 1 *royal headband, crown*
**ἐκλέγομαι** 1 • 15 *to select someone/something for oneself*
**ἐνειλέω** 1 • 1 *to confine in*
**ἐπιβάλλω** 1 • 3 *to fall to, belong to*
**μεγάλως** 1 • 9 *greatly*
**μίμημα, τό** 1 • 1 *copy, image*
**προπέμπω** 1 • 1 *to send on one's way*
**συγχαίρω** 1 • 7 *to rejoice with*
2 **ᾅδης, ὁ** 1 • 3 *the nether world, Hades*
**ἀρχαῖος** 1 • 12 *ancient*
**βέβαιος** 1 • 9 *abiding*
**διαμένω** 1 • 9 *to remain*
**καρποφορέω** 1 • 7 *to bear fruit*
**καταγγέλλω** 1 • 3 *to proclaim, announce*
**καταντάω** 1 • 4 *to arrive at, attain, meet*
**μέχρι** 1 • 23 *until*
**ῥίζα, ἡ** 1 • 8 *root*
**ὑπομένω** 2 • 32 *to stand one's ground, hold out, endure*
**ὠδίν, ἡ** 1 • 1 *great pain (as in giving birth)*
3 **ἀνεκλάλητος** 1 • 2 *inexpressible*
**ἐπιθυμέω** 1 • 17 *to desire, long for*

## Chapter 2

1 **ἀναζώννυμι** 1 • 1 *to bind up, gird up*
**ἀπειθέω** 1 • 5 *to disobey, be disobedient*
**ἀπολείπω** 2 • 6 *to put aside, give up*
**δουλεύω** 2 • 42 *to (perform the duties of a slave) serve, obey*
**ἐκζητέω** 1 • 16 *to look for, seek*
**ἐπίγειος** 1 • 12 *earthly*
**ἐπουράνιος** 1 • 11 *heavenly, in heaven*
**κενός** 3 • 26 *empty*
**κριτής, ὁ** 1 • 6 *a judge*
**λατρεύω** 1 • 3 *to serve*
**ματαιολογία, ἡ** 1 • 1 *empty talk, fruitless talk*
**ὀσφύς, ἡ** 1 • 2 *waist, loins*
**πλάνη, ἡ** 1 • 11 *error, delusion, deceit, deception*
**πνοή** 1 • 3 *breath;*
  **πᾶσα πνόη** *every living thing, every breathing creature, everything that has breath*
2 **ἀδικία, ἡ** 1 • 7 *wrongdoing*
**ἀντί** [4] 4 • 15 *for, as, in the place of*
**ἀπέχω** 4 • 35 *to keep away, abstain, refrain from*
**γρόνθος, ὁ** [2] 2 • 2 *fist;*
  **γρόνθον ἀντὶ γρόνθου** *blow for blow*

**καταλαλιά, ἡ** 2 • 13 *evil speech, slander, defamation, detraction*
**κατάρα, ἡ** [2] 2 • 4 *curse, imprecation*
**λοιδορία, ἡ** [2] 2 • 2 *abuse, reproach, reviling*
**πλεονεξία, ἡ** 1 • 7 *greediness, insatiableness, avarice, covetousness*
**φιλαργυρία, ἡ** 4 • 5 *love of money, avarice, miserliness*
**ψευδομαρτυρία, ἡ** 2 • 4 *false witness*
3 **ἀντιμετρέω** 1 • 1 *to measure in return*
**ἐλεάω** [2] 2 • 4 *to have mercy on*
**ἕνεκα** 1 • 15 *because of, on account of, for the sake of*
**μετρέω** 1 • 5 *to give out, deal out, apportion*
**μέτρον, τό** 1 • 3 *measure*
**μνημονεύω** 1 • 25 *to remember, keep in mind, think of, mention*

## Chapter 3

1 **ἐπεί** 1 • 35 *because, since, for*
**ἐπιτρέπω** 1 • 11 *to allow, permit;* **οὐκ ἐμαυτῷ ἐπιτρέψας** *not of my own initiative*
**προεπικαλέω** 1 • 1 *to request*
2 **ἀκριβῶς** 1 • 8 *accurately, carefully, well*
**ἄπειμι** 1 • 5 *to be absent/away*
**βεβαίως** 1 • 3 *certainly, truly, reliably*
**ἐγκύπτω** 1 • 5 *to examine*
**ἔνδοξος** 1 • 54 *glorious, splendid*
**ἐπιστολή, ἡ** 3 • 13 *letter, epistle*
**κατακολουθέω** 1 • 1 *to follow*
3 **ἐντός** 1 • 3 *inside, within, within the limits of*
**ἐπακολουθέω** 1 • 4 *to follow;* **ἐπακολουθούσης τῆς ἐλπίδος, προαγούσης τῆς ἀγάπης** (gen. absolutes in mid-sentence) *while hope follows and love leads*
**μακράν** 3 • 15 *far (away)*
**πλησίον** 1 • 17 *near;* subst. *neighbor, fellow human being*
**προάγω** 1 • 3 *to go before, lead the way, precede*

## Chapter 4

1 **εἰσφέρω** 2 • 4 *to bring in*
**ἐκφέρω** 1 • 3 *to carry/bring out*
**ὁπλίζω** 1 • 1 *to equip, arm*
**ὅπλον, τό** 1 • 5 *weapon*
**φιλαργυρία, ἡ** 4 • 5 *love of money, avarice, miserliness*
**χαλεπός** 1 • 5 *hard, difficult*
2 **ἁγνεία, ἡ** 2 • 13 *purity, chastity*
**ἐγκράτεια, ἡ** 1 • 14 *self-control*
**ἔπειτα** 1 • 4 *then, thereupon*
**ἴσος** 1 • 3 *equal*
**παιδεία, ἡ** 1 • 11 *upbringing, training, instruction, discipline, correction*
**παιδεύω** 1 • 13 *to practice discipline, correct, give guidance*
**στέργω** 1 • 2 *to love, feel affection for*
**ἐν πάσῃ ἀληθείᾳ** *in all fidelity*
3 **ἀδιαλείπτως** 2 • 6 *constantly, unceasingly*
**διαβολή, ἡ** 1 • 1 *slander*
**ἔννοια, ἡ** 1 • 4 *thought, knowledge, insight*
**ἐντυγχάνω** 1 • 8 *to pray*
**θυσιαστήριον, τό** 1 • 15 *altar*
**καταλαλιά, ἡ** 2 • 13 *evil speech, slander, defamation, detraction*
**κρυπτόν, τό** 1 • 4 *something hidden*
**λανθάνω** 1 • 7 *to escape notice, be hidden*
**λογισμός, ὁ** 1 • 4 *calculation, reasoning, reflection, thought*
**μακράν** 3 • 15 *far (away)*
**μωμοσκοπέομαι** 1 • 2 *to examine for blemishes*
**σωφρονέω** 1 • 2 *to be reasonable, be sensible, be serious, keep one's head*
**φιλαργυρία, ἡ** 4 • 5 *love of money, avarice, miserliness*
**χήρα, ἡ** 2 • 13 *widow*
**ψευδομαρτυρία, ἡ** 2 • 4 *false testimony*

## Chapter 5

1 **ἀξίως** 2 • 5 *worthily, in a manner of, suitably*

**μυκτηρίζω** 1 • 3 *to turn up the nose at, treat with contempt*
2 **ἄμεμπτος** 2 • 4 *blameless, faultless*
**ἀξίως** 2 • 5 *worthily, in a manner worthy of, suitably*
**ἀπολαμβάνω** 1 • 17 *to receive*
**ἀφιλάργυρος** 1 • 2 *not loving money, not greedy*
**διάκονος, ὁ** [3] 4 • 29 *assistant*
**δίλογος** 1 • 1 *insincere*
**ἐγκρατής** 1 • 3 *self-controlled, disciplined*
**εἴγε** 1 • 1 *if indeed, inasmuch as*
**ἐπιμελής** 1 • 1 *careful, attentive*
**εὐαρεστέω** 1 • 6 *to please, be pleasing*
**εὔσπλαγχνος** 2 • 4 *tenderhearted, compassionate*
**κατενώπιον** 1 • 1 *before*
**πολιτεύομαι** 1 • 10 *to live, lead one's life*
**συμβασιλεύω** 1 • 1 *to rule (as a king) with someone*
**ὑπισχνέομαι** 1 • 1 *to promise*
3 **ἁγνεία, ἡ** 2 • 13 *purity, chastity*
**ἁγνός** 1 • 11 *pure, holy*
**ἄμεμπτος** 2 • 4 *blameless, faultless*
**ἄμωμος** 1 • 17 *blameless*
**ἀνακόπτω** 1 • 1 *to hinder, restrain*
**ἀπέχω** 4 • 35 *to keep away, abstain, refrain from*
**ἀρσενοκοίτης, ὁ** 1 • 1 *pederast, a male who engages in sexual activity with a person of own sex*
**ἄτοπος** 1 • 2 *evil, wrong, improper*
**διάκονος, ὁ** 4 • 29 *assistant*
**κληρονομέω** 1 • 11 *to acquire, obtain, come into possession of*
**μαλακός** 1 • 1 *effeminate, being passive in a same-sex relationship*
**νέος** 1 • 16 *young*
**παρθένος, ἡ** 1 • 62 *virgin, chaste person*
**πόρνος, ὁ** 1 • 1 *fornicator*
**προνοέω** 2 • 3 *to take thought for, take into consideration, have regard for*
**στρατεύω** 1 • 4 *to wage battle, fight*
**χαλιναγωγέω** 1 • 2 *to bridle, hold in check*

## Chapter 6

1 **ἄδικος** 1 • 14 *unjust*
**ἀεί** 1 • 7 *always*
**ἀμελέω** 1 • 3 *to neglect, be unconcerned*
**ἀπέχω** 4 • 35 *to keep away, abstain, refrain from*
**ἀποπλανάω** 2 • 8 *to mislead*
**ἀπότομος** 1 • 1 *relentless*
**ἀσθενής** 2 • 12 *sick, ill*
**ἐλεήμων** 1 • 4 *merciful, sympathetic, compassionate*
**ἐπισκέπτομαι** 1 • 8 *to visit*
**εὔσπλαγχνος** 2 • 4 *tenderhearted, compassionate*
**μακράν** 3 • 15 *far (away)*
**ὀρφανός** 1 • 9 *without parents, orphan*
**ὀφειλέτης, ὁ** 1 • 2 *one under obligation, one liable for*
**πένης** 1 • 16 *poor, needy*
**προνοέω** 2 • 3 *to take thought for, take into consideration, have regard for*
**προσωποληψία/προσωπολημψία, ἡ** 1 • 1 *partiality*
**ταχέως** 1 • 4 *too quickly, too easily, hastily*
**φιλαργυρία, ἡ** 4 • 5 *love of money, avarice, miserliness*
**χήρα, ἡ** 2 • 13 *widow*
2 **ἀπέναντι** 1 • 3 *opposite*
**βῆμα, τό** 1 • 1 *tribunal*
**δέομαι** 1 • 7 *to ask, request*
3 **ἀπέχω** 4 • 35 *to keep away, abstain, refrain from*
**ἀποπλανάω** 2 • 8 *to mislead*
**δουλεύω** 2 • 42 *to (perform the duties of a slave) serve, obey*
**ἔλευσις, ἡ** 1 • 2 *coming, arrival*
**ἐντέλλω** 2 • 29 *to command, order, give orders*
**εὐλάβεια, ἡ** 1 • 1 *awe, fear of God*
**ζηλωτής, ὁ** 1 • 3 *enthusiast, adherent, loyalist*
**κενός** 3 • 26 *empty*
**προκηρύσσω** 1 • 1 *to proclaim publicly*
**σκάνδαλον, τό** 1 • 5 *temptation to sin, enticement*
**ὑπόκρισις** 1 • 13 *play-acting, pretense, outward show, dissembling*

**ψευδάδελφος, ὁ** 1 • 1 *false brother, false member*

## Chapter 7

1 **ἀντίχριστος, ὁ** 1 • 1 *antichrist*
**λόγιον, τό** 1 • 11 *a saying*
**μαρτύριον, τό** 1 • 16 *testimony, proof*
**μεθοδεύω** 1 • 1 *to defraud, deceive, pervert, tamper with*
**ὁμολογέω** [2] 2 • 18 *to acknowledge, claim, profess, praise*
**πρωτότοκος** 1 • 4 *firstborn*
**Σατανᾶς/Σατάν, ὁ** 1 • 5 *Satan, adversary*
**σταυρός, ὁ** 1 • 17 *the cross*
2 **ἀπολείπω** 2 • 6 *to put aide, give up*
**ἀσθενής** 2 • 12 *weak*
**δέησις, ἡ** 1 • 6 *prayer*
**εἰσφέρω** 2 • 4 *to bring in*
**εὐχή, ἡ** 1 • 5 *prayer*
**ματαιότης, ἡ** 1 • 3 *emptiness, futility, purposelessness, transitoriness*
**νηστεία, ἡ** 1 • 25 *fast*
**νήφω** 1 • 3 *to be well-balanced, be self-controlled*
**παντεπόπτης, ὁ** 1 • 3 *one who sees all, one who is all-seeing*
**πειρασμός, ὁ** 1 • 4 *temptation, enticement to sin*
**πρόθυμος** 1 • 4 *ready, willing, eager*
**προσκαρτερέω** 2 • 2 *to busy oneself with, be busily engaged in, be devoted to*
**ψευδοδιδασκαλία, ἡ** 1 • 1 *false, spurious teaching*

## Chapter 8

1 **ἀδιαλείπτως** 2 • 6 *constantly, unceasingly*
**ἀναφέρω** 1 • 8 *to offer up*
**ἀρραβών, ὁ** 1 • 1 *first installment, deposit, down payment, pledge*
**δόλος, ὁ** 1 • 8 *deceit, cunning, treachery*
**ξύλον, τό** 1 • 23 *tree, cross*
**προσκαρτερέω** 2 • 2 *to hold fast to, continue in, preserve in*
**ὑπομένω** 2 • 32 *to stand one's ground, hold out, endure*
2 **μιμητής, ὁ** 1 • 12 *imitator*
**ὑπογραμμός, ὁ** 1 • 4 *example*

## Chapter 9

1 **ἀσκέω** 1 • 6 *to practice, engage in*
**Ζώσιμος, ὁ** 1 • 1 *Zosimus*
**Ἰγνάτιος, ὁ** 3 • 10 *Ignatius*
**πειθαρχέω** 1 • 3 *to obey*
**Ῥοῦφος, ὁ** 1 • 1 *Rufus*
2 **κενός** 3 • 26 *in vain*
**συμπάσχω** 1 • 4 *to suffer with, suffer the same thing as*
**τρέχω** 1 • 2 *to exert oneself, run*

## Chapters 10–12[1]

## Chapter 13

1 **ἀποκομίζω** 1 • 1 *to take along*
**γράμμα, τό** 1 • 8 *a document, piece of writing*
**εὔθετος** 1 • 1 *fit, suitable, usable, convenient*
**Ἰγνάτιος, ὁ** 3 • 10 *Ignatius*
**ὅσπερ** 1 • 10 *which indeed*
**πρεσβεύω** 1 • 2 *to be an ambassador/envoy, travel/work as an ambassador*
**Συρία, ἡ** 1 • 17 *Syria*
2 **ἀνήκω** 1 • 10 *to refer, relate, belong*
**ἐντέλλω** 2 • 29 *to command, order, give orders*
**ἐπιστολή, ἡ** 3 • 13 *letter, epistle*
**Ἰγνάτιος, ὁ** 3 • 10 *Ignatius*
**οἰκοδομή, ἡ** 1 • 103 *building, construction*
**περιέχω** 1 • 4 *to contain*
**ὠφελέω** 1 • 8 *to help, aid, benefit, be of use (to)*
**ὑποτεταγμέναι** *to be attached to* (referring to one document attached to another [cf. BDAG s.v. ὑποτάσσω 2])

---

1. Chapters 10–12 are not extant in Greek.

# The Martyrdom of Polycarp

## Preface

**ἔλεος, τό** 1 • 19 *pity, clemency*
**καθολικός** 4 • 6 *general, universal*
**παροικέω** [2] 2 • 6 *to be a stranger*
**παροικία, ἡ** 1 • 3 *congregation, parish*
**πληθύνω** 1 • 11 *to be multiplied, grow, increase;*
**πληθυνθείη** (voluntative optative) *may it be multiplied*
**Σμύρνα, ἡ** 5 • 14 *Smyrna*
**Φιλομήλιον, τό** 1 • 1 *Philomelium*

## Chapter 1

1 **ἄνωθεν** 1 • 8 *again, anew*
**διωγμός, ὁ** 1 • 2 *persecution*
**ἐπιδείκνυμι** 2 • 11 *to show, point out*
**ἐπισφραγίζω** 1 • 1 *to seal*
**καταπαύω** 2 • 7 *to stop, bring to an end*
**μαρτύριον, τό** 5 • 16 *martyrdom*
**Πολύκαρπος, ὁ** 28 • 39 *Polycarp*
**προάγω** 1 • 3 *to go before, lead the way, precede*
**σχεδόν** 3 • 4 *nearly, almost*
2 **ἀληθής** 1 • 16 *real, genuine, not imaginary*
**βέβαιος** 1 • 9 *abiding*
**μιμητής, ὁ** 2 • 12 *imitator*
**πέλας** 1 • 1 *near;*
**τὸ καθ᾽ ἑαυτοὺς ἀλλὰ καὶ τὸ κατὰ τοὺς πέλας** *(your) own interests, but also the interests of (your) neighbors*
**περιμένω** 1 • 2 *to wait for*
**σκοπέω** 1 • 2 *to look (out) for, notice*

## Chapter 2

1 **ἀνατίθημι** 1 • 1 *to ascribe, attribute*
**γενναῖος** 3 • 8 *noble, illustrious*
**εὐλαβής** 1 • 1 *devout, God-fearing*
**μαρτύριον, τό** 5 • 16 *martyrdom*
2 **ἀποδημέω** 1 • 2 *to go on a journey*
**ἀρτηρία, ἡ** 1 • 1 *artery*
**βασανίζω** 2 • 18 *to torture*
**γενναῖος** 3 • 8 *noble, illustrious*
**γενναιότης, ἡ** 2 • 2 *nobility, bravery*
**γρύζω** 1 • 1 *to mutter, complain*
**ἐλεέω** 1 • 16 *to have compassion/ mercy/pity*
**ἐπιδείκνυμι** 2 • 11 *to demonstrate, show*
**ἔσω** 1 • 4 *inside, within*
**καταξαίνω** 1 • 1 *to tear to shreds*
**μάστιξ, ἡ** 1 • 8 *whip, lash*
**μέχρι** 1 • 23 *as far as*
**ὀδύρομαι** 1 • 1 *to mourn, lament*
**οἰκονομία, ἡ** 1 • 6 *arrangement, order, plan*
**ὁμιλέω** 1 • 3 *to speak, converse, address*
**περιίστημι** 1 • 1 *to stand around*
**στενάζω** 2 • 3 *to sigh, groan*
**τοσοῦτος** 5 • 38 *so great/strong, to such extent*
**ὑπομένω** 4 • 32 *to stand one's ground, hold out, endure*
**ὑπομονητικός** 1 • 1 *patient, showing endurance*
**φιλοδέσποτος** 1 • 1 *loving one's master*
**φλέψ, ἡ** 1 • 1 *vein*
3 **ἀναβλέπω** 3 • 7 *to look up*
**ἀπάνθρωπος** 1 • 1 *inhuman*
**βασανιστής, ὁ** 1 • 1 *oppressive jailer*
**βάσανος, ἡ** 2 • 18 *torture, torment*
**ἐξαγοράζω** 1 • 1 *to buy off*
**καταφρονέω** 2 • 9 *to care nothing for, disregard, be unafraid of*
**κόλασις, ἡ** 4 • 11 *punishment*
**κοσμικός** 1 • 4 *earthly*
**μηδέποτε** 1 • 5 *never*
**μηκέτι** 1 • 16 *no longer, not from now*

ὅσπερ 2 • 10 *which indeed*
προσέχω 1 • 25 *to pay attention to, give heed to, follow*
σβέννυμι 2 • 5 *to extinguish, put out*
ὑποδείκνυμι 1 • 3 *to indicate, point out*
ὑπομένω 4 • 32 *to stand one's ground, hold out, endure*
φεύγω 1 • 20 *to escape*
ψυχρός 1 • 2 *cold*
4 ἄρνησις, ἡ 1 • 3 *repudiation, rejection*
βάσανος, ἡ 2 • 18 *torture, torment*
δεινός 2 • 7 *fearful, terrible*
ἐπίμονος 1 • 2 *lasting*
ἰδέα, ἡ 1 • 9 *form, kind*
κατακρίνω 1 • 6 *to pronounce a sentence on*
κῆρυξ, ὁ 3 • 4 *trumpet-shell*
κόλασις, ἡ [2] 4 • 11 *punishment*
κολαφίζω 1 • 1 *to strike with the fist, beat, cuff*
μηχανάομαι 1 • 1 *to devise, contrive*
ποικίλος 1 • 22 *diversified, manifold*
τρέπω 1 • 2 *to turn, direct*
ὑπομένω 4 • 32 *to stand one's ground, hold out, endure*
ὑποστρωννύω/ὑποστρώννυμι 1 • 2 *to spread out underneath*

## Chapter 3

1 ἄδικος 2 • 14 *unjust*
ἀνθύπατος, ὁ 7 • 7 *proconsul*
ἄνομος 3 • 17 *lawless*
ἀπαλλάσσω 1 • 3 *to leave, depart*
βίος, ὁ 1 • 13 *life*
γενναῖος 3 • 8 *noble, illustrious*
Γερμανικός, ὁ 1 • 1 *Germanicus*
δειλία, ἡ 1 • 2 *cowardice*
ἐπιρρώννυμι 1 • 1 *to strengthen, encourage*
ἐπισήμως 1 • 1 *in an outstanding manner*
ἐπισπάω 1 • 4 *to draw to oneself*
ἡλικία, ἡ 3 • 4 *age, time of life*
θηριομαχέω 1 • 4 *to fight with wild animals*
ἰσχύω 2 • 9 *to have power, be mighty*
κατοικτείρω/κατοικτίρω 1 • 1 *to have pity on something*
προσβιάζομαι 1 • 2 *to compel, use force*
ταχύς 2 • 18 *quickly*
2 ἄθεος 3 • 5 *god-denier, atheist*
γενναιότης, ἡ 2 • 2 *nobility, bravery*
γένος, τό 3 • 16 *nation, people*
ἐπιβοάω 4 • 4 *to cry out loudly*
θεοσεβής 1 • 2 *god-fearing, devout*
θεοφιλής 1 • 1 *loving God*
Πολύκαρπος, ὁ 28 • 39 *Polycarp*
Χριστιανός, ὁ 4 • 24 *Christ-follower, Christian*

## Chapter 4

1 ἀνθύπατος, ὁ 7 • 7 *proconsul*
δειλιάω 1 • 1 *to be cowardly/fearful*
ἐκλιπαρέω 1 • 1 *to beg, entreat*
ἑκών 1 • 4 *willing(ly), glad(ly)*
ἐπαινέω 1 • 6 *to praise*
ἐπειδή 2 • 17 *(just) because*
ἐπιθύω 2 • 2 *to offer a sacrifice*
Κόϊντος, ὁ 1 • 1 *Quintus*
ὀμνύω 5 • 9 *to swear, take an oath*
παραβιάζομαι 1 • 1 *to urge strongly, prevail upon*
προδίδωμι 3 • 5 *to betray*
προσφάτως 1 • 1 *recently*
Φρυγία, ἡ 1 • 1 *Phrygia*
Φρύξ, ὁ 1 • 1 *a Phrygian*

## Chapter 5

1 ἀγρίδιον, τό 2 • 2 *a little farm, country house*
ἀπέχω 1 • 35 *to be distant*
διατρίβω 1 • 5 *to spend time*
θαυμάσιος 2 • 4 *wonderful, remarkable, admirable*
μακράν 1 • 15 *far (away)*
οἰκουμένη, ἡ 3 • 6 *the inhabited earth, the world*
ὅσπερ 2 • 10 *which indeed*
Πολύκαρπος, ὁ 28 • 39 *Polycarp*
συνήθης 2 • 2 *habitual, customary, usual*
ταράσσω 2 • 4 *to stir up, disturb, unsettle, throw into confusion*

**ὑπεξέρχομαι** [2] 2 • 2 *to go out quietly/secretly*
**κατὰ πόλιν** here probably *in town*
2 **καίω** 6 • 11 *to burn (up)*
**κατακαίω** 2 • 4 *to burn down, burn up, consume*
**ὀπτασία, ἡ** 2 • 2 *trance*
**προσκεφάλαιον, τό** 2 • 2 *pillow*
**στρέφω** 1 • 5 *to turn around, turn toward*
**συλλαμβάνω** 5 • 11 *to seize, grasp, apprehend*

## Chapter 6

1 **ἀγρίδιον, τό** 2 • 2 *a little farm or country house*
**βασανίζω** 2 • 18 *to torture*
**ἐπιμένω** 4 • 16 *to continue, persist in, persevere*
**ἐφίστημι** 1 • 5 *to stand at/near*
**μεταβαίνω** 1 • 2 *to go/pass over*
**ὁμολογέω** 3 • 18 *to grant, admit, confess*
**παιδάριον, τό** 2 • 2 *young slave*
**συλλαμβάνω** 5 • 11 *to seize, arrest*
2 **ἀδύνατος** 1 • 11 *impossible*
**ἀπαρτίζω** 1 • 7 *to finish, complete*
**εἰρήναρχος, ὁ** 2 • 2 *chief of police, police captain*
**εἰσάγω** 2 • 6 *to bring or lead in/into*
**ἐπεί** 2 • 35 *because, since, for*
**ἐπιλέγω** 1 • 1 *to call/name (in addition)*
**'Ιούδα/'Ιούδας, ὁ** 1 • 2 *Judas*
**κλῆρος, ὁ** 1 • 8 *lot, destiny*
**κληρόω** 1 • 2 *to obtain by lot*
**κοινωνός, ὁ/ἡ** 1 • 7 *companion, partner, sharer*
**λανθάνω** 1 • 7 *to escape notice, be hidden*
**οἰκεῖος** 1 • 2 *members of a household*
**προδίδωμι** [2] 3 • 5 *to betray*
**σπεύδω** 1 • 4 *to hurry, hasten*
**στάδιον, τό** 6 • 9 *arena, stadium*
**τιμωρία, ἡ** 1 • 13 *punishment*
**ὑπέχω** 1 • 1 *to undergo punishment;*
**ὑπόσχοιεν** (oblique optative used after secondary tense; cf. *ExSyn* 483) *might undergo punishment*

## Chapter 7

1 **δεῖπνον, τό** 1 • 4 *dinner, supper*
**διωγμίτης, ὁ** 1 • 1 *detective*
**δωμάτιον, τό** 1 • 1 *a little room upstairs*
**ἱππεύς, ὁ** 1 • 1 *horse rider, cavalryman*
**κἀκεῖθεν** 1 • 1 *and from there*
**κατάκειμαι** 1 • 2 *to lie down*
**λῃστής, ὁ** 1 • 2 *revolutionary, insurrectionist, guerilla*
**ὅπλον, τό** 1 • 5 *weapon*
**ὀψέ** 1 • 3 *late*
**παιδάριον, τό** 2 • 2 *young slave*
**παρασκευή, ἡ** 1 • 2 *day of preparation*
**συνεπέρχομαι** 1 • 1 *to come together against, attack together*
**συνήθης** 2 • 2 *habitual, customary, usual*
**τρέχω** 1 • 2 *to run, rush, advance*
**ὑπερῷον, τό** 1 • 2 *upper story, room upstairs*
**χωρίον, τό** 1 • 5 *place, piece of land, field*
2 **ἀδεῶς** 1 • 2 *without fear/disturbance*
**διαλέγομαι** 1 • 1 *to converse, discuss, argue*
**ἐξαιτέω** 1 • 1 *to ask*
**εὐσταθής** 1 • 1 *stable, firm, calm*
**ἡλικία, ἡ** 3 • 4 *age, time of life*
**κελεύω** 2 • 44 *to command, order, urge*
**παρατίθημι** 1 • 6 *to set before*
**πάρειμι** [2] 4 • 17 *to be present*
**πρεσβύτης, ὁ** 2 • 3 *old man, aged man*
**σπουδή, ἡ** 3 • 4 *eagerness, earnestness, diligence, willingness, zeal*
**συλλαμβάνω** 5 • 11 *to seize, grasp, apprehend*
**τοσοῦτος** 5 • 38 *so great/strong, to such extent*
3 **ἐκπλήσσω** 1 • 4 *to be amazed, be overwhelmed*

**ἐπιτρέπω** 1 • 11 *to allow, permit*
**θεοπρεπής** 1 • 6 *worthy of God, revered, venerable, godly*
**πλήρης** 1 • 20 *filled, full*
**πρεσβύτης, ὁ** 2 • 3 *old man, aged man*
**σιγάω** 1 • 6 *to stop speaking, become silent*

## Chapter 8

1 **ἄδοξος** 1 • 2 *without reputation, obscure*
**ἔνδοξος** 1 • 54 *honored, distinguished, eminent*
**ἔξειμι** 1 • 1 *to go out, go away*
**ἐπεί** 2 • 35 *when, after*
**καθολικός** 4 • 6 *general, universal*
**καταπαύω** 2 • 7 *to stop, bring to an end*
**μνημονεύω** 2 • 25 *to remember, keep in mind, think of, mention*
**οἰκουμένη, ἡ** 3 • 6 *the inhabited earth, the world*
**ὄνος, ὁ/ἡ** 1 • 1 *(domesticated) ass, donkey*
**ποτέ** 3 • 15 *at last, finally*
**πώποτε** 1 • 2 *ever, at any time*
**συμβάλλω** 1 • 4 *to meet, fall in with*
2 **ἀκόλουθος** 3 • 8 *following*
**διασῴζω** 1 • 4 *to bring safely through, save, rescue*
**εἰρήναρχος, ὁ** 2 • 2 *chief of police, police captain*
**ἐπιθύω** 2 • 2 *to offer a sacrifice*
**ἐπιμένω** 4 • 16 *to continue, persist in, persevere*
**Καῖσαρ, ὁ** 4 • 4 *emperor, Caesar*
**καροῦχα, ἡ** 2 • 2 *carriage*
**μετατίθημι** 2 • 9 *to put in another place, transfer*
**Νικήτης, ὁ** 1 • 2 *Nicetes*
**παρακαθέζομαι** 1 • 1 *to sit beside*
**συμβουλεύω** 1 • 3 *to advise*
**ὑπαντάω** 1 • 2 *to meet*
3 **ἀντικνήμιον, τό** 1 • 1 *shin*
**ἀποσύρω** 1 • 1 *to tear/scrape off*
**ἀποτυγχάνω** 1 • 3 *to fail*
**δεινός** 2 • 7 *fearful, terrible*
**θόρυβος, ὁ** 2 • 4 *noise, clamor*
**καθαιρέω** 1 • 7 *to take down, bring down, lower*
**καροῦχα, ἡ** 2 • 2 *carriage*
**κάτειμι** 1 • 1 *to come down, get down*
**προθύμως** 2 • 5 *willingly, eagerly, freely*
**σπουδή, ἡ** [2] 3 • 4 *eagerness, earnestness, diligence, willingness, zeal*
**στάδιον, τό** [2] 6 • 9 *arena, stadium*
**τηλικοῦτος** 1 • 6 *so great/important/mighty*

## Chapter 9

1 **ἀνδρίζομαι** 1 • 4 *to conduct oneself in a courageous way*
**εἴσειμι** 1 • 1 *to go in/into*
**ἡμέτερος** 2 • 13 *our*
**θόρυβος, ὁ** 2 • 4 *noise, clamor*
**ἰσχύω** 2 • 9 *to have power, be mighty*
**πάρειμι** 4 • 17 *to be present*
**Πολύκαρπος, ὁ** [3] 28 • 39 *Polycarp*
**προσάγω** 2 • 7 *to bring (forward)*
**στάδιον, τό** 6 • 9 *arena, stadium*
**συλλαμβάνω** 5 • 11 *to seize, grasp, apprehend*
2 **ἄθεος** [2] 3 • 5 *god-denier, atheist*
**αἰδέομαι** 1 • 2 *to respect*
**ἀκόλουθος** 3 • 8 *following*
**ἀναβλέπω** 3 • 7 *to look up*
**ἀνερωτάω** 1 • 1 *to ask*
**ἀνθύπατος, ὁ** 7 • 7 *proconsul*
**ἄνομος** 3 • 17 *lawless*
**ἔθος, τό** 3 • 4 *habit, usage*
**ἐμβλέπω** 1 • 5 *to look at, gaze on*
**ἐμβριθής** 1 • 1 *dignified, serious*
**ἐπισείω** 1 • 1 *to shake at/against*
**ἡλικία, ἡ** 3 • 4 *age, time of life*
**Καῖσαρ, ὁ** 4 • 4 *emperor, Caesar*
**κἄν** 1 • 8 *even if*
**ὀμνύω** 5 • 9 *to swear, take an oath*
**ὁμολογέω** 3 • 18 *to grant, admit, confess*
**Πολύκαρπος, ὁ** [2] 28 • 39 *Polycarp*
**προσάγω** 2 • 7 *to bring (forward)*
**στάδιον, τό** 6 • 9 *arena, stadium*
**στενάζω** 2 • 3 *to sigh, groan*
**τύχη, ἡ** 3 • 3 *fortune*
3 **ἀδικέω** 1 • 7 *to do wrong*

**ἀνθύπατος, ὁ** 7 • 7 *proconsul*
**δουλεύω** 1 • 42 *to (perform the duties of a slave) serve, obey*
**ἔγκειμαι** 1 • 2 *to insist, warn urgently*
**ἕξ** 1 • 22 *six*
**λοιδορέω** 1 • 2 *to revile, abuse*
**ὀγδοήκοντα** 1 • 1 *eighty*
**ὀμνύω** 5 • 9 *to swear, take an oath*
**Πολύκαρπος, ὁ** 28 • 39 *Polycarp*

## Chapter 10

1 **ἀγνοέω** 3 • 11 *to not to know, be ignorant (of)*
**ἐπιμένω** 4 • 16 *to continue, persist in, persevere*
**Καῖσαρ, ὁ** [2] 4 • 4 *emperor, Caesar*
**κενοδοξέω** 1 • 1 *to vainly imagine*
**μανθάνω** 3 • 26 *to learn, appropriate to oneself*
**ὀμνύω** 5 • 9 *to swear, take an oath*
**προσποιέω** 1 • 1 *to make/act as though, pretend*
**τύχη, ἡ** [2] 3 • 3 *fortune*
**Χριστιανισμός, ὁ** 1 • 6 *the Christian way, Christianity*
**Χριστιανός, ὁ** 4 • 24 *Christ-follower, Christian*
2 **ἀνθύπατος, ὁ** 7 • 7 *proconsul*
**ἀξιόω** 2 • 14 *to consider worthy, deserving*
**ἀπολογέομαι** 1 • 1 *to defend oneself*
**ἀπονέμω** 1 • 3 *to assign, show pity, pay, accord*
**βλάπτω** 1 • 3 *to harm, injure*
**δῆμος, ὁ** 1 • 1 *people, populace, crowd*
**ἡγέομαι** 1 • 25 *to lead, guide*
**Πολύκαρπος, ὁ** 28 • 39 *Polycarp*
**προσήκω** 1 • 3 *to be fitting, be suitable, be proper, be one's duty*
**τάσσω** 1 • 4 *to arrange, put in place*

## Chapter 11

1 **ἀμετάθετος** 1 • 1 *impossible*
**ἀνθύπατος, ἡ** 7 • 7 *proconsul*
**κρείττων** 1 • 8 *more prominent, higher in rank, preferable, better*
**μετάνοια, ἡ** 1 • 72 *repentance, turning about, conversion*
**μετατίθημι** 2 • 9 *to change one's mind, turn away, desert*
**παραβάλλω** 1 • 3 *to throw to*
**χαλεπός** 1 • 5 *hard, difficult*
**χείρων** 1 • 4 *worse, more severe*
2 **ἀγνοέω** 3 • 11 *to not to know, be ignorant (of)*
**ἀπειλέω** 1 • 1 *to threaten, warn*
**ἀσεβής** 1 • 14 *irreverent, impious, ungodly*
**βραδύνω** 1 • 2 *to hesitate, delay*
**δαπανάω** 2 • 7 *to wear out, destroy*
**καίω** 6 • 11 *to light, have/keep burning*
**καταφρονέω** 2 • 9 *to care nothing for, disregard, be unafraid of*
**κόλασις, ἡ** 4 • 11 *punishment*
**Πολύκαρπος, ὁ** 28 • 39 *Polycarp*
**σβέννυμι** 2 • 5 *to extinguish, put out*

## Chapter 12

1 **ἀνθύπατος, ὁ** 7 • 7 *proconsul*
**ἐμπίμπλημι/ἐμπίπλημι** 1 • 3 *to fill*
**ἐναντίον** 1 • 5 *on the other hand*
**ἐξίστημι** 1 • 2 *to be amazed, be astonished*
**θάρσος, τό** 1 • 2 *courage*
**κῆρυξ, ὁ** 3 • 4 *herald*
**ὁμολογέω** 3 • 18 *to grant, admit, confess*
**Πολύκαρπος, ὁ** 28 • 39 *Polycarp*
**στάδιον, τό** 6 • 9 *arena, stadium*
**συμπίπτω** 1 • 3 *to collapse*
**ταράσσω** 2 • 4 *to stir up, disturb, unsettle, throw into confusion*
**τρίς** 1 • 3 *three times, thrice*
**Χριστιανός, ὁ** 4 • 24 *Christ-follower, Christian*
2 **ἀκατάσχετος** 1 • 1 *uncontrollable*
**Ἀσία, ἡ** 1 • 10 *Asia*
**Ἀσιάρχης, ὁ** 1 • 1 *Asiarch*
**ἐπαφίημι** 1 • 1 *to let loose upon*
**ἐπειδή** 2 • 17 *(just) because*
**ἐπιβοάω** [2] 4 • 4 *to cry out loudly*
**ἡμέτερος** 2 • 13 *our*

**θυμός, ὁ** 1 • 6 *anger, wrath, rage, indignation*
**θύω** 1 • 3 *to sacrifice*
**καθαιρέτης, ὁ** 1 • 1 *destroyer*
**κῆρυξ, ὁ** 3 • 4 *herald*
**κυνηγέσιον, τό** 1 • 1 *animal hunt*
**λέων, ὁ** 1 • 3 *lion*
**Πολύκαρπος, ὁ** 28 • 39 *Polycarp*
**Σμύρνα, ἡ** 5 • 14 *Smyrna*
**Χριστιανός, ὁ** 4 • 24 *Christ-follower, Christian*
**πεπληρώκει** (pluperfect of πληρόω) *had fulfilled, brought to a close*
3 **ἐπιβοάω** 4 • 4 *to cry out loudly*
**καίω** [2] 6 • 11 *to burn (up)*
**κατακαίω** 2 • 4 *to burn down, burn up, consume*
**ὁμοθυμαδόν** 1 • 1 *with one mind/purpose/impulse*
**ὀπτασία, ἡ** 2 • 2 *a vision, celestial sight*
**Πολύκαρπος, ὁ** 28 • 39 *Polycarp*
**προσκεφάλαιον, τό** 2 • 2 *cushion*
**προφητικῶς** 1 • 1 *prophetically*

## Chapter 13

1 **βαλανεῖον, τό** 1 • 1 *bathhouse*
**ἔθος, τό** 3 • 4 *habit, usage*
**ἐργαστήριον, τό** 1 • 1 *workshop*
**μάλιστα** 1 • 14 *most of all, above all, especially, particularly*
**ξύλον, τό** 1 • 23 *wood*
**παραχρῆμα** 1 • 2 *immediately*
**προθύμως** 2 • 5 *willingly, eagerly, freely*
**ταχέως** 1 • 4 *more quickly, faster;* **θᾶττον** Attic form of **ταχέως**
**τάχος, τό** 1 • 7 *speed, quickness, swiftness, haste*
**ταχύς** 2 • 18 *eager, quick*
**τοσοῦτος** 5 • 38 *so great/strong, to such extent*
**ὑπουργέω** 1 • 1 *to be helpful, assist;*
**ὑπουργούντων** (pres. participle of purpose; cf. *ExSyn* 635–37) *to be helpful, assist*
**φρύγανον, τό** 1 • 2 *pieces of dry wood/brushwood*
2 **ἀεί** 1 • 7 *continually, constantly*
**ἀποτίθημι** 2 • 13 *to take off*
**ἕνεκα** 2 • 15 *because of, on account of, for the sake of*
**ζώνη, ἡ** 1 • 1 *belt, girdle*
**κοσμέω** 1 • 10 *to adorn, decorate;* **ἐκεκόσμητο** (pluperfect pass.) *he had been adorned*
**πειράω** 1 • 2 *to try, attempt, endeavor*
**πολιά, ἡ** 1 • 1 *old age*
**πολιτεία, ἡ** 2 • 5 *way of life, conduct*
**πρότερος** 1 • 47 *earlier, formerly, in former times*
**πυρκαϊά, ἡ** 1 • 1 *funeral pyre*
**σπουδάζω** 1 • 14 *to hurry, hasten*
**ταχύς** 2 • 5 *quick*
**ὑπολύω** 1 • 1 *to take off one's sandals/shoes*
**χρώς, ὁ** 1 • 1 *skin*
3 **ἁρμόζω** 1 • 23 *to join*
**ἄσκυλτος** 1 • 1 *unmoved, without moving*
**ἀσφαλεία, ἡ** 1 • 1 *security*
**ἐπιμένω** 4 • 16 *to stay, remain*
**ἧλος, ὁ** 1 • 1 *nail*
**ὄργανον, τό** 1 • 3 *tool*
**περιτίθημι** 1 • 6 *to put/place around/on*
**προσηλόω** 1 • 1 *to nail (fast)*
**πυρά, ἡ** [2] 2 • 2 *fire*
**ὑμέτερος** 1 • 4 *belonging to, incumbent upon you*
**ὑπομένω** 4 • 32 *to stand one's ground, hold out, endure*

## Chapter 14

1 **ἀναβλέπω** 3 • 7 *to look up*
**γένος, τό** 3 • 16 *nation, people*
**δεκτός** 1 • 9 *pleasing, acceptable*
**ἐπίγνωσις, ἡ** 1 • 3 *knowledge, recognition*
**ἐπίσημος** 2 • 2 *splendid, prominent, outstanding*
**εὐλογητός** 1 • 3 *blessed, praised*
**καθηλόω** 1 • 4 *to nail on*
**κριός, ὁ** 1 • 1 *male sheep, ram*
**κτίσις, ἡ** 1 • 19 *that which is created*
**ὁλοκαύτωμα, τό** 1 • 7 *whole burnt offering, holocaust*
**παῖς, ὁ/ἡ** 3 • 20 *child, as 'son' or 'daughter'*

**παντοκράτωρ, ὁ** 2 • 12 *Almighty, All-powerful, Omnipotent (One)*
**ποίμνιον, τό** 1 • 1 *flock*
**προσδέω** [2] 2 • 3 *to tie, bond*
**προσφορά, ἡ** 1 • 6 *offering*
2 **ἀληθινός** 1 • 14 *true, trustworthy*
**ἀριθμός, ὁ** 1 • 14 *number*
**ἀφθαρσία, ἡ** 3 • 12 *incorruptibility, immortality*
**ἀψευδής** 1 • 2 *truthful, trustworthy*
**θυσία, ἡ** 1 • 22 *sacrifice, offering*
**καταξιόω** 1 • 14 *to consider worthy*
**πίων** 1 • 1 *fat*
**προετοιμάζω** 1 • 5 *to prepare beforehand*
**προσδεκτός** 1 • 3 *acceptable*
**προσδέχομαι** 1 • 10 *to receive in a friendly manner*;
  **προσδεχθείην** (voluntative optative) *I might be received/ welcomed*
**προφανερόω** 1 • 5 *to reveal beforehand/in advance*
3 **αἰνέω** 1 • 2 *to praise*
**ἐπουράνιος** 3 • 11 *heavenly, in heaven*
**παῖς, ὁ/ἡ** 3 • 20 *child, as 'son' or 'daughter'*

## Chapter 15

1 **ἀναγγέλλω** 1 • 8 *to disclose, announce, proclaim, teach*
**ἀναπέμπω** 1 • 3 *to send up*
**ἐκλάμπω** 1 • 2 *to shine (out)*
**ἐξάπτω** 1 • 1 *to light, kindle*
**εὐχή, ἡ** 1 • 5 *prayer*
**θαῦμα, τό** 1 • 2 *wonder*
**φλόξ, ἡ** 1 • 2 *flame*
2 **ἀντιλαμβάνω** 1 • 2 *to perceive, notice*
**ἄργυρος, ὁ** 1 • 3 *silver*
**ἄρωμα, τό** 1 • 2 *fragrant spice/ salve/oil/perfume*
**εἶδος, τό** 1 • 6 *form, outward appearance*
**εὐωδία, ἡ** 1 • 2 *aroma, fragrance*
**καίω** 6 • 11 *to burn (up)*
**καμάρα, ἡ** 1 • 1 *arch, vault, vaulted room*
**κάμινος, ἡ** 1 • 3 *oven, furnace*
**κύκλῳ** 1 • 18 *around*
**λιβανωτός, ὁ** 1 • 1 *(frank)incense*
**ὀθόνη, ἡ** 1 • 1 *linen cloth, sheet*
**ὀπτάω** 1 • 1 *to bake*
**περιτειχίζω** 1 • 3 *to surround*
**πνέω** 1 • 2 *to breathe out*
**πυρόω** 1 • 2 *to make red hot, cause to glow, heat thoroughly*
**τίμιος** 2 • 2 *costly, precious*
**τοσοῦτος** 5 • 38 *so great/strong, to such extent*
**χρυσός, ὁ** 1 • 3 *gold*

## Chapter 16

1 **ἄνομος** 3 • 17 *lawless*
**ἄπιστος** 1 • 8 *without faith, disbelieving, unbelieving*
**γοῦν** 2 • 4 *hence, then*
**δαπανάω** 2 • 7 *to wear out, destroy*
**διαφορά, ἡ** 1 • 3 *difference*
**ἐκλεκτός** 4 • 30 *chosen*
**κατασβέννυμι** 1 • 1 *to put out, quench*
**κελεύω** 2 • 44 *to command, order, urge*
**κομφέκτωρ, ὁ** 1 • 1 *executioner*
**μεταξύ** 1 • 10 *between*
**ξιφίδιον, τό** 1 • 1 *short sword, dagger*
**παραβύω** 1 • 1 *to plunge into*
**πέρας, τό** 1 • 13 *end, limit boundary*;
  **πέρας γοῦν** (adverbial marker of time or logical summation) *finally, in conclusion, further(more)*
**τοσοῦτος** 5 • 38 *so much, so great*
2 **ἀποστολικός** 1 • 4 *apostolic*
**ἐπίσκοπος, ὁ** 2 • 76 *overseer, supervisor*
**θαυμάσιος** 2 • 4 *wonderful, remarkable, admirable*
**Πολύκαρπος, ὁ** 28 • 39 *Polycarp*
**προφητικός** 1 • 3 *prophetic*
**Σμύρνα, ἡ** 5 • 14 *Smyrna*
**τελειόω** [2] 2 • 14 *to fulfill*

## Chapter 17

1 **ἀναντίρρητος** 1 • 1 *not to be contradicted, undeniable*

**ἀνεπίληπτος/ἀνεπίλημπτος** 1 • 1 *irreproachable*
**ἀντίζηλος, ὁ** 1 • 1 *jealous one, adversary*
**ἀντίκειμαι** 1 • 2 *to be in opposition to*
**ἀποφέρω** 1 • 9 *to carry off, win*
**ἀφθαρσία, ἡ** 3 • 12 *incorruptibility, immortality*
**βάσκανος, ὁ** 1 • 1 *envious one*
**βραβεῖον, τό** 1 • 2 *prize, reward*
**γένος, τό** 3 • 16 *nation, people*
**ἐπιθυμέω** 2 • 17 *to desire, long for*
**ἐπιτηδεύω** 1 • 1 *to take care*
**καίπερ** 1 • 7 *although*
**κοινωνέω** 1 • 2 *to share, have a share*
**μέγεθος, τό** 1 • 5 *greatness*
**πολιτεία, ἡ** 2 • 5 *way of life, conduct*
**σαρκίον, τό** 1 • 1 *piece of flesh, bit of flesh*
**στέφανος, ὁ** 2 • 7 *prize, reward*
**στεφανόω** 2 • 8 *to prize, reward*
**σωμάτιον, τό** 1 • 1 *little body,* especially *poor little body*

2 **ἀγνοέω** 3 • 11 *to not to know, be ignorant of*
**Ἄλκη, ἡ** 1 • 3 *Alce*
**ἄμωμος** 1 • 17 *blameless*
**γοῦν** 2 • 4 *hence, then*
**ἐνισχύω** 1 • 2 *to strengthen*
**ἐντυγχάνω** 1 • 8 *to approach, appeal*
**καταλείπω** 1 • 12 *to leave (behind)*
**Νικήτης, ὁ** 2 • 2 *Nicetes*
**ποτέ** 3 • 15 *at any time, ever*
**σέβω** [2] 2 • 6 *to worship*
**ὑποβάλλω** [2] 2 • 2 *to instigate (secretly), suborn*

3 **ἀνυπέρβλητος** 1 • 2 *unsurpassable, unexcelled*
**ἀξίως** 1 • 5 *worthily, in a manner worthy of, suitably*
**ἕνεκα** 2 • 15 *because of, on account of, for the sake of*
**εὔνοια, ἡ** 1 • 3 *favor, affection, benevolence*
**μιμητής, ὁ** 2 • 12 *imitator*
**συγκοινωνός, ὁ** 1 • 1 *participant, partner*
**συμμαθητής, ὁ** 1 • 1 *fellow-pupil, fellow-disciple*

## Chapter 18

1 **ἔθος, τό** 3 • 4 *habit, usage*
**καίω** 6 • 11 *to burn (up)*
**κεντυρίων, ὁ** 1 • 1 *centurion*
**φιλονεικία, ἡ** 1 • 1 *contentiousness*

2 **ἀκόλουθος** 3 • 8 *following*
**ἀναιρέω** 1 • 10 *to take away*
**ἀποτίθημι** 2 • 13 *to put away, lay down*
**δόκιμος** 1 • 1 *precious*;
  **δοκιμώτερα ὑπέρ** (preposition is marker of degree) *more precious than*
**ὀστέον, τό** 1 • 6 *bone*
**πολυτελής** 1 • 3 *(very) expensive, costly*
**τίμιος** 2 • 3 *of great worth/value, precious*
**ὕστερος** 1 • 3 *in the second place, later, then, thereafter*
**χρυσίον, τό** 1 • 3 *gold*

3 **ἀγαλλίασις, ἡ** 1 • 5 *exultation*
**ἄσκησις, ἡ** 1 • 1 *practice*
**γενέθλιος** 1 • 1 *birthday*
**ἔνθα** 1 • 2 *there*
**ἐπιτελέω** 1 • 15 *to complete, accomplish, perform, bring about*
**ἑτοιμασία, ἡ** 1 • 1 *readiness, preparation*
**μαρτύριον, τό** 5 • 16 *martyrdom*
**μνήμη, ἡ** 1 • 3 *recollection, memory*
**παρέχω** 1 • 18 *to grant, show*
**προαθλέω** 1 • 1 *to compete in former times*

## Chapter 19

1 **δωδέκατος** 1 • 3 *twelfth*
**ἔξοχος** 1 • 2 *prominent*
**ἐπιθυμέω** 2 • 17 *to desire, long for*
**ἐπίσημος** 2 • 2 *splendid, prominent, outstanding*
**μαρτύριον, τό** 5 • 16 *martyrdom*
**μιμέομαι** 1 • 4 *to imitate, emulate, follow*
**μνημονεύω** 2 • 25 *to remember, keep in mind, think of, mention*
**παντοκράτωρ, ὁ** 2 • 12 *Almighty, All-powerful, Omnipotent (One)*
**Πολύκαρπος, ὁ** 28 • 39 *Polycarp*

**Σμύρνα, ἡ** 5 • 14 *Smyrna*
**Φιλαδελφία, ἡ** 1 • 4 *Philadelphia*
2 **ἀγαλλιάω** 1 • 11 *to exult, be glad, overjoyed*
**ἄδικος** 2 • 14 *unjust, crooked*
**ἀπολαμβάνω** 1 • 17 *to receive*
**ἀφθαρσία, ἡ** 3 • 12 *incorruptibility, immortality*
**καθολικός** 4 • 6 *general, universal*
**καταγωνίζομαι** 1 • 1 *to conquer, defeat, overcome*
**κυβερνήτης, ὁ** 1 • 2 *pilot*
**οἰκουμένη, ἡ** 3 • 6 *the inhabited earth, the world*
**ποιμήν, ὁ** 1 • 54 *shepherd*
**στέφανος, ὁ** 2 • 7 *wreath, crown*
**σωτήρ, ὁ** 1 • 14 *savior, deliverer, preserver*

## Chapter 20

1 **ἀξιόω** 2 • 14 *to consider worthy, deserving*
**δηλόω** 2 • 49 *to reveal, make clear, show*
**διαπέμπω** 1 • 1 *to send on*
**ἐκλογή, ἡ** 1 • 3 *selection, choice, election*
**ἐπέκεινα** 1 • 1 *farther on, beyond*
**ἐπιστολή, ἡ** 1 • 13 *letter, epistle*
**κεφάλαιον, τό** 1 • 2 *main thing, main point*
**μανθάνω** 3 • 26 *to learn*
**μηνύω** 1 • 1 *to inform, make known, reveal*
**Μαρκίων, ὁ** 3 • 3 *Marcion*
**πάρειμι** 4 • 17 *to be present*
2 **δωρεά, ἡ** 1 • 1 *gift, bounty*
**εἰσάγω** 2 • 6 *to bring* or *lead in/into*
**ἐπουράνιος** 3 • 11 *heavenly, in heaven*
**Εὐάρεστος, ὁ** 1 • 1 *Evarestus*
**κράτος, τό** 1 • 7 *power, rule, sovereignty*
**μεγαλωσύνη, ἡ** 2 • 10 *majesty*
**μονογενής** 1 • 3 *unique (in kind)*
**παῖς, ὁ/ἡ** 3 • 20 *child, as 'son' or 'daughter'*
**πανοικεί/πανοικί** 1 • 1 *with one's whole household*
**προσαγορεύω** [2] 2 • 5 *to greet*

## Chapter 21

1 **ἀνθυπατεύω** 1 • 1 *to be proconsul*
**βασιλεύω** 1 • 4 *to be king, rule*
**καλάνδαι, αἱ** 1 • 2 *the calends*
**Κοδράτος, ὁ** 1 • 2 *Quadratus*
**μεγαλωσύνη, ἡ** 2 • 10 *majesty*
**μήν, ὁ** 1 • 2 *month*
**Μάρτιος, ὁ** 1 • 1 *March*
**Ξανθικός, ὁ** 1 • 1 *Xanthicus;* a month in the Macedonian calendar; the second of the month would be February 22 or 23, the date of Polycarp's martyrdom.
**ὄγδοος** 1 • 5 *eighth;*
**ὥρᾳ ὀγδόῃ** *eighth hour—that is, 2 PM*
**Πολύκαρπος, ὁ** 28 • 39 *Polycarp*
**Στάτιος, ὁ** 1 • 1 *Statius*
**συλλαμβάνω** 5 • 11 *to seize, grasp, apprehend*
**Τραλλιάνος, ὁ** 1 • 1 *Trallian, from Tralles*

## Chapter 22

1 **ἐκλεκτός** 4 • 30 *chosen*
**εὔχομαι** 1 • 16 *to wish*
**ἴχνος, τό** 1 • 2 *footprint;*
**πρὸς τὰ ἴχνη** *in (whose) steps*
**Πολύκαρπος, ὁ** 28 • 39 *Polycarp*
**ῥώννυμι** 1 • 10 *to strengthen;*
**Ἐρρῶσθαι** (perfect pass.) *farewell, goodbye*
**στοιχέω** 1 • 1 *to hold to, agree with, follow, conform to*
2 **ἀντίγραφον, τό** 3 • 4 *a copy*
**Γάϊος, ὁ** [2] 5 • 5 *Gaius*
**Εἰρηναῖος, ὁ** [2] 8 • 19 *Irenaeus*
**Κόρινθος, ἡ** 2 • 3 *Corinth*
**μεταγράφω** 3 • 5 *to copy, transcribe*
**Πολύκαρπος, ὁ** 28 • 39 *Polycarp*
**συμπολιτεύομαι** 2 • 2 *to live in the same state, be a fellow-citizen/compatriot*
**Σωκράτης, ὁ** 1 • 1 *Socrates*
3 **ἀναζητέω** 1 • 1 *to look or search (for someone)*
**ἀποκάλυψις, ἡ** 2 • 18 *revelation, disclosure*

δηλόω 2 • 49 *to reveal, make clear, show*
ἐκλεκτός 4 • 30 *chosen*
καθεξῆς 1 • 2 *in order, one after the other*
κάμνω 2 • 3 *to be weary, be fatigued*
οὐράνιος 1 • 1 *heavenly*
Πιόνιος, ὁ 2 • 2 *Pionius*
Πολύκαρπος, ὁ 28 • 39 *Polycarp*
προγράφω 1 • 4 *to write before(hand)*
σχεδόν 3 • 4 *nearly, almost*

## Chapter 23

1 Γάϊος, ὁ 5 • 5 *Gaius*
Εἰρηναῖος, ὁ [2] 8 • 19 *Ireneaus*
μεταγράφω 3 • 5 *to copy, transcribe*
Πολύκαρπος, ὁ 28 • 39 *Polycarp*
σύγγραμμα, τό 4 • 6 *book, (written) work*
συμπολιτεύομαι 2 • 2 *to live in the same state, be a fellow-citizen/ compatriot*
2 αἵρεσις, ἡ 1 • 6 *sect, party, school, faction*
Εἰρηναῖος, ὁ 8 • 19 *Irenaeus*
ἐκκλησιαστικός 1 • 4 *to the (universal) church*
ἐλέγχω 1 • 16 *to reprove, correct*
ἐπίσκοπος, ὁ 2 • 76 *overseer, supervisor*
καθολικός 4 • 6 *general, universal*
κανών, ὁ 1 • 4 *rule, standard*
μανθάνω 3 • 26 *to learn*
μαρτύριον, τό 5 • 16 *martyrdom*
μιμνῄσκομαι 1 • 9 *to make mention of someone*
ὀρθός 1 • 5 *correct, true*
Πολύκαρπος, ὁ [2] 28 • 39 *Polycarp*
Ῥώμη, ἡ 1 • 8 *Rome*
σύγγραμμα, τό 4 • 6 *book, (written) work*
3 Μαρκίων, ὁ [2] 3 • 3 *Marcion*
Μαρκιωνιστής, ὁ 1 • 1 *Marcionite*
Πολύκαρπος, ὁ [2] 28 • 39 *Polycarp*
ποτέ 3 • 15 *at some time or other, once*
πρωτότοκος 1 • 4 *firstborn*
Σατανᾶς/Σατάν, ὁ 1 • 5 *Satan, adversary*
4 Πολύκαρπος, ὁ [2] 28 • 39 *Polycarp*
Ῥωμαῖος 1 • 3 *Roman*
σάλπιγξ, ἡ 1 • 2 *trumpet*
Σμύρνα, ἡ 5 • 14 *Smyrna*
σύγγραμμα, τό 4 • 6 *book, (written) work*
5 ἀντίγραφον, τό [2] 3 • 4 *a copy*
ἀποκάλυψις, ἡ 2 • 18 *revelation, disclosure*
Γάϊος, ὁ [2] 5 • 5 *Gaius*
Εἰρηναῖος, ὁ 8 • 19 *Irenaeus*
ἐκλεκτός 4 • 30 *chosen*
ἐπουράνιος 3 • 11 *heavenly, in heaven*
Ἰσοκράτης, ὁ [2] 2 • 2 *Isocrates*
κάμνω 2 • 3 *to be weary, be fatigued*
Κόρινθος, ἡ 2 • 3 *Corinth*
μεταγράφω 3 • 5 *to copy, transcribe*
Πιόνιος, ὁ 2 • 2 *Pionius*
Πολύκαρπος, ὁ 28 • 39 *Polycarp*
προλέγω 1 • 16 *to state beforehand/earlier*
σύγγραμμα, τό 4 • 6 *book, (written) work*
σχεδόν 3 • 4 *nearly, almost*

# The Didache

## Preface

διδαχή, ἡ [2] 6 • 14 *teaching*

## Chapter 1

1 διαφορά, ἡ 1 • 3 *difference*
μεταξύ 1 • 10 *between*
2 πλησίον 3 • 17 *near, close;* subst. *neighbor, fellow human being*
3 διδαχή, ἡ 6 • 14 *teaching*
καταράομαι 1 • 5 *to curse, execrate*
νηστεύω 4 • 23 *to fast*
4 ἀγγαρεύω 1 • 1 *to requisition, press into service, force, compel*
ἀπαιτέω 2 • 4 *to ask for, demand (back)*
ἀπέχω 1 • 35 *to keep away, abstain, refrain from*
μίλιον, τό 1 • 1 *mile*
ῥάπισμα, τό 1 • 2 *a slap in the face*
σαρκικός 1 • 10 *(merely) human, fleshly*
σιαγών, ἡ 1 • 2 *cheek*
σός 3 • 9 *your, yours*
στρέφω 4 • 5 *to turn*
σωματικός 1 • 1 *body-related, bodily*
τέλειος 2 • 25 *perfect, fully developed*
χιτών, ὁ 1 • 3 *tunic, shirt*
5 ἀθῷος [2] 2 • 7 *innocent*
ἀπαιτέω 2 • 4 *to ask for, demand*
δίκη, ἡ 1 • 3 *punishment, penalty*; δίδωμι δίκην *pay a penalty*; here possibly *give an account*
ἐξετάζω 1 • 3 *to question, examine*
ἱνατί 2 • 6 *why, for what reason?*
κοδράντης, ὁ 1 • 1 *quadrans, penny*
μέχρι 2 • 23 *until*
συνοχή, ἡ 1 • 1 *prison*; here possibly *place of exclusion* (from the Eucharist?)
χάρισμα, τό 1 • 6 *favor bestowed, gift*
6 ἐλεημοσύνη, ἡ 2 • 5 *alms*
ἱδρόω 1 • 1 *to sweat, perspire*
μέχρι 2 • 23 *until*

## Chapter 2

1 διδαχή, ἡ 6 • 14 *teaching*
2 ἐπιθυμέω 1 • 17 *to desire, long for*
κλέπτω 1 • 3 *to steal*
μαγεύω 1 • 1 *to practice magic*
μοιχεύω 1 • 3 *to commit adultery*
παιδοφθορέω 1 • 2 *to commit sodomy, sexually molest (children)*
πλησίον 3 • 17 *near, close*; subst. *neighbor, fellow human being;* τὰ τοῦ πλησίον *(your) neighbor's possessions* (lit., 'the things of the neighbor'; cf. BDF §266.3)
πορνεύω 1 • 2 *to engage in illicit sex, fornicate, whore*
φαρμακεύω 1 • 1 *to practice magic*
φθορά, ἡ 1 • 4 *abortion*
φονεύω [2] 2 • 4 *to murder, kill*
3 ἐπιορκέω 1 • 1 *to swear falsely, perjure oneself*
κακολογέω 1 • 1 *to speak evil of, revile, insult*
μνησικακέω 1 • 9 *to remember evil, bear malice, bear a grudge*
ψευδομαρτυρέω 1 • 1 *to bear false witness, give false testimony*
4 διγλωσσία, ἡ 1 • 1 *duplicity, insincerity* (or *double tongue)*
δίγλωσσος 1 • 2 *insincere, deceitful* (or *double-tongued)*
διγνώμων 1 • 2 *double-minded, fickle*
παγίς, ἡ 1 • 2 *trap, snare*
5 κενός 1 • 27 *empty*
μεστόω 1 • 1 *to fill*
πρᾶξις, ἡ 2 • 50 *act, action, deed*
ψευδής 1 • 4 *false, lying*

6 **ἅρπαξ** 1 • 1 *rapacious, ravenous;* subst. *robber*
**βουλή, ἡ** 1 • 19 *resolution, decision*
**κακοήθης** 1 • 1 *malicious, spiteful*
**πλεονέκτης, ὁ** 1 • 3 *a greedy person*
**πλησίον** 3 • 17 *near, close;* subst. *neighbor, fellow human being*
**ὑπερήφανος** 1 • 6 *arrogant, haughty, proud*
**ὑποκριτής, ὁ** 3 • 6 *pretender, dissembler*
7 **ἐλέγχω** 3 • 16 *to reprove, correct*
**ὑπὲρ τὴν ψυχήν σου** *more than your soul, more than your own life* (comparative use of ὑπέρ; cf. *ExSyn* 383)

## Chapter 3

1 **φεύγω** 1 • 20 *to flee from, avoid, shun*
2 **ἐριστικός** 1 • 1 *contentious, quarrelsome*
**ζηλωτής, ὁ** 1 • 3 *a jealous person*
**θυμικός** 1 • 1 *hot-tempered, irascible*
**ὁδηγέω** 5 • 5 *to lead, guide, conduct*
**ὀργίλος** 1 • 1 *inclined to anger, quick-tempered*
**φόνος, ὁ** [2] 3 • 4 *murder, killing*
3 **αἰσχρολόγος, ὁ** 1 • 1 *a foul-mouthed person*
**ἐπιθυμητής, ὁ** 1 • 1 *one who is lustful*
**μοιχεία, ἡ** 2 • 9 *adultery*
**ὁδηγέω** 5 • 5 *to lead, guide, conduct*
**πορνεία, ἡ** 2 • 5 *prostitution, unchastity, fornication*
**ὑψηλόφθαλμος** 1 • 1 *lifting up the eyes* (in lust)
4 **εἰδωλολατρία, ἡ** [2] 3 • 3 *image-worship, idolatry*
**ἐπαοιδός, ὁ** 1 • 1 *enchanter*
**ἐπειδή** 3 • 17 *(just) because*
**μαθηματικός** 1 • 1 *astrologer*
**ὁδηγέω** 5 • 5 *to lead, guide, conduct*
**οἰωνοσκόπος, ὁ** 1 • 1 *soothsayer, augur*
**περικαθαίρω** 1 • 1 *to purify completely;* here *practice magic*
5 **ἐπειδή** 3 • 17 *(just) because*
**κενόδοξος** 1 • 1 *conceited, boastful*
**κλοπή, ἡ** [2] 3 • 3 *theft, stealing*
**ὁδηγέω** 5 • 5 *to lead, guide, conduct*
**φιλάργυρος** 1 • 1 *fond of money, avaricious*
**ψεῦσμα, τό** 1 • 3 *lying, untruthfulness, undependability*
**ψεύστης, ὁ** 1 • 2 *liar*
6 **αὐθάδης** 1 • 5 *self-willed, stubborn, arrogant*
**βλασφημία, ἡ** [2] 2 • 7 *reviling, denigration, disrespect, slander*
**γόγγυσος** 1 • 1 *complaining;* subst. *grumbler*
**ἐπειδή** 3 • 17 *(just) because*
**ὁδηγέω** 5 • 5 *to lead, guide, conduct*
**πονηρόφρων** 1 • 1 *evil-minded*
7 **ἐπεί** 2 • 35 *because, since, for*
**κληρονομέω** 1 • 11 *to acquire, obtain, come into possession of*
**πραΰς** [2] 3 • 8 *gentle, humble, considerate, meek*
8 **ἄκακος** 1 • 7 *innocent, guileless*
**ἐλεήμων** 1 • 4 *merciful, sympathetic, compassionate*
**ἡσύχιος** 1 • 7 *quiet, well-ordered*
**μακρόθυμος** 1 • 9 *patient, forbearing, tolerant, even-tempered*
**τρέμω** 1 • 3 *to tremble, be in awe*
9 **ἀναστρέφω** 1 • 8 *to associate (with someone)*
**θράσος, τό** 1 • 3 *arrogance, shamelessness*
**κολλάω** 2 • 32 *to cling to, attach to*
**ταπεινός** 1 • 8 *humble*
**ὑψηλός** 1 • 12 *exalted, proud, haughty*
**ὑψόω** 1 • 4 *to exalt*
10 **ἄτερ** 1 • 6 *without*
**ἐνέργημα, τό** 1 • 2 *experience*
**προσδέχομαι** 1 • 10 *to receive*
**συμβαίνω** 1 • 7 *to happen, come about*

## Chapter 4

1 **κυριότης, ἡ** 1 • 2 *the Lord's nature*; here possibly *his lordship*
**μιμνῄσκομαι** 2 • 9 *to remember, think of, care for, be concerned about, keep in mind*
**ὅθεν** 1 • 16 *from where, whence, from which*
**τιμάω** 2 • 12 *to honor, revere*
2 **ἐκζητέω** 1 • 16 *to seek out, search for*
**ἐπαναπαύομαι** 1 • 3 *to find rest, comfort, support*
3 **δικαίως** 1 • 12 *justly, in an upright manner*
**εἰρηνεύω** 1 • 17 *to reconcile*
**ἐλέγχω** 3 • 16 *to reprove, correct*
**μάχομαι** 1 • 2 *to fight, quarrel, dispute*
**παράπτωμα, τό** 3 • 10 *offense, wrongdoing, sin*
**σχίσμα, τό** 1 • 10 *division, dissension, schism*
4 **διψυχέω** 1 • 25 *to be undecided, be changeable, doubt*
**πότερος** 1 • 3 *whether*
5 **ἐκτείνω** 1 • 7 *to stretch out*
**συσπάω** 1 • 2 *to draw together*
6 **λύτρωσις, ἡ** 1 • 2 *ransom; ransom(-money)*
7 **ἀνταποδότης, ὁ** 1 • 2 *recompenser, paymaster*
**γογγύζω** 1 • 1 *to grumble, murmur*
**διστάζω** 1 • 10 *to hesitate*
**μισθός, ὁ** 2 • 22 *recompense*
8 **ἀθάνατος** 1 • 5 *immortal*
**ἀποστρέφω** 2 • 8 *to reject, repudiate*
**ἐνδέω** 2 • 5 *to be in want*
**θνητός** 1 • 5 *mortal*
**κοινωνός, ὁ/ἡ** 1 • 7 *companion, partner, sharer*
**πόσος** 1 • 10 *how great?*
**συγκοινωνέω** 1 • 1 *to share*
9 **θυγάτηρ, ἡ** 1 • 10 *daughter*
**νεότης, ἡ** 1 • 3 *youth*
10 **ἀμφότεροι** 2 • 21 *both*
**ἐπιτάσσω** 1 • 7 *to order, command*
**μήποτε** 1 • 22 *that ... not*
**παιδίσκη, ἡ** 1 • 3 *female slave*
**πικρία, ἡ** 1 • 7 *bitterness, animosity, anger, harshness*
11 **αἰσχύνη, ἡ** 1 • 2 *modesty, reverence*
**τύπος, ὁ** 1 • 26 *copy, image*
12 **ἀρεστός** 1 • 2 *pleasing*
**ὑπόκρισις, ἡ** 2 • 13 *play-acting, pretense, outward show, dissembling*
13 **ἀφαιρέω** 1 • 8 *to take away, do away with, remove*
**ἐγκαταλείπω** 1 • 8 *to forsake, abandon, desert*
**προστίθημι** 2 • 22 *to add, put to*
14 **ἐξομολογέω** 1 • 15 *to confess, admit*
**παράπτωμα, τό** 3 • 10 *offense, wrongdoing, sin*

## Chapter 5

1 **αἰσχρολογία, ἡ** 1 • 1 *obscene speech, dirty talk*
**ἀλαζονεία, ἡ** 1 • 10 *pretension, arrogance*
**ἁρπαγή, ἡ** 1 • 3 *robbery, plunder*
**αὐθάδεια, ἡ** 1 • 6 *arrogance, willfulness, stubbornness*
**διπλοκαρδία, ἡ** 1 • 2 *duplicity*
**δόλος, ὁ** 1 • 8 *deceit, cunning, treachery*
**εἰδωλολατρία, ἡ** 3 • 3 *image-worship, idolatry*
**ζηλοτυπία, ἡ** 1 • 1 *jealousy*
**θρασύτης, ἡ** 1 • 2 *boldness, arrogance*
**κακία, ἡ** 1 • 9 *malice, ill-will, malignity*
**κατάρα, ἡ** 1 • 4 *curse, imprecation*
**κλοπή, ἡ** 3 • 3 *theft, stealing*
**μαγεία, ἡ** 1 • 3 *magic*
**μεστός** 1 • 4 *filled (with something)*
**μοιχεία, ἡ** 2 • 9 *adultery*
**πλεονεξία, ἡ** 1 • 7 *greediness, insatiableness, avarice, covetousness*
**πορνεία, ἡ** 2 • 5 *prostitution, unchastity, fornication*
**ὑπερηφανία, ἡ** 1 • 8 *arrogance, haughtiness, pride*

**ὑπόκρισις, ἡ** 2 • 13 *play-acting, pretense, outward show, dissembling*
**ὕψος, τό** 1 • 7 *pride, arrogance*
**φαρμακία/φαρμακεία, ἡ** 1 • 2 *sorcery, magic*
**φόνος, ὁ** 3 • 4 *murder, killing*
**ψευδομαρτυρία, ἡ** 1 • 4 *false testimony*
2 **ἀγρυπνέω** 1 • 2 *to look after, care for*
**ἄνομος** 1 • 17 *lawless*
**ἀνταπόδομα, τό** 1 • 3 *repayment, reward*; here possibly *recompense*
**ἀποστρέφω** 2 • 8 *to reject, repudiate*
**διώκτης, ὁ** 1 • 2 *persecutor*
**ἐλεέω** 1 • 16 *to have compassion/mercy/pity*
**ἐνδέω** 2 • 5 *to be in want*
**θλίβω** 1 • 25 *to oppress, afflict*
**καταπονέω** [2] 2 • 4 *to subdue, torment, wear out, oppress*
**κολλάω** 2 • 32 *to cling to*
**κριτής, ὁ** 1 • 6 *a judge*
**μακράν** 1 • 15 *far (away)*
**μάταιος** 1 • 14 *idle, empty, fruitless, useless, powerless, lacking truth*
**μισθός, ὁ** 2 • 22 *recompense*
**πανθαμαρτητός** 1 • 1 *altogether sinful*
**παράκλητος, ὁ** 1 • 3 *mediator, intercessor, helper*
**πένης** 1 • 16 *poor, needy*
**πλάσμα, τό** 1 • 3 *image, figure*
**πλούσιος** 1 • 22 *rich, wealthy*
**πονέω** 1 • 2 *to toil, undergo trouble*
**πραΰτης, ἡ** 1 • 8 *gentleness, humility, courtesy, considerateness, meekness*
**ῥύομαι** 3 • 19 *to save, rescue, deliver, preserve*;
**ῥυσθείητε** (voluntative optative) *May you be delivered*
**φθορεύς, ὁ** 2 • 4 *seducer*
**φονεύς, ὁ** 1 • 2 *murderer*
**ψεῦδος, τό** 1 • 6 *a lie, falsehood*

## Chapter 6

1 **διδαχή, ἡ** 6 • 14 *teaching*
**ἐπεί** 2 • 35 *because, since, for*
**παρεκτός** 1 • 1 *apart from, except for*
2 **βαστάζω** 2 • 24 *to carry, bear*
**ζυγός, ὁ** 1 • 3 *yoke*
**τέλειος** 2 • 25 *perfect*
3 **βαστάζω** 2 • 24 *to carry, bear*
**βρῶσις, ἡ** 1 • 4 *food*
**εἰδωλόθυτος** 1 • 1 *offered to a cultic image/idol*
**λατρεία, ἡ** 1 • 2 *service/worship (of God)*
**λίαν** 1 • 48 *very (much), exceedingly*
**προσέχω** 2 • 25 *to be concerned about, care for, take care*

## Chapter 7

1 **βάπτισμα, τό** 2 • 6 *plunging, dipping, washing, water-rite, baptism*
**προλέγω** 2 • 16 *to tell beforehand/in advance*
2 **θερμός** 1 • 1 *warm*
**ψυχρός** 1 • 2 *cold*
3 **ἀμφότεροι** 2 • 21 *both*
**ἐκχέω/ἐκχύννω** 1 • 6 *to pour out*
**τρίς** 2 • 3 *three times, thrice*
4 **βάπτισμα, τό** 2 • 6 *plunging, dipping, washing, water-rite, baptism*
**κελεύω** 2 • 44 *to command, order, urge*;
**κελεύεις** *you shall command* (the pres. indicative is probably a textual corruption of the future indicative κελεύσεις, an imperatival future [see *ExSyn* 569–70])
**νηστεύω** 4 • 23 *to fast*
**προνηστεύω** 1 • 1 *to fast beforehand*

## Chapter 8

1 **νηστεία, ἡ** 1 • 25 *fast*
**νηστεύω** [2] 4 • 23 *to fast*
**παρασκευή, ἡ** 1 • 2 *the day of preparation, Friday*
**πέμπτος** 1 • 5 *fifth, Thursday*

**τετράς, ἡ** 1 • 1 (the) *fourth* (day of the week), *Wednesday*
**ὑποκριτής, ὁ** 3 • 6 *pretender, dissembler*
2 **ἁγιάζω** 2 • 16 *to reverence*
**εἰσφέρω** 1 • 4 *to bring in*
**ἐπιούσιος** 1 • 1 *for the current day, for today; necessary for existence; for the following day*
**κελεύω** 2 • 44 *to command, order, urge*
**ὀφειλέτης, ἡ** 1 • 1 *debtor*
**ὀφειλή, ἡ** 1 • 1 *duty*
**πειρασμός, ὁ** 1 • 4 *temptation, enticement*
**ῥύομαι** 3 • 19 *to save, rescue, deliver, preserve*
**ὑποκριτής, ὁ** 3 • 6 *pretender, dissembler*
3 **τρίς** 2 • 3 *three times, thrice;* **τρὶς τῆς ἡμέρας** *three times during the day* (gen. of time)

## Chapter 9

1 **εὐχαριστία, ἡ** 2 • 7 *Lord's Supper, Eucharist*
2 **ἄμπελος, ἡ** 1 • 16 *vine, grapevine*
**γνωρίζω** 3 • 18 *to make known, reveal*
**παῖς, ὁ/ἡ** [2] 5 • 20 *slave, servant*
3 **γνωρίζω** 3 • 18 *to make known, reveal*
**γνῶσις, ἡ** 3 • 32 *knowledge*
**κλάσμα, τό** 2 • 2 *fragment, piece, crumb*; here *broken bread*
**παῖς, ὁ/ἡ** 5 • 20 *slave, servant*
4 **διασκορπίζω** 1 • 1 *to scatter, disperse*
**ἐπάνω** 2 • 8 *above, over*
**κλάσμα, τό** 2 • 2 *fragment, piece, crumb*; here *broken bread*
**πέρας, τό** 1 • 13 *end, limit, boundary*
**σός** 3 • 9 *your, yours*
5 **εὐχαριστία, ἡ** 2 • 7 *Lord's Supper, Eucharist*
**κύων, ὁ** 1 • 2 *dog;* fig. *an unqualified person*

## Chapter 10

1 **ἐμπίμπλημι/ἐμπίπλημι** 1 • 3 *to satisfy*
2 **ἀθανασία, ἡ** 1 • 3 *immortality*
**γνωρίζω** 3 • 18 *to make known, reveal*
**γνῶσις, ἡ** 3 • 32 *knowledge*
**κατασκηνόω** 1 • 3 *to cause to dwell*
**παῖς, ὁ/ἡ** [2] 5 • 20 *slave, servant*
3 **ἀπόλαυσις, ἡ** 1 • 6 *enjoyment*
**δεσπότης, ὁ** 1 • 52 *lord, master*
**ἕνεκα** 1 • 15 *because of, on account of, for the sake of*
**κτίζω** 1 • 25 *to create*
**παῖς, ὁ/ἡ** 5 • 20 *slave, servant*
**παντοκράτωρ, ὁ** 1 • 12 *Almighty, All-powerful, Omnipotent (One)*
**πνευματικός** 1 • 19 *spiritual, pertaining to the divine spirit*
**ποτόν, τό** [2] 2 • 3 *drink*
**τροφή, ἡ** [2] 4 • 12 *nourishment, food*
**χαρίζομαι** 1 • 5 *to give graciously*
5 **ἁγιάζω** 2 • 16 *to consecrate, dedicate, sanctify*
**ἄνεμος, ὁ** 1 • 4 *the four directions or cardinal points*
**μιμνῄσκομαι** 2 • 9 *to remember, think of, care for, be concerned about, keep in mind*
**ῥύομαι** 3 • 19 *to save, rescue, deliver, preserve*
**σός** 3 • 9 *your, yours*
**τελειόω** 2 • 14 *to make perfect*
**τέσσαρες** 1 • 12 *four*
6 **μαραναθά** 1 • 1 *Lord, come!*
**παρέρχομαι** 1 • 12 *to pass away, disappear*
**ὡσαννά** 1 • 1 *hosanna*
7 **ἐπιτρέπω** 1 • 11 *to allow, permit*

## Chapter 11

1 **προλέγω** 2 • 16 *to tell beforehand/in advance*
2 **γνῶσις, ἡ** 3 • 32 *knowledge*
**διδαχή, ἡ** 6 • 14 *teaching*
**καταλύω** 1 • 2 *to abolish, annul, make invalid*
**προστίθημι** 2 • 22 *to add, put to*

**στρέφω** 4 • 5 *to turn, change, pervert*
3 **δόγμα, τό** 1 • 10 *ordinance, decision, command*
5 **ψευδοπροφήτης, ὁ** 6 • 11 *false/ bogus prophet*
6 **ἀργύριον, τό** 3 • 3 *silver money, money*
**αὐλίζομαι** 1 • 2 *to spend the night*
**ψευδοπροφήτης, ὁ** 6 • 11 *false/ bogus prophet*
7 **διακρίνω** 1 • 7 *to pass judgment on*
8 **τρόπος, ὁ** [2] 2 • 17 *ways, customs, kind of life*
**ψευδοπροφήτης, ὁ** 6 • 11 *false/ bogus prophet*
9 **εἰ δὲ μήγε** 1 • 2 *otherwise*
**ὁρίζω** 1 • 10 *to determine, appoint, fix, set*
**τράπεζα, ἡ** 1 • 3 *a meal, food*
**ψευδοπροφήτης, ὁ** 6 • 11 *false/ bogus prophet*
10 **ψευδοπροφήτης, ὁ** 6 • 11 *false/ bogus prophet*
11 **ἀληθινός** 3 • 57 *genuine, authentic, real*
**ἀρχαῖος** 1 • 12 *ancient*
**δοκιμάζω** 3 • 19 *to test, approve*
**κοσμικός** 1 • 4 *earthly*
**μυστήριον, τό** 1 • 11 *transcendent/ ultimate reality, secret*
**ὡσαύτως** 3 • 7 *(in) the same (way), similarly, likewise*
12 **ἀργύριον, τό** 3 • 3 *silver money, money*
**ὑστερέω** 1 • 11 *to be needy, lack*

## Chapter 12

1 **ἀριστερός** 1 • 5 *left (*here *false* as opposed to δεξιός which here means *true)*
**δοκιμάζω** 3 • 19 *to put to the test, examine*
**ἔπειτα** 1 • 4 *then, thereupon*
**σύνεσις, ἡ** 2 • 22 *understanding*
2 **ἀνάγκη, ἡ** 1 • 11 *necessity, pressure*
**βοηθέω** 1 • 4 *to furnish aid*
**παρόδιος** 1 • 1 subst. *one who is traveling by*
3 **τεχνίτης, ὁ** 1 • 4 *craftsperson, artisan, designer*
4 **ἀργός** 1 • 6 *unemployed, idle*
**προνοέω** 1 • 3 *to take thought for, take into consideration, have regard for*
**σύνεσις, ἡ** 2 • 22 *intelligence, acuteness, shrewdness*
**τέχνη, ἡ** 1 • 3 *skill, trade*
**Χριστιανός, ὁ** 1 • 24 *Christ-follower, Christian*
5 **προσέχω** 2 • 25 *to beware of, be on one's guard against*
**χριστέμπορος, ὁ** 1 • 1 *Christmonger* ["one who carries on a cheap trade in (the teachings of) Christ"[1]]

## Chapter 13

1 **ἀληθινός** 3 • 14 *genuine, authentic, real*
**τροφή, ἡ** 4 • 12 *nourishment, food*
2 **ἀληθινός** 3 • 14 *genuine, authentic, real*
**ἐργάτης, ὁ** 1 • 3 *worker, laborer*
**τροφή, ἡ** 4 • 12 *nourishment, food*
**ὡσαύτως** 3 • 7 *(in) the same (way), similarly, likewise*
3 **ἅλων, ἡ** 1 • 3 *threshing floor*
**ἀπαρχή, ἡ** [2] 5 • 9 *first fruits, first portion*
**βοῦς, ἡ** 1 • 1 cow; pl. *cattle*
**γέννημα, τό** 1 • 1 *child, offspring;* here *produce*
**ληνός, ἡ** 1 • 1 *wine-press*
5 **ἀπαρχή, ἡ** 5 • 9 *first fruits, first portion*
**σιτία, ἡ** 1 • 1 *dough;*
**ἐὰν σιτίαν ποιῇς** *if you make bread*
6 **ἀπαρχή, ἡ** 5 • 9 *first fruits, first portion*
**ἔλαιον, τό** 1 • 4 *olive oil*
**κεράμιον, τό** 1 • 8 *an earthenware vessel, jar*
**ὡσαύτως** 3 • 7 *(in) the same (way), similarly, likewise*
7 **ἀπαρχή, ἡ** 5 • 9 *first fruits, first portion*

1. BDAG s.v. χριστέμπορος.

**ἀργύριον, τό** 3 • 3 *silver money, money*
**ἱματισμός, ὁ** 1 • 8 *clothing, apparel*
**κτῆμα, τό** 1 • 2 *possession*

## Chapter 14

1 **θυσία, ἡ** 3 • 22 *sacrifice, offering*
**καθαρός** 2 • 45 *pure*
**κλάω** 1 • 2 *to break*
**κυριακός** 1 • 9 *the Lord's*
**παράπτωμα, τό** 3 • 10 *offense, wrongdoing, sin*
**προεξομολογέομαι** 1 • 1 *to confess (one's sins) beforehand*
2 **ἀμφιβολία, ἡ** 1 • 1 *a quarrel*
**διαλλάσσομαι** 1 • 1 *to reconcile*
**ἑταῖρος, ὁ** 1 • 4 *comrade, companion*
**θυσία, ἡ** 3 • 22 *sacrifice, offering*
**κοινόω** 1 • 1 *to make common* or *impure; defile*
**συνέρχομαι** 1 • 4 *to assemble, gather, come together*
3 **καθαρός** 2 • 45 *pure*
**θαυμαστός** 1 • 13 *wonderful, marvelous, remarkable*
**θυσία, ἡ** 3 • 22 *sacrifice, offering*

## Chapter 15

1 **ἀληθής** 1 • 16 *truthful, righteous, honest*
**ἀφιλάργυρος** 1 • 2 *not loving money, not greedy*
**διάκονος, ὁ** 1 • 29 *assistant*
**δοκιμάζω** 3 • 19 *to prove, approve*
**λειτουργέω** 1 • 11 *to serve, render service*
**λειτουργία, ἡ** 1 • 11 *service*
**πραΰς** 3 • 8 *gentle, humble, considerate, meek*
**χειροτονέω** 1 • 4 *to choose*
2 **τιμάω** 2 • 12 *honor, revere*
**ὑπεροράω** 1 • 3 *to disdain, despise*
3 **ἀστοχέω** 1 • 2 *to miss, fail, deviate, depart*
**ἐλέγχω** 3 • 16 *to reprove, correct*
4 **ἐλεημοσύνη, ἡ** 2 • 5 *alms, charitable giving*
**εὐχή, ἡ** 1 • 5 *prayer*
**πρᾶξις, ἡ** 2 • 50 *act, action, deed*

## Chapter 16

1 **γρηγορέω** 1 • 2 *to be on the alert*
**ἐκλύω** 1 • 1 *to become weary, give out, be ungirded*
**ἕτοιμος** 1 • 9 *ready*
**λύχνος, ὁ** 1 • 2 *lamp*
**ὀσφύς, ἡ** 1 • 2 *the loins*
**σβέννυμι** 1 • 5 *to extinguish, put out*
2 **ἀνήκω** 1 • 10 *to refer, relate, belong*
**πυκνῶς** 1 • 3 *frequently, often*
**τελειόω** 2 • 14 *to make perfect*
**ὠφελέω** 1 • 8 *to help, aid, benefit, be of use (to)*
3 **λύκος, ὁ** 1 • 5 *wolf*
**μῖσος, τό** 1 • 2 *hate, hatred*
**πληθύνω** 1 • 11 *to grow, increase, multiply*
**στρέφω** [2] 4 • 5 *to turn, change*
**φθορεύς, ὁ** 2 • 4 *seducer, corrupter*
**ψευδοπροφήτης, ὁ** 6 • 11 *false, bogus prophet*
4 **ἀθέμιτος** 1 • 3 *wanton, disgusting, unseemly;*
**ποιεῖν ἀθέμιτα** *to commit lawless acts*
**ἀνομία, ἡ** 1 • 33 *lawlessness*
**αὐξάνω/αὔξω** 1 • 7 *to grow, increase*
**κοσμοπλανής, ὁ** 1 • 1 *deceiver of the world*
**οὐδέποτε** 1 • 6 *never*
**τέρας, τό** 1 • 4 *prodigy, portent, omen, wonder*
5 **δοκιμασία, ἡ** 1 • 1 *testing, examination*
**ἥκω** 2 • 11 *to have come, be present*
**κατάθεμα, τό** 1 • 1 *accursed thing*; BDAG: "D 16:5 is (perhaps purposely) obscure: σωθήσονται ὑπ' αὐτοῦ τοῦ κ. *they will be saved by the accursed one himself* (i.e. by Christ who, in the minds of those offended by him, is accursed; cp. also Gal 3:13 κατάρα...)"
**κτίσις, ἡ** 1 • 19 *that which is created*

**πύρωσις, ἡ** 1 • 1 *burning ordeal;* **τὴν πύρωσιν τῆς δοκιμασίας** *the fiery test* (attributed gen.; see *ExSyn* 89–91)
**σκανδαλίζω** 1 • 4 *to cause to sin;* pass. *be led into sin, let oneself be led into sin* (on permissive pass., see *ExSyn* 440–41)
**ὑπομένω** 1 • 32 *to stand one's ground, hold out, endure*
6 **εἶτα** 1 • 48 *then, next*
**ἐκπέτασις, ἡ** 1 • 1 *spreading out, opening*
**σάλπιγξ, ἡ** 1 • 2 *trumpet*
7 **ἥκω** 2 • 11 *to have come, be present*
8 **ἐπάνω** 2 • 8 *above, over*
**νεφέλη, ἡ** 1 • 1 *cloud*

# The Letter of Barnabas

## Chapter 1

1 **θυγάτηρ, ἡ** 2 • 10 *daughter*
2 **δικαίωμα, τό** 8 • 12 *righteous deed*
**δωρεά, ἡ** 1 • 7 *gift, bounty*
**ἔμφυτος** 2 • 2 *implanted*
**ἔνδοξος** 1 • 54 *glorious, splendid*
**πλούσιος** 5 • 22 *abound (in), rich (in)*
**πνευματικός** 3 • 19 *spiritual, caused by* or *filled with the divine spirit, pertaining to the divine spirit*
**ὑπερβολή, ἡ** 1 • 2 *excess, extraordinary quality/character*; **καθ᾽ ὑπερβολήν** *to an extraordinary degree, beyond measure, utterly*
**ὑπερευφραίνομαι** 1 • 1 *to rejoice exceedingly*
3 **ἀληθῶς** 4 • 23 *truly, in truth, really, actually*
**ἐκπλήσσω** 3 • 4 *to amaze, astound, overwhelm*
**ἐκχέω/ἐκχύννω** 1 • 6 *to pour out*
**ἐπιπόθητος** 1 • 2 *longed for, desired*
**ὄψις, ἡ** 1 • 6 *seeing, sight*
**πηγή, ἡ** 2 • 7 *fountainhead*
**πλούσιος** 5 • 22 *abound (in), rich (in)*;
subst. *riches*
**συγχαίρω** 1 • 7 *to congratulate*
4 **ἀναγκάζω** 1 • 3 *to compel, force*
**ἐγκατοικέω** 1 • 1 *to live, reside*
**ἐπίσταμαι** 1 • 7 *to know, be acquainted with*
**πάντως** 1 • 9 *altogether, totally*
**συνοδεύω** 1 • 1 *to travel together with*
**σύνοιδα** 1 • 2 *to know, be conscious of*
5 **γνῶσις, ἡ** 10 • 32 *knowledge*
**μέλει** 2 • 5 *it is a care/concern, is of interest to someone*
**μεταδίδωμι** 1 • 3 *to give (a part of), impart, share*
**μισθός, ὁ** 6 • 22 *recompense*
**σπουδάζω** 3 • 16 *to be zealous/eager, take pains, make every effort, be conscientious*
**τέλειος** 6 • 25 *perfect*
**ὑπηρετέω** 1 • 5 *to serve, be helpful*
6 **ἀγαλλίασις, ἡ** 1 • 5 *exultation*
**δόγμα, τό** 5 • 10 *command, ordinance, decision*
**εὐφροσύνη, ἡ** 4 • 5 *joy, gladness, cheerfulness*
7 **ἀπαρχή, ἡ** 1 • 9 *first fruits, first portion*
**γεῦσις, ἡ** 1 • 1 *taste*
**γνωρίζω** 2 • 18 *to make known, reveal*
**δεσπότης, ὁ** 2 • 52 *lord, master*
**ἐνεργέω** 2 • 4 *to work, be at work, be active, operate, be effective*
**ἐνίστημι** 4 • 6 *to be now, happen now*;
subst. *things of the present*
**παρέρχομαι** 2 • 12 *to pass*;
subst. participle *things of the past*
**πλουσίως** 1 • 1 *richly, abundantly*
**προσάγω** 4 • 7 *to bring (forward)*
**ὑψηλός** 4 • 12 *noble, sublime*
8 **εὐφραίνω** 4 • 15 *to be glad, enjoy oneself, rejoice, celebrate*
**πάρειμι** 2 • 17 *to be present*
**ὑποδείκνυμι** 1 • 3 *to show, give direction, prove, set forth*

## Chapter 2

1 **δικαίωμα, τό** 8 • 12 *righteous requirement, commandment*
**ἐκζητέω** 7 • 16 *to seek out, search for*
**ἐνεργέω** 2 • 4 *to be at work*
**προσέχω** 11 • 25 *to take care, be on guard*

2 **βοηθός** 1 • 4 *helpful;* subst. *helper*
**ἐγκράτεια, ἡ** 1 • 14 *self-control*
**μακροθυμία, ἡ** 1 • 15 *patience, forbearance*
**συμμαχέω** 1 • 1 *to be an ally, assist*
3 **ἁγνῶς** 1 • 6 *purely*
**γνῶσις, ἡ** 10 • 32 *knowledge*
**ἐπιστήμη, ἡ** 2 • 5 *understanding, knowledge*
**σύνεσις, ἡ** 3 • 22 *understanding, insight*
**συνευφραίνω** 1 • 1 *to rejoice together*
4 **θυσία, ἡ** 5 • 22 *sacrifice*
**ὁλοκαύτωμα, τό** 4 • 7 *whole burnt offering*
**ὁτέ** 6 • 21 *at one point*
**προσφορά, ἡ** 2 • 6 *offering*
**χρῄζω** 1 • 7 *to have need*
5 **ἀνέχομαι** 2 • 4 *to endure, put up with*
**ἀρνός, ὁ** 1 • 1 *lamb*
**αὐλή, ἡ** 1 • 1 *court*
**βδέλυγμα, τό** 1 • 1 *something detestable, loathsome*
**ἐκζητέω** 7 • 16 *to desire*
**θυμίαμα, τό** 1 • 1 *incense*
**θυσία, ἡ** 5 • 22 *sacrifice*
**μάταιος** 4 • 14 *vain, useless*
**νεομηνία, ἡ** 2 • 2 *new moon*
**ὁλοκαύτωμα, τό** 4 • 7 *whole burnt offering*
**πατέω** 1 • 2 *to tread on*
**πλήρης** 2 • 20 *full*
**προστίθημι** 2 • 22 *to add;* idiomatically: *to continue, do again*
**σεμίδαλις, ἡ** 1 • 1 *fine flour*
**στέαρ, τό** 1 • 2 *fat*
**ταῦρος, ὁ** 1 • 1 *bull*
**τράγος, ὁ** 6 • 6 *goat*
6 **ἀνάγκη, ἡ** 1 • 11 *necessity*
**ἄνευ** 2 • 12 *without*
**ἀνθρωποποίητος** 1 • 1 *made by man, something of human origin*
**ζυγός, ὁ** 1 • 3 *yoke*
**καταργέω** 5 • 6 *to abolish, nullify*
**προσφορά, ἡ** 2 • 6 *offering*
7 **Αἴγυπτος, ἡ** 3 • 9 *Egypt*
**ἐντέλλω** 7 • 29 *to command*
**θυσία, ἡ** 5 • 22 *sacrifice*
**ὁλοκαύτωμα, τό** 4 • 7 *whole burnt offering*
8 **ἐντέλλω** 7 • 29 *to command*
**κακία, ἡ** 2 • 9 *malice, ill-will*
**μνησικακέω** 2 • 9 *to remember evil, bear malice, bear a grudge*
**ὅρκος, ὁ** 1 • 2 *oath*
**πλησίον** 5 • 17 *near, close;* subst. *neighbor*
**ψευδής** 1 • 4 *false*
9 **ἀγαθωσύνη, ἡ** 1 • 1 *generosity, goodness*
**αἰσθάνομαι** 4 • 5 *to perceive, understand*
**ἀσύνετος** 2 • 16 *without understanding*
**γνώμη, ἡ** 2 • 20 *intention, mind-set*
**προσάγω** 4 • 9 *to approach*
10 **ἀκριβεύω** 1 • 1 *to pay strict attention*
**ἐκσφενδονάω** 1 • 1 *to hurl away*
**εὐωδία, ἡ** 1 • 2 *fragrant aroma*
**θυσία, ἡ** 5 • 22 *sacrifice*
**ὀσμή, ἡ** 1 • 3 *smell, aroma*
**παρείσδυσις, ἡ** 2 • 2 *a slipping in (stealthily), sneaking in*
**πλάνη, ἡ** 4 • 11 *error*
**πλάσσω** 2 • 8 *to form*
**συντρίβω** 5 • 10 pass. *to be broken*

## Chapter 3

1 **ἐκλέγομαι** 4 • 15 *to choose, select*
**κραυγή, ἡ** 1 • 2 *a loud cry or shout*
**νηστεία, ἡ** 5 • 25 *fast, fasting*
**νηστεύω** 5 • 24 *to fast*
**ταπεινόω** 3 • 8 *to humiliate, mortify*
2 **δεκτός** 3 • 9 *acceptable, pleasing*
**ἐνδύω** 1 • 32 *to wear, put on*
**κάμπτω** 1 • 5 *to bend, bow*
**κρίκος, ὁ** 1 • 1 *ring*
**νηστεία, ἡ** 5 • 25 *fast, fasting*
**σάκκος, ὁ** 2 • 4 *sackcloth*
**σποδός, ἡ** 3 • 4 *ashes*
**τράχηλος, ὁ** 2 • 3 *neck*
**ὑποστρώννυμι** 1 • 2 *to spread out underneath*
3 **ἀδικία, ἡ** 1 • 7 *injustice, unrighteousness*
**ἄδικος** 1 • 14 *unjust*
**ἄστεγος** 1 • 1 *homeless, roofless*

**ἄφεσις, ἡ** 7 • 13 *release;*
**ἀπόστελλε τεθραυσμένους ἐν ἀφέσει** *set free those who are oppressed*
**βίαιος** 1 • 1 *violent, forced*
**γυμνός** 1 • 3 *naked, inadequately clothed*
**διαθρύπτω** 1 • 1 *to break in pieces*
**διαλύω** 1 • 3 *to destroy, loose, dissolve*
**διασπάω** 1 • 2 *to tear apart, tear up*
**εἰσάγω** 3 • 6 *to bring in, lead in*
**ἐκλέγομαι** 4 • 15 *to choose, select*
**θραύω** 1 • 5 *to oppress, weaken, break down*
**νηστεία, ἡ** 5 • 25 *fast, fasting*
**οἰκεῖος** 1 • 2 *member of a household*
**πεινάω** 3 • 6 *to hunger, be hungry*
**περιβάλλω** 1 • 2 *to clothe*
**στραγγαλιά, ἡ** 1 • 1 *knot*
**συγγραφή, ἡ** 1 • 1 *document, contract*
**συνάλλαγμα, τό** 1 • 1 *contract, agreement*
**σύνδεσμος, ὁ** 1 • 2 *bond, chain, fetter*
**ταπεινός** 3 • 8 *lowly, being of low status*
**ὑπεροράω** 1 • 3 *to disdain, despise*
4 **ἀνατέλλω** 2 • 6 *to rise, spring up, dawn*
**ἴαμα, τό** 1 • 1 *healing*
**περιστέλλω** 1 • 1 *to cover all around, clothe*
**προπορεύομαι** 1 • 1 *to go on before*
**πρώϊμος** 1 • 1 *early rain; early morning*
**ῥήγνυμι** 1 • 2 *to break out, break loose*
**ταχέως** 1 • 4 *quickly, at once, without delay, soon*
5 **ἀφαιρέω** 4 • 8 *to take away, do away with, remove*
**βοάω** 2 • 5 *to call, shout, cry out*
**γογγυσμός, ὁ** 1 • 1 *utterance made in a low tone of voice, grumbling, complaint*
**ἐλεέω** 2 • 16 *to have compassion/ mercy/pity*
**ἐπακούω** 2 • 3 *to hear, listen to*
**πάρειμι** 2 • 18 *to be present*
**πεινάω** 3 • 6 *to hunger, be hungry*
**σύνδεσμος, ὁ** 1 • 2 *bond, chain, fetter*
**ταπεινόω** 3 • 8 *to humble, make humble*
**χειροτονία, ἡ** 1 • 1 *scornful gesture*
6 **ἀκεραιοσύνη, ἡ** 2 • 2 *purity*
**ἐπήλυτος** 1 • 1 of one who is new to a thing, *coming lately, coming after;*
subst. *one who is new to something*
**μακρόθυμος** 1 • 9 *patient, forbearing, tolerant, even-tempered*
**προβλέπω** 3 • 3 *to see beforehand, foresee*
**προσρήσσω** 1 • 1 *to break into pieces, shatter, wreck*
**προφανερόω** 4 • 5 *to reveal beforehand/in advance*

## Chapter 4

1 **ἀνομία, ἡ** [2] 9 • 33 *lawlessness*
**ἐκζητέω** 7 • 16 *to seek out, search for*
**ἐνίστημι** 4 • 6 *to be present, be now, happen now*
**ἐπιπολύ** 1 • 1 *to a great extent, carefully*
**ἐραυνάω** 1 • 1 *to search, examine, investigate*
**καταλαμβάνω** 1 • 5 *to seize, overtake, come upon*
**μήποτε** 5 • 22 *lest*
**πλάνη, ἡ** 4 • 11 *error, delusion, deceit, deception*
**τελείως** 3 • 8 *fully, perfectly, completely, altogether*
**φεύγω** 2 • 30 *to flee from, avoid, shun*
2 **ἄνεσις, ἡ** 1 • 1 *rest, relaxation, relief*
**μήποτε** 5 • 22 *lest*
**ὁμοιόω** 6 • 7 *to make like;*
pass. *be like*
**συντρέχω** 1 • 6 *to be in league with, go with, associate with*
3 **δεσπότης, ὁ** 2 • 54 *master, lord*
**Ἐνώχ, ὁ** 1 • 2 *Enoch*
**ἥκω** 3 • 32 *to come*
**κληρονομία, ἡ** 2 • 6 *inheritance*

**σκάνδαλον, τό** 2 • 5 *temptation, enticement*
**συντέμνω** 1 • 1 *to cut short, shorten, limit*
**ταχύνω** 1 • 1 *to hasten, hurry, come quickly*
**τέλειος** 6 • 25 *perfect, full*
4 **βασιλεύω** 1 • 5 *to reign*
**δέκα** 4 • 22 *ten*
**ἐξανίστημι** 1 • 3 *to rise up*
**ὄπισθεν** 1 • 1 *after*
**ταπεινόω** 3 • 8 *to humble, humiliate, abase*
5 **ἀνατέλλω** 2 • 6 *to rise up, spring forth*
**Δανιήλ, ὁ** 1 • 3 *Daniel*
**δέκα** 4 • 22 *ten*
**ἰσχυρός** 3 • 21 *strong, mighty*
**κέρας, τό** [3] 3 • 4 *horn*
**παραφυάδιον, τό** 1 • 1 *offshoot*
**ταπεινόω** 3 • 8 *to humble, humiliate, abase*
**τέταρτος** 1 • 9 *fourth*
**χαλεπός** 1 • 5 *troublesome, dangerous, difficult*
6 **ἐπισωρεύω** 1 • 1 *to heap up, accumulate*
**ἰδίως** 1 • 1 *in a special way, especially*
**ὁμοιόω** 6 • 7 *to make like*; pass. *be like*
**προσέχω** 11 • 25 *to take care, be on guard*
**συνίημι** 7 • 21 *to understand, comprehend*
7 **δάκτυλος, ὁ** 2 • 4 *finger*
**λίθινος** 2 • 3 *made of stone*
**νηστεύω** 5 • 24 *to fast*
**πλάξ, ἡ** 5 • 5 *tablet*
**τεσσαράκοντα** [2] 4 • 6 *forty*
8 **Αἴγυπτος, ἡ** 3 • 9 *Egypt*
**ἀνομέω** 2 • 5 *to be lawless, sin*
**ἐγκατασφραγίζω** 1 • 1 *to seal*
**εἴδωλον, τό** 2 • 3 *idol*
**ἐξάγω** 3 • 7 *to lead out, bring out*
**πλάξ, ἡ** 5 • 5 *tablet*
**ῥίπτω** 3 • 22 *to throw*
**συνίημι** 7 • 21 *to understand, comprehend*
**συντρίβω** 5 • 10 *to smatter, smash, crush*
**τάχος, τό** 2 • 7 *quickly, without delay*
9 **ἀνθίστημι** 6 • 24 *to resist*
**ἄνομος** 4 • 20 *lawless*
**ἐλλείπω** 3 • 3 *to leave off*
**μέλας** 2 • 20 *black*; subst. *the devil, 'the black one'*
**παρείσδυσις, ἡ** 2 • 2 *a slipping in (stealthily), sneaking in*
**περίψημα, τό** 2 • 4 *dirt, scum*; fig. *humble servant*
**πρέπω** 2 • 16 *to be fitting, be seemly, be suitable*
**προσέχω** 11 • 25 *to take care, be on guard*
**σκάνδαλον, τό** 2 • 5 *temptation, enticement*
**σπουδάζω** 3 • 16 *to be zealous, eager, take pains, make every effort, be conscientious*
**ὠφελέω** 1 • 8 *to help, aid, benefit, be of use to*
10 **ἐνδύνω** 1 • 1 *to retire within, go within*
**κοινός** 1 • 15 *communal, common*
**ματαιότης, ἡ** 1 • 3 *emptiness, futility*
**μονάζω** 1 • 2 *to live alone, separate oneself*
**συζητέω** 1 • 2 *to discuss*
**συμφέρω** 1 • 3 *to help, confer a benefit, be profitable, useful*
**συνέρχομαι** 1 • 4 *to assemble, gather, come together*
**τελείως** 3 • 8 *fully, perfectly, completely, altogether*
**φεύγω** 2 • 30 *to flee*
11 **ἀγωνίζομαι** 1 • 8 *to fight, struggle, strive*
**δικαίωμα, τό** 8 • 12 *righteous requirement, commandment*
**ἐπιστήμων** 2 • 2 *expert, learned, understanding*
**εὐφραίνω** 5 • 16 *to be glad, rejoice, celebrate*
**μελετάω** 5 • 6 *to practice, cultivate*
**πνευματικός** 3 • 19 *filled with the divine spirit; spiritual*
**συνετός** 3 • 23 *intelligent, sagacious, wise, with good sense*
**τέλειος** 6 • 25 *perfect*
12 **ἀπροσωπολήμπτως** 1 • 2 *impartially*
**κομίζω** 1 • 7 *to receive, get*
**μισθός, ὁ** 6 • 22 *reward, recompense*

**πονηρία, ἡ** 2 • 41 *wickedness, baseness, maliciousness, sinfulness*
**προηγέομαι** 1 • 4 *to go before, lead the way, precede*
13 **ἀπωθέω** 1 • 2 *to reject, repudiate, force out*
**ἐπαναπαύομαι** 1 • 3 *to rest, take one's rest*
**ἐπικαθυπνόω** 1 • 1 *to fall asleep over*
**κλητός** 3 • 6 *called, invited*
**μήποτε** 5 • 22 *never*
14 **ἐγκαταλείπω** 3 • 8 *to forsake, abandon, desert*
**ἐκλεκτός** 2 • 31 *chosen, selected*
**κλητός** 3 • 6 *called, invited*
**μήποτε** 5 • 22 *lest*
**νοέω** 7 • 46 *to consider, take note of*
**προσέχω** 11 • 25 *to take care, be on guard*
**τέρας, τό** 2 • 4 *portent, omen, wonder*
**τηλικοῦτος** 2 • 6 *so great, important, mighty*

## Chapter 5

1 **ἁγνίζω** 2 • 4 *to purify*
**ἄφεσις, ἡ** 7 • 13 *forgiveness, pardon, cancellation*
**καταφθορά, ἡ** 2 • 5 *destruction, downfall*
**ῥάντισμα, τό** 1 • 1 *sprinkling*
**ὑπομένω** 6 • 32 *to endure, submit to, suffer*
2 **ἀμνός, ὁ** 1 • 2 *lamb*
**ἀνομία, ἡ** 9 • 33 *lawless deed, transgression*
**ἄφωνος** 1 • 2 *silent, mute*
**ἐναντίον** 1 • 5 *before*
**ἰάομαι** 3 • 11 *to heal, restore*
**κείρω** 1 • 2 *to shear*
**μαλακίζω** 1 • 2 *to be weak, be discouraged, be sick, be made to suffer*
**μώλωψ, ὁ** 1 • 2 *wound, welt, bruise*
**σφαγή, ἡ** 2 • 3 *slaughter*
**τραυματίζω** 1 • 2 *to wound*
3 **ἀσύνετος** 2 • 16 *void of understanding, senseless, foolish*
**γνωρίζω** 2 • 18 *to make known, reveal*
**ἐνίστημι** 4 • 6 *to be now, happen now;*
subst. participle *things of the present*
**οὐκοῦν** 8 • 10 *therefore, so, accordingly*
**παρέρχομαι** 2 • 12 *to pass;*
subst. participle *things past, the past*
**σοφίζω** 2 • 3 *to make wise, give wisdom*
**ὑπερευχαριστέω** 1 • 1 *to give heartiest thanks, be exceedingly thankful*
4 **ἀδίκως** 1 • 2 *unjustly*
**ἀποσυνέχω** 1 • 1 *to hold, keep, ensnare*
**γνῶσις, ἡ** 10 • 32 *knowledge*
**δικαίως** 3 • 12 *justly, rightly*
**δίκτυον, τό** 1 • 1 *net*
**ἐκτείνω** 3 • 7 *to stretch out*
**πτερωτός** 1 • 1 *feathered, winged;*
subst. *birds, winged creatures*
5 **εἰκών, ἡ** 2 • 5 *image, form*
**ἡμέτερος** 2 • 13 *our*
**καταβολή, ἡ** 1 • 2 *foundation*
**μανθάνω** 10 • 26 *to learn*
**ὁμοίωσις, ἡ** 2 • 3 *likeness, resemblance*
**ὑπομένω** [2] 6 • 32 *to endure, submit to, suffer*
6 **καταργέω** 5 • 6 *to invalidate, make powerless*
**προφητεύω** 5 • 9 *to prophesy, foretell*
**ὑπομένω** 6 • 32 *to endure, submit to, suffer*
7 **ἐπιδείκνυμι** 2 • 11 *to demonstrate, show*
8 **γέ** 6 • 18 *indeed;*
**πέρας γέ τοι** *and furthermore*
**πέρας** 6 • 13 *finally, in conclusion, furthermore*
**τέρας, τό** 2 • 4 *portent, omen, wonder*
**τηλικοῦτος** 2 • 6 *so great, important, mighty*
**τοί** 6 • 7 *and furthermore, besides*
**ὑπεραγαπάω** 1 • 1 *to love most dearly*
9 **ἄνομος** 4 • 20 *lawless*
**ἐκλέγομαι** 4 • 15 *to select*

10 **ἀκτίς, ἡ** 1 • 1 *ray, beam*
**ἀντοφθαλμέω** 1 • 2 *to look directly at*
**ἐμβλέπω** 1 • 5 *to look at, gaze upon*
**ἰσχύω** 1 • 9 *to be able, be competent, be strong*
11 **ἀνακεφαλαιόω** 1 • 1 *to sum up, recapitulate*
**οὐκοῦν** 8 • 10 *therefore, so, accordingly*
**τέλειος** 6 • 25 *perfect, full measure*
12 **οὐκοῦν** 8 • 10 *therefore, so, accordingly*
**πατάσσω** 1 • 2 *to strike down, slay*
**πληγή, ἡ** 2 • 5 *wound, bruise*
**ποιμήν, ὁ** 1 • 54 *shepherd*
**ποίμνη, ἡ** 1 • 1 *flock*
**ὑπομένω** 6 • 32 *to endure, submit to, suffer*
13 **ἐπανίστημι** 1 • 1 *to rise up*
**καθηλόω** 1 • 4 *to nail*
**ξύλον, τό** 8 • 23 *tree, cross*
**πονηρεύομαι** 2 • 15 *to do wrong, commit sin*
**προφητεύω** 5 • 9 *to prophesy, foretell*
**ῥομφαία, ἡ** 1 • 1 *sword*
**φείδομαι** 1 • 3 *to spare*
14 **μάστιξ, ἡ** 1 • 8 *whip, lash*
**νῶτος, ὁ** 1 • 1 *back*
**πέτρα, ἡ** 4 • 20 *rock*
**ῥάπισμα, τό** 1 • 2 *slap, blow*
**σιαγών, ἡ** 1 • 2 *cheek*
**στερεός** 2 • 2 *firm, hard, solid, strong*

## Chapter 6

1 **ἀνθίστημι** 6 • 24 *to oppose, set oneself against*
**παῖς, ὁ** 4 • 20 *servant*
2 **ἀκρογωνιαῖος** 1 • 1 *cornerstone*
**ἐκλεκτός** 2 • 30 *choice, excellent*
**ἐμβάλλω** 2 • 4 *to put, set*
**ἔντιμος** 1 • 2 *precious, valuable*
**ἐπεί** 5 • 35 *since, because, for*
**θεμέλιον, τό** 1 • 4 *foundation*
**ἰσχυρός** 3 • 21 *strong, mighty, solid*
**κατεσθίω** 1 • 3 *to eat up, consume, devour, swallow*
**παλαιόω** 1 • 3 *to become old*
**πολυτελής** 1 • 3 *expensive, costly*
**σής, ὁ** 1 • 6 *moth*
**Σιών, ἡ** 1 • 1 *Zion*
**συντριβή, ἡ** 1 • 1 *crushing, destruction*
3 **εἶτα** 6 • 48 *furthermore, then, next*
**ἐπεί** 5 • 35 *since, because, for*
**ἰσχύς, ἡ** 2 • 11 *strength, power, might*
**πέτρα, ἡ** 4 • 20 *rock*
**στερεός** 2 • 2 *firm, hard, solid, strong*
4 **ἀποδοκιμάζω** 1 • 5 *to reject*
**γωνία, ἡ** 1 • 5 *cornerstone*
**θαυμαστός** 1 • 13 *marvelous, wonderful, remarkable*
5 **ἁπλοῦς** 2 • 4 *simple, guileless, straightforward*
**περίψημα, τό** 2 • 4 *dirt, scum;* fig. *humble servant*
**συνίημι** 7 • 21 *to understand, comprehend*
6 **ἱματισμός, ὁ** 1 • 8 *clothing, apparel*
**κηρίον, τό** 1 • 1 *honeycomb*
**κλῆρος, ὁ** 1 • 8 *lot*
**κυκλόω** 1 • 3 *to surround, encircle*
**μέλισσα, ἡ** 1 • 1 *bee*
**περιέχω** 1 • 4 *to surround, encircle*
**πονηρεύομαι** 2 • 15 *to do wrong, commit sin*
**ὡσεί** 1 • 17 *like, as*
7 **βουλεύω** 1 • 6 *to resolve, decide, plot*
**βουλή, ἡ** 4 • 19 *counsel, plan, purpose, intention*
**δύσχρηστος** 1 • 1 *inconvenient, annoying, irritating*
**πάθος, τό** 1 • 18 *suffering*
**προφανερόω** 4 • 5 *to reveal beforehand/in advance*
8 **γάλα, τό** 5 • 5 *milk*
**Ἰακώβ, ὁ** 9 • 13 *Jacob*
**Ἰσαάκ, ὁ** 5 • 7 *Isaac*
**κατακληρονομέω** 1 • 1 *to take possession of, occupy*
**μέλι, τό** 5 • 12 *honey*
**ὅδε** 3 • 7 *this*

**ὀμνύω** 2 • 9 *to swear, take an oath, confirm with an oath*
**ῥέω** 3 • 3 *to overflow with*
9 **Ἀδάμ, ὁ** 1 • 4 *Adam*
**γνῶσις, ἡ** 10 • 32 *knowledge*
**μανθάνω** 10 • 26 *to learn*
**πλάσις, ἡ** 1 • 1 *formation, molding, creation*
10 **γάλα, τό** 5 • 5 *milk*
**ἐπιστήμων** 2 • 2 *expert, learned, understanding*
**εὐλογητός** 1 • 3 *blessed, praised*
**κρύφιος** 1 • 4 *hidden, secret;* subst. *hidden* or *secret things*
**μέλι, τό** 5 • 12 *honey*
**νοῦς, ὁ** 1 • 12 *understanding, mind*
**ῥέω** 3 • 3 *to overflow with*
**σοφός** 1 • 8 *wise*
11 **ἀνακαινίζω** 1 • 3 *to renew, restore, make new*
**ἀναπλάσσω** 2 • 3 *to form anew, remold*
**ἄφεσις, ἡ** 7 • 13 *forgiveness, pardon, cancellation*
**δή** 1 • 6 *indeed*
**ἐπεί** 5 • 35 *since, because, for*
**τύπος, ὁ** 13 • 26 *form, figure, pattern*
12 **αὐξάνω/αὔξω** 2 • 7 *to grow, increase*
**εἰκών, ἡ** 2 • 5 *image, form*
**ἰχθύς, ὁ** 5 • 5 *fish*
**ὁμοίωσις, ἡ** 2 • 3 *likeness, resemblance*
**πετεινόν, τό** 4 • 6 *bird*
**πλάσμα, τό** 2 • 3 *creation, image, formation*
**πληθύνω** 2 • 11 *to multiply, grow, increase*
13 **γάλα, τό** 5 • 5 *milk*
**ἐπιδείκνυμι** 2 • 11 *to show, demonstrate*
**κατακυριεύω** 2 • 15 *to rule, be master, be lord over*
**μέλι, τό** 5 • 12 *honey*
**πλάσις, ἡ** 1 • 1 *formation, molding, creation*
**ῥέω** 3 • 3 *to overflow with*
14 **ἀναπλάσσω** 2 • 3 *to form anew, remold*
**ἐμβάλλω** 2 • 4 *to put, set*
**ἐξαιρέω** 1 • 4 *to take out, tear out*
**λίθινος** 2 • 3 *made of stone*
**προβλέπω** 3 • 3 *to see beforehand, foresee*
**σάρκινος** 1 • 1 *material, physical, human, fleshly*
**τουτέστιν** 2 • 5 *that is*
15 **κατοικητήριον, τό** 3 • 3 *dwelling place, habitat*
16 **ἀναμέσον** 1 • 1 *in the middle*
**εἰσάγω** 3 • 6 *to bring in, lead in*
**ἐξομολογέω** 2 • 15 *to praise, confess, profess*
**οὐκοῦν** 8 • 10 *therefore, so, accordingly*
**ψάλλω** 1 • 1 *to sing, sing praise*
17 **γάλα, τό** [2] 5 • 5 *milk*
**εἶτα** 6 • 48 *then, next*
**ζωοποιέω** [2] 5 • 10 *to keep alive, sustain life, nourish*
**κατακυριεύω** 2 • 15 *to rule, be master, be lord over*
**μέλι, τό** [2] 5 • 12 *honey*
18 **αἰσθάνομαι** 4 • 5 *to understand, comprehend*
**αὐξάνω/αὔξω** 2 • 7 *to grow, increase*
**ἐπάνω** 1 • 8 *above*
**ἐπιτάσσω** 2 • 7 *to command, order, give orders*
**ἰχθύς, ὁ** [2] 5 • 5 *fish*
**κυριεύω** 3 • 5 *to rule*
**πετεινόν, τό** 4 • 6 *bird*
**πληθύνω** 2 • 11 *to multiply, grow, increase*
**προλέγω** 1 • 16 *to state beforehand/earlier*
19 **κληρονόμος, ὁ** 2 • 3 *beneficiary, heir*
**πότε** 2 • 6 *when?*
**τελειόω** 2 • 14 *to make perfect*

## Chapter 7

1 **αἰνέω** 1 • 2 *to praise*
**εὐφροσύνη, ἡ** 4 • 5 *joy, gladness, cheerfulness*
**νοέω** 7 • 46 *to perceive, apprehend, understand, gain an insight into*
**οὐκοῦν** 8 • 10 *therefore, so, accordingly*
**προφανερόω** 4 • 5 *to reveal beforehand/in advance*

2 **ζωοποιέω** 5 • 10 *to make alive, give life to*
**πληγή, ἡ** 2 • 5 *wound, bruise*
3 **ἐντέλλω** 7 • 29 *to command, order, give orders*
**ἐξολεθρεύω** 1 • 5 *to eliminate by destruction, destroy utterly, root out*
**ἐπεί** 5 • 35 *since, because, for*
**ἡμέτερος** 2 • 13 *our*
**θυσία, ἡ** 5 • 22 *sacrifice, offering*
**θυσιαστήριον, τό** 2 • 15 *altar*
**Ἰσαάκ, ὁ** 5 • 7 *Isaac*
**νηστεία, ἡ** 5 • 25 *fast, fasting*
**νηστεύω** 5 • 24 *to fast*
**ὄξος, τό** 3 • 4 *sour wine, vinegar*
**ποτίζω** 2 • 7 *to give a drink*
**σκεῦος, τό** 3 • 9 *instrument, vessel*
**τελέω** 1 • 23 *to carry out, accomplish, perform, fulfill, keep*
**τύπος, ὁ** 13 • 26 *type, pattern, model*
**χολή, ἡ** 2 • 2 *gall*
4 **ἀκριβῶς** 1 • 8 *accurately, carefully, well*
**ἄπλυτος** 1 • 1 *unwashed*
**ἔντερον, τό** 1 • 1 *entrails*
**νηστεία, ἡ** 5 • 25 *fast, fasting*
**ὄξος, τό** 3 • 4 *sour wine, vinegar*
**προσέχω** 11 • 25 *to pay attention to, give heed to, follow*
**τράγος, ὁ** 6 • 6 *goat*
5 **ἐπειδή** 3 • 17 *since, because*
**κόπτω** 1 • 12 *to mourn, lament*
**νηστεύω** 5 • 24 *to fast*
**ὄξος, τό** 3 • 4 *sour wine, vinegar*
**ποτίζω** 2 • 7 *to give a drink*
**σάκκος, ὁ** 2 • 4 *sackcloth*
**σποδός, ἡ** 3 • 4 *ashes*
**χολή, ἡ** 2 • 2 *gall*
6 **ἐντέλλομαι** 7 • 29 *to command, order, give orders*
**ὁλοκαύτωμα, τό** 4 • 7 *whole burnt offering*
**προσέχω** 11 • 25 *to pay attention to, give heed to, follow*
**τράγος, ὁ** 6 • 6 *goat*
7 **ἐπικατάρατος** 4 • 4 *cursed*
**προσέχω** 11 • 25 *to pay attention to, give heed to, follow*
**τύπος, ὁ** 13 • 26 *type, pattern, model*
8 **ἀφαιρέω** 4 • 8 *to take away, remove*
**βαστάζω** 1 • 24 *to bear, carry*
**βλαστός, ὁ** 1 • 3 *sprout, bud*
**γλυκύς** 1 • 6 *sweet*
**εἴωθα** 1 • 2 *to be accustomed*
**ἐμπτύω** 2 • 2 *to spit upon*
**ἔριον, τό** [2] 8 • 10 *wool*
**κατακεντέω** 1 • 1 *to pierce, stab*
**κόκκινος** 5 • 7 *red, scarlet*
**περιτίθημι** 2 • 6 *to put on, place on*
**ῥαχή, ἡ** [2] 2 • 2 *a certain species of shrub*; possibly *a blackberry bush*
**τράγος, ὁ** 6 • 6 *goat*
**τρώγω** 3 • 4 *to eat, chew*
**φρύγανον, τό** 1 • 2 *bush, shrub*
**χώρα, ἡ** 1 • 6 *field, country*
9 **ἀληθῶς** 4 • 23 *truly, in truth, really, actually*
**ἐμπτύω** 2 • 2 *to spit upon*
**ἐξουθενέω** 1 • 2 *to treat with contempt, insult*
**ἐπειδή** 3 • 17 *because, since, for*
**ἐπικατάρατος** 4 • 4 *cursed*
**θυσιαστήριον, τό** 2 • 15 *altar*
**κατακεντέω** 1 • 1 *to pierce, stab*
**κόκκινος** 5 • 7 *red, scarlet*
**ποδήρης, ὁ** 1 • 1 *foot-length robe*
**ποτέ** 4 • 15 *once, formerly*
**προσέχω** 11 • 25 *to pay attention to, give heed to, follow*
**στεφανόω** 1 • 12 *to crown, wreathe*
10 **ἐκπλήσσω** 3 • 4 *to be amazed, be overwhelmed*
**ἴσος** 1 • 3 *equal*
**ὁμοιός** 4 • 29 *of the same nature, like, similar*
**ὁμοιότης, ἡ** 1 • 2 *likeness, similarity, agreement*
**οὐκοῦν** 8 • 10 *therefore, so, accordingly*
**τράγος, ὁ** [2] 6 • 6 *goat*
**τύπος, ὁ** 13 • 26 *type, pattern, model*
11 **ἄκανθα, ἡ** [2] 3 • 9 *thorn-plant*
**ἔριον, τό** [2] 8 • 10 *wool*
**θλίβω** [2] 3 • 25 *to oppress, afflict*
**κόκκινος** 5 • 7 *red, scarlet*
**κυριεύω** 3 • 5 *to rule, master, gain*
**τύπος, ὁ** 13 • 26 *type, pattern, model*

**φοβερός** 1 • 2 *causing fear, fearful, terrible, frightful*

## Chapter 8

1 **ἄγγος, τό** 1 • 2 *vessel, container*
**ἁγνίζω** 2 • 4 *to purify*
**δάμαλις, ἡ** 1 • 1 *heifer, young cow*
**ἐντέλλω** 7 • 29 *to command*
**ἔριον, τό** [2] 8 • 10 *wool*
**κατακαίω** 1 • 4 *to burn up, consume*
**κόκκινος** [2] 5 • 7 *red, scarlet*
**ξύλον, τό** 8 • 23 *wood, tree*
**περιτίθημι** 2 • 6 *to put on, place on*
**ῥαντίζω** 3 • 4 *to sprinkle*
**σποδός, ἡ** 3 • 4 *ashes*
**σταυρός, ὁ** 9 • 17 *cross*
**σφάζω** 1 • 1 *to slaughter*
**τέλειος** 6 • 25 *perfect, complete*
**τύπος, ὁ** [2] 13 • 26 *type, pattern, model*
**ὕσσωπον, ὁ** 3 • 3 *hyssop*
2 **ἁπλότης** 2 • 15 *simplicity, sincerity, uprightness, frankness*
**εἶτα** 6 • 48 *then, next*
**μόσχος, ὁ** 1 • 2 *calf, young bull*
**νοέω** 7 • 46 *to consider, take note of*
**σφαγή, ἡ** 2 • 3 *slaughter*
3 **ἁγνισμός, ὁ** 1 • 1 *purification*
**ἄφεσις, ἡ** 7 • 13 *forgiveness, pardon, cancellation*
**δεκαδύο** [2] 2 • 2 *twelve*
**μαρτύριον, τό** 3 • 16 *testimony, proof*
**παῖς, ὁ** 4 • 20 *child*
**ῥαντίζω** 3 • 4 *to sprinkle*
4 **διατί** 2 • 29 *why?*
**Ἰακώβ, ὁ** 9 • 13 *Jacob*
**Ἰσαάκ, ὁ** 5 • 7 *Isaac*
**μαρτύριον, τό** 3 • 16 *testimony, proof*
**παῖς, ὁ** 4 • 20 *child*
**ῥαντίζω** 3 • 4 *to sprinkle*
5 **ἔριον, τό** 8 • 10 *wool*
**ξύλον, τό** [2] 8 • 23 *wood, tree*
6 **ἀλγέω** 1 • 2 *to suffer, feel pain, be ill*
**ἅμα** 1 • 12 *together, at the same time*
**διατί** 2 • 29 *why?*
**ἔριον, τό** 8 • 10 *wool*
**ἰάομαι** 3 • 11 *to heal, cure*
**ῥυπαρός** 1 • 3 *dirty, filthy, soiled, foul*
**ῥύπος, ὁ** 2 • 3 *juice*
**ὕσσωπον, ὁ** [2] 3 • 3 *hyssop*
7 **σκοτεινός** 2 • 2 *dark, obscure*
**φανερός** 2 • 9 *readily known, visible, clear, plainly to be seen, open, plain, evident*

## Chapter 9

1 **ἀκοή, ἡ** 5 • 8 *hearing, listening*
**περιτέμνω** [2] 9 • 9 *to circumcise*
**πόρρωθεν** 1 • 1 *from a distance*
**ὑπακούω** 1 • 9 *to obey, follow, be subject to*
**ὠτίον, τό** [2] 2 • 2 *ear*
2 **ἀκοή, ἡ** 5 • 8 *ear*
**ὅδε** 3 • 7 *this*
**παῖς, ὁ** 4 • 20 *servant*
**προφητεύω** 5 • 9 *to prophesy, proclaim an inspired revelation*
3 **βοάω** 2 • 5 *to cry out, call, shout*
**ἐνωτίζομαι** 1 • 1 *to give ear, pay attention to*
**μαρτύριον, τό** 3 • 16 *testimony, proof*
4 **ἀκοή, ἡ** 5 • 8 *ear*
**καταργέω** 5 • 6 *to invalidate, make powerless*
**οὐκοῦν** 8 • 10 *therefore, so, accordingly*
**παραβαίνω** 1 • 3 *to transgress, break*
**περιτέμνω** 9 • 9 *to circumcise*
**σοφίζω** 2 • 3 *to make wise, teach, instruct;* negatively *to beguile*
5 **ἄκανθα, ἡ** 3 • 9 *thorn-plant*
**ἀκροβυστία, ἡ** 2 • 2 *foreskin*
**ἀπερίτμητος** [2] 2 • 2 *uncircumcised*
**ὅδε** 3 • 7 *this*
**περιτέμνω** [2] 9 • 9 *to circumcise*
**σκληροκαρδία, ἡ** 1 • 2 *an unyielding frame of mind, hardness of heart, coldness, obstinacy, stubbornness*
**σκληρύνω** 1 • 4 *to make hard, stiffen*
**σπείρω** 1 • 5 *to sow*
**τράχηλος, ὁ** 2 • 3 *neck, throat*

6 **Αἰγύπτιος** 1 • 2 *Egyptian*
**Ἄραψ, ὁ** 1 • 1 *Arab, Arabian*
**εἴδωλον, τό** 2 • 3 *idol*
**μήν** 1 • 10 *indeed, surely, yet*
**περιτέμνω** 9 • 9 *to circumcise*
**Σύρος, ὁ** 1 • 1 *Syrian*
**σφραγίς, ἡ** 1 • 16 *seal, mark;* fig. *attestation, confirmation, certification*
7 **γράμμα, τό** 2 • 8 *letter (of the alphabet)*
**δόγμα, τό** 5 • 10 *instruction, ordinance, decision, command*
**μανθάνω** 10 • 26 *to learn*
**περιτέμνω** 9 • 9 *to circumcise*
**πλουσίως** 1 • 1 *richly, abundantly*
**προβλέπω** 3 • 3 *to see beforehand, foresee*
8 **γνῶσις, ἡ** 10 • 32 *knowledge*
**γράμμα, τό** 2 • 8 *letter (of the alphabet)*
**δέκα** 4 • 22 *ten*
**δεκαοκτώ** [3] 3 • 3 *eighteen*
**δηλόω** 2 • 49 *to reveal, make clear, show*
**διάστημα, τό** 1 • 1 *interval*
**ή** 1 • 1 8, the numerical sign for eight
**ί** 1 • 6 10, the numerical sign for ten
**μανθάνω** 10 • 26 *to learn*
**ὀκτώ** 1 • 1 *eight*
**περιτέμνω** 9 • 9 *to circumcise*
**σταυρός, ὁ** [2] 9 • 17 *cross*
**τριακόσιοι** [3] 3 • 3 *three hundred*
9 **γνήσιος** 1 • 2 *genuine, reliable*
**δωρεά, ἡ** 1 • 7 *gift, bounty*
**ἔμφυτος** 2 • 2 *implanted*
**μανθάνω** 10 • 26 *to learn*

## Chapter 10

1 **ἀετός, ὁ** 2 • 2 *eagle*
**δόγμα, τό** 5 • 10 *instruction, ordinance, decision, command*
**ἰχθύς, ὁ** 5 • 5 *fish*
**κόραξ, ὁ** 2 • 2 *raven, crow*
**λεπίς, ἡ** 1 • 1 *scale*
**ὀξύπτερος, ὁ** 2 • 2 *hawk*
**σύνεσις, ἡ** 3 • 22 *correct understanding, comprehension*
**χοῖρος, ὁ** 4 • 4 *pig, swine*
2 **γέ** 6 • 18 *indeed* θνβολδ
πέρας γέ τοι *and furthermore*
**Δευτερονόμιον, τό** 1 • 1 *Deuteronomy*
**διατίθημι** 2 • 2 *to decree, ordain*
**δικαίωμα, τό** 8 • 12 *righteous requirement, commandment*
**πέρας** 6 • 13 *finally, in conclusion, furthermore*
**τοί** 6 • 7 *and furthermore, besides*
**τρώγω** 3 • 4 *to eat*
3 **ἐπιλανθάνομαι** 1 • 8 *to forget*
**κολλάω** 7 • 32 *to join oneself to, join, cling to, associate with*
**κραυγάζω** 1 • 2 *to utter a loud sound (ordinarily of harsh texture), cry out* (here the squealing or grunting of a hungry pig)
**πεινάω** 3 • 6 *to hunger, be hungry*
**σιωπάω** 1 • 5 *to become quiet, stop speaking*
**σπαταλάω** 1 • 3 *to live luxuriously/voluptuously*
**τουτέστιν** 2 • 5 *that is*
**τρώγω** 3 • 4 *to eat*
**ὑστερέω** 1 • 11 *to lack, be lacking, go without, come short of*
**χοιρίον, τό** 1 • 1 *swine*
**χοῖρος, ὁ** [2] 4 • 4 *pig, swine*
4 **ἀετός, ὁ** 2 • 2 *eagle*
**ἀκεραιοσύνη, ἡ** 2 • 2 *purity*
**ἀλλότριος** [2] 2 • 14 *not one's own, strange, another's;* subst. *property belonging to another*
**ἀνομία, ἡ** 9 • 33 *lawlessness*
**ἀργός** 1 • 6 *idle, lazy*
**ἁρπάζω** 1 • 3 *to steal, carry off, drag away*
**ἐκδύω** 1 • 1 *to strip, plunder*
**ἐκζητέω** 7 • 16 *to seek out, search for*
**ἐπιτηρέω** 1 • 2 *to look out for or watch for, watch carefully, lie in wait*
**ἱδρώς, ὁ** 1 • 1 *sweat, perspiration*
**ἰκτίν, ὁ** 1 • 1 *hawk, kite* (type of bird)
**κολλάω** 7 • 32 *to join oneself to, join, cling to, associate with*
**κόπος, ὁ** 1 • 8 *work, labor, toil*
**κόραξ, ὁ** 2 • 2 *raven, crow*
**λοιμός, ὁ** 2 • 3 *pestilential, diseased*
**ὁμοιόω** 6 • 7 *to make like;* pass. *be like*

**ὀξύπτερος, ὁ** 2 • 2 *hawk*
**ὄρνεον, τό** 1 • 3 *bird*
**περιβλέπω** 1 • 1 *to be on the lookout for, look for, hunt*
**πλεονεξία, ἡ** 2 • 7 *greediness, insatiableness, avarice, covetousness*
**πονηρία, ἡ** 2 • 41 *wickedness, baseness, maliciousness, sinfulness*
**πορίζω** [2] 2 • 2 *to procure, provide*
**τροφή, ἡ** [2] 3 • 12 *food, nourishment*
5 **ἀσεβής** 6 • 14 *irreverent, impious, ungodly*
**βυθός, ὁ** [2] 2 • 14 *deep sea, deep water*
**ἐπικατάρατος** 4 • 4 *cursed*
**ἰχθύδιον, τό** 1 • 1 *fish*
**κάτω** 1 • 3 *below, at the bottom*
**κολυμβάω** 1 • 1 *to swim up and down, dive*
**νήχομαι** 1 • 1 *to swim*
**ὁμοιόω** 6 • 7 *to make like;* pass. *be like*
**πώλυψ, ὁ** 1 • 1 *octopus*
**σηπία, ἡ** 1 • 1 *cuttle-fish, sepia*
**σμύραινα, ἡ** 1 • 1 *sea-eel*
**εἰς τέλος** (adverbial marker of intensity) *utterly, finally*
6 **ἀφόδευσις, ἡ** 1 • 1 *anus*
**δασύπους, ὁ** 1 • 1 *hare*
**ἐνιαυτός, ὁ** 3 • 7 *year*
**λαγωός, ὁ** 1 • 1 *hare*
**ὁμοιόω** 6 • 7 *to make like;* pass. *be like*
**παιδοφθόρος, ὁ** 1 • 1 *pedophile,* one who rapes/sodomizes a boy
**πλεονεκτέω** 1 • 1 *to increase the number of*
**τοσοῦτος** 1 • 38 *so much, so great*
**τρύπη, ἡ** 1 • 1 *hole, opening*
7 **ἀλλάσσω** 2 • 5 *to change, alter*
**ἄρσην** 1 • 8 *male*
**ἐνιαυτός, ὁ** 3 • 7 *year*
**ζῷον, τό** 2 • 8 *living creature, animal*
**θῆλυς** 1 • 9 *female*
**μοιχός, ὁ** 1 • 3 *adulterer*
**ὁμοιόω** 6 • 7 *to make like;* pass. *be like*
**ποτέ** [2] 4 • 15 *at some time, now*
**ὕαινα, ἡ** 1 • 1 *hyena*
**φθορεύς, ὁ** 2 • 4 *seducer*
**φῦσις, ἡ** 1 • 4 *nature, natural characteristic/disposition*
8 **ἀκαθαρσία, ἡ** 2 • 2 *immorality, vileness* (especially of sexual sins)
**ἀνομία, ἡ** [2] 9 • 33 *a lawless deed*
**γαλή, ἡ** 1 • 1 *weasel*
**ζῷον, τό** 2 • 8 *living creature, animal*
**κολλάω** 7 • 32 *to join oneself to, join, cling to, associate with*
**κύω** 1 • 1 *to conceive, become pregnant*
**οἷος** 1 • 10 *of what sort*
9 **βρῶμα, τό** 1 • 4 *food*
**βρῶσις, ἡ** 2 • 4 *eating*
**δόγμα, τό** 5 • 10 *instruction, ordinance, decision, command*
**προσδέχομαι** 3 • 10 *to receive*
10 **ἁρπαγή, ἡ** 2 • 3 *robbery, plunder*
**ἀσεβής** 6 • 14 *irreverent, impious, ungodly*
**βάθος, τό** 1 • 4 *depth*
**βουλή, ἡ** 4 • 19 *counsel, plan, purpose, intention*
**βρῶσις, ἡ** 2 • 4 *eating*
**γνῶσις, ἡ** 10 • 32 *knowledge*
**δόγμα, τό** 5 • 10 *instruction, ordinance, decision, command*
**ἰχθύς, ὁ** 5 • 5 *fish*
**καθέδρα, ἡ** 1 • 11 *chair, seat*
**λοιμός, ὁ** 2 • 3 *pestilential, diseased*
**πετεινόν, τό** 4 • 6 *bird*
**τελείως** 3 • 8 *fully, perfectly, completely, altogether*
**χοῖρος, ὁ** 4 • 4 *pig, swine*
11 **ἀναμαρυκάομαι** 1 • 1 *to ruminate, think on again and again*
**ἀναπαύω** 1 • 13 *to rest, take one's rest*
**διάσταλμα, τό** 1 • 1 *distinguishing feature, special message*
**δικαίωμα, τό** 8 • 12 *righteous requirement, commandment*
**διχηλέω** [2] 2 • 2 *to have a divided hoof*
**ἐκδέχομαι** 1 • 5 *to expect, wait for*
**εὐφραίνω** 4 • 15 *to be glad, enjoy oneself, rejoice, celebrate*
**εὐφροσύνη, ἡ** 4 • 5 *joy, gladness, cheerfulness*

**κολλάω** 7 • 32 *to join oneself to, join, cling to, associate with*
**μαρυκάομαι** 1 • 2 *to ruminate*
**μελετάω** 5 • 6 *to think about, meditate upon*
**μελέτη, ἡ** 1 • 1 *meditation, study*
**νομοθετέω** 1 • 2 *to legislate, function as a lawgiver*
**τρέφω** 1 • 3 *to feed, nourish, support*
**τροφή, ἡ** 3 • 12 *food, nourishment*
12 **ἀκοή, ἡ** 5 • 8 *ear*
**δικαίως** 3 • 12 *correctly, justly, rightly*
**νοέω** [2] 7 • 46 *to perceive, apprehend, understand, gain an insight into*
**περιτέμνω** 9 • 9 *to circumcise*
**πόθεν** 2 • 6 *how? in what way?*
**συνίημι** [2] 7 • 21 *to understand, comprehend*

## Chapter 11

1 **ἄφεσις, ἡ** 7 • 13 *forgiveness, pardon, cancellation*
**βάπτισμα, τό** 1 • 6 *washing, baptism*
**μέλει** 2 • 5 *it is a care/concern, is of interest to someone*
**προσδέχομαι** 3 • 10 *to receive*
**προφανερόω** 4 • 5 *to reveal beforehand/in advance*
**σταυρός, ὁ** 9 • 17 *cross*
2 **βόθρος, ὁ** 1 • 1 *hole, pit, cistern*
**ἐγκαταλείπω** 3 • 8 *to forsake, abandon, desert*
**ἐξίστημι** 1 • 2 *to be amazed, be astonished*
**ὀρύσσω** 1 • 2 *to dig out, prepare by digging*
**πηγή, ἡ** 2 • 7 *fountainhead*
**φρίσσω** 1 • 2 *to tremble, shudder*
3 **ἀνίπταμαι** 1 • 1 *to fly up, flutter about*
**ἀφαιρέω** 4 • 8 *to take away*
**νοσσιά, ἡ** 1 • 1 *nest*
**νοσσός, ὁ** 1 • 1 *the young of a bird*
**πετεινόν, τό** 4 • 6 *bird*
**πέτρα, ἡ** 4 • 20 *rock*
**Σινᾶ** 3 • 3 *Sinai* (indecl.)
4 **ἀόρατος** 1 • 13 *invisible, unseen*
**ἀπόκρυφος** 1 • 1 *hidden*
**θησαυρός, ὁ** 1 • 1 *treasure*
**μοχλός, ὁ** 1 • 1 *bar, bolt*
**ὁμαλίζω** 1 • 1 *to make level*
**πύλη, ἡ** 1 • 37 *gate*
**σιδηροῦς** 1 • 1 *made of iron*
**σκοτεινός** 2 • 2 *dark*
**συνκλάω** 1 • 1 *to shatter, break*
**συντρίβω** 5 • 10 *to shatter, smash, crush*
**χαλκοῦς** 2 • 2 *made of copper/brass/bronze*
5 **ἰσχυρός** 3 • 21 *solid, mighty*
**μελετάω** 5 • 6 *to practice, cultivate*
**πέτρα, ἡ** 4 • 20 *rock*
**σπήλαιον, τό** 1 • 2 *hideout, refuge*
**ὑψηλός** 4 • 12 *high, tall, lofty*
6 **ἀπορρέω** 2 • 2 *to fall down*
**διέξοδος, ἡ** 1 • 1 *a spring* (the place where water from an underground source wells up)
**κατευοδόω** 1 • 2 *to prosper*
**ξύλον, τό** 8 • 23 *tree*
**φύλλον, τό** 2 • 5 *foliage, leaf*
**φυτεύω** 1 • 16 *to plant*
7 **ἄνεμος, ὁ** 1 • 4 *wind*
**ἀσεβής** [3] 6 • 14 *irreverent, impious, ungodly*
**βουλή, ἡ** 4 • 19 *council meeting*
**ἐκρίπτω** 1 • 2 *to drive away, blow away*
**χνοῦς, ὁ** 1 • 1 *dust, chaff*
8 **αἰσθάνομαι** 4 • 5 *to notice, perceive, understand*
**ἀπορρέω** 2 • 2 *to fall down*
**ἐπιστροφή, ἡ** 1 • 2 *conversion*
**μισθός, ὁ** 6 • 22 *reward, recompense*
**ὁρίζω** 3 • 10 *to define, explain, set limits to*
**σταυρός, ὁ** [2] 9 • 17 *cross*
**φύλλον, τό** 2 • 5 *foliage, leaf*
9 **ἐπαινέω** 1 • 6 *to praise*
**Ἰακώβ, ὁ** 9 • 13 *Jacob*
**σκεῦος, τό** 3 • 9 *instrument, vessel*
10 **δένδρον, τό** 1 • 28 *tree*
**εἶτα** 6 • 48 *furthermore, then, next*
**ἕλκω** 1 • 3 *to flow*
**ποταμός, ὁ** 1 • 4 *river, stream*
**ὡραῖος** 1 • 1 *beautiful, fair, lovely, pleasant*
11 **γέμω** 1 • 4 *to be full*
**καρποφορέω** 1 • 7 *to bear fruit*

ῥύπος, ὁ 2 • 3 *uncleanness, dirt*

### Chapter 12

1 κλίνω 1 • 1 *to fall over, lean over*
ξύλον, τό [2] 8 • 23 *tree*
ὁρίζω 3 • 10 *to define, explain, set limits to*
πότε 2 • 6 *when?*
στάζω 1 • 2 *to drip, trickle*
σταυρός, ὁ [2] 9 • 17 *cross*
συντελέω 6 • 15 *to carry out, fulfill, accomplish*
2 ἀλλόφυλος 1 • 4 *foreign, alien*
εἶτα 6 • 48 *then, next*
ἐκτείνω 3 • 7 *to stretch out*
θανατόω 1 • 7 *to put to death*
καθαιρέω 3 • 7 *to take down, bring down, lower*
ὅπλον, ὁ 1 • 5 *weapon, shield*
ὁπόταν 1 • 1 *whenever*
πολεμέω [3] 4 • 7 *to wage war;* pass. *be warred upon, attacked*
πυγμή, ἡ 1 • 1 *fight*
σταυρός, ὁ 9 • 17 *cross*
τύπος, ὁ 13 • 26 *type, pattern, model*
ὑπομιμνήσκω 1 • 4 *to remind*
ὑψηλός 4 • 12 *tall, high*
4 ἀντιλέγω 1 • 3 *to oppose, refuse*
ἀπειθής 1 • 1 *disobedient*
ἐκπετάννυμι 1 • 2 *to spread, hold out*
5 δάκνω 2 • 2 *to bite*
ἐλέγχω 2 • 16 *to convict, convince*
ἐπειδή 3 • 17 *since, because*
Εὕα, ἡ 1 • 2 *Eve*
ζωοποιέω 5 • 10 *to make alive, give life to*
ὄφις, ὁ [2] 4 • 9 *snake, serpent*
παράβασις, ἡ [2] 3 • 4 *transgression, overstepping*
τύπος, ὁ 13 • 26 *type, pattern, model*
6 γέ 6 • 18 *indeed;*
πέρας γέ τοι *and furthermore*
γλυπτός 1 • 1 *carved;* subst. *carved image*
ἐνδόξως 3 • 5 *splendor, place of honor*
ἐντέλλω 7 • 29 *to command*
κήρυγμα, τό 1 • 5 *proclamation, official announcement*
ὄφις, ὁ 4 • 9 *snake, serpent*
πέρας 6 • 13 *finally, in conclusion, furthermore*
τοί 6 • 7 *and furthermore, besides*
τύπος, ὁ 13 • 26 *type, pattern, model*
χαλκοῦς 2 • 2 *made of copper/brass/bronze*
χωνευτός 1 • 1 *cast, poured;* subst. *an image made of cast metal*
7 ἀναφέρω 1 • 8 *to offer up*
δάκνω 2 • 2 *to bite*
δέησις, ἡ 1 • 6 *prayer, urgent request to meet a need*
δέομαι 2 • 7 *to ask, request*
ἐπίκειμαι 1 • 6 *to lie on*
ζωοποιέω 5 • 10 *to make alive, give life to*
ἴασις, ἡ 1 • 7 *healing, cure*
ξύλον, τό 8 • 23 *pole, wooden pole*
ὄφις, ὁ 4 • 9 *snake, serpent*
παραχρῆμα 1 • 2 *immediately, at once*
8 Ναυή, ὁ 2 • 3 *Nun*
9 Ἀμαλήκ, ὁ 1 • 1 *Amalek*
ἐκκόπτω 1 • 3 *to cut off, exterminate*
κατάσκοπος, ὁ 1 • 3 *a spy*
Ναυή, ὁ 2 • 3 *Nun*
ὁπότε 1 • 1 *when*
ῥίζα, ἡ 1 • 8 *root*
10 ἐπεί 5 • 35 *since, because, for*
πλάνη, ἡ 4 • 11 *error, delusion, deceit, deception*
προφητεύω 5 • 9 *to prophesy, foretell*
συνίημι 7 • 21 *to understand, comprehend*
τύπος, ὁ 13 • 26 *type, pattern, model*
ὑποπόδιον, τό 2 • 3 *footstool*
11 διαρρήσσω 1 • 1 *to shatter, destroy*
ἐπακούω 2 • 3 *to heed, obey;*
ἐπακούω ἔμπροσθέν τινος *to act appropriately before someone;* i.e., *obey someone*
Ἠσαΐας, ὁ 1 • 2 *Isaiah*
ἰσχύς, ἡ 2 • 11 *strength, power, might*

## Chapter 13

1 **κληρονομέω** 2 • 11 *to inherit, be an heir*
2 **γαστήρ, ἡ** 1 • 2 *womb*
**δέομαι** 2 • 7 *to ask, request*
**δουλεύω** 2 • 42 *to be a slave, be subjected*
**εἶτα** 6 • 48 *then, next*
**ἐλάσσων** 2 • 6 *younger*
**Ἰσαάκ, ὁ** 5 • 7 *Isaac*
**κοιλία, ἡ** 1 • 1 *womb, uterus*
**πυνθάνομαι** 1 • 2 *to inquire, ask*
**Ῥεβέκκα, ἡ** [2] 3 • 3 *Rebecca*
**στεῖρα, ἡ** 1 • 4 *barren, infertile*
**συλλαμβάνω** 1 • 11 *to conceive, become pregnant*
**ὑπερέχω** 2 • 7 *to rule over, have power over, be in authority over*
3 **αἰσθάνομαι** 4 • 5 *to perceive, understand*
**Ἰσαάκ, ὁ** 5 • 7 *Isaac*
**Ῥεβέκκα, ἡ** 3 • 3 *Rebecca*
4 **Ἰακώβ, ὁ** 9 • 13 *Jacob*
**προφητεία, ἡ** 1 • 4 *prophecy, prophetic utterance*
**στερέω** 1 • 1 *to deprive*
**φανερός** 2 • 9 *readily known, visible, clear, plainly to be seen, open, plain, evident*
5 **δουλεύω** 2 • 42 *to be a slave, be subjected*
**ἐλάσσων** 2 • 6 *younger*
**ἐναλλάξ** 1 • 2 *crossways*
**Ἐφραίμ, ὁ** [2] 2 • 2 *Ephraim*
**Ἰακώβ, ὁ** [6] 9 • 13 *Jacob*
**Μανασσῆ, ὁ** [3] 3 • 3 *Manasseh*
**μεταξύ** 1 • 10 *afterward, next, yet to come*
**μετατίθημι** 1 • 9 *to transfer*
**νέος** 1 • 16 *young, younger*
**προσάγω** [2] 4 • 7 *to bring (forward)*
**πρωτότοκος** 1 • 4 *firstborn*
**τύπος, ὁ** 13 • 26 *type, pattern, model*
6 **κληρονόμος, ὁ** 2 • 3 *beneficiary, heir*
7 **ἀκροβυστία, ἡ** 2 • 2 *uncircumcision*
**ἀπέχω** 1 • 35 *to receive in full*
**γνῶσις, ἡ** 10 • 32 *knowledge*
**μιμνήσκω** 1 • 1 *to think of and call attention to (something or someone), make mention of (someone)*
**τέλειος** 6 • 25 *perfect, full measure of*

## Chapter 14

1 **ναί** 1 • 8 *yes, indeed*
**ὀμνύω** 2 • 9 *to swear, take an oath*
2 **δάκτυλος, ὁ** 2 • 4 *finger*
**καταφέρω** 1 • 1 *to bring down*
**νηστεύω** 5 • 24 *to fast*
**πλάξ, ἡ** 5 • 5 *tablet*
**Σινᾶ** 3 • 3 *Sinai* (indecl.)
**τεσσαράκοντα** [2] 4 • 6 *forty*
3 **Αἴγυπτος, ἡ** 3 • 9 *Egypt*
**ἀνομέω** 2 • 5 *to be lawless, sin*
**ἐξάγω** 3 • 7 *to lead out, bring out*
**πλάξ, ἡ** [2] 5 • 5 *tablet*
**ῥίπτω** 3 • 22 *to throw*
**συνίημι** 7 • 21 *to understand, comprehend*
**συντρίβω** 5 • 10 *to shatter, smash, crush*
**τάχος, τό** 2 • 7 *quickly, without delay*
**χώνευμα, τό** 1 • 2 *image made of cast metal, cast image*
4 **θεράπων, ὁ** 1 • 6 *servant, attendant, aide*
**κληρονομία, ἡ** 2 • 6 *inheritance*
**μανθάνω** 10 • 26 *to learn*
**ὑπομένω** 6 • 32 *to hold out, endure*
5 **ἁμάρτημα, τό** 1 • 8 *sin, transgression*
**ἀνομία, ἡ** 9 • 33 *lawlessness*
**δαπανάω** 1 • 7 *to spend, spend freely*
**διατίθημι** 2 • 2 *to decree, ordain*
**κληρονομέω** 2 • 11 *to inherit, be an heir*
**λυτρόω** 5 • 11 *to set free, rescue, redeem*
**πλάνη, ἡ** 4 • 11 *error, delusion, deceit, deception*
**τελειόω** 2 • 14 *to make perfect*
**φαίνω** 1 • 37 *to make one's appearance, show oneself*
6 **ἐντέλλω** 7 • 29 *to command*
**λυτρόω** 5 • 11 *to set free, rescue, redeem*

7 **γένος, τό** 1 • 16 *nation, people*
**δεσμός, ὁ** 1 • 14 *bond, fetter*
**ἐνισχύω** 1 • 2 *to strengthen*
**ἐξάγω** 3 • 7 *to lead out, free*
**λυτρόω** 5 • 11 *to set free, rescue, redeem*
**πεδάω** 1 • 1 *to bind, fetter, shackle*
**πόθεν** 2 • 6 *from where? from what place?*
8 **λυτρόω** 5 • 11 *to set free, rescue, redeem*
9 **αἰχμάλωτος, ὁ** 1 • 1 *captive*
**ἀνάβλεψις, ἡ** 1 • 1 *recovering of sight*
**ἀνταπόδοσις, ἡ** 1 • 1 *reward, recompense*
**ἄφεσις, ἡ** 7 • 13 *release*
**δεκτός** 3 • 9 *favorable*
**εἵνεκα** 1 • 3 *because of, on account of, for the sake of*
**ἐνιαυτός, ὁ** 3 • 7 *year*
**ἰάομαι** 3 • 11 *to heal, restore*
**πενθέω** 1 • 2 *to grieve, mourn, be sad*
**συντρίβω** 5 • 10 pass. *to be broken*
**ταπεινός** 3 • 8 *lowly, humble*
**χρίω** 1 • 2 *to anoint*

## Chapter 15

1 **ἁγιάζω** 8 • 16 *to reverence, treat as holy*
**δέκα** 4 • 22 *ten*
**καθαρός** [2] 5 • 45 *pure, free from moral guilt*
**Σινᾶ** 3 • 3 *Sinai* (indecl.)
2 **ἔλεος, τό** 1 • 19 *mercy, compassion, pity*
3 **ἁγιάζω** 8 • 16 *to reverence, treat as holy*
**ἕβδομος** 3 • 6 *seventh*
**ἕξ** 3 • 22 *six*
**καταπαύω** 5 • 7 *to rest, stop*
**κτίσις, ἡ** 1 • 19 *creation, world*
**συντελέω** 6 • 15 *to bring to an end, complete, finish, close*
4 **ἕξ** [2] 3 • 22 *six*
**ἑξακισχίλιοι** [2] 2 • 2 *six thousand*
**οὐκοῦν** 8 • 10 *therefore, so, accordingly*
**προσέχω** 11 • 25 *to pay attention, be alert, notice*
**σημαίνω** 1 • 2 *to mean, signify*
**σύμπας** [2] 2 • 3 *all together, whole*
**συντελέω** [3] 6 • 15 *to bring to an end, complete, finish, close*
**χίλιοι** [2] 2 • 3 *thousand*
5 **ἀλλάσσω** 2 • 5 *to change, alter*
**ἄνομος** 4 • 20 *lawless;* subst. *the lawless one*
**ἀσεβής** 6 • 14 *irreverent, impious, ungodly*
**ἀστήρ, ὁ** 1 • 7 *star*
**ἕβδομος** [2] 3 • 6 *seventh*
**καταπαύω** [2] 5 • 7 *to rest, stop*
**καταργέω** 5 • 6 *to put an end to, abolish, wipe out, set aside*
**σελήνη, ἡ** 1 • 7 *moon*
6 **ἁγιάζω** [3] 8 • 16 *to reverence, treat as holy*
**γέ** 6 • 18 *indeed;*
**πέρας γέ τοι** *and furthermore*
**καθαρός** [3] 5 • 45 *pure, free from moral guilt*
**πέρας** 6 • 13 *finally, in conclusion, furthermore*
**τοί** 6 • 7 *and furthermore, besides*
7 **ἁγιάζω** [3] 8 • 16 *to reverence, treat as holy*
**ἀνομία, ἡ** 9 • 33 *lawlessness*
**ἀπολαμβάνω** 1 • 17 *to receive*
**καταπαύω** 5 • 7 *to rest, stop*
**μηκέτι** 1 • 16 *no longer, not from now on*
8 **ἀνέχομαι** 2 • 4 *to endure, put up with, bear*
**γέ** 6 • 18 *indeed;*
**πέρας γέ τοι** *and furthermore*
**δεκτός** 3 • 9 *pleasing, acceptable*
**καταπαύω** 5 • 7 *to rest, stop*
**νεομηνία, ἡ** 2 • 2 *new moon, first of the month*
**ὄγδοος** 2 • 5 *eighth*
**πέρας** 6 • 13 *finally, in conclusion, furthermore*
**τοί** 6 • 7 *and furthermore, besides*
9 **εὐφροσύνη, ἡ** 4 • 5 *joy, gladness, cheerfulness*
**ὄγδοος** 2 • 5 *eighth*

## Chapter 16

1 **οἰκοδομή, ἡ** 1 • 103 *building, edifice*

**ταλαίπωρος** 1 • 5 *miserable, wretched, distressed*
2 **ἀφιερόω** 1 • 1 *to consecrate*
**δράξ, ἡ** 1 • 1 *hand*
**κατάπαυσις, ἡ** 1 • 1 *rest*
**καταργέω** 5 • 6 *to invalidate, make powerless*
**μανθάνω** 10 • 26 *to learn*
**μάταιος** 4 • 14 *idle, empty, fruitless, useless, powerless*
**μετρέω** 1 • 5 *to measure*
**σπιθαμή, ἡ** 1 • 1 *span*
**σχεδόν** 1 • 4 *almost, nearly*
**ὑποπόδιον, τό** 2 • 3 *footstool*
3 **γέ** 6 • 18 *indeed;*
**πέρας γέ τοι** *and furthermore*
**καθαιρέω** 3 • 7 *to tear down*
**πέρας** 6 • 13 *finally, in conclusion, furthermore*
**τοί** 6 • 7 *and furthermore, besides*
4 **ἀνοικοδομέω** 1 • 1 *to build up again, rebuild*
**καθαιρέω** 3 • 7 *to tear down*
**πολεμέω** 4 • 7 *to wage war, make war*
**ὑπηρέτης, ὁ** 1 • 5 *helper, assistant, servant*
5 **καταφθορά, ἡ** 2 • 5 *destruction, downfall, corruption*
**μάνδρα, ἡ** 1 • 1 *sheep-fold*
**νομή, ἡ** 1 • 2 *pasturage*
**πύργος, ὁ** 1 • 148 *tower*
6 **ἑβδομάς, ἡ** 1 • 1 *week*
**ἐνδόξως** 3 • 5 *in splendor*
**καταρτίζω** 1 • 6 *to prepare, make, create, outfit*
**συντελέω** 6 • 15 *to bring to an end, complete, finish, close*
7 **ἀληθῶς** 4 • 23 *truly, in truth, really, actually*
**ἀσθενής** 1 • 12 *weak*
**εἰδωλολατρεία, ἡ** 2 • 2 *idolatry, image worship*
**ἐναντίος** 1 • 4 *opposed, contrary*
**κατοικητήριον, τό** 3 • 3 *dwelling place, habitat*
**μανθάνω** 10 • 26 *to learn*
**οἰκοδομητός** 1 • 1 *built*
**πλήρης** 2 • 20 *full, filled*
**φθαρτός** 2 • 10 *perishable, subject to decay/destruction*
8 **ἀληθῶς** 4 • 23 *truly, in truth, really, actually*
**ἄφεσις, ἡ** 7 • 13 *forgiveness, pardon, cancellation*
**ἐνδόξως** 3 • 5 *in splendor*
**κατοικητήριον, τό** 3 • 3 *dwelling place, habitat*
**κτίζω** 1 • 25 *to create, bring into existence*
**μανθάνω** 10 • 26 *to learn*
**προσέχω** 11 • 25 *to pay attention, be alert, notice*
9 **ἄφθαρτος** 2 • 7 *imperishable, immortal, incorruptible*
**δικαίωμα, τό** 8 • 12 *righteous requirement, commandment*
**δουλόω** 1 • 2 *to enslave*
**εἰσάγω** 3 • 6 *to bring in, lead in*
**κλῆσις, ἡ** 1 • 4 *call, calling*
**μετάνοια, ἡ** 1 • 72 *repentance, turning about, conversion*
**προφητεύω** 5 • 9 *to prophesy, proclaim an inspired revelation*
10 **ἐκπλήσσω** 3 • 4 *to be amazed, be overwhelmed*
**ἐπιθυμέω** 2 • 17 *to desire, long for*
**μηδέποτε** 1 • 5 *never*
**πνευματικός** 3 • 19 *spiritual, caused by* or *filled with the divine spirit, pertaining to the divine spirit*
**ποθέω** 1 • 4 *to desire, wish (for), be anxious, strive after*
**ποτέ** 4 • 15 *ever, at any time*

## Chapter 17

1 **ἀνήκω** 1 • 10 *to refer, relate, belong*
**ἁπλότης** 2 • 15 *simplicity, sincerity, uprightness, frankness*
**δηλόω** 2 • 49 *to explain, clarify*
**παραλείπω** 1 • 2 *to leave out, omit*
2 **ἐνίστημι** 4 • 6 *to be now, happen now;*
subst. *things of the present*
**κεῖμαι** 1 • 24 *to occur, appear, be found*
**νοέω** 7 • 46 *to perceive, apprehend, understand, gain insight into*

## Chapter 18

1 **γνῶσις, ἡ** 10 • 32 *knowledge*

**διαφορά, ἡ** 1 • 3 *difference*
**μεταβαίνω** 1 • 2 *to pass, pass on*
**Σατανᾶς, ὁ** 1 • 5 *Satan*
**τάσσω** 1 • 4 *to arrange, put in place*
**φωταγωγός** 1 • 1 *light-bringing, light-giving*
2 **ἀνομία, ἡ** 9 • 33 *lawlessness*

## Chapter 19

1 **ὁδεύω** 1 • 3 *to go, travel, make one's way*
**ὁρίζω** 3 • 10 *to determine, appoint, fix, set*
**σπεύδω** 1 • 4 *to be zealous, exert oneself, be industrious*
2 **ἁπλοῦς** 2 • 4 *guileless, sincere, straightforward*
**ἀρεστός** 1 • 2 *pleasing, satisfying*
**ἐγκαταλείπω** 3 • 8 *to forsake, abandon, desert*
**κολλάω** 7 • 32 *to join oneself to, join, cling to, associate with*
**λυτρόω** 5 • 11 *to set free, rescue, redeem*
**πλάσσω** 2 • 8 *to form, mold*
**πλούσιος** 5 • 22 *rich in, abounding in*
**ὑπόκρισις, ἡ** 3 • 13 *hypocrisy, pretense, outward show*
3 **βουλή, ἡ** 4 • 19 *resolution, decision*
**θράσος, τό** 1 • 3 *arrogance, shamelessness*
**πλησίον** 5 • 17 *near, close;* subst. *neighbor*
**ταπεινόφρων** 1 • 4 *humble*
**ὑψόω** 1 • 4 *to exalt*
4 **ἀκαθαρσία, ἡ** 2 • 2 *immorality, vileness, impurity (especially of sexual sins)*
**ἐλέγχω** 2 • 16 *to reprove, correct*
**ἡσύχιος** 1 • 7 *quiet, well-ordered*
**μνησικακέω** 2 • 9 *to remember evil, bear malice, bear a grudge*
**μοιχεύω** 1 • 3 *to commit adultery*
**παιδοφθορέω** 1 • 2 *to molest (children), sodomize (young boys)*
**παράπτωμα, τό** 1 • 10 *offense, wrongdoing, sin*
**πορνεύω** 1 • 2 *to engage in sexual immorality, engage in illicit sex, fornicate*
**πραΰς** 1 • 8 *gentle, humble, considerate, meek*
**τρέμω** 1 • 3 *to tremble, be in awe*
5 **διψυχέω** 1 • 25 *to be undecided, be changeable, doubt*
**θυγάτηρ, ἡ** 2 • 10 *daughter*
**μάταιος** 4 • 14 *vain, idle, empty, fruitless, useless, powerless*
**νεότης, ἡ** 1 • 3 *youth*
**πλησίον** 5 • 17 *near, close;* subst. *neighbor*
**πότερος** 1 • 3 *whether*
**φθορά, ἡ** 1 • 4 *abortion*
**φονεύω** 1 • 4 *to murder, kill*
6 **ἀναστρέφω** 1 • 8 *to associate with, be involved with*
**ἄνευ** 2 • 12 *without*
**ἐνέργημα, τό** 1 • 2 *experience*
**ἐπιθυμέω** 2 • 17 *to desire, long for*
**κολλάω** 7 • 32 *to join oneself to, join, cling to, associate with*
**πλεονέκτης, ὁ** 1 • 3 *a greedy person, one who desires to have more than is due*
**πλησίον** 5 • 17 *near, close;* subst. *neighbor*
**προσδέχομαι** 3 • 10 *to receive*
**συμβαίνω** 1 • 7 *to happen, come about*
**ταπεινός** 3 • 8 *humble*
**ὑψηλός** 4 • 12 *exalted, proud, haughty*
7 **αἰσχύνη, ἡ** 1 • 2 *modesty, reverence, shame*
**ἀμφότεροι** 1 • 21 *both*
**δίγλωσσος** 1 • 2 *double-tongued, insincere, deceitful*
**διγνώμων** 1 • 2 *double-minded, fickle*
**ἐπιτάσσω** 2 • 7 *to command, order, give orders*
**μήποτε** 5 • 22 *lest*
**παιδίσκη, ἡ** 1 • 3 *female slave*
**πικρία, ἡ** 1 • 7 *bitterness, animosity, anger, harshness*
**τύπος, ὁ** 13 • 26 *copy, image*
8 **ἁγνεύω** 1 • 1 *to be pure*
**ἄφθαρτος** 2 • 7 *imperishable, immortal, incorruptible*
**κοινωνέω** 1 • 2 *to share, contribute a share*
**κοινωνός, ὁ** 1 • 7 *sharer, companion, partner*
**παγίς, ἡ** 1 • 2 *snare, trap*

**πλησίον** 5 • 17 *near, close;* subst. *neighbor*
**πόσος** 1 • 10 *how great?* (with **μᾶλλον**, *how much more?*)
**πρόγλωσσος** 1 • 1 *hasty of tongue, talkative*
**φθαρτός** 2 • 10 *perishable, subject to decay/destruction*
9 **ἐκτείνω** 3 • 7 *to stretch out*
**κόρη, ἡ** 1 • 1 *pupil;* fig. of something held dear, *favorite, apple of the eye*
**συσπάω** 1 • 2 *to draw together, pull back*
10 **ἐκζητέω** 7 • 16 *to seek out, search for*
**κοπιάω** 1 • 4 *to labor, work hard, toil, strive, struggle*
**λύτρον, τό** 1 • 2 *price of release, ransom*
**μελετάω** 5 • 6 *to take care, endeavor*
**μιμνήσκομαι** 1 • 9 *to give careful consideration to, remember, think of, care for, be concerned about, keep in mind*
11 **ἀνταποδότης, ὁ** 1 • 2 *paymaster, recompenser*
**ἀφαιρέω** 4 • 8 *to take away, do away with, remove*
**γόγγυσις, ἡ** 1 • 1 *murmuring, muttering*
**δικαίως** 3 • 12 *justly, in an upright manner, fairly*
**διστάζω** 1 • 10 *to hesitate*
**μισθός, ὁ** 6 • 22 *reward, recompense*
**προστίθημι** 2 • 22 *to add*
**εἰς τέλος** (adverbial marker of intensity) *utterly, finally*
12 **εἰρηνεύω** 1 • 17 *to cause others to live in peace, reconcile*
**ἐξομολογέω** 2 • 15 *to confess, admit*
**μάχομαι** 1 • 2 *to fight, quarrel, dispute*
**προσήκω** 1 • 3 *to come to, approach*
**σχίσμα, τό** 1 • 10 *division, dissension, schism*

## Chapter 20

1 **ἁρπαγή, ἡ** 2 • 3 *robbery, plunder*
**αὐθάδεια, ἡ** 1 • 6 *arrogance, willfulness, stubbornness*
**ἀφοβία, ἡ** 1 • 1 *lack of reverence*
**διπλοκαρδία, ἡ** 1 • 2 *double-heartedness, duplicity*
**δόλος, ὁ** 1 • 8 *deceit, cunning, treachery*
**εἰδωλολατρεία, ἡ** 2 • 2 *idolatry, image worship*
**θρασύτης, ἡ** 1 • 2 *boldness, arrogance*
**κακία, ἡ** 2 • 9 *malice, ill-will*
**κατάρα, ἡ** 1 • 4 *curse, imprecation*
**μαγεία, ἡ** 1 • 3 *magic*
**μέλας** 2 • 20 *black;* subst. *the devil, 'the black one'*
**μεστός** 1 • 4 *filled with, thoroughly characterized by (something)*
**μοιχεία, ἡ** 1 • 9 *adultery*
**παράβασις, ἡ** 3 • 4 *transgression, overstepping*
**πλεονεξία, ἡ** 2 • 7 *greediness, insatiableness, avarice, covetousness*
**σκολιός** 1 • 2 *crooked*
**τιμωρία, ἡ** 1 • 13 *punishment*
**ὑπερηφανία, ἡ** 1 • 8 *arrogance, haughtiness, pride*
**ὑπόκρισις, ἡ** 3 • 13 *hypocrisy, pretense, outward show*
**ὕψος, τό** 1 • 7 *pride, arrogance*
**φαρμακεία, ἡ** 1 • 1 *sorcery, magic*
**φόνος, ὁ** 1 • 4 *murder, killing*
2 **ἀγρυπνέω** 1 • 2 *to look after, care for*
**ἄνομος** 4 • 20 *lawless*
**ἀνταπόδομα, τό** 2 • 3 *repayment, reward*
**ἀποστρέφω** 1 • 8 *to turn away from, reject*
**διώκτης, ὁ** 1 • 2 *persecutor*
**ἐλεέω** 2 • 16 *to have compassion, mercy, pity*
**ἐνδέω** 1 • 5 *to be in want, be in need*
**εὐχερής** 1 • 2 *easily inclined, prone, reckless*
**θλίβω** 3 • 25 *to oppress, afflict*
**καταλαλιά, ἡ** 1 • 13 *evil speech, slander, defamation, detraction*

**καταπονέω** 2 • 4 *to subdue, torment, wear out, oppress*
**κολλάω** 7 • 32 *to join oneself to, join, cling to, associate with*
**κριτής, ὁ** 1 • 6 *judge*
**μακράν** 1 • 15 *far away, distant*
**μάταιος** 4 • 14 *idle, empty, fruitless, useless, powerless, lacking truth*
**μισθός, ὁ** 6 • 22 *reward*
**ὀρφανός** 1 • 9 *orphaned, without parents*
**πανταμάρτηρος** 1 • 1 *altogether sinful*
**παράκλητος, ὁ** 1 • 3 *mediator, intercessor, helper, advocate*
**πένης** 1 • 16 *poor, needy*
**πλάσμα, τό** 2 • 3 *that which is formed or molded;*
**φθορεῖς πλάσματος θεοῦ** possibly "*those who destroy what God has formed* in the womb, by abortion"[1]
**πλούσιος** 5 • 22 *rich, wealthy*
**πονέω** 1 • 2 *to work hard, toil*
**πόρρω** 1 • 8 *far away*
**πραΰτης, ἡ** 1 • 8 *gentleness, humility, courtesy, considerateness, meekness*
**προσέχω** 11 • 25 *to be concerned about, care for, take care*
**φθορεύς, ὁ** 2 • 4 *seducer, corruptor*
**φονεύς, ὁ** 1 • 2 *murderer*
**χήρα, ἡ** 1 • 13 *widow*
**ψεῦδος, τό** 1 • 6 *lie, falsehood*

## Chapter 21

1 **ἀνταπόδομα, τό** 2 • 3 *recompense*
**δικαίωμα, τό** 8 • 12 *righteous requirement, commandment*
**ἐκλέγομαι** 4 • 15 *to choose, select*
**μανθάνω** 10 • 26 *to learn*
**συναπόλλυμι** 2 • 2 *to destroy with*
2 **γνώμη, ἡ** 2 • 20 *purpose, intention, mind, mind-set, will, motive*
**ἐλλείπω** 3 • 3 *to leave off, fail, be deficient* or *inadequate*
**συμβουλία, ἡ** 1 • 2 *advice, counsel*
**ὑπερέχω** 2 • 7 *to rule over, have power over, be in authority over*
3 **μισθός, ὁ** 6 • 22 *reward*
**συναπόλλυμι** 2 • 2 *to destroy with*
4 **νομοθέτης, ὁ** 1 • 1 *lawgiver*
**σύμβουλος, ὁ** 1 • 8 *adviser, counselor*
**ὑπόκρισις, ἡ** 3 • 13 *hypocrisy, pretense, outward show*
5 **γνῶσις, ἡ** 10 • 32 *knowledge*
**δικαίωμα, τό** 8 • 12 *righteous requirement, commandment*
**ἐπιστήμη, ἡ** 2 • 5 *understanding, knowledge*
**κυριεύω** 3 • 5 *to rule*
**σύνεσις, ἡ** 3 • 22 *understanding, insight*
6 **ἐκζητέω** 7 • 16 *to seek out, search for*
**θεοδίδακτος** 1 • 1 *taught/ instructed by God*
7 **ἀγρυπνία, ἡ** 1 • 1 *care*
**μελετάω** 5 • 6 *to practice, cultivate*
**μνεῖα, ἡ** 1 • 3 *remembrance, memory*
**μνημονεύω** 1 • 25 *to remember, keep in mind, think of*
**χωρέω** 1 • 15 *to lead to, reach*
8 **ἀναπληρόω** 1 • 4 *to fulfill*
**ἐκζητέω** 7 • 16 *to seek out, search for*
**ἐλλείπω** 3 • 3 *to leave off, fail, be deficient* or *inadequate*
**κεῦος, τό** 3 • 9 *instrument, vessel*
**συνεχῶς** 1 • 1 *continually, unremittingly*
9 **εὐφραίνω** 4 • 15 *to gladden, cheer up*
**σπουδάζω** 3 • 16 *to be zealous, be eager, take pains, make every effort, be conscientious*

1. BDAG s.v. **πλάσμα**.

# The Shepherd of Hermas

## VISION ONE

### Chapter 1 (Hv 1.1)

1 **ἀδελφή, ἡ** 6 • 10 *sister*
**ἀναγνωρίζω** 1 • 1 *to see again*
**πιπράσκω** 1 • 1 *to sell*
**Ῥόδη, ἡ** 1 • 1 *Rhoda*
**Ῥώμη, ἡ** 1 • 8 *Rome*
**τρέφω** 2 • 3 *to rear, bring up, train*

2 **βουλεύω** 5 • 6 *to deliberate, consider*
**διαλογίζομαι** 6 • 6 *to consider, ponder, reason*
**ἐξάγω** 1 • 7 *to lead out, bring out*
**ἐπιδίδωμι** 60 • 62 *to give, hand over, deliver*
**κάλλος, τό** 4 • 5 *beauty*
**λούω** 1 • 2 *to wash, bathe*
**ποταμός, ὁ** 3 • 4 *river, stream*
**Τίβερις, ὁ** 1 • 1 *Tiber River*
**τρόπος, ὁ** 5 • 17 *ways, customs, kind of life*

3 **ἀνοδία, ἡ** 5 • 5 *a wayless area, roadless place*
**ἀπορρήγνυμι** 1 • 1 *to break up*
**ἀποφέρω** 8 • 9 *to carry, take away*
**ἀφυπνόω** 1 • 1 *to fall asleep*
**γόνυ, τό** 3 • 4 *knee*
**διαβαίνω** 1 • 1 *to go through, cross*
**ἐκπρεπής** 2 • 2 *remarkable, outstanding*
**ἐξομολογέω** 5 • 15 *to confess, admit*
**Κοῦμαι** 2 • 2 *Cumae*
**κρημνώδης** 2 • 2 *steep, precipitous*
**κτίσις, ἡ** 13 • 19 *creature, created work*
**ὁδεύω** 2 • 3 *to go, travel, make a trip, walk*
**ὁμαλός** 5 • 5 *level, smooth, even*
**ποταμός, ὁ** 3 • 4 *river, stream*

4 **ἐπιθυμέω** 7 • 17 *to desire*
**Ἑρμᾶς, ὁ** 13 • 13 *Hermas*

5 **ἀναλαμβάνω** 3 • 10 *to take up*
**ἐλέγχω** 1 • 16 *to expose*
**κυρία, ἡ** 24 • 24 *lady, mistress*

6 **αὐξάνω/αὔξω** 2 • 7 *to grow something, cause to grow, increase*
**ἔλεγχος, ὁ** 1 • 3 *accusation*
**ἕνεκα** 8 • 15 *because of, on account of, for the sake of*
**κτίζω** 14 • 25 *to create*
**ὀργίζω** 3 • 3 *to be angry*
**πληθύνω** 2 • 11 *to increase, multiply*

7 **ἀδελφή, ἡ** 6 • 10 *sister*
**αἰσχρός** 1 • 3 *shameful, base*
**ἐντρέπω** 2 • 9 *to respect*
**ἡγέομαι** 7 • 25 *to think, consider, regard*
**θεά, ἡ** 1 • 1 *goddess*
**πότε** 3 • 6 *when?*
**τρόπος, ὁ** 5 • 17 *manner, way, kind guise;*
**ποίῳ τρόπῳ** *how?*
**ὦ** 1 • 8 *o, oh!*

8 **αἰχμαλωτισμός, ὁ** 1 • 1 *captivity*
**ἀντέχομαι** 1 • 1 *to hold fast to*
**βουλεύω** 5 • 6 *to deliberate, consider*
**γαυριάω** 1 • 1 *to be proud, exult, glory*
**γέ** 3 • 18 *indeed*
**γελάω** 2 • 2 *to laugh*
**ἐπισπάω** 3 • 4 *to bring upon*
**εὐκατάλλακτος** 1 • 1 *easily placated, favorable*
**κατορθόω** 5 • 5 *to set straight, complete, bring to a successful conclusion*
**μάλιστα** 5 • 14 *most of all, above all, especially, particularly*
**περιποιέω** 8 • 9 *to acquire, obtain, gain for oneself*

**πλοῦτος, ὁ** 14 • 15 *wealth*
**πονηρία, ἡ** 36 • 41 *evil*
**πρᾶγμα, τό** [2] 19 • 23 *thing, matter, affair*
9 **ἁμάρτημα, τό** 4 • 8 *sin, transgression*
**ἀπογινώσκω** 3 • 3 *to despair*
**ἰάομαι** 4 • 11 *to heal*

## Chapter 2 (Hv 1.2)

1 **ἀναγράφω** 1 • 2 *to record, register*
**ἐξιλάσκομαι** 1 • 2 *to appease*
**ἱλατεύομαι** 1 • 1 *to be gracious*
**κλείω** 1 • 2 *to close*
**λυπέω** 13 • 17 *to be sad, be sorrowful*
**τέλειος** 2 • 25 *perfect*
**φρίσσω** 1 • 2 *to tremble, shudder*
2 **διακρίνω** 3 • 7 *to evaluate, judge*
**ἔριον, τό** 1 • 10 *wool*
**Ἑρμᾶς, ὁ** 13 • 13 *Hermas*
**ἱματισμός, ὁ** 6 • 8 *clothing, apparel*
**καθέδρα, ἡ** 10 • 11 *chair, seat*
**κατέναντι** 3 • 3 *opposite, before*
**κυρία, ἡ** 24 • 24 *lady, mistress*
**λαμπρός** 14 • 14 *bright, shining*
**λευκός** 24 • 24 *white*
**λυπέω** 13 • 17 *to be sad, be sorrowful*
**πρεσβῦτις, ἡ** 1 • 1 *older woman, elderly woman*
**συμβουλεύω** 1 • 3 *to meditate on, consider*
**χιόνινος** 1 • 1 *snowy, snow-white*
3 **ἀστομάχητος** 1 • 1 *not easily angered*
**γελάω** 2 • 2 *to laugh*
**Ἑρμᾶς, ὁ** 13 • 13 *Hermas*
**ἰδέα, ἡ** 8 • 9 *appearance*
**ἱλαρός** 24 • 34 *joyful*
**κατηφής** 1 • 1 *downcast*
**μακρόθυμος** 5 • 9 *patient, forbearing, tolerant, even-tempered*
**στυγνός** 1 • 1 *gloomy, sad*
4 **ἀκακία, ἡ** 8 • 10 *innocence, guilelessness*
**ἀπέχω** 21 • 35 *to keep away, abstain, refrain from*
**ἁπλότης, ἡ** 12 • 15 *ingenuousness, simplicity, sincerity, uprightness, frankness*
**βουλή, ἡ** 8 • 19 *plan, purpose, intention*
**δοκιμάζω** 10 • 19 *to prove, approve*
**ἐγκρατής** 1 • 3 *self-controlled, disciplined*
**ἔκπληκτος** 1 • 1 *shocking, frightful*
**ἐπιθυμέω** 7 • 17 *to desire, long for*
**ἐπιφέρω** 2 • 3 *to bring on/about, inflict*
**Ἑρμᾶς, ὁ** 13 • 13 *Hermas*
**μάλιστα** 5 • 14 *most of all, above all, especially, particularly*
**μηδαμῶς** 1 • 4 *by no means, certainly not, no*
**πάνσεμνος** 1 • 1 *greatly revered*
**πάντως** 7 • 9 *of course*
**πλήρης** 13 • 20 *filled, full*
**πρᾶγμα, τό** 19 • 23 *thing, matter, affair*; here with negative connotation *difficulties, troubles*

## Chapter 3 (Hv 1.3)

1 **ἀνομέω** 1 • 5 *to be lawless, sin*
**ἀνόμημα, τό** 1 • 2 *lawless action, iniquity*
**βιωτικός** 4 • 4 *belonging to daily life*;
  **τῶν βιωτικῶν πράξεων** *affairs/cares of daily life*
**γονεύς, ὁ** 3 • 3 pl. *parents*
**δεινῶς** 2 • 2 *terribly*;
  **καταφθαρῆναι δεινῶς** *to become disgustingly corrupt*
**ἕνεκα** 8 • 15 *because of, on account of, for the sake of;* here *for this reason*
**ἰάομαι** 4 • 11 *to heal*
**καταφθείρω** [2] 8 • 8 *to ruin, corrupt*
**νουθετέω** 5 • 9 *to admonish, warn, instruct*
**ὀργίζω** 3 • 3 *to be angry*
**πρᾶξις, ἡ** 44 • 50 *affairs, cares*
**προγίνομαι** 1 • 2 *to happen/be done before*

**φιλότεκνος** 1 • 1 *loving one's children;* here *indulgent*
2 **βίβλος, ἡ** 2 • 5 *record-book*
**διαλείπω** 3 • 3 *to stop, cease*
**ἐγγράφω** 4 • 5 *to write in, record*
**ἐλεέω** 1 • 16 *to have compassion, mercy, pity*
**εὐψυχέω** 1 • 1 *to have courage*
**θεμελιόω** 6 • 6 *to establish, strengthen*
**ἰσχυροποιέω** [2] 7 • 7 *to strengthen*
**καθημερινός** 1 • 1 *daily*
**νουθετέω** 5 • 9 *to admonish, warn, instruct*
**περιγίνομαι** [2] 2 • 2 *to overcome*
**πολυσπλαγχνία, ἡ** 3 • 3 *sympathy, compassion, mercy*
**πονηρία, ἡ** 36 • 41 *wickedness, baseness, maliciousness, sinfulness*
**πρᾶγμα, τό** 19 • 23 *thing, matter, affair*
**ῥᾳθυμέω** 1 • 1 *to be unconcerned, be idle, relax*
**σφυροκοπέω** 1 • 1 *to beat with a hammer*
**χαλκεύς, ὁ** 1 • 2 *blacksmith, metalworker*
3 **ἀκροατής, ὁ** 1 • 4 *a hearer*
**βαστάζω** 18 • 24 *to bear, endure*
**ἔκφρικτος** 1 • 1 *frightening*
**ἥμερος** 2 • 3 *kind*
**θαυμαστῶς** 3 • 3 *wonderfully*
**ἰσχύω** 4 • 9 *to have power, be competent, be able*
**κυρία, ἡ** 24 • 24 *lady, mistress*
**μεγάλως** 5 • 9 *greatly*
**μνημονεύω** [2] 7 • 25 *to retain in one's memory*
**παύω** 8 • 12 *to stop (oneself), cease*
**σύμφορος** 6 • 6 *beneficial, advantageous, profitable*
**οὖν** (here possibly adversative; BDAG s.v. **οὖν** 4) *however*
4 **ἀόρατος** 2 • 13 *unseen, invisible*
**βουλή, ἡ** 8 • 19 *resolution, decision,* here with reference to the divine will
**βουνός, ὁ** 1 • 1 *hill*
**ἐκλεκτός** 9 • 30 *chosen*
**ἔνδοξος** 43 • 54 *glorious, splendid*
**ἐπαγγέλλω** 6 • 7 *to promise*
**εὐπρέπεια** 1 • 1 *beauty*
**θεμελιόω** 6 • 6 *to found*
**ἰσχυρός** 14 • 21 *mighty*
**κραταιός** 1 • 3 *powerful, mighty*
**κτίζω** [2] 14 • 25 *to create*
**κτίσις, ἡ** 13 • 19 *creation, world*
**μεθιστάνω** 1 • 1 *to remove*
**νόμιμος** 1 • 4 *lawful;* subst. *commandment*
**ὁμαλός** 5 • 5 *level*
**περιτίθημι** 1 • 6 *to put/place around/on*
**πήγνυμι** 1 • 1 *to make firm, fix*
**πρόνοια, ἡ** 1 • 3 *forethought, foresight, providence*
**σύνεσις, ἡ** 13 • 22 *wisdom*

### Chapter 4 (Hv 1.4)

1 **ἀνατολή, ἡ** 2 • 6 *east*
**καθέδρα, ἡ** 10 • 11 *chair, seat*
**νεανίας, ὁ** 1 • 1 *youth, young man;* here *servant* is possible
**τελέω** 22 • 23 *to bring to an end, finish, complete*
**τέσσαρες** 11 • 12 *four*
2 **ἀνάγνωσις, ἡ** 1 • 1 *reading*
**ἀποστάτης, ὁ** 3 • 3 *deserter, rebel*
**ἅπτω** 4 • 10 *to touch*
**ἀρέσκω** [2] 6 • 12 *to please, accommodate*
**κυρία, ἡ** 24 • 24 *lady, mistress*
**προσκαλέω** 3 • 5 *to summon, call on, call to oneself, invite*
**πρότερος** [2] 40 • 47 *former, earlier*
**σκληρός** 9 • 9 *hard, harsh, unpleasant*
**στῆθος, τό** 1 • 2 *chest, breast*
**χαλεπός** 2 • 5 *hard, difficult*
3 **ἀγκών, ὁ** 1 • 1 *arm*
**ἀνατολή, ἡ** 2 • 6 *east*
**ἀνδρίζομαι** 3 • 4 *to conduct oneself in a courageous way, act like a man*
**Ἑρμᾶς, ὁ** 13 • 13 *Hermas*
**ἱλαρός** 24 • 34 *cheerful, glad, happy*
**καθέδρα, ἡ** 10 • 11 *chair, seat*
**φαίνω** 12 • 37 *to make one's appearance, show oneself*

## VISION TWO

### Chapter 5 (Hv 2.1)

1 **ἀναμιμνῄσκω** 1 • 1 *to remind, cause to remember*
**ἀποφέρω** 8 • 9 *to carry, take away*
**Κοῦμαι** 2 • 2 *Cumae*
**ὅρασις, ἡ** 10 • 13 *vision*
**πέρυσι** [2] 3 • 3 *last year*
**περυσινός** 2 • 2 *of last year, of the previous year*
2 **γνωρίζω** 10 • 18 *to make known, reveal*
**γόνυ, τό** 3 • 4 *knee*
**ἡγέομαι** 7 • 25 *to think, consider, regard*
**πρότερος** 40 • 47 *former, earlier*
3 **ἀναγγέλλω** 2 • 8 *to disclose, announce, proclaim, teach*
**ἀπέναντι** 1 • 3 *before*
**βιβλαρίδιον, τό** 2 • 2 *little scroll/roll*
**βιβλίδιον, τό** 4 • 5 *brief document*
**ἐκλεκτός** 9 • 30 *chosen*
**κυρία, ἡ** 24 • 24 *lady, mistress*
**μεταγράφω** 2 • 5 *to copy, transcribe*
**μνημονεύω** 7 • 25 *to retain in one's memory*
**πέρυσι** 3 • 3 *last year*
**τοσοῦτος** 9 • 38 *so much*
4 **ἀναχωρέω** 7 • 7 *to withdraw, retire, take refuge*
**ἁρπάζω** 1 • 3 *to snatch away, take away*
**βιβλίδιον, τό** [2] 4 • 5 *brief document*
**γράμμα, τό** [2] 2 • 14 *letter (of the alphabet)*
**ἐξαίφνης** 3 • 6 *suddenly, unexpectantly*
**μεταγράφω** 2 • 5 *to copy, transcribe*
**συλλαβή, ἡ** 1 • 1 *syllable*
**τελέω** 22 • 23 *to bring to an end, finish, complete*

### Chapter 6 (Hv 2.2)

1 **ἀποκαλύπτω** 18 • 23 *to disclose*
**γνῶσις, ἡ** 1 • 32 *knowledge, grasp*
**δέκα** 3 • 10 *ten*
**νηστεύω** 14 • 23 *to fast*
2 **ἀθετέω** 2 • 4 *to commit an offense*
**ἀνομία, ἡ** 9 • 33 *lawless deeds, transgressions*
**ἀσέλγεια, ἡ** 3 • 3 *licentiousness*
**γονεύς, ὁ** [2] 3 • 3 pl. *parents*; **ἤκουσαν προδόται γονέων** (see BDAG s.v. **ἀκούω** 6: 'be called') *they were called betrayers of their parents*
**Ἑρμᾶς, ὁ** 13 • 13 *Hermas*
**πίμπλημι** 2 • 3 *to fill, fulfill*
**πονηρία, ἡ** [2] 36 • 41 *wickedness, baseness, maliciousness, sinfulness*
**προδίδωμι** [2] 2 • 5 *to betray*
**προδότης, ὁ** 5 • 6 *traitor, betrayer*
**προστίθημι** 13 • 22 *to add, put to*
**συμφυρμός, ὁ** 1 • 1 *improper sexual activities*
**ὠφελέω** 2 • 8 *to give help, benefit*
3 **ἀδελφή, ἡ** 6 • 10 *sister*
**ἀπέχω** [2] 21 • 35 *to keep away, abstain, refrain from, control*
**γνωρίζω** 10 • 18 *to make known, reveal*
**ἔλεος, τό** 4 • 19 *mercy*
**πονηρεύομαι** 13 • 15 *to do wrong, commit sin*
**σύμβιος** 1 • 3 *living together*; subst. *husband, wife*
4 **ἀποκαλύπτω** 18 • 23 *to reveal, disclose, bring to light, make fully known*
**γνωρίζω** 10 • 18 *to make known, reveal*
**δεσπότης, ὁ** 24 • 54 *lord, master*
**διψυχία, ἡ** 17 • 18 *indecision, doubt*
**ἐντέλλω** 17 • 29 *to command, order, give orders*
**μέχρι** 7 • 23 *until*
**πρότερος** 40 • 47 *former, earlier*
5 **ἁμάρτησις, ἡ** 1 • 1 *sin, sinning*
**δεσπότης, ὁ** 24 • 54 *lord, master*
**ἐκλεκτός** 9 • 30 *chosen*
**μετάνοια, ἡ** [3] 58 • 72 *repentance, turning about, conversion*
**ὀμνύω** 2 • 9 *to take an oath*
**ὁρίζω** 1 • 10 *to determine, appoint, fix, set*
6 **ἀπολαμβάνω** 6 • 17 *to receive*

**κατορθόω** 5 • 5 *to carry out*
**πλήρης** 13 • 20 *filled, full*
**προηγέομαι** 2 • 4 *to preside*
7 **ἐμμένω** 7 • 8 *to persevere, stand firm*
**διψυχέω** 21 • 25 *to be undecided, be changeable, doubt*
**πάροδος, ἡ** 2 • 3 *way, passage, thoroughfare;*
**ἡ πάροδος μετὰ τῶν ἀγγέλων** *the entrance with the angels, the way to the angels*
**ὑπομένω** 1 • 32 *to stand one's ground, hold out, endure*
8 **ἀπογνωρίζω** 1 • 1 *to dispossess*
**ἵλεως** 2 • 5 *gracious, forgiving*
**ὀμνύω** 2 • 9 *to take an oath*
**πολυσπλαγχνία, ἡ** 3 • 3 *sympathy, compassion, mercy*
**πρότερος** 40 • 47 *former, earlier*

## Chapter 7 (Hv 2.3)

1 **ἀδελφή, ἡ** 6 • 10 *sister*
**ἐάω** 5 • 13 *to let, permit*
**Ἑρμᾶς, ὁ** 13 • 13 *Hermas*
**ἰδιωτικός** 1 • 1 *private, of one's own*
**κατεργάζομαι** 3 • 7 *to bring about, produce, create*
**μέλει** 2 • 5 *it is a care/concern, is of interest to someone*
**μηκέτι** 12 • 16 *no longer, not from now on, ever*
**μνησικακέω** [2] 5 • 9 *to remember evil, bear malice, bear a grudge*
**μνησικακία, ἡ** 4 • 4 *bearing a grudge, vengefulness*
**παιδεία, ἡ** 3 • 11 *discipline, correction*
**παιδεύω** 3 • 13 *to discipline, correct, give guidance*
**παράβασις, ἡ** 1 • 4 *transgression, overstepping*
**παρενθυμέω** 4 • 4 *to disregard, neglect, forget*
**πραγματεία, ἡ** 11 • 11 *activity, occupation;*
pl. *undertakings, business, affairs*
**πρότερος** 40 • 47 *former, earlier*
**συναναφύρω** 1 • 1 *to entangle, involve*

2 **ἀκακία, ἡ** 8 • 10 *innocence, guilelessness*
**ἁπλότης, ἡ** [2] 12 • 15 *ingenuousness, sincerity, uprightness, frankness, simplicity*
**ἀφίστημι** 19 • 19 *to fall away, go away, withdraw*
**ἐγκράτεια, ἡ** 7 • 14 *self-control*
**ἐμμένω** 7 • 8 *to persevere, stand firm*
**κατισχύω** 2 • 2 *to win a victory over, prevail*
**παραμένω** 6 • 9 *to endure, remain, stay (on)*
**πονηρία, ἡ** 36 • 41 *wickedness, baseness, maliciousness, sinfulness*
3 **διαφθείρω** 8 • 12 *to destroy, spoil*
4 **Ἐλδάδ, ὁ** 1 • 1 *Eldad*
**Μάξιμος, ὁ** 1 • 1 *Maximus*
**Μωδάτ, ὁ** 1 • 1 *Modad*
**προφητεύω** 4 • 9 *to prophesy*
**φαίνω** 12 • 37 *to seem*

## Chapter 8 (Hv 2.4)

1 **ἀποκαλύπτω** 18 • 23 *to reveal, disclose, bring to light, make fully known*
**βιβλίδιον, τό** 4 • 5 *brief document*
**διατί** 27 • 29 *why?*
**εὐειδής** 3 • 3 *handsome*
**καταρτίζω** 2 • 6 *to prepare, make, create, outfit*
**κοιμάω** 8 • 12 *to sleep, fall asleep*
**κτίζω** 14 • 25 *to create*
**νεανίσκος, ὁ** 11 • 11 *youth, young man*
**Σίβυλλα, ἡ** 1 • 1 *the Sibyl*
2 **ἀποτελέω** 4 • 4 *to finish, bring to completion*
**γνωρίζω** 10 • 18 *to make known, reveal*
**ἐκλεκτός** 9 • 30 *chosen*
**μετέπειτα** 1 • 1 *afterwards*
**ὅρασις, ἡ** 10 • 13 *vision*
**προστίθημι** 13 • 22 *to add, put to*
3 **βιβλαρίδιον, τό** 2 • 2 *a little scroll/roll*
**Γραπτή, ὁ** 2 • 2 *Grapte*
**ἐπιτρέπω** 3 • 11 *to entrust to, be (one's) duty*

**Κλήμης, ὁ** 2 • 6 *Clement*
**νουθετέω** 5 • 9 *to admonish, warn, instruct*
**ὀρφανός** 5 • 9 *without parents, orphan*
**προΐστημι** 1 • 2 *to rule, direct, be at the head of*
**χήρα, ἡ** 6 • 13 *widow*

## VISION THREE

### Chapter 9 (Hv 3.1)

2 **ἀποκάλυψις, ἡ** 13 • 18 *revelation, disclosure*[1]
**δέομαι** 2 • 7 *to pray, ask, request*
**ἐμφανίζω** 2 • 2 *to make visible*
**ἐνδεής** 4 • 4 *poorly instructed*
**ἐπαγγέλλω** 6 • 7 *to promise*
**ἐπεί** 10 • 35 *because, since, for*
**νηστεύω** 14 • 23 *to fast*
**πέμπτος** 3 • 5 *fifth*
**πολλάκις** 1 • 2 *many times, often, frequently*
**σπουδαῖος** 1 • 3 *eager, zealous, earnest, diligent*
**χονδρίζω** 1 • 1 *to make coarsely crushed grain, make groats*
3 **ἀναχωρέω** 7 • 7 *to go away;* subst. *secluded place*
**ἐκλέγομαι** 5 • 15 *to select someone/something for oneself*
**ἥκω** 1 • 11 *to have come, be present*
**κυρία, ἡ** 24 • 24 *lady, mistress*
**πρίν** 4 • 7 *before*
4 **διατάσσω** 1 • 8 *to make arrangements, arrange*
**ἐλεφάντινος** 1 • 1 *of ivory*
**ἐξαπλόω** 1 • 1 *to unfold, spread out*
**ἐπάνω** 5 • 8 *on, over, above*
**καρπάσινος** 1 • 1 *made of fine flax*
**κεῖμαι** [2] 22 • 24 *to lie* (on something)
**κερβικάριον, τό** 1 • 1 *pillow*
**λέντιον, τό** 1 • 1 *linen cloth*
**λινοῦς** 4 • 4 *(made of) linen*
**συμψέλιον, τό** 8 • 8 *bench*
**συμψηφίζω** 1 • 1 *to count*
5 **γόνυ, τό** 3 • 4 *knee*
**ἔκθαμβος** 1 • 1 *utterly astonished*
**ἐξομολογέω** 5 • 15 *to confess, admit*
**θάρσος, τό** 1 • 2 *courage*
**θρίξ, ἡ** 7 • 7 *hair*
**κεῖμαι** 22 • 24 *to lie* (on something)
**μιμνῄσκομαι** 2 • 9 *to remember, recollect, remind oneself*
**ὀρθός** 4 • 5 *straight up, upright*
**πρότερος** 40 • 47 *former, earlier*
**τρόμος, ὁ** 1 • 2 *trembling, quivering*
**φρίκη, ἡ** 1 • 1 *a shudder*
**ὡσεί** [2] 16 • 17 *as, like*
6 **ἅπτω** 4 • 10 *to touch*
**ἕξ** 16 • 23 *six*
**ἐξομολογέω** 5 • 15 *to confess, admit*
**Ἑρμᾶς, ὁ** 13 • 13 *Hermas*
**ἐφίστημι** 2 • 5 *to approach, stand at/near;* the aorist pass. ἐπεστάθη has an intransitive force
**κατακροάομαι** 1 • 1 *to listen attentively*
**νεανίσκος, ὁ** 11 • 11 *youth, young man*
**παύω** 8 • 12 *to stop (oneself), cease*
**πρότερος** 40 • 47 *formerly, earlier*
7 **ἐξεγείρω** 2 • 3 *to raise up*
**νεανίσκος, ὁ** 11 • 11 *youth, young man*
**συμψέλιον, τό** 8 • 8 *bench*
8 **ἀναχωρέω** 7 • 7 *to go away*
**κυρία, ἡ** 24 • 24 *lady, mistress*
**νεανίσκος, ὁ** 11 • 11 *youth, young man*
9 **ἁπλότης, ἡ** 12 • 15 *sincerity*
**ἀριστερός** 4 • 5 *left*
**διαλογίζομαι** 6 • 6 *to consider, ponder, reason*
**ἐάω** [2] 5 • 13 *to let, permit*
**εἵνεκα** 2 • 3 *because of, on account of, for the sake of*
**ἐμμένω** 7 • 8 *to persevere in, stand by*
**ἐννεύω** 1 • 1 *to motion*
**Ἑρμᾶς, ὁ** 13 • 13 *Hermas*

1. BDAG s.v. ἀποκάλυψις 1.b.: "In the visions of Hermas the ἀ. are not only transcendent rev. for eye and ear, but also the interpretations given to such rev. The ἀ. is ὁλοτελής *complete* only when it is explained and understood…"

**εὐαρεστέω** 2 • 6 *to please, be pleasing*
**λείπω** 2 • 5 *to fall short, lack*
**λυπέω** [2] 13 • 17 *to grieve, be hurt, be sad, be distressed*
**ὑποφέρω** [2] 9 • 12 *to submit to, endure*

## Chapter 10 (Hv 3.2)

1 **ἁγίασμα, τό** 1 • 1 *sanctuary*
**ἀμφότεροι** 14 • 21 *both*
**ἀριστερός** 4 • 5 *left*
**δῶρον, τό** 1 • 4 *gift, present*
**εἵνεκα** 2 • 3 *on account of, because of, for the sake of*
**μάστιξ, ἡ** 3 • 8 *lash, whip*
**σταυρός, ὁ** 1 • 17 *cross*
**ὑποφέρω** 9 • 12 *to submit to, endure*
2 **ἁμάρτημα, τό** 4 • 8 *sin, transgression*
**διψυχέω** 21 • 25 *to waver, be undecided, be changeable, doubt*
**κατεπίθυμος** 2 • 2 *very eager, desirous*
**ὑστέρημα, τό** [2] 2 • 4 *lack, shortcoming*
3 **ἐπαγγέλλομαι** 6 • 7 *to promise, offer*
**ἐπιδείκνυμι** 2 • 11 *to show, point out*
**ὅραμα, τό** 5 • 5 *vision*
4 **ἐπαίρω** 1 • 6 *to lift up, hold up*
**ἐπιλαμβάνομαι** 2 • 2 *to take hold of, grasp, catch*
**εὐώνυμος** 2 • 2 *left*
**καθέζομαι** 2 • 2 *to sit down*
**κατέναντι** 3 • 3 *opposite, before*
**κυρία, ἡ** 24 • 24 *lady, mistress*
**λαμπρός** [2] 14 • 14 *gleaming, bright*
**πρᾶγμα, τό** 19 • 23 *thing, matter, affair*
**πύργος, ὁ** 147 • 148 *tower*
**ῥάβδος, ἡ** 58 • 62 *rod, staff, stick*
**συμψέλιον, τό** 8 • 8 *bench*
**τετράγωνος** 9 • 9 *(four)square*
5 **βυθός, ὁ** 12 • 14 *sea, deep water*
**ἕξ** [2] 16 • 23 *six*
**ἐπιδίδωμι** 60 • 62 *to give, hand over, deliver*
**μυριάς, ἡ** 1 • 2 *myriad*
**νεανίσκος, ὁ** [2] 11 • 11 *youth, young man*
**παραφέρω** 6 • 7 *to bring up*
**πύργος, ὁ** 147 • 148 *tower*
**τετράγωνος** 9 • 9 *(four)square*
6 **ἁρμογή, ἡ** [2] 6 • 6 *joint*
**ἁρμόζω** 20 • 23 *to join*
**βυθός, ὁ** 12 • 14 *sea, deep water*
**ἕλκω** 2 • 3 *to drag, draw*
**κολλάω** 12 • 32 *to join to, cling to, attach to*
**οἰκοδομή, ἡ** [2] 100 • 103 *building, edifice*
**συμφωνέω** 7 • 7 *to fit together*
7 **ἀποβάλλω** 32 • 36 *to throw away, reject*
**κατακόπτω** 2 • 2 *to break into pieces*
**μακράν** 9 • 15 *far away*
**ξηρός** 46 • 47 *dry, dried up*; subst. *dry land*
**οἰκοδομή, ἡ** 100 • 103 *building, edifice*
**πύργος, ὁ** 147 • 148 *tower*
**ῥίπτω** 8 • 11 *to throw*
8 **ἁρμόζω** 20 • 23 *to fit, fit in*
**κεῖμαι** 22 • 24 *to lie*
**κολοβόω** 3 • 3 *to shorten*
**κύκλῳ** 17 • 18 *around*
**λευκός** 24 • 24 *white*
**οἰκοδομή, ἡ** [2] 100 • 103 *building, edifice*
**πύργος, ὁ** 147 • 148 *tower*
**στρογγύλος** 10 • 10 *round*
**σχισμή, ἡ** 25 • 25 *crack, fissure*
**χράομαι** 7 • 18 *to make use of, employ*
**ψωριάω** 5 • 5 *to have a rough surface*
9 **ἀνοδία, ἡ** 5 • 5 *a wayless area, roadless place*
**ἐμπίπτω** 3 • 5 *to fall (in, into)*
**καίπερ** 3 • 7 *although*
**καίω** 4 • 11 *to burn (up)*
**κυλίω** [2] 5 • 5 *to roll*
**μακράν** 9 • 15 *far (away)*
**πύργος, ὁ** 147 • 148 *tower*
**ῥίπτω** 8 • 11 *to throw*

## Chapter 11 (Hv 3.3)

1 **ἀναγγέλλω** 2 • 8 *to disclose, announce, proclaim, teach*

**ἀποτρέχω** 1 • 1 *to hurry away, run away*
**ἱλαρός** 24 • 34 *cheerful, glad, happy*
**κυρία, ἡ** [2] 24 • 24 *lady, mistress*
**ναί** 6 • 8 *certainly, indeed, quite so*
**ὄφελος, τό** 1 • 2 *benefit, good*
**πανοῦργος** 2 • 2 *crafty, clever, sly*
**πρᾶγμα, τό** 19 • 23 *thing, matter, affair*
**πύργος, ὁ** 147 • 148 *tower*
2 **ἀναιδής** 2 • 2 *shameless, bold*
**ἀποκαλύπτω** 18 • 23 *to reveal, disclose, bring to light, make fully known*
**ἀποκάλυψις, ἡ** [3] 13 • 18 *revelation, disclosure*
**κόπος, ὁ** 6 • 8 *trouble, difficulty*
**μηκέτι** 12 • 16 *no longer, not from now on*
**παρέχω** 3 • 18 *to cause, bring about*
**παύω** 8 • 12 *to stop (oneself), cease*
**πύργος, ὁ** 147 • 148 *tower*
3 **ἀποκαλύπτω** 18 • 23 *to reveal, disclose, bring to light, make fully known*
**πρότερος** 40 • 47 *formerly, earlier*
**πύργος, ὁ** [2] 147 • 148 *tower*
4 **ἅπαξ** 2 • 4 *once*
**ἀποκαλύπτω** [4] 18 • 23 *to reveal, disclose, bring to light, make fully known*
**διψυχέω** 21 • 25 *to doubt, be undecided, be changeable*
**ἐνδέχομαι** 2 • 2 *to be possible, be permitted*
**ἐπεί** 10 • 35 *since, because, for*
**ἡγέομαι** 7 • 25 *to think, consider, regard*
**κυρία, ἡ** 24 • 24 *lady, mistress*
5 **ἀόρατος** 2 • 13 *unseen, invisible*
**δεσπότης, ὁ** 24 • 54 *lord, master*
**διατί** [2] 27 • 29 *why?*
**ἐκζητέω** [2] 3 • 16 *to search for, seek out*
**ἔνδοξος** 43 • 54 *glorious, splendid*
**ἐπιμελῶς** 5 • 9 *carefully, diligently*
**θεμελιόω** 6 • 6 *to establish*
**κυρία, ἡ** 24 • 24 *lady, mistress*
**παντοκράτωρ, ὁ** 1 • 12 *the Almighty, All-Powerful, Omnipotent (One)*
**πρότερος** 40 • 47 *former*
**πύργος, ὁ** [3] 147 • 148 *tower*

## Chapter 12 (Hv 3.4)

1 **αὐξάνω/αὔξω** 2 • 7 *to grow, cause to grow, increase*
**δεσπόζω** 1 • 1 *to be lord, master*
**ἕξ** 16 • 23 *six*
**θαυμαστῶς** 3 • 3 *wonderful*
**κτίζω** 14 • 25 *to create*
**κτίσις, ἡ** [2] 13 • 19 *creation, world*
**κυρία, ἡ** [2] 24 • 24 *lady, mistress*
**μεγάλως** 5 • 9 *great*
**νεανίσκος, ὁ** 11 • 11 *youth, young man*
**οἰκοδομή, ἡ** 100 • 103 *building, edifice*
**πρᾶγμα, τό** 19 • 23 *thing, matter, affair*
**πύργος, ὁ** 147 • 148 *tower*
**τελέω** 22 • 23 *to bring to an end, finish, complete*
2 **ἕξ** 16 • 23 *six*
**εὐφραίνω** 6 • 15 *to be glad, enjoy oneself, rejoice, celebrate*
**κύκλῳ** 17 • 18 *around*
**οἰκοδομή, ἡ** [2] 100 • 103 *building, edifice*
**ὁμοῦ** 3 • 5 *together at the same time (as), in company (with)*
**παραφέρω** 6 • 7 *to bring up*
**πύργος, ὁ** [3] 147 • 148 *tower*
**συντελέω** 9 • 15 *to bring to an end, complete, finish, close*
**τελέω** 22 • 23 *to bring to an end, finish, complete*
**ὑπερέχω** 5 • 7 *to be better than, surpass, excel*
3 **ἀληθής** 6 • 16 *true*
**ἀποκαλύπτω** [4] 18 • 23 *to reveal, disclose, bring to light, make fully known*
**βέβαιος** 1 • 9 *reliable*
**βελτίων** 3 • 6 *better*
**διαλογίζομαι** 6 • 6 *to consider, ponder, reason*
**δίψυχος** 20 • 23 *doubting, hesitating;* lit. *double-minded*

ἔξοδος, ἡ 1 • 1 *course, fate, destination*
ἔξωθεν 1 • 3 *outside, apart from*
θεμελιόω 6 • 6 *to establish, strengthen*
ἰσχυρός 14 • 21 *secure*
κυρία, ἡ 24 • 24 *lady, mistress*
ὅραμα, τό 5 • 5 *vision*
οὐθείς 2 • 3 *nothing*
ποταπός 5 • 5 *of what sort? of what kind?*
πρότερος 40 • 47 *superior, preferable, more prominent*

## Chapter 13 (Hv 3.5)

1 ἁγνῶς 5 • 6 *in sincerity, sincerely, purely*
ἁρμογή, ἡ [2] 6 • 6 *joint*
διάκονος, ὁ 3 • 29 *assistant*
ἐκλεκτός 9 • 30 *chosen*
ἐπισκοπέω 1 • 3 *to serve as overseer*
ἐπίσκοπος, ὁ 3 • 76 *overseer, supervisor*
κοιμάω 8 • 12 *to sleep, be dead*
λευκός 24 • 24 *white*
οἰκοδομή, ἡ [2] 100 • 103 *building, edifice*
πύργος, ὁ 147 • 148 *tower*
σεμνότης, ἡ 11 • 12 *holiness*
σεμνῶς 3 • 4 *honorably, worthily, in a manner above reproach*
συμφωνέω [3] 7 • 7 *to fit together* (first and third instance); *to be in agreement, be in harmony* (second instance)
τετράγωνος 9 • 9 *(four)square*
2 ἁρμογή, ἡ 6 • 6 *joint*
βυθός, ὁ 12 • 14 *sea, deep water*
ἕλκω 2 • 3 *to drag, draw*
ἕνεκα 8 • 15 *because of, on account of, for the sake of*
οἰκοδομή, ἡ 100 • 103 *building, edifice*
συμφωνέω 7 • 7 *to fit together*
εἰς τέλος (adverbial marker of intensity) *utterly, completely*
3 δοκιμάζω 10 • 19 *to accept as proved, approve*
εὐθύτης, ἡ 1 • 2 *uprightness, righteousness*
κατορθόω 5 • 5 *to carry out, set straight, complete, bring to a successful conclusion*
κυρία, ἡ 24 • 24 *lady, mistress*
λατομέω 15 • 15 *to hew, shape*
ξηρός 46 • 47 *dry, dried up*; subst. *dry land*
οἰκοδομή, ἡ 100 • 103 *building, edifice*
4 ἀγαθοποιέω 4 • 6 *to do what is right, be a good citizen*
διότι 2 • 3 *because*
νέος 7 • 16 *novice*
νουθετέω 5 • 9 *to admonish, warn, instruct*
οἰκοδομή, ἡ 100 • 103 *building, edifice*
πονηρία, ἡ 36 • 41 *wickedness, baseness, maliciousness, sinfulness*
5 ἀποβάλλω 32 • 36 *to throw away, reject*
ἀπορίπτω 2 • 2 *to throw away*
ἔκβολος 1 • 1 *excluded, rejected*
εὔχρηστος 13 • 14 *useful, serviceable*
ἰσχυρός 14 • 21 *strong, mighty*
κεῖμαι 22 • 24 *to lie*
μακράν 9 • 15 *far (away)*
οἰκοδομή, ἡ [2] 100 • 103 *building, edifice*
πύργος, ὁ [3] 147 • 148 *tower*
ῥίπτω 8 • 11 *to throw*
τελέω 22 • 23 *to bring to an end, finish, complete*

## Chapter 14 (Hv 3.6)

1 ἀνομία, ἡ 9 • 33 *lawlessness*
ἀπορίπτω 2 • 2 *to throw away*
ἀφίστημι 19 • 19 *to depart, withdraw, go away*
εὔχρηστος 13 • 14 *useful, serviceable*
κατακόπτω 2 • 2 *to break into pieces*
μακράν 9 • 15 *far (away)*
οἰκοδομή, ἡ 100 • 103 *building, edifice*
παροργίζω 1 • 1 *to make angry*
πονηρία, ἡ [2] 36 • 41 *wickedness, baseness, maliciousness, sinfulness*

πόρρω 1 • 8 *far (away)*
πύργος, ὁ 147 • 148 *tower*
ῥίπτω 8 • 11 *to throw*
συγκόπτω 3 • 3 *to break*
ὑπόκρισις, ἡ 5 • 13 *insincerely, pretense, outward show, dissembling*
2 ἄχρηστος 4 • 6 *useless, worthless*
ἐπιμένω 10 • 16 *to continue, persist in, persevere*
κεῖμαι 22 • 24 *to lie*
κολλάω 12 • 32 *to join oneself to, join, cling to, associate with*
οἰκοδομή, ἡ 100 • 103 *building, edifice*
ψωριάω 5 • 5 *to have a rough surface*
3 ἀποχωρέω 3 • 3 *to go away*
εἰρηνεύω 6 • 17 *to keep the peace*
ἐμμένω 7 • 8 *to stay/remain (in)*
πονηρία, ἡ 36 • 41 *wickedness, baseness, maliciousness, sinfulness*
σχισμή, ἡ [2] 25 • 25 *crack, fissure*
πρόσωπον εἰρήνης ἔχοντες *having a face of peace;* fig. *having an outward countenance or appearance of peace*
4 ἀνομία, ἡ 9 • 33 *a lawless deed*
κολοβός 5 • 5 *mutilated;* in imagery of hewn stones: *with some part broken off*
κολοβόω 3 • 3 *to shorten*
ὁλοτελής 5 • 5 *in every way complete, quite perfect*
5 ἀπαρνέομαι 5 • 6 *to deny*
ἁρμόζω 20 • 23 *to fit, fit in*
ἀσύνετος 11 • 16 *without understanding, senseless, foolish*
κυρία, ἡ 24 • 24 *lady, mistress*
λευκός 24 • 24 *white*
μωρός 11 • 12 *foolish, stupid;* ἕως πότε μωρὸς εἶ *How long will you be foolish?*
νοέω 30 • 46 *to comprehend, perceive, apprehend, understand, gain insight into*
οἰκοδομή, ἡ 100 • 103 *building, edifice*
πλοῦτος, ὁ [2] 14 • 15 *wealth*
πότε 3 • 6 *when?;* ἕως πότε *How long?*
πραγματεία, ἡ 11 • 11 *activity, occupation;* pl. *undertakings, business, affairs*
στρογγύλος 10 • 10 *round*
6 ἀποβάλλω 32 • 36 *to lose*
εὔχρηστος [3] 13 • 14 *useful, serviceable*
κυρία, ἡ 24 • 24 *lady, mistress*
οἰκοδομή, ἡ 100 • 103 *building, edifice*
περικόπτω [2] 4 • 5 *to cut off, cut away, take away*
πλουτέω 4 • 6 *to have riches, be rich*
πλοῦτος, ὁ [2] 14 • 15 *wealth*
πότε 3 • 6 *when?*
στρογγύλος 10 • 10 *round*
τετράγωνος 9 • 9 *(four)square*
ψυχαγωγέω 1 • 1 *to beguile, attract, lead away*
7 ἄχρηστος 4 • 6 *useless, worthless*
εὔχρηστος [2] 13 • 14 *useful, serviceable*
πλουτέω 4 • 6 *to have riches, be rich*
χράομαι 7 • 18 *to make use of, employ*
ὠφέλιμος 1 • 3 *useful, beneficial, advantageous*

## Chapter 15 (Hv 3.7)

1 ἀληθινός 3 • 14 *true*
ἀνοδία, ἡ 5 • 5 *a wayless area, roadless place*
βελτίων 3 • 6 *better*
διψυχία, ἡ 17 • 18 *doubt, indecision*
κυλίω 5 • 5 *to roll (oneself)*
μακράν 9 • 15 *far (away)*
πύργος, ὁ 147 • 148 *tower*
ῥίπτω 8 • 11 *to throw*
ταλαιπωρέω 3 • 4 *to endure sorrow/distress, be miserable*
2 ἀσέλγεια, ἡ 3 • 3 *licentiousness, self-abandonment*
ἀφίστημι 19 • 19 *to fall away, become a backslider*
καίω 4 • 11 *to burn (up)*
πονηρία, ἡ 36 • 41 *wickedness, baseness, maliciousness, sinfulness*
3 ἁγνότης, ἡ 2 • 2 *purity, sincerity*

εἶτα 30 • 48 *then, next*
κυλίω 5 • 5 *to roll (oneself)*
μνεῖα, ἡ 1 • 3 *recollection, remembrance, memory*
4 ἐξήγησις, ἡ 1 • 6 *explanation, interpretation*
πύργος, ὁ 147 • 148 *tower*
τελέω 22 • 23 *to bring to an end, finish, complete*
5 ἀναιδεύω 1 • 1 *to be unabashed, be bold*
ἀποβάλλω 32 • 36 *to throw away, reject*
ἁρμόζω [2] 20 • 23 *to fit, fit in*
μετάνοια, ἡ [2] 58 • 72 *repentance, turning about, conversion*
οἰκοδομή, ἡ 100 • 103 *building, edifice*
πύργος, ὁ [3] 147 • 148 *tower*
6 ἁρμόζω 20 • 23 *to fit, fit in*
βασανίζω 15 • 18 *to torment, harass*
βάσανος, ἡ 11 • 18 *torture, torment*
ἐκπληρόω 2 • 2 *to fulfill*, here *atone fully*
ἐλάσσων 4 • 6 *inferior*
μεταλαμβάνω 2 • 12 *to have a share in*
μετατίθημι 2 • 9 *to remove, transfer, put in another place*
σκληροκαρδία, ἡ 1 • 2 *hardness of heart, coldness, obstinacy, stubbornness*
συμβαίνω 2 • 7 *to happen, come about*

## Chapter 16 (Hv 3.8)

1 θεάομαι 1 • 4 *to see, look at, behold*
κατεπίθυμος 2 • 2 *very eager, desirous*
παύω 8 • 12 *to stop (oneself), cease*
περιχαρής 2 • 2 *very glad*
2 βαστάζω 18 • 24 *to carry, bear*
ἐμβλέπω 2 • 5 *to look at, gaze on*
ἐπιταγή, ἡ 1 • 1 *command, order, injunction*
κύκλῳ 17 • 18 *around*
κυρία, ἡ 24 • 24 *lady, mistress*
πύργος, ὁ [2] 147 • 148 *tower*
ὑπομειδιάω 1 • 1 *to smile a bit*
3 ἐκλεκτός 9 • 30 *chosen*
ἐνέργεια, ἡ 8 • 8 *function, working, operation, action*
4 ἀνδρίζομαι 3 • 4 *to be of manly appearance, act courageously*
ἀπέχω [2] 21 • 35 *to keep away, abstain, refrain from*
ἐγκράτεια, ἡ 7 • 14 *self-control*
θυγάτηρ, ἡ 4 • 10 *daughter*
κληρονομέω 1 • 11 *to acquire, obtain, come into possession of, receive, share in*
περιζώννυμι 6 • 6 *to gird about*
5 ἀκακία, ἡ 8 • 10 *innocence, guilelessness*
ἁπλότης, ἡ 12 • 15 *simplicity, sincerity, uprightness, frankness*
ἐπιστήμη, ἡ 3 • 5 *understanding, knowledge*
θυγάτηρ, ἡ 4 • 10 *daughter*
κυρία, ἡ 24 • 24 *lady, mistress*
σεμνότης, ἡ 11 • 12 *dignity, seriousness, probity, holiness*
6 κυρία, ἡ 24 • 24 *lady, mistress*
7 ἁγνός 1 • 11 *pure, holy*
ἀκακία, ἡ 8 • 10 *innocence, guilelessness*
ἁπλότης, ἡ [2] 12 • 15 *simplicity, sincerity, uprightness, frankness*
ἐγκράτεια, ἡ 7 • 14 *self-control*
ἐπιστήμη, ἡ 3 • 5 *understanding, knowledge*
θεῖος 10 • 16 *divine*
σεμνός 7 • 13 *honorable, worthy, venerable, holy, above reproach*
σεμνότης, ἡ [2] 11 • 12 *dignity, seriousness, probity, holiness*
8 δουλεύω 25 • 42 *to serve, obey, (perform the duties of a slave)*
ἰσχύω 4 • 9 *to be strong, have power, be competent, be able*
κατοίκησις, ἡ 3 • 3 *living (quarters), dwelling*
πύργος, ὁ 147 • 148 *tower*
9 ἀνακαίνωσις, ἡ 1 • 1 *renewal*
ἀνακράζω 1 • 1 *to cry out*
ἀρκετός 3 • 4 *enough, sufficient, adequate*
ἀσύνετος 11 • 16 *senseless, foolish*
ἐποικοδομέω 2 • 2 *to build onto*
μηκέτι 12 • 16 *no longer, not from now on*
πύργος, ὁ [2] 147 • 148 *tower*

**συντέλεια, ἡ** 2 • 3 *completion, close, end*
**συντελέω** 9 • 15 *to bring to an end, complete, finish, close*
**ταχύς** 11 • 18 *soon, in a short time*
**ὑπόμνησις, ἡ** 1 • 1 *reminding*
10 **ἀποκαλύπτω** 18 • 23 *to reveal, disclose, bring to light, make fully known, give (someone) a revelation*
**δηλόω** 32 • 49 *to reveal, make clear, show*
11 **ἐντέλλω** 17 • 29 *to command, order, give orders*
**Ἑρμᾶς, ὁ** 13 • 13 *Hermas*
**νοέω** 30 • 46 *to understand, perceive, apprehend, gain insight into*
**πονηρία, ἡ** 36 • 41 *wickedness, baseness, maliciousness, sinfulness*

## Chapter 17 (Hv 3.9)

1 **ἁγιάζω** 1 • 16 *to purify*
**ἀκακία, ἡ** 8 • 10 *innocence, guilelessness*
**ἁπλότης, ἡ** 12 • 15 *ingenuousness, simplicity, sincerity, uprightness, frankness*
**ἐκτρέφω** 1 • 1 *to rear, bring up*
**ἔλεος, τό** 4 • 19 *mercy, compassion, pity, clemency*
**παύω** 8 • 12 *to stop (oneself), cease*
**πονηρία, ἡ** [2] 36 • 41 *wickedness, baseness, maliciousness, sinfulness*
**σεμνότης, ἡ** 11 • 12 *dignity, seriousness, probity, holiness*
**σκολιότης, ἡ** 1 • 1 *crookedness, perversity, deceit*
**στάζω** 1 • 2 *to instill*
2 **ἀντιλαμβάνω** 1 • 2 *to help, take part, come to the aid of*
**εἰρηνεύω** 6 • 17 *to keep the peace*
**ἐπισκέπτομαι** 6 • 8 *to visit*
**κατάχυμα, τό** 1 • 1 *sauce, broth, soup*; fig. perhaps *abundance, surplus*[2]
**κτίσμα, τό** 3 • 4 *that which is created, creature*
**μεταδίδωμι** 2 • 3 *to give (a part of), impart, share*
**μεταλαμβάνω** 2 • 12 *to take possession of, receive*
**ὑστερέω** 7 • 11 *to be needy, lack, be poor*
3 **ἀρκετός** 3 • 4 *adequate, enough, sufficient*
**ἀσθένεια, ἡ** 6 • 7 *sickness, disease*
**διαφθείρω** 8 • 12 *to waste away*
**ἔδεσμα, τό** [2] 12 • 12 *food*
**ἐπισπάω** 3 • 4 *to bring upon*
**λυμαίνω** 4 • 4 *to injure, cause harm to, damage, spoil, ruin, destroy*
**τροφή, ἡ** 1 • 12 *nourishment, food*
4 **ἀσυγκρασία, ἡ** 1 • 1 *lack of sharing, lack of community spirit*
**βλαβερός** 5 • 5 *harmful*
**μεταδίδωμι** 2 • 3 *to give (a part of), impart, share*
**ὑστερέω** 7 • 11 *to be needy, lack, be poor*
5 **ἀγαθοποιέω** 4 • 6 *to do what is right, be a good citizen*
**ἐκζητέω** 3 • 16 *to seek out, visit*
**ἐπέρχομαι** 6 • 8 *to come (on), approach*
**οὔπω** 2 • 3 *not yet*
**πεινάω** 1 • 6 *to hunger, be hungry*
**πύργος, ὁ** [2] 147 • 148 *tower*
**τελέω** [2] 22 • 23 *to bring to an end, finish, complete*
**ὑπερέχω** 5 • 7 *to be better off (economically)*
6 **γαυρόομαι** 1 • 1 *to pride oneself*
**ἐκκλείω** 2 • 2 *to shut out, exclude*
**μήποτε** 13 • 22 *lest*
**πλοῦτος, ὁ** 14 • 15 *wealth*
**στεναγμός, ὁ** 1 • 2 *sigh, groan, groaning*
**στενάζω** 1 • 3 *to sigh, groan*
**ὑστερέω** 7 • 11 *to be needy, lack, be poor*
7 **βαστάζω** 18 • 24 *to carry, bear*
**ἰός, ὁ** 2 • 4 *poison, venom*
**προηγέομαι** 2 • 4 *to be in a position of leadership, preside*

2. BDAG s.v. κατάχυμα: "ἐκ καταχύματος μεταλαμβάνειν *to fish out of the soup*, i.e. get everything for oneself…"

**πρωτοκαθεδρίτης, ὁ** 1 • 1 *congregation leader, one who occupies a seat of honor*
**πυξίς, ἡ** 1 • 1 *box, container*
**φάρμακον, τό** 2 • 5 *drug, poison*
**φαρμακός, ὁ** 2 • 2 *poisoner, sorcerer, magician*
8 **ἔλεος, τό** 4 • 19 *mercy, compassion, pity, clemency*
**ἐνσκιρόω** 1 • 1 *to harden, make callous*
**καθαρός** 25 • 45 *pure, free*
**συγκεράννυμι** 1 • 1 *to unite*
**φρόνησις, ἡ** 6 • 7 *way of thinking, (frame of) mind*
9 **ἀποστερέω** 1 • 2 *to rob, steal, despoil, defraud*
**διχοστασία, ἡ** 4 • 6 *dissension*
**μήποτε** 13 • 22 *lest*
10 **εἰρηνεύω** 6 • 17 *to keep the peace*
**ἐκλεκτός** 9 • 30 *chosen*
**ἱλαρός** 24 • 34 *cheerful, glad, happy*
**κατέναντι** 3 • 3 *opposite, before*
**παιδεία, ἡ** 3 • 11 *training*
**παιδεύω** 3 • 13 *to correct, give guidance*

## Chapter 18 (Hv 3.10)

1 **ἀποστρέφω** 2 • 8 *to turn away*
**ἀποφέρω** 8 • 9 *to carry, take away*
**ἕξ** 16 • 23 *six*
**νεανίσκος, ὁ** 11 • 11 *youth, young man*
**παύω** 8 • 12 *to stop (oneself), cease*
**πύργος, ὁ** [2] 147 • 148 *tower*
**συμψέλιον, τό** 8 • 8 *bench*
**τέσσαρες** 11 • 12 *four*
2 **ἀποκαλύπτω** [2] 18 • 23 *to reveal, disclose, bring to light, make fully known*
**ἐμφανίζω** 2 • 2 *to make visible*
**μορφή, ἡ** 6 • 8 *form, outward appearance, shape*
3 **καθέδρα, ἡ** 10 • 11 *chair, seat*
**λίαν** 43 • 48 *exceedingly, very (much)*
**ὅρασις, ἡ** 10 • 13 *vision*
**περυσινός** 2 • 2 *of last year*
4 **θρίξ, ἡ** 7 • 7 *hair*
**ἱλαρός** 24 • 34 *cheerful, glad, happy*
**νέος** 7 • 16 *young;* comparative *more youthful*
**ὅρασις, ἡ** 10 • 13 *vision*
**ὄψις, ἡ** 3 • 6 *outward appearance, aspect*
**πρότερος** 40 • 47 *former, earlier*
5 **ἐκπρεπής** 2 • 2 *remarkable, outstanding*
**θρίξ, ἡ** 7 • 7 *hair*
**ἱλαρός** 24 • 34 *cheerful, glad, happy*
**κάλλος, τό** 4 • 5 *beauty*
**νέος** 7 • 16 *young*
**ὅρασις, ἡ** 10 • 13 *vision*
**συμψέλιον, τό** 8 • 8 *bench*
**εἰς τέλος** (adverbial marker of intensity) *extremely, quite*
6 **ἀποκάλυψις, ἡ** 13 • 18 *revelation, disclosure*
**ἐρώτησις, ἡ** 1 • 1 *request*
**λίαν** 43 • 48 *extremely*
**νηστεύω** 14 • 23 *to fast*
**ὅραμα, τό** 5 • 5 *vision*
**περίλυπος** 1 • 2 *very sad, deeply grieved, very unhappy*
**ταπεινοφροσύνη, ἡ** 3 • 9 *humility*
**χρῄζω** 1 • 7 *to have need of*
7 **ἀποκάλυψις, ἡ** 13 • 18 *revelation, disclosure*
**βλάπτω** 1 • 3 *to harm, injure*
**δέησις, ἡ** 1 • 6 *prayer*
**μήποτε** 13 • 22 *lest*
**νεανίσκος, ὁ** 11 • 11 *youth, young man*
**νηστεύω** 14 • 23 *to fast*
**ὑπὸ χεῖρα** *continually*
8 **ἀποκάλυψις, ἡ** [2] 13 • 18 *revelation, disclosure*
**ἀρκέω** 2 • 5 *to be enough, be sufficient, be adequate*
**ἰσχυρός** 14 • 21 *meaningful*
**μήτι** 3 • 3 *not*
9 **ἀποκάλυψις, ἡ** 13 • 18 *revelation, disclosure*
**ἀσύνετος** 11 • 16 *senseless, foolish*
**διψυχία, ἡ** 17 • 18 *indecision, doubt*
**μέχρι** 7 • 23 *how long?*
**μορφή, ἡ** 6 • 8 *form, outward appearance, shape*
**ὁλοτελής** 5 • 5 *in every way complete, quite perfect*
10 **ἀκριβής** 2 • 2 *exact, strict*

## Chapter 19 (Hv 3.11)

1 **ἐπιζητέω** 5 • 9 *to make an inquiry, inquire, want to know*
**μορφή, ἡ** 6 • 8 *form, outward appearance, shape*
2 **διατί** 27 • 29 *why?*
**διψυχία, ἡ** 17 • 18 *indecision, doubt*
**καθέδρα, ἡ** 10 • 11 *chair, seat*
**μαλακία, ἡ** 2 • 3 *faint-heartedness, despondency, lack of energy*
**μαραίνω** 4 • 4 *to wither, die out, fade, disappear*
**ὅρασις, ἡ** 10 • 13 *vision*
3 **ἀκηδία, ἡ** 1 • 1 *apathy, melancholy*
**ἀνανεόω** 5 • 5 *to become young again*
**βιωτικός** 4 • 4 *belonging to (daily) life*
**διάνοια, ἡ** 6 • 22 *mind, thought, disposition*
**ἐπιρίπτω** 1 • 1 *to cast upon*
**θραύω** 2 • 4 *to break, weaken, oppress*
**κοίμησις, ἡ** 2 • 2 *sleep, death*
**λύπη, ἡ** 23 • 24 *sorrow, grief, affliction*
**μαλακίζομαι** 1 • 1 *to be/become weak, be discouraged, be sick*
**μέριμνα, ἡ** 3 • 3 *anxiety, worry, care*
**μηκέτι** 12 • 16 *no longer, not from now on*
**παλαιόω** 1 • 3 *to make or become old*
**πρᾶγμα, τό** 19 • 23 *task, undertaking, occupation*
**προσδοκάω** 1 • 8 *to wait for, look for, expect*
4 **ἀσθένεια, ἡ** 6 • 7 *weakness*
**ἀσθενής** 4 • 12 *weak*
**διατί** 27 • 29 *why?*
**καθέδρα, ἡ** 10 • 11 *chair, seat*
**καθέζομαι** 2 • 2 *to sit down*
**ὅρασις, ἡ** 10 • 13 *vision*
**συγκρατέω** 1 • 1 *to support, hold upright*
**τύπος, ὁ** 10 • 26 *symbol, type*

## Chapter 20 (Hv 3.12)

1 **θρίξ, ἡ** 7 • 7 *hair*
**ἱλαρός** 24 • 34 *cheerful, glad, happy*
**νέος** 7 • 16 *young;* comparative *more youthful*
**ὅρασις, ἡ** 10 • 13 *vision*
**ὄψις, ἡ** 3 • 6 *outward appearance*
**πρότερος** 40 • 47 *first, former*
2 **ἀνάκειμαι** 1 • 1 *to lie, recline*
**ἀνανεόω** 5 • 5 *to renew*
**ἀνδρίζομαι** 3 • 4 *to conduct oneself in a courageous way*
**ἀπελπίζω** 1 • 2 *to despair*
**ἀποκαλύπτω** 18 • 23 *to impart a revelation (to someone)*
**ἀποκάλυψις, ἡ** 13 • 18 *revelation, disclosure*
**ἀσθένεια, ἡ** 6 • 7 *weakness*
**εἶτα** 30 • 48 *then, next*
**ἐνδύω** 29 • 32 *to clothe oneself in, put on, wear;* fig. *take on the characteristics/ virtues/intentions of*
**ἐξαίφνης** 3 • 6 *suddenly, unexpectantly*
**ἐξεγείρω** 2 • 3 *to raise up;* pass. with act. sense *rise up*
**ἰσχύς, ἡ** 2 • 11 *strength, power, might*
**καταλείπω** 6 • 12 *to leave behind*
**κληρονομία, ἡ** 2 • 6 *inheritance*
**περιχαρής** 2 • 2 *very glad*
**πρᾶξις, ἡ** 44 • 50 *condition, state, situation*
**προσδέχομαι** 2 • 10 *to wait for, await*
**πρότερος** 40 • 47 *former, earlier*
**πτωχότης, ἡ** 1 • 1 *poverty*
**φθείρω** 2 • 10 *to destroy, ruin;* pass. *be degenerated, be ruined, be doomed to destruction*
3 **ἀνανεόω** 5 • 5 *to renew*
**ἀποτίθημι** 7 • 13 *to lay aside, rid oneself*
**δηλόω** [2] 32 • 49 *to reveal, make clear, show*
**εἰρηνεύω** 6 • 17 *to keep the peace*
**ἐνδυναμόω** 12 • 14 *to become strong, grow strong*
**ἰσχυροποίησις, ἡ** 1 • 1 *strengthening*

**ἰσχυρότης, ἡ** 2 • 2 *power, (inward) strength*
**μαλακία, ἡ** 2 • 3 *faint-heartedness, despondency, lack of energy*
**οἰκοδομή, ἡ** 100 • 103 *building, edifice*
**πύργος, ὁ** 147 • 148 *tower*
**σπλαγχνίζομαι** 8 • 9 *to have pity, feel sympathy*

## Chapter 21 (Hv 3.13)

1 **ἱλαρός** 24 • 34 *cheerful, glad, happy*
**μορφή, ἡ** 6 • 8 *form, outward appearance, shape*
**νέος** 7 • 16 *young*
**ὅρασις, ἡ** 10 • 13 *vision*
2 **ἀγγελία, ἡ** [2] 2 • 2 *message, news*
**ἀνανεόω** 5 • 5 *to renew*
**ἀνανέωσις, ἡ** 2 • 2 *renewal*
**ἐπιλανθάνομαι** 5 • 8 *to forget*
**ἰσχυροποιέω** 7 • 7 *to strengthen*
**λυπέω** 13 • 17 *to be sad, be sorrowful, be distressed, grieve*
**λύπη, ἡ** 23 • 24 *sorrow, grief, affliction*
**προσδέχομαι** 2 • 10 *to wait for, await*
**πρότερος** 40 • 47 *former, earlier*
3 **θέσις, ἡ** 1 • 1 *position*
**ἰσχυρός** 14 • 21 *secure*
**ἰσχυρῶς** 5 • 5 *firmly, strongly, dependably*
**στοιχεῖον, τό** 1 • 3 *elements*
**συμψέλιον, τό** [2] 8 • 8 *bench*
**τέσσαρες** [2] 11 • 12 *four*
4 **ἀπέχω** 21 • 35 *to receive in full*
**ἀποκαλύπτω** 18 • 23 *to reveal, disclose, bring to light, make fully known*
**ἀποκάλυψις, ἡ** [2] 13 • 18 *revelation, disclosure*
**θεμελιόω** 6 • 6 *to establish, strengthen*
**μηκέτι** 12 • 16 *no longer, not from now on*
**νέος** 7 • 16 *young*
**ὁλοτελής** 5 • 5 *in every way complete, quite perfect*
**ὁλοτελῶς** 1 • 1 *fully, wholly, altogether*

# VISION FOUR

## Chapter 22 (Hv 4.1)

1 **εἴκοσι** 1 • 1 *twenty*
**ἐπέρχομαι** 6 • 8 *to come (on), approach*
**ὅρασις, ἡ** 10 • 13 *vision*
**πρότερος** 40 • 47 *former, earlier*
**τύπος, ὁ** 10 • 26 *type, symbol, foreshadowing*
2 **δέκα** 3 • 10 *ten*
**δημόσιος** 1 • 1 *public*
**Καμπανός, ἡ** 1 • 1 *Campanian*
**ὁδεύω** 2 • 3 *to go, travel, make a trip, walk*
**ῥᾳδίως** 1 • 2 *easily, readily*
**στάδιον, τό** 2 • 9 *stade* (about one-eighth mile or 192 meters)
**ὡσεί** 16 • 17 *about*
3 **ἀξιόω** 1 • 14 *to request, ask*
**ἀποκάλυψις, ἡ** 13 • 18 *revelation, disclosure*
**ἔνδοξος** 43 • 54 *glorious, splendid*
**ἡγέομαι** 7 • 25 *to think, consider, regard*
**θαυμάσιος** 1 • 4 *wonderful things, wonders*
**ἰσχυροποιέω** 7 • 7 *to strengthen*
**μετάνοια, ἡ** 58 • 72 *repentance, turning about, conversion*
**ὅραμα, τό** 5 • 5 *vision*
**σκανδαλίζω** 2 • 4 *to be led into sin*
**τελειόω** 3 • 14 *to bring to full measure, fill the measure of*
4 **διαλογίζομαι** 6 • 6 *to consider, ponder, reason*
**διψυχέω** [2] 21 • 25 *to be doubtful, be undecided, be changeable*
**ἔνδοξος** 43 • 54 *glorious, splendid*
**Ἑρμᾶς, ὁ** 13 • 13 *Hermas*
**ἦχος, ὁ** 1 • 1 *sound, tone, noise*; **ὡς ἦχος φωνῆς** lit. *a sound of a voice*, possibly *a sound like an echo*[3]
**θεμελιόω** 6 • 6 *to establish, strengthen*
**πρᾶγμα, τό** 19 • 23 *thing, matter, affair*

---

3. Carolyn Osiek, *Shepherd of Hermas: A Commentary* (Minneapolis: Fortress, 1999) 92.

5 **κονιορτός, ὁ** [2] 3 • 3 *dust*
**κτῆνος, τό** 4 • 4 *livestock*
**μήποτε** 13 • 22 *that…not*
**προσβαίνω** 1 • 1 *to draw close, approach*
**στάδιον, τό** 2 • 9 *stade* (about one-eighth mile or 192 meters)
6 **ἀκρίς, ἡ** 1 • 1 *locust*
**ἐκλάμπω** 1 • 2 *to shine (out)*
**θεῖος** 10 • 16 *supernatural, other-worldly*
**κέραμος, ὁ** 2 • 2 *clay, earthenware vessel*
**κῆτος, τό** 2 • 2 *sea monster*
**κονιορτός, ὁ** 3 • 3 *dust*
**μῆκος, τό** 1 • 1 *length* (dimension)
**πύρινος** 1 • 1 *fiery*
**ρ´** 1 • 1 numerical sign for one-hundred, *100*
**ὑπονοέω** 1 • 1 *to suspect, suppose*
**ὡσεί** [2] 16 • 17 *as, like*
7 **διψυχέω** 21 • 25 *to be undecided, be changeable, doubt*
**ἐπαναμιμνῄσκω** 1 • 1 *to remind*; pass. *call to mind, remember (something) again*
**Ἑρμᾶς, ὁ** 13 • 13 *Hermas*
**λυτρόω** 2 • 11 *to set free, rescue, redeem*
8 **ἐνδύω** 29 • 32 *to clothe oneself in, put on, wear*; fig. *take on the characteristics/virtues/intentions of*
**θαρσέω** 1 • 1 *to be enheartened, be courageous*
**λυμαίνω** 4 • 4 *to destroy, cause harm to, injure, damage, spoil, ruin*
**μεγαλεῖος** 3 • 6 subst. *greatness, sublimity*; *mighty deed*
**μιμνῄσκομαι** 2 • 9 *to remember, recollect, remind oneself*
**ῥοίζος, ὁ** or **ἡ** 1 • 1 *a whoosh*
9 **ἐκτείνω** 1 • 7 *to stretch out*
**κῆτος, τό** 2 • 2 *sea monster*
**κινέω** 1 • 3 *to move, move around*
**μέχρι** 7 • 23 *until*
**ὅλως** 30 • 31 *completely, wholly, everywhere*; with a negative *not at all*
**παρέρχομαι** 4 • 12 *to go by, pass by*
**προβάλλω** 1 • 2 *to put forward, thrust out*
**τηλικοῦτος** 3 • 6 *so great, so large*
**χαμαί** 6 • 6 *on the ground*
10 **αἱματώδης** 2 • 2 *blood-red, dark red*
**εἶτα** [3] 30 • 48 *then, next*
**λευκός** 24 • 24 *white*
**μέλας** 17 • 20 *black*
**πυροειδής** 2 • 2 *red as fire, bright red*
**τέσσαρες** 11 • 12 *four*
**χρυσοῦς** 2 • 2 *golden*
**χρῶμα, τό** 3 • 5 *color*

## Chapter 23 (Hv 4.2)

1 **θρίξ, ἡ** 7 • 7 *hair*
**κατακαλύπτω** 1 • 1 *to cover, veil*
**κατακάλυψις, ἡ** 1 • 1 *covering*
**κοσμέω** 3 • 10 *to adorn, decorate*
**λ´** 1 • 1 numerical sign for thirty, *30*
**λευκός** [3] 24 • 24 *white*
**μέτωπον, τό** 1 • 1 *forehead*
**μίτρα, ἡ** 1 • 1 *turban, snood, head-covering*
**νυμφών, ὁ** 1 • 1 *bridal chamber*
**παρέρχομαι** 4 • 12 *to go by, pass by*
**παρθένος, ἡ** 58 • 62 *virgin*
**προέρχομαι** 1 • 5 *to go forward, advance, proceed*
**ὑπαντάω** 1 • 2 *to meet*
**ὑπόδημα, τό** 1 • 1 *sandal*
**ὡσεί** 16 • 17 *about*
2 **ἀντασπάζομαι** 2 • 2 *to greet in return*
**ἱλαρός** 24 • 34 *cheerful, glad, happy*
**κυρία, ἡ** 24 • 24 *lady, mistress*
**ὅραμα, τό** 5 • 5 *vision*
**πρότερος** 40 • 47 *former, earlier*
3 **ἀπαντάω** 1 • 1 *to meet someone*
**διαφθείρω** 8 • 12 *to destroy, spoil*
**ἐκφεύγω** 5 • 6 *to escape*
**κυρία, ἡ** 24 • 24 *lady, mistress*
**πολυσπλαγχνία, ἡ** 3 • 3 *sympathy, compassion, mercy*
**τηλικοῦτος** 3 • 6 *so great, so large*
4 **διψυχέω** 21 • 25 *to be undecided, be changeable, doubt*
**ἐκφεύγω** [2] 5 • 6 *to escape*
**ἐμφράσσω** 1 • 1 *to stop (up), shut*
**ἔνδοξος** 43 • 54 *glorious, splendid*

**ἐπιρίπτω** 3 • 3 *to cast upon*
**Θεγρί, ὁ** 1 • 1 *Thegri*
**λυμαίνω** 4 • 4 *to hurt someone, cause harm to, injure, damage, spoil, ruin, destroy*
**μέριμνα, ἡ** 3 • 3 *anxiety, worry, care*
**τηλικοῦτος** 3 • 6 *so great, so large*
5 **ἀμέμπτως** 2 • 6 *blamelessly*
**ἄμωμος** 1 • 17 *blameless*
**δουλεύω** 25 • 42 *to serve, obey, (perform the duties of a slave)*
**ἐκλεκτός** 9 • 30 *chosen*
**ἐκφεύγω** 5 • 6 *to escape*
**ἐξηγέομαι** 1 • 2 *to relate, tell, report, describe*
**ἐπιρίπτω** 3 • 3 *to cast upon*
**καθαρός** 25 • 45 *pure, clean*
**κατορθόω** 5 • 5 *to set straight, complete, bring to a successful conclusion*
**μεγαλεῖος** 3 • 6 subst. *greatness, sublimity; mighty deed*
**μέριμνα, ἡ** 3 • 3 *anxiety, worry, care*
**προετοιμάζω** 1 • 5 *to prepare beforehand*
**τύπος, ὁ** 10 • 26 *type, symbol, foreshadowing*
6 **αἱρετός** 1 • 1 *better, desirable*
**ἀποστρέφω** 2 • 8 *to turn away, turn*
**δίψυχος** 20 • 23 *doubting, hesitating*
**ἐξαποστέλλω** 3 • 4 *to send, dispatch*
**μάστιξ, ἡ** 3 • 8 *torment, suffering*
**παρακούω** 1 • 5 *to refuse to listen to, disobey*

## Chapter 24 (Hv 4.3)

1 **γνωρίζω** 10 • 18 *to make known, reveal*
**κυρία, ἡ** 24 • 24 *lady, mistress*
**ναί** 6 • 8 *certainly, indeed, quite so*
**περίεργος** 1 • 1 *inquisitive, meddlesome, officious, curious*
**πρᾶγμα, τό** 19 • 23 *thing, matter, affair*
**τέσσαρες** 11 • 12 *four*
**χρῶμα, τό** 3 • 5 *color*
2 **μέλας** 17 • 20 *black*
3 **αἱματώδης** 2 • 2 *blood-red, dark red*
**πυροειδής** 2 • 2 *red as fire, bright red*
4 **ἀποβάλλω** [2] 32 • 36 *to take off, doff, shed*
**δοκιμάζω** 10 • 19 *to prove by testing*
**ἐκφεύγω** [2] 5 • 6 *to shun, avoid, escape*
**εὔχρηστος** 13 • 14 *useful, serviceable*
**λύπη, ἡ** 23 • 24 *sorrow, grief, affliction*
**οἰκοδομή, ἡ** 100 • 103 *building, edifice*
**πύργος, ὁ** 147 • 148 *tower*
**πυρόω** 1 • 2 *to make red hot, cause to glow, heat thoroughly*
**σκωρία, ἡ** 1 • 1 *slag, dross*
**στενοχωρία, ἡ** 2 • 2 *distress, difficulty, anguish, trouble*
**χρήσιμος** 1 • 2 *useful, beneficial, advantageous*
**χρυσίον, τό** [2] 2 • 3 *gold*
**χρυσοῦς** 2 • 2 *golden*
5 **ἄσπιλος** 2 • 3 *pure, without spot*
**ἐκλέγομαι** 5 • 15 *to select someone/something for oneself*
**ἐκλεκτός** 9 • 30 *chosen*
**ἐπέρχομαι** 6 • 8 *to happen, come about*
**καθαρός** 25 • 45 *pure*
**λευκός** 24 • 24 *white*
6 **διαλείπω** 3 • 3 *to stop, cease*
**μνημονεύω** 7 • 25 *to remember, keep in mind, think of*
**προγράφω** 2 • 4 *to write before(hand)*
**τύπος, ὁ** 10 • 26 *type, symbol, foreshadowing*
7 **ψόφος, ὁ** 1 • 1 *noise, sound*

# VISION FIVE

## Chapter 25 (Hv 5)

1 **ἀντασπάζομαι** 2 • 2 *to greet in return*
**δέρμα, τό** 2 • 3 *skin, hide*
**ἔνδοξος** 43 • 54 *distinguished*

**κλίνη, ἡ** 1 • 1 *bed, couch*
**λευκός** 24 • 24 *white*
**ὄψις, ἡ** 3 • 6 *outward appearance*
**περίκειμαι** 2 • 4 *to wear, have something on*
**πήρα, ἡ** 3 • 3 *knapsack, shepherd's bag*
**ποιμενικός** 1 • 1 *pertaining to a shepherd*
**ῥάβδος, ἡ** 58 • 62 *shepherd's staff*
**σχῆμα, τό** 1 • 1 *outward appearance, form, shape*
**ὦμος, ὁ** 5 • 5 *shoulder*
2 **οἰκέω** 2 • 6 *to live, dwell*
**παρακαθίζω** 1 • 1 *to sit down beside*
**σεμνός** 7 • 13 *worthy of reverence, august, sublime, holy*
3 **ἐκπειράζω** 3 • 4 *to tempt*
**πάρειμι** 3 • 17 *to come, be present*
**ποιμήν, ὁ** 51 • 55 *shepherd*
4 **ἀλλοιόω** 3 • 5 *to change*
**ἀφρόνως** 1 • 1 *foolishly*
**ἰδέα, ἡ** 8 • 9 *appearance*
**λύπη, ἡ** 23 • 24 *sorrow, grief, affliction*
**πονηρῶς** 1 • 1 *wickedly, basely*
**συγκόπτω** 3 • 3 *to be overcome*
**συγχέω** 4 • 4 *to confuse, confound, trouble, stir up*
5 **ἐντέλλω** [2] 17 • 29 *to command, order, give orders*
**ἰσχυροποιέω** 7 • 7 *to strengthen*
**κεφάλαιον, τό** 1 • 2 *main point, main thing*
**πρότερος** 40 • 47 *formerly, earlier*
**συγχέω/συγχύν(ν)ω** 4 • 4 *to confuse, confound, trouble, stir up*
**σύμφορος** 6 • 6 *beneficial, advantageous, profitable*
6 **ἐντέλλω** 17 • 29 *to command, order, give orders*
7 **ἀπολαμβάνω** [2] 6 • 17 *to receive*
**ἐναντίος** 1 • 4 *opposed, contrary;* subst. *the opposite*
**ἐντέλλω** 17 • 29 *to command, order, give orders*
**ἐπαγγέλλω** 6 • 7 *to promise*
**καθαρός** 25 • 45 *pure, free*
**μετάνοια, ἡ** 58 • 72 *repentance, turning about, conversion*
**ποιμήν, ὁ** 50 • 54 *shepherd*
**προστίθημι** 13 • 22 *to add to, increase*

## COMMANDMENT ONE

### Chapter 26 (Hm 1)

1 **ἀχώρητος** 2 • 2 *uncontained*
**καταρτίζω** 2 • 6 *to prepare, make, create, outfit;* perhaps *put in order*
**κτίζω** 14 • 25 *to create*
**χωρέω** 3 • 15 *to hold, contain*
2 **ἀποβάλλω** 32 • 36 *to take off, doff*
**ἀρετή, ἡ** 5 • 6 *uprightness, excellence of character, exceptional civic virtue*
**ἐγκρατεύομαι** 24 • 25 *to control oneself, abstain*
**ἐνδύω** 29 • 32 *to clothe oneself in, put on, wear;* fig. *take on the characteristics/virtues/intentions of*
**πονηρία, ἡ** 36 • 41 *wickedness, baseness, maliciousness, sinfulness*

## COMMANDMENT TWO

### Chapter 27 (Hm 2)

1 **ἄκακος** 5 • 8 *innocent, guileless*
**ἁπλότης, ἡ** 12 • 15 *simplicity, sincerity, uprightness, frankness*
**νήπιος** 2 • 4 *infant, child*
**πονηρία, ἡ** 36 • 41 *wickedness*
2 **ἔνοχος** [2] 3 • 3 *liable, answerable, guilty*
**ἡδέως** 7 • 10 *gladly*
**καταλαλέω** [4] 4 • 6 *to speak evil*
**καταλαλιά, ἡ** 7 • 13 *slander, evil speech, defamation, detraction*
3 **ἀκατάστατος** 1 • 1 *restless, unstable*
**ἀπέχω** 21 • 35 *to keep away, abstain, refrain from*
**διχοστασία, ἡ** 4 • 6 *dissension*
**εἰρηνεύω** 6 • 17 *to keep the peace*
**εὐθηνία, ἡ** 2 • 2 *good relation, rapport, well-being*
**καταλαλιά, ἡ** 7 • 13 *slander, evil speech, defamation, detraction*
**μηδέποτε** 3 • 5 *never*
4 **ἁπλῶς** 4 • 6 *simply, above board, sincerely, openly*

διστάζω 5 • 10 *to doubt, waver*
δώρημα, τό 2 • 2 *gift*
ἐνδύω 29 • 32 *to clothe oneself in, put on, wear;*
fig. *take on the characteristics/ virtues/intentions of*
ἱλαρός 24 • 34 *cheerful, glad, happy*
κόπος, ὁ 6 • 8 *labor, work, toil*
ὁμαλός 5 • 5 *level*
πρόσκομμα, τό 2 • 2 *cause for offense, cause for making a misstep*
σεμνότης, ἡ 11 • 12 *dignity, seriousness, probity, holiness*
ὑστερέω 7 • 11 *to be needy, lack, be poor*
5 διατί 27 • 29 *why?*
δικάζω 1 • 1 *to judge, condemn*
δίκη, ἡ 2 • 3 *punishment, penalty*
θλίβω 19 • 25 *to afflict, cause distress*
τίνω 2 • 2 *to pay, undergo a penalty*
ὑπόκρισις, ἡ 5 • 13 *insincerely, play-acting, pretense, outward show, dissembling*
6 ἀθῷος 1 • 7 *guiltless, innocent*
ἁπλῶς [3] 4 • 6 *without reservation, simply, above board, sincerely, openly*
διακρίνω 3 • 7 *to distinguish*
ἔνδοξος 43 • 54 *esteemed, honored, distinguished, eminent*
μηθείς 1 • 3 *not*
τελέω [3] 22 • 23 *to carry out, accomplish, perform, fulfill, keep*
7 ἄκακος 5 • 8 *innocent, guileless*
ἀμίαντος 3 • 5 *undefiled, pure*
ἁπλότης, ἡ 12 • 15 *sincerity, simplicity, uprightness, frankness*
καθαρός 25 • 45 *pure, free*
μετάνοια, ἡ 58 • 72 *repentance, turning about, conversion*

## COMMANDMENT THREE

### Chapter 28 (Hm 3)

1 ἀληθής 6 • 16 *real, genuine, not imaginary*
ἀληθινός 3 • 14 *true, trustworthy*
ψεῦδος, τό 4 • 6 *lie, falsehood*
2 ἀθετέω 2 • 4 *to reject, not recognize, disallow*
ἀποστερητής, ὁ [2] 3 • 3 *defrauder, cheat*
ἄψευστος 1 • 1 *free from lies, truthful*
μιαίνω 14 • 14 *to defile*
παρακαταθήκη, ἡ 1 • 1 *deposit*
ψευδής 2 • 4 *false, lying*
ψεύδομαι 1 • 1 *to lie*
3 ἀληθής [2] 6 • 16 *true*
ἀντιλέγω 1 • 3 *to speak against, contradict*
διατί 27 • 29 *why?*
ἐπιδείκνυμι 2 • 11 *to represent*
λίαν 43 • 48 *bitterly, exceedingly, very (much)*
οὐδέποτε 4 • 6 *never*
οὐδέπω 1 • 1 *not yet, still not*
πανούργως 1 • 1 *deceitfully*
ψεῦδος, τό 4 • 6 *lie, falsehood*
4 ἀκριβῶς 5 • 8 *accurately, carefully, well*
ἀληθής 6 • 16 *true*
ἀληθῶς 1 • 23 *truly, in truth, really, actually*
ἐπάγω 1 • 1 *to bring on, bring upon*
λύπη, ἡ 23 • 24 *grief, sorrow, affliction*
οὐδέποτε 4 • 6 *never*
σεμνός 7 • 13 *honorable, worthy, venerable, holy, above reproach*
συνείδησις, ἡ 1 • 11 *conscience, moral consciousness*
φρονέω 5 • 17 *to judge, form/hold an opinion*
5 ἀληθινός 3 • 14 *true*
ἀπέχω 21 • 35 *to keep away, abstain, refrain from*
περιποιέω 8 • 9 *to acquire, obtain, gain for oneself*
πραγματεία, ἡ 11 • 11 *activity, occupation;*
pl. *undertakings, business, affairs*
πρότερος 40 • 47 *former, earlier*
ψευδής 2 • 4 *false, lying*
ψεῦσμα, τό 2 • 3 *lying, untruthfulness, undependability*

## COMMANDMENT FOUR

### Chapter 29 (Hm 4.1)

1 **ἁγνεία, ἡ** 7 • 13 *purity, chastity*
**ἀλλότριος** 5 • 14 *another's, not one's own, strange*
**διαμαρτάνω** 3 • 5 *to miss the mark badly, be quite wrong, sin*
**ἐντέλλω** 17 • 29 *to command, order, give orders*
**μνημονεύω** 7 • 25 *to remember, keep in mind, think of*
**ὁμοίωμα, τό** 2 • 3 *likeness*
**οὐδέποτε** 4 • 6 *never*
**πορνεία, ἡ** 3 • 5 *prostitution, fornication, unchastity*
**σός** 4 • 9 *your, yours*
2 **διαμαρτάνω** 3 • 5 *to fail, miss the mark badly, be quite wrong, sin*
**ἐνθύμησις, ἡ** [2] 4 • 5 *idea, thought, reflection*
**κατεργάζομαι** 3 • 7 *to bring about*
3 **ἀνομία, ἡ** 9 • 33 *lawlessness*
**ἀπέχω** 21 • 35 *to keep away, abstain, refrain from*
**ἐνθύμησις, ἡ** 4 • 5 *thought, reflection, idea*
**σεμνότης, ἡ** 11 • 12 *dignity, seriousness, probity, holiness*
4 **ἐπιτρέπω** 3 • 11 *to allow, permit*
**μοιχεία, ἡ** 4 • 9 *adultery*
**συζάω** 5 • 5 *to live with*
5 **ἄγνοια, ἡ** 2 • 3 *ignorance, unawareness;*
**ἄχρι τῆς ἀγνοίας** *as long as he is ignorant of it*
**ἔνοχος** 3 • 3 *liable, answerable, guilty*
**ἐπιμένω** 10 • 16 *to continue, persist in, persevere*
**μοιχεία, ἡ** 4 • 9 *adultery*
**πορνεία, ἡ** 3 • 5 *prostitution, unchastity, fornication*
**συζάω** 5 • 5 *to live with*
6 **γαμέω** 5 • 8 *to marry, take someone as wife*
**ἐπιμένω** 10 • 16 *to continue, persist in, persevere*
**μοιχάω** 2 • 3 *to be caused to commit adultery, be an adulterer/adulteress, commit adultery*
**πάθος, τό** 2 • 18 *passion*
7 **παραδέχομαι** 4 • 9 *to take back, receive, accept*
8 **γαμέω** 5 • 8 *to marry, enter matrimony*
**ἐπισπάομαι** 1 • 1 *to bring upon*
**κεῖμαι** 22 • 24 *to be given, exist, be valid*
**μετάνοια, ἡ** [2] 58 • 72 *repentance, turning about, conversion*
**μήν** 2 • 10 *indeed*
**παραδέχομαι** [2] 4 • 9 *to take back, receive, accept*
**πρᾶξις, ἡ** 44 • 50 *way of acting, course of action*
**μὴ ἐπὶ πολὺ δέ** *but not repeatedly, not often*
9 **ἀπέχω** 21 • 35 *to keep away, abstain, refrain from*
**ἐμμένω** 7 • 8 *to persevere in, stand by*
**μέτοχος** 1 • 3 *sharing in, participating in*
**μιαίνω** 14 • 14 *to defile*
**μοιχάω** 2 • 3 *to commit adultery, be unfaithful*
**μοιχεία, ἡ** 4 • 9 *adultery*
**ὁμοίωμα, τό** 2 • 3 *similar to, likeness*
**συζάω** 5 • 5 *to live with*
10 **μετάνοια, ἡ** 58 • 72 *repentance, turning about, conversion*
**προστάσσω** 3 • 8 *to command, order, give instructions, determine*
11 **ἀφορμή, ἡ** 2 • 5 *occasion, opportunity*
**ἴασις, ἡ** 6 • 7 *forgiveness, cure deliverance*
**μηκέτι** 12 • 16 *no longer, not from now on*
**πρᾶξις, ἡ** 44 • 50 *way of acting, course of action*
**πρότερος** 40 • 47 *former, earlier*
**συντελέω** 9 • 15 *to find application, carry out, fulfill, accomplish*

### Chapter 30 (Hm 4.2)

1 **ἀνέχω** 1 • 7 *to put up with, endure, bear*
**ἄφρων** 11 • 17 *foolish, ignorant*

**ἐπεί** [2] 10 • 35 *since, because, for*
**ἡγέομαι** 7 • 25 *to think, consider, regard*
**λίαν** 43 • 48 *exceedingly, very (much)*
**νοέω** 30 • 46 *to understand*
**ὅλως** 30 • 31 *completely, wholly, everywhere;* with a negative *not at all*
**οὐθείς** 2 • 3 *nothing*
**πρᾶξις, ἡ** 44 • 50 *evil or disgraceful deed*
**πρότερος** 40 • 47 *former, earlier*
**πωρόω** 2 • 2 *to make dull/obtuse/blind, close the mind*
**συνετίζω** 1 • 2 *to cause to understand*
**συνίημι** 13 • 21 *to understand, comprehend*
2 **βασανίζω** 15 • 18 *to torment, harass*
**μετάνοια, ἡ** [2] 58 • 72 *repentance, turning about, conversion*
**πολυτελῶς** 1 • 1 *lavishly, abundantly*
**πρᾶξις, ἡ** 44 • 50 *evil or disgraceful deed*
**σύνεσις, ἡ** [4] 13 • 22 *understanding*
**συνίημι** 13 • 21 *to understand, comprehend*
**ταπεινόω** 1 • 8 *to constrain, mortify*
3 **ἀγνοέω** 2 • 11 *to be ignorant, be uninformed, not know*
**εἶτα** 30 • 48 *then, next*
**ἐξακριβάζομαι** 2 • 2 *to ask exactly, inquire exactly*
**ποικίλος** 20 • 22 *diversified, manifold*

## Chapter 31 (Hm 4.3)

1 **ἄφεσις, ἡ** 5 • 13 *forgiveness, pardon*
**μετάνοια, ἡ** 58 • 72 *repentance, turning about, conversion*
**προστίθημι** 13 • 22 *to add, put to*
**πρότερος** 40 • 47 *former, earlier*
2 **ἁγνεία, ἡ** 7 • 13 *purity, chastity*
**ἄφεσις, ἡ** 5 • 13 *forgiveness, pardon, cancellation*
**μηκέτι** 12 • 16 *no longer, not from now on*
3 **ἄφεσις, ἡ** 5 • 13 *forgiveness, pardon, cancellation*
**ἀφορμή, ἡ** 2 • 5 *excuse, occasion, opportunity*
**δηλόω** 32 • 49 *to explain, clarify*
**ἐξακριβάζομαι** 2 • 2 *to ask exactly, inquire exactly*
**ἐπεί** 10 • 35 *since, because, for*
**μετάνοια, ἡ** 58 • 72 *repentance, turning about, conversion*
**πρότερος** 40 • 47 *former, earlier*
4 **ἀσθένεια, ἡ** 6 • 7 *weakness, moral deficiency*
**καρδιογνώστης, ὁ** 1 • 1 *one who knows the hearts*
**μετάνοια, ἡ** 58 • 72 *repentance, turning about, conversion*
**πολυπλοκία, ἡ** 1 • 1 *cunning, craftiness*
**πονηρεύομαι** 13 • 15 *to act wickedly toward someone, do harm to someone*
**προγινώσκω** 2 • 2 *to have foreknowledge (of)*
5 **μετάνοια, ἡ** [2] 58 • 72 *repentance, turning about, conversion*
**ποίησις, ἡ** 2 • 3 *work, creation*
**πολυεύσπλαγχνος** 2 • 2 *rich in compassion*
**σπλαγχνίζομαι** 8 • 9 *to have pity, feel sympathy*
6 **ἀσύμφορος** 6 • 7 *harmful, disadvantageous*
**δυσκόλως** 7 • 7 *hardly, with difficulty*
**ἐκπειράζω** 3 • 4 *to tempt*
**κλῆσις, ἡ** 2 • 4 *call, calling, invitation*
**σεμνός** 7 • 13 *honorable, worthy, venerable, holy, above reproach*
**ὑπὸ χεῖρα ἁμαρτάνῃ** *he sins repeatedly*
7 **ἀκριβῶς** 5 • 8 *accurately, carefully, well*
**ζωοποιέω** 3 • 10 *to make alive, give life to*
**μηκέτι** 12 • 16 *no longer, not from now on*
**προστίθημι** 13 • 22 *to add to, increase*

## Chapter 32 (Hm 4.4)

1 **ἀνέχομαι** 1 • 4 *to endure, bear, put up with*
**ἅπαξ** 2 • 4 *once*
**γαμέω** 5 • 8 *to marry*
**δηλόω** 32 • 49 *to explain, make clear*
**ἐπεί** 10 • 35 *since, because, for*
**κοιμάω** 8 • 12 *to fall asleep, die, pass away*
**μήτι** 3 • 3 *perhaps, not*
2 **γαμέω** [2] 5 • 8 *to marry*
**περιποιέω** 8 • 9 *to acquire, obtain, gain for oneself*
**περισσός** 2 • 5 *abundant;* comparative *greater, more, even more*
3 **ἁγνεία, ἡ** 7 • 13 *purity, chastity*
**σεμνότης, ἡ** 11 • 12 *dignity, seriousness, probity, holiness*
4 **ἁγνότης, ἡ** 2 • 2 *purity, sincerity*
**ἄφεσις, ἡ** 5 • 13 *forgiveness, pardon, cancellation*
**παράπτωμα, τό** 2 • 10 *offense, wrongdoing, sin*
**πρότερος** 40 • 47 *former, earlier*

# COMMANDMENT FIVE

## Chapter 33 (Hm 5.1)

1 **κατακυριεύω** 13 • 15 *to become master, gain dominion over, subdue, gain power over*
**μακρόθυμος** 5 • 9 *patient, forbearing, tolerant, even-tempered*
**συνετός** 4 • 7 *intelligent, sagacious, wise, with good sense*
2 **ἀγαλλιάω** 6 • 11 *to exult, be glad, be overjoyed*
**ἐπισκοτέω** 2 • 2 *to obscure*
**εὐθηνία, ἡ** 2 • 2 *good relation, rapport, well-being*
**εὐρύχωρος** 1 • 1 *broad, spacious, roomy*
**εὐφραίνω** 6 • 15 *to be glad, enjoy oneself, rejoice, celebrate*
**ἱλαρότης, ἡ** 4 • 4 *cheerfulness, gladness, wholeheartedness, graciousness*
**καθαρός** 25 • 45 *pure, free*
**λειτουργέω** 4 • 11 *to serve, render service*
**μακρόθυμος** 5 • 9 *patient, forbearing, tolerant, even-tempered*
**σκεῦος, τό** 2 • 9 *vessel, instrument*
3 **ἀφίστημι** 19 • 19 *to go away, withdraw*
**ἐπέρχομαι** 6 • 8 *to come upon, approach*
**καθαρός** 25 • 45 *pure, free*
**λειτουργέω** 4 • 11 *to serve, render service*
**μακροθυμία, ἡ** 9 • 15 *forbearance, patience*
**μιαίνω** 14 • 14 *to defile*
**ὀξυχολία, ἡ** [3] 17 • 17 *irritability, bad temper*
**πνίγω** 4 • 4 *to choke*
**στενοχωρέω** 1 • 2 *to be distressed*
**τρυφερός** 4 • 4 *delicate, gentle, subdued*
4 **ἀμφότεροι** 14 • 21 *both*
**ἀσύμφορος** 6 • 7 *harmful, disadvantageous*
5 **ἀφανίζω** 1 • 2 *to be spoiled*
**ἀψίνθιον, τό** [3] 3 • 3 *wormwood*
**γλυκύς** 3 • 6 *sweet*
**γλυκύτης, ἡ** 1 • 2 *sweetness*
**δεσπότης, ὁ** [2] 24 • 54 *owner*
**ἐλάχιστος** 13 • 16 *very little*
**ἐπιχέω** 1 • 1 *to pour in*
**εὔχρηστος** 13 • 14 *useful, serviceable*
**κεράμιον, τό** 7 • 8 *jar, an earthenware vessel*
**λίαν** 43 • 48 *exceedingly, very (much)*
**μέλι, τό** 7 • 12 *honey*
**οὐχί** 1 • 6 *not*
**πικραίνω** 2 • 2 *to make bitter*
**τοσοῦτος** 9 • 38 *so great, so much*
**χρῆσις, ἡ** 1 • 5 *usefulness*
6 **ἄχρηστος** 4 • 6 *useless, worthless*
**γλυκύς** 3 • 6 *sweet*
**ἔντευξις, ἡ** 15 • 18 *prayer*
**εὔχρηστος** [2] 13 • 14 *useful, serviceable*
**μακροθυμία, ἡ** [3] 9 • 15 *forbearance, patience*
**μέλι, τό** 7 • 12 *honey*
**μιαίνω** 14 • 14 *to defile*

**μίγνυμι** 4 • 4 *to mix, blend*
**ὀξυχολία, ἡ** [2] 17 • 17 *irritability, bad temper*
**πικρός** 5 • 5 *bitter, embittered, harsh*
7 **ἀπέχω** 21 • 35 *to keep away, abstain, refrain from*
**ἐνέργεια, ἡ** 8 • 8 *way of working*
**μήν** 2 • 10 *indeed*
**ὀξυχολία, ἡ** 17 • 17 *irritability, bad temper*
**σεμνός** 7 • 13 *worthy of reverence, august, sublime, holy*
**συντηρέω** 3 • 3 *to protect, defend*

## Chapter 34 (Hm 5.2)

1 **ἀπόκενος** 6 • 6 *quite empty*
**ἀποπλανάω** [3] 6 • 8 *to mislead*
**δίψυχος** 20 • 23 *doubting, hesitating, double-minded*
**ἐνέργεια, ἡ** [2] 8 • 8 *way of working*
**ἐνεργέω** 1 • 4 *to influence*
**καταστρέφω** 3 • 5 *to turn away, mislead, divert, ruin*
**ὀξυχολία, ἡ** 17 • 17 *irritability, bad temper*
**πλήρης** 13 • 20 *full, filled*
2 **ἀσύμφορος** 6 • 7 *harmful, disadvantageous*
**ἄφρων** 11 • 17 *foolish, ignorant*
**βιωτικός** 4 • 4 *belonging to (daily) life*
**δόσις, ἡ** 1 • 1 *giving*
**ἔδεσμα, τό** 12 • 12 *food*
**ἕνεκα** 8 • 15 *because of, on account of, for the sake of*
**εὐσταθέω** 3 • 4 *to lead a quiet life, be stable, be tranquil, be at rest*
**κενός** 20 • 27 *vain, empty*
**λῆψις, ἡ** 1 • 1 *receiving*
**μικρολογία, ἡ** 1 • 1 *trifle*
**μωρός** [2] 11 • 12 *foolish, stupid*
**παρεμβάλλω** 1 • 1 *to insinuate*
**πικρία, ἡ** 5 • 7 *embittered*
**πρᾶγμα, τό** [2] 19 • 23 *undertaking, occupation, task*
**φίλος** 5 • 8 *loving*; subst. *friend*
**ἐκ τοῦ μηδενός** *for no reason at all*
3 **ἀγαλλιάω** 6 • 11 *to exult, be glad, be overjoyed*
**ἀμέριμνος** 1 • 1 *free from care*
**εὐθηνέω** 3 • 3 *to thrive, flourish, be in good condition*
**ἡσύχιος** 4 • 7 *quiet, well-ordered*
**ἱλαρός** 24 • 34 *cheerful, glad, happy*
**ἰσχυρός** 14 • 21 *strong, mighty*
**μακροθυμία, ἡ** [2] 9 • 15 *forbearance, patience*
**ὁλόκληρος** 1 • 1 *undiminished, whole, complete, undamaged, intact, blameless*
**ὀχυρός** 1 • 1 *strong, firm, sturdy*
**παραμένω** 6 • 9 *to remain, continue in an occupation/office*
**πικρός** 5 • 5 *bitter, embittered, harsh*
**πλατυσμός, ὁ** 1 • 2 *amplitude, extent*
**πρᾶος** 1 • 1 *gentle, humble, considerate, meek*
**στιβαρός** 1 • 1 *stout, sturdy*
4 **ἀνίατος** 1 • 1 *unforgivable, incurable*
**ἀφροσύνη, ἡ** 7 • 11 *foolishness, lack of sense*
**ἄφρων** 11 • 17 *foolish, ignorant*
**εἶτα** [2] 30 • 48 *then, next*
**ἐλαφρός** 3 • 3 *impetuous*
**θυμός, ὁ** [2] 2 • 6 *anger, wrath, rage, indignation*
**μῆνις, ἡ** [2] 2 • 2 *implacable anger, vengefulness*
**μωρός** 11 • 12 *foolish, stupid*
**ὀξυχολία, ἡ** 17 • 17 *irritability, bad temper*
**πικρία, ἡ** [2] 5 • 7 *bitterness, animosity, anger, harshness*
**συνίστημι** 1 • 3 *to consist*
**τοσοῦτος** 9 • 38 *so much*
5 **ἀγγεῖον, τό** 1 • 1 *vessel*
**ἄγγος, τό** 1 • 2 *vessel, flask, container*
**ὑπερπλεονάζω** 1 • 1 *to run over, overflow*
**χωρέω** 3 • 15 *to hold, contain*
6 **ἀποχωρέω** 3 • 3 *to withdraw*
**ἡσυχία, ἡ** 1 • 3 *quietness, rest*
**πραότης, ἡ** 2 • 4 *gentleness, humility, courtesy, considerateness, meekness*
**σκληρότης, ἡ** 1 • 1 *harshness, roughness, hardness of heart, stubbornness*

**συνήθεια, ἡ** 1 • 3 *custom, habit, usage*
**τρυφερός** 4 • 4 *delicate, gentle, subdued*

7 **ἀκαταστατέω** 2 • 2 *to be unsettled, be vacillating*
**ἀποτυφλόω** 1 • 1 *to blind*
**ἀφίστημι** 19 • 19 *to go away, withdraw*
**διάνοια, ἡ** 6 • 22 *understanding, intelligence, mind*
**εἶτα** 30 • 48 *then, next*
**κενός** 20 • 27 *empty*
**ὅλως** 30 • 31 *completely, wholly, everywhere*; with a negative *not at all*
**ὀξύχολος** 3 • 3 *irritable, irascible, bad-tempered*
**περισπάω** 3 • 3 *to be pulled/ dragged away*
**πρᾶξις, ἡ** 44 • 50 *acting, activity, function*
**συμβαίνω** 2 • 7 *to happen, come about*
**ὧδε κἀκεῖ** *here and there*

8 **ἀνθίστημι** 6 • 8 *to resist, set oneself against, oppose*
**ἀπέχω** 21 • 35 *to keep away, abstain, refrain from*
**ἐνδυναμόω** [2] 12 • 14 *to become strong*
**ἐνδύω** 29 • 32 *to clothe oneself in, put on, wear*; fig. *take on the characteristics/ virtues/intentions of*
**ἐντέλλω** 17 • 29 *to command, order, give orders*
**ἰσχυρόω** 1 • 1 *to be strong, strengthen*
**κυριεύω** 2 • 5 *to master, rule; make (one's) own*
**μακροθυμία, ἡ** 9 • 15 *forbearance, patience*
**μήποτε** 13 • 22 *lest*
**ὀξυχολία, ἡ** [2] 17 • 17 *irritability, bad temper*
**παρενθυμέω** 4 • 4 *to disregard, neglect, forget*
**πικρία, ἡ** 5 • 7 *bitterness, animosity, anger, harshness*
**σεμνότης, ἡ** 11 • 12 *dignity, seriousness, probity, holiness*

## COMMANDMENT SIX

### Chapter 35 (Hm 6.1)

1 **ἄδικος** 3 • 14 *unjust, crooked*
**δηλόω** 32 • 49 *to explain, clarify*
**διπλοῦς** 4 • 4 *two kinds, double, two-fold*
**ἐγκράτεια, ἡ** 7 • 14 *self-control*
**ἐνέργεια, ἡ** [2] 8 • 8 *way of working*
**ἐντέλλω** 17 • 29 *to command, order, give orders*
**κεῖμαι** 22 • 24 *to exist (for something), relate* or *apply to something*
**ναί** 6 • 8 *certainly, indeed, quite so*
**νοέω** 30 • 46 *to perceive, apprehend, understand, gain insight into*

2 **ἄδικος** 3 • 14 *unjust, crooked*
**ἐάω** 5 • 13 *to avoid, let go, leave alone*
**ὁμαλός** 5 • 5 *level*
**ὀρθός** [2] 4 • 5 *straight, in a straight line*
**στρεβλός** [2] 3 • 4 *crooked, perverse*

3 **ἀκανθώδης** 4 • 4 *thorny*
**ἀνοδία, ἡ** 5 • 5 *a wayless area, roadless place*
**βλαβερός** 5 • 5 *harmful*
**πρόσκομμα, τό** 2 • 2 *obstacle, hindrance, cause for stumbling*
**στρεβλός** 3 • 4 *crooked, perverse*
**τραχύς** 6 • 6 *rough, uneven*
**τρίβος, ἡ** 2 • 2 *path*

4 **ἀκανθώδης** 4 • 4 *thorny*
**ἀπροσκόπως** 1 • 3 *without stumbling*
**ὁμαλῶς** 1 • 1 *smoothly, evenly*
**ὀρθός** 4 • 5 *straight, in a straight line*
**σύμφορος** 6 • 6 *beneficial, advantageous, profitable*
**τραχύς** 6 • 6 *rough, uneven*

5 **ἀρέσκω** 6 • 12 *to please, accommodate*
**ἐπιστρέφω** 3 • 11 *to turn back, return*

## Chapter 36 (Hm 6.2)

1 **πονηρία, ἡ** 36 • 41 *wickedness, baseness, maliciousness, sinfulness*
2 **ἀμφότεροι** 14 • 21 *both*
**ἐνέργεια, ἡ** 8 • 8 *way of working*
3 **ἁγνεία, ἡ** 7 • 13 *purity, chastity*
**αἰσχυντηρός** 1 • 1 *modest*
**ἀρετή, ἡ** 5 • 6 *uprightness, excellence of character, exceptional civic virtue*
**αὐτάρκεια, ἡ** 2 • 2 *contentment, self-sufficiency*
**ἔνδοξος** 43 • 54 *glorious, splendid*
**ἡσύχιος** 4 • 7 *quiet, well-ordered*
**πραΰς** 2 • 8 *gentle, humble, considerate, meek*
**σεμνότης, ἡ** 11 • 12 *dignity, seriousness, probity, holiness*
**συνίημι** 13 • 21 *to understand, comprehend*
**τρυφερός** 4 • 4 *delicate, gentle, subdued*
4 **ἄφρων** 11 • 17 *foolish, ignorant*
**καταστρέφω** 3 • 5 *to turn away, mislead, divert, ruin*
**ὀξύχολος** 3 • 3 *irritable, irascible, bad-tempered*
**πικρός** 5 • 5 *bitter, embittered, harsh*
**πονηρία, ἡ** 36 • 41 *wickedness, baseness, maliciousness, sinfulness*
5 **ἀλαζονεία, ἡ** 2 • 10 *pretension, arrogance*
**ἔδεσμα, τό** 12 • 12 *food*
**εἶτα** 30 • 48 *then, next*
**ἐπίσταμαι** 1 • 7 *to know, be acquainted with*
**κραιπάλη, ἡ** 1 • 1 *drinking bout, carousing*
**μεθύσμα, τό** 3 • 3 *intoxicating drink*
**νοέω** 30 • 46 *to understand, perceive, apprehend, gain an insight into*
**ὀξυχολία, ἡ** 17 • 17 *irritability, bad temper*
**παραπλήσιος** 1 • 1 *coming near, resembling, similar*
**πικρία, ἡ** 5 • 7 *bitterness, animosity, anger, harshness*
**πλεονεξία, ἡ** 2 • 7 *greediness, insatiableness, avarice, covetousness*
**ποικίλος** 20 • 22 *diversified, manifold*
**πολυτέλεια, ἡ** 6 • 6 *extravagance, luxury, richness*
**πονηρία, ἡ** 36 • 41 *wickedness, baseness, maliciousness, sinfulness*
**πρᾶξις, ἡ** 44 • 50 *undertaking, business*
**προσπίπτω** 1 • 3 *to come over, fall upon, strike against*
**τρυφή, ἡ** 19 • 22 *indulgence, reveling*
**ὑπερηφανία, ἡ** 3 • 8 *arrogance, haughtiness, pride*
6 **ἀμφότεροι** 14 • 21 *both*
**ἀσύμφορος** 6 • 7 *harmful, disadvantageous*
**ἀφίστημι** 19 • 19 *to go away, withdraw*
**ἐνέργεια, ἡ** 8 • 8 *way of working*
**συνίημι** 13 • 21 *to understand, comprehend*
7 **ἀφίστημι** 19 • 19 *to go away, withdraw*
**ἐνθύμησις, ἡ** 4 • 5 *idea, thought, reflection*
**ἐξαμαρτάνω** 2 • 2 *to violate a law or command, commit an offense, do wrong, sin*
**πονηρία, ἡ** 36 • 41 *wickedness, baseness, maliciousness, sinfulness*
8 **ἀνάγκη, ἡ** 8 • 11 *necessity, pressure*
9 **ἀποτάσσω** 1 • 5 *to say farewell (to), take leave (of)*
**πονηρία, ἡ** 36 • 41 *wickedness, baseness, maliciousness, sinfulness*
10 **δηλόω** 32 • 49 *to explain, clarify*
**πονηρία, ἡ** 36 • 41 *wickedness, baseness, maliciousness, sinfulness*
**χαλεπός** 2 • 5 *evil, hard, difficult*

## COMMANDMENT SEVEN

### Chapter 37 (Hm 7)

1 **ἀσύγκριτος** 1 • 2 *incomparable, beyond compare*
**πρᾶξις, ἡ** [2] 44 • 50 *function, acting, activity*
2 **ἔνδοξος** 43 • 54 *glorious, splendid*
**κατακυριεύω** 13 • 15 *to become master, gain dominion over, subdue, gain power over*
**καταφρονέω** 3 • 9 *to look down on, despise, scorn, treat with contempt*
3 **ἀπέχω** 21 • 35 *to keep away, abstain, refrain from*
4 **δισσός** 1 • 2 *two kinds, double*
**ἔνδοξος** 43 • 54 *glorious, splendid*
**ἰσχυρός** 14 • 21 *productive, mighty*
5 **διατί** 27 • 29 *why?*
**κτίσις, ἡ** 13 • 19 *creation, world*

## COMMANDMENT EIGHT

### Chapter 38 (Hm 8)

1 **διπλοῦς** [2] 4 • 4 *two kinds, double, two-fold*
**ἐγκράτεια, ἡ** 7 • 14 *self-control*
**ἐγκρατεύομαι** 24 • 25 *to control oneself, abstain*
**κτίσμα, τό** 3 • 4 *that which is created, creature*
2 **γνωρίζω** 10 • 18 *to make known, reveal*
**ἐγκρατεύομαι** [6] 24 • 25 *to control oneself, abstain*
**πονηρία, ἡ** 36 • 41 *wickedness, baseness, maliciousness, sinfulness*
3 **ἀνομία, ἡ** 9 • 33 *lawlessness, wanton;*
**μεθύσματος ἀνομίας** (gen. of destination; cf. *ExSyn* 99) *intoxicating drink that leads to lawlessness*
**βλασφημία, ἡ** 2 • 7 *blasphemy, abusive speech, reviling, denigration, disrespect, slander*
**ἐγκρατεύομαι** 24 • 25 *to control oneself, abstain*
**ἔδεσμα, τό** 12 • 12 *food*
**καταλαλιά, ἡ** 7 • 13 *evil speech, slander, defamation, detraction*
**καύχησις, ἡ** 1 • 3 *boasting*
**μεθύσμα, τό** 3 • 3 *intoxicating drink*
**μνησικακία, ἡ** 4 • 4 *bearing a grudge, vengefulness*
**μοιχεία, ἡ** 4 • 9 *adultery*
**πλοῦτος, ὁ** 14 • 15 *wealth*
**πολυτέλεια, ἡ** 6 • 6 *extravagance, luxury, richness*
**πονηρία, ἡ** 36 • 41 *wickedness, baseness, maliciousness, sinfulness*
**πορνεία, ἡ** 3 • 5 *prostitution, fornication, unchastity*
**ποταπός** 5 • 5 *of what sort? of what kind?*
**τρυφή, ἡ** 19 • 22 *indulgence, reveling*
**ὑπερηφανία, ἡ** 3 • 8 *arrogance, haughtiness, pride*
**ὑπόκρισις, ἡ** 5 • 13 *play-acting, pretense, outward show, dissembling*
**ὑψηλοφροσύνη, ἡ** 2 • 2 *pride, haughtiness*
**ψεῦσμα, τό** 2 • 3 *lying, untruthfulness, undependability*
4 **ἀκόλουθος** 3 • 8 *following*
**ἐγκρατεύομαι** [2] 24 • 25 *to control oneself, abstain*
5 **ἀλαζονεία, ἡ** 2 • 10 *pretension, arrogance*
**ἀπάτη, ἡ** 13 • 16 *deception, deceitfulness*
**ἀποστέρησις, ἡ** 1 • 1 *fraud*
**γέ** 3 • 18 *even*
**ἐγκρατεύομαι** 24 • 25 *to control oneself, abstain*
**κενοδοξία, ἡ** 2 • 5 *vanity, conceit, excessive ambition*
**κλέμμα, τό** 1 • 1 *stealing, theft*
**πλεονεξία, ἡ** 2 • 7 *greediness, insatiableness, avarice, covetousness*
**ψευδομαρτυρία, ἡ** 1 • 4 *false witness*
**ψεῦδος, τό** 4 • 6 *a lie, falsehood*
6 **δουλεύω** 25 • 42 *to (perform the duties of a slave) serve, obey*

ἐγγράφω 4 • 5 *to write in, record*
ἐγκρατεύομαι [4] 24 • 25 *to control oneself, abstain*
λίαν 43 • 48 *exceedingly, very (much)*
7 ἐγκρατεύομαι [2] 24 • 25 *to control oneself, abstain*
8 δηλόω 32 • 49 *to explain, clarify*
δουλεύω 25 • 42 *to (perform the duties of a slave) serve, obey*
ἐγκρατεύομαι 24 • 25 *to control oneself, abstain*
9 ἐγκρατεύομαι 24 • 25 *to control oneself, abstain*
ὁμόνοια, ἡ 2 • 24 *oneness of mind, unanimity, concord, harmony*
10 ἀγαθοποίησις, ἡ 2 • 2 *doing good*
ἀδελφότης, ἡ 1 • 2 *familial affection*
ἀκόλουθος 3 • 8 *following*
ἀνάγκη, ἡ 8 • 11 *distress, calamity, pressure*
ἀντιτάσσω 2 • 7 *to oppose, resist*
ἀποβάλλω 32 • 36 *to reject*
ἀσκέω 1 • 6 *to practice, engage in*
εἶτα 30 • 48 *then, next*
ἐνδεής [2] 4 • 4 *poor, impoverished*
ἐπισκέπτομαι 6 • 8 *to visit*
εὔθυμος 1 • 2 *cheerful, in good spirits*
ἡσύχιος 4 • 7 *quiet, well-ordered*
θλίβω 19 • 25 *to oppress, afflict*
κάμνω 1 • 3 *to be weary, be fatigued*
λυτρόω 2 • 11 *to set free, rescue, redeem*
μακρόθυμος 5 • 9 *patient, forbearing, tolerant, even-tempered*
μνησικακία, ἡ 4 • 4 *bearing a grudge, vengefulness*
νουθετέω 5 • 9 *to admonish, warn, instruct*
ὀρφανός 5 • 9 *without parents, orphan*
ποτέ 4 • 15 *presumably*
πρεσβύτης, ὁ 1 • 3 *old man, aged man*
σέβω 1 • 6 *to show reverence, show respect*
σκανδαλίζω 2 • 4 *to lead into sin*
συντηρέω 3 • 3 *to keep in mind, be concerned about*
ὕβρις, ἡ 2 • 4 *shame, insult, mistreatment*
ὑπηρετέω 2 • 5 *to serve, be helpful*
ὑποφέρω 9 • 12 *to bear up under, submit to, endure*
ὑστερέω 7 • 11 *to be needy, be poor, lack*
φιλοξενία, ἡ 1 • 5 *hospitality*
φιλόξενος 2 • 3 *hospitable*
χήρα, ἡ 6 • 13 *widow*
χρεώστης, ὁ 1 • 1 *debtor*
11 ἐγκρατεύομαι 24 • 25 *to control oneself, abstain*
12 ἐγκρατεύομαι [2] 24 • 25 *to control oneself, abstain*

## COMMANDMENT NINE

### Chapter 39 (Hm 9)

1 διψυχέω 21 • 25 *to hesitate, be undecided, be changeable, doubt*
διψυχία, ἡ 17 • 18 *doubt, indecision*
ὅλως 30 • 31 *completely, wholly, everywhere;* with a negative *not at all*
τοσοῦτος 9 • 38 *so many, so much;* perhaps *so seriously*
2 ἀδιστάκτως 8 • 8 *confidently, without doubting, without hesitating*
αἴτημα, τό 10 • 10 *petition, request*
διαλογίζομαι 6 • 6 *to consider, ponder, reason*
ἐγκαταλείπω 2 • 8 *to forsake, abandon, desert*
πληροφορέω 3 • 9 *to fulfill*
πολυευσπλαγχνία, ἡ 2 • 2 *richness in mercy*
3 ἀμνησίκακος 1 • 2 *bearing no malice, forgiving*
μνησικακέω 5 • 9 *to hold a grudge, remember evil, bear malice*
ποίησις, ἡ 2 • 3 *work, creation*
σπλαγχνίζομαι 8 • 9 *to have pity, feel sympathy*
4 ἀδιστάκτως 8 • 8 *confidently, without doubting, without hesitating*
αἴτημα, τό 10 • 10 *request*

**ἀνυστέρητος** 1 • 2 *not lacking*
**ἀπολαμβάνω** 6 • 17 *to receive*
**ματαίωμα, τό** 2 • 2 *emptiness, worthlessness*
**προλέγω** 5 • 16 *to state beforehand/earlier*
5 **αἴτημα, τό** [2] 10 • 10 *request*
**διστάζω** [2] 5 • 10 *to doubt, waver*
**δίψυχος** 20 • 23 *doubting, hesitating, double-minded*
**ἐπιτυγχάνω** 2 • 23 *to obtain, attain to, reach*
**ὅλως** 30 • 31 *completely, wholly, everywhere*;
with a negative *not at all*
6 **ἀδιστάκτως** 8 • 8 *confidently, without doubting, without hesitating*
**διψυχέω** 21 • 25 *to waver, be undecided, be changeable, doubt*
**δίψυχος** 20 • 23 *doubting, hesitating, double-minded*
**δυσκόλως** 7 • 7 *with difficulty, hardly*
**ὁλοτελής** 5 • 5 *in every way complete, quite perfect*
7 **ἀγνοέω** 2 • 11 *to not know, be ignorant (of)*
**αἴτημα, τό** [4] 10 • 10 *request*
**βραδύς** [2] 4 • 5 *slow, rather slowly*
**διψυχέω** 21 • 25 *to be undecided, be changeable, doubt*
**διψυχία, ἡ** 17 • 18 *doubt, indecision*
**ἐνδύω** 29 • 32 *to clothe oneself in, put on, wear;*
fig. *take on the characteristics/ virtues/intentions of*
**ἰσχυρός** 14 • 21 *productive, mighty*
**πάντως** 7 • 9 *surely, by all means, certainly, probably, doubtless*
**παράπτωμα, τό** 2 • 10 *offense, wrongdoing, sin*
**πειρασμός, ὁ** 1 • 4 *test, trial*
**ποτέ** 7 • 21 *once, at some time or other*
**ταχύς** 11 • 18 *without delay, quickly, at once*
8 **αἴτημα, τό** 10 • 10 *request*
**αἰτιάομαι** 2 • 2 *to blame, accuse*
**διαλείπω** 3 • 3 *to stop, cease*
**διψυχέω** 21 • 25 *to be undecided, be changeable, doubt*
**ἐκκακέω** 1 • 1 *to lose heart*
9 **ἀσύνετος** 11 • 16 *senseless, foolish*
**γέ** 3 • 18 *even, indeed*
**διψυχία, ἡ** [2] 17 • 18 *doubt, indecision*
**ἐκριζόω** 1 • 2 *to uproot, utterly destroy*
**θυγάτηρ, ἡ** 4 • 10 *daughter*
**ἰσχυρός** 14 • 21 *productive, mighty*
**λίαν** [2] 43 • 48 *exceedingly, very (much)*
**πονηρεύομαι** 13 • 15 *to act wickedly toward someone, do harm to someone*
10 **ἀποτυγχάνω** 2 • 3 *to fail*
**διψυχία, ἡ** [2] 17 • 18 *doubt, indecision*
**ἐνδύω** 29 • 32 *to clothe oneself in, put on, wear;*
fig. *take on the characteristics/ virtues/intentions of*
**ἐπαγγέλλομαι** 1 • 7 *to promise*
**ἰσχυρός** 14 • 21 *productive, mighty*
**κατακυριεύω** 13 • 15 *to master, gain dominion over, subdue, gain power over*
**καταπιστεύω** 1 • 1 *to trust*
**καταφρονέω** 3 • 9 *to look down on, despise, scorn, treat with contempt*
**πρᾶγμα, τό** 19 • 23 *thing, matter, affair*
**τελειόω** 3 • 14 *to fulfill*
11 **ἄνωθεν** 6 • 8 *from above*
**διψυχία, ἡ** 17 • 18 *doubt, indecision*
**ἐπίγειος** 7 • 12 *earthly*
12 **ἀπέχω** 21 • 35 *to keep away, abstain, refrain from*
**διψυχία, ἡ** 17 • 18 *doubt, indecision*
**δουλεύω** 25 • 42 *to (perform the duties of a slave) serve, obey*
**φρονέω** 5 • 17 *to judge, think, form/hold an opinion*

## COMMANDMENT TEN

### Chapter 40 (Hm 10.1)

1 **ἀδελφή, ἡ** 6 • 10 *sister*
**διψυχία, ἡ** 17 • 18 *doubt, indecision*
**λύπη, ἡ** 23 • 24 *grief, sorrow, affliction*
**ὀξυχολία, ἡ** 17 • 17 *irritability, bad temper*
2 **ἀδελφή, ἡ** 6 • 10 *sister*
**ἀσύνετος** 11 • 16 *senseless, foolish*
**δεινός** 2 • 7 *very bad, fearful, terrible*
**διψυχία, ἡ** 17 • 18 *doubt, indecision*
**ἐκτρίβω** 6 • 6 *to drive out*
**καταφθείρω** 8 • 8 *to ruin, corrupt*
**λύπη, ἡ** [2] 23 • 24 *grief, sorrow, affliction*
**νοέω** 30 • 46 *to perceive, apprehend, understand, gain an insight into*
**ὀξυχολία, ἡ** 17 • 17 *irritability, bad temper*
3 **ἀσύνετος** 11 • 16 *senseless, foolish*
**ἐκτρίβω** 6 • 6 *to wear out, drive out*
**νοέω** 30 • 46 *to understand, perceive, apprehend, gain an insight into*
**συνίημι** 13 • 21 *to understand, comprehend*
4 **ἐθνικός** 1 • 1 *unbelieving, worldly, polytheistic;*
subst. *unbeliever*
**ἐμφύρω** 6 • 6 *to mix up, involve*
**ἐπιζητέω** 5 • 9 *to inquire about, want to know*
**ἐπισκοτέω** 2 • 2 *to prevent/block from seeing*
**ἐρευνάω/ἐραυνάω** 2 • 3 *to search, examine, investigate*
**θεότης, ἡ** [2] 8 • 8 *deity;*
**τὰς παραβολὰς τῆς θεότητος** (likely an attributive gen.) *the divine parables*
**καταφθείρω** 8 • 8 *to ruin, corrupt*
**μηδέποτε** 3 • 5 *never*
**νοέω** 30 • 46 *to understand, perceive, apprehend, gain an insight into*
**πλοῦτος, ὁ** 14 • 15 *wealth*
**πραγματεία, ἡ** [2] 11 • 11 *activity, occupation;*
pl. *undertakings, business, affairs*
**πρᾶξις, ἡ** 44 • 50 *undertaking, business*
**πρόσκειμαι** 1 • 1 *to be involved in, be absorbed in, be devoted to*
**φιλία, ἡ** 1 • 1 *friendship, love*
**χερσόω** 3 • 3 *to make dry and barren*
5 **ἄκανθα, ἡ** 6 • 9 *thorn-plant*
**ἀμελεία, ἡ** 2 • 2 *neglect*
**ἀμπελών, ὁ** 20 • 20 *vineyard*
**ἀποπλανάω** 6 • 8 *to mislead, wander away*
**βοτάνη, ἡ** 27 • 30 *weed*
**διάνοια, ἡ** 6 • 22 *understanding, intelligence, mind*
**ἐμπίπτω** 3 • 5 *to get in, fall (into/among)*
**θεότης, ἡ** 8 • 8 *deity, divine character/nature, divinity*
**καταγίνομαι** 1 • 1 *to be taken up with something*
**νοέω** [2] 30 • 46 *to understand, perceive, apprehend, gain an insight into*
**νοῦς, ὁ** 5 • 12 *mind*
**ὅλως** [2] 30 • 31 *completely, wholly, everywhere;*
with a negative *not at all*
**ποικίλος** 20 • 22 *diversified, manifold*
**πρᾶξις, ἡ** [2] 44 • 50 *undertaking, business*
**προλέγω** 5 • 16 *to state beforehand/earlier*
**τυγχάνω** 2 • 15 *to meet, attain, gain, find, experience*
**χερσόω** 3 • 3 *to become barren* or *wild*
6 **ἐρευνάω/ἐραυνάω** 2 • 3 *to search, examine, investigate*
**θεότης, ἡ** 8 • 8 *deity, divine character/nature, divinity*
**κολλάω** 12 • 32 *to join oneself to, join, cling to, associate with*
**νοέω** [2] 30 • 46 *to understand, perceive, apprehend, gain an insight into*
**σύνεσις, ἡ** 13 • 22 *understanding*
**συνίημι** [2] 13 • 21 *to understand, comprehend*

**ταχύς** 11 • 18 *quickly, soon, without delay*

## Chapter 41 (Hm 10.2)

1 **ἀνόητος** 1 • 4 *unintelligent, foolish, dull-witted*
**ἐκτρίβω** 6 • 6 *to wear out, drive out*
**λύπη, ἡ** 23 • 24 *grief, sorrow, affliction*
2 **ἀποτυγχάνω** 2 • 3 *to fail*
**διψυχία, ἡ** 17 • 18 *doubt, indecision*
**δίψυχος** 20 • 23 *doubting, hesitating, double-minded*
**εἰσπορεύομαι** 3 • 3 *to come in, enter*
**ἐκτρίβω** 6 • 6 *to wear out, drive out*
**ἐπιβάλλω** 2 • 3 *to take something upon oneself, undertake*
**λυπέω** 13 • 17 *to vex, irritate, offend, insult*
**λύπη, ἡ** 23 • 24 *grief, sorrow, affliction*
**πρᾶξις, ἡ** 44 • 50 *act, action, deed*
3 **εἰσπορεύομαι** 3 • 3 *to come in, enter*
**εἶτα** 30 • 48 *then, next*
**κολλάω** 12 • 32 *to attach to*
**λίαν** 43 • 48 *exceedingly, very (much)*
**λυπέω** 13 • 17 *to grieve, be sad, be depressed*
**λύπη, ἡ** 23 • 24 *grief, sorrow, affliction*
**ὀξυχολέω** 1 • 1 *to be easily moved to anger*
**ὀξυχολία, ἡ** 17 • 17 *irritability, bad temper*
**πικραίνω** 2 • 2 *to embitter, make bitter*
**πρᾶγμα, τό** 19 • 23 *thing, matter, affair*
**πρᾶξις, ἡ** 44 • 50 *act, action, deed*
4 **ἀμφότεροι** [2] 14 • 21 *both*
**διψυχία, ἡ** [2] 17 • 18 *doubt, indecision*
**ἐπιτυγχάνω** 2 • 23 *to obtain, attain to, reach*
**λυπέω** [2] 13 • 17 *to vex, irritate, offend, insult*
**λύπη, ἡ** 23 • 24 *grief, sorrow, affliction*
**λυπηρός** 3 • 3 *painful, distressing*
**ὀξυχολία, ἡ** [2] 17 • 17 *irritability, bad temper*
**πρᾶξις, ἡ** [2] 44 • 50 *act, action, deed*
5 **ἀφίστημι** 19 • 19 *to go away, withdraw*
**ἐντυγχάνω** 4 • 8 *to approach, appeal*
**θλίβω** 19 • 25 *to oppress, afflict*
**λύπη, ἡ** 23 • 24 *grief, sorrow, affliction*
**μήποτε** 13 • 22 *lest*
6 **λύπη, ἡ** 23 • 24 *grief, sorrow, affliction*
**στενοχωρία, ἡ** 2 • 2 *distress, difficulty, anguish, trouble*
**ὑποφέρω** 9 • 12 *to submit to, endure*

## Chapter 42 (Hm 10.3)

1 **ἐνδύω** 29 • 32 *to clothe oneself in, put on, wear;* fig. *take on of characteristics/virtues/intentions of*
**ἐντρυφάω** 1 • 1 *to indulge in, delight in*
**εὐπρόσδεκτος** 2 • 5 *acceptable*
**ἱλαρός** 24 • 34 *cheerful, glad, happy*
**ἱλαρότης, ἡ** 4 • 4 *cheerfulness, gladness, wholeheartedness, graciousness*
**καταφρονέω** 3 • 9 *to look down on, despise, scorn, treat with contempt*
**λύπη, ἡ** 23 • 24 *grief, sorrow, affliction*
**φρονέω** 5 • 17 *to set one's mind on, be intent on*
2 **ἀνομία, ἡ** 9 • 33 *a lawless deed, lawlessness*
**ἔντευξις, ἡ** 15 • 18 *prayer,*
**ἐντυγχάνω** 4 • 8 *to pray, power of intercession*
**ἐξομολογέω** 5 • 15 *to praise*
**θυσιαστήριον, τό** 4 • 15 *incense altar*
**ἱλαρός** 24 • 34 *cheerful, glad, happy*

**λυπέω** [2] 13 • 17 *to vex, irritate, offend, insult*
**λυπηρός** 3 • 3 *sad, mournful, downcast*
**πονηρεύομαι** [2] 13 • 15 *to do wrong, commit sin*
3 **διατί** 27 • 29 *why?*
**ἐγκάθημαι** 1 • 1 *to reside, dwell*
**ἔντευξις, ἡ** [4] 15 • 18 *prayer, power of intercession*
**ἡδονή, ἡ** 5 • 12 *pleasant/agreeable taste*
**θυσιαστήριον, τό** [2] 4 • 15 *incense altar*
**καθαρός** 25 • 45 *pure, free*
**λυπέω** 13 • 17 *to mourn, be sad, be distressed, grieve*
**λύπη, ἡ** [3] 23 • 24 *grief, sorrow, affliction*
**μίγνυμι** [3] 4 • 4 *to mix, mingle*
**ὄξος, τό** 1 • 4 *sour wine, wine vinegar*
4 **ἀποβάλλω** 32 • 36 *to take off, doff*
**ἐνδύω** 29 • 32 *to clothe oneself in, put on, wear;*
fig. *take on characteristics/ virtues, intentions of*
**ἱλαρότης, ἡ** 4 • 4 *cheerfulness, gladness, wholeheartedness, graciousness*
**λύπη, ἡ** [2] 23 • 24 *grief, sorrow, affliction*

## COMMANDMENT ELEVEN

### Chapter 43 (Hm 11)

1 **ἀπολλύω** 5 • 5 *to destroy, ruin*
**διάνοια, ἡ** 6 • 22 *understanding, intelligence, mind*
**δίψυχος** 20 • 23 *doubting, hesitating, double-minded*
**καθέδρα, ἡ** [2] 10 • 11 *chair, seat*
**συμψέλλιον, τό** [2] 2 • 2 *bench*
**ψευδοπροφήτης, ὁ** 5 • 11 *false/ bogus prophet*
2 **δίψυχος** 20 • 23 *doubting, hesitating, double-minded*
**ἐπερώτημα, τό** 1 • 1 *question*
**θεῖος** 10 • 16 *divine*
**μάντις, ὁ** 1 • 1 *soothsayer, diviner, prophet*
**πονηρία, ἡ** 36 • 41 *evil*
**ψευδοπροφήτης, ὁ** 5 • 11 *false/ bogus prophet*
3 **ἀληθής** 6 • 16 *true*
**κενός** [3] 20 • 27 *empty*
**κένωμα, τό** 1 • 1 *empty space, emptiness;*
**πρὸς τὸ κένωμα** *in accordance with the emptiness*
**ῥήγνυμι** 1 • 2 *to break, tear*
4 **ἀπέχω** 21 • 35 *to keep away, abstain, refrain from*
**ἄφρων** 11 • 17 *foolish, ignorant*
**δίψυχος** 20 • 23 *doubting, hesitating, double-minded*
**εἰδωλολατρέω** 2 • 2 *to be/become an image-worshiper/idolater*
**εἰδωλολάτρης, ὁ** 1 • 1 *image-worshiper/idolater*
**ἐνδύω** 29 • 32 *to clothe oneself in, put on, wear;*
fig. *take on characteristics/ virtues, intentions of*
**ἐπιφέρω** 2 • 3 *to bring on/about, inflict*
**ἰσχυρός** 14 • 21 *strong, mighty*
**κενός** 20 • 27 *empty, vain*
**κολλάω** 12 • 32 *to have something to do with, join oneself to, join, cling to, associate with*
**μαντεύομαι** 1 • 1 *to consult an oracle*
**πρᾶξις, ἡ** 44 • 50 *plan of action, undertaking*
**πυκνῶς** 1 • 3 *frequently, often*
**ψευδοπροφήτης, ὁ** 5 • 11 *false/ bogus prophet*
5 **ἄνωθεν** 6 • 8 *from above*
**θεῖος** 10 • 16 *divine*
**θεότης, ἡ** 8• 8 *deity, divine character/nature, divinity*
6 **ἐλαφρός** 3 • 3 *frivolous, fickle, vacillating*
**ἐπίγειος** 7 • 12 *earthly*
**ὅλως** 30 • 31 *completely, wholly, everywhere;*
with a negative *not at all*
7 **ἀμφότεροι** 14 • 21 *both*
**δοκιμάζω** [2] 10 • 19 *to put to the test, examine, evaluate*
**θεῖος** 10 • 16 *divine*
**ψευδοπροφήτης, ὁ** [2] 5 • 11 *false/ bogus prophet*
8 **ἄνωθεν** 6 • 8 *from above*

**ἀπέχω** 21 • 35 *to keep away, abstain, refrain from*
**ἐνδεής** 4 • 4 *needy, poor*
**ἡσύχιος** 4 • 7 *quiet, well-ordered*
**θεῖος** 10 • 16 *divine*
**μάταιος** 6 • 14 *futile, worthless*
**πονηρία, ἡ** 36 • 41 *wickedness, baseness, maliciousness, sinfulness*
**πραΰς** 2 • 8 *gentle, humble, considerate, meek*
**ταπεινόφρων** 1 • 4 *humble*
9 **ἔντευξις, ἡ** 15 • 18 *prayer*
**θεῖος** [2] 10 • 16 *divine*
**κεῖμαι** 22 • 24 *to be very close to someone*
**πίμπλημι** 2 • 3 *to fill, fulfill*
**πλῆθος, τό** 4 • 19 *fellowship, community, congregation, church*
**προφητικός** 1 • 3 *prophetic*
10 **θεότης, ἡ** [2] 8• 8 *deity, divine character/nature, divinity*
**φανερός** 4 • 9 *visible, clear, plainly to be seen, open, plain, evident, known*
11 **ἐπίγειος** 7 • 12 *earthly*
**κενός** 20 • 27 *empty, without content/basis/truth/power*
**μωρός** 11 • 12 *foolish, stupid*
12 **ἀναιδής** 2 • 2 *shameless, bold*
**ἀναστρέφω** 3 • 8 *to act, behave, conduct oneself, live*
**ἀπάτη, ἡ** 13 • 16 *fraud, deceit, treachery*
**ἐνδέχομαι** 2 • 2 *it is possible*
**ἐπίγειος** 7 • 12 *earthly*
**θεῖος** 10 • 16 *divine*
**ἰταμός** 1 • 1 *bold, impetuous*
**μισθός, ὁ** [2] 5 • 22 *payment, wages*
**πολύλαλος** 1 • 1 *talkative, garrulous*
**προφητεία, ἡ** 1 • 4 *prophetic activity*
**προφητεύω** [2] 4 • 9 *to prophesy*
**πρωτοκαθεδρία, ἡ** 1 • 1 *seat of honor, best seat*
**τρυφή, ἡ** 19 • 22 *indulgence, reveling*
**ὑψόω** 2 • 4 *to exalt, consider better (than others)*
13 **ἀπατάω** 8 • 9 *to deceive, mislead*
**ἀποφεύγω** 1 • 1 *to avoid, shun*
**γωνία, ἡ** 4 • 5 *corner*
**δίψυχος** 20 • 23 *doubting, hesitating, double-minded*
**εἶτα** 30 • 48 *furthermore, then, next*
**θραύω** 2 • 4 *to break*
**κενός** [4] 20 • 27 *empty, vain, senseless*
**κενῶς** 1 • 1 *in an empty manner, idly, in vain*
**κολλάω** 12 • 32 *to join oneself to, join, cling to, associate with*
**ὅλως** 30 • 31 *completely, wholly, everywhere;* with a negative *not at all*
**προφητεύω** 4 • 9 *to foretell, prophesy*
**σκεῦος, τό** 2 • 9 *vessel, jar, dish*
**συμφωνέω** 7 • 7 *to harmonize, match in sound*
**συντίθημι** 1 • 2 *to place beside, put/place with*
14 **ἔντευξις, ἡ** 15 • 18 *prayer, intercession*
**ἐπίγειος** 7 • 12 *earthly*
**θεότης, ἡ** 8• 8 *deity, divine character/nature, divinity*
**κενόω** 2 • 2 *to empty*
**κωφόω** 1 • 2 *to be rendered speechless*
**ὅλως** 30 • 31 *completely, wholly, everywhere;* with a negative *not at all*
**πλήρης** 13 • 20 *filled, full*
**συνθραύω** 1 • 1 *to be broken, be shattered*
**φεύγω** 4 • 20 *to flee*
15 **ἀποθήκη, ἡ** [2] 2 • 2 *cellar, storehouse, barn*
**ἀποστιβάζω** 1 • 1 *to make empty*
**ἔλαιον, τό** 1 • 4 *olive oil*
**κενός** [4] 20 • 27 *empty*
**κεράμιον, τό** [2] 7 • 8 *jar, earthen vessel*
**ὁποῖος** 1 • 2 *of what sort, as*
**στιβάζω** 1 • 1 *to store (up)*
16 **ἀμφότεροι** 14 • 21 *both*
**δοκιμάζω** 10 • 19 *to put to the test, examine, evaluate*
**πνευματοφόρος** 1 • 2 *bearing the divine Spirit*
17 **ἐπίγειος** 7 • 12 *earthly*
**κενός** 20 • 27 *empty, without content/basis/truth/power*

18 **ἅπτω** 4 • 10 *to touch, take hold of, hold*
**σίφων, ὁ** 1 • 1 *(water) pump*
**σιφωνίζω** 1 • 1 *to squirt*
**τρυπάω** 2 • 2 *to make a hole in, bore through*
19 **ἀδρανής** 1 • 1 *powerless*
**ἀδύνατος** [3] 4 • 11 first and second instance: *impossible*; third instance: *powerless, impotent*
**ἀμφότεροι** 14 • 21 *both*
**ἐπίγειος** 7 • 12 *earthly*
20 **ἄνωθεν** 6 • 8 *from above*
**ἐλάχιστος** 13 • 16 *very small/short*
**ἐπιπίπτω** 1 • 2 *to fall on*
**κέραμος, ὁ** 2 • 2 *roof tile, roof*
**κοκκάριον, τό** 1 • 1 *little grain*
**παρέχω** 3 • 18 *to cause, make happen*
**πόνος, ὁ** 1 • 6 *pain, hurt, distress, affliction*
**σταγών, ἡ** 1 • 1 *drop*
**τρυπάω** 2 • 2 to *make a hole in, bore through*
**χάλαζα, ἡ** 1 • 1 *hailstone*
**χαμαί** 6 • 6 *to the ground*
21 **ἄνωθεν** [2] 6 • 8 *from above*
**ἀπέχω** 21 • 35 *to keep away, abstain, refrain from*
**ἐλάχιστος** 13 • 16 *very small, short*
**θεῖος** 10 • 16 *divine*

## COMMANDMENT TWELVE

### Chapter 44 (Hm 12.1)

1 **ἐνδύω** [2] 29 • 32 *to clothe oneself in, put on, wear;*
fig. *take on the characteristics/virtues/intentions of*
**σεμνός** 7 • 13 *honorable, worthy, venerable, holy, above reproach*
**χαλιναγωγέω** 1 • 2 *to bridle, hold in check*
2 **ἄγριος** 5 • 8 *uncontrolled, savage, fierce*
**ἀγριότης, ἡ** 1 • 1 *wildness, savagery*
**δαπανάω** [3] 4 • 7 *to wear out, destroy*
**δεινῶς** 2 • 2 *dreadfully, terribly*
**δυσκόλως** 7 • 7 *hardly, with difficulty*
**ἐμπίπτω** 3 • 5 *to get into, fall (into/among)*
**ἐμφύρω** 6 • 6 *to mix up, involve*
**ἔνδυμα, τό** 5 • 5 *covering, garment*
**ἡμερόω** 1 • 1 *to tame*
**λίαν** 43 • 48 *exceedingly, (very) much*
**μάλιστα** 5 • 14 *most of all, above all, especially, particularly*
**συνετός** 4 • 7 *intelligent, sagacious, wise, with good sense*
**φοβερός** 1 • 2 *causing fear, fearful, terrible, frightful*
3 **ἀπέχω** 21 • 35 *to keep away, abstain, refrain from*
**γνωρίζω** 10 • 18 *to make known, reveal*
**θανατόω** 3 • 7 *to bring death*

### Chapter 45 (Hm 12.2)

1 **ἀλλότριος** 5 • 14 *another's, not one's own, strange*
**ἔδεσμα, τό** 12 • 12 *food*
**κενός** [2] 20 • 27 *vain, empty*
**μάταιος** 6 • 14 *needless*
**μεθύσμα, τό** 3 • 3 *intoxicating drink*
**μωρός** [2] 11 • 12 *foolish, stupid*
**πλοῦτος, ὁ** 14 • 15 *wealth*
**πολυτέλεια, ἡ** 6 • 6 *extravagance, luxury, richness*
**προέχω** 1 • 1 *to be above all, be first*
**τρυφή, ἡ** [2] 19 • 22 *indulgence, reveling*
2 **ἀπέχω** [2] 21 • 35 *to keep away, abstain, refrain from*
**θανατόω** 3 • 7 *to bring death*
**θυγάτηρ, ἡ** 4 • 10 *daughter*
3 **ἀνθίστημι** 6 • 8 *to set oneself against, oppose*
**θανατώδης** 1 • 1 *deadly, fatal*
**κατακυριεύω** 13 • 15 *to master, gain dominion over;*
pass. *let oneself be overcome by something*
4 **ἀνθίστημι** [2] 6 • 8 *to set oneself against, oppose*

**ἐνδύω** 29 • 32 *to clothe oneself in, put on, wear;* fig. *take on characteristics/ virtues, intentions of*
**καθοπλίζω** [2] 2 • 2 *to arm, equip oneself*
**μακράν** 9 • 15 *far (away)*
**ὅπλον, τό** 1 • 5 *weapon*
**φεύγω** 4 • 20 *to flee*
5 **δουλεύω** [2] 25 • 42 *to (perform the duties of a slave) serve, obey*
**κατακυριεύω** 13 • 15 *to master, become master, gain dominion over, subdue, gain power over*
**νῖκος, τό** [2] 2 • 2 *prize of victory*
**στεφανόω** 5 • 12 *to crown, honor, reward*

## Chapter 46 (Hm 12.3)

1 **ἀρετή, ἡ** 5 • 6 *excellence of character, exceptional civic virtue*
**δουλεύω** [2] 25 • 42 *to (perform the duties of a slave) serve, obey*
**εὐάρεστος** 3 • 9 *pleasing, acceptable*
**πραότης, ἡ** 2 • 4 *gentleness, humility, courtesy, considerateness, meekness*
**τρόπος, ὁ** 5 • 17 *manner, way, kind, guise*
2 **καθαρός** 25 • 45 *pure, free*
**μετάνοια, ἡ** 58 • 72 *repentance, turning about, conversion*
**συντελέω** 9 • 15 *to bring to an end, complete, finish, close*
3 **ἀναγκάζω** 1 • 3 *to compel, force*
**ἐκτελέω** 1 • 1 *to finish*
**ἐπιμελῶς** 5 • 9 *carefully, diligently*
4 **διότι** 2 • 3 *because*
**ἔνδοξος** 43 • 54 *glorious, splendid*
**εὐφραίνω** 6 • 15 *to gladden, cheer (up)*
**λίαν** 43 • 48 *exceedingly, very (much)*
**σκληρός** 9 • 9 *hard, difficult*
5 **εὐκόπως** 1 • 1 *easily*
**προτίθημι** 1 • 1 *to set before someone as a task/duty*
**σκληρός** 9 • 9 *hard, difficult*
6 **ἐπεί** 10 • 35 *since, because, for*
**παρενθυμέω** 4 • 4 *to disregard, neglect, forget*

## Chapter 47 (Hm 12.4)

1 **ἀλλοιόω** 3 • 5 *to change*
**λίαν** [2] 43 • 48 *exceedingly, very (much), vehemently*
**μορφή, ἡ** 6 • 8 *appearance, form, outward appearance, shape*
**ὀργίλως** 1 • 1 *angrily*
**συγχέω** 4 • 4 *to confuse, confound, trouble, stir up*
**ὑποφέρω** 9 • 12 *to submit to, endure*
2 **ἀσύνετος** 11 • 16 *senseless, foolish*
**ἄφρων** 11 • 17 *foolish, ignorant*
**δίψυχος** 20 • 23 *doubting, hesitating, double-minded*
**ἕνεκα** 8 • 15 *because of, on account of, for the sake of*
**ἐπιεικής** 1 • 4 *yielding, gentle, kind, courteous, tolerant*
**θαυμαστός** 2 • 13 *wonderful, marvelous, remarkable*
**ἱλαρός** 24 • 34 *cheerful, glad, happy*
**ἰσχυρός** 14 • 21 *strong, mighty*
**κατακυριεύω** 13 • 15 *to be master, lord it (over), rule*
**κτίζω** 14 • 25 *to create*
**κτίσις, ἡ** 13 • 19 *creation, world*
**νοέω** 30 • 46 *to understand, perceive, apprehend, gain an insight into*
**συγχέω** 4 • 4 *to confuse, confound, trouble, stir up*
**ταράσσω** 1 • 4 *to trouble, frighten, terrify*
3 **κατακυριεύω** [3] 13 • 15 *to be master, lord it (over), rule*
**κτίσμα, τό** 3 • 4 *that which is created, creature*
4 **δύσβατος** 1 • 1 *impassible, hard to walk in*
**μακράν** 9 • 15 *far (away)*
**πωρόω** 2 • 2 *to make dull/obtuse/ blind, close the mind*
**σκληρός** 9 • 9 *hard, difficult*
**χεῖλος, τό** 2 • 11 *the lips*
5 **γλυκύς** 3 • 6 *sweet*
**ἐλαφρός** 3 • 3 *frivolous, fickle, vacillating*

**εὔκολος** 1 • 1 *easy*
**ἥμερος** 2 • 3 *kind*
**κενός** 20 • 27 *foolish, senseless, empty*
6 **ἄγριος** 5 • 8 *uncontrolled, savage, fierce*
**ἀσελγής** 1 • 1 *lewd, licentious*
**δύσκολος** 3 • 5 *hard, difficult*
**πικρός** 5 • 5 *bitter, embittered, harsh*
7 **κατακυριεύω** 13 • 15 *to become master, gain dominion over, subdue, gain power over*
**μετάνοια, ἡ** 58 • 72 *repentance, turning about, conversion*
**τόνος, ὁ** 1 • 1 *force, lasting quality*
**φεύγω** 4 • 20 *to flee*

## Chapter 48 (Hm 12.5)

1 **ἐνδυναμόω** 12 • 14 *to become strong*
**καταδυναστεύω** 2 • 3 *to oppress, exploit, dominate*
**πρόθυμος** 2 • 4 *ready, willing, eager*
**σκληρός** 9 • 9 *hard, strict, harsh, cruel, merciless*
**ὑποταγή, ἡ** 1 • 4 *submissiveness, subjection, subordination*
2 **ἀνθίστημι** 6 • 8 *to set oneself against, oppose*
**ἀντιπαλαίω** 1 • 1 *to wrestle*
**ἀπόκενος** 6 • 6 *quite empty*
**καταδυναστεύω** 2 • 3 *to oppress, exploit, dominate*
**καταισχύνω** 1 • 1 *to put to shame*
**καταπαλαίω** 1 • 1 *to win a victory over, defeat (in wrestling)*
**νικάω** 2 • 8 *to conquer, beat*
**φεύγω** 4 • 20 *to flee*
3 **ἀπόκενος** [3] 6 • 6 *quite empty*
**γεμίζω** 1 • 1 *to fill*
**ἡδονή, ἡ** 5 • 12 *pleasant taste, agreeable taste*
**κατανοέω** [2] 21 • 26 *to pay attention to, consider, contemplate*
**κεράμιον, τό** [4] 7 • 8 *jar, earthen vessel*
**μήποτε** 13 • 22 *lest*
**ὀξίζω** [2] 2 • 2 *to become sour, turn sour, taste of vinegar*
**πλήρης** [2] 13 • 20 *filled, full*
**ταχύς** 11 • 18 *in a short time, soon*
4 **ἀνθίστημι** 6 • 8 *to set oneself against, oppose*
**ἀπόκενος** 6 • 6 *quite empty*
**ἀποχωρέω** 3 • 3 *to withdraw, go away, leave*
**εἰσπορεύομαι** 3 • 3 *to go into, enter*
**ἐκπειράζω** 3 • 4 *to tempt*
**ἰσχυρῶς** 5 • 5 *strongly, dependably*
**πλήρης** 13 • 20 *filled, full*
**ὑπόδουλος** 1 • 1 *enslaved, subject as a slave*

## Chapter 49 (Hm 12.6)

1 **ἰσχυροποιέω** 7 • 7 *to strengthen*
**μετάνοια, ἡ** 58 • 72 *repentance, turning about, conversion*
2 **ἁμάρτημα, τό** 4 • 8 *sin, transgression*
**ἀπειλή, ἡ** 1 • 2 *threat*
**ἀπογινώσκω** 3 • 3 *to despair*
**ἄτονος** 1 • 1 *powerless, slack*
**δουλεύω** 25 • 42 *to (perform the duties of a slave) serve, obey*
**ἴασις, ἡ** 6 • 7 *forgiveness, cure, deliverance, cure*
**καταβαρύνω** 1 • 1 *to make someone's life hard, weigh down, burden, oppress*
**κατακυριεύω** 13 • 15 *to become master, gain dominion over, subdue, gain power over*
**νεῦρον, τό** 1 • 1 *sinew*
**ὅλως** 30 • 31 *completely, wholly, everywhere;* with a negative *not at all*
**ὀρθῶς** 3 • 8 *rightly, correctly*
**προστίθημι** 13 • 22 *to add to, increase*
**πρότερος** 40 • 47 *former, earlier*
4 **δικαίωμα, τό** 1 • 12 *regulation, requirement, commandment*
**ἐνδυναμόω** [2] 12 • 14 *to become strong*
**ἐντέλλω** 17 • 29 *to command, order, give orders*
**κατακυριεύω** 13 • 15 *to become master, gain dominion over, subdue, gain power over*

**κατισχύω** 2 • 2 *to win a victory over*
**συγκόπτω** 3 • 3 *to break, destroy*
5 **καθαρός** 25 • 45 *pure*
**μάταιος** 6 • 14 *futile, worthless*

## PARABLE ONE

### Chapter 50 (Hs 1)

1 **μακράν** 9 • 15 *far (away)*
**μάταιος** 6 • 14 *futile, worthless, empty, fruitless, useless;* here of things that will pass away
**ξένος** 2 • 8 *strange, foreign;* subst. *a foreign country*
**οἴκημα, τό** 1 • 1 *room, apartment*
**οἰκοδομή, ἡ** 100 • 103 *building, edifice*
**παράταξις, ἡ** 3 • 3 *furnishings, establishments*
**πολυτελής** 1 • 3 *costly, (very) expensive*
2 **διανοέομαι** 1 • 1 *to consider*
**ἐπανακάμπτω** 3 • 3 *to return*
3 **ἀλλότριος** 5 • 14 *another's, not one's own, strange*
**ἄφρων** 11 • 17 *foolish, ignorant*
**δίψυχος** 20 • 23 *doubting, hesitating, double-minded*
**νοέω** 30 • 46 *to perceive, apprehend, understand, gain an insight into*
**ταλαίπωρος** 1 • 5 *miserable, wretched, distressed*
**χράομαι** 7 • 18 *to make use of, employ, live in accordance with*
4 **δικαίως** 2 • 12 *uprightly, justly, in (all) justice*
**ἐκχωρέω** 1 • 4 *to go out, go away, depart*
**οἴκησις, ἡ** 1 • 3 *house, dwelling*
**ὕπαρξις, ἡ** 2 • 2 *possessions, belongings, property*
**χράομαι** 7 • 18 *to make use of, employ, live in accordance with*
**χώρα, ἡ** [2] 2 • 6 *country, district, region, place*
5 **ἀπαρνέομαι** [3] 5 • 6 *to deny*
**ἀσύμφορος** 6 • 7 *harmful, disadvantageous*
**ἐκκλείω** 2 • 2 *to shut out, exclude*
**ἕνεκα** 8 • 15 *because of, on account of, for the sake of*
**ἐπανακάμπτω** 3 • 3 *to return*
**πάντως** 7 • 9 *totally, altogether*
**παραδέχομαι** 4 • 9 *to receive, accept*
**σός** 4 • 9 *your, yours*
**ὕπαρξις, ἡ** 2 • 2 *property, possession*
6 **ἀγαλλιάω** 6 • 11 *to exult, be glad, be overjoyed*
**ἀντιτάσσω** 2 • 7 *to oppose, resist*
**ἀνυβρίστως** 1 • 1 *without insolence, decorously*
**ἀρκετός** 3 • 4 *adequate, sufficient, enough;*
**τὴν αὐτάρκειαν τὴν ἀρκετήν σοι** *self-sufficient, what is sufficient for you*
**αὐτάρκεια, ἡ** 2 • 2 *sufficiency, a competence*
**δεσπότης, ὁ** 24 • 54 *lord, master*
**ἕτοιμος** 3 • 9 *ready, prepared*
**ξένος** 2 • 8 *strange, foreign;* subst. *a foreign country*
**σός** 4 • 9 *your, yours*
**χράομαι** 7 • 18 *to make use of, employ, live in accordance with*
7 **δουλεύω** 25 • 42 *to (perform the duties of a slave) serve, obey*
**ἐπαγγέλλω** 6 • 7 *to promise*
**μνημονεύω** 7 • 25 *to remember, keep in mind, think of*
8 **ἀντί** 4 • 15 *instead of, in place of*
**δαπανάω** 4 • 7 *to spend something for/on something*
**ἐπισκέπτομαι** 6 • 8 *to visit*
**θλίβω** 19 • 25 *to distress, oppress, afflict*
**καθά** 1 • 2 *just as*
**ὀρφανός** 5 • 9 *without parents, orphan*
**παραβλέπω** 1 • 1 *to overlook, neglect, despise*
**παράταξις, ἡ** 3 • 3 *possessions*
**πλοῦτος, ὁ** 14 • 15 *wealth*
**χήρα, ἡ** 6 • 13 *widow*
9 **βελτίων** 3 • 6 *better*
**δεσπότης, ὁ** 24 • 54 *lord, master*
**ἐπιδημέω** 1 • 1 *to return/go home*
**κτῆμα, τό** 1 • 2 *possessions*
**πλουτίζω** 2 • 5 *to make wealthy*
**τελέω** 22 • 23 *to carry out, accomplish, perform, fulfill, keep*

10 **ἀσύμφορος** 6 • 7 *harmful, disadvantageous*
**ἱλαρός** 24 • 34 *joyful, cheerful, glad, happy*
**λύπη, ἡ** 23 • 24 *pain, grief, sorrow, affliction*
**πολυτέλεια, ἡ** [2] 6 • 6 *extravagance, luxury, richness*
11 **ἀλλότριος** [2] 5 • 14 *not one's own;* subst. *other people's property, what belongs to another*
**ἅπτω** 4 • 10 *to touch, take hold of, hold*
**ἐπιθυμέω** [2] 7 • 17 *to desire, long for*
**παραχαράσσω** 1 • 1 *to debase/ counterfeit*
**πολυτέλεια, ἡ** 6 • 6 *extravagance, luxury, richness*
**σός** 4 • 9 *your, yours*

## PARABLE TWO

### Chapter 51 (Hs 2)

1 **ἄμπελος, ἡ** 13 • 16 *vine, grapevine*
**διακρίνω** 3 • 7 *to make a distinction, differentiate*
**εὐπρεπής** 6 • 7 *suited, well suited*
**κατανοέω** 21 • 26 *to notice, observe*
**ποιμήν, ὁ** 51 • 55 *shepherd*
**πτελέα, ἡ** [2] 13 • 13 *elm tree*
**συζητέω** 1 • 2 *to reflect, meditate*
2 **ἄμπελος, ἡ** 13 • 16 *vine, grapevine*
**δένδρον, τό** [2] 26 • 28 *tree*
**κεῖμαι** 22 • 24 *to be appointed, be set, be destined*
**πτελέα, ἡ** 13 • 13 *elm tree*
**τύπος, ὁ** [2] 10 • 26 *type*
3 **ἄκαρπος** 3 • 3 *unfruitful, fruitless*
**ἄμπελος, ἡ** [3] 13 • 16 *vine, grapevine*
**ἐπιρίπτω** 3 • 3 *to throw;* pass. *be attached to*
**καρποφορέω** 4 • 7 *to bear fruit/ crops*
**κρεμάννυμι** 2 • 2 *to hang, hang on*
**ξύλον, τό** 2 • 23 *tree*
**πτελέα, ἡ** [5] 13 • 13 *elm tree*
**ῥίπτω** 8 • 11 *to put/lay something down*
**σήπω** 1 • 4 *to rot, decay*
**χαμαί** 6 • 6 *on the ground*
4 **ἄμπελος, ἡ** [2] 13 • 16 *vine, grapevine*
**ἐλάσσων** 4 • 6 *less*
**κεῖμαι** 22 • 24 *to be given, exist*
**κρεμάννυμι** 2 • 2 *to hang, hang on*
**πλούσιος** 13 • 22 *rich, wealthy*
**πτελέα, ἡ** [2] 13 • 13 *elm tree*
**ῥίπτω** 8 • 11 *to put/lay something down*
**σαπρός** 3 • 3 *spoiled, rotten*
**χαμαί** 6 • 6 *on the ground*
5 **ἀδιστάκτως** 8 • 8 *without hesitating, without doubting*
**ἄνω** 1 • 3 *above*
**βληχρός** 2 • 2 *feeble*
**γνωρίζω** 10 • 18 *to make known, reveal*
**ἔντευξις, ἡ** [3] 15 • 18 *intercessory prayer*
**ἐξομολόγησις, ἡ** [2] 2 • 2 *praise*
**ἐπαναπαύομαι** 1 • 3 *to find rest, comfort, support*
**ἐπιχορηγέω** 3 • 5 *to support, give, grant; help afterwards*
**λίαν** 43 • 48 *exceedingly, very (much)*
**μισθός, ὁ** 5 • 22 *reward*
**πένης** [4] 12 • 16 *poor, needy*
**περισπάω** 3 • 3 *to become/be distracted, be quite busy, be overburdened*
**πλούσιος** [4] 13 • 22 *rich, wealthy*
**πλοῦτος, ὁ** 14 • 15 *wealth*
**πτωχεύω** 1 • 2 *to be (extremely) poor*
**χορηγέω** 3 • 6 *to provide, supply (in abundance)*
**χρῆμα, τό** 1 • 1 *property, wealth, means*
6 **ἀδιάλειπτος** 2 • 3 *lacking nothing*
**ἔντευξις, ἡ** 15 • 18 *prayer, intercession*
**ἐντυγχάνω** 4 • 8 *to pray*
**ἐπισπουδάζω** 1 • 1 *to be more zealous*
**ἐπιχορηγέω** 3 • 5 *to support*
**πένης** [3] 12 • 16 *poor, needy*
**πλούσιος** [2] 13 • 22 *rich, wealthy*
**προσδεκτός** 1 • 3 *acceptable*

7 **ἀδιστάκτως** 8 • 8 *without hesitating, without doubting*
**ἀμφότεροι** 14 • 21 *both*
**δεκτός** 5 • 9 *pleasing, acceptable*
**δώρημα, τό** 2 • 2 *gift, present*
**ἔντευξις, ἡ** 15 • 18 *prayer*
**ἐπιχορηγέω** 3 • 5 *to give, grant*
**ὀρθῶς** 3 • 8 *properly, rightly, correctly*
**παρέχω** 3 • 18 *to give up, offer, present*
**πένης** [3] 12 • 16 *poor, needy*
**πλούσιος** 13 • 22 *rich, wealthy*
**πλουτέω** 4 • 6 *to be rich*
**πλοῦτος, ὁ** [2] 14 • 15 *wealth*
**συνίημι** 13 • 21 *to show understanding, understand, comprehend*
**τελέω** [2] 22 • 23 *to carry out, accomplish, perform, fulfill, keep*
**ὡσαύτως** 3 • 7 *(in) the same (way), similarly, likewise*
8 **ἀβροχία, ἡ** 1 • 1 *drought*
**ἀδιάλειπτος** 2 • 3 *without failing, unceasing, constant*
**ἄμπελος, ἡ** [2] 13 • 16 *vine, grapevine*
**διπλοῦς** 4 • 4 *double, two-fold*
**ἐντυγχάνω** 4 • 8 *to pray*
**νοέω** 30 • 46 *to perceive, apprehend, understand, gain an insight into*
**πένης** [2] 12 • 16 *poor, needy*
**πληροφορέω** [2] 3 • 9 *to fill out, complement, aid*
**πλούσιος** [2] 13 • 22 *rich, wealthy*
**πλοῦτος, ὁ** 14 • 15 *wealth*
**πτελέα, ἡ** [3] 13 • 13 *elm tree*
**τρέφω** 2 • 3 *to feed, nourish, support*
**χορηγέω** 3 • 6 *to provide, supply (in abundance)*
9 **ἀμφότεροι** 14 • 21 *both*
**βίβλος, ἡ** 2 • 5 *record-book*
**ἐγκαταλείπω** 2 • 8 *to forsake, abandon, desert*
**ἐπιγράφω** 1 • 4 *to enroll, record*
**κοινωνός, ὁ** 3 • 7 *companion, partner, sharer*
10 **πλουτίζω** 2 • 5 *to make wealthy;* pass. *receive riches*
**συνίημι** [2] 13 • 21 *to understand, comprehend*

## PARABLE THREE

### Chapter 52 (Hs 3)

1 **δένδρον, τό** [3] 26 • 28 *tree*
**ξηρός** [2] 46 • 47 *dry, dried up*
**φύλλον, τό** 2 • 5 *leaf, foliage*
**ὡσεί** 16 • 17 *as, like*
2 **διατί** 27 • 29 *why?*
**ξηρός** 46 • 47 *dry, dried up*
**φαίνω** [2] 12 • 37 *to be apparent, be recognized, be revealed*
**χειμών, ὁ** 3 • 3 *winter*
**ὡσεί** 16 • 17 *as, like*
3 **ἀποβάλλω** 32 • 36 *to shed*
**δένδρον, τό** 26 • 28 *tree*
**ξηρός** 46 • 47 *dry, dried up*
**φαίνω** [2] 12 • 37 *to be apparent, be recognized, be revealed*
**φύλλον, τό** 2 • 5 *leaf, foliage*
**χειμών, ὁ** 3 • 3 *winter*

## PARABLE FOUR

### Chapter 53 (Hs 4)

1 **βλαστάνω** [2] 3 • 5 *to bud, sprout*
**δένδρον, τό** [2] 26 • 28 *tree*
**ξηρός** [2] 46 • 47 *dry, dried up*
2 **βλαστάνω** 3 • 5 *to bud, sprout*
**δένδρον, τό** 26 • 28 *tree*
**δουλεύω** 25 • 42 *to (perform the duties of a slave) serve, obey*
**ἔλεος, τό** 4 • 19 *mercy, compassion, pity, clemency*
**ἐπιλάμπω** 1 • 2 *to shine forth, shine out*
**θερεία, ἡ** 3 • 3 *summertime*
**χειμών, ὁ** 3 • 3 *winter*
3 **δένδρον, τό** 26 • 28 *tree*
**εὐθαλής** 5 • 5 *flourishing, thriving*
**θερεία, ἡ** 3 • 3 *summertime*
**ποταπός** 5 • 5 *of what sort? of what kind?*
**φανερός** 4 • 9 *visible, clear, plainly to be seen, open, plain, evident, known*
4 **ἄκαρπος** 3 • 3 *unfruitful, fruitless*
**δένδρον, τό** 26 • 28 *tree*
**καίω** [2] 4 • 11 *to burn (up)*

**κατακαίω** 1 • 4 *to burn down, burn up, consume*
**κτίζω** 14 • 25 *to create*
**ξηρός** [2] 46 • 47 *dry, dried up*
**ξύλον, τό** 2 • 23 *wood*
**πρᾶξις, ἡ** 44 • 50 *acting, activity, function*
**φανερός** 4 • 9 *visible, clear, plainly to be seen, open, plain, evident, known*
5 **ἀπέχω** 21 • 35 *to keep away, abstain, refrain from*
**διαμαρτάνω** 3 • 5 *to sin, miss the mark badly, be quite wrong*
**δουλεύω** 25 • 42 *to (perform the duties of a slave) serve, obey*
**θερεία, ἡ** 3 • 3 *summertime*
**καρποφορέω** 4 • 7 *to bear fruit*
**περισπάω** 3 • 3 *to become/be distracted, be quite busy, be overburdened*
**πραγματεία, ἡ** 11 • 11 *activity, occupation;* pl. *undertakings, business, affairs*
**πρᾶξις, ἡ** 44 • 50 *undertaking, business*
6 **αἴτημα, τό** 10 • 10 *request*
**δουλεύω** [3] 25 • 42 *to (perform the duties of a slave) serve, obey*
7 **διάνοια, ἡ** [2] 6 • 22 *disposition, thought, mind*
**διαφθείρω** 8 • 12 *to corrupt*
**δουλεύω** [2] 25 • 42 *to (perform the duties of a slave) serve, obey*
**καθαρός** 25 • 45 *pure, free*
**πρᾶξις, ἡ** 44 • 50 *undertaking, business*
8 **καρποφορέω** [2] 4 • 7 *to bear fruit*

## PARABLE FIVE

### Chapter 54 (Hs 5.1)

1 **νηστεύω** 14 • 23 *to fast*
**ὀρθρινός** 1 • 1 *early in the morning*
**παρακάθημαι** 2 • 2 *to sit beside*
**ποιμήν, ὁ** 51 • 55 *shepherd*
**στατίων, ἡ** 2 • 2 *post, station, keep a fast*
2 **εἴωθα** 1 • 1 *to be accustomed*
**νηστεία, ἡ** 14 • 25 *fast*
**νηστεύω** [3] 14 • 23 *to fast, observe a fast*
**στατίων, ἡ** 2 • 2 *post, station, keep a fast*
3 **ἀνωφελής** 1 • 2 *useless*
**δεκτός** [2] 5 • 9 *pleasing, acceptable*
**διατί** 27 • 29 *why?*
**ναί** 6 • 8 *yes, certainly, indeed, quite so*
**νηστεία, ἡ** [4] 14 • 25 *fast*
**νηστεύω** [3] 14 • 23 *to fast, observe a fast*
**πλήρης** 13 • 20 *complete*
4 **μάταιος** 6 • 14 *useless, futile, worthless, empty, fruitless*
**νηστεία, ἡ** [2] 14 • 25 *fast*
**νηστεύω** [2] 14 • 23 *to fast*
5 **δεκτός** 5 • 9 *pleasing, acceptable*
**δουλεύω** 25 • 42 *to (perform the duties of a slave) serve, obey*
**ἐγκρατεύομαι** 24 • 25 *to control oneself, abstain*
**καθαρός** 25 • 45 *pure, free*
**νηστεία, ἡ** 14 • 25 *fast*
**πονηρεύομαι** 13 • 15 *to do evil, do wrong, commit sin*
**πρᾶγμα, τό** 19 • 23 *thing, matter, affair*
**πρόσταγμα, τό** 1 • 10 *order, commandment, injunction*
**τελέω** 22 • 23 *to carry out, accomplish, perform, fulfill, keep*

### Chapter 55 (Hs 5.2)

1 **ἀνήκω** 1 • 10 *to have to do with, refer, relate, belong*
**νηστεία, ἡ** 14 • 25 *fast, fasting*
2 **ἀμπελών, ὁ** [3] 20 • 20 *vineyard*
**ἀποδημέω** 1 • 2 *to go on a journey*
**ἀποδημία, ἡ** 2 • 2 *journey*
**δεσπότης, ὁ** 24 • 54 *lord, master*
**ἐκλέγομαι** 5 • 15 *to select someone/something for oneself*
**ἐλεύθερος** 1 • 3 *free*
**εὐάρεστος** 3 • 9 *pleasing, acceptable, well thought of*
**προσκαλέω** 2 • 2 *to summon, call on, call to oneself, invite*
**φυτεύω** [2] 10 • 16 *to plant*
**χαρακόω** 4 • 4 *to fence in (with stakes)*

3 **ἀμπελών, ὁ** [3] 20 • 20 *vineyard*
**βοτάνη, ἡ** 27 • 30 *weed*
**πλήρης** 13 • 20 *filled, full*
**τελέω** 22 • 23 *to finish, bring to an end, complete*
**χαρακόω** 4 • 4 *to fence in (with stakes)*
**χαράκωσις, ἡ** 1 • 1 *fencing in*
4 **ἀμπελών, ὁ** [4] 20 • 20 *vineyard*
**βοτάνη, ἡ** [4] 27 • 30 *weed*
**ἐκτίλλω** 5 • 5 *to pull out*
**εὐθαλής** 5 • 5 *flourishing, thriving*
**εὐπρεπής** [2] 6 • 7 *looking well/ better*
**πνίγω** [2] 4 • 4 *to choke*
**σκάπτω** [3] 5 • 5 *to dig (up), spade (up)*
**τελέω** 22 • 23 *to carry out, accomplish, perform, fulfill, keep*
5 **ἄμπελος, ἡ** 13 • 16 *vine, grapevine*
**ἀμπελών, ὁ** [2] 20 • 20 *vineyard*
**βοτάνη, ἡ** 27 • 30 *weed*
**δεσπότης, ὁ** 24 • 54 *lord, master*
**ἐκτίλλω** 5 • 5 *to pull out*
**εὐθαλής** 5 • 5 *flourishing, thriving*
**εὐπρεπῶς** 2 • 2 *attractively*
**λίαν** 43 • 48 *exceedingly, very (much)*
**σκάπτω** 5 • 5 *to dig (up), spade (up)*
**χαρακόω** 4 • 4 *to fence in (with stakes)*
6 **δεσπότης, ὁ** 24 • 54 *lord, master*
**ἐντέλλω** 17 • 29 *to command, order, give orders*
**κληρονόμος, ὁ** 1 • 3 *heir*
**προσκαλέω** 3 • 5 *to summon, call on, call to oneself, invite*
**συγχαίρω** 1 • 7 *to congratulate*
**σύμβουλος, ὁ** 6 • 8 *adviser, counselor*
**φίλος** 5 • 8 *loving;* subst. *friend*
7 **ἀμπελών, ὁ** 20 • 20 *vineyard*
**ἀντί** 4 • 15 *because of, for the purpose of*
**ἀρέσκω** 6 • 12 *to please, accommodate*
**ἐλευθερία, ἡ** 1 • 2 *freedom, liberty*
**ἐντέλλω** 17 • 29 *to command, order, give orders*
**ἐπαγγέλλω** 6 • 7 *to promise, offer*
**λίαν** 43 • 48 *exceedingly, very (much)*
**παρενθυμέω** 4 • 4 *to disregard, neglect, forget*
**προστίθημι** 13 • 22 *to do, provide, give, grant*
**συγκληρονόμος** 3 • 3 *co-heir*
**τελέω** 22 • 23 *to carry out, accomplish, perform, fulfill, keep*
**φρονέω** 5 • 17 *to set one's mind on, be intent on*
8 **γνώμη, ἡ** 1 • 20 *proposal, declaration, decision, resolution*
**δεσπότης, ὁ** 24 • 54 *lord, master*
**συγκληρονόμος** 3 • 3 *co-heir*
**συνευδοκέω** 2 • 5 *to agree with, approve of, consent to, sympathize with*
9 **ἀρκέω** 2 • 5 *to be enough, be sufficient, be adequate*
**δεῖπνον, τό** 3 • 4 *feast, dinner*
**δεσπότης, ὁ** 24 • 54 *lord, master*
**διαδίδωμι** 1 • 1 *to distribute, give*
**ἔδεσμα, τό** [2] 12 • 12 *food*
**οἰκοδεσπότης, ὁ** 1 • 2 *master of the house, householder*
**σύνδουλος, ὁ** 2 • 6 *fellow-slave*
10 **δεσπότης, ὁ** 24 • 54 *lord, master*
**ἔδεσμα, τό** 12 • 12 *food*
**εὔχομαι** 2 • 16 *to pray*
**σύνδουλος, ὁ** 2 • 6 *fellow-slave*
**χράομαι** 7 • 18 *to treat a person in a certain way*
11 **δεσπότης, ὁ** [2] 24 • 54 *lord, master*
**ἔδεσμα, τό** 12 • 12 *food*
**λίαν** 43 • 48 *exceedingly, very (much)*
**πρᾶξις, ἡ** [2] 44 • 50 *act, action, deed*
**συγκαλέω** 1 • 2 *to summon*
**συγκληρονόμος** 3 • 3 *co-heir*
**συνευδοκέω** 2 • 5 *to agree with, approve of, consent to, sympathize with*
**φίλος** 5 • 8 *loving;* subst. *friend*

## Chapter 56 (Hs 5.3)

1 **ἐπιλύω** 8 • 8 *to explain, interpret*

**νοέω** 30 • 46 *to understand, perceive, apprehend, gain an insight into*
2 **ἀριθμός, ὁ** 2 • 14 *number*
**ἐγγράφω** 4 • 5 *to enroll, write in, record*
**ἐπιλύω** 8 • 8 *to explain, interpret*
**εὐάρεστος** 3 • 9 *pleasing, acceptable*
3 **ἐκτός** 1 • 3 *apart, outside, beyond*
**ἔνδοξος** 43 • 54 *honorable, honored, distinguished, eminent*
**λειτουργία, ἡ** 2 • 11 *service*
**περιποιέω** 8 • 9 *to acquire, obtain, gain for oneself*
**περισσός** 2 • 5 *greater, more, even more*
**προστίθημι** 13 • 22 *to add, put to*
4 **ἀγαθοποίησις, ἡ** 2 • 2 *doing good*
**ἐντέλλω** 17 • 29 *to command, order, give orders*
**προθυμία, ἡ** [2] 2 • 6 *zeal, willingness, readiness, goodwill*
5 **λίαν** 43 • 48 *exceedingly, very (much)*
**νηστεία, ἡ** [2] 14 • 25 *fast, fasting*
6 **ματαίωμα, τό** 2 • 2 *emptiness, worthlessness*
**νηστεία, ἡ** 14 • 25 *fast*
**τέλειος** 2 • 25 *perfect*
7 **γεύομαι** 1 • 3 *to taste, partake of*
**δαπάνη, ἡ** 1 • 1 *expense, cost*
**ἔδεσμα, τό** 12 • 12 *food*
**ἐμπίμπλημι** 1 • 3 *to satisfy*
**εὔχομαι** 2 • 16 *to pray*
**νηστεύω** 14 • 23 *to fast*
**ὀρφανός** 5 • 9 *without parents, orphan*
**ποσότης, ἡ** 1 • 2 *quantity, amount*
**συνοψίζω** 1 • 1 *to calculate, estimate, count*
**συντελέω** 9 • 15 *to carry out, fulfill, accomplish*
**ταπεινοφρονέω** 3 • 14 *to be modest, be unassuming*
**ταπεινοφροσύνη, ἡ** 3 • 9 *humility, modesty*
**τρώγω** 1 • 4 *to eat*
**ὑστερέω** 7 • 11 *to be needy, be poor, lack*
**χήρα, ἡ** 6 • 13 *widow*
8 **ἔγγραφος** 1 • 2 *recorded*
**ἐντέλλω** 17 • 29 *to command, order, give orders*
**εὐπρόσδεκτος** 2 • 5 *acceptable*
**θυσία, ἡ** 1 • 22 *sacrifice, offering*
**ἱλαρός** 24 • 34 *joyful, cheerful, glad, happy*
**λειτουργία, ἡ** 2 • 11 *service*
**νηστεία, ἡ** [2] 14 • 25 *fast*
**τελέω** 22 • 23 *to carry out, accomplish, perform, fulfill, keep*

## Chapter 57 (Hs 5.4)

1 **ἀμπελών, ὁ** [2] 20 • 20 *vineyard*
**βοτάνη, ἡ** 27 • 30 *weed*
**δέομαι** 2 • 7 *to ask, request*
**δεσπότης, ὁ** 24 • 54 *lord, master*
**δηλόω** 32 • 49 *to explain, clarify*
**ἐκτίλλω** 5 • 5 *to pull out*
**σύμβουλος, ὁ** 6 • 8 *adviser, counselor*
**συνίημι** 13 • 21 *to understand, comprehend*
**φίλος** 5 • 8 *loving;* subst. *friend*
**χαρακόω** 4 • 4 *to fence in (with stakes)*
**χάραξ, ὁ** 2 • 2 *stake*
2 **αὐθάδης** 3 • 5 *self-willed, stubborn, arrogant*
**δηλόω** [3] 32 • 49 *to explain, clarify*
**ἐπιλύω** 8 • 8 *to explain, interpret*
**λίαν** 43 • 48 *exceedingly, very (much)*
**μάτην** [2] 5 • 5 *in vain, to no end*
**νοέω** 30 • 46 *to perceive, apprehend, understand, gain an insight into*
**ὅλως** 30 • 31 *completely, wholly, everywhere;* with a negative *not at all*
**ὡσαύτως** 3 • 7 *(in) the same (way), similarly, likewise*
3 **ἀργός** 2 • 5 *neglectful, careless*
**βληχρός** 2 • 2 *weak, feeble*
**γνωστός** 2 • 3 *intelligible, capable of being known*
**διστάζω** 5 • 10 *to hesitate*
**ἔντευξις, ἡ** 15 • 18 *intercessory prayer*
**ἐπιλύω** 8 • 8 *to explain, interpret*
**σύνεσις, ἡ** 13 • 22 *understanding*
4 **ἀδιαλείπτως** 3 • 6 *constantly, unceasingly*

**ἀργός** 2 • 5 *neglectful, careless*
**διατί** 27 • 29 *why?*
**ἐνδυναμόω** 12 • 14 *to strengthen*
**ἔντευξις, ἡ** 15 • 18 *power of intercession*
**πολυεύσπλαγχνος** 2 • 2 *rich in compassion*
**σύνεσις, ἡ** 13 • 22 *understanding*
5 **ἀνάγκη, ἡ** 8 • 11 *necessity, pressure*
**ἄτερ** 5 • 6 *without*
**δεικνύω** 3 • 3 *to point out, show, make known*
**δηλόω** 32 • 49 *to explain, clarify*

## Chapter 58 (Hs 5.5)

1 **αὐθάδης** 3 • 5 *self-willed, stubborn, arrogant*
**γνωστός** 2 • 3 *known*
**ἐπειδή** 3 • 17 *because*
**ἐπίλυσις, ἡ** 6 • 6 *explanation, interpretation*
**ἐπιλύω** 8 • 8 *to explain, interpret*
**πανοῦργος** 2 • 2 *crafty, clever, sly*
**παράμονος** 3 • 5 *stubborn, persistent*
**συνίημι** 13 • 21 *to understand, comprehend*
2 **ἄμπελος, ἡ** 13 • 16 *vine, grapevine*
**ἀπαρτίζω** 1 • 7 *to perfect, finish, complete*
**ἐνδυναμόω** 12 • 14 *to strengthen*
**κτίζω** 14 • 25 *to create*
**φυτεύω** 10 • 16 *to plant*
3 **ἀμπελών, ὁ** 20 • 20 *vineyard*
**ἀνομία, ἡ** 9 • 33 *lawless deeds, transgressions*
**ἀποδημία, ἡ** 2 • 2 *absence, journey*
**βοτάνη, ἡ** 27 • 30 *weed*
**δεῖπνον, τό** 3 • 4 *feast, dinner*
**δεσπότης, ὁ** 24 • 54 *lord, master*
**ἔδεσμα, τό** 12 • 12 *food*
**ἐκτίλλω** 5 • 5 *to pull out*
**κτίζω** 14 • 25 *to create*
**παρουσία, ἡ** 1 • 4 *coming, advent*
**συγκρατέω** 3 • 3 *to surround (and protect)*
**σύμβουλος, ὁ** 6 • 8 *adviser, counselor*
**φίλος** 5 • 8 *loving;* subst. *friend*
**χάραξ, ὁ** 2 • 2 *stake*
4 **δηλόω** 32 • 49 *to explain, clarify*
**ἐνδόξως** 2 • 5 *glorious, in splendor*
**θαυμαστῶς** 3 • 3 *wonderfully*
**κἄν** 1 • 8 *even if*
**λίαν** 43 • 48 *exceedingly, very (much)*
**μεγάλως** 5 • 9 *greatly*
**νοέω** [2] 30 • 46 *to perceive, apprehend, understand, gain an insight into*
**συνετός** 4 • 7 *intelligent, sagacious, wise, with good sense*
5 **διατί** 27 • 29 *why?*
**κεῖμαι** 22 • 24 *to appear*
**τρόπος, ὁ** 5 • 17 *manner, way, kind, guise*

## Chapter 59 (Hs 5.6)

1 **κεῖμαι** [2] 22 • 24 *to appear*
**κυριότης, ἡ** 1 • 2 *ruling power, lordship, dominion*
**νοέω** 30 • 46 *to understand, perceive, apprehend, gain an insight into*
**τρόπος, ὁ** 5 • 17 *manner, way, kind, guise*
2 **ἀμπελών, ὁ** [2] 20 • 20 *vineyard*
**ἀναντλέω** 1 • 2 *to bear patiently*
**ἄτερ** 5 • 6 *without*
**καθίστημι** 2 • 8 *to appoint, put in charge*
**κοπιάω** 2 • 4 *to work hard, toil, strive, struggle*
**κόπος, ὁ** [2] 6 • 8 *hardship, trouble, difficulty*
**κτίζω** 14 • 25 *to create*
**μόχθος, ὁ** 1 • 1 *labor, exertion, hardship*
**σκάπτω** 5 • 5 *to dig (up), spade (up)*
**συντηρέω** 3 • 3 *to protect, defend*
**φυτεύω** 10 • 16 *to plant*
3 **τρίβος, ἡ** 2 • 2 *path*
4 **ἔνδοξος** 43 • 54 *glorious, splendid*
**κληρονομία, ἡ** 2 • 6 *inheritance*
**σύμβουλος, ὁ** 6 • 8 *adviser, counselor*
5 **ἁγνεία, ἡ** 7 • 13 *purity, chastity*

**δουλεύω** 25 • 42 *to (perform the duties of a slave) serve, obey*
**κατοικίζω** [2] 3 • 3 *to cause to dwell, establish, settle*
**κτίζω** 14 • 25 *to create*
**κτίσις, ἡ** 13 • 19 *creation, world*
**μιαίνω** 14 • 14 *to defile*
**ὅλως** 30 • 31 *completely, wholly, everywhere;* with a negative *not at all*
**πρόειμι** 1 • 1 *to be preexistent*
**σεμνότης, ἡ** 11 • 12 *dignity, seriousness, probity, holiness*

6 **ἁγνῶς** 5 • 6 *purely, sincerely*
**αἱρέω** 1 • 1 mid. *to choose*
**ἀναστρέφω** 3 • 8 *to conduct oneself, act, behave, live*
**ἀνδρείως** 2 • 2 *bravely, manly*
**ἀρέσκω** 6 • 12 *to please, accommodate*
**ἰσχυρῶς** 5 • 5 *dependably, strongly*
**κοινωνός, ὁ** 3 • 7 *companion, partner, sharer*
**μιαίνω** 14 • 14 *to defile*
**πολιτεύομαι** 1 • 10 *to live, lead one's life*
**πορεία, ἡ** 1 • 3 *conduct*
**πρᾶγμα, τό** 19 • 23 *thing, matter, affair*
**συγκοπιάω** 1 • 2 *to labor together*
**συνεργέω** 1 • 1 *to be helpful, work together with, assist*

7 **ἀμέμπτως** 2 • 6 *blamelessly*
**ἀμίαντος** 3 • 5 *undefiled, pure*
**ἀπολαμβάνω** 6 • 17 *to receive*
**ἄσπιλος** 2 • 3 *pure, without fault*
**δουλεία, ἡ** 1 • 3 *servility, slavery*
**δουλεύω** 25 • 42 *to (perform the duties of a slave) serve, obey*
**ἔνδοξος** 43 • 54 *glorious, splendid*
**κατασκήνωσις, ἡ** 1 • 1 *a place to dwell, taking up lodging*
**κατοικίζω** 3 • 3 *to cause to dwell, establish, settle*
**μισθός, ὁ** [2] 5 • 22 *reward*
**σύμβουλος, ὁ** 6 • 8 *adviser, counselor*

8 **ἐπίλυσις, ἡ** 6 • 6 *explanation, interpretation*

## Chapter 60 (Hs 5.7)

1 **ἀμίαντος** 3 • 5 *undefiled, pure*
**ἐπίλυσις, ἡ** 6 • 6 *explanation, interpretation*
**εὐφραίνω** 6 • 15 *to be glad, enjoy oneself, rejoice, celebrate*
**καθαρός** 25 • 45 *pure, free*

2 **μήποτε** 13 • 22 *that...not*
**μιαίνω** [3] 14 • 14 *to defile*
**μιασμός, ὁ** 1 • 1 *defilement*
**παραχράομαι** 1 • 1 *to misuse*
**φθαρτός** 2 • 10 *perishable*

3 **ἀγνόημα, τό** 2 • 2 *sin committed in ignorance/unintentionally*
**ἄγνοια, ἡ** 2 • 3 *ignorance, unawareness, lack of discernment*
**ἴασις, ἡ** 6 • 7 *forgiveness*
**μιαίνω** 14 • 14 *to defile*
**πρίν** 4 • 7 *before*
**πρότερος** [2] 40 • 47 *former, earlier*

4 **ἀγνόημα, τό** 2 • 2 *sin committed in ignorance/unintentionally*
**ἀμφότεροι** [2] 14 • 21 *both*
**ἄτερ** 5 • 6 *without*
**ἴασις, ἡ** 6 • 7 *forgiveness*
**καθαρός** 25 • 45 *pure, free*
**κοινός** 1 • 15 *common, communal, belonging together*
**μιαίνω** [2] 14 • 14 *to defile*
**πάντως** 7 • 9 *of course, by all means, certainly, probably, doubtless*
**πολύσπλαγχνος** 1 • 1 *sympathetic, compassionate, merciful*
**πρότερος** 40 • 47 *former, earlier*

# PARABLE SIX

## Chapter 61 (Hs 6.1)

1 **ἔνδοξος** 43 • 54 *glorious, splendid*
**ἱλαρός** 24 • 34 *cheerful, glad, happy*
**συζητέω** 1 • 2 *to reflect, meditate*

2 **διψυχέω** [2] 21 • 25 *to be in doubt about something*
**ἐνδυναμόω** 12 • 14 *to make someone strong in something*

ἐνδύω 29 • 32 *to clothe oneself in, put on, wear;*
fig. *take on the characteristics/ virtues/intentions of*
ἐντέλλω 17 • 29 *to command, order, give orders*
ἐξαίφνης 3 • 6 *suddenly, unexpectantly*
ὅλως 30 • 31 *completely, wholly, everywhere;*
with a negative *not at all*
παρακάθημαι 2 • 2 *to sit beside*
3 μάτην 5 • 5 *in vain, to no end*
μετάνοια, ἡ 58 • 72 *repentance, turning about, conversion*
σύμφορος 6 • 6 *beneficial, advantageous, profitable*
4 ἀποβάλλω 32 • 36 *to take off, doff*
ἀρετή, ἡ 5 • 6 *excellence of character, exceptional civic virtue*
ἐκτρίβω 6 • 6 *to ruin, destroy*
ἐνδύω 29 • 32 *to clothe oneself in, put on, wear;*
fig. *take on the characteristics/ virtues/intentions of*
κόπτω 11 • 12 *to cut (off)*
μηκέτι 12 • 16 *no longer, not from now on*
πονηρία, ἡ 36 • 41 *wickedness, baseness, maliciousness, sinfulness*
προστίθημι [2] 13 • 22 *to add to, increase*
πρότερος 40 • 47 *former, earlier*
5 δεικνύω 3 • 3 *to show, point out, make known*
ἐνδύω 29 • 32 *to clothe oneself in, put on, wear*
κροκώδης 1 • 1 *saffron-yellow*
νεανίσκος, ὁ 11 • 11 *youth, young man*
πεδίον, τό 15 • 17 *level place, plain, field*
ποιμήν, ὁ [2] 51 • 55 *shepherd*
σύνθεσις, ἡ 1 • 1 *combination, collection, suit*
χρῶμα, τό 3 • 5 *color*
6 βόσκω 4 • 4 *to herd, tend*
ἰδέα, ἡ 8 • 9 *appearance*
ἱλαρός [3] 24 • 34 *joyful, cheerful, glad, happy*
λίαν [3] 43 • 48 *exceedingly, very (much)*
πάνυ 1 • 5 *altogether, very*
περιτρέχω 2 • 2 *to run about, go about in*
ποιμήν, ὁ [2] 51 • 55 *shepherd*
ποίμνιον, τό 2 • 7 *flock*
σκιρτάω 4 • 5 *to leap, spring about*
σπαταλάω 2 • 3 *to be sportive*
τρυφάω 12 • 12 *to be contented, be well fed*
ὡσεί 16 • 17 *as, like*
ὧδε κἀκεῖ *here and there*

## Chapter 62 (Hs 6.2)

1 ἀπατάω 8 • 9 *to deceive, mislead*
ἀπάτη, ἡ 13 • 16 *fraud, deceit, treachery*
ἐκτρίβω 6 • 6 *to ruin, destroy*
καταστρέφω 3 • 5 *to turn away, mislead, divert, ruin*
ποιμήν, ὁ 51 • 55 *shepherd*
τρυφή, ἡ 19 • 22 *indulgence, reveling*
2 ἀπάτη, ἡ 13 • 16 *fraud, deceit, treachery*
ἐπιλανθάνομαι 5 • 8 *to forget, disregard, put out of mind*
καταφθορά, ἡ 3 • 5 *destruction, downfall, corruption*
μάταιος 6 • 14 *idle, empty, fruitless, useless, powerless, lacking truth*
τρυφή, ἡ 19 • 22 *indulgence, reveling*
3 ἀποσπάω 1 • 2 *to tear oneself away*
βλασφημία, ἡ 2 • 7 *reviling, denigration, disrespect, slander*
ἱλαρός 24 • 34 *cheerful, glad, happy*
καταφθορά, ἡ 3 • 5 *destruction, downfall, corruption*
μετάνοια, ἡ 58 • 72 *repentance, turning about, conversion*
προστίθημι 13 • 22 *to add to, increase*
σκιρτάω 4 • 5 *to leap, spring about*
4 ἀνανέωσις, ἡ 2 • 2 *renewal*
ἀπάτη, ἡ 13 • 16 *fraud, deceit, treachery*
ἀπώλεια, ἡ 1 • 3 *annihilation, ruin*

**βόσκω** 4 • 4 *to graze, feed*
**καταφθείρω** 8 • 8 *to ruin, corrupt*
**καταφθορά, ἡ** 3 • 5 *destruction, downfall, corruption*
**μετάνοια, ἡ** 58 • 72 *repentance, turning about, conversion*
**σκιρτάω** 4 • 5 *to leap, spring about*
**τρυφή, ἡ** 19 • 22 *indulgence, reveling*
5 **ἄγριος** 5 • 8 *wild*
**αἴγειος** 1 • 2 *of a goat*
**βλέμμα, τό** [2] 2 • 2 *look, mien, expression of countenance*
**δεικνύω** 3 • 3 *to show, point out, make known*
**δέρμα, τό** 2 • 3 *skin, hide*
**ἰδέα, ἡ** 8 • 9 *appearance*
**λευκός** 24 • 24 *white*
**λίαν** 43 • 48 *exceedingly, very (much)*
**μάστιξ, ἡ** 3 • 8 *whip, lash*
**ὄζος, ὁ** 1 • 1 *the knot (on a tree branch)*
**περίκειμαι** 2 • 4 *to wear, have something on*
**περίπικρος** 1 • 1 *very bitter*
**πήρα, ἡ** 3 • 3 *knapsack, traveler's bag, shepherd's bag*
**ποιμήν, ὁ** 51 • 55 *shepherd*
**προβαίνω** 1 • 1 *to go ahead, advance*
**ῥάβδος, ἡ** 58 • 62 *shepherd's staff, rod, stick*
**σκληρός** 9 • 9 *hard, rough*
**ὦμος, ὁ** 5 • 5 *shoulder*
**ὡσεί** 16 • 17 *as, like*
6 **ἄκανθα, ἡ** [2] 6 • 9 *thorn-plant*
**ἀκανθώδης** 4 • 4 *thorny*
**ἐκπλέκω** 2 • 2 *to disentangle (oneself)*
**ἐμπλέκω** 2 • 2 *to be entangled*
**κρημνώδης** 2 • 2 *steep, precipitous*
**νεανίσκος, ὁ** 11 • 11 *youth, young man*
**ποιμήν, ὁ** [2] 51 • 55 *shepherd*
**σκιρτάω** 4 • 5 *to leap, spring about*
**σπαταλάω** 2 • 3 *to be sportive*
**τρίβολος, ὁ** [2] 7 • 7 *thistle*
**τριβολώδης** 1 • 1 *full of thistles*
**τρυφάω** 12 • 12 *to be contented, be well fed*
7 **ἄκανθα, ἡ** 6 • 9 *thorn-plant*
**ἀνάπαυσις, ἡ** 1 • 3 *rest, relief*
**βόσκω** 4 • 4 *to graze, feed*
**δέρω** 1 • 2 *to beat, whip*
**ἐμπλέκω** 2 • 2 *to be entangled*
**εὐσταθέω** 3 • 4 *to have peace, be stable, be tranquil, be at rest*
**λίαν** 43 • 48 *exceedingly, very (much)*
**ὅλως** 30 • 31 *completely, wholly, everywhere;* with a negative *not at all*
**περιελαύνω** 1 • 1 *to drive about*
**ταλαιπωρέω** 3 • 4 *to endure sorrow/distress, be miserable*
**τρίβολος, ὁ** 7 • 7 *thistle*

## Chapter 63 (Hs 6.3)

1 **ἀνοχή, ἡ** 3 • 3 *relief*
**βασανίζω** 15 • 18 *to torment, harass*
**λυπέω** 13 • 17 *to grieve, be sad, be depressed*
**μαστιγόω** 1 • 4 *to afflict, torment, mistreat*
**ὅλως** 30 • 31 *completely, wholly, everywhere;* with a negative *not at all*
**ταλαιπωρέω** 3 • 4 *to endure sorrow/distress, be miserable*
2 **ἄσπλαγχνος** 1 • 1 *ruthless, merciless*
**κεῖμαι** 22 • 24 *to be in charge of, be appointed, be set, be destined*
**ὅλως** 30 • 31 *completely, wholly, everywhere;* with a negative *not at all*
**πικρός** 5 • 5 *bitter, embittered, harsh*
**ποιμήν, ὁ** [2] 51 • 55 *shepherd*
**σπλαγχνίζομαι** 8 • 9 *to have pity, feel sympathy*
**τιμωρία, ἡ** [2] 10 • 13 *punishment*
3 **ἀπάτη, ἡ** 13 • 16 *fraud, deceit, treachery*
**ἀποπλανάω** 6 • 8 *to mislead;* pass. *wander away*
**δεινός** 2 • 7 *fearful, terrible*
**ποικίλος** 20 • 22 *diversified, manifold*
**τιμωρέω** 5 • 5 *to punish*
**τιμωρία, ἡ** 10 • 13 *punishment*

4 **ἀκαταστασία, ἡ** 1 • 4 *disturbance, tumult*
**ἀνάξιος** 1 • 4 *unworthy*
**ἀσθένεια, ἡ** 6 • 7 *sickness, disease*
**βάσανος, ἡ** [2] 11 • 18 *torture, torment*
**βιωτικός** 4 • 4 *belonging to (daily) life*
**ζημία, ἡ** 1 • 1 *damage, disadvantage, loss, forfeit*
**ποικίλος** [3] 20 • 22 *diversified, manifold*;
pl. *many/various kinds*
**ποταπός** 5 • 5 *of what sort? of what kind?*
**πρᾶξις, ἡ** 44 • 50 *state, condition, situation*
**τιμωρέω** 5 • 5 *to punish*
**τιμωρία, ἡ** [2] 10 • 13 *punishment*
**ὑβρίζω** 1 • 5 *to mistreat, scoff at, insult*
**ὑστέρησις, ἡ** 1 • 1 *need, lack, poverty*;
pl. *deprivations*

5 **αἰτιάομαι** 2 • 2 *to blame, accuse*
**ἀκαταστατέω** 2 • 2 *to be vacillating, be unsettled*
**βουλή, ἡ** 8 • 19 *resolution, decision*
**ἐπιβάλλω** 2 • 3 *to take something upon oneself, undertake*
**εὐοδόω** 2 • 2 *to succeed, prosper*
**ὅλως** 30 • 31 *completely, wholly, everywhere*;
with a negative *not at all*
**πρᾶξις, ἡ** 44 • 50 *undertaking, business*
**προχωρέω** 1 • 1 *to turn out, succeed*

6 **δικαίως** 2 • 12 *uprightly, justly, in (all) justice*
**δουλεύω** [2] 25 • 42 *to (perform the duties of a slave) serve, obey*
**εὐοδόω** 2 • 2 *to succeed, prosper*
**θλίβω** 19 • 25 *to oppress, afflict;*
**θλιβῶσι πάσῃ θλίψει** (a cognate dat. of means; cf. *ExSyn* 168–69) *they are afflicted with every affliction*
**ἰσχυροποιέω** 7 • 7 *to strengthen*
**καθαρός** [2] 25 • 45 *pure, free*
**κριτής, ὁ** 1 • 6 *a judge*
**παιδεία, ἡ** 3 • 11 *instruction*
**πρᾶξις, ἡ** [2] 44 • 50 *act, action, deed*

## Chapter 64 (Hs 6.4)

1 **ἀπατάω** [2] 8 • 9 *to deceive, be deceitful, mislead*
**βασανίζω** [2] 15 • 18 *to torment, harass*
**δηλόω** 32 • 49 *to give information, explain, clarify*
**ἐπιζητέω** 5 • 9 *to inquire, want to know*
**τρυφάω** [2] 12 • 12 *to live for pleasure, revel, carouse*

2 **βασανίζω** [2] 15 • 18 *to torment, harass*
**ἐλάχιστος** 13 • 16 *very short*
**ἐπιλανθάνομαι** 5 • 8 *to forget*
**ἑπταπλασίως** 1 • 1 *sevenfold*
**τρυφάω** 12 • 12 *to live for pleasure, revel, carouse*

3 **ἀμφότεροι** 14 • 21 *both*
**ἄφρων** 11 • 17 *foolish, ignorant*
**βάσανος, ἡ** 11 • 18 *torture, torment*
**δηλόω** 32 • 49 *to give information, explain, clarify*
**νοέω** [2] 30 • 46 *to understand, perceive, apprehend, gain an insight into*

4 **ἀπατάω** 8 • 9 *to deceive, mislead*
**ἀπάτη, ἡ** [2] 13 • 16 *fraud, deceit, treachery*
**βασανίζω** [2] 15 • 18 *to torment, harass*
**βάσανος, ἡ** [3] 11 • 18 *torture, torment*
**ἐλάχιστος** 13 • 16 *very short*
**ἐνιαυτός, ὁ** [2] 4 • 7 *year*
**ἰσχύω** 4 • 9 *to have the value of, be equal to*
**τιμωρία, ἡ** 10 • 13 *punishment*
**τοσοῦτος** 9 • 38 *so many*
**τριάκοντα** 1 • 2 *thirty*
**τρυφάω** [2] 12 • 12 *to live for pleasure, revel, carouse*
**τρυφή, ἡ** [2] 19 • 22 *indulgence, reveling*

## Chapter 65 (Hs 6.5)

1 **ἀπάτη, ἡ** 13 • 16 *fraud, deceit, treachery*
**βάσανος, ἡ** 11 • 18 *torture, torment*

**δηλόω** 32 • 49 *to explain, clarify*
**ἐπεί** 10 • 35 *because, since, for*
**νοέω** 30 • 46 *to understand, perceive, apprehend, gain an insight into*
**ὅλως** 30 • 31 *completely, wholly, everywhere*;
with a negative *not at all*
**τηλαυγής** 1 • 1 *more clearly*
**τρυφή, ἡ** 19 • 22 *indulgence, reveling*

2 **ἀφροσύνη, ἡ** 7 • 11 *foolishness, lack of sense*
**ἄφρων** 11 • 17 *foolish, ignorant*
**δουλεύω** 25 • 42 *to (perform the duties of a slave) serve, obey*
**μήποτε** 13 • 22 *lest*
**νοέω** 30 • 46 *to understand. perceive, apprehend, gain an insight into*
**παράμονος** 3 • 5 *lasting, constant, enduring*

3 **ἀπατάω** 8 • 9 *to deceive, be deceitful, mislead*
**ἀπάτη, ἡ** 13 • 16 *fraud, deceit, treachery*
**αὔριον** 2 • 2 *next day*
**ἀφροσύνη, ἡ** [2] 7 • 11 *foolishness, lack of sense*
**βασανίζω** 15 • 18 *to torment, harass*
**βάσανος, ἡ** [2] 11 • 18 *torture, torment*
**ἐνδύω** [2] 29 • 32 *to clothe oneself in, put on, wear;*
fig. *take on the characteristics/ virtues/intentions of*
**ἐνιαυτός, ὁ** 4 • 7 *year*
**ἐπιλανθάνομαι** 5 • 8 *to forget*
**κολλάω** 12 • 32 *to join to, join, cling to, associate with*
**μέχρι** 7 • 23 *until*
**μνήμη, ἡ** [2] 2 • 3 *remembrance, memorial*
**νοέω** 30 • 46 *to understand, perceive, apprehend, gain an insight into*
**πρᾶξις, ἡ** 44 • 50 *act, action, deed*
**τιμωρέω** 5 • 5 *to punish*
**τιμωρία, ἡ** [2] 10 • 13 *punishment*
**τρυφάω** 12 • 12 *to live for pleasure, revel, carouse*
**τρυφή, ἡ** 19 • 22 *indulgence, reveling*

4 **ἀπατάω** 8 • 9 *to deceive, be deceitful*
**ἀπάτη, ἡ** 13 • 16 *fraud, deceit, treachery*
**βασανίζω** [2] 15 • 18 *to torment, harass*
**ἐνιαυτός, ὁ** 4 • 7 *year*
**μνημονεύω** 7 • 25 *to remember, keep in mind, think of*
**τιμωρέω** 5 • 5 *to punish*
**τρυφάω** 12 • 12 *to live for pleasure, revel, carouse*
**τρυφή, ἡ** 19 • 22 *indulgence, reveling*

5 **ἀποστερητής, ὁ** 3 • 3 *defrauder, cheat*
**βλαβερός** 5 • 5 *harmful*
**ἡδέως** 7 • 10 *gladly*
**κατάλαλος, ὁ** 3 • 3 *slanderer*
**μέθυσος, ὁ** 1 • 1 *drunkard*
**μοιχός, ὁ** 1 • 3 *adulterer*
**νόσος, ἡ** 1 • 2 *disease*
**ὀξύχολος** 3 • 3 *irritable, irascible, bad-tempered*
**πάθος, τό** 2 • 18 *passion*
**πλεονέκτης, ὁ** 1 • 3 *greedy person*
**πρᾶξις, ἡ** [2] 44 • 50 *act, action, deed*
**τρυφάω** [2] 12 • 12 *to live for pleasure, revel, carouse*
**τρυφή, ἡ** [2] 19 • 22 *indulgence, reveling*
**ψεύστης, ὁ** 1 • 2 *liar*

6 **ἀπάτη, ἡ** 13 • 16 *fraud, deceit, treachery*
**βασανίζω** 15 • 18 *to torment, harass*
**βλαβερός** 5 • 5 *harmful*
**τιμωρέω** 5 • 5 *to punish*
**τρυφή, ἡ** 19 • 22 *indulgence, reveling*

7 **βάσανος, ἡ** 11 • 18 *torture, torment*
**βλαβερός** 5 • 5 *harmful*
**ἐπιμένω** 10 • 16 *to persist in, continue, persevere*
**ἡδονή, ἡ** 5 • 12 *desire, pleasure, delight, enjoyment, pleasantness*
**περιποιέω** [3] 8 • 9 *to bring about*
**προλέγω** 5 • 16 *to state beforehand/earlier*
**σύμφορος** 6 • 6 *beneficial, advantageous, profitable*
**τιμωρία, ἡ** 10 • 13 *punishment*

**τρυφάω** 12 • 12 *to live for pleasure, revel;* here in a positive sense *to revel in doing good*
**τρυφή, ἡ** [3] 19 • 22 *indulgence, reveling*

## PARABLE SEVEN

### Chapter 66 (Hs 7)

1 **ἔνδοξος** 43 • 54 *glorious, splendid*
**ἐπιζητέω** 5 • 9 *to want, wish, wish for*
**θλίβω** [2] 19 • 25 *to oppress, afflict;* pass. *suffer*
**κελεύω** 32 • 44 *to command, order, urge*
**λίαν** 43 • 48 *exceedingly, very (much)*
**πάρειμι** 3 • 17 *to come, be present*
**πεδίον, τό** 15 • 17 *level place, plain, field*
**ποιμήν, ὁ** [2] 51 • 55 *shepherd*
**προστάσσω** 3 • 8 *to give orders*
**τιμωρητής, ὁ** 2 • 2 *avenger, punisher*
2 **ἀνομία, ἡ** 9 • 33 *lawlessness*
**ἀφίστημι** 19 • 19 *to keep away*
**ἔνδοξος** 43 • 54 *glorious, splendid*
**θλίβω** 19 • 25 *to oppress, afflict;* pass. *suffer*
**κελεύω** 32 • 44 *to command, order, urge*
**παραπικραίνω** 2 • 2 *to embitter, make angry, provoke*
**τιμωρία, ἡ** 10 • 13 *punishment*
**τοσοῦτος** 9 • 38 *so much, so great*
3 **ἄλλως** 6 • 6 *otherwise, in another way*
**ἀνάγκη, ἡ** 8 • 11 *necessity, pressure*
**ἔνδοξος** 43 • 54 *glorious, splendid*
**εὐσταθέω** 3 • 4 *to be stable, be tranquil, be at rest*
**θλίβω** [4] 19 • 25 *to oppress, afflict;* pass. *suffer*
**παραπικραίνω** 2 • 2 *to embitter, make angry, provoke*
4 **βασανίζω** 15 • 18 *to torment, harass*
**ἐνδυναμόω** 12 • 14 *to strengthen*
**ἐπέρχομαι** 6 • 8 *to come upon, approach*
**θλίβω** 19 • 25 *to oppress, afflict;* pass. *suffer*
**ἴασις, ἡ** 6 • 7 *forgiveness, cure, deliverance*
**ἰσχυρῶς** 5 • 5 *extremely, strongly, dependably*
**κτίζω** 14 • 25 *to create*
**παντελῶς** 1 • 1 *fully, completely, altogether;*
with **οὐ** *not at all, by no means*
**πάντως** 7 • 9 *of course, by all means, certainly, probably, doubtless*
**ποικίλος** 20 • 22 *many kinds, diversified, manifold*
**πρᾶξις, ἡ** 44 • 50 *act, action, deed*
**σπλαγχνίζομαι** 8 • 9 *to have pity, feel sympathy*
**ταπεινοφρονέω** 3 • 14 *to be humble, be modest, be unassuming*
**ὑποφέρω** 9 • 12 *to submit to, endure*
5 **ἡγέομαι** 7 • 25 *to think, consider, regard*
**θλίβω** [2] 19 • 25 *to oppress, afflict;* pass. *suffer*
**ἰσχυρῶς** 5 • 5 *bravely, strongly, dependably*
**καθαρός** 25 • 45 *pure, free*
**πάντως** 7 • 9 *by all means, certainly, probably, doubtless, especially so*
**πρᾶγμα, τό** 19 • 23 *thing, matter, affair*
**προγινώσκω** 2 • 2 *to have foreknowledge (of)*
**προδηλόω** 1 • 2 *to reveal*
**προστάσσω** 3 • 8 *to command, order, give instructions, determine*
**σύμφορος** 6 • 6 *beneficial, advantageous, profitable*
**ὑποφέρω** 9 • 12 *to submit to, endure*
6 **ἀποκαθίστημι** 1 • 4 *to restore, bring back, give back*
**ἐλαφρός** 1 • 1 *having little weight, light;*
comparative adverb **ἐλαφροτέρως** *more lightly*

**ἐντέλλω** 17 • 29 *to command, order, give orders*
**θλίβω** [2] 19 • 25 *to oppress, afflict;* pass. *suffer*
**ἰσχυρός** 14 • 21 *mighty, productive*
**καθαρός** [2] 25 • 45 *pure, free*
**λειτουργέω** 4 • 11 *to serve, render service*
**μετάνοια, ἡ** 58 • 72 *repentance, turning about, conversion*
**παραμένω** 6 • 9 *to continue in an occupation/office*
**ταπεινοφρονέω** 3 • 14 *to be modest, be unassuming*
**τιμωρητής, ὁ** 2 • 2 *avenger, punisher*
**ὑποφέρω** 9 • 12 *to submit to, endure*
7 **ἀφίστημι** [2] 19 • 19 *to depart, withdraw*

## PARABLE EIGHT

### Chapter 67 (Hs 8.1)

1 **ἰτέα, ἡ** [2] 6 • 6 *willow tree*
**πεδίον, τό** 15 • 17 *level place, plain, field*
**σκεπάζω** 6 • 8 *to cover*
**σκέπη, ἡ** 3 • 3 *shade*
2 **δρέπανον, τό** 2 • 2 *sickle*
**ἔνδοξος** 43 • 54 *glorious, splendid*
**ἐπιδίδωμι** [2] 60 • 62 *to give, hand over, deliver*
**ἰτέα, ἡ** 6 • 6 *willow tree*
**κλάδος, ὁ** 5 • 6 *branch*
**κόπτω** 11 • 12 *to cut (off)*
**λίαν** 43 • 48 *exceedingly, very (much)*
**πηχυαῖος** 1 • 1 *a cubit long (about eighteen inches)*
**ῥαβδίον, τό** 3 • 3 *stick, twig*
**σκεπάζω** 6 • 8 *to cover*
**ὑψηλός** 5 • 12 *tall, high*
**ὡσεί** 16 • 17 *about*
3 **δένδρον, τό** 26 • 28 *tree*
**δρέπανον, τό** 2 • 2 *sickle*
**οἷος** 8 • 10 *as, such as, of what sort*
**ῥαβδίον, τό** 3 • 3 *stick, twig*
**ὑγιής** 9 • 9 *sound, undamaged*
4 **δένδρον, τό** [2] 26 • 28 *tree*
**δηλόω** 32 • 49 *to explain, clarify*
**κλάδος, ὁ** [2] 5 • 6 *branch*
**κόπτω** [2] 11 • 12 *to cut off*
**ποιμήν, ὁ** 51 • 55 *shepherd*
**τοσοῦτος** [2] 9 • 38 *so many, so much*
**ὑγιής** [2] 9 • 9 *sound, undamaged*
5 **ἀπαιτέω** 1 • 4 *to ask for, demand back*
**ἐπιδίδωμι** 60 • 62 *to give, hand over, deliver*
**κατανοέω** 21 • 26 *to inspect, consider, contemplate*
**ῥάβδος, ἡ** [2] 58 • 62 *rod, stick, staff*
6 **βιβρώσκω** 7 • 8 *to eat, gnaw*
**ἐπιδίδωμι** 60 • 62 *to give, hand over, deliver*
**κελεύω** 32 • 44 *to command, order, urge*
**ξηρός** 46 • 47 *dry, dried up*
**ῥάβδος, ἡ** [2] 58 • 62 *rod, stick, staff*
**σής, ὁ** 4 • 6 *worm, moth*
7 **βιβρώσκω** 7 • 8 *to eat, gnaw*
**ἐπιδίδωμι** 60 • 62 *to give, hand over, deliver*
**κελεύω** 32 • 44 *to command, order, urge*
**ξηρός** 46 • 47 *dry, dried up*
**σής, ὁ** 4 • 6 *worm, moth*
8 **ἐπιδίδωμι** 60 • 62 *to give, hand over, deliver*
**ἡμίξηρος** 11 • 11 *half dry, half withered*
9 **ἐπιδίδωμι** 60 • 62 *to give, hand over, deliver*
**ἡμίξηρος** 11 • 11 *half dry, half withered*
**ῥάβδος, ἡ** 58 • 62 *rod, stick, staff*
**σχισμή, ἡ** 25 • 25 *crack, fissure*
10 **ἐπιδίδωμι** 60 • 62 *to give, hand over, deliver*
**ῥάβδος, ἡ** 58 • 62 *rod, stick, staff*
**σχισμή, ἡ** 25 • 25 *crack, fissure*
**χλωρός** 44 • 44 *green, fresh*
11 **ἐπιδίδωμι** 60 • 62 *to give, hand over, deliver*
**ἥμισυς** [2] 11 • 11 *one-half;* subst. *the half*
**ξηρός** 46 • 47 *dry, dried up*
**ῥάβδος, ἡ** 58 • 62 *rod, stick, staff*
**χλωρός** 44 • 44 *green, fresh*

12 ξηρός 46 • 47 *dry, dried up*
ῥάβδος, ἡ [2] 58 • 62 *rod, stick, staff*
χλωρός 44 • 44 *green, fresh*
13 ἐπιδίδωμι 60 • 62 *to give, hand over, deliver*
ξηρός 46 • 47 *dry, dried up*
χλωρός 44 • 44 *green, fresh*
14 ἄκρον, τό 3 • 3 *tip, high point, top*
ἐλάχιστος 13 • 16 *very small*
ἐπιδίδωμι 60 • 62 *to give, hand over, deliver*
ξηρός 46 • 47 *dry, dried up*
ῥάβδος, ἡ [2] 58 • 62 *rod, stick, staff*
σχισμή, ἡ 25 • 25 *crack, fissure*
χλωρός 44 • 44 *green, fresh*
15 ἐλάχιστος 13 • 16 *very small*
ξηρός 46 • 47 *dry, dried up*
ῥάβδος, ἡ 58 • 62 *rod, stick, staff*
χλωρός 44 • 44 *green, fresh*
16 ἐπιδίδωμι 60 • 62 *to give, hand over, deliver*
λίαν 43 • 48 *exceedingly, very (much)*
ῥάβδος, ἡ [2] 58 • 62 *rod, stick, staff*
χλωρός 44 • 44 *green, fresh*
17 ἐπιδίδωμι 60 • 62 *to give, hand over, deliver*
ἱλαρός 24 • 34 *cheerful, glad, happy*
λίαν 43 • 48 *exceedingly, very (much)*
παραφυάς, ἡ 13 • 14 *offshoot, side growth*
ῥάβδος, ἡ 58 • 62 *rod, stick, staff*
χλωρός 44 • 44 *green, fresh*
18 ἀγαλλιάω 6 • 11 *to exult, be glad, be overjoyed*
ἐπιδίδωμι 60 • 62 *to give, hand over, deliver*
ἱλαρός [2] 24 • 34 *cheerful, glad, happy*
λίαν [2] 43 • 48 *exceedingly, very (much)*
παραφυάς, ἡ [2] 13 • 14 *offshoot, side growth*
ποιμήν, ὁ 51 • 55 *shepherd*
ῥάβδος, ἡ [2] 58 • 62 *rod, stick, staff*
χλωρός 44 • 44 *green, fresh*
ὡσεί 16 • 17 *as, like*

## Chapter 68 (Hs 8.2)

1 ἐπιδίδωμι 60 • 62 *to give, hand over, deliver*
κελεύω 32 • 44 *to command, order, urge*
παραφυάς, ἡ 13 • 14 *offshoot, side growth*
πύργος, ὁ 147 • 148 *tower*
ῥάβδος, ἡ 58 • 62 *rod, stick, staff*
στέφανος, ὁ [2] 2 • 7 *wreath, crown*
στεφανόω 5 • 12 *to wreathe, crown*
φοῖνιξ, ὁ 1 • 2 *palm-branch, palm-leaf*
ὡσεί 16 • 17 *as, like*
2 ἐπιδίδωμι 60 • 62 *to give, hand over, deliver*
παραφυάς, ἡ [2] 13 • 14 *offshoot, side growth*
πύργος, ὁ 147 • 148 *tower*
ῥάβδος, ἡ 58 • 62 *rod, stick, staff*
σφραγίς, ἡ 12 • 16 *mark*
χλωρός 44 • 44 *green, fresh*
3 ἱματισμός, ὁ 6 • 8 *clothing, apparel*
λευκός 24 • 24 *white*
πύργος, ὁ 147 • 148 *tower*
χιών, ἡ 1 • 3 *snow*
ὡσεί 16 • 17 *as, like*
4 ἐπιδίδωμι 60 • 62 *to give, hand over, deliver*
ἱματισμός, ὁ 6 • 8 *clothing, apparel*
λευκός 24 • 24 *white*
ῥάβδος, ἡ 58 • 62 *rod, stick, staff*
σφραγίς, ἡ 12 • 16 *mark*
χλωρός 44 • 44 *green, fresh*
5 δοκιμάζω 10 • 19 *to put to the test, examine, evaluate*
ἐπιμελῶς [2] 5 • 9 *carefully, diligently*
θυσιαστήριον, τό 4 • 15 *altar*
κατανοέω [2] 21 • 26 *to inspect, consider, contemplate*
παρέρχομαι [2] 4 • 12 *to get by unnoticed, escape notice*
ποιμήν, ὁ 51 • 55 *shepherd*
ῥάβδος, ἡ 58 • 62 *rod, stick, staff*
τεῖχος, τό 4 • 4 *wall*
τελέω 22 • 23 *to bring to an end, finish, complete*
6 ξηρός 46 • 47 *dry, dried up*

**ποιμήν, ὁ** 51 • 55 *shepherd*
**ῥάβδος, ἡ** 58 • 62 *rod, stick, staff*
**φυτεύω** 10 • 16 *to plant*
7 **ἀμελής** 2 • 2 *careless, negligent*
**γένος, τό** 8 • 16 *species, class, kind*
**δένδρον, τό** 26 • 28 *tree*
**εἶτα** 30 • 48 *then, next*
**ἰκμάς, ἡ** 2 • 3 *moisture*
**ἰτέα, ἡ** 6 • 6 *willow tree*
**παραχέω** 2 • 2 *to pour near/on*
**ῥάβδος, ἡ** 58 • 62 *rod, stick, staff*
**συνχαίρω/συγχαίρω** 1 • 1 *to rejoice with/in*
**φιλόζωος** 2 • 2 *tenacious of life, loving life*
**φυτεύω** 10 • 16 *to plant*
8 **ἐπιδίδωμι** 60 • 62 *to give, hand over, deliver*
**κελεύω** 32 • 44 *to command, order, urge*
**παραχέω** 2 • 2 *to pour near/on*
**ποιμήν, ὁ** [3] 51 • 55 *shepherd*
**ῥάβδος, ἡ** [3] 58 • 62 *rod, stick, staff*
**τάγμα, τό** [3] 13 • 16 *class, group*
**τάγματα τάγματα** (distributive acc.) *group by group, row by row*
**φυτεύω** [2] 10 • 16 *to plant*
9 **δένδρον, τό** [2] 26 • 28 *tree*
**ἐπανέρχομαι** 1 • 1 *to return*
**ἐπισκέπτομαι** 6 • 8 *to look at, examine, inspect*
**ἰκμάς, ἡ** 2 • 3 *moisture*
**κλάδος, ὁ** 5 • 6 *branch*
**κτίζω** 14 • 25 *to create*
**ποτίζω** 5 • 7 *to water*
**ῥαβδίον, τό** 3 • 3 *stick, twig*
**ῥάβδος, ἡ** [2] 58 • 62 *rod, stick, staff*

## Chapter 69 (Hs 8.3)

1 **ἀπορέω** [2] 2 • 2 *to be at a loss, be in doubt, be uncertain*
**γνωρίζω** 10 • 18 *to make known, reveal*
**δένδρον, τό** [2] 26 • 28 *tree*
**κλάδος, ὁ** 5 • 6 *branch*
**κόπτω** [2] 11 • 12 *to cut (off)*
**ὅλως** 30 • 31 *completely, wholly, everywhere*; with a negative *not at all*
**τοσοῦτος** 9 • 38 *so many, so much*
**ὑγιής** 9 • 9 *sound, undamaged*
**φαίνω** 12 • 37 *to have the appearance, seem*
2 **δένδρον, τό** 26 • 28 *tree*
**κήρυγμα, τό** 3 • 5 *proclamation*
**πεδίον, τό** 15 • 17 *level place, plain, field*
**πέρας, τό** 1 • 13 *end, limit, boundary*
**σκεπάζω** 6 • 8 *to cover*
**σκέπη, ἡ** 3 • 3 *shade*
3 **διακυβερνάω** 1 • 1 *to direct, govern*
**ἔνδοξος** 43 • 54 *glorious, splendid*
**ἐπισκέπτομαι** 6 • 8 *to look at, examine, inspect*
**Μιχαήλ, ὁ** 1 • 1 *Michael*
4 **ἀχρειόω** 1 • 1 *to make useless*
**κατοικία, ἡ** 10 • 10 *dwelling-place, habitation*
**ῥάβδος, ἡ** [3] 58 • 62 *rod, stick, staff*
5 **διατί** 27 • 29 *why?*
**εὐαρεστέω** 2 • 6 *to be pleased, take delight*
**καταλείπω** [2] 6 • 12 *to leave behind*
**μετάνοια, ἡ** 58 • 72 *repentance, turning about, conversion*
**παραβαίνω** 1 • 3 *to transgress, break*
**πύργος, ὁ** 147 • 148 *tower*
6 **νικάω** 2 • 8 *to be victor, conquer, overcome, prevail*
**παλαίω** 1 • 1 *to wrestle*
**πύργος, ὁ** 147 • 148 *tower*
**στεφανόω** [2] 5 • 12 *to wreathe, crown*
7 **ἐπιδίδωμι** 60 • 62 *to give, hand over, deliver*
**θλίβω** 19 • 25 *to persecute, oppress, afflict*
**παραφυάς, ἡ** 13 • 14 *offshoot, side growth*
**ῥάβδος, ἡ** 58 • 62 *rod, stick, staff*
**χλωρός** 44 • 44 *green, fresh*
8 **ἐπιδίδωμι** 60 • 62 *to give, hand over, deliver*
**καθαρός** 25 • 45 *pure, free*

**κατανοέω** 21 • 26 *to inspect, consider, contemplate*
**λίαν** 43 • 48 *exceedingly, very (much)*
**οἷος** 8 • 10 *as, such as, of what sort*
**ποτίζω** 5 • 7 *to water*
**ῥάβδος, ἡ** 58 • 62 *rod, stick, staff*
**σεμνός** 7 • 13 *worthy of respect/honor, noble, dignified, serious*
**φυτεύω** 10 • 16 *to plant*
**χλωρός** 44 • 44 *green, fresh*

## Chapter 70 (Hs 8.4)

1 **καθαρός** 25 • 45 *clean, pure*
**περιζώννυμι** [2] 6 • 6 mid. *to gird/bind oneself with something*
**ποιμήν, ὁ** 51 • 55 *shepherd*
**σάκκος, ὁ** 1 • 4 *sack, sackcloth*
**ὠμόλινον, τό** [2] 2 • 2 *apron, towel*
2 **ἐπιδίδωμι** 60 • 62 *to give, hand over, deliver*
**ἕτοιμος** 3 • 9 *ready, prepared*
**πεδίον, τό** 15 • 17 *level place, plain, field*
**περιζώννυμι** 6 • 6 *to gird about*
**ῥάβδος, ἡ** [2] 58 • 62 *rod, stick, staff*
**τάγμα, τό** [3] 13 • 16 *class, group*; **τάγματα τάγματα** (distributive acc.) *group by group, row by row*
**φυτεύω** 10 • 16 *to plant*
3 **ἐκτίλλω** 5 • 5 *to pull out*
**ῥάβδος, ἡ** 58 • 62 *rod, stick, staff*
4 **ἐπιδίδωμι** 60 • 62 *to give, hand over, deliver*
**κελεύω** 32 • 44 *to command, order, urge*
**κόπτω** [2] 11 • 12 *to cut (off)*
**ξηρός** [2] 46 • 47 *dry, dried up*
**ὡσαύτως** 3 • 7 *(in) the same (way), similarly, likewise*
5 **εἶτα** 30 • 48 *then, next*
**ἐπιδίδωμι** [3] 60 • 62 *to give, hand over, deliver*
**κελεύω** [2] 32 • 44 *to command, order, urge*
**κόπτω** [3] 11 • 12 *to cut (off)*
**ξηρός** [3] 46 • 47 *dry, dried up*
**ῥάβδος, ἡ** [2] 58 • 62 *rod, stick, staff*
**σής, ὁ** 4 • 6 *worm, moth*
**χλωρός** [2] 44 • 44 *green, fresh*
6 **ἄβρωτος** 1 • 1 *not eaten*
**βιβρώσκω** 7 • 8 *to eat, gnaw*
**εἶτα** 30 • 48 *then, next*
**ἐπιδίδωμι** [3] 60 • 62 *to give, hand over, deliver*
**ἡμίξηρος** 11 • 11 *half dry, half withered*
**ἥμισυς** 11 • 11 *one-half*
**κελεύω** 32 • 44 *to command, order, urge*
**ξηρός** [3] 46 • 47 *dry, dried up*
**οἷος** [2] 8 • 10 *as, such as, of what sort*
**παραφυάς, ἡ** [2] 13 • 14 *offshoot, side growth*
**πύργος, ὁ** 147 • 148 *tower*
**στεφανόω** 5 • 12 *to wreathe, crown*
**σχισμή, ἡ** [3] 25 • 25 *crack, fissure*
**τάγμα, τό** 13 • 16 *class, group*
**χλωρός** [2] 44 • 44 *green, fresh*

## Chapter 71 (Hs 8.5)

1 **ἀλλοιόω** 3 • 5 *to change*
**ἀποτίθημι** 7 • 13 *to lose, lay aside, rid oneself*
**εἶτα** 30 • 48 *then, next*
**ἐπιδίδωμι** [2] 60 • 62 *to give, hand over, deliver*
**ποιμήν, ὁ** 51 • 55 *shepherd*
**ῥάβδος, ἡ** 58 • 62 *rod, stick, staff*
**σχισμή, ἡ** 3 • 10 *crack, fissure*
**τάγμα, τό** 13 • 16 *class, group*
**χλωρός** [2] 44 • 44 *green, fresh*
2 **βιβρώσκω** 7 • 8 *to eat, gnaw*
**ἐπιδίδωμι** 60 • 62 *to give, hand over, deliver*
**ἡμίξηρος** 11 • 11 *half dry, half withered*
**ἥμισυς** [2] 11 • 11 *one-half*; subst. *the half*
**ξηρός** [2] 46 • 47 *dry, dried up*
**ὁλοτελής** 5 • 5 *quite perfect, in every way complete, very*
**παραφυάς, ἡ** 13 • 14 *offshoot, side growth*
**ῥάβδος, ἡ** 58 • 62 *rod, stick, staff*
**τάγμα, τό** 13 • 16 *class, group*
**χλωρός** [3] 44 • 44 *green, fresh*
3 **βιβρώσκω** 7 • 8 *to eat, gnaw*
**εἶτα** 30 • 48 *then, next*

ἐπιδίδωμι [2] 60 • 62 *to give, hand over, deliver*
ἡμίξηρος 11 • 11 *half dry, half withered*
ξηρός [2] 46 • 47 *dry, dried up*
τάγμα, τό 13 • 16 *class, group*
χλωρός [2] 44 • 44 *green, fresh*
4 βιβρώσκω 7 • 8 *to eat, gnaw*
ἐλάχιστος 13 • 16 *very little, very few*
ἐπιδίδωμι [3] 60 • 62 *to give, hand over, deliver*
ἡμίξηρος [2] 11 • 11 *half dry, half withered*
ξηρός [2] 46 • 47 *dry, dried up*
ῥάβδος, ἡ 58 • 62 *rod, stick, staff*
σχισμή, ἡ 25 • 25 *crack, fissure*
τάγμα, τό 13 • 16 *class, group*
χλωρός [2] 44 • 44 *green, fresh*
5 ἐλάχιστος 13 • 16 *very small, short*
ἐπιδίδωμι [2] 60 • 62 *to give, hand over, deliver*
ξηρός 46 • 47 *dry, dried up*
παραφυάς, ἡ 13 • 14 *offshoot, side growth*
ῥάβδος, ἡ 58 • 62 *rod, stick, staff*
σχισμή, ἡ 25 • 25 *crack, fissure*
τάγμα, τό 13 • 16 *class, group*
χλωρός [3] 44 • 44 *green, fresh*
6 εἶτα 30 • 48 *then, next*
ἐλάχιστος 13 • 16 *very small, very little, short*
ἐπιδίδωμι 60 • 62 *to give, hand over, deliver*
μεγάλως 5 • 9 *greatly*
ξηρός 46 • 47 *dry, dried up*
παραφυάς, ἡ [2] 13 • 14 *offshoot, side growth*
ποιμήν, ὁ 51 • 55 *shepherd*
ῥάβδος, ἡ [2] 58 • 62 *rod, stick, staff*
τάγμα, τό 13 • 16 *class, group*
χλωρός [3] 44 • 44 *green, fresh*

## Chapter 72 (Hs 8.6)

1 δένδρον, τό 26 • 28 *tree*
ἔνδοξος 43 • 54 *glorious, splendid*
κατανοέω 21 • 26 *to inspect, consider, contemplate*
μετάνοια, ἡ 58 • 72 *repentance, turning about, conversion*
ποιμήν, ὁ 51 • 55 *shepherd*
πολυευσπλαγχνία, ἡ 2 • 2 *richness in mercy*
πόσος 1 • 9 *how many?*
ῥάβδος, ἡ 58 • 62 *rod, stick, staff*
φιλόζωος 2 • 2 *tenacious of life, loving life*
2 βεβηλόω 1 • 1 *to violate sanctity, desecrate, profane*
δολιότης, ἡ 2 • 3 *deceit*
δουλεύω 25 • 42 *to (perform the duties of a slave) serve, obey*
καθαρός 25 • 45 *pure, free*
μετάνοια, ἡ [2] 58 • 72 *repentance, turning about, conversion*
μήποτε 13 • 22 *lest*
πονηρία, ἡ 36 • 41 *wickedness, baseness, maliciousness, sinfulness*
ὑπόκρισις, ἡ 5 • 13 *insincerity, play-acting, pretense, outward show, dissembling*
3 ἀνακαινίζω 2 • 3 *to renew, restore*
δηλόω 32 • 49 *to explain, clarify*
ἐξαποστέλλω 3 • 4 *to send away, send off, send out*
ἐπιδίδωμι 60 • 62 *to give, hand over, deliver*
θλάω 1 • 1 *to break*
κατοικία, ἡ 10 • 10 *dwelling-place, habitation*
ποταπός 5 • 5 *of what sort? of what kind?*
ῥάβδος, ἡ 58 • 62 *rod, stick, staff*
σπλαγχνίζομαι 8 • 9 *to have pity, feel sympathy*
σφραγίς, ἡ [2] 12 • 16 *attestation, confirmation, certification;* here as a term referring to baptism
ὑγιής 9 • 9 *unbroken, uncorrupted, correct*
4 ἀποστάτης, ὁ 3 • 3 *deserter, rebel*
ἀφίστημι 19 • 19 *to depart, withdraw*
βιβρώσκω 7 • 8 *to eat, gnaw*
ἐντέλλω 17 • 29 *to command, order, give orders*
ἐπαισχύνομαι 3 • 5 *to be ashamed*
καίπερ 3 • 7 *although*
ξηρός 46 • 47 *dry, dried up*
προδότης, ὁ 5 • 6 *traitor, betrayer*
ῥάβδος, ἡ 58 • 62 *rod, stick, staff*
σής, ὁ 4 • 6 *worm, moth*

5 **ἄσηπτος** 1 • 1 *not rotten, not worm-eaten*
**εἰσφέρω** 1 • 4 *to introduce, bring in*
**ἐκστρέφω** 1 • 1 *to turn aside, pervert*
**ἐπιδίδωμι** 60 • 62 *to give, hand over, deliver*
**μάλιστα** 5 • 14 *most of all, above all, especially, particularly*
**μωρός** 11 • 12 *foolish, stupid*
**ξηρός** 46 • 47 *dry, dried up*
**ὑποκριτής, ὁ** 3 • 6 *play-actor, pretender, dissembler*
6 **κατοικία, ἡ** 10 • 10 *dwelling-place, habitation*
**μετάνοια, ἡ** 58 • 72 *repentance, turning about, conversion*
**πύργος, ὁ** 147 • 148 *tower*
**τεῖχος, τό** 4 • 4 *wall*

## Chapter 73 (Hs 8.7)

1 **δίψυχος** 20 • 23 *doubting, hesitating, double-minded*
**ἐπιδίδωμι** 60 • 62 *to give, hand over, deliver*
**ἡμίξηρος** [2] 11 • 11 *half dry, half withered*
**θνήσκω** 5 • 5 *to die*
**ῥάβδος, ἡ** 58 • 62 *rod, stick, staff*
**σχισμή, ἡ** 25 • 25 *crack, fissure*
2 **διχοστατέω** 2 • 3 *to disagree, dissent*
**δίψυχος** 20 • 23 *doubting, hesitating, double-minded*
**εἰρηνεύω** 6 • 17 *to keep the peace*
**ἐπίκειμαι** 1 • 6 *to be open*
**ἡμίξηρος** 11 • 11 *half dry, half withered*
**κατάλαλος, ὁ** 3 • 3 *slanderous*
**μετάνοια, ἡ** [2] 58 • 72 *repentance, turning about, conversion*
**μηδέποτε** 3 • 5 *never*
**σχισμή, ἡ** 25 • 25 *crack, fissure*
3 **βραδύς** 4 • 5 *slow*
**ἐμμένω** 7 • 8 *to persevere in, stand by*
**κατοικία, ἡ** 10 • 10 *dwelling-place, habitation*
**πρᾶξις, ἡ** 44 • 50 *act, action, deed*
**πύργος, ὁ** 147 • 148 *tower*
**τεῖχος, τό** 4 • 4 *wall*
4 **ἐπιδίδωμι** 60 • 62 *to give, hand over, deliver*
**ζῆλος, ὁ** [2] 2 • 25 *jealousy, envy*
**μωρός** 11 • 12 *foolish, stupid*
**πρωτεῖος** [2] 3 • 3 *of first quality/rank, preeminence*
**ῥάβδος, ἡ** 58 • 62 *rod, stick, staff*
**σχισμή, ἡ** 25 • 25 *crack, fissure*
**χλωρός** 44 • 44 *green, fresh*
5 **διχοστασία, ἡ** 4 • 6 *dissension*
**κατοίκησις, ἡ** 3 • 3 *a home, dwelling, living quarters*
**πύργος, ὁ** [2] 147 • 148 *tower*
**ταχύς** 11 • 18 *in a short time, soon*
6 **διχοστάτης, ὁ** 1 • 1 *one who causes dissensions*
**μακροθυμία, ἡ** 9 • 15 *patience, steadfastness, endurance*
**παράνομος** 1 • 2 *lawless*; subst. *evil-doer*
**πρωτεῖος** 3 • 3 *of first quality/rank, preeminence*
**ταπεινοφροσύνη, ἡ** 3 • 9 *humility*

## Chapter 74 (Hs 8.8)

1 **ἐμφύρω** 6 • 6 *to mix up, involve*
**ἐπιδίδωμι** 60 • 62 *to give, hand over, deliver*
**ἥμισυς** [4] 11 • 11 *one-half*; subst. *the half*
**κολλάω** 12 • 32 *join oneself to, join, cling to, associate with*
**ξηρός** 46 • 47 *dry, dried up*
**πραγματεία, ἡ** 11 • 11 *activity, occupation*; pl. *undertakings, business, affairs*
**ῥάβδος, ἡ** 58 • 62 *rod, stick, staff*
**χλωρός** 44 • 44 *green, fresh*
2 **ἀπαρνέομαι** 5 • 6 *to deny*
**ἀφίστημι** 19 • 19 *to go away, withdraw*
**γοῦν** 1 • 4 *hence, then*
**κατοικία, ἡ** 10 • 10 *dwelling-place, habitation*
**μετάνοια, ἡ** 58 • 72 *repentance, turning about, conversion*
**πονηρία, ἡ** 36 • 41 *wickedness, baseness, maliciousness, sinfulness*

**πραγματεία, ἡ** 11 • 11 *activity, occupation;* pl. *undertakings, business, affairs*
**πύργος, ὁ** 147 • 148 *tower*
3 **βραδύς** 4 • 5 *slow*
**διψυχέω** 21 • 25 *to be undecided, be changeable, doubt*
**κατοικία, ἡ** 10 • 10 *dwelling-place, habitation*
**μετάνοια, ἡ** 58 • 72 *repentance, turning about, conversion*
**πύργος, ὁ** 147 • 148 *tower*
**ταχύς** 11 • 18 *in a short time, soon*
**τεῖχος, τό** 4 • 4 *wall*
4 **ἄρνησις, ἡ** 2 • 3 *repudiation, rejection*
**ἐπιδίδωμι** 60 • 62 *to give, hand over, deliver*
**ξηρός** 46 • 47 *dry, dried up*
**ποικίλος** 20 • 22 *diversified, manifold*
**χλωρός** 44 • 44 *green, fresh*
5 **ἀφίστημι** 19 • 19 *to fall away, go away, withdraw*
**διχοστατέω** 2 • 3 *to disagree, dissent*
**διψυχέω** 21 • 25 *to be undecided, be changeable, doubt*
**ἐπιμένω** [2] 10 • 16 *to continue, persist in, persevere*
**ἡδονή, ἡ** 5 • 12 *pleasure, delight, enjoyment, pleasantness*
**κατεργάζομαι** 3 • 7 *to bring about, produce, create*
**μετάνοια, ἡ** 58 • 72 *repentance, turning about, conversion*
**πρᾶξις, ἡ** 44 • 50 *act, action, deed*
**πύργος, ὁ** 147 • 148 *tower*
**ταχύς** 11 • 18 *in a short time, soon*

## Chapter 75 (Hs 8.9)

1 **ἀφίστημι** 19 • 19 *to fall away, go away, withdraw*
**ἐμμένω** 7 • 8 *to persevere in, stand by*
**ἔνδοξος** 43 • 54 *honored, distinguished, eminent*
**ἐνδύω** 29 • 32 *to clothe oneself in, put on, wear;* fig. *take on the characteristics/virtues/intentions of*
**ἐπιδίδωμι** 60 • 62 *to give, hand over, deliver*
**ἡδύς** 1 • 1 *suitable, pleasant*
**καταλείπω** 6 • 12 *to abandon*
**κολλάω** 12 • 32 *to join oneself to, join, cling to, associate with*
**ξηρός** 46 • 47 *dry, dried up*
**πλουτέω** 4 • 6 *to be rich*
**ῥάβδος, ἡ** 58 • 62 *rod, stick, staff*
**συζάω** 5 • 5 *to live with*
**ὑπερηφανία, ἡ** 3 • 8 *arrogance, haughtiness, pride*
**ὑψηλόφρων** 1 • 1 *proud, haughty*
**χλωρός** 44 • 44 *green, fresh*
2 **κατοίκησις, ἡ** 3 • 3 *home, dwelling, living quarters*
**πύργος, ὁ** 147 • 148 *tower*
3 **ἀφίστημι** 19 • 19 *to fall away, go away, withdraw*
**κενοδοξία, ἡ** 2 • 5 *illusion, delusion, error*
**πρᾶξις, ἡ** 44 • 50 *act, action, deed*
**συζάω** 5 • 5 *to live with*
**φθείρω** 2 • 10 *to ruin, corrupt*
**εἰς τέλος** (adverbial marker of intensity) *entirely, utterly*
4 **διψυχέω** [3] 21 • 25 *to be undecided, be changeable, doubt*
**ἐπιμένω** 10 • 16 *to continue, persist in, persevere*
**ἡδονή, ἡ** 5 • 12 *pleasure, delight, enjoyment, pleasantness*
**κατοικία, ἡ** 10 • 10 *dwelling-place, habitation*
**μετάνοια, ἡ** [2] 58 • 72 *repentance, turning about, conversion*
**πρᾶξις, ἡ** [2] 44 • 50 *act, action, deed*
**πύργος, ὁ** 147 • 148 *tower*
**σχίσμα, τό** 3 • 10 *division, dissension, schism*
**ταχινός** 3 • 3 *coming soon, imminent, swift, soon*

## Chapter 76 (Hs 8.10)

1 **ἄκρον, τό** 3 • 3 *tip, high point, top*

**ἐλάχιστος** 13 • 16 *very small; a little*
**ἔνδοξος** 43 • 54 *glorious, splendid*
**ἐξαμαρτάνω** 2 • 2 *to miss the mark (of God's expectation), violate a law or command, commit an offense, do wrong, sin*
**ἐπιδίδωμι** 60 • 62 *to give, hand over, deliver*
**κατοικία, ἡ** 10 • 10 *dwelling-place, habitation*
**ξηρός** 46 • 47 *dry, dried up*
**πύργος, ὁ** 147 • 148 *tower*
**ῥάβδος, ἡ** 58 • 62 *rod, stick, staff*
**σχισμή, ἡ** 25 • 25 *crack, fissure*
**ταχύς** 11 • 18 *in a short time, soon*
**χλωρός** 44 • 44 *green, fresh*
2 **διχοστασία, ἡ** 4 • 6 *dissension*
**διψυχέω** [2] 21 • 25 *to be undecided, be changeable, doubt*
**δυσκόλως** 7 • 7 *with difficulty, hardly*
**μετάνοια, ἡ** 58 • 72 *repentance, turning about, conversion*
3 **ἀδιστάκτως** 8 • 8 *without delay, without doubting, without hesitating*
**ἀνομία, ἡ** 9 • 33 *lawless deeds, lawlessness*
**ἀρετή, ἡ** 5 • 6 *excellence of character, exceptional civic virtue*
**ἀφίστημι** 19 • 19 *to fall away, go away, withdraw*
**βαστάζω** 18 • 24 *to carry, bear*
**ἐλάχιστος** 13 • 16 *very small*
**ἐπιδίδωμι** 60 • 62 *to give, hand over, deliver*
**ἡδέως** [2] 7 • 10 *gladly*
**μετάνοια, ἡ** 58 • 72 *repentance, turning about, conversion*
**ξηρός** 46 • 47 *dry, dried up*
**οὐδέποτε** 4 • 6 *never*
**ῥάβδος, ἡ** 58 • 62 *rod, stick, staff*
**ὑποδέχομαι** 2 • 3 *to receive, welcome, entertain as a guest*
**χλωρός** 44 • 44 *green, fresh*
4 **ἡδέως** 7 • 10 *gladly*
**θλίβω** 19 • 25 *to oppress, afflict*
**κατοικία, ἡ** 10 • 10 *dwelling-place, habitation*
**πρᾶξις, ἡ** 44 • 50 *act, action, deed*
**πύργος, ὁ** 147 • 148 *tower*

## Chapter 77 (Hs 8.11)

1 **ἐπίλυσις, ἡ** 6 • 6 *explanation, interpretation*
**καίπερ** 3 • 7 *although*
**κλῆσις, ἡ** 2 • 4 *call, calling, invitation*
**μακρόθυμος** 5 • 9 *patient, forbearing, tolerant, even-tempered*
**μετάνοια, ἡ** 58 • 72 *repentance, turning about, conversion*
**ῥάβδος, ἡ** 58 • 62 *rod, stick, staff*
**σπλαγχνίζομαι** 8 • 9 *to have pity, feel sympathy*
**συντελέω** 9 • 15 *to bring to an end, complete, finish, close*
3 **διψυχέω** 21 • 25 *to be in doubt, be undecided, be changeable*
**ἴασις, ἡ** 6 • 7 *forgiveness, cure, deliverance*
**κατακρίνω** 1 • 6 *to pronounce a sentence on*
**μηκέτι** 12 • 16 *no longer, not from now on*
**πονηρία, ἡ** 36 • 41 *wickedness, baseness, maliciousness, sinfulness*
**προλέγω** 5 • 16 *to state beforehand/earlier*
**προστίθημι** [2] 13 • 22 *to add to, increase*
**πρότερος** 40 • 47 *former, earlier*
4 **ὀρθῶς** 3 • 8 *rightly, correctly*

# PARABLE NINE

## Chapter 78 (Hs 9.1)

1 **μετάνοια, ἡ** 58 • 72 *repentance, turning about, conversion*
**μορφή, ἡ** 6 • 8 *form, outward appearance, shape*
**ποιμήν, ὁ** 51 • 55 *shepherd*
2 **ἀσθενής** 4 • 12 *weak*
**δηλόω** 32 • 49 *to reveal, make clear, show*
**ἐνδυναμόω** 12 • 14 *to become strong, grow strong*
**ἐπειδή** 3 • 17 *because, since*
**ἰσχύς, ἡ** 2 • 11 *strength, might, power*

**ἰσχύω** 4 • 9 *to have power, be competent, be able*
**οἰκοδομή, ἡ** 100 • 103 *building, edifice*
**παρθένος, ἡ** 58 • 62 *virgin;*
**ὡς ὑπὸ παρθένου** *as from a young girl*
**πύργος, ὁ** 147 • 148 *tower*
**σεμνῶς** 3 • 4 *honorably, worthily, in a manner above reproach*
3 **ἀκριβής** 2 • 2 *exact, strict*
**δειλαίνω** 1 • 2 *to be cowardly, be fearful*
**δυνατῶς** 1 • 1 *strongly, keenly*
**ἔνδοξος** 43 • 54 *glorious, splendid*
**μανθάνω** 1 • 26 *to learn*
**πρότερος** 40 • 47 *the first time*
4 **ἄκρον, τό** 3 • 3 *high point, top*
**ἀπάγω** 2 • 4 *to lead off, take away*
**Ἀρκαδία, ἡ** 1 • 1 *Arcadia*
**ἰδέα, ἡ** 8 • 9 *appearance*
**κύκλῳ** 17 • 18 *around*
**μαστώδης** 1 • 1 *breast-shaped, rounded*
**πεδίον, τό** [2] 15 • 17 *level place, plain, field*
5 **ἀκανθώδης** 4 • 4 *thorny*
**ἀσβόλη, ἡ** 2 • 2 *soot*
**βοτάνη, ἡ** 27 • 30 *herb, plant*
**μέλας** 17 • 20 *black*
**πλήρης** 13 • 20 *filled, full*
**τρίβολος, ὁ** 7 • 7 *thistle*
**ψιλός** 2 • 2 *bare*
6 **βοτάνη, ἡ** [3] 27 • 30 *herb, plant*
**ἐπάνω** 5 • 8 *on, over, above;* subst. *the upper part*
**ἐπικαίω** 1 • 1 *to scorch;*
**ἐπικεκαύκει** (pluperfect act. indicative) *had scorched*
**ἡμίξηρος** 11 • 11 *half dry, half withered*
**ξηρός** [2] 46 • 47 *dry, dried up*
**ῥίζα, ἡ** 4 • 8 *root*
**τέταρτος** 4 • 9 *fourth*
**χλωρός** 44 • 44 *green, fresh*
7 **βοτάνη, ἡ** [3] 27 • 30 *herb, plant*
**γέμω** 1 • 4 *to be full*
**ἕκτος** 2 • 3 *sixth*
**εὐθαλής** 5 • 5 *flourishing, thriving*
**λίαν** [2] 43 • 48 *exceedingly, very (much)*
**μαραίνω** 4 • 4 *to wither, die out, fade, disappear*
**πέμπτος** 3 • 5 *fifth*
**σχισμή, ἡ** [2] 25 • 25 *crack, fissure*
**τραχύς** 6 • 6 *rough, uneven*
**χλωρός** 44 • 44 *green, fresh*
8 **βόσκω** 4 • 4 *to graze, feed*
**βοτάνη, ἡ** [2] 27 • 30 *herb, plant*
**γένος, τό** [2] 8 • 16 *class, kind*
**ἕβδομος** 2 • 6 *seventh*
**εὐθηνέω** 3 • 3 *to thrive, flourish, be in good condition*
**θάλλω** 1 • 1 *to grow up, flourish*
**ἱλαρός** 24 • 34 *cheerful, glad, happy, blooming*
**κτῆνος, τό** [2] 4 • 4 *livestock*
**κτίσις, ἡ** 13 • 19 *that which is created, creature*
**νέμω** 3 • 3 *to feed, graze*
**ὄγδοος** 2 • 5 *eighth*
**ὄρνις, τό** 1 • 1 *bird, hen*
**πετεινόν, τό** 2 • 6 *bird*
**πηγή, ἡ** [2] 4 • 7 *spring, fountain*
**πλήρης** 13 • 20 *filled, full*
**ποτίζω** 5 • 7 *to water*
9 **ἀναπαύω** 4 • 13 *to rest*
**δέκατος** 2 • 2 *tenth*
**δένδρον, τό** 26 • 28 *tree*
**διαφθείρω** 8 • 12 *to spoil, destroy*
**ἔνατος** 2 • 2 *ninth*
**ἐρημώδης** 3 • 3 *desert-like*
**ἑρπετόν, τό** 2 • 2 *snake, reptile*
**θανάσιμος** 1 • 2 *deadly, death-dealing*
**κατάκειμαι** 1 • 2 *to rest, lie down*
**κατάσκιος** 1 • 1 *shaded*
**μαρυκάομαι** 1 • 2 *to ruminate, chew the cud*
**ὅλως** 30 • 31 *completely, wholly, everywhere;*
with a negative *not at all*
**σκέπη, ἡ** 3 • 3 *shade*
10 **δένδρον, τό** 26 • 28 *tree*
**δωδέκατος** 2 • 3 *twelfth*
**ἑνδέκατος** 2 • 2 *eleventh*
**ἐπιθυμέω** 7 • 17 *to desire, long for*
**εὐπρεπής** 6 • 7 *beautiful, looking well*
**ἱλαρός** 24 • 34 *cheerful, glad, happy*
**κατάκαρπος** 1 • 1 *very fruitful*
**κοσμέω** 3 • 10 *to adorn*
**λευκός** 24 • 24 *white*
**λίαν** [2] 43 • 48 *exceedingly, very (much)*

**πρόσοψις, ἡ** 1 • 1 *appearance, aspect*
**σύνδενδρος** 1 • 1 *covered with trees, forested*

## Chapter 79 (Hs 9.2)

1 **λευκός** 24 • 24 *white*
**πεδίον, τό** [2] 15 • 17 *level place, plain, field*
**πέτρα, ἡ** [2] 15 • 20 *rock*
**τετράγωνος** 9 • 9 *(four)square, shaped like a cube*
**ὑψηλός** 5 • 12 *tall, high*
**χωρέω** 3 • 15 *to hold, contain*
2 **ἐκκόλαψις, ἡ** 1 • 1 *the chiseling out*
**ἐκκόπτω** 1 • 3 *to hew out, cut off/down*
**λαμπηδών, ἡ** 1 • 1 *brightness, brilliance*
**παλαιός** 3 • 7 *old*
**πέτρα, ἡ** 15 • 20 *rock*
**πρόσφατος** 1 • 1 *new, recent*
**πύλη, ἡ** [4] 32 • 37 *gate, door*
**στίλβω** 1 • 1 *to shine, be radiant*
3 **ἀνά** [2] 3 • 4 *in the middle, between*
**γωνία, ἡ** 4 • 5 *corner*
**ἔνδοξος** [2] 43 • 54 *glorious, splendid*
**κύκλῳ** 17 • 18 *around*
**παρθένος, ἡ** [2] 58 • 62 *virgin*
**πύλη, ἡ** [2] 32 • 37 *gate, door*
**τέσσαρες** [2] 11 • 12 *four*
4 **βαστάζω** 18 • 24 *to carry, bear*
**ἐνδύω** 29 • 32 *to clothe oneself in, put on, wear*
**ἕτοιμος** 3 • 9 *ready*
**εὐπρεπῶς** 2 • 2 *fittingly, appropriately*
**ἱλαρός** 24 • 34 *cheerful, glad, happy*
**λίαν** 43 • 48 *exceedingly, very (much)*
**λινοῦς** 4 • 4 *linen, (made of) linen*
**περιζώννυμι** 6 • 6 *to gird about*
**πρόθυμος** 2 • 4 *willing, eager, ready*
**φορτίον, τό** 1 • 1 *load*
**χιτών, ὁ** 2 • 3 *tunic, shirt*
**ὦμος, ὁ** 5 • 5 *shoulder*
5 **ἀνδρείως** 2 • 2 *bravely, manly;* with reference to women *firm*
**βαστάζω** 18 • 24 *to carry, bear*
**διαπορέω** 2 • 2 *to be greatly perplexed, be at a loss*
**ἔνδοξος** 43 • 54 *glorious, splendid*
**παρθένος, ἡ** 58 • 62 *virgin*
**πρᾶγμα, τό** 19 • 23 *thing, matter, affair*
**τρυφερός** 4 • 4 *delicate, gentle, subdued*
6 **διαλογίζομαι** 6 • 6 *to consider, ponder, reason*
**διαπορέω** 2 • 2 *to be greatly perplexed, be at a loss*
**ἐπισπάω** 3 • 4 *to bring upon*
**ἐπιχειρέω** 1 • 1 *to attempt, endeavor, try*
**λύπη, ἡ** 23 • 24 *sorrow, grief, affliction*
**νοέω** [2] 30 • 46 *to perceive, apprehend, understand, gain an insight into*
**ποιμήν, ὁ** 51 • 55 *shepherd*
**σύνεσις, ἡ** 13 • 22 *understanding, wisdom*
**συνετός** 4 • 7 *intelligent, sagacious, wise, with good sense*
7 **δηλόω** 32 • 49 *to explain, clarify*
**ἐάω** 5 • 13 *to avoid, let go, leave alone*
**ἐμβλέπω** 2 • 5 *to look at, gaze on*
**κατακυριεύω** 13 • 15 *to become master, gain dominion over, subdue, gain power over*
**περιεργάζομαι** 1 • 1 *to concern oneself, be a busybody, meddler*
**στρεβλόω** 1 • 1 *to trouble, torture, torment*

## Chapter 80 (Hs 9.3)

1 **ἔνδοξος** 43 • 54 *glorious, splendid*
**ἕξ** [2] 16 • 23 *six*
**ἐπάνω** 5 • 8 *above, over*
**θόρυβος, ὁ** 1 • 4 *turmoil, excitement, uproar*
**ἰδέα, ἡ** 8 • 9 *appearance*
**κἀκεῖσε** 1 • 1 *and there*
**κελεύω** 32 • 44 *to command, order, urge*
**κύκλῳ** 17 • 18 *around*

**περιτρέχω** 2 • 2 *to run/move around*
**πέτρα, ἡ** 15 • 20 *rock*
**πύλη, ἡ** 32 • 37 *gate, door*
**πύργος, ὁ** [2] 147 • 148 *tower*
**ὑψηλός** [2] 5 • 12 *tall, high*
2 **ἐκπετάννυμι** 1 • 2 *to spread/hold out;*
**ἐκπεπετάκεισαν** (pluperfect act.) *had spread out*
**παρθένος, ἡ** [2] 58 • 62 *virgin*
**πύλη, ἡ** 32 • 37 *gate, door*
**πύργος, ὁ** 147 • 148 *tower*
**σπεύδω** 1 • 4 *to make haste, hasten, hurry*
3 **βυθός, ὁ** 12 • 14 *sea, deep water*
**ἕξ** 16 • 23 *six*
**ι´** 5 • 6 numerical sign for ten, *10*
**κελεύω** 32 • 44 *to command, order, urge*
**λαμπρός** 14 • 14 *gleaming, bright*
**λατομέω** 15 • 15 *to hew, shape*
**οἰκοδομή, ἡ** 100 • 103 *building, edifice*
**πύργος, ὁ** 147 • 148 *tower*
**τετράγωνος** 9 • 9 *(four)square*
4 **βαστάζω** 18 • 24 *to carry, bear*
**δέκα** 3 • 10 *ten*
**διαπορεύομαι** 1 • 1 *to go, walk through*
**ἕξ** 16 • 23 *six*
**ἐπιδίδωμι** 60 • 62 *to give, hand over, deliver*
**κελεύω** 32 • 44 *to command, order, urge*
**οἰκοδομή, ἡ** 100 • 103 *building, edifice*
**παρθένος, ἡ** 58 • 62 *virgin*
**πύλη, ἡ** 32 • 37 *gate, door*
**πύργος, ὁ** [2] 147 • 148 *tower*
5 **βαστάζω** 18 • 24 *to carry, bear*
**βυθός, ὁ** 12 • 14 *sea, deep water*
**δέκα** 3 • 10 *ten*
**ὁμοῦ** 3 • 5 *together at the same time (as), in company (with)*
**παρθένος, ἡ** 58 • 62 *virgin*

## Chapter 81 (Hs 9.4)

1 **βαστάζω** [2] 18 • 24 *to carry, bear*
**γωνία, ἡ** 4 • 5 *corner*
**διαφέρω** 4 • 5 *to carry through*
**ἐπιδίδωμι** 60 • 62 *to give, hand over, deliver*
**κελεύω** 32 • 44 *to command, order, urge*
**κύκλῳ** 17 • 18 *around*
**ὁμοῦ** 3 • 5 *together*
**πλευρά, ἡ** 1 • 1 *side*
**πύλη, ἡ** [2] 32 • 37 *gate, door*
**πύργος, ὁ** 147 • 148 *tower*
**ὑποδύομαι** [2] 2 • 2 *to get under, take one's place under;*
**ὑποδεδύκεισαν** (pluperfect act.) *had got under*
2 **ἀναπίμπλημι** 1 • 1 *to cover*
**ἁρμόζω** 20 • 23 *to join*
**βαστάζω** 18 • 24 *to support, carry, bear*
**ἐπάνω** 5 • 8 *on, above, over*
**θεμέλιος, ὁ** 3 • 4 *foundation*
**ι´** 5 • 6 numerical sign for ten, *10*
**οἰκοδομή, ἡ** [2] 100 • 103 *building, edifice*
**πέτρα, ἡ** [3] 15 • 20 *rock*
**πύλη, ἡ** [2] 32 • 37 *gate, door*
**πύργος, ὁ** [3] 147 • 148 *tower*
3 **ἁρμόζω** [2] 20 • 23 *to join*
**βαστάζω** 18 • 24 *to carry, bear*
**βυθός, ὁ** 12 • 14 *sea, deep water*
**θεμέλιος, ὁ** 3 • 4 *foundation*
**ι´** 5 • 6 numerical sign for ten, *10*
**κε´** 3 • 3 numerical sign for twenty-five, *25*
**λε´** 3 • 3 numerical sign for thirty-five, *35*
**μ´** 4 • 4 numerical sign for forty, *40*
**οἰκοδομή, ἡ** [2] 100 • 103 *building, edifice*
**παρθένος, ἡ** 58 • 62 *virgin*
**πρότερος** 40 • 47 *former, earlier*
**πύργος, ὁ** [4] 147 • 148 *tower*
**στοῖχος, ὁ** 1 • 1 *row, course*
**τέσσαρες** 11 • 12 *four*
4 **βυθός, ὁ** 12 • 14 *sea, deep water*
**ἕξ** 16 • 23 *six*
**ἐπιτάσσω** 2 • 7 *to order, command*
**οἰκοδομή, ἡ** 100 • 103 *building, edifice*
**παραφέρω** 6 • 7 *to bring up*
**παύω** [2] 8 • 12 *to stop (oneself), cease*
**πύργος, ὁ** 147 • 148 *tower*
5 **ἀλλάσσω** 3 • 5 *to change, alter*
**διαφέρω** 4 • 5 *to carry through*

**ἐπιδίδωμι** [2] 60 • 62 *to give, hand over, deliver*
**λατομέω** 15 • 15 *to hew, shape*
**λευκός** 24 • 24 *white*
**οἰκοδομή, ἡ** [2] 100 • 103 *building, edifice*
**παραφέρω** 6 • 7 *to bring up*
**παρθένος, ἡ** [2] 58 • 62 *virgin*
**ποικίλος** [2] 20 • 22 first instance: *diversified, manifold;* second instance: *many-colored, variegated*
**πρότερος** 40 • 47 *former, earlier*
**πύλη, ἡ** 32 • 37 *gate, door*
**πύργος, ὁ** 147 • 148 *tower*
**χρόα, ἡ** [2] 6 • 6 *color*
6 **ἀπρεπής** 2 • 2 *unsuitable*
**ἐπιδίδωμι** [2] 60 • 62 *to give, hand over, deliver*
**λαμπρός** 14 • 14 *gleaming, bright*
**οἰκοδομή, ἡ** [2] 100 • 103 *building, edifice*
**οἷος** 8 • 10 *of what sort, such as*
**παραφέρω** 6 • 7 *to bring up*
**παρθένος, ἡ** 58 • 62 *virgin*
**πύλη, ἡ** 32 • 37 *gate, door*
**πύργος, ὁ** 147 • 148 *tower*
7 **ἀπάγω** 2 • 4 *to lead off, take away*
**ἀπρεπής** 2 • 2 *unsuitable*
**ἕξ** 16 • 23 *six*
**κάτω** 1 • 3 *downwards, down*
**κελεύω** 32 • 44 *to command, order, urge*
**ὅθεν** 4 • 16 *from where, whence, from which*
**οἰκοδομή, ἡ** 100 • 103 *building, edifice*
8 **ἀλλάσσω** 3 • 5 *to change, alter*
**διαφέρω** 4 • 5 *to carry through*
**ἐπιδίδωμι** [2] 60 • 62 *to give, hand over, deliver*
**κοπιάω** 2 • 4 *to work hard, toil, strive, struggle*
**μάτην** 5 • 5 *in vain, to no end*
**οἰκοδομή, ἡ** [2] 100 • 103 *building, edifice*
**ὅλως** 30 • 31 *completely, wholly, everywhere;* with a negative *not at all*
**παραφέρω** 6 • 7 *to bring up*
**παρεμφέρω** 1 • 1 *to bring in*
**παρθένος, ἡ** [2] 58 • 62 *virgin*
**πύλη, ἡ** [2] 32 • 37 *gate, door*
**πύργος, ὁ** 147 • 148 *tower*
**χρόα, ἡ** 6 • 6 *color*

## Chapter 82 (Hs 9.5)

1 **ἀναπαύω** 4 • 13 *to rest*
**ἀναχωρέω** [2] 7 • 7 *to go away*
**ἀνοχή, ἡ** 3 • 3 *pause*
**ἀποτελέω** 4 • 4 *to bring to completion, finish*
**ἕξ** 16 • 23 *six*
**ἐπιτάσσω** 2 • 7 *to order, command*
**ἐποικοδομέω** 2 • 2 *to build onto*
**καταλείπω** 6 • 12 *to cease, leave to one side, give up*
**κελεύω** 32 • 44 *to command, order, urge*
**οἰκοδομή, ἡ** [2] 100 • 103 *building, construction*
**παρθένος, ἡ** [2] 58 • 62 *virgin*
**πύργος, ὁ** [3] 147 • 148 *tower*
**τελέω** 22 • 23 *to bring to an end, finish, complete*
2 **ἀλλάσσω** 3 • 5 *to exchange*
**ἀναπαύω** 4 • 13 *to rest*
**ἀναχωρέω** 7 • 7 *to go away*
**ἀποτελέω** 4 • 4 *to bring to completion, finish*
**δοκιμάζω** 10 • 19 *to put to the test, examine, evaluate*
**οἰκοδομή, ἡ** [2] 100 • 103 *building, edifice*
**οὔπω** 2 • 3 *not yet*
**ποιμήν, ὁ** 51 • 55 *shepherd*
**πύργος, ὁ** [3] 147 • 148 *tower*
**σαπρός** 3 • 3 *of poor quality, unusable, unfit, bad*
**συντελέω** 9 • 15 *to bring to an end, complete, finish, close*
3 **βυθός, ὁ** 12 • 14 *sea, deep water*
**λατομέω** 15 • 15 *to hew, shape*
**οἰκοδομή, ἡ** [2] 100 • 103 *building, edifice*
**παρθένος, ἡ** 58 • 62 *virgin*
**πέτρα, ἡ** 15 • 20 *rock*
**πύλη, ἡ** 32 • 37 *gate, door*
**πύργος, ὁ** 147 • 148 *tower*
4 **ἀναπαύω** 4 • 13 *to set at rest, cause to rest, give rest, refresh, revive*
**ἀποτίθημι** 7 • 13 *to put back, put away, lay down*

γνωρίζω 10 • 18 *to make known, reveal*
διατί 27 • 29 *why?*
εἶτα [3] 30 • 48 *then, next*
θεμέλιον, τό 3 • 4 *foundation, basis*
ί 5 • 6 numerical sign for ten, *10*
κέ 3 • 3 numerical sign for twenty-five, *25*
λέ 3 • 3 numerical sign for thirty-five, *35*
μ΄ 4 • 4 numerical sign for forty, *40*
οἰκοδομή, ἡ 100 • 103 *building, edifice*

5 ἀκριβῶς 5 • 8 *accurately, carefully, well*
ἐνθάδε 1 • 5 *here, to this place*
ἐπέρχομαι 6 • 8 *to come (on), approach*
κενόσπουδος 1 • 1 *concerning oneself about worthless things*
πύργος, ὁ 147 • 148 *tower*

6 αὐθέντης, ὁ 1 • 1 *master*
κατανοέω 21 • 26 *to inspect, consider, contemplate*
ὅλως 30 • 31 *completely, wholly, everywhere;*
with a negative *not at all*
παρθένος, ἡ 58 • 62 *virgin*
πύργος, ὁ [3] 147 • 148 *tower*

7 δεσπότης, ὁ 24 • 54 *lord, master*
κατανοέω 21 • 26 *to inspect, consider, contemplate*
οἰκοδομή, ἡ 100 • 103 *building, edifice*
παρθένος, ἡ 58 • 62 *virgin*
ποιμήν, ὁ 51 • 55 *shepherd*
πύργος, ὁ 147 • 148 *tower*

## Chapter 83 (Hs 9.6)

1 μέγεθος, τό 1 • 5 *size*
παράταξις, ἡ 3 • 3 *array, procession*
πύργος, ὁ 147 • 148 *tower*
ὑπερέχω 5 • 7 *to rise above, surpass, excel*
ὑψηλός 5 • 12 *tall, high*

2 ἀριστερός 4 • 5 *left*
ἔνδοξος 43 • 54 *glorious, splendid*
ἕξ 16 • 23 *six*
ἐφίστημι 2 • 5 *to be over, be in charge of*
καταφιλέω 3 • 3 *to kiss*
κύκλῳ [2] 17 • 18 *around*
οἰκοδομή, ἡ [2] 100 • 103 *building, edifice*
παρθένος, ἡ 58 • 62 *virgin*
προστρέχω 1 • 1 *to run up (to)*
πύργος, ὁ [2] 147 • 148 *tower*

3 ἀκριβῶς 5 • 8 *accurately, carefully, well*
κατανοέω 21 • 26 *to inspect, consider, contemplate*
οἰκοδομή, ἡ 100 • 103 *building, edifice*
ῥάβδος, ἡ 58 • 62 *rod, stick, staff*
τύπτω 1 • 2 *to strike*
ψηλαφάω 1 • 3 *to touch, handle*

4 ἀσβόλη, ἡ 2 • 2 *soot*
κολοβός 5 • 5 *mutilated, broken*
λευκός 24 • 24 *white*
μέλας [2] 17 • 20 *black*
οἰκοδομή, ἡ 100 • 103 *building, edifice*
πατάσσω 1 • 2 *to touch, strike*
ποικιλία, ἡ 3 • 3 *many-colored appearance, variety, diversity*
σαπρός 3 • 3 *of poor quality, unusable, unfit, bad*
σπίλος, ὁ 3 • 3 *spot, stain, blemish*
συμφωνέω 7 • 7 *to fit in with, match with, agree with*
σχισμή, ἡ 25 • 25 *crack, fissure*
τραχύς 6 • 6 *rough, uneven*
ψωριάω 5 • 5 *to have a rough surface*
ὡσεί 16 • 17 *as, like*

5 ἐμβάλλω 2 • 4 *to throw, set*
κελεύω 32 • 44 *to command, order, urge*
μεταφέρω 2 • 2 *to carry away*
πύργος, ὁ [2] 147 • 148 *tower*

6 ἐμβάλλω 2 • 4 *to throw, set*
κελεύω [2] 32 • 44 *to command, order, urge*
πεδίον, τό 15 • 17 *level place, plain, field*

7 βαστάζω 18 • 24 *to carry, bear*
λαμπρός 14 • 14 *gleaming, bright*
ὀρύσσω 1 • 2 *to dig up*
παρθένος, ἡ 58 • 62 *virgin*
πεδίον, τό [2] 15 • 17 *level place, plain, field*
ποτέ 4 • 15 *ever;*
ὅσοι ποτέ *whatever*
πύλη, ἡ 32 • 37 *gate, door*

στρογγύλος 10 • 10 *round*
τετράγωνος 9 • 9 *(four)square*
8 βραδέως 1 • 1 *slowly*
λαμπρός 14 • 14 *gleaming, bright*
λατομέω [3] 15 • 15 *to hew, shape*
λίαν 43 • 48 *exceedingly, very (much)*
οἰκοδομή, ἡ [2] 100 • 103 *building, edifice*
πύργος, ὁ 147 • 148 *tower*
σκληρός 9 • 9 *hard, rough*
στρογγύλος 10 • 10 *round*
τετράγωνος 9 • 9 *(four)square*

## Chapter 84 (Hs 9.7)

1 ἀποβάλλω 32 • 36 *to throw away, reject*
ἔνδοξος 43 • 54 *glorious, splendid*
κεῖμαι 22 • 24 *to lie*
οἰκοδομή, ἡ 100 • 103 *building, edifice*
ποιμήν, ὁ 51 • 55 *shepherd*
προσκαλέομαι 2 • 2 *to summon, call on, call to oneself, invite*
πύργος, ὁ [2] 147 • 148 *tower*
συντελέω 9 • 15 *to bring to an end, complete, finish, close*
2 ἁρμόζω [2] 20 • 23 *to fit, fit in*
ἐπιμελῶς 5 • 9 *carefully, diligently*
μακράν 9 • 15 *far (away)*
οἰκοδομή, ἡ 100 • 103 *building, edifice*
πύργος, ὁ [2] 147 • 148 *tower*
ῥίπτω 8 • 11 *to throw, throw away*
3 κελεύω 32 • 44 *to command, order, urge*
κύκλῳ 17 • 18 *around*
παρθένος, ἡ 58 • 62 *virgin*
ποιμήν, ὁ 51 • 55 *shepherd*
πύργος, ὁ [2] 147 • 148 *tower*
4 ἀποδοκιμάζω 3 • 5 *to reject*
ἁρμόζω 20 • 23 *to fit, fit in*
λατομέω 15 • 15 *to hew, shape*
οἰκοδομή, ἡ [2] 100 • 103 *building, edifice*
ποιμήν, ὁ 51 • 55 *shepherd*
πύργος, ὁ 147 • 148 *tower*
5 ἐξώτερος 5 • 5 *outside*
οἰκοδομή, ἡ 100 • 103 *building, edifice*
περικόπτω 4 • 5 *to hew all around*
συγκρατέω 3 • 3 *to hold together*
6 ἀμελής 2 • 2 *careless, negligent*
δεσπότης, ὁ [2] 24 • 54 *lord, master*
ἐξάπινα 1 • 1 *unexpectedly*
κύκλῳ 17 • 18 *around*
μήποτε 13 • 22 *lest*
οἰκοδομή, ἡ [2] 100 • 103 *building, edifice*
προσοχθίζω 1 • 1 *to be angry, be offended, be provoked*
πύργος, ὁ [3] 147 • 148 *tower*
ῥυπαρός 1 • 3 *filthy, soiled*
7 κατανοέω [2] 21 • 26 *to inspect, consider, contemplate*
οἰκοδομή, ἡ 100 • 103 *building, edifice*
πύργος, ὁ 147 • 148 *tower*

## Chapter 85 (Hs 9.8)

1 κατανοέω 21 • 26 *to inspect, consider, contemplate*
κελεύω 32 • 44 *to command, order, urge*
μέλας 17 • 20 *black*
μεταφέρω 2 • 2 *to carry away*
οἰκοδομή, ἡ 100 • 103 *building, edifice*
οἷος 8 • 10 *of what sort, such as*
ποιμήν, ὁ 51 • 55 *shepherd*
πύργος, ὁ 147 • 148 *tower*
χωρίζω 1 • 1 *to be taken away, take one's departure, go away*
2 εἶτα 30 • 48 *then, next*
κατανοέω 21 • 26 *to inspect, consider, contemplate*
κελεύω [2] 32 • 44 *to command, order, urge*
λατομέω [2] 15 • 15 *to hew, shape*
μέλας [2] 17 • 20 *black*
οἰκοδομή, ἡ [2] 100 • 103 *building, edifice*
παρθένος, ἡ [2] 58 • 62 *virgin*
πύργος, ὁ 147 • 148 *tower*
ψωριάω 5 • 5 *to have a rough surface*
3 αἰτία, ἡ 1 • 5 *cause, reason*
ἀποβάλλω 32 • 36 *to throw away, reject*
ἀποφέρω 8 • 9 *to carry, take away*
εἶτα 30 • 48 *then, next*
ἐξώτερος 5 • 5 *outside*

**κατανοέω** 21 • 26 *to inspect, consider, contemplate*
**κελεύω** 32 • 44 *to command, order, urge*
**λατομέω** 15 • 15 *to hew, shape*
**οἰκοδομή, ἡ** [2] 100 • 103 *building, edifice*
**παρθένος, ἡ** 58 • 62 *virgin*
**πύργος, ὁ** 147 • 148 *tower*
**σχίσμα, τό** 3 • 10 *tear, crack*
**σχισμή, ἡ** 25 • 25 *crack, fissure*
**ὑγιής** 9 • 9 *sound, undamaged*
4 **ἀποβάλλω** 32 • 36 *to throw away, reject*
**ἁρμόζω** 20 • 23 *to join*
**ἀσθενής** 4 • 12 *weak*
**εἶτα** 30 • 48 *then, next*
**κατανοέω** 21 • 26 *to inspect, consider, contemplate*
**κελεύω** [2] 32 • 44 *to command, order, urge*
**κολοβός** 5 • 5 *mutilated, broken*
**λατομέω** 15 • 15 *to hew, shape*
**μέλας** 17 • 20 *black*
**οἰκοδομή, ἡ** [2] 100 • 103 *building, edifice*
**παρθένος, ἡ** 58 • 62 *virgin*
**πύργος, ὁ** 147 • 148 *tower*
**σχισμή, ἡ** 25 • 25 *crack, fissure*
5 **ἀποβάλλω** 32 • 36 *to throw away, reject*
**ἁρμόζω** 20 • 23 *to join*
**εἶτα** 30 • 48 *then, next*
**ἐξώτερος** 5 • 5 *outside*
**ἥμισυς** [2] 11 • 11 *one-half*
**κατανοέω** 21 • 26 *to inspect, consider, contemplate*
**κελεύω** 32 • 44 *to command, order, urge*
**κολοβόω** 3 • 3 *to shorten*
**λευκός** [2] 24 • 24 *white*
**μέλας** [2] 17 • 20 *black*
**οἰκοδομή, ἡ** 100 • 103 *building, edifice*
**ὅλως** 30 • 31 *completely, wholly, everywhere;* with a negative *not at all*
**παρθένος, ἡ** [2] 58 • 62 *virgin*
**ὑγιής** 9 • 9 *sound, undamaged*
6 **ἀποβάλλω** 32 • 36 *to throw away, reject*
**ἁρμόζω** 20 • 23 *to join*
**ἀσθενής** 4 • 12 *weak*
**εἶτα** 30 • 48 *then, next*
**κατανοέω** 21 • 26 *to inspect, consider, contemplate*
**λατομέω** [2] 15 • 15 *to hew, shape*
**λίαν** 43 • 48 *exceedingly, very (much)*
**οἰκοδομή, ἡ** 100 • 103 *building, edifice*
**παρθένος, ἡ** 58 • 62 *virgin*
**πύργος, ὁ** 147 • 148 *tower*
**σκληρός** [2] 9 • 9 *hard, rough*
**τραχύς** 6 • 6 *rough, uneven*
7 **ἀποβάλλω** 32 • 36 *to throw away, reject*
**ἁρμόζω** 20 • 23 *to join*
**εἶτα** 30 • 48 *then, next*
**ἐλάχιστος** 13 • 16 *very few, very small/short*
**ἐξώτερος** 5 • 5 *outside*
**ἰσχυρότης, ἡ** 2 • 2 *solidity, strength*
**κατανοέω** 21 • 26 *to inspect, consider, contemplate*
**λαμπρός** 14 • 14 *gleaming, bright*
**μελανέω** 1 • 1 *to turn black*
**οἰκοδομή, ἡ** 100 • 103 *building, edifice*
**παρθένος, ἡ** 58 • 62 *virgin*
**σπίλος, ὁ** 3 • 3 *spot, stain, blemish*
**ὑγιής** 9 • 9 *sound, undamaged*

## Chapter 86 (Hs 9.9)

1 **εἶτα** 30 • 48 *then, next*
**ἐπινοέω** 1 • 2 *to notice*
**κατανοέω** 21 • 26 *to inspect, consider, contemplate*
**λευκός** 24 • 24 *white*
**στρογγύλος** 10 • 10 *round*
2 **ἀνάγκη, ἡ** 8 • 11 *necessity, pressure*
**ἀποκόπτω** 1 • 1 *to cut off, cut away*
**λατόμος, ὁ** 1 • 1 *stonecutter, stonemason*
**λίαν** 43 • 48 *exceedingly, very (much)*
**νοέω** 30 • 46 *to understand, perceive, apprehend, gain an insight into*
**οἰκοδομή, ἡ** 100 • 103 *building, edifice*
**στρογγύλος** 10 • 10 *round*
**τετράγωνος** 9 • 9 *(four)square*

**τέχνη, ἡ** 1 • 3 *skill, trade*
3 **ἀνάγκη, ἡ** 8 • 11 *necessity, pressure*
**ἁρμόζω** [2] 20 • 23 *to fit, fit in*
**βασανίζω** 15 • 18 *to torment*
**ἐκλέγομαι** [2] 5 • 15 *to choose (for oneself)*
**ἐξώτερος** 5 • 5 *outside*
**λαμπρός** 14 • 14 *gleaming, bright*
**λατομέω** 15 • 15 *to hew, shape*
**οἰκοδομή, ἡ** [2] 100 • 103 *building, edifice*
**παρθένος, ἡ** 58 • 62 *virgin*
4 **ἀποβάλλω** 32 • 36 *to throw away, reject*
**ἀποτίθημι** 7 • 13 *to put away, lay down*
**ἁρμόζω** 20 • 23 *to join*
**δεσπότης, ὁ** 24 • 54 *lord, master*
**λαμπρός** 14 • 14 *gleaming, bright*
**λείπω** 2 • 5 *to lack*
**λίαν** 43 • 48 *exceedingly, very (much)*
**ὅθεν** 4 • 16 *from where, whence, from which*
**οἰκοδομή, ἡ** 100 • 103 *building, edifice*
**πάντως** 7 • 9 *by all means, certainly, probably, doubtless*
**πεδίον, τό** 15 • 17 *level place, plain, field*
**πύργος, ὁ** [2] 147 • 148 *tower*
5 **ἄγριος** 5 • 8 *wild*
**ἀποβάλλω** 32 • 36 *to throw away, reject*
**ἀποφέρω** 8 • 9 *to carry, take away*
**ἐνδύω** 29 • 32 *to clothe oneself in, put on, wear*
**εὐειδής** 3 • 3 *beautiful, well-formed*
**θρίξ, ἡ** 7 • 7 *hair*
**κελεύω** 32 • 44 *to command, order, urge*
**μέλας** 17 • 20 *black*
**ὅθεν** 4 • 16 *from where, whence, from which*
**οἰκοδομή, ἡ** 100 • 103 *building, edifice*
**περιζώννυμι** 6 • 6 *to gird about*
**ποιμήν, ὁ** 51 • 55 *shepherd*
**χαρακτήρ, ὁ** 1 • 5 *outward appearance, outward aspect, form*
**ὦμος, ὁ** 5 • 5 *shoulder*
6 **ἀποφέρω** 8 • 9 *to carry, take away*
**ἐλάττωμα, τό** 1 • 1 *defect*
**ἱλαρός** 24 • 34 *cheerful, glad, happy*
**κεῖμαι** 22 • 24 *to lie*
**κυκλεύω** 1 • 1 *to go around*
**κυκλόω** 1 • 3 *to go around, circle round*
**κύκλῳ** 17 • 18 *around*
**μηκέτι** 12 • 16 *no longer, not from now on*
**ὅθεν** 4 • 16 *from where, whence, from which*
**ποιμήν, ὁ** 51 • 55 *shepherd*
**πύργος, ὁ** [2] 147 • 148 *tower*
7 **ἁρμογή, ἡ** 6 • 6 *joint*
**ἐκκολάπτω** 1 • 1 *to chisel out*
**ἐπιθυμέω** 7 • 17 *to desire, long for*
**εὐπρεπής** 6 • 7 *magnificent, looking well*
**ἱλαρός** 24 • 34 *cheerful, glad, happy*
**λίαν** 43 • 48 *exceedingly, very (much)*
**μονόλιθος** 2 • 2 *made of a single stone*
**οἰκοδομή, ἡ** [2] 100 • 103 *building, edifice*
**πέτρα, ἡ** 15 • 20 *rock*
**ποιμήν, ὁ** 51 • 55 *shepherd*
**πύργος, ὁ** [2] 147 • 148 *tower*
**ὡσάν** 1 • 2 *as if, as if were, so to speak*

## Chapter 87 (Hs 9.10)

1 **ἀναπληρόω** 1 • 4 *to fill a gap, replace, fill up*
**ἄσβεστος** 1 • 3 *inextinguishable;* subst. *unslaked lime*
**ἱλαρός** 24 • 34 *cheerful, glad, happy*
**κύκλῳ** 17 • 18 *around*
**λεπτός** 1 • 1 *small, thin, light*
**οἰκοδομή, ἡ** 100 • 103 *building, edifice*
**ὁμαλός** 5 • 5 *level, smooth, even*
**ὄστρακον, τό** 1 • 2 *baked clay, pottery*
**ποιμήν, ὁ** 51 • 55 *shepherd*
**πύργος, ὁ** 147 • 148 *tower*
**τύπος, ὁ** 10 • 26 *mark, trace*
2 **καθαρός** 25 • 45 *clean, pure*

**κελεύω** [2] 32 • 44 *to command, order, urge*
**κύκλῳ** 17 • 18 *around*
**οἰκοδομή, ἡ** 100 • 103 *building, edifice*
**πύργος, ὁ** 147 • 148 *tower*
**σαρόω** 2 • 2 *to sweep*
**τελέω** 22 • 23 *to bring to an end, finish, complete*
**τύπος, ὁ** 10 • 26 *mark, trace*
**ὑπηρετέω** 2 • 5 *to serve, be helpful*
3 **εὐπρεπής** 6 • 7 *attractive, looking well*
**ἱλαρός** 24 • 34 *cheerful, glad, happy*
**κόπριον, τό** 1 • 1 *dirt, filth*
**παρθένος, ἡ** 58 • 62 *virgin*
**πύργος, ὁ** [2] 147 • 148 *tower*
**ῥαίνω** 1 • 1 *to sprinkle*
**σάρος, ὁ** 1 • 1 *broom*
**σαρόω** 2 • 2 *to sweep*
4 **ἐπισκέπτομαι** 6 • 8 *to look at, examine, inspect*
**καθαίρω** 2 • 3 *to make clean*
**μέμφομαι** 3 • 4 *to find fault with, blame*
**ποιμήν, ὁ** 51 • 55 *shepherd*
**πύργος, ὁ** 147 • 148 *tower*
5 **ἀκαιρέομαι** 1 • 1 *to be busy, have no opportunity, have no time*
**ἐκδέχομαι** 2 • 5 *to wait*
**ἐπιλαμβάνομαι** 2 • 2 *to take hold of, grasp, catch*
**ἐπιλύω** [2] 8 • 8 *to explain, interpret*
**ὁρκίζω** 1 • 1 *to adjure, implore*
**πήρα, ἡ** 3 • 3 *knapsack, traveler's bag, shepherd's bag*
6 **παρατίθημι** 1 • 6 *to entrust (someone) to the care/protection of (someone)*
**παρθένος, ἡ** 58 • 62 *virgin*
**ποιμήν, ὁ** 51 • 55 *shepherd*
**προσκαλέω** 3 • 5 *to summon, call on, call to oneself, invite*
7 **ἔνδοξος** 43 • 54 *glorious, splendid*
**εὖ** 1 • 4 *well-disposed, gracious*
**ἱλαρός** 24 • 34 *cheerful, glad, happy*
**μάλιστα** 5 • 14 *most of all, above all, especially, particularly*
**παρθένος, ἡ** 58 • 62 *virgin*
**τέσσαρες** 11 • 12 *four*

## Chapter 88 (Hs 9.11)

1 **μέχρι** 7 • 23 *until*
**ὀψέ** 2 • 3 *late in the day, evening*
**παρθένος, ἡ** 58 • 62 *virgin*
**περιμένω** 1 • 2 *to wait for*
**ποιμήν, ὁ** 51 • 55 *shepherd*
2 **ἀναχωρέω** 7 • 7 *to go away*
**ἐκδέχομαι** 2 • 5 *to wait*
**ἐπανήκω** 1 • 1 *to come back again*
**ὀψέ** 2 • 3 *late in the day, evening*
**πρωΐ** 1 • 1 *early, early in the morning*
3 **αἰσχύνω** 1 • 3 *to be ashamed*
**ἡμέτερος** 2 • 13 *our*
**κοιμάω** 8 • 12 *to sleep, fall asleep*
**λίαν** 43 • 48 *exceedingly, very (much)*
4 **καταφιλέω** [2] 3 • 3 *to kiss*
**κύκλῳ** 17 • 18 *around*
**παίζω** 2 • 3 *to play, amuse oneself*
**περιάγω** 1 • 1 *to go around, go about*
**περιπλέκω** [2] 2 • 3 *to embrace*
**πύργος, ὁ** 147 • 148 *tower*
5 **ᾄδω** 1 • 6 *to sing (in praise)*
**ἱλαρός** 24 • 34 *cheerful, glad, happy*
**κύκλῳ** 17 • 18 *around*
**νέος** 7 • 16 *young*
**ὀρχέομαι** 1 • 1 *to dance in chorus*
**παίζω** 2 • 3 *to play, amuse oneself*
**πύργος, ὁ** 147 • 148 *tower*
**σιγή, ἡ** 1 • 3 *silence, quiet*
**χορεύω** 1 • 1 *to dance in chorus*
**ὡσεί** 16 • 17 *as, like*
6 **κατέχω** 1 • 4 *to hold back, hinder, prevent from going away*
**κοιμάω** 8 • 12 *to sleep, fall asleep*
**ὄψιος** 1 • 1 *evening*
**πύργος, ὁ** 147 • 148 *tower*
7 **ἀδιαλείπτως** 3 • 6 *constantly, unceasingly*
**ἀνακλίνω** 1 • 1 *to cause to lie down, lay down, lay*
**αὔριον** 2 • 2 *next day*
**ἐλάσσων** 4 • 6 *less*
**λινοῦς** 4 • 4 *linen, made of linen*
**μέχρι** 7 • 23 *until*
**ὅλως** 30 • 31 *completely, wholly, everywhere*; with a negative *not at all*
**παρθένος, ἡ** [3] 58 • 62 *virgin*
**στρώννυμι** 1 • 1 *to spread*

**χαμαί** 6 • 6 *on the ground*
**χιτών, ὁ** 2 • 3 *tunic, shirt*
8 **δειπνέω** [2] 2 • 2 *to eat, dine*
**εἶτα** 30 • 48 *then, next*
**εὐφραίνω** 6 • 15 *to be glad, enjoy oneself, rejoice, celebrate*
**ναί** 6 • 8 *yes, certainly, indeed, it's true that*
**πάρειμι** 3 • 17 *to come, be present*
**παρθένος, ἡ** 58 • 62 *virgin*
**ποιμήν, ὁ** 51 • 55 *shepherd*
**ὕβρις, ἡ** 2 • 4 *harm, shame, insult, mistreatment*
9 **ἀποκρύπτω** 1 • 1 *to keep secret*
**δηλόω** 32 • 49 *to explain, clarify*
**ἐπιλύω** 8 • 8 *to explain, interpret*
**ὅλως** 30 • 31 *completely, wholly, everywhere;* with a negative *not at all*

### Chapter 89 (Hs 9.12)

1 **ἀσύνετος** 11 • 16 *senseless, foolish*
**δηλόω** 32 • 49 *to explain, clarify*
**παλαιός** 3 • 7 *old*
**πέτρα, ἡ** [3] 15 • 20 *rock*
**πύλη, ἡ** [3] 32 • 37 *gate, door*
**συνίημι** 13 • 21 *to understand, comprehend*
2 **διατί** 27 • 29 *why?*
**κτίσις, ἡ** [2] 13 • 19 *creative work, creation, world; act of creation*
**παλαιός** 3 • 7 *old*
**πέτρα, ἡ** 15 • 20 *rock*
**προγενής** 1 • 1 *primeval;* comparative *older*
**πύλη, ἡ** 32 • 37 *gate, door*
**σύμβουλος, ὁ** 6 • 8 *adviser, counselor*
3 **πύλη, ἡ** 32 • 37 *gate, door*
**συντέλεια, ἡ** 2 • 3 *consummation, last, completion, close, end*
**φανερός** 4 • 9 *visible, clear, plainly to be seen, open, plain, evident, known*
4 **ἀποβάλλω** 32 • 36 *to put back, throw away, reject*
**οἰκοδομή, ἡ** 100 • 103 *building, edifice*
**πύλη, ἡ** 32 • 37 *gate, door*
**πύργος, ὁ** 147 • 148 *tower*
5 **ἄλλως** [2] 6 • 6 *otherwise, in another way*
**κύκλῳ** 17 • 18 *around*
**μήτι** 3 • 3 *not, no*
**περιτειχίζω** 2 • 3 *to wall around, surround with a wall*
**πύλη, ἡ** [3] 32 • 37 *gate, door*
6 **ἄλλως** 6 • 6 *otherwise, in another way*
**εἴσοδος, ἡ** 1 • 1 *entrance*
**ἔνδοξος** 43 • 54 *glorious, splendid*
**περιτειχίζω** 2 • 3 *to surround*
**πύλη, ἡ** 32 • 37 *gate, door*
**πύργος, ὁ** 147 • 148 *tower*
7 **ἀποδοκιμάζω** 3 • 5 *to reject*
**ἔνδοξος** 43 • 54 *glorious, splendid*
**ἕξ** 16 • 23 *six*
**οἰκοδομή, ἡ** 100 • 103 *building, edifice*
**πύργος, ὁ** 147 • 148 *tower*
8 **ἄτερ** 5 • 6 *without*
**ἔνδοξος** [3] 43 • 54 *glorious, splendid*
**ἕξ** 16 • 23 *six*
**εὐώνυμος** 2 • 2 *left*
**συγκρατέω** 3 • 3 *to surround (and protect)*

### Chapter 90 (Hs 9.13)

1 **πύργος, ὁ** [2] 147 • 148 *tower*
2 **ἄλλως** 6 • 6 *otherwise, in another way*
**ἔνδυμα, τό** [2] 5 • 5 *covering, garment*
**ἐνδύω** 29 • 32 *to dress, clothe*
**μάτην** 5 • 5 *in vain, to no end*
**παρθένος, ἡ** [2] 58 • 62 *virgin*
**φορέω** [3] 17 • 18 *to bear*
**ὠφελέω** 2 • 8 *to help, aid, benefit, be of use (to)*
3 **ἀποβάλλω** 32 • 36 *to throw away, reject*
**ἐνδύω** 29 • 32 *to clothe oneself in, put on, wear*
**ἱματισμός, ὁ** [3] 6 • 8 *clothing, apparel*
**παρθένος, ἡ** [2] 58 • 62 *virgin*
**φορέω** [4] 17 • 18 *to bear*
4 **ἐνδύω** 29 • 32 *to dress, clothe*
**ἐπιδίδωμι** 60 • 62 *to give, hand over, deliver*
**οἰκοδομή, ἡ** [2] 100 • 103 *building, edifice*

**παρθένος, ἡ** 58 • 62 *virgin*
**πύργος, ὁ** 147 • 148 *tower*
5 **ἐνδιδύσκω** 1 • 1 *to dress, put on*
**κατοικία, ἡ** 10 • 10 *dwelling-place, habitation*
**μονόλιθος** 2 • 2 *made of a single stone*
**παρθένος, ἡ** 58 • 62 *virgin*
**πέτρα, ἡ** 15 • 20 *rock*
**πύργος, ὁ** [2] 147 • 148 *tower*
**φορέω** 17 • 18 *to bear*
**χρόα, ἡ** 6 • 6 *color*
6 **ἀκριβῶς** 5 • 8 *accurately, carefully, well*
**ἀποβάλλω** [3] 32 • 36 *to throw away, reject*
**διατί** 27 • 29 *why?*
**ἐξετάζω** 2 • 3 *to scrutinize, examine, inquire*
**ἐπειδή** 3 • 17 *because, since*
**μέλει** 2 • 5 *it is a care/concern, it is of interest (to someone);*
**πάντα σοι μέλει** *everything interests you*
**οἰκοδομή, ἡ** 100 • 103 *building, edifice*
**παρθένος, ἡ** 58 • 62 *virgin*
**πύλη, ἡ** 32 • 37 *gate, door*
**πύργος, ὁ** 147 • 148 *tower*
7 **ἔνδυμα, τό** 5 • 5 *covering, garment*
**ἐνδυναμόω** 12 • 14 *to become strong, grow strong*
**παρθένος, ἡ** 58 • 62 *virgin*
**φρονέω** 5 • 17 *to think, form/hold an opinion, judge*
8 **ἀναπείθω** 1 • 1 *to incite, induce*
**ἀποδύομαι** 1 • 1 *to take off*
**ἔνδυμα, τό** 5 • 5 *covering, garment*
**ἐνδύω** [2] 29 • 32 *to clothe oneself in, put on, wear*
**ἐπιθυμέω** 7 • 17 *to desire*
**εὔμορφος** 1 • 1 *well-formed, beautiful*
**θρίξ, ἡ** 7 • 7 *hair*
**μέλας** 17 • 20 *black*
**παρθένος, ἡ** 58 • 62 *virgin*
**ὦμος, ὁ** 5 • 5 *shoulder*
9 **ἀπατάω** 8 • 9 *to lead astray, deceive, mislead*
**ἀποβάλλω** [2] 32 • 36 *to throw away, reject*
**ἐπίλυσις, ἡ** 6 • 6 *explanation, interpretation*
**κάλλος, τό** 4 • 5 *beauty*

## Chapter 91 (Hs 9.14)

1 **ἀποβάλλω** 32 • 36 *to take off, doff*
**ἐπανακάμπτω** 3 • 3 *to return*
**παρθένος, ἡ** 58 • 62 *virgin*
2 **ἀναλαμβάνω** 3 • 10 *to take back, take to one's self, adopt*
**ἀνοχή, ἡ** 3 • 3 *pause*
**ἀποβάλλω** 32 • 36 *to take off, doff*
**οἰκοδομή, ἡ** [2] 100 • 103 *building, construction*
**παρθένος, ἡ** 58 • 62 *virgin*
**πύργος, ὁ** 147 • 148 *tower*
3 **ἀνακαινίζω** 2 • 3 *to renew, restore*
**ἀνανεόω** 5 • 5 *to restore, renew*
**ἐξαποστέλλω** 3 • 4 *to send away, send off, send out*
**καταφθείρω** 8 • 8 *to ruin, corrupt*
**μετάνοια, ἡ** 58 • 72 *repentance, turning about, conversion*
**σπλαγχνίζομαι** 8 • 9 *to have pity, feel sympathy*
4 **ἀνάγκη, ἡ** 8 • 11 *necessity, pressure*
**ἀσύνετος** 11 • 16 *senseless, foolish*
**ἄφρων** 11 • 17 *foolish, ignorant*
**δηλόω** 32 • 49 *to explain, clarify*
**διατί** 27 • 29 *why?*
**δυσνόητος** 1 • 1 *hard to understand*
**ἔνδοξος** 43 • 54 *glorious, splendid*
**νοέω** 30 • 46 *to comprehend, perceive, apprehend, understand, gain an insight into*
**ὅλως** 30 • 31 *completely, wholly, everywhere;*
with a negative *not at all*
**πέτρα, ἡ** 15 • 20 *rock*
**πύλη, ἡ** 32 • 37 *gate, door*
**πύργος, ὁ** 147 • 148 *tower*
**χαμαί** 6 • 6 *on the ground*
5 **ἀχώρητος** 2 • 2 *illimitable, incomprehensible*
**βαστάζω** [2] 18 • 24 *to support, carry, bear*
**κτίσις, ἡ** 13 • 19 *creation, world*
**φορέω** 17 • 18 *to bear*
6 **βαστάζω** [2] 18 • 24 *to support, carry, bear*

**ἐπαισχύνομαι** 3 • 5 *to be ashamed*
**ἡδέως** 7 • 10 *gladly*
**θεμέλιος, ὁ** 3 • 4 *foundation*
**φορέω** [2] 17 • 18 *to bear*

## Chapter 92 (Hs 9.15)

1 **γωνία, ἡ** 4 • 5 *corner*
**δηλόω** 32 • 49 *to reveal, make clear, show*
**ἐνδύω** 29 • 32 *to clothe oneself in, put on, wear*
**ἰσχυρός** 14 • 21 *strong*
**μέλας** 17 • 20 *black*
**παρθένος, ἡ** [2] 58 • 62 *virgin*
2 **ἁγνεία, ἡ** 7 • 13 *purity, chastity*
**ἀκακία, ἡ** 8 • 10 *innocence, guilelessness*
**ἀνά** 3 • 4 *in the middle, between*
**ἁπλότης, ἡ** 12 • 15 *sincerity, simplicity, uprightness, frankness*
**ἐγκράτεια, ἡ** 7 • 14 *self-control*
**ἱλαρότης, ἡ** 4 • 4 *cheerfulness, gladness, wholeheartedness, graciousness*
**μακροθυμία, ἡ** 9 • 15 *patience, steadfastness, endurance*
**ὁμόνοια, ἡ** 2 • 24 *oneness of mind, unanimity, concord, harmony*
**σύνεσις, ἡ** 13 • 22 *understanding*
**τέταρτος** 4 • 9 *fourth*
**φορέω** 17 • 18 *to bear*
3 **ἀκόλουθος** 3 • 8 *following*
**ἀκρασία, ἡ** 1 • 1 *lack of self-control, self-indulgence*
**ἀπάτη, ἡ** 13 • 16 *deception, deceitfulness*
**ἀπείθεια, ἡ** 1 • 1 *disobedience, disbelief*
**ἀπιστία, ἡ** 1 • 4 *lack of belief, unbelief*
**ἀσέλγεια, ἡ** 3 • 3 *licentiousness, self-abandonment*
**ἀφροσύνη, ἡ** 7 • 11 *foolishness, lack of sense*
**καταλαλιά, ἡ** 7 • 13 *evil speech, slander, defamation, detraction*
**λύπη, ἡ** 23 • 24 *grief, sorrow, affliction*
**μέλας** 17 • 20 *black*
**μῖσος, τό** 1 • 2 *hate*
**ὀξυχολία, ἡ** 17 • 17 *irritability, bad temper*
**πονηρία, ἡ** 36 • 41 *wickedness, baseness, maliciousness, sinfulness*
**τέσσαρες** 11 • 12 *four*
**τέταρτος** 4 • 9 *fourth*
**φορέω** 17 • 18 *to bear*
**ψεῦδος, τό** 4 • 6 *a lie, falsehood*
4 **ἁρμόζω** 20 • 23 *to join*
**βυθός, ὁ** 12 • 14 *sea, deep water*
**διάκονος, ὁ** 3 • 29 *agent, intermediary, courier*
**θεμέλιον, τό** 3 • 4 *foundation, basis*
**ι´** 5 • 6 numerical sign for ten, *10*
**κέ** 3 • 3 numerical sign for twenty-five, *25*
**κήρυγμα, τό** 3 • 5 *proclamation*
**λέ** 3 • 3 numerical sign for thirty-five, *35*
**μ´** 4 • 4 numerical sign for forty, *40*
**οἰκοδομή, ἡ** 100 • 103 *building, edifice*
5 **διατί** 27 • 29 *why?*
**διαφέρω** 4 • 5 *to carry through*
**ἐπιδίδωμι** 60 • 62 *to give, hand over, deliver*
**οἰκοδομή, ἡ** 100 • 103 *building, edifice*
**παρθένος, ἡ** 58 • 62 *virgin*
**πύλη, ἡ** 32 • 37 *gate, door*
**πύργος, ὁ** 147 • 148 *tower*
6 **ἀφίστημι** 19 • 19 *to go away, withdraw*
**εὔχρηστος** 13 • 14 *useful, serviceable*
**κοίμησις, ἡ** 2 • 2 *sleep, death*
**μέχρι** 7 • 23 *until*
**οἰκοδομή, ἡ** 100 • 103 *building, edifice*
**ὅλως** 30 • 31 *completely, wholly, everywhere*; with a negative *not at all*
**παραμένω** 6 • 9 *to remain/stay with someone*
**πύργος, ὁ** 147 • 148 *tower*
**φορέω** 17 • 18 *to bear*

## Chapter 93 (Hs 9.16)

1 **βυθός, ὁ** 12 • 14 *sea, deep water*
**δηλόω** 32 • 49 *to explain, clarify*

**διατί** 27 • 29 *why?*
**ἐπιζητέω** 5 • 9 *to inquire, want to know*
**οἰκοδομή, ἡ** 100 • 103 *building, edifice*
**φορέω** 17 • 18 *to bear*
2 **ἄλλως** 6 • 6 *otherwise, in another way*
**ἀνάγκη, ἡ** 8 • 11 *necessity, pressure*
**ἀποτίθημι** 7 • 13 *to lay aside, rid oneself*
**ζωοποιέω** 3 • 10 *to make alive, give life to*
**νέκρωσις, ἡ** 2 • 2 *deadness, mortification*
**πρότερος** 40 • 47 *former, earlier*
3 **ἀναλαμβάνω** 3 • 10 *to receive, take to oneself, adopt*
**ἀποτίθημι** 7 • 13 *to lay aside, rid oneself*
**κοιμάω** 8 • 12 *to fall asleep, die, pass away*
**νέκρωσις, ἡ** 2 • 2 *deadness, mortification*
**πρίν** 4 • 7 *before*
**σφραγίς, ἡ** [2] 12 • 16 *attestation, confirmation, certification*; here as a term referring to baptism
**φορέω** 17 • 18 *to bear*
4 **σφραγίς, ἡ** [2] 12 • 16 *attestation, confirmation, certification*; here as a term referring to baptism
**χράομαι** 7 • 18 *to make use of, employ*
5 **βυθός, ὁ** 12 • 14 *sea, deep water*
**διατί** 27 • 29 *why?*
**κήρυγμα, τό** 3 • 5 *proclamation*
**κοιμάω** 8 • 12 *to fall asleep, die, pass away*
**μ´** 4 • 4 numerical sign for forty, *40*
**προκοιμάω** 2 • 2 *to fall asleep before/earlier, die before now*
**σφραγίς, ἡ** [2] 12 • 16 *attestation, confirmation, certification*; here as a term referring to baptism
6 **προκοιμάω** 2 • 2 *to fall asleep before/earlier, die before now*
7 **ἁγνεία, ἡ** 7 • 13 *purity, chastity*
**ἀλατόμητος** 1 • 1 *uncut*
**ἐπίλυσις, ἡ** 6 • 6 *explanation, interpretation*
**ζωοποιέω** 3 • 10 *to make alive, give life to*
**κοιμάω** 8 • 12 *to fall asleep, die, pass away*
**οἰκοδομή, ἡ** 100 • 103 *building, edifice*
**πύργος, ὁ** 147 • 148 *tower*
**συναναβαίνω** 1 • 1 *to come/go up with*
**συναρμόζω** 1 • 2 *to fit in (with)*
**συνοικοδομέω** 1 • 1 *to build in*
**σφραγίς, ἡ** 12 • 16 *attestation, confirmation, certification*; here as a term referring to baptism

## Chapter 94 (9.17)

1 **δηλόω** 32 • 49 *to explain, clarify*
**διατί** 27 • 29 *why?*
**ἰδέα, ἡ** 8 • 9 *appearance*
**ποικίλος** 20 • 22 *diversified, manifold*
2 **δηλόω** [2] 32 • 49 *to explain, clarify*
**διατί** 27 • 29 *why?*
**ἰδέα, ἡ** 8 • 9 *appearance*
**νοῦς, ὁ** [2] 5 • 12 *understanding, mind*
**οἷος** 8 • 10 *of what sort (such)*
**ποικιλία, ἡ** 3 • 3 *many-colored appearance, variety, diversity*
**ποικίλος** [3] 20 • 22 *diversified, manifold*
**πρᾶξις, ἡ** 44 • 50 *acting, activity, function*
**φρόνησις, ἡ** [2] 6 • 7 *way of thinking, frame of mind*
3 **βυθός, ὁ** 12 • 14 *sea, deep water*
**δηλόω** 32 • 49 *to explain, clarify*
**διατί** 27 • 29 *why?*
**λαμπρός** 14 • 14 *gleaming, bright*
**οἰκοδομή, ἡ** 100 • 103 *building, edifice*
**ποικίλος** 20 • 22 *diversified, manifold*
**χρόα, ἡ** 6 • 6 *color*
4 **λαμπρός** 14 • 14 *bright*
**νοῦς, ὁ** 5 • 12 *attitude, way of thinking*
**οἰκοδομή, ἡ** 100 • 103 *building, edifice*
**παρθένος, ἡ** 58 • 62 *virgin*
**πύργος, ὁ** 147 • 148 *tower*
**σφραγίς, ἡ** 12 • 16 *attestation, confirmation, certification*; here as a term referring to baptism

**φορέω** 17 • 18 *to bear*
**φρόνησις, ἡ** 6 • 7 *way of thinking, frame of mind*
**χρόα, ἡ** 6 • 6 *color*
5 **γένος, τό** 8 • 16 *nation, people*
**μιαίνω** 14 • 14 *to defile*
**οἷος** 8 • 10 *of what sort (such)*
**πρότερος** 40 • 47 *former, earlier*
**χείρων** 2 • 4 *worse, more severe*

## Chapter 95 (Hs 9.18)

1 **ἀγαθοποιέω** 4 • 6 *to do what is right, be a good citizen*
**κόλασις, ἡ** 1 • 11 *punishment*
**πονηρεύομαι** [2] 13 • 15 *to do wrong, commit sin*
**πονηρία, ἡ** 36 • 41 *wickedness, baseness, maliciousness, sinfulness*
**χείρων** 2 • 4 *worse, more severe*
2 **ἀγαθοποιέω** 4 • 6 *to do what is right, be a good citizen*
**δισσῶς** 1 • 1 *doubly*
**κολάζω** 2 • 9 *to punish, penalize*
**μεγαλεῖος** 3 • 6 subst. *greatness, sublimity; mighty deed*
**πονηρεύομαι** [3] 13 • 15 *to do wrong, commit sin*
**πονηρία, ἡ** 36 • 41 *wickedness, baseness, maliciousness, sinfulness*
3 **ἀποβάλλω** 32 • 36 *to reject*
**βλάσφημος** 3 • 3 *defaming, denigrating, demeaning*; of persons: *slanderer*
**δίψυχος** 20 • 23 *doubting, hesitating, double-minded*
**καθαίρω** 2 • 3 *to purify, make clean*
**ποικίλος** 20 • 22 *diversified, manifold*
**πονηρεύομαι** 13 • 15 *to do wrong, commit sin*
**πονηρία, ἡ** 36 • 41 *wickedness, baseness, maliciousness, sinfulness*
**πύργος, ὁ** [2] 147 • 148 *tower*
**ὑποκριτής, ὁ** 3 • 6 *actor, pretender, dissembler*
4 **ἀγαλλιάω** 6 • 11 *to exult, be glad, be overjoyed*
**ἀποβάλλω** 32 • 36 *to reject*
**ἀπολαμβάνω** 6 • 17 *to take back, recover, get back*
**ἐνδόξως** 2 • 5 *glorious, in splendor*
**εὐφραίνω** 6 • 15 *to be glad, enjoy oneself, rejoice, celebrate*
**καθαρός** 25 • 45 *pure, free*
**μεγάλως** 5 • 9 *greatly*
**νοῦς, ὁ** 5 • 12 *attitude, way of thinking*
**φρόνησις, ἡ** 6 • 7 *way of thinking, frame of mind*
5 **δηλόω** 32 • 49 *to reveal, make clear, show*
**ἔνδοξος** 43 • 54 *glorious, splendid*
**θαυμαστός** 2 • 13 *wonderful, marvelous, remarkable*
**ποικιλία, ἡ** 3 • 3 *many-colored appearance, variety, diversity*
**πρᾶξις, ἡ** 44 • 50 *acting, activity, function*

## Chapter 96 (Hs 9.19)

1 **ἄνομος** 1 • 17 *wicked, lawless*
**ἀποστάτης, ὁ** 3 • 3 *deserter, rebel*
**βλάσφημος** 3 • 3 *defaming, denigrating, demeaning*; of persons: *slanderer*
**γένος, τό** 8 • 16 *nation, people*
**μέλας** [2] 17 • 20 *black*
**μετάνοια, ἡ** 58 • 72 *repentance, turning about, conversion*
**προδότης, ὁ** 5 • 6 *traitor, betrayer*
2 **ἄκαρπος** 3 • 3 *unfruitful, fruitless, barren*
**βραδύνω** 1 • 2 *to hesitate, delay*
**κεῖμαι** 22 • 24 *to be given, exist, be valid*
**κενός** 20 • 27 *empty*
**μετάνοια, ἡ** 58 • 72 *repentance, turning about, conversion*
**πονηρία, ἡ** 36 • 41 *wickedness, baseness, maliciousness, sinfulness*
**πρότερος** [2] 40 • 47 *former, earlier*
**ταχύς** 11 • 18 *in a short time, soon*
**ὑποκριτής, ὁ** 3 • 6 *actor, pretender, dissembler*
**ψιλός** 2 • 2 *bare*

3 **βλάσφημος** 3 • 3 *defaming, denigrating, demeaning;* of persons: *slanderer*
**διατί** 27 • 29 *why?*
**δίκη, ἡ** 2 • 3 *punishment, penalty*
**κεῖμαι** [2] 22 • 24 *to be given, exist, be valid*
**λῆμμα, τό** 1 • 1 *gain*
**μετάνοια, ἡ** [3] 58 • 72 *repentance, turning about, conversion*
**πρᾶξις, ἡ** 44 • 50 *way of acting, course of action*
**προδότης, ὁ** [2] 5 • 6 *traitor, betrayer*
**τίνω** 2 • 2 *to pay, undergo a penalty*
**ὑποκρίνομαι** 1 • 1 *to play a role, act a part, dissemble*

### Chapter 97 (Hs 9.20)

1 **ἄκανθα, ἡ** [2] 6 • 9 *thorn-plant*
**ἐμφύρω** [2] 6 • 6 *to mix up, involve*
**πλούσιος** [2] 13 • 22 *rich, wealthy*
**ποικίλος** 20 • 22 *diversified, manifold*
**πραγματεία, ἡ** [2] 11 • 11 *activity, occupation;* pl. *undertakings, business, affairs*
**τρίβολος, ὁ** [2] 7 • 7 *thistle*
2 **αἰτίζω** 1 • 1 *to beg*
**ἀποπλανάω** 6 • 8 *to lead into error, mislead*
**δυσκόλως** [2] 7 • 7 *hardly, with difficulty*
**ἐμφύρω** 6 • 6 *to mix up, involve*
**κολλάω** [2] 12 • 32 *to join oneself to, join, cling to, associate with*
**πλούσιος** 13 • 22 *rich, wealthy*
**πνίγω** 4 • 4 *to choke*
**ποικίλος** 20 • 22 *diversified, manifold*
**πραγματεία, ἡ** 11 • 11 *activity, occupation;* pl. *undertakings, business, affairs*
**πρᾶξις, ἡ** 44 • 50 *undertaking, business*
3 **γυμνός** 1 • 3 *naked, stripped, bare*
**δύσκολος** [2] 3 • 5 *hard, difficult*
**τρίβολος, ὁ** 7 • 7 *thistle*
4 **ἀνατρέχω** 1 • 1 *to make up for, make amends for*
**ἐπιμένω** 10 • 16 *to continue, persist in, persevere*
**θανατόω** 3 • 7 *to bring death*
**μετάνοια, ἡ** 58 • 72 *repentance, turning about, conversion*
**πρᾶξις, ἡ** 44 • 50 *act, action, deed*
**πρότερος** 40 • 47 *former, earlier*
**ταχινός** 3 • 3 *soon, coming soon, imminent, swift*

### Chapter 98 (Hs 9.21)

1 **βοτάνη, ἡ** [2] 27 • 30 *herb, plant*
**δίψυχος** 20 • 23 *doubting, hesitating, double-minded*
**ἐπάνω** 5 • 8 *over, above;* subst. *upper part*
**ξηραίνω** 2 • 2 *to dry, dry up;* pass. *to become dry, dry up, wither*
**ξηρός** 46 • 47 *dry, dried up*
**ῥίζα, ἡ** 4 • 8 *root*
**τέταρτος** 4 • 9 *fourth*
**χεῖλος, τό** 2 • 11 *the lips*
**χλωρός** 44 • 44 *green, fresh*
2 **δίψυχος** 20 • 23 *doubting, hesitating, double-minded*
**θεμέλιον, τό** 3 • 4 *foundation, basis*
**θνήσκω** [2] 5 • 5 *to die*
**ξηρός** [2] 46 • 47 *dry, dried up*
**χλωρός** 44 • 44 *green, fresh*
3 **βοτάνη, ἡ** 27 • 30 *herb, plant*
**δειλία, ἡ** 1 • 2 *cowardice*
**δίψυχος** 20 • 23 *doubting, hesitating, double-minded*
**εἰδωλολατρέω** 2 • 2 *to be/become an image-worshiper/idolater*
**ἐπαισχύνομαι** 3 • 5 *to be ashamed*
**ξηραίνω** 2 • 2 *to dry, dry up;* pass. *become dry, dry up, wither*
4 **ἀποφέρω** 8 • 9 *to take away*
**θνήσκω** 5 • 5 *to die*
**ταχύς** 11 • 18 *in a short time, soon*

### Chapter 99 (Hs 9.22)

1 **ἀρέσκω** 6 • 12 *to please, accommodate*
**αὐθάδης** 3 • 5 *self-willed, stubborn, arrogant*
**βοτάνη, ἡ** 27 • 30 *herb, plant*

δυσμαθής 1 • 1 *obtuse, slow to learn, hard to teach*
ὅλως 30 • 31 *completely, wholly, everywhere*; with a negative *not at all*
πέμπτος 3 • 5 *fifth*
τραχύς 6 • 6 *rough, uneven*
χλωρός 44 • 44 *green, fresh*
2 αὐθάδεια, ἡ 2 • 6 *arrogance, willfulness, stubbornness*
ἀφίστημι 19 • 19 *to depart, withdraw*
ἀφροσύνη, ἡ 7 • 11 *foolishness, lack of sense*
ἄφρων 11 • 17 *foolish, ignorant*
ἐθελοδιδάσκαλος, ὁ 1 • 1 *self-made/self-proclaimed teacher*
ἐπαινέω 1 • 6 *to praise*
μωρός 11 • 12 *foolish, stupid*
σύνεσις, ἡ [2] 13 • 22 *understanding, intelligence, acuteness, shrewdness*
3 ἀποβάλλω 32 • 36 *to reject*
αὐθάδεια, ἡ 2 • 6 *arrogance, willfulness, stubbornness*
ἀφροσύνη, ἡ 7 • 11 *foolishness, lack of sense*
κενός 20 • 27 *vain, empty, without content/basis/truth/power*
κενόω 2 • 2 *to empty, turn into a fool*
πεποίθησις, ἡ 1 • 7 *self-confidence, trust*
σύνεσις, ἡ 13 • 22 *understanding, intelligence, acuteness, shrewdness*
ὑψηλοφροσύνη, ἡ 2 • 2 *pride, haughtiness*
ὑψόω 2 • 4 *to exalt*
4 ἀσύνετος 11 • 16 *without understanding, senseless, foolish*
κεῖμαι 22 • 24 *to be given, exist, be valid*
μετάνοια, ἡ 58 • 72 *repentance, turning about, conversion*
μωρός 11 • 12 *foolish, stupid*
πονηρεύομαι 13 • 15 *to act wickedly toward someone, do harm to someone*

## Chapter 100 (Hs 9.23)

1 βοτάνη, ἡ 27 • 30 *herb, plant*
ἕκτος 2 • 3 *sixth*
μαραίνω 4 • 4 *to die out, fade, disappear, wither*
σχισμή, ἡ [2] 25 • 25 *crack, fissure*
2 καταλαλιά, ἡ [2] 7 • 13 *evil speech, slander, defamation*
μαραίνω 4 • 4 *to die out, fade, disappear, wither*
σχισμή, ἡ 25 • 25 *crack, fissure*
ταχύς 11 • 18 *in a short time, soon*
3 ἀποδοκιμάζω 3 • 5 *to reject*
ἀπορρίπτω 1 • 3 *to throw away*
δυσκόλως 7 • 7 *hardly, with difficulty*
καταλαλιά, ἡ 7 • 13 *evil speech, slander, defamation, detraction*
μηνιάω 1 • 1 *to cherish anger, rage*
μνησίκακος 1 • 1 *vengeful*
οἰκοδομή, ἡ 100 • 103 *building, edifice*
παράμονος 3 • 5 *stubborn, persistent*
πύργος, ὁ 147 • 148 *tower*
σχισμή, ἡ 25 • 25 *crack, fissure*
4 ἐξομολογέω 5 • 15 *to praise*
ἵλεως 2 • 5 *merciful, gracious*
κτίσις, ἡ 13 • 19 *creation, world*
κυριεύω 2 • 5 *to rule*
μνησικακέω [2] 5 • 9 *to remember evil, bear malice, bear a grudge*
πλήρης 13 • 20 *filled, full*
φθαρτός 2 • 10 *perishable, mortal*
5 αἵρεσις, ἡ 1 • 6 *a way of thinking, opinion, dogma*
ἁμάρτημα, τό 4 • 8 *sin, transgression*
ἀποτίθημι 7 • 13 *to give up, lay aside, rid oneself of*
ἰάομαι 4 • 11 *to restore, heal*
μετάνοια, ἡ 58 • 72 *repentance, turning about, conversion*
πρότερος 40 • 47 *former, earlier*

## Chapter 101 (Hs 9.24)

1 βοτάνη, ἡ [3] 27 • 30 *herb, plant*
γένος, τό 8 • 16 *class, kind*
ἕβδομος 2 • 6 *seventh*
εὐθαλής 5 • 5 *flourishing, thriving*
εὐθηνέω 3 • 3 *to thrive, flourish, be in good condition*

ἱλαρός 24 • 34 *cheerful, glad, happy*
κτῆνος, τό 4 • 4 *livestock*
νέμω [2] 3 • 3 *to feed, graze*
πετεινόν, τό 2 • 6 *bird*
χλωρός 44 • 44 *green, fresh*
2 ἀγαλλιάω 6 • 11 *to exult, be glad, be overjoyed*
ἀδιστάκτως 8 • 8 *without doubting, without hesitating*
ἄκακος 4 • 7 *innocent, guileless*
ἀνονειδίστως 1 • 1 *without reproaching*
ἁπλοῦς 1 • 4 *single, without guile, sincere, straightforward*
ἐνδύω 29 • 32 *to clothe oneself in, put on, wear;*
fig. *take on the characteristics/ virtues/intentions of*
κόπος, ὁ 6 • 8 *work, labor, toil*
παρθένος, ἡ 58 • 62 *virgin*
σπλάγχνον, τό 1 • 5 *mercy, love, affection*
χορηγέω 3 • 6 *to provide, supply (in abundance)*
3 ἁπλότης, ἡ 12 • 15 *ingenuousness, simplicity, sincerity, uprightness, frankness*
κόπος, ὁ 6 • 8 *work, labor toil*
νηπιότης, ἡ 3 • 3 *childlikeness, innocence*
πληθύνω 2 • 11 *to increase, multiply, give abundance*
πρᾶξις, ἡ 44 • 50 *act, action, deed*
χαριτόω 1 • 1 *to bestow favor on, favor highly, bless*
4 ἀριθμός, ὁ 2 • 14 *number*
διαμένω 6 • 9 *to remain*
δοκιμάζω 10 • 19 *to accept as proved, approve*
ἐγγράφω 4 • 5 *to enroll, write in, record*
ἐξαλείφω 2 • 8 *to remove, destroy, obliterate*
ἡμέτερος 2 • 13 *our*
μετάνοια, ἡ 58 • 72 *repentance, turning about, conversion*

## Chapter 102 (Hs 9.25)

1 κτίσις, ἡ 13 • 19 *creation, world*
ὄγδοος 2 • 5 *eighth*
πηγή, ἡ 4 • 7 *spring, fountain*
ποτίζω 5 • 7 *to drink*
2 ἁγνῶς 5 • 6 *purely, sincerely*
νοσφίζω 1 • 1 *to keep back, reserve*
ὅλως 30 • 31 *completely, wholly, everywhere;*
with a negative *not at all*
πάροδος, ἡ 2 • 3 *passage, thoroughfare*
σεμνῶς 3 • 4 *honorably, worthily, in a manner above reproach*

## Chapter 103 (Hs 9.26)

1 διαφθείρω 8 • 12 *to spoil, destroy*
ἔνατος 2 • 2 *ninth*
ἐρημώδης 3 • 3 *desert-like*
ἑρπετόν, τό 2 • 2 *reptile*
2 ἁγνῶς 5 • 6 *purely, sincerely*
διάκονος, ὁ 3 • 29 *assistant*
διαρπάζω 1 • 2 *to steal, plunder thoroughly;*
διαρπάσαντες τὴν ζωὴν *plundering the livelihood*
ἐπιμένω 10 • 16 *to continue, persist in, persevere*
κακῶς 1 • 1 *wrongly, wickedly*
ὀρφανός 5 • 9 *without parents;*
subst. *orphan*
περιποιέω 8 • 9 *to enrich oneself, acquire, obtain, gain for oneself*
σπίλος, ὁ 3 • 3 *spot, stain, blemish*
τελειόω 3 • 14 *to complete, bring to an end, finish, accomplish*
χήρα, ἡ 6 • 13 *widow*
3 ἀπολλύω 5 • 5 *to kill, put to death, destroy, ruin*
ἐρημώδης 3 • 3 *desert-like*
κολλάω 12 • 32 *to join oneself to, join, cling to, associate with*
μονάζω 1 • 2 *to live alone, separate oneself*
χερσόω 3 • 3 *to make dry and barren*
ψωριάω 5 • 5 *to have a rough surface*
4 ἄγριος 5 • 8 *wild*
ἀγριόω 1 • 1 *to become wild/ uncontrolled*
ἀμελεία, ἡ 2 • 2 *neglect*
ἄμπελος, ἡ 13 • 16 *vine, grapevine*
ἀπογινώσκω 3 • 3 *to despair*
ἄχρηστος 4 • 6 *useless, worthless*

βοτάνη, ἡ 27 • 30 *weed*
δεσπότης, ὁ 24 • 54 *lord, master*
ἐρημόω 1 • 1 *to lay waste*
εὔχρηστος 13 • 14 *useful, serviceable*
καταλείπω 6 • 12 *to set to one side, neglect*
καταφθείρω 8 • 8 *to ruin, corrupt*
τυγχάνω 2 • 15 *to meet, attain, gain, find, experience*
φραγμός, ὁ 1 • 1 *fence, hedge*
5 μετάνοια, ἡ 58 • 72 *repentance, turning about, conversion*
6 ἀδύνατος 4 • 11 *impossible*
ἀποτελέω 4 • 4 *to bring to completion, finish*
καταφθείρω 8 • 8 *to ruin, corrupt*
κεῖμαι 22 • 24 *to be given, exist, be valid*
μετάνοια, ἡ [2] 58 • 72 *repentance, turning about, conversion*
πάλαι 1 • 2 *long ago, formerly, time past*
πρίν 4 • 7 *before*
πύργος, ὁ 147 • 148 *tower*
ταχινός 3 • 3 *quick, in haste*
7 ἀπολλύω [2] 5 • 5 *to kill, put to death, ruin, destroy*
διαφθείρω [2] 8 • 12 *to spoil, destroy*
δόλιος 1 • 3 *deceitful, treacherous*
ἰός, ὁ 2 • 4 *poison, venom*
κατάλαλος 3 • 3 *slanderous;* subst. *slanderer*
κολοβός 5 • 5 *mutilated, broken*
8 κολοβός 5 • 5 *mutilated, damaged*
πρᾶξις, ἡ 44 • 50 *state, condition, situation*

## Chapter 104 (Hs 9.27)

1 δέκατος 2 • 2 *tenth*
δένδρον, τό 26 • 28 *tree*
σκεπάζω 6 • 8 *to cover, protect, shelter*
2 ἁγνῶς 5 • 6 *purely, sincerely*
ἀδιαλείπτως 3 • 6 *constantly, unceasingly*
ἀναστρέφω 3 • 8 *to act, behave, conduct oneself, live*
ἄτερ 5 • 6 *without*
ἐπίσκοπος, ὁ [2] 3 • 76 *overseer, supervisor*
ἡδέως 7 • 10 *gladly*
σκεπάζω 6 • 8 *to protect, shelter*
ὑποδέχομαι 2 • 3 *to receive, welcome, entertain as a guest*
ὑπόκρισις, ἡ 5 • 13 *pretense, play-acting, outward show, dissembling*
ὑστερέω 7 • 11 *to be needy, be poor, lack*
φιλόξενος 2 • 3 *hospitable*
χήρα, ἡ 6 • 13 *widow*
3 διαπαντός 2 • 2 *always, continually, constantly*
ἔνδοξος 43 • 54 *glorious, splendid*
ἐπιμένω 10 • 16 *to continue, persist in, persevere*
λειτουργέω 4 • 11 *to serve, render service*
σκεπάζω 6 • 8 *to protect, shelter*

## Chapter 105 (Hs 9.28)

1 δένδρον, τό 26 • 28 *tree*
ἐνδέκατος 2 • 2 *eleventh*
κοσμέω 3 • 10 *to adorn*
πλήρης 13 • 20 *filled, full*
2 προθύμως 2 • 5 *readily, willingly, eagerly, freely*
3 ἀφαιρέω 1 • 8 *to do away with, remove;* pass. *be taken away*
δένδρον, τό 26 • 28 *tree*
διατί [2] 27 • 29 *why?*
ἔνδοξος 43 • 54 *glorious, splendid*
εὐειδής 3 • 3 *well-formed, beautiful*
ποικίλος 20 • 22 *diversified, manifold*
ποτέ 4 • 15 *ever;* ὅσοι ποτέ *whoever*
ὑπερέχω 5 • 7 *to be more excellent, be superior*
4 βουλή, ἡ [2] 8 • 19 *purpose, counsel, plan, intention*
δειλός 1 • 1 *cowardly, timid*
δισταγμός, ὁ 1 • 2 *doubt, uncertain*
ἐλάσσων 4 • 6 *inferior*
ἔνδοξος 43 • 54 *glorious, splendid*
ἐξετάζω 2 • 3 *to question, examine*

ὁμολογέω 2 • 18 *to confess, acknowledge, claim, profess, praise*
πότερος 1 • 3 *whether*
προθύμως 2 • 5 *readily, willingly, eagerly, freely*
ὑπερέχω 5 • 7 *to be more excellent, be superior*
5 βαστάζω 18 • 24 *to carry, bear*
βουλεύω 5 • 6 *to deliberate, consider*
βουλή, ἡ 8 • 19 *purpose, counsel, plan, intention*
διαμένω 6 • 9 *to remain*
ἕνεκα 8 • 15 *because of, on account of, for the sake of*
ἡγέομαι 7 • 25 *to think, consider, regard*
ἰάομαι 4 • 11 *to heal, restore*
μήποτε 13 • 22 *lest*
6 ἕνεκα 8 • 15 *because of, on account of, for the sake of*
θνήσκω 5 • 5 *to die*
καταβαρέω 1 • 1 *to weigh heavily, burden, be a burden to*
μακαρίζω 1 • 5 *to call/consider blessed, happy, fortunate*
νοέω 30 • 46 *to perceive, apprehend, understand, gain an insight into*
οὐκοῦν 1 • 10 *therefore, so, accordingly*
χαρίζομαι 1 • 5 *to give graciously*
7 ἄρνησις, ἡ 2 • 3 *repudiation, rejection*
δεσμωτήριον, τό 1 • 1 *prison, jail*
διστάζω 5 • 10 *to doubt, waver*
μήποτε 13 • 22 *(in order) that... not*
ὁμολογέω 2 • 18 *to confess, acknowledge, claim, profess, praise*
ὁμολόγησις, ἡ 1 • 1 *confessing*
8 βουλή, ἡ 8 • 19 *purpose, counsel, plan, intention*
διαπαντός 2 • 2 *always, continually, constantly*
κολάζω 2 • 9 *to punish, penalize*

## Chapter 106 (Hs 9.29)

1 βρέφος, τό 3 • 3 *baby, infant*
διαμένω 6 • 9 *to remain, continue (in something)*
δωδέκατος 2 • 3 *twelfth*
κακία, ἡ 2 • 9 *baseness, depravity, wickedness, vice*
λευκός 24 • 24 *white*
νήπιος 2 • 4 *infant, child*
νηπιότης, ἡ 3 • 3 *childlikeness, innocence*
πονηρία, ἡ 36 • 41 *wickedness, baseness, maliciousness, sinfulness*
2 ἀδιστάκτως 8 • 8 *unquestionably, beyond doubt, surely*
διαμένω 6 • 9 *to remain*
μιαίνω 14 • 14 *to defile*
νηπιότης, ἡ 3 • 3 *childlikeness, innocence*
πρᾶγμα, τό 19 • 23 *thing, matter, affair*
φρόνησις, ἡ 6 • 7 *way of thinking, frame of mind*
3 ἀκακία, ἡ 8 • 10 *innocence, guilelessness*
βρέφος, τό [2] 3 • 3 *baby, infant*
διαμένω 6 • 9 *to remain*
ἔνδοξος [2] 43 • 54 *glorious, splendid*
ἐνδύω 29 • 32 *to clothe oneself in, put on, wear;*
fig. *take on the characteristics/ virtues/intentions of*
κακία, ἡ 2 • 9 *baseness, depravity, wickedness, vice*
πονηρία, ἡ 36 • 41 *wickedness, baseness, maliciousness, sinfulness*
προλέγω 5 • 16 *to state beforehand/earlier*
4 ἀντί 4 • 15 *instead of, in place of*
δηλόω 32 • 49 *to explain, clarify*
οἰκοδομή, ἡ [2] 100 • 103 *building, edifice*
πεδίον, τό 15 • 17 *level place, plain, field*
πύργος, ὁ 147 • 148 *tower*
στρογγύλος [2] 10 • 10 *round*
συντελέω 9 • 15 *to bring to an end, finish, complete, close*

## Chapter 107 (Hs 9.30)[4]

1 **ἀντί** 4 • 15 *in place of, instead of*
**ἀποβάλλω** 32 • 36 *to throw away, reject*
**λευκός** 24 • 24 *white*
**οἰκοδομή, ἡ** 100 • 103 *building, edifice*
**πεδίον, τό** 15 • 17 *level place, plain, field*
**πύργος, ὁ** 147 • 148 *tower*
**ῥίζα, ἡ** 4 • 8 *root*; here the *foot* of the mountain
2 **ἄκακος** 5 • 8 *innocent, guileless*
**διαμένω** 6 • 9 *to remain, stay*
**ἐπεί** 10 • 35 *because, since, for*
**κελεύω** 32 • 44 *to command, order, urge*
**λαμπρός** 14 • 14 *gleaming, bright*
**λευκός** 24 • 24 *white*
**μελανέω** 1 • 1 *to turn black*
**οἰκοδομή, ἡ** [2] 100 • 103 *building, edifice*
**πύργος, ὁ** [3] 147 • 148 *tower*
**ῥίζα, ἡ** 4 • 8 *root*; here the *foot* of the mountain
3 **ἄκακος** 5 • 8 *innocent, guileless*
**γένος, τό** [2] 8 • 16 *nation, people*
4 **λαμπρός** 14 • 14 *gleaming, bright*
**λευκός** 24 • 24 *white*
**στρογγύλος** 10 • 10 *round*

## Chapter 108 (Hs 9.31)[5]

5 **διαπίπτω** [2] 4 • 4 *to fall away, slip away*; pass. *be scattered*
**ποιμήν, ὁ** 51 • 55 *shepherd*
**ὑγιής** 9 • 9 *healthy, sound, undamaged*
6 **δεσπότης, ὁ** 24 • 54 *lord, master*
**διαπίπτω** [2] 4 • 4 *to fall away, slip away*; pass. *be scattered*
**κολάζω** 3 • 10 *to penalize, punish*
**ποιμήν, ὁ** [2] 51 • 55 *shepherd*
**ποίμνιον, τό** 3 • 8 *flock*
**πρᾶγμα, τό** 20 • 24 *thing, matter, affair*

## Chapter 109 (Hs 9.32)[6]

## Chapter 110 (Hs 9.33)

1 **δολιότης, ἡ** 2 • 3 *deceit*
**κατορθόω** 5 • 5 *to set straight, complete, bring to a successful conclusion*
**μετάνοια, ἡ** 58 • 72 *repentance, turning about, conversion*
**μνησικακία, ἡ** 4 • 4 *bearing a grudge, vengefulness*
**παραμένω** 6 • 9 *to continue in an occupation/office, persist*
**ποιμήν, ὁ** 51 • 55 *shepherd*
**προγράφω** 2 • 4 *to write beforehand*
2 **ἐκπληρόω** 2 • 2 *to fulfill*
**ἐπιλανθάνομαι** 5 • 8 *to forget*
**ναί** 6 • 8 *yes, certainly, indeed, it's true that*
**οἰκοδομή, ἡ** 100 • 103 *building, edifice*
**ποιμήν, ὁ** 51 • 55 *shepherd*
**τύπος, ὁ** 10 • 26 *mark, trace*
3 **ἐξαλείφω** 2 • 8 *to remove, destroy, obliterate*
**ἐξομαλίζω** 1 • 1 *to smooth away, smooth out, make smooth*
**ἐπεί** 10 • 35 *when, after*
**καθαρός** 25 • 45 *pure, free*
**κελεύω** 32 • 44 *to command, order, urge*
**μετάνοια, ἡ** [2] 58 • 72 *repentance, turning about, conversion*
**μηκέτι** 12 • 16 *no longer, not from now on*
**παραμένω** 6 • 9 *to continue in an occupation/office*
**πρότερος** 40 • 47 *former, earlier*
**τύπος, ὁ** 10 • 26 *mark, trace*

4. Portions of Chapter 107 are extant in Latin only.
5. Portions of Chapter 108 are extant in Latin only.
6. Chapter 109 is extant in Latin only.

## PARABLE TEN

### Chapter 111 (Hs 10.1)[7]

### Chapter 112 (Hs 10.2)[8]

### Chapter 113 (Hs 10.3)[9]

3 **μέμφομαι** [2] 3 • 4 *to find fault with, blame*
4 **καθαρότης, ἡ** 1 • 1 *purity*
**καθίστημι** 2 • 8 *to make, cause*
**παρθένος, ἡ** 58 • 62 *virgin*
**ποιμήν, ὁ** 51 • 55 *shepherd*
5 **παρθένος, ἡ** 58 • 62 *virgin*
**ποιμήν, ὁ** 51 • 55 *shepherd*

### Chapter 114 (Hs 10.4)[10]

7. Chapter 111 is extant only in Latin.
8. Chapter 112 is extant only in Latin.
9. Portions of Chapter 113 are extant only in Latin.
10. Chapter 114 is extant only in Latin.

# The Letter to Diognetus

## Chapter 1

1 **βίος, ὁ** 4 • 13 *life*
**γένος, τό** 1 • 16 *nation, people*
**δεισιδαιμονία, ἡ** 2 • 2 *religious scruple, religiosity*
**Διόγνητος, ὁ** 1 • 1 *Diognetus*
**Ἕλλην, ὁ** 3 • 4 *gentile, polytheist, Greco-Roman*
**ἐπειδή** 1 • 17 *(just) because*
**ἐπιμελῶς** 2 • 9 *carefully, diligently*
**ἐπιτήδευμα, τό** 1 • 1 *pursuit, way of living*
**θεοσέβεια, ἡ** 5 • 6 *piety, godliness*
**θρησκεύω** 2 • 3 *to worship*
**καταφρονέω** 3 • 9 *to care nothing for, disregard, be unafraid of*
**κράτιστος** 1 • 1 *most noble, most excellent*
**μανθάνω** 5 • 26 *to learn*
**νομίζω** 6 • 10 *to think, believe, hold, consider*
**πάνυ** 1 • 5 *altogether, very*
**πρότερος** 1 • 47 *earlier, formerly, in former times*
**πυνθάνομαι** 1 • 2 *to learn*
**σαφῶς** 2 • 5 *clearly, exactly, very well*
**ὑπεροράω** 1 • 3 *to disdain, despise*
**ὑπερσπουδάζω** 1 • 1 *to take great pains, be very eager;*
  **ὁρῶ ὑπερεσπουδακότα σε** (object-complement with predicate participle) *I see that you are very eager*
**φιλοστοργία, ἡ** 1 • 1 *heartfelt love, strong affection*
**Χριστιανός, ὁ** 14 • 24 *Christ-follower, Christian*
2 **ἀποδέχομαι** 2 • 6 *to recognize, acknowledge, praise*
**βελτίων** 1 • 6 *better*
**γέ** 5 • 18 *at least, even, indeed*
**λυπέω** 2 • 17 *to become sad, be sorrowful, be distressed*
**μάλιστα** 2 • 14 *most of all, above all, especially, particularly*
**προθυμία, ἡ** 1 • 6 *willingness, readiness, goodwill*
**χορηγέω** 3 • 6 *to provide, supply (in abundance)*

## Chapter 2

1 **ἀκροατής, ὁ** 1 • 4 *a hearer*
**ἀπατάω** 1 • 9 *to deceive, mislead*
**ἀποσκευάζω** 1 • 1 *to lay aside, get rid of*
**δή** 1 • 6 *now, then, therefore*
**διάνοια, ἡ** 1 • 22 *understanding, intelligence, mind*
**εἶδος, τό** 1 • 6 *form, outward appearance*
**ἴδε** 1 • 10 *look! see!*
**καθαίρω** 1 • 3 *to make clean*
**καθάπερ** 3 • 3 *just as*
**λογισμός, ὁ** 2 • 4 *calculation, reasoning, reflection, thought*
**νομίζω** 6 • 10 *to think, believe, hold, consider*
**ὁμολογέω** 1 • 18 *to grant, admit, confess*
**προκατέχω** 1 • 1 *to gain possession of previously or occupy previously*
**συνήθεια, ἡ** 1 • 3 *custom, habit, usage*
**τυγχάνω** 5 • 15 *to meet, attain, gain, find, experience*
**ὑπόστασις, ἡ** 1 • 1 *substantial nature, essence, actual being, reality*
**φρόνησις, ἡ** 1 • 7 *understanding, insight, intelligence*
2 **ἄργυρος, ὁ** 1 • 3 *silver*
**ἄτιμος** 1 • 3 *insignificant*
**διαφθείρω** 1 • 12 *to spoil, destroy*
**εὐπρεπής** 1 • 7 *looking well*
**ἰός, ὁ** 1 • 4 *corrosion, rust*

**κατασκευάζω** 1 • 1 *to build, construct, erect, create*
**κλέπτω** 2 • 3 *to steal*
**κρείττων** 2 • 8 *more prominent, higher in rank, preferable, better*
**ξύλον, τό** 7 • 23 *wood*
**ὄστρακον, τό** 1 • 2 *baked clay, pottery*
**πατέω** 1 • 2 *to tread, walk*
**σήπω** 2 • 4 *to decay, rot*
**σίδηρος, ὁ** 2 • 3 *iron*
**σκεῦος, τό** 3 • 9 *thing, object*
**ὑπηρεσία, ἡ** 1 • 2 *service*
**χαλκεύω** 2 • 2 *to forge*
**χαλκός, ὁ** 1 • 2 *brass, bronze*
**χρῄζω** 2 • 7 *to (have) need of*
**χρῆσις, ἡ** 2 • 5 *use, usage*
3 **ἀργυροκόπος, ὁ** 1 • 1 *silversmith*
**ἐκτυπόω** 1 • 1 *to shape*
**κεραμεύς, ὁ** 1 • 2 *potter*
**λιθοξόος, ὁ** 1 • 1 *sculptor*
**μεταμορφόω** 1 • 1 *to be transfigured*
**μορφή, ἡ** 1 • 8 *form, outward appearance, shape*
**πλάσσω** 2 • 8 *to form, mold*
**πρίν** 2 • 7 *before*
**σίδηρος, ὁ** 2 • 3 *iron*
**σκεῦος, τό** 3 • 9 *thing, object*
**τέχνη, ἡ** 1 • 3 *skill, trade*
**τεχνίτης, ὁ** 2 • 4 *craftsperson, artisan, designer*
**τυγχάνω** 5 • 15 *to happen, turn out;*
**γένοιτ' ἄν, εἰ τύχοι** (fourth class condition, with optatives in apodosis and protasis; cf. *ExSyn* 483–84)
**ὕλη, ἡ** [2] 2 • 4 *material, matter, stuff*
**φθαρτός** 3 • 10 *perishable*
**χαλκεύς, ὁ** 1 • 2 *(black)smith, metalworker*
**χαλκεύω** 2 • 2 *to forge*
4 **ἀκίνητος** 1 • 4 *unable to move*
**ἀναίσθητος** 2 • 2 *without feeling/perception*
**ἄψυχος** 1 • 1 *inanimate, lifeless*
**κωφός** 3 • 3 *deaf and mute*
**σήπω** 2 • 4 *to decay, rot*
**σκεῦος, τό** 3 • 9 *thing, object*
**φθείρω** 2 • 10 *to destroy, ruin, corrupt, spoil*
5 **δουλεύω** 1 • 42 *to (perform the duties of a slave) serve, obey*
**ἐξομοιόω** 1 • 1 *to become just like/similar, resemble fully*
**τέλειος** 1 • 25 *attaining an end* or *purpose, complete*
6 **ἡγέομαι** 5 • 25 *to think, consider, regard*
**Χριστιανός, ὁ** 14 • 24 *Christ-follower, Christian*
7 **ἀργυροῦς** 1 • 1 *silver*
**ἀφυλάκτως/ἀφύλάκτος** 1 • 1 *without guarding*
**ἐγκλείω** 3 • 4 *to lock up, shut up, enclose*
**καταφρονέω** 3 • 9 *to look down on, despise, scorn, treat with contempt*
**κλέπτω** 2 • 3 *to steal*
**λίθινος** 1 • 3 *(made of) stone*
**νομίζω** 6 • 10 *to think, believe, hold, consider*
**ὀστρακίνος** 1 • 1 *made of earth/clay*
**παρακαθίστημι** 1 • 1 *to post*
**σέβω** [2] 3 • 6 *to worship*
**ὑβρίζω** 2 • 5 *to mistreat, scoff at, insult*
**φύλαξ, ὁ** 1 • 1 *guard, sentinel*
**χλευάζω** 1 • 2 *to mock, scoff at, sneer at*
**χρυσός, ὁ** 1 • 3 *gold*
8 **αἰσθάνομαι** 1 • 5 *to notice*
**ἀναισθητέω** 2 • 3 *to be unfeeling, be insensible*
**ἐλέγχω** 4 • 16 *to bring to light, expose, set forth*
**θρησκεύω** 2 • 3 *to worship*
**κνῖσα, ἡ** 2 • 2 *the odor of burning fat*
**κολάζω** 6 • 9 *to penalize, punish*
9 **αἴσθησις, ἡ** [2] 2 • 2 *perception, sensation*
**ἀναισθητέω** 2 • 3 *to be unfeeling, be insensible*
**ἀνέχω** [3] 4 • 7 *to endure, bear with, put up with*
**ἑκών** 1 • 4 *willing(ly), glad(ly)*
**ἐλέγχω** 4 • 16 *to bring to light, expose, set forth*
**κόλασις, ἡ** 3 • 11 *punishment*
**λογισμός, ὁ** 2 • 4 *reasoning power, wisdom*

**οὐκοῦν** 1 • 10 *therefore, so, accordingly*
**ὑπομένω** 3 • 32 *to stand one's ground, hold out, endure*
10 **δουλόω** 1 • 2 *to cause to be like a slave*
**ἡγέομαι** 5 • 25 *to think, consider, regard*
**κἄν** 1 • 8 *even if*
**περισσός** 2 • 5 *abundant, profuse*
**Χριστιανός, ὁ** 14 • 24 *Christ-follower, Christian*

## Chapter 3

1 **ἑξῆς** 1 • 2 *in the next place*
**θεοσεβέω** 1 • 1 *to worship God*
**μάλιστα** 2 • 14 *most of all, above all, especially, particularly*
**οἴομαι** 4 • 11 *to think, suppose, expect*
**ποθέω** 3 • 4 *to desire, wish (for), be anxious, strive after*
2 **ἀξιόω** 3 • 14 *to deem, hold an opinion*
**ἀπέχω** 2 • 35 *to keep away, abstain, refrain from*
**δεσπότης, ὁ** 2 • 52 *lord, master*
**διαμαρτάνω** 1 • 5 *to miss the mark badly, be quite wrong*
**θρησκεία, ἡ** 1 • 3 *worship*
**λατρεία, ἡ** 1 • 2 *service/worship (of God)*
**ὁμοιοτρόπως** 1 • 1 *in the same way*
**προλέγω** [2] 2 • 16 *to tell beforehand/in advance*
**προσάγω** 1 • 7 *to bring (forward)*
**σέβω** [2] 3 • 6 *to worship*
**τοίνυν** 1 • 2 *hence, so, well (then), indeed*
**φρονέω** 1 • 17 *to think, form/hold an opinion, judge*
3 **ἀναίσθητος** 2 • 2 *without feeling/perception*
**ἀφροσύνη, ἡ** 2 • 11 *foolishness, lack of sense*
**δεῖγμα, τό** 3 • 3 *example*
**εἰκός** 1 • 2 *probable, reasonable*
**Ἕλλην, ὁ** 3 • 4 *gentile, polytheist, Greco-Roman*
**ἡγέομαι** 5 • 25 *to think, consider, regard*
**θεοσέβεια, ἡ** 5 • 6 *piety, godliness*
**καθάπερ** 3 • 3 *just as*
**κωφός** 3 • 3 *deaf and mute*
**μωρία, ἡ** 1 • 1 *foolishness*
**παρέχω** [2] 7 • 18 *to grant, show*
**προσδέομαι** 4 • 4 *to need*
4 **οἴομαι** 4 • 11 *to think, suppose, expect*
**παρέχω** 7 • 18 *to grant, show*
**προσδέομαι** [2] 4 • 4 *to need*
**χορηγέω** 3 • 6 *to provide, supply (in abundance)*
5 **γέ** 5 • 18 *at least, even indeed*
**γεραίρω** 1 • 1 *to honor*
**διαφέρω** 1 • 5 *to differ, be different*
**ἐνδείκνυμι** 2 • 4 *to show, demonstrate*
**ἐπιτελέω** 1 • 15 *to complete, accomplish, perform, bring about*
**θυσία, ἡ** 1 • 22 *sacrifice, offering*
**κνῖσα, ἡ** 2 • 2 *the odor of burning fat*
**κωφός** 3 • 3 *deaf and mute*
**μεταλαμβάνω** 1 • 12 *to have a share in*
**οἴομαι** 4 • 11 *to think, suppose, expect*
**ὁλοκαύτωμα, τό** 1 • 7 *whole burnt offering, holocaust*
**παρέχω** 7 • 18 *to grant, show*
**προσδέομαι** 4 • 4 *to need*
**φιλοτιμία, ἡ** 1 • 1 *generous zeal*

## Chapter 4

1 **ἀλαζονεία, ἡ** 2 • 10 *pretension, arrogance*
**βρῶσις, ἡ** 1 • 4 *food*
**γέ** 5 • 18 *at least, even, indeed*
**δεισιδαιμονία, ἡ** 2 • 2 *religious scruple, religiosity*
**εἰρωνεία, ἡ** 1 • 1 *pretense, posturing*
**καταγέλαστος** 1 • 1 *ridiculous*
**μανθάνω** 5 • 26 *to learn*
**μήν** 2 • 8 *on the other hand*
**νηστεία, ἡ** 1 • 25 *fast*
**νομίζω** 6 • 10 *to think, believe, hold, consider*
**νουμηνία/νεομηνία, ἡ** 1 • 1 *new moon, first of the month*
**χρῄζω** 2 • 7 *to need*
**ψοφοδεής** 1 • 1 *timid, anxious*

2 **ἀθέμιτος** 1 • 3 *wanton, disgusting, unseemly*
**ἄχρηστος** 1 • 6 *useless, worthless*
**κτίζω** [2] 4 • 25 *to create*
**παραδέχομαι** 1 • 9 *to accept*
**παραιτέομαι** 1 • 1 *to decline, refuse, avoid, reject*
**περισσός** 2 • 5 *abundant, profuse*
**χρῆσις, ἡ** 2 • 5 *use, usage*
3 **ἀσεβής** 2 • 14 *irreverent, impious, ungodly*
**καταψεύδομαι** 1 • 1 *to tell lies (against)*
**κωλύω** 2 • 3 *to hinder, prevent, forbid*
4 **ἀλαζονεύομαι** 1 • 3 *to boast, be boastful*
**ἐκλογή, ἡ** 1 • 3 *selection, choice, election*
**ἐξαιρέτως** 1 • 3 *especially*
**μαρτύριον, τό** 1 • 16 *testimony, proof*
**μείνωσις/μείωσις, ἡ** 1 • 1 *lessening, diminution*
**χλεύη, ἡ** 1 • 1 *scorn, ridicule*
5 **ἀλλαγή, ἡ** 1 • 1 *a change*
**ἄστρον, τό** 2 • 3 *star, constellation, single star*
**ἀφροσύνη, ἡ** 2 • 11 *foolishness, lack of sense*
**δεῖγμα, τό** 1 • 3 *indicator, proof*
**ἑορτή, ἡ** 1 • 1 *festival, celebration*
**ἡγέομαι** 5 • 25 *to think, consider, regard*
**θεοσέβεια, ἡ** 5 • 6 *piety, godliness*
**καταδιαιρέω** 1 • 1 *to divide, make a distinction between*
**μήν, ὁ** 1 • 2 *month*
**οἰκονομία, ἡ** 2 • 6 *arrangement, order, plan*
**ὁρμή, ἡ** 1 • 1 *impulse, inclination, desire*
**παρατήρησις, ἡ** 1 • 1 *observance*
**παρεδρεύω** 1 • 1 *to apply oneself to, concern oneself with*
**πένθος, τό** 1 • 1 *grief, sadness, mourning*
**σελήνη, ἡ** 3 • 7 *moon*
6 **ἀλαζονεία, ἡ** 2 • 10 *pretension, arrogance*
**ἀπάτη, ἡ** 2 • 16 *deception, deceitfulness*
**ἀπέχω** 2 • 35 *to keep away, abstain, refrain from*
**ἀρκούντως** 1 • 1 *sufficiently*
**εἰκαιότης, ἡ** 1 • 1 *silliness*
**θεοσέβεια, ἡ** 5 • 6 *piety, godliness*
**κοινός** 2 • 15 *communal, common*
**μανθάνω** [2] 5 • 26 *to learn*
**μυστήριον, τό** 7 • 11 *transcendent/ultimate reality, secret*
**νομίζω** 2 • 10 *to think, believe, hold, consider*
**ὀρθῶς** 3 • 8 *rightly, correctly*
**πολυπραγμοσύνη, ἡ** 1 • 1 *fussiness*
**προσδοκάω** 4 • 8 *to wait for, look for, expect*
**Χριστιανός, ὁ** 14 • 24 *Christ-follower, Christian*

## Chapter 5

1 **διακρίνω** 2 • 7 *to make a distinction, differentiate*
**ἐσθής, ἡ** 2 • 2 *clothing*
**Χριστιανός, ὁ** 14 • 24 *Christ-follower, Christian*
2 **ἀσκέω** 2 • 6 *to practice, engage in*
**βίος, ὁ** 4 • 13 *life*
**διάλεκτος, ἡ** 1 • 2 *language*
**παραλλάσσω** 1 • 1 *to change*
**παράσημος** 1 • 1 *peculiar, odd*
**πού** 1 • 7 *somewhere*
**χράομαι** 3 • 18 *to make use of, employ*
3 **ἀνθρώπινος** 2 • 7 *human*
**δόγμα, τό** 1 • 10 *doctrine, dogma*
**ἔνιοι** 1 • 4 *some, several*
**ἐπίνοια, ἡ** 2 • 2 *thought, conception*
**μάθημα, τό** 1 • 1 *knowledge, teaching*
**μήν** 2 • 8 *indeed*
**πολυπράγμων** 1 • 1 *inquisitive*
**προΐστημι** 1 • 2 *to show concern for, care for, give aid*
**φροντίς, ἡ** 1 • 3 *reflection, thought, care, concern*
4 **βάρβαρος** 1 • 1 *not Hellenic*
**βίος, ὁ** 4 • 13 *means of subsistence*
**δίαιτα, ἡ** 1 • 3 *food, diet*
**ἐγχώριος** 1 • 1 *local*
**ἔθος, τό** 1 • 4 *custom*
**Ἑλληνίς, ἡ** 1 • 1 *Greek*

**ἐνδείκνυμι** 2 • 4 *to show, demonstrate*
**ἐσθής, ἡ** 2 • 2 *clothing*
**θαυμαστός** 1 • 13 *wonderful, marvelous, remarkable*
**κατάστασις, ἡ** 1 • 1 *state of being/ character*
**κληρόω** 1 • 2 *to appoint by lot*
**ὁμολογουμένως** 1 • 1 *uncontestable, undeniably, most certainly, beyond question*
**παράδοξος** 1 • 4 *strange, wonderful, remarkable*
**πολιτεία, ἡ** 1 • 5 *way of life, conduct*
5 **μετέχω** 2 • 4 *to share, have a share, participate*
**ξένος** [3] 4 • 8 *strange;* **ἡ ξένη** *a foreign country*
**οἰκέω** 3 • 6 *to inhabit, dwell in*
**πάροικος, ὁ** 1 • 1 *stranger, alien*
**πατρίς, ἡ** [3] 3 • 4 *fatherland, homeland*
**πολίτης, ὁ** 1 • 2 *citizen*
**ὑπομένω** 3 • 32 *to stand one's ground, hold out, endure*
6 **γαμέω** 1 • 8 *to marry*
**ῥίπτω/ῥιπτέω** 1 • 11 *to throw*
**τεκνογονέω** 1 • 1 *to bear/beget children*
7 **κοινός** 2 • 15 *communal, common*
**κοίτη, ἡ** 1 • 1 *marriage-bed*
**παρατίθημι** 1 • 6 *to set before*
**τράπεζα, ἡ** 1 • 3 *a meal, food*
8 **τυγχάνω** 5 • 15 *to happen to be, turn out*
9 **διατρίβω** 1 • 5 *to spend time*
**πολιτεύομαι** 2 • 10 *to have one's citizenship/home*
10 **βίος, ὁ** 4 • 13 *life*
**νικάω** 2 • 8 *to outstrip, excel*
**ὁρίζω** 1 • 10 *to determine, appoint, fix, set*
12 **ἀγνοέω** 1 • 11 *to not know, be ignorant (of)*
**ζωοποιέω** 2 • 10 *to make alive, give life to*
**θανατόω** 1 • 7 *to put to death*
**κατακρίνω** 2 • 6 *to pronounce a sentence on*
13 **πλουτίζω** 2 • 5 *to make rich*
**πτωχεύω** 1 • 2 *to be (extremely) poor*
**ὑστερέω** 1 • 11 *to lack, be lacking, go without, come short of*
14 **ἀτιμία, ἡ** 1 • 1 *dishonor*
**ἀτιμόω** 1 • 1 *to dishonor*
15 **λοιδορέω** 1 • 2 *to revile, abuse*
**τιμάω** 1 • 12 *to honor, revere*
**ὑβρίζω** 2 • 5 *to mistreat, scoff at, insult*
16 **ἀγαθοποιέω** 1 • 6 *to do what is right, be a good citizen*
**ζωοποιέω** 2 • 10 *to make alive, give life to*
**κολάζω** [2] 6 • 9 *to penalize, punish*
17 **αἰτία, ἡ** 1 • 5 *cause, reason*
**ἀλλόφυλος** 1 • 4 *alien, foreign*
**Ἕλλην** 3 • 4 *gentile, polytheist, Greco-Roman*
**ἔχθρα, ἡ** 1 • 1 *enmity*
**πολεμέω** 2 • 7 *to be hostile*

## Chapter 6

1 **ἁπλῶς** 1 • 6 *in short, in a word;* **Ἁπλῶς εἰπεῖν** lit. *to speak simply*
**ὅσπερ** 1 • 10 *which indeed*
**Χριστιανός, ὁ** 14 • 24 *Christ-follower, Christian*
2 **σπείρω** 1 • 5 *to scatter, disperse*
**Χριστιανός, ὁ** 14 • 24 *Christ-follower, Christian*
3 **οἰκέω** [2] 3 • 6 *to live, dwell*
**Χριστιανός, ὁ** 14 • 24 *Christ-follower, Christian*
4 **ἀόρατος** [2] 3 • 13 *unseen, invisible*
**θεοσέβεια, ἡ** 5 • 6 *piety, godliness*
**ὁρατός** 1 • 5 *visible*
**φρουρέω** 1 • 1 *to detain, confine*
**Χριστιανός, ὁ** 14 • 24 *Christ-follower, Christian*
5 **ἀδικέω** [2] 2 • 7 *to do wrong*
**ἀντιτάσσω** 1 • 7 *to oppose, resist*
**διότι** 1 • 3 *because*
**ἡδονή, ἡ** 3 • 12 *pleasure, delight, enjoyment, pleasantness*
**κωλύω** 2 • 3 *to hinder, prevent, forbid*
**πολεμέω** 2 • 7 *to be hostile*
**χράομαι** 3 • 18 *to make use of, employ*
**Χριστιανός, ὁ** 14 • 24 *Christ-follower, Christian*

6 **Χριστιανός, ὁ** 14 • 24 *Christ-follower, Christian*
7 **ἐγκλείω** 3 • 4 *to lock up, shut up, enclose*
**κατέχω** 2 • 4 *to confine*
**συνέχω** 2 • 4 *to hold together, sustain*
**φρουρά, ἡ** 1 • 1 *prison*
**Χριστιανός, ὁ** 14 • 24 *Christ-follower, Christian*
8 **ἀθάνατος** 2 • 5 *immortal*
**ἀφθαρσία, ἡ** 1 • 12 *incorruptibility, immortality*
**θνητός** 3 • 5 *mortal*
**παροικέω** 1 • 6 *to be a stranger*
**προσδέχομαι** 1 • 10 *to wait for*
**σκήνωμα, τό** 1 • 1 *habitation*
**φθαρτός** 3 • 10 *perishable*
**Χριστιανός, ὁ** 14 • 24 *Christ-follower, Christian*
9 **βελτιόω** 1 • 1 *to become better*
**κακουργέω** 1 • 1 *to treat badly*
**κολάζω** 6 • 9 *to penalize, punish*
**πλεονάζω** 2 • 3 *to be/become more, be/become great, be present in abundance, grow, increase*
**ποτόν, τό** 1 • 1 *drink;*
**σιτίοις καὶ ποτοῖς** (dat. of reference) *with reference to food and drink*
**σιτίον, τό** 1 • 1 *food*
**Χριστιανός, ὁ** 14 • 24 *Christ-follower, Christian*
10 **θεμιτός** 1 • 2 *allowed, permitted, right*
**παραιτέομαι** 1 • 1 *to reject, avoid*
**τάξις, ἡ** 2 • 6 *position, post*
**τοσοῦτος** 2 • 38 *so great/strong, to such extent*

## Chapter 7

1 **ἀνθρώπινος** 2 • 7 *human*
**ἀξιόω** 3 • 14 *to deem, hold an opinion*
**ἐπίγειος** 2 • 12 *earthly*
**ἐπιμελῶς** 2 • 9 *carefully, diligently*
**ἐπίνοια, ἡ** 2 • 2 *thought, conception*
**εὕρημα, τό** 1 • 1 *discovery, invention*
**θνητός** 3 • 5 *mortal*
**μυστήριον, τό** 7 • 11 *transcendent/ultimate reality, secret*
**οἰκονομία, ἡ** 2 • 6 *management*
2 **ἄβυσσος, ἡ** 1 • 4 *depth, abyss*
**ἀήρ, ὁ** 1 • 1 *air*
**ἀληθῶς** 2 • 3 *truly, in truth, really, actually*
**ἀόρατος** 3 • 13 *unseen, invisible*
**ἀπερινόητος** 1 • 1 *incomprehensible*
**ἄστρον, τό** 2 • 3 *star, constellation, single star*
**βάθος, τό** 1 • 4 *depth*
**δημιουργός, ὁ** 2 • 7 *builder, maker, creator*
**διατάσσω** 1 • 8 *to order*
**διέπω** 1 • 3 *to conduct, administer*
**διοίκησις, ἡ** 1 • 2 *administration, management*
**διορίζω** 1 • 1 *to set limits to*
**δρόμος, ὁ** [2] 2 • 5 *course, race*
**ἐγκαταστηρίζω** 1 • 1 *to establish*
**ἐγκλείω** 3 • 4 *to lock up, shut up, enclose*
**εἰκάζω** 1 • 1 *to suppose, imagine*
**ἐνιδρύω** 1 • 1 *to place/establish in*
**ἐπίγειος** 2 • 12 *earthly*
**καθάπερ** 3 • 3 *just as*
**κελεύω** 2 • 44 *to command, order, urge*
**κτίζω** 4 • 25 *to create*
**μεταξύ** 1 • 10 *between, in the middle, next*
**μέτρον, τό** 1 • 3 *quantity, number*
**μυστήριον, τό** 7 • 11 *transcendent/ultimate reality, secret*
**ὅρος, ὁ** 1 • 66 *boundary, limit*
**παντοκράτωρ, ὁ** 1 • 12 *Almighty, all-powerful, Omnipotent (One)*
**παντοκτίστης, ὁ** 1 • 1 *creator of the universe*
**πειθαρχέω** 2 • 3 *to obey*
**πιστῶς** 1 • 1 *faithfully*
**σελήνη, ἡ** [2] 3 • 7 *moon*
**στοιχεῖον, τό** 2 • 3 *heavenly bodies*
**τεχνίτης, ὁ** 2 • 4 *artisan, designer*
**ὑπηρέτης, ὁ** 1 • 5 *helper, assistant*
**ὕψος, τό** 1 • 7 *height*
3 **ἆρα** 1 • 18 *then*
**γέ** 5 • 18 *at least, even indeed*

**καταπλήσσω** 1 • 3 *to amaze, astound*
**τυραννίς, ἡ** 1 • 1 *despotic rule, tyranny*
4 **βία, ἡ** 1 • 1 *force*
**βιάζω** 2 • 2 *to use force*
**ἐπιείκεια, ἡ** 1 • 9 *clemency, gentleness, graciousness, courtesy, indulgence, tolerance*
**πραΰτης, ἡ** 1 • 8 *gentleness, humility, courtesy, considerateness, meekness*
**πρόσειμι** 1 • 1 *to belong to, be present with, be an attribute/custom of*
**οὐ μὲν οὖν** *certainly not!*
6 **παρουσία, ἡ** 2 • 4 *coming, advent*
**ὑφίστημι** 1 • 2 *to resist, face, endure*
7 **νικάω** 2 • 8 *to vanquish, overcome*
**παραβάλλω** 1 • 3 *to throw to*
8 **κολάζω** 6 • 9 *to penalize, punish*
**πλεονάζω** 2 • 3 *to be/become more, be/become great, be present in abundance, grow, increase*
**τοσοῦτος** 2 • 38 *so much, as much*
9 **δεῖγμα, τό** 3 • 3 *indicator, proof*
**παρουσία, ἡ** 2 • 4 *coming, advent*

## Chapter 8

1 **ἐπίσταμαι** 1 • 7 *to know, be acquainted with*
**ὅλως** 1 • 31 *completely, wholly, everywhere*
**ποτέ** 1 • 15 *at some time or other*
**πρίν** 2 • 7 *before*
2 **ἀξιόπιστος** 1 • 4 *betraying confidence, pretentious, specious*
**ἀποδέχομαι** 2 • 6 *to accept*
**κενός** 1 • 26 *to empty*
**κτίζω** 4 • 25 *to create*
**ληρώδης** 1 • 1 *foolish, silly, frivolous*
**στοιχεῖον, τό** 2 • 3 *elements*
**φιλόσοφος, ὁ** 1 • 3 *philosopher*
**χωρέω** 2 • 15 *to go, go out/away, reach*
3 **ἀπόδεκτος** 1 • 1 *acceptable, welcome, and pleasing*
**ἀποφαίνω/ἀποφαίνομαι** 1 • 1 *to show, declare, pronounce*
**γέ** 5 • 18 *at least, even, indeed*
**καίτοι/καίτοιγε** 1 • 1 *and yet*
**κτίσμα, τό** 1 • 4 *that which is created (by God), creature (created by God)*
4 **γόης, ὁ** 1 • 1 *swindler, cheat*
**τερατεία, ἡ** [2] 2 • 2 *illusion, humbug*
5 **γνωρίζω** 1 • 18 *to know*
**ἐπιδείκνυμι** 3 • 13 *to demonstrate, show*
6 **ἐπιδείκνυμι** 3 • 13 *to demonstrate, show*
**συγχωρέω** 1 • 2 *to grant, permit*
7 **δεσπότης, ὁ** 2 • 52 *lord, master*
**δημιουργός, ὁ** 2 • 7 *builder, maker, creator*
**διακρίνω** 2 • 7 *to separate, arrange*
**μακρόθυμος** 1 • 9 *patient, forbearing, tolerant, even tempered*
**τάξις, ἡ** 2 • 6 *order, proper procedure*
**φιλάνθρωπος** 1 • 1 *loving humanity, benevolent*
8 **ἀεί** 3 • 7 *always*
**ἀληθής** 4 • 16 *truthful, righteous, honest*
**ἀόργητος** 1 • 3 *free from anger*
**χρηστός** 1 • 2 *kind, loving, benevolent*
9 **ἀνακοινόω** 1 • 1 *to communicate (something) to someone*
**ἄφραστος** 1 • 1 *too wonderful for words*
**ἐννοέω** 1 • 1 *to have in mind, consider*
**ἔννοια, ἡ** 1 • 4 *thought, knowledge, insight*
**παῖς, ὁ/ἡ** 3 • 20 *slave, servant*
10 **ἀμελέω** 1 • 3 *to neglect, be unconcerned*
**ἀφροντιστέω** 1 • 1 *to be careless, be unconcerned*
**βουλή, ἡ** 1 • 19 *resolution, decision*
**διατηρέω** 1 • 1 *to keep*
**κατέχω** 2 • 4 *to prevent, hinder, restrain*
**μυστήριον, τό** 7 • 11 *transcendent/ultimate reality, secret*
**σοφός** 1 • 8 *wise*
11 **ἅμα** 1 • 12 *at the same time*

**ἀποκαλύπτω** 2 • 23 *to reveal, disclose, bring to light, make fully known*
**ἐπεί** 2 • 35 *when, after*
**εὐεργεσία, ἡ** 2 • 5 *good deed, benefit, a kindness*
**μετέχω** 2 • 4 *to share, have a share, participate*
**νοέω** 2 • 46 *to perceive, apprehend, understand, gain an insight to*
**παῖς, ὁ/ἡ** 3 • 20 *slave, servant*
**παρέχω** 7 • 18 *to grant, show*
**προσδοκάω** 4 • 8 *to wait for, look for, expect*
**πώποτε** 1 • 2 *ever, at any time*

## Chapter 9

1 **ἀδικία, ἡ** 2 • 7 *unrighteousness, wickedness, injustice*
**ἀδύνατος** 3 • 11 *powerless, impotent*
**ἁμάρτημα, τό** 1 • 8 *sin, transgression*
**ἀνάξιος** 1 • 4 *unworthy*
**ἀνέχω** 1 • 4 *to endure, bear with, put up with*
**ἀξιόω** 3 • 14 *to consider worthy, deserving*
**ἀπάγω** 1 • 4 pass. *to be misled, be carried away*
**ἄτακτος** 1 • 1 *undisciplined*
**δημιουργέω** 1 • 3 *to create*
**ἐάω** 1 • 13 *to let, permit*
**ἐλέγχω** 4 • 16 *to convict, convince*
**ἐφήδομαι** 1 • 1 *to (take) delight in*
**ἡδονή, ἡ** 3 • 12 *pleasure, delight, enjoyment, pleasantness*
**μέχρι** 2 • 23 *until*
**οἰκονομέω** 1 • 1 *to manage, regulate, administer, plan*
**παῖς, ὁ/ἡ** 3 • 20 *slave, servant*
**πάντως** 1 • 9 *not at all*
**πρόσθεν** 2 • 4 *earlier, former*
**συνευδοκέω** 1 • 5 *to agree with, approve of, consent to, sympathize with*
**φορά, ἡ** 1 • 1 *impulse, passion*
**χρηστότης, ἡ** 4 • 9 *goodness, kindness, generosity*

2 **ἀδικία, ἡ** 2 • 7 *unrighteousness, wickedness, injustice*
**ἄδικος** 1 • 14 *unjust, crooked*
**ἀθάνατος** 2 • 5 *immortal*
**ἄκακος** 1 • 7 *innocent, guileless*
**ἀναδέχομαι** 2 • 2 *to accept, receive*
**ἀνέχω** 4 • 7 *to endure, bear with, put up with*
**ἄνομος** 3 • 17 *lawless*
**ἀπωθέω** 1 • 2 *to reject, repudiate*
**ἄφθαρτος** 1 • 7 *imperishable, incorruptible, immortal*
**ἐλεέω** 1 • 16 *to have compassion/ mercy/pity*
**ἐπεί** 2 • 35 *when, after*
**ἡμέτερος** [2] 3 • 13 *our*
**θνητός** 3 • 5 *mortal*
**κόλασις, ἡ** 3 • 11 *punishment*
**λύτρον, τό** 1 • 2 *price of release, ransom*
**μακροθυμέω** 1 • 3 *to be patient, be forbearing*
**μισθός, ὁ** 1 • 22 *recompense*
**μνησικακέω** 1 • 9 *to remember evil, bear malice, bear a grudge*
**προσδοκάω** 4 • 8 *to wait for, expect, look for, expect*
**προστίθημι** 1 • 22 *to add, put to*
**τελείως** 1 • 8 *fully, perfectly, completely, altogether*
**ὑπερβάλλω** 1 • 4 *to go beyond, surpass, outdo*
**φθαρτός** 3 • 10 *perishable*
**φιλανθρωπία, ἡ** 1 • 1 *(loving) kindness*
**χρηστότης, ἡ** 4 • 9 *goodness, kindness, generosity*
**ὦ** 4 • 8 *o, oh, how!*
**πεπλήρωτο** (pluperfect pass. of πληρόω) *had been fulfilled*
**πεφανέρωτο** (pluperfect pass. of φανερόω) *had become clear*

3 **καλύπτω** 1 • 3 *to hide, conceal, keep secret*

4 **ἄνομος** 3 • 17 *lawless*
**ἀσεβής** 2 • 14 *irreverent, impious, ungodly*

5 **ἀνεξιχνίαστος** 1 • 2 *inscrutable, incomprehensible*
**ἀνομία, ἡ** 1 • 33 *lawlessness*
**ἄνομος** 3 • 17 *lawless*
**ἀνταλλαγή, ἡ** 1 • 1 *exchange*
**ἀπροσδόκητος** 1 • 1 *unexpected*
**γλυκύς** 1 • 6 *sweet*
**δημιουργία, ἡ** 1 • 2 *creative act*

**εὐεργεσία, ἡ** 2 • 5 *good deed, benefit, a kindness*
**κρύπτω** 1 • 4 *to hide*
**ὦ** [3] 4 • 8 *o, oh, how!*
6 **ἀδύνατος** [2] 3 • 11 *powerless, impotent*
**ἀμφότεροι** 1 • 21 *both*
**ἐλέγχω** 4 • 16 *to bring to light, expose, set forth*
**ἔνδυσις, ἡ** 1 • 1 *clothing*
**ἡγέομαι** 5 • 25 *to think, consider, regard*
**ἡμέτερος** 3 • 13 *our*
**ἰατρός, ὁ** 1 • 3 *physician of the soul*
**ἰσχύς, ἡ** 1 • 11 *strength, power, might*
**μεριμνάω** 1 • 1 *to have anxiety, be anxious, be (unduly) concerned*
**νοῦς, ὁ** 3 • 12 *understanding, mind*
**πρόσθεν** 2 • 4 *earlier, former*
**σύμβουλος, ὁ** 1 • 8 *adviser, counselor*
**σωτήρ, ὁ** 1 • 14 *savior, deliverer, preserver*
**τροφεύς, ὁ** 1 • 1 *nourisher*
**τροφή, ἡ** 1 • 12 *nourishment, food*
**τυγχάνω** 5 • 15 *to meet, attain, gain, find, experience*
**φῦσις, ἡ** 1 • 4 *natural characteristic/disposition*
**χρηστότης, ἡ** 4 • 9 *goodness, kindness, generosity*

## Chapter 10

1 **ἐπίγνωσις, ἡ** 1 • 5 *knowledge, recognition*
**καταλαμβάνω** 1 • 5 *to win, attain*
**ποθέω** 3 • 4 *to desire, wish (for), be anxious, strive after*
2 **ἄνω** 1 • 3 *upwards(s), up*
**εἰκών, ἡ** 1 • 5 *form, appearance*
**ἐπαγγέλλω** 1 • 7 *to promise*
**ἐπιτρέπω** 1 • 11 *to allow, permit*
**μονογενής** 1 • 3 *unique (in kind)*
**νοῦς, ὁ** 3 • 12 *understanding, mind*
**πλάσσω** 2 • 8 *to form, mold*
3 **οἴομαι** 4 • 11 *to think, suppose, expect*
**προαγαπάω** 1 • 1 *to love before, love first*
4 **μιμητής, ὁ** [2] 3 • 12 *imitator*
**χρηστότης, ἡ** 4 • 9 *goodness, kindness, generosity*
5 **ἀσθενής** 1 • 12 *weak*
**βιάζω** 2 • 2 *to dominate, constrain*
**ἐκτός** 1 • 6 *outside*
**εὐδαιμονέω** 1 • 1 *to be happy, be fortunate*
**καταδυναστεύω** 1 • 3 *to oppress, exploit, dominate*
**μεγαλειότης, ἡ** 1 • 3 *impressiveness*
**μιμέομαι** 1 • 4 *to imitate, emulate, follow*
**πλησίον** 3 • 17 *near;* subst. *neighbor, fellow human being*
**πλουτέω** 1 • 6 *to be rich*
**ὑποδεής** 1 • 2 *inferior*
6 **ἀναδέχομαι** 2 • 2 *to accept, receive*
**βάρος, τό** 1 • 1 *burden*
**ἐλαττόω** 1 • 1 *to be worse off, be in need*
**ἐπιδέομαι** 1 • 1 *to need, be in need*
**εὐεργετέω** 1 • 3 *to do good to, benefit*
**κρείττων** 2 • 8 *more prominent, higher in rank, preferable, better*
**μιμητής, ὁ** 3 • 12 *imitator*
**πλησίον** 3 • 17 *near;* subst. *neighbor, fellow human being*
**χορηγέω** 3 • 6 *to provide, supply (in abundance)*
7 **ἀληθῶς** 2 • 23 *truly, in truth, really, actually*
**ἀπάτη, ἡ** 2 • 16 *deception, deceitfulness*
**ἐνθάδε** 1 • 5 *here*
**θεάομαι** 1 • 4 *to see, behold, perceive*
**καταγινώσκω** 1 • 1 *to condemn, convict*
**κατακρίνω** 2 • 6 *to pronounce a sentence on*
**καταφρονέω** 3 • 9 *to care nothing for, disregard, be unafraid of*
**κολάζω** 6 • 9 *to penalize, punish*
**κόλασις, ἡ** 3 • 11 *punishment*
**μέχρι** 2 • 23 *to the point of*

**μυστήριον, τό** 7 • 11 *transcendent/ultimate reality, secret*
**ὄντως** 1 • 1 *really, certainly, in truth*
**πλάνη, ἡ** 3 • 11 *error, delusion, deceit, deception*
**πολιτεύομαι** 2 • 10 *to rule*
**τυγχάνω** 5 • 15 *to happen to be*
8 **μακαρίζω** 1 • 5 *to call/consider blessed, happy, fortunate*
**πρόσκαιρος** 1 • 1 *temporary, transitory*
**ὑπομένω** 3 • 32 *to stand one's ground, hold out, endure*

## Chapter 11

1 **ἀξίως** 1 • 5 *worthily, in a manner worthy of, suitably*
**ξένος** 4 • 8 *strange*
**ὁμιλέω** 2 • 3 *to speak, converse, address*
**παραλόγως** 1 • 1 *in an unreasonable manner*
**ὑπηρετέω** 1 • 5 *to serve, be helpful*
2 **ἄπιστος** 1 • 8 *without faith, disbelieving, unbelieving*
**διηγέομαι** 1 • 4 *to tell, relate, describe*
**ἐπιζητέω** 3 • 9 *to wish, wish for*
**μανθάνω** 5 • 26 *to learn*
**μυστήριον, τό** 7 • 11 *transcendent/ultimate reality, secret*
**νοέω** 2 • 46 *to perceive, apprehend, understand, gain an insight into*
**ὀρθῶς** 3 • 8 *rightly, correctly*
**προσφιλής** 1 • 1 *pleasing, agreeable, lovely, amiable*
**σαφῶς** 2 • 5 *clearly, exactly, very well*
**φανερῶς** 1 • 2 *clearly, plainly*
3 **ἀτιμάζω** 1 • 8 *to dishonor, shame*
**χάριν** 1 • 4 *for the sake of, on behalf of, on account of*
4 **νέος** 1 • 16 *new, fresh*
**παλαιός** 1 • 7 *old*
5 **ἀεί** 3 • 7 *always;*
**οὗτος ὁ ἀεί** *the eternal one*
**ἁπλόω** 1 • 1 *to make single, unfold*
**διαγγέλλω** 1 • 1 *to announce, report*
**δωρέω/δωρέομαι** 1 • 1 *to present, bestow*
**ἐπιζητέω** 3 • 9 *to wish, wish for*
**θραύω** 1 • 4 *to break*
**μυστήριον, τό** 7 • 11 *transcendent/ultimate reality, secret*
**νοῦς, ὁ** 3 • 12 *understanding, mind*
**ὅριον, τό** 1 • 2 *boundary*
**ὅρκιον, τό** 1 • 1 *oath, vow, pledge*
**παρέχω** 7 • 18 *to grant, show*
**παρορίζω** 1 • 1 *to overstep, transgress*
**πληθύνω** 1 • 11 *to be multiplied, grow, increase*
**πλουτίζω** 2 • 5 *to make rich*
6 **ᾄδω** 1 • 6 *to sing (in praise)*
**εἶτα** 1 • 48 *furthermore, then, next*
**ἱδρύω** 1 • 2 *to be seated, sit, be established*
**παράδοσις, ἡ** 1 • 7 *tradition*
**σκιρτάω** 1 • 5 *to leap, spring about*
7 **λυπέω** 2 • 17 *to irritate, offend, insult*
**ὁμιλέω** 2 • 3 *to speak, converse, address*
8 **ἀποκαλύπτω** 2 • 23 *to reveal, disclose, bring to light, make fully known*
**ἐξαγορεύω/ἐξεῖπον** 1 • 4 *to express, proclaim*
**κελεύω** 2 • 44 *to command, order, urge*
**κινέω** 1 • 3 *to move, cause*
**κοινωνός, ὁ/ἡ** 1 • 7 *sharer*
**πόνος, ὁ** 1 • 6 *(hard) labor, toil*

## Chapter 12

1 **ἀνατέλλω** 1 • 6 *to cause to spring/rise up*
**ἐντυγχάνω** 1 • 8 *to read*
**εὐθαλέω** 1 • 1 *to flourish, thrive*
**κοσμέω** 1 • 10 *to adorn, decorate*
**ξύλον, τό** 7 • 23 *tree*
**ὀρθῶς** 3 • 8 *rightly, correctly*
**πάγκαρπος** 1 • 1 *bearing much fruit*

**παράδεισος, ὁ** 2 • 8 *paradise*
**παρέχω** 7 • 18 *to grant, show*
**ποικίλος** 1 • 22 *diversified, manifold*
**σπουδή, ἡ** 1 • 4 *eagerness, earnestness, diligence, willingness, zeal*
**τρυφή, ἡ** 1 • 22 *enjoyment, joy, delight*
2 **ἀναιρέω** [2] 2 • 10 *to do away with, destroy*
**γνῶσις, ἡ** [2] 10 • 32 *knowledge*
**ξύλον, τό** [2] 7 • 23 *tree*
**παρακοή, ἡ** 1 • 1 *unwillingness to hear, disobedience*
**φυτεύω** 4 • 16 *to plant*
**χωρίον, τό** 1 • 5 *to place, piece of land, field*
3 **ἄσημος** 1 • 1 *obscure, unclear*
**γνῶσις, ἡ** [2] 10 • 32 *knowledge*
**γυμνόω** 1 • 1 *to strip, lay bare*
**ἐπιδείκνυμι** 3 • 11 *to demonstrate, show*
**καθαρῶς** 1 • 1 *in purity*
**ξύλον, τό** [2] 7 • 23 *tree*
**ὄφις, ὁ** 3 • 9 *serpent*
**παράδεισος, ὁ** 2 • 8 *paradise*
**πλάνη, ἡ** 3 • 11 *error, delusion, deceit, deception*
**φυτεύω** 4 • 16 *to plant*
**χράομαι** 3 • 18 *to make use of, employ*
4 **ἀληθής** 4 • 16 *real, genuine, not imaginary*
**ἄνευ** [2] 4 • 12 *without*
**ἀσφαλής** 1 • 4 *certain*
**γνῶσις, ἡ** [2] 10 • 32 *knowledge*
**διό** 1 • 14 *therefore, for this reason*
**ἑκάτερος** 1 • 2 *each of two, both*
**πλησίον** 3 • 17 *nearby, near, close*
**φυτεύω** 4 • 16 *to plant*
5 **ἄνευ** 4 • 12 *without*
**ἀσκέω** 2 • 6 *to practice, engage in*
**γνῶσις, ἡ** [2] 10 • 32 *knowledge*
**ἐνοράω** 1 • 1 *to see, perceive*
**μέμφομαι** 1 • 4 *to find fault with, blame*
**πρόσταγμα, τό** 1 • 10 *order, command(ment), injunction*
**φυσιόω** 1 • 6 *to puff up, make proud*
6 **ἀληθής** 4 • 16 *true*
**ἄνευ** 4 • 12 *without*
**γνῶσις, ἡ** 10 • 32 *knowledge*
**ἐπιζητέω** 3 • 9 *to wish, wish for*
**νομίζω** 6 • 10 *to think, believe, hold, consider*
**ὄφις, ὁ** 3 • 9 *serpent*
**προσδοκάω** 4 • 8 *to wait for, look for, expect*
**φυτεύω** 4 • 16 *to plant*
7 **ἀληθής** 4 • 16 *true*
**γνῶσις, ἡ** 10 • 32 *knowledge*
**χωρέω** 2 • 15 *to hold, contain*
8 **ἀεί** 3 • 7 *always*
**Εὔα, ἡ** 1 • 2 *Eve*
**ξύλον, τό** 7 • 23 *tree*
**ὄφις, ὁ** 3 • 9 *serpent*
**παρθένος, ἡ** 1 • 62 *virgin, chaste person*
**πλάνη, ἡ** 3 • 11 *error, delusion, deceit, deception*
**ποθέω** 3 • 4 *to desire, wish (for), be anxious, strive after*
**συγχρωτίζομαι** 1 • 1 *to defile by touching*
**τρυγάω** 1 • 2 *to harvest (grapes)*
**φθείρω** 2 • 10 *to ruin, corrupt*
9 **ἁρμόζω** 1 • 23 *to join*
**εὐφραίνω** 1 • 15 *to be glad, enjoy oneself, rejoice, celebrate*
**κλῆρος, ὁ** 1 • 8 *portion, share;* perhaps *congregation, group*
**πάσχα, τό** 1 • 1 *the Easter festival*
**προέρχομαι** 1 • 5 *to go forward, advance, proceed*
**συνετίζω** 1 • 2 *to cause to understand*

# The Fragment of Quadratus

1 **Ἁδριανός, ὁ** 1 • 2 *Hadrian*
**Αἴλιος, ὁ** 1 • 1 *Aelius*
**ἀναδίδωμι** 1 • 1 *to deliver, hand over*
**ἀπολογία, ἡ** 1 • 1 *defense, reply*
**ἀποστολικός** 1 • 5 *apostolic*
**διαδέχομαι** 1 • 2 *to receive (in turn) from a former owner, succeed to*
**διανοία, ἡ** 1 • 23 *understanding, intelligence, mind*
**εἴκοσι** 1 • 2 *twenty*
**ἐνοχλέω** 1 • 2 *to trouble, annoy*
**ἕξ** 1 • 23 *six*
**ἡγεμονία, ἡ** 1 • 3 *chief command, direction, management of the imperial government*
**ἡμέτερος** 2 • 15 *our*
**θεοσέβεια, ἡ** 1 • 7 *reverence for God, piety, religion*
**καθοράω** 1 • 1 *to, see, behold, regard*
**Κοδράτος, ὁ** 1 • 2 *Quadratus*
**λαμπρός** 1 • 15 *clear, transparent*
**μήν, ὁ** 1 • 11 *month*
**ὀρθοτομία, ἡ** 1 • 1 *orthodoxy*
**πειράω** 1 • 3 *to try, attempt, endeavor*
**προσφωνέω** 1 • 1 *to call out, address*
**σύγγραμμα, τό** 1 • 7 *writing, book, work*
**συντάσσω, ἡ** 1 • 5 *to order, organize, compose*
**τεκμήριον, τό** 1 • 1 *proof*
**Τραϊανός, ὁ** 1 • 3 *Trajan*

2 **ἀεί** [2] 2 • 9 *always*
**ἀπαλλάσσω** 1 • 4 *to leave, depart*
**ἀρχαιότης, ἡ** 1 • 2 *antiquity*
**ἀφικνέομαι** 1 • 2 *to reach (become known to), remain alive, survive*
**ἐπιδημέω** 1 • 2 *to live;*
**οὐδὲ ἐπιδημοῦντος μόνον τοῦ σωτῆρος** *not only while the Savior was (with us)*
**ἡμέτερος** 2 • 15 *our*
**ἱστορέω** 1 • 9 *to give an account of what one has learned, record*
**παραφαίνω** 1 • 1 *to show, demonstrate, give a glimpse*
**πάρειμι** [2] 2 • 19 *to be present*
**σωτήρ, ὁ** [2] 2 • 14 *savior*

# The Fragments of Papias

## Chapter 1

1 **ἀκουστής, ὁ** 4 • 4 *hearer*
**βίος, ὁ** 2 • 13 *life*
**γνωρίζω** 2 • 18 *to make known, reveal*
**Εἰρηναῖος, ὁ** 11 • 19 *Irenaeus*
**ἐπίσκοπος, ὁ** 9 • 76 *overseer, supervisor*
**θεολόγος, ὁ** 4 • 4 *God's herald*
**Ἱεραπολίτης, ὁ** 5 • 5 *inhabitant of Hierapolis*
**ἱστορέω** 8 • 9 *to narrate/record (what one has learned)*
**Παπίας, ὁ** 28 • 28 *Papias*
**παραμένω** 2 • 9 *to remain, stay (on)*
**Πολύκαρπος, ὁ** 5 • 39 *Polycarp*
**Σμύρνα, ἡ** 2 • 14 *Smyrna*
**Τραϊανός, ὁ** 2 • 2 *Trajan*

## Chapter 2

1 **Ἀσία, ἡ** 5 • 10 *Asia*
**αὐτόπτης, ὁ** 3 • 3 *eyewitness*
**γέ** 3 • 18 *at least, even, indeed*
**γνωρίζω** 2 • 18 *to make known, reveal*
**διαπρέπω** 1 • 1 *to appear prominent, conspicuous*
**ἐγχειρίζω** 1 • 1 *to put into one's hands, entrust*
**ἐπισκοπή, ἡ** 1 • 5 *position, assignment*
**ἐπίσκοπος, ὁ** 9 • 76 *overseer or supervisor*
**Ἱεράπολις, ἡ** 7 • 7 *Hierapolis*
**μήν** 3 • 8 *surely, certainly*
**ὁμιλητής, ὁ** 1 • 1 *disciple*
**Παπίας, ὁ** 28 • 28 *Papias*
**παροικία, ἡ** 1 • 3 *congregation, parish*
**Πολύκαρπος, ὁ** 5 • 39 *Polycarp*
**Σμύρνα, ἡ** 2 • 14 *Smyrna*
**ὑπηρέτης, ὁ** 1 • 5 *helper, assistant*

## Chapter 3

1 **ἀκουστής, ὁ** 4 • 4 *hearer*
**ἀριθμός** 6 • 14 *number*
**ἀρχαῖος** 8 • 12 *ancient;* **ἀρχαῖος ἀνήρ** *a man of the early period (of the Christian faith)*
**ἐγγράφως** 2 • 2 *in writing*
**Εἰρηναῖος, ὁ** 11 • 19 *Irenaeus*
**ἐξήγησις, ἡ** 4 • 6 *explanation, interpretation*
**ἐπιγράφω** 1 • 4 *to write on/in*
**ἐπιμαρτυρέω** 2 • 2 *to bear witness, attest*
**ἑταῖρος, ὁ** 3 • 4 *comrade, companion*
**κυριακός** 7 • 9 *the Lord's*
**λόγιον, τό** 5 • 11 *a saying*
**μνημονεύω** 7 • 25 *to retain in one's memory*
**Παπίας, ὁ** [2] 28 • 28 *Papias*
**Πολύκαρπος, ὁ** 5 • 39 *Polycarp*
**σύγγραμμα, τό** 2 • 6 *book, (written) work*
**συντάσσω** 4 • 4 *to write, compose, compile*
**τέταρτος** 4 • 9 *fourth*
2 **ἀκροατής, ὁ** 2 • 4 *a hearer*
**αὐτόπτης, ὁ** 3 • 3 *eyewitness*
**γέ** 3 • 18 *at least, even, indeed*
**γνώριμος** 1 • 1 *acquainted with*
**Εἰρηναῖος, ὁ** 11 • 19 *Irenaeus*
**ἐμφαίνω/ἐμφαίζω** 1 • 1 *to make clear, explain, inform, make a report*
**ἱερός** 2 • 5 *holy*
**λέξις** 3 • 3 *expressly, in the very words*
**μήν** 3 • 8 *and indeed*
**οὐδαμῶς** 1 • 1 *by no means*
**Παπίας, ὁ** 28 • 28 *Papias*
**προοίμιον, τό** 1 • 1 *prelude, preface*
3 **ἀληθής** 2 • 16 *true*
**ἀλλότριος** 1 • 14 *not one's own, strange*

**διαβεβαιόω/διαβεβαιόομαι** 2 • 2 *to speak confidently, insist*
**ἑρμηνεία, ἡ** 2 • 2 *interpretation, exposition*
**μανθάνω** 2 • 26 *to learn*
**μνημονεύω** [2] 7 • 25 *to retain in one's memory*
**ὀκνέω** 1 • 1 *to hesitate, delay*
**ποτέ** 1 • 15 *at some time or other;* **ὅσα ποτέ** *whatever, everything*
**συγκατατάσσω** 1 • 1 *to set forth things along with*
4 **ἀνακρίνω** 1 • 1 *to question, examine*
**Ἀνδρέας, ὁ** 1 • 1 *Andrew*
**Ἀριστίων, ὁ** 5 • 5 *Aristion*
**Θωμᾶς, ὁ** 3 • 3 *Thomas*
**Ματθαῖος, ὁ** 6 • 6 *Matthew*
**παρακολουθέω** 3 • 3 *to follow*
**πού** 1 • 7 *somewhere;* **εἰ δέ που** *and if by chance*
**τοσοῦτος** 6 • 38 *so much, as much*
**ὑπολαμβάνω** 2 • 3 *to assume, think, believe, be of the opinion (that), suppose*
**ὠφελέω** 1 • 8 *to help, aid, benefit, be of use (to)*
5 **ἀριθμός, ὁ** 6 • 14 *number*
**Ἀριστίων, ὁ** 5 • 5 *Aristion*
**δηλόω** 6 • 49 *to reveal, make clear, show*
**διαστέλλω** 1 • 1 *to distinguish, differentiate between*
**δίς** 1 • 2 *twice*
**ἔνθα** 1 • 2 *there, where*
**εὐαγγελιστής, ὁ** 3 • 3 *proclaimer of the gospel, evangelist*
**ἐφίστημι** 1 • 5 *to fix one's mind on, be attentive to*
**καταριθμέω** 1 • 2 *to count, list, enumerate*
**κατατάσσω** 1 • 1 *to place, refer to*
**Ματθαῖος, ὁ** 6 • 6 *Matthew*
**προτάσσω** 1 • 1 *to fix, determine, allot (beforehand)*
**πρότερος** 4 • 47 *former, earlier*
**σαφῶς** 2 • 2 *clearly, exactly, very well*
**συγκαταλέγω** 1 • 1 *to number together with, reckon among*
6 **ἀληθής** 2 • 16 *true*
**ἀναγκαῖος** 2 • 4 *necessary*
**ἀποδείκνυμι** 1 • 3 *to prove*
**ἀποκάλυψις, ἡ** 3 • 18 *Revelation*
**Ἀσία, ἡ** 5 • 10 *Asia*
**εἰκός** 1 • 2 *probable, reasonable*
**ἑκάτερος** 1 • 2 *each of two, both*
**Ἔφεσος, ἡ** 3 • 4 *Ephesus*
**ἱστορία, ἡ** 4 • 4 *account, story*
**μνῆμα, τό** 1 • 1 *grave, tomb*
**νοῦς, ὁ** 2 • 12 *mind, thought, opinion, decree*
**ὁμωνυμία, ἡ** 1 • 1 *having the same name, verbal identity*
**ὀνομάζω** 1 • 1 *to call, name*
**προσέχω** 1 • 25 *to pay attention to, give heed to, follow*
**σαφῶς** 2 • 5 *clearly, exactly, very well*
**χράομαι** 2 • 18 *to make use of, employ*
**ἐθέλοι** (present optative of θέλω, from Attic form ἐθέλω) *he might prefer*
7 **Ἀριστίων, ὁ** 5 • 5 *Aristion*
**αὐτήκοος** 1 • 1 *ear-witness*
**ἄχρηστος** 1 • 6 *useless, worthless*
**γοῦν** 1 • 4 *hence, then*
**δηλόω** 6 • 49 *to explain, clarify*
**μνημονεύω** 7 • 25 *to retain in one's memory*
**ὁμολογέω** 1 • 18 *to acknowledge, claim, profess, praise*
**ὀνομαστί** 1 • 1 *by name*
**Παπίας, ὁ** 28 • 28 *Papias*
**παράδοσις, ἡ** 5 • 7 *tradition*
**παρακολουθέω** 3 • 3 *to follow*
**πολλάκις** 1 • 2 *many times, often, frequently*
**σύγγραμμα, τό** 1 • 6 *book, (written) work*
8 **ἱστορέω** 8 • 9 *to narrate/record (what one has learned);* **παράδοξά τινα ἱστορεῖ καὶ ἄλλα** (acc. direct object with appositional accs. coming in v. 9) *he narrates some other remarkable things as well*
**λέξις** 3 • 3 *expressly, in the very words*
**Παπίας, ἡ** 28 • 28 *Papias*
**παράδοξος** 2 • 4 *strange, wonderful, remarkable*
**παράδοσις, ἡ** 5 • 7 *tradition*
**προσάπτω** 1 • 1 *to attribute*
9 **ἀηδής** 2 • 2 *unpleasant, odious*
**ἅμα** 1 • 12 *together*

**αὖ** 1 • 1 *again, anew, afresh, once more*
**Βαρσαβᾶς, ὁ** 2 • 2 *Barsabbas*
**δηλητήριος** 1 • 1 *noxious*
**δηλόω** 6 • 49 *to reveal, make clear, show*
**διατρίβω** 3 • 5 *to spend time*
**διήγησις, ἡ** 3 • 3 *narrative, account*
**ἐμπίνω** 1 • 1 *to drink*
**θαυμάσιος** 1 • 4 *wonderful, remarkable, admirable*
**θυγάτηρ, ἡ** [2] 3 • 10 *daughter*
**Ἱεράπολις, ἡ** 7 • 7 *Hierapolis*
**Ἰοῦστος, ὁ** 4 • 4 *Justus*
**ἱστορέω** 8 • 9 *to narrate/record (what one has learned)*
**μνημονεύω** 7 • 25 *to remember, keep in mind, think of, mention*
**Παπίας, ὁ** 28 • 28 *Papias;*
  **κατὰ τοὺς αὐτοὺς ὁ Παπίας γενόμενος** *since Papias was their contemporary*
**παράδοξος** 2 • 4 *strange, wonderful, remarkable*
**πρόσθεν** 2 • 4 *earlier, former*
**σημειωτέον** 1 • 1 *one must note*
**ὑπομένω** 1 • 32 *to stand one's ground, hold out, endure*
**φάρμακον, τό** 1 • 5 *poison*
10 **ἀνάληψις, ἡ** 1 • 1 *ascension*
**ἀναπλήρωσις, ἡ** 2 • 2 *filling up, means of filling up*
**ἀντί** 2 • 15 *for, as, in place of*
**ἀριθμός, ὁ** 6 • 14 *number, total*
**Βαρσαββᾶς, ὁ** 1 • 1 *Barsabbas*
**ἐπεύχομαι** 1 • 1 *to pray*
**ἱερός** 2 • 5 *holy*
**Ἰούδας, ὁ** 1 • 2 *Judas*
**Ἰοῦστος, ὁ** [2] 4 • 4 *Justus*
**ἱστορέω** 8 • 9 *to narrate/record (what one has learned);*
  **πως ἱστορεῖ γραφή** *how the scripture reads, how the passage goes*
**κλῆρος, ὁ** 1 • 8 *lot*
**Ματθίας, ὁ** [2] 2 • 2 *Matthias*
**πρᾶξις, ἡ** 2 • 50 *act, action, deed*
**προδότης, ὁ** 1 • 6 *traitor, betrayer*
**σωτήρ, ὁ** 3 • 14 *savior, deliverer, preserver*
11 **ἄγραφος** 2 • 2 *unwritten*
**διδασκαλία, ἡ** 4 • 6 *teaching, instruction*
**ἥκω** 1 • 11 *to come*
**μυθικός** 1 • 1 *fictional*
**ξένος** 1 • 8 *strange*
**παράδοσις, ἡ** 5 • 7 *tradition*
**παρατίθημι** 2 • 6 *to demonstrate, point out*
**σωτήρ, ὁ** 3 • 14 *savior, deliverer, preserver*
**ὡσάν** 1 • 2 *as if, as if it were, so to speak*
12 **ἀποστολικός** 2 • 4 *apostolic*
**διήγησις, ἡ** 3 • 3 *narrative, account*
**ἡγέομαι** 2 • 25 *to think, consider, regard*
**μυστικῶς** 1 • 1 *secretly*
**οὑτοσί** 1 • 1 *this (here)*
**παρεκδέχομαι** 1 • 1 *to misinterpret*
**συνοράω** 1 • 1 *to comprehend, realize*
**σωματικῶς** 1 • 1 *bodily, corporeally*
**ὑπόδειγμα, τό** 2 • 8 *example, model, pattern*
**ὑπολαμβάνω** 2 • 3 *to assume, think, believe, be of the opinion (that), suppose*
**ὑφίστημι** 1 • 2 *to take (structured) shape*
**χιλιάς, ἡ** 1 • 3 *a thousand*
13 **ἀναφαίνω** 1 • 1 *to show forth, make known, display*
**ἀρχαιότης, ἡ** 1 • 1 *antiquity, ancient date*
**Εἰρηναῖος, ὁ** 11 • 19 *Irenaeus*
**ἐκκλησιαστικός** 3 • 4 *to the (universal) church*
**νοῦς, ὁ** 2 • 12 *mind, intellect*
**παραίτιος** 1 • 1 *sharing*
**προβάλλω** 1 • 2 *to put forward*
**σφόδρα** 1 • 1 *very (much), extremely, greatly*
**τεκμαίρομαι** 1 • 1 *to judge, conjecture*
**τοί** 1 • 7 *let me tell you, surely*
**φαίνω** 2 • 37 *to have the appearance, seem*
**φρονέω** 1 • 17 *to think, form/hold an opinion, judge*
14 **ἀναγκαίως** 2 • 2 *necessary*
**ἀναπέμπω** 1 • 3 *to send*
**Ἀριστίων, ὁ** 5 • 5 *Aristion*

**δηλόω** 6 • 49 *to reveal, make clear, show*
**διήγησις, ἡ** 3 • 3 *narrative, account*
**ἐκτίθημι** 3 • 3 *to explain, abound*
**Μᾶρκος, ὁ** 8 • 8 *Mark*
**παράδοσις, ἡ** [2] 5 • 7 *tradition*
**προεκτίθημι** 1 • 1 *to set out before*
**πρόσθεν** 2 • 4 *earlier, former*
**προστίθημι** 1 • 22 *to add, put to*
**φιλομαθής** 1 • 1 *fond of learning, eager after knowledge*
15 **ἀκριβῶς** 1 • 8 *accurately, carefully, well*
**ἀπομνημονεύω** 1 • 1 *to remember*
**διδασκαλία, ἡ** 4 • 6 *teaching, instruction*
**ἔνιοι** 2 • 4 *some, several*
**ἑρμηνευτής, ὁ** 1 • 1 *translator*
**ἱστορέω** 8 • 9 *to narrate/record (what one has learned)*;
**Ταῦτα ἱστόρηται τῷ Παπίᾳ** (dat. of agency with perfect pass. verb; cf. *ExSyn* 164)
**κυριακός** 7 • 9 *the Lord's*
**λόγιον, τό** 5 • 11 *a saying*
**Μᾶρκος, ὁ** [3] 8 • 8 *Mark*
**μέντοι** 2 • 2 *though, to be sure, indeed*
**μνημονεύω** 7 • 25 *to retain in one's memory*
**Παπίας, ὁ** 28 • 28 *Papias*
**παρακολουθέω** 3 • 3 *to follow*
**παραλείπω** 1 • 2 *to leave out, omit*
**πρόνοια, ἡ** 1 • 3 *forethought, foresight, providence*
**σύνταξις, ἡ** 1 • 1 *an organized account*
**τάξις, ἡ** 2 • 6 *fixed succession, order*
**ὕστερος** 2 • 3 *in the second place, later, then, thereafter*
**ψεύδομαι** 2 • 7 *to lie*
16 **διάλεκτος, ἡ** 1 • 2 *language*
**Ἑβραΐς, ἡ** 1 • 1 *the Hebrew language*
**ἑρμηνεύω** 1 • 2 *to translate*
**λόγιον, τό** 5 • 11 *a saying*
**Ματθαῖος, ὁ** [2] 6 • 6 *Matthew*
**συντάσσω** 4 • 4 *to write, compose, compile, organize*
17 **ἀναγκαίως** 2 • 2 *necessary*
**διαβάλλω** 1 • 1 *to bring charges, inform*
**Ἑβραῖος, ὁ** 1 • 1 *Hebrew*
**ἐκτίθημι** [2] 3 • 3 *to explain, expound*
**ἐπιστολή, ἡ** 3 • 13 *letter, epistle*
**ἐπιτηρέω** 1 • 2 *to watch carefully, lie in wait*
**ἱστορία, ἡ** 4 • 4 *account, story*
**περιέχω** 1 • 4 *to contain*
**πρότερος** 4 • 47 *superior, preferable, more prominent*
**χράομαι** 2 • 18 *to make use of, employ*

## Chapter 4

1 **ἔλαιον, τό** 1 • 4 *olive oil*
2 **ὄρθρος, ὁ** 1 • 1 *dawn, early morning*
4 **αὐτόφωρος** 1 • 1 *(caught) in the act*
**ἐκπειράζω** 1 • 4 *to entrap*
**καταλαμβάνω** 2 • 5 *to catch*
**κατηγορία, ἡ** 1 • 1 *accusation*
**μοιχεύω** 1 • 3 *to commit adultery*
5 **κελεύω** 1 • 44 *to command, order, urge*
**λιθάζω** 1 • 3 *to stone*
6 **δάκτυλος, ὁ** 2 • 4 *finger*
**καταγράφω** 2 • 2 *to write, draw figures*
**κάτω** 1 • 3 *below*
**κύπτω** 1 • 1 *to bend (oneself) down*
7 **ἀνακύπτω** 2 • 2 *to stand erect, straighten oneself*
**ἀναμάρτητος** 1 • 1 *without sin*
**ἐπιμένω** 1 • 16 *to persist in, persevere*
8 **δάκτυλος, ὁ** 2 • 4 *finger*
**καταγράφω** 2 • 2 *to write, draw figures*
**κατακύπτω** 1 • 1 *to bend down*
9 **καταλαμβάνω** 2 • 5 *to catch*
10 **ἀνακύπτω** 2 • 2 *to stand erect, straighten oneself*
**κατακρίνω** 2 • 6 *to pronounce a sentence on*
11 **κατακρίνω** 2 • 6 *to pronounce a sentence on*
**μηκέτι** 1 • 16 *no longer, not from now on*

## Chapter 5

1 **ἀκουστής, ὁ** 4 • 4 *hearer*
**ἐπίσκοπος, ὁ** 9 • 76 *overseer, supervisor*
**ἑταῖρος, ὁ** 3 • 4 *comrade, companion*
**θεολόγος, ὁ** 4 • 4 *God's herald*
**Ἱεράπολις, ἡ** 7 • 7 *Hierapolis*
**κυριακός** 7 • 9 *the Lord's*
**λόγιον, τό** 5 • 11 *saying*
**Παπίας, ὁ** 28 • 28 *Papias*
**Πολύκαρπος, ὁ** 5 • 39 *Polycarp*
2 **ἀναγράφω** 1 • 2 *to record, register*
**ἀπαρίθμησις, ἡ** 1 • 1 *counting*
**Ἀριστίων, ὁ** 5 • 5 *Aristion*
**Θωμᾶς, ὁ** 3 • 3 *Thomas*
**Ματθαῖος, ὁ** 6 • 6 *Matthew*
3 **ἀποκάλυψις, ἡ** 3 • 18 *Revelation*
**ἀρχαῖος** 8 • 12 *ancient*
**ἐγκρίνω** 1 • 1 *to class, classify*
**ἐπιστολή, ἡ** 3 • 13 *letter, epistle*
**καθολικός** 1 • 6 *general, universal*
**νομίζω** 1 • 10 *to think, believe, hold, consider*
**οἴομαι** 2 • 11 *to think, suppose, expect*
4 **Εἰρηναῖος, ὁ** 11 • 19 *Irenaeus*
**Παπίας, ὁ** 28 • 28 *Papias*
**σφάλλω** 2 • 2 *to slip, stumble, fall*
**χιλιονταετηρίς, ἡ** 2 • 2 *period of the millennium*
5 **ἀναιρέω** 2 • 10 *to do away with, destroy*
**θεολόγος, ὁ** 4 • 4 *God's herald*
**Παπίας, ὁ** 28 • 28 *Papias*
6 **ἀπαθής** 1 • 3 *without suffering, uninjured*
**ἄπιστος** 1 • 8 *without faith, disbelieving, unbelieving*
**Βαρσαβᾶς, ὁ** 2 • 2 *Barsabbas*
**διαφυλάσσω** 1 • 2 *to guard, protect*
**δοκιμάζω** 1 • 19 *to put to the test*
**ἔχιδνα, ἡ** 1 • 1 *snake*
**θυγάτηρ, ἡ** 3 • 10 *daughter*
**ἰός, ὁ** 1 • 4 *poison, venom*
**Ἰοῦστος, ὁ** 4 • 4 *Justus*
**ἱστορέω** 8 • 9 *to narrate/record (what one has learned)*
**Παπίας, ὁ** 28 • 28 *Papias*
7 **θαῦμα, τό** 1 • 2 *wonder*
**ἱστορέω** 8 • 9 *to narrate/record (what one has learned)*
**μάλιστα** 1 • 14 *most of all, above all, especially, particularly*
**Μαναΐμος, ὁ** 1 • 1 *Manaimos*
8 **Ἀδριανός, ὁ** 1 • 2 *Hadrian*

## Chapter 6

1 **ἀνακαλέω** 1 • 1 *to recall*
**βασιλεύω** 1 • 4 *to be king, rule*
**Δομετιανός, ὁ** 1 • 1 *Domitian*
**Ἔφεσος, ὁ** 3 • 4 *Ephesus*
**Νερούας, ὁ** 1 • 1 *Nerva*
**νῆσος, ἡ** 1 • 1 *island*
**οἰκέω** 1 • 6 *to live, dwell*
2 **βίος, ὁ** 2 • 13 *life*
**καταξιόω** 2 • 14 *to consider worthy*
**μαρτύριον, τό** 2 • 16 *martyrdom*
**περίειμι** 1 • 1 *to be over and above;*
pres. participle *chosen, especial*
**συγγράφω** 1 • 1 *to write down, compose*
3 **ἀναιρέω** 2 • 10 *to do away with, destroy*
**αὐτόπτης, ὁ** 3 • 3 *eyewitness*
**δηλαδή** 2 • 2 *obviously, plainly*
**ἐπίσκοπος, ὁ** 9 • 76 *overseer, supervisor*
**Ἱεράπολις, ἡ** 7 • 7 *Hierapolis*
**κυριακός** 7 • 9 *the Lord's*
**λόγιον, τό** 5 • 11 *a saying*
**ὁμολογία, ἡ** 1 • 1 *confession, acknowledgment that one makes*
**Παπίας, ὁ** 28 • 28 *Papias*
**πρόρρησις, ἡ** 1 • 1 *prediction*
**συγκατάθεσις, ἡ** 1 • 1 *agreement, union*
**φάσκω** 1 • 1 *to say, assert, claim*
4 **βάπτισμα, τό** 1 • 6 *plunging, dipping, washing, water-rite, baptism*
**κατανεύω** 1 • 1 *to signal*
**προθύμως** 1 • 5 *willingly, eagerly, freely*
**συντίθημι** 1 • 2 *to agree*
5 **ἀδύνατος** 1 • 11 *impossible*
**εἰκότως** 1 • 1 *reasonable*
**ψεύδομαι** 2 • 6 *to lie*
6 **διαβεβαιόω** 2 • 2 *to confirm*
**διάδοχος, ὁ** 1 • 1 *successor*
**ἑρμηνεία, ἡ** 2 • 2 *interpretation, exposition*

**μανθάνω** 2 • 26 *learn*
**Ματθαῖος, ὁ** 6 • 6 *Matthew*
**πολυμαθής** 1 • 1 *very learned, knowledgeable*
**ὑποσημαίνω** 1 • 1 *to indicate*
**Ὠριγένης, ὁ** 1 • 1 *Origen*
7 **Ἀσία, ἡ** 5 • 10 *Asia*
**δή** 2 • 6 *indeed*
**διατρίβω, ὁ** 1 • 5 *to make one's residence*
**ἐκκλησιαστικός** 3 • 6 *to the (universal) church*
**Εὐσέβιος, ὁ** 2 • 2 *Eusebius*
**Ἔφεσος, ὁ** 3 • 4 *Ephesus*
**Θωμᾶς, ὁ** 3 • 3 *Thomas*
**ἱστορία, ἡ** 4 • 4 *account, story*
**λαγχάνω** 1 • 1 *to receive, obtain*
**Παρθία, ἡ** 1 • 1 *Parthia*
**πολυΐστωρ** 1 • 1 *well-informed, very learned*
**τελευτάω** 3 • 8 *to die*

## Chapters 7–9[1]

## Chapter 10

1 **ἀξιόπιστος** 1 • 4 *trustworthy*
**ἀποκάλυψις, ἡ** 3 • 18 *Revelation*
**ἀρχαῖος** 8 • 12 *ancient;*
**τῶν ἀρχαιοτέρων Παπίου, Εἰρηναίου, Μεθοδίου καὶ Ἱππολύτου** (gens. of simple apposition) *the earlier ones/older generation, namely, Papias, Irenaeus, Methodius, and Hyppolytus*
**βίβλος, ἡ** 1 • 5 *book*
**Γρηγόριος, ὁ** 1 • 1 *Gregory*
**Εἰρηναῖος, ὁ** 11 • 19 *Irenaeus*
**θεολόγος, ὁ** 4 • 4 *God's herald*
**Ἱππόλυτος, ὁ** 1 • 1 *Hippolytus*
**Κύριλλος, ὁ** 1 • 1 *Cyril*
**μέντοι** 2 • 2 *though, to be sure, indeed*
**μηκύνω** 1 • 1 *to make long*
**Παπίας, ὁ** 28 • 28 *Papias*
**περισσός** 1 • 5 *abundant, profuse*
**προσέτι** 1 • 1 *over and above, besides*
**προσμαρτυρέω** 1 • 1 *to bear witness in addition, bear additional witness to, confirm*

## Chapter 11

1 **ἀρχαῖος** 8 • 12 *ancient*
**δέον** 1 • 1 *necessary*
**δηλαδή** 2 • 2 *obviously, plainly*
**διακόσμησις, ἡ** 1 • 1 *regulation, orderly arrangement*
**δράκων, ὁ** 1 • 1 *dragon, serpent*
**ἔνιοι** 2 • 4 *some, several*
**ἑξῆς** 1 • 2 *in the next place*
**θεῖος** 3 • 16 *divine, supernatural*
**λέξις** 3 • 3 *expressly, in the very words*
**οἰκουμένη, ἡ** 2 • 6 *the inhabited earth, the world*
**ὄφις, ὁ** 1 • 9 *snake, serpent*
**πάλαι** 1 • 2 *long ago, formerly*
**Παπίας, ὁ** 28 • 28 *Papias*
**παρεγγυάω** 1 • 1 *to exhort, command*
**Σατανᾶς, ὁ** 1 • 5 *Satan*
**συμβαίνω** 1 • 7 *to happen, come about*
**τάξις, ἡ** 2 • 6 *position, post*
**τελευτάω** 3 • 8 *to come to an end*

## Chapter 12

1 **Ἀλεξανδρεύς, ὁ** 2 • 2 *an Alexandrian*
**Ἀμμώνιος, ὁ** 1 • 1 *Ammonius*
**ἀρχαῖος** 8 • 12 *ancient*
**ἀφορμή, ἡ** 1 • 5 *occasion, opportunity*
**ἑξαήμερος, ὁ** 1 • 1 *six days*
**ἐξηγητής, ὁ** 1 • 1 *expounder, interpreter*
**ἐπιστήθιος, ὁ** 1 • 1 *bosom-friend*
**Ἱεραπολίτης, ὁ** 5 • 5 *inhabitant of Hierapolis*
**Κλήμης, ὁ** 4 • 6 *Clement*
**νοέω** 1 • 46 *to perceive, apprehend, understand, gain an insight into*
**Πανταῖνος, ὁ** 2 • 2 *Pantaenus*
**πάνυ** 2 • 5 *altogether, very*
**Παπίας, ὁ** 28 • 28 *Papias*
**σοφός** 1 • 8 *wise*

1. Chapters 7–9 are not extant in Greek.

**συνῳδός** 1 • 1 *in unison with*
**φοιτάω** 1 • 2 *to go back and forth, move about (regularly)*

## Chapter 13

1 **Ἀλεξάνδρεια, ἡ** 1 • 1 *Alexandria*
**ἀμφί** 1 • 1 *persons grouped about one*
**ἀναφέρω** 1 • 8 *to refer*
**ἀρχαῖος** 8 • 12 *ancient*
**δή** 2 • 6 *indeed*
**Εἰρηναῖος, ὁ** 11 • 19 *Irenaeus*
**ἐξηγητικός** 1 • 1 *expository works, commentaries*
**εὐαγγελιστής, ὁ** 3 • 3 *proclaimer of the gospel, evangelist*
**Ἱεραπολίτης, ὁ** 5 • 5 *inhabitant of Hierapolis*
**Ἰουστῖνος, ὁ** 1 • 1 *Justin*
**Κλήμης, ὁ** 4 • 6 *Clement*
**Λουγδουνεύς, ὁ** 1 • 1 *inhabitant of Lyons*
**ὁμόχρονος** 1 • 1 *contemporary, contemporaneous*
**Πανταῖνος, ὁ** 2 • 2 *Pantaenus*
**Παπίας, ὁ** 28 • 28 *Papias*
**παράδεισος, ὁ** 6 • 8 *paradise*
**πνευματικῶς** 1 • 4 *spiritually, in a spiritual manner/in a manner caused by or filled with the Spirit*
**Στρωματεύς, ὁ** 1 • 1 *Stromateus*
**φιλόσοφος, ὁ** [2] 2 • 3 *philosopher*
**Φίλων, ὁ** 1 • 4 *Philo*
**φοιτητής, ὁ** 1 • 1 *pupil, disciple*

## Chapter 14[2]

6 **ἀκουστής, ὁ** 4 • 4 *hearer*
**ἀρχαῖος** 8 • 12 *ancient;*
**ἀρχαῖος ἀνήρ** *a man of the early period (of the Christian faith)*
**ἐγγράφως** 2 • 2 *in writing*
**ἐπιμαρτυρέω** 2 • 2 *to bear witness, attest*
**ἑταῖρος, ὁ** 3 • 4 *comrade, companion*
**Παπίας, ὁ** 28 • 28 *Papias*
**Πολύκαρπος, ὁ** 5 • 39 *Polycarp*

2. Verses 1–5 and 7–8 are not extant in Greek.

**συντάσσω** 4 • 4 *to write, compose, compile*
**τέταρτος** 4 • 9 *fourth*

## Chapter 15

1 **ἀκακία, ἡ** 1 • 10 *innocence, guilelessness;*
**κατὰ θεὸν ἀκακίαν** *godly innocence*
**Ἀλεξανδρεύς, ὁ** 2 • 2 *an Alexandrian*
**ἀσκέω** 1 • 6 *to practice, engage in*
**δηλόω** 6 • 49 *to reveal, make clear, show*
**ἐξήγησις, ἡ** 4 • 6 *explanation, interpretation*
**Κλήμης, ὁ** 4 • 6 *Clement*
**κυριακός** 7 • 9 *the Lord's*
**παιδαγωγός, ὁ** 1 • 1 *guardian, leader, guide*
**παῖς, ὁ/ἡ** 1 • 20 *child*
**Παπίας, ὁ** 28 • 28 *Papias*

## Chapter 16

1 **αἰνίσσομαι** 1 • 1 *to hint, signify obscurely*
**αἵρεσις, ἡ** 2 • 6 *sect, party, school, faction*
**ἀπόλαυσις, ἡ** 2 • 6 *enjoyment*
**Ἀπολλινάριος, ὁ** 1 • 1 *Apollinarius*
**Ἀσία, ἡ** 5 • 10 *Asia*
**βρῶμα, τό** 2 • 4 *food*
**δόγμα, τό** 2 • 10 *doctrine, dogma*
**Εἰρηναῖος, ὁ** 11 • 19 *Irenaeus*
**ἐξήγησις, ἡ** 4 • 6 *explanation, interpretation*
**ἐπίσκοπος, ὁ** 9 • 76 *overseer, supervisor*
**εὐαγγελιστής, ὁ** 3 • 3 *proclaimer of the gospel, evangelist*
**θεῖος** 3 • 16 *holy, divine*
**Ἱεράπολις, ἡ** 7 • 7 *Hierapolis*
**κυριακός** 7 • 9 *the Lord's*
**Λουγδοῦνος, ὁ** 3 • 3 *Lyons*
**οἴομαι** 2 • 11 *to think, suppose, expect*
**ὅσπερ** 1 • 10 *which indeed*
**Παπίας, ὁ** [3] 28 • 28 *Papias*

**παράγω** 1 • 2 *to introduce, bring in beside*
**πέμπτος** 1 • 5 *fifth*
**συνακμάζω** 1 • 1 *to flourish at the same time*
**τέταρτος** 4 • 9 *fourth*
**χιλιονταετηρίς, ἡ** 2 • 2 *period of the millennium*

## Chapter 17

1 **αἰσθητός** 1 • 1 *sensible, perceptible by the senses*
**ἀποδέχομαι** 1 • 6 *to accept, welcome*
**ἀπόλαυσις, ἡ** 2 • 6 *enjoyment*
**βρῶμα, τό** 2 • 4 *food*
**Εἰρηναῖος, ὁ** 11 • 19 *Irenaeus*
**ἐπίσκοπος, ὁ** [2] 9 • 76 *overseer, supervisor*
**Ἱεράπολις, ἡ** 7 • 7 *Hierapolis*
**Λουγδοῦνος, ὁ** 3 • 3 *Lyons*
**μήν** 3 • 8 *indeed*
**ὅσιος** 1 • 10 *holy*
**Παπίας, ὁ** 28 • 28 *Papias*
**Στέφανος, ὁ** 1 • 1 *Stephen*

## Chapter 18

1 **ἀγχόνη, ἡ** 1 • 1 *means of strangling, halter*
**Ἀπολινάριος, ὁ** 1 • 1 *Apollinarius*
**ἀποπνίγω** 1 • 1 *to choke*
**ἐπιβιόω** 1 • 1 *to live after, survive*
**καθαιρέω** 1 • 7 *to take down, bring down, lower*
2 **δηλόω** 6 • 49 *to reveal, make clear, show*
**ἐκχέω/ἐκχύννω** 1 • 6 *to pour out*
**λακάω** 1 • 1 *to burst apart, burst open*
**πρᾶξις, ἡ** 2 • 50 *act, action, deed*
**πρηνής** 1 • 1 *forward, prostrate, head first, headlong*
**σπλάγχνον, τό** 1 • 5 *inward parts, entrails*
3 **ἐξήγησις, ἡ** 4 • 6 *explanation, interpretation*
**ἱστορέω** 8 • 9 *to narrate/record (what one has learned)*
**κυριακός** 7 • 9 *the Lord's*
**Παπίας, ὁ** 28 • 28 *Papias*
**σαφής** 1 • 1 *clearly, exactly, very well*
**τέταρτος** 4 • 9 *fourth*
4 **ἅμαξα, ἡ** 1 • 1 *wagon*
**ἀσέβεια, ἡ** 1 • 3 *impiety*
**ὄγκος, ὁ** 1 • 1 *bulk*
**ὁπόθεν** 1 • 1 *where*
**πρήθω** 1 • 1 *to swell up*
**ῥᾳδίως** 1 • 2 *readily, easily*
**τοσοῦτος** 6 • 38 *so great/strong, to such extent*
**ὑπόδειγμα, τό** 2 • 8 *example, model, pattern*
5 **βάθος, τό** 1 • 4 *depth*
**βλέφαρον, τό** 1 • 1 *eyelid*
**διόπτρα, ἡ** 1 • 1 *optical instrument*
**ἐξοιδέω** 1 • 1 *to swell, be swollen up*
**ἔξωθεν** 1 • 3 *having to do with the outside, the external*
**ἐπιφανεία, ἡ** 1 • 3 *surface appearance*
**ἰατρός, ὁ** 1 • 3 *physician*
**καθόλου** 1 • 1 *entirely, completely*
**τοσοῦτος** [2] 6 • 38 *so great/ strong, to such extent*
6 **ἀηδής** 2 • 2 *unpleasant, odious*
**αἰδοῖον, τό** 1 • 1 *private parts*
**ἀναγκαῖος** 2 • 4 *necessary*
**ἀσχημοσύνη, ἡ** 1 • 1 *genitals*
**ἰχώρ, ὁ** 1 • 1 *serious discharge, pus*
**σκώληξ, ὁ** 1 • 5 *worm*
**συρρέω** 1 • 1 *to flow together*
**ὕβρις, ἡ** 1 • 4 *shame, insult, mistreatment*
7 **ἀοίκητος** 1 • 1 *uninhabited, uninhabitable*
**βάσανος, ἡ** 1 • 18 *severe pain, torment*
**ἔκρυσις, ἡ** *outflow, efflux*
**ἐπιφράσσω** 1 • 1 *to close*
**μέχρι** [2] 3 • 23 *to the point of*
**ὀσμή, ἡ** 1 • 3 *odor, smell*
**παρέρχομαι** 1 • 12 *to go by, pass by*
**ῥίς, ἡ** 1 • 1 *nose, nostrils*
**τελευτάω** 3 • 8 *to die*
**τιμωρία, ἡ** 1 • 13 *punishment*
**τοσοῦτος** 6 • 38 *so great/strong, to such extent*
**χωρέω** 2 • 15 *to go, go out/away, reach*

**χωρίον, τό** [2] 2 • 5 *place, piece of land, field*

## Chapter 19[3]

## Chapter 20

1 **αἵρεσις, ἡ** 2 • 6 *sect, party, school, faction*
**ἀνά** 1 • 4 *among, in the midst of*
**ἀναπλήρωσις, ἡ** 2 • 2 *completion, fulfillment*
**ἀναφύω** 1 • 1 *to cause to spring up*
**βροντή, ἡ** 1 • 1 *thunder*
**γηραλέος** 1 • 1 *aged, old*
**δεινός** 1 • 7 *fearful, terrible*
**διαδοχή, ἡ** 1 • 1 *succession*
**Εἰρηναῖος, ὁ** 11 • 19 *Irenaeus*
**εὐβίωτος** 1 • 1 *leading an honest life, respectable*
**Εὐσέβιος, ὁ** 2 • 2 *Eusebius*
**Ἱεραπολίτης, ὁ** 5 • 5 *inhabitant of Hierapolis*
**ἱστορικός** 1 • 1 *historical*
**μετακαλέω** 1 • 1 *to call by a different name*
**οἰκουμένη, ἡ** 2 • 6 *the inhabited earth, the world*
**πάνυ** 2 • 5 *altogether, very*
**Παπίας, ὁ** 28 • 28 *Papias*
**ὑπαγορεύω** 1 • 1 *to dictate*
**ὕστερος** 2 • 3 *the second one*

## Chapter 21

1 **ἄγραφος** 2 • 2 *unwritten*
**αἴτιος, ὁ** 1 • 1 *cause*
**ἀκοή, ἡ** 1 • 8 *hearing*
**ἀκόλουθος** 1 • 8 *following*
**ἀκροατής, ὁ** 2 • 4 *a hearer*
**ἄνειμι** 1 • 1 *to go back, return*
**ἅπαξ** 1 • 4 *once and for all*
**ἀρκέω** 1 • 5 pass. *to be satisfied/content (with something)*
**διάνοια, ἡ** 1 • 22 *disposition, thought, mind*
**διδασκαλία, ἡ** [2] 4 • 6 *teaching, instruction*
**ἐπιλάμπω** 1 • 2 *to shine out, shine forth*
**εὐσέβεια, ἡ** 1 • 6 *devoutness, piety, godliness*
**θεῖος** 3 • 16 *divine*
**ἱκανῶς** 1 • 2 *sufficiently, of number*
**καταλείπω** 1 • 12 *to leave (behind)*
**κατεργάζομαι** 1 • 7 *to prepare someone*
**κήρυγμα, τό** 1 • 5 *something proclaimed aloud, proclamation*
**λιπαρέω** 1 • 1 *to beseech*
**Μᾶρκος, ὁ** [2] 8 • 8 *Mark*
**παντοῖος** 1 • 1 *every kind of, all sorts of*
**παράκλησις, ἡ** 1 • 1 *encouragement, exhortation*
**πρότερος** 4 • 47 *earlier, formerly, in former times*
**τοσοῦτος** 6 • 38 *so great/strong, to such extent*
**ὑπόμνημα, τό** 1 • 1 *record*
**φέγγος, τό** 1 • 1 *light, radiance*
2 **ἀποκαλύπτω** 1 • 23 *to reveal, disclose, bring to light, make fully known*
**Βαβυλών, ἡ** [2] 2 • 2 *Babylon*
**ἕκτος** 1 • 6 *sixth*
**ἔντευξις, ἡ** 1 • 18 *reading*
**ἐπίσκοπος, ὁ** 9 • 76 *overseer, supervisor*
**ἐπιστολή, ἡ** 3 • 13 *letter, epistle*
**ἥδομαι** 1 • 2 *to be pleased with, delight in*
**Ἱεραπολίτης, ὁ** 5 • 5 *inhabitant of Hierapolis*
**ἱστορία, ἡ** 4 • 4 *account, story*
**Κλήμης, ὁ** 4 • 6 *Clement*
**κυρόω** 1 • 1 *to confirm, ratify*
**Μᾶρκος, ὁ** [2] 8 • 8 *Mark*
**μνημονεύω** 7 • 25 *to remember, keep in mind, think of, mention*
**Παπίας, ὁ** 28 • 28 *Papias*
**παρατίθημι** 2 • 6 *to demonstrate, point out*
**προθυμία, ἡ** 1 • 6 *willingness, readiness, goodwill*
**προσλέγω** 1 • 1 *to answer, reply*
**πρότερος** 4 • 47 *earlier, formerly, in former times*
**Ῥώμη, ἡ** 1 • 8 *Rome*
**σημαίνω** 1 • 2 *to indicate, suggest, intimate*

3. Chapter 19 is not extant in Greek.

**συνεκλεκτός** 1 • 1 *chosen together*
**συνεπιμαρτυρέω** 1 • 3 *to testify at the same time*
**συντάσσω** 4 • 4 *to write, compose, compile*
**τροπικός** 1 • 1 *figurative*
**Ὑποτυπώσεις, αἱ** 1 • 1 pl. proper noun *Hypotyposes (name of a book)*

## Chapter 22

1 **ἀναδέω** 1 • 1 *to bind, tie up, crown;*
**τὸν στέφανον ἀναδησάμενον** (cognate acc. functioning as retained object with pass. verb; cf. *ExSyn* 189–90, 197) *crowned with the crown*
**ἀπεναντίον** 1 • 1 *against, contrary to*
**ἀποστολικός** 2 • 4 *apostolic*
**γέ** 3 • 18 *at least, even, indeed*
**δόγμα, τό** 2 • 10 *doctrine, dogma*
**Εἰρηναῖος, ὁ** 11 • 19 *Irenaeus*
**ἐκκλησιαστικός** 3 • 4 *pertaining to the universal church*
**ἐπίσκοπος, ὁ** 9 • 76 *overseer, supervisor*
**ἕπω** 1 • 1 *to conduct, administer*
**Ἱεράπολις, ἡ** 7 • 7 *Hierapolis*
**κοινός** 1 • 15 *communal, common*
**Λουγδοῦνος** 3 • 3 *Lyons*
**μαρτύριον, τό** 2 • 16 *martyrdom*
**Μεθόδιος, ὁ** 2 • 2 *Methodius*
**ὀλιγωρέω** 1 • 1 *to think lightly, make light of something*
**οὐμενοῦν** 1 • 1 *not at all, by no means*
**Παπίας, ὁ** 28 • 28 *Papias*
**παραφέρω** 1 • 7 *to take/carry away*
**πατρικός** 1 • 1 *derived/handed down by one's father, paternal*
**περικόπτω** 1 • 5 *to cut away, take away*
**στέφανος, ὁ** 2 • 7 *wreath, crown*
**φθέγγομαι** 1 • 1 *to speak, utter, proclaim*

## Chapters 23–28[4]

4. Chapters 23–28 are not extant in Greek.

# The Traditions of the Elders

## Chapter 1

1 Ἀσία, ἡ 1 • 10 *Asia*
**μέχρι** 1 • 23 *until*
**παραδίδωμι** 1 • 61 *to hand down, deliver*
**παραμένω** 1 • 9 *to remain*
**συμβάλλω** 1 • 4 *to meet, assist, live*
**Τραϊανός, ὁ** 1 • 3 *Trajan*

## Chapter 2

1 **ἀνατολή, ἡ** 1 • 6 *east*
**ἄρρητος** 1 • 1 *unutterable*
**ἀφθαρσία, ἡ** 1 • 12 *immortality*
**δηλονότι** 1 • 2 *quite clearly, obviously*
**Ἐδέμ** 1 • 1 *Eden*
**εἰσκομίζω** 1 • 1 *to carry*
**ἐκεῖσε** 2 • 2 *there, to that place*
**μετατίθημι** [3] 3 • 9 *to translate, transfer*
**ὅδε** 1 • 7 *this*
**παράδεισος, ὁ** [3] 5 • 8 *paradise*
**παρακούω** 1 • 5 *to disobey*
**πάρειμι** 1 • 19 *to be present*
**πλάσσω** 1 • 8 *to form, mold, create*
**πνευματοφόρος** 1 • 2 *bearing the spirit;*
subst. *inspired person, person bearing the spirit*
**προοιμιάζομαι** 1 • 1 *to serve as a prelude/preamble, make a prelude/ preamble*
**συντέλεια, ἡ** 1 • 3 *consummation*
**φυτεύω** 1 • 16 *to plant*

## Chapter 3

1 **ἀθετέω** 1 • 4 *to take liberties with, reject, disallow*
**ἀντί** 1 • 15 *instead of, in place of*
**ἀντίγραφον, τό** 1 • 4 *copy (of a book)*
**ἀριθμός, ὁ** [3] 3 • 14 *number*
**ἀρχαῖος** 1 • 12 *old, ancient*
**γράμμα, τό** 1 • 8 *letter (of the alphabet)*
**δεκάς, ἡ** [2] 2 • 2 *group of ten, decad, ten*
**ἕξ** [2] 2 • 23 *six*
**ἑξακόσιοι** 1 • 2 *six hundred*
**ἑξήκοντα** 2 • 2 *sixty*
**ἐπακολουθέω** 1 • 4 *to follow;*
**τινες ἐπακολουθήσαντες ἰδιωτισμῷ** *some have followed/ adopted a particular (reading)*
**ἰδιωτισμός** 1 • 1 *unique, particular, peculiar*
**κεῖμαι** 1 • 24 *to be found*
**ν´** 1 • 1 *fifty*
**ὄψις, ἡ** 1 • 6 *face;*
**κατ᾽ ὄψιν** *face to face, with their own eyes*
**σπουδαῖος** 1 • 3 *carefully produced, good*
**σφάλλω** 1 • 2 *to err, stumble*
**ὑφαιρέω** 1 • 1 *to subtract*
**ψήφισμα, τό** 1 • 1 *count, value, amount*
**ψῆφος, ἡ** 1 • 1 *reckoning, computation*

## Chapter 4[1]

## Chapter 5

1 **ἀπολαύω** 1 • 1 *to enjoy, have the benefit of*
**διατριβή, ἡ** 1 • 1 *life, spending time, abode*
**ἐκεῖσε** 2 • 2 *there*
**καταξιόω** 1 • 14 *to consider/deem worthy*
**κατέχω** 1 • 4 *to possess*

1. Chapter 4 is not extant in Greek.

**λαμπρότης, ἡ** 1 • 2 *splendor, brilliance, brightness*
**πανταχοῦ** 1 • 2 *everywhere, in every place*
**παράδεισος, ὁ** 5 • 8 *paradise*
**σωτήρ, ὁ** 1 • 14 *savior*
**τρυφή, ἡ** 1 • 22 *delight, joy, enjoyment*
**χωρέω** 1 • 15 *to go, reach*
2 **ἀναλαμβάνω** 1 • 10 *to take up*
**ἁρμόζω** 1 • 23 *to fit, be an appropriate part of*
**διαστολή, ἡ** 1 • 1 *difference, distinction*
**διατρίβω** 1 • 5 *to stay, spend time, dwell*
**ἑξήκοντα** 2 • 2 *sixty*
**μονή, ἡ** 1 • 1 *room, abode, dwelling place*
**οἴκησις, ἡ** [2] 2 • 3 *dwelling, habitation, residence*
**παράδεισος, ὁ** 5 • 8 *paradise*
**παρέχω** 1 • 18 *to grant, give, offer*
**τριάκοντα** 1 • 2 *thirty*